New Perspectives on

E-COMMERCE

Comprehensive

GARY P. SCHNEIDER
University of San Diego

COURSE
TECHNOLOGY
THOMSON LEARNING

Australia • Canada • Mexico • Singapore • Spain • United Kingdom • United States

COURSE TECHNOLOGY
THOMSON LEARNING

New Perspectives on E-Commerce—Comprehensive
is published by Course Technology.

Managing Editor:
Greg Donald

Senior Editor:
Donna Gridley

Series Technology Editor:
Rachel Crapser

Senior Product Manager:
Kathy Finnegan

Technology Product Manager:
Amanda Young

Editorial Assistant:
Jessica Engstrom

Marketing Manager:
Sean Teare

Developmental Editor:
Jessica Evans
Jane Pedicini

Production Editor:
Karen Jacot

Composition:
GEX Publishing Services

Text Designer:
Meral Dabcovich

Cover Designer:
Efrat Reis

Preface

New Perspectives

Course Technology is the world leader in information technology education. The New Perspectives Series is an integral part of Course Technology's success. Visit our Web site to see a whole new perspective on teaching and learning solutions.

File Edit View Favorites Tools Help

Back | Forward | Stop | Refresh | Home | Search | Favorites | History | Mail | Print | Edit | Discuss

Address http://www.course.com/newperspectives/ Go Links »

COURSE TECHNOLOGY
THOMSON LEARNING ™

Series | Student Downloads | Instructor Resources | Bookstore | Support
Home | About Us | Contact | Find Your Rep | search

NEW PERSPECTIVES

Home
Catalog
Teacher's Lounge
Student Union
Tech Center
Contact Us
Photo Contest

Building Computer Skills Has Never Been This Real...

Engaging, Real, Dynamic, Interactive — these are just a few of the qualities that the New Perspectives Series can add to your class.

Critical thinking and **problem solving** — without them, computer skills are learned but soon forgotten. With its case-based approach the New Perspectives series challenges you to apply what you've learned to real-life situations. Become a member of the New Perspectives community and join the large number of users who understand *why* they're learning *what* they're learning.

New Perspectives—Building Computer Skills Has Never Been This Real

Why New Perspectives will work for you.

Critical thinking and **problem solving**—without them, computer skills are learned but soon forgotten. With its **case-based** approach, the New Perspectives Series challenges students to apply what they've learned to real-life situations. Become a member of the New Perspectives community and watch your students not only **master** computer skills, but also **retain** and carry this **knowledge** into the world.

New Perspectives catalog
Our online catalog is never out of date! Go to the Catalog button on our Web site to check out our available titles, request a desk copy, download a book preview, or locate online files.

Complete system of offerings
Whether you're looking for a Brief book, an Advanced book, or something in between, we've got you covered. Go to the Catalog button on our Web site to find the level of coverage that's right for you.

Instructor materials
We have all the tools you need—data files, solution files, figure files, a sample syllabus, and ExamView, our powerful testing software package.

How well do your students know Microsoft Office?
Find out with performance-based testing software that measures your students' proficiency in the application. Click the Tech Center button to learn more.

Get certified
If you want to get certified, we have the titles for you. Find out more by clicking the Teacher's Lounge button.

Interested in online learning?
Enhance your course with any one of our online learning platforms. Go to the Teacher's Lounge to find the platform that's right for you.

Your link to the future is at
www.course.com/NewPerspectives

What you need to know about this book.

- Student Online Companion takes students to the Web for additional work.

- ExamView testing software gives you the option of generating a printed test, LAN-based test, or test over the Internet.

- The tutorials and exercises use realistic and relevant cases, including those from traditional large and small businesses, as well as e-commerce businesses and not-for-profit organizations.

- Students learn what e-commerce is and how it relates to the Internet.

- Students have an opportunity to create an online store with products to sell.

- Students learn about security on the Web. Students will learn what security entails and how it can be maintained.

- Students learn how they can protect themselves from breaches on security and invasion of their privacy when using the Web.

- Students learn how electronic payment systems work on the Web and how companies try to secure the information submitted by customers.

- Students will also learn the international, legal, and ethical issues that face Web users.

CASE	TROUBLE?	SESSION 1.1	QUICK CHECK	RW
Tutorial Case Each tutorial begins with a problem presented in a case that is meaningful to students. The case sets the scene to help students understand what they will do in the tutorial.	**TROUBLE? Paragraphs** These paragraphs anticipate the mistakes or problems that students may have and help them continue with the tutorial.	**Sessions** Each tutorial is divided into sessions designed to be completed in about 45 minutes each. Students should take as much time as they need and take a break between sessions.	**Quick Check Questions** Each session concludes with conceptual Quick Check questions that test students' understanding of what they learned in the session.	**Reference Windows** Reference Windows are succinct summaries of the most important tasks covered in a tutorial. They preview actions students will perform in the steps to follow.

TABLE OF CONTENTS

Tutorial 2   EC 2.01

Creating a Successful Web Presence

Designing the User Interface and Promoting the Electronic Commerce Web Site

Tutorial 5   EC 5.01

Electronic Payment Systems

Accepting and Processing Customer Payments

Appendix A   EC A.01

Careers in Electronic Commerce

Acknowledgments

Creating a textbook is a collaborative effort between author and publisher working as a team to provide the highest quality book possible. I want to acknowledge the outstanding work of the editorial team at Course Technology: Greg Donald, Managing Editor; Donna Gridley, Senior Editor, and Rachel Crapser, Series Technology Manager. Donna and Rachel embraced the idea for this book early on and encouraged its development. Other key people at Course Technology I want to thank for their work and dedication to the project are Amanda Young, Technology Product Manager; Jessica Engstrom, Editorial Assistant; Karen Jacot, Production Editor; Sean Teare, Marketing Manager; and the Quality Assurance Group: John Bosco, John Freitas, Nicole Ashton, and Harris Bierhoff. Thanks to Shirley Kaiser, the Web site designer who created the Online Companion for the book. Special thanks goes to the Development Editors, Jessica Evans and Jane Pedicini, who contributed so much to this book.

Many of my colleagues on the faculty at University of San Diego deserve my gratitude for their help. Special thanks go to Tom Buckles, who provided many insights about Internet marketing and strategy issues. Tom spent many late hours working with me long after everyone else in the building had gone home.

I want to thank the following reviewers for their insightful comments and excellent suggestions at various stages of this book's development: David J. Oscarson, Brevard Community College; Paul Redig, Milwaukee Area Technical College; and Andrea Watcher, Point Park College.

Finally, I want to express my deep appreciation for the continuous support and encouragement provided by my wife, Cathy Cosby. I also want to thank our children for tolerating my absence while I was occupied with the writing of this book.

Gary Schneider

New Perspectives on

E-COMMERCE

Read This Before You Begin

To the Student

Using Your Own Computer

If you are going to work through this book using your own computer, you need:

- **Computer System** Microsoft Internet Explorer version 5.0 or higher or Netscape Navigator version 4.7 or higher must be installed on your computer. If you use lower versions of these browsers, some Web pages might look slightly different from what you see in the figures. This book assumes a complete installation of the browser. You can download current browser versions from www.microsoft.com or www.netscape.com.

- **Internet Connection** You must connect to the Internet to complete the tutorials in this book. For some tutorials, you must have an e-mail address. If you do not have an e-mail address, you can obtain one for free at www.hotmail.com, www.altavista.com, www.email.com, mail.yahoo.com, or any other Internet site that provides free e-mail accounts.

What to Do If a Web Site Looks Different from What Is Printed in the Book

Because companies change their Web sites occasionally, the Web sites that you visit in the tutorials might look different from the Web pages that appear in the figures in this book. Important content is pointed out in the tutorial or in the figure's callouts. If you cannot find a hyperlink on the page, try scrolling the page to see if the link appears in a different location, or look for a link with a similar name.

Using the Student Online Companion

The Student Online Companion for this book contains the links that you need to complete the tutorial steps and case problems. The URL is www.course.com/NewPerspectives/EC. The Student Online Companion also contains links to sites that are set in the tutorial in bold, blue, sans serif type. Although you are not directed to visit these sites in the tutorial steps, you can link to them using the Student Online Companion page to broaden your experiences while learning about electronic commerce. These links might include resources for important topics or different examples of electronic commerce sites. The Student Online Companion page also includes updated tutorial material to keep the tutorials current in a constantly changing Web environment.

Visit Our World Wide Web Site

Additional materials designed especially for you are available on the World Wide Web. Go to http://www.course.com.

OBJECTIVES

In this tutorial you will:

- Investigate the differences between traditional commerce and electronic commerce

- Examine the features of the Internet and the World Wide Web that make electronic commerce possible

- Analyze value chains to identify electronic commerce opportunities

- Identify how businesses sell products and services on the Web

- Identify purchasing, logistic, and business support activities on the Web

- Learn about the new types of business opportunities that electronic commerce makes possible

WHAT IS ELECTRONIC COMMERCE?

Value Chains and Using the Web to Sell Products and Services

CASE

The Daily Metropolitan

Ben Beeler, editor of *The Daily Metropolitan*, hired you several months ago as the newspaper's technology reporter. The paper reports local business news, and Ben saw an increasing need for coverage of computer technologies because they were becoming a more important part of many businesses. He was right—your weekly columns and other news reports have been a big hit with readers. Ben stopped by your office this morning and asked you to begin work on a new series of columns on electronic commerce. Ben said that electronic commerce seemed to be something that everyone was talking about but that nobody really understood. He would like you to write about the technologies and business strategies that companies use to implement electronic commerce. As you think about your assignment, you realize that most people who are working in electronic commerce are either technologists or businesspersons. In writing for the newspaper, you have interviewed many of these people and have found that the technologists understand the hardware and software issues and the businesspersons understand the marketing and management strategies. You have not met very many people who are conversant in both aspects of electronic commerce. You decide that a good theme for your series would be the convergence of technology and business strategy and begin to outline your first draft.

SESSION 1.1

In this session, you will learn what electronic commerce is and how it is enabled by the Web. You will also learn what value chains are and how you can use value chain analysis to identify electronic commerce opportunities.

Defining Electronic Commerce

You decide to begin your first column by providing a definition of electronic commerce. As you interview Ron Delbeq, the president of a local Internet service provider, he tells you that many people think of electronic commerce solely in terms of shopping on the part of the Internet called the World Wide Web (the Web). Although consumer shopping on the Web is expected to exceed $300 billion by 2003, electronic commerce is much broader and encompasses many more business activities than just Web shopping.

Some people and businesses use the term **electronic business** (or **e-business**) when they are discussing electronic commerce in this broader sense. However, most people use the terms electronic commerce and electronic business interchangeably. Many not-for-profit organizations conduct "business" activities. For example, a museum might sell tickets for an upcoming special exhibition on its Web site. In this book, the term **electronic commerce** (or **e-commerce**) is used in its broadest sense; that is, the conduct of selling, buying, logistics, or other organization-management activities via the Web.

In 1994, Jeff Bezos, a young financial analyst and fund manager who had become intrigued by the rapid growth of the Internet, founded one of the most successful retail electronic commerce sites. Bezos listed 20 products that might sell well on the Internet. After some intense analysis, he determined that books were at the top of his list. Bezos had no experience in the book-selling business, but he realized that books were small-ticket commodity items that would be easy and inexpensive to ship. He knew many customers would be willing to buy books without inspecting them in person and that books could be impulse purchase items if properly promoted.

Bezos believed that buying books from an online seller could be more attractive than a visit to the local bookstore. He envisioned his Web site's software tracking customer's purchases and recommending similar titles. He wanted to give his customers the option of requesting notification when a particular author publishes a new book. By relentlessly paying attention to every process involved in buying, promoting, selling, and shipping books, and by working to improve each process continuously, Bezos and Amazon.com have become one of the first highly visible success stories in electronic commerce.

As it has grown, Amazon.com has continued to identify strategic opportunities. In 1998, it began selling music CDs. More recently, it has added consumer electronics, toys, auctions, and hardware to its list of offerings. Five years after opening its Web site, Amazon.com had reached annual sales of over $1 billion.

To visit the Amazon.com retail electronic commerce site:

1. Start your Web browser, and then go to the Student Online Companion page, or the Online Companion, by entering the URL **http://www.course.com/NewPerspectives/EC** in the appropriate location of your Web browser. Click the **Tutorial 1** link, and then click the **Session 1.1** link. Click the **Amazon.com** link and wait while your browser loads the Amazon.com home page. Note that Amazon.com has expanded from its beginnings as an online bookstore; the tabs across the top of the home page are hyperlinks to books, music, video, and other categories of products now sold by Amazon.com.

2. Click the **Books** hyperlink on the left side of the page to open the Books Web page shown in Figure 1-1. A new set of hyperlinks appear just under the tabs that let you search for a specific book, browse categories of books, or go directly to the week's bestsellers. Return visitors, who have purchased books from the site or who have registered their preferences, will find that the ads for books and other items that appear on the home page and the category pages are tailored to match the types of books they have purchased or the preferences they have expressed.

Figure 1-1	AMAZON.COM BOOKS PAGE

tabs to different products sold by Amazon.com, including music and videos

click to request notification of new releases

TROUBLE? Because companies change their Web sites regularly, the sites you visit might look different from the figures shown in the book.

3. Use the hyperlinks on this page to explore the offerings of Amazon.com. You can click your browser's Back button to return to the home page and explore other categories of products offered. Note the way Amazon.com has combined the technologies it uses to generate each product's Web page with the business strategies that underlie the way each product is presented on the site.

As you consider this combination of technology and business strategy, you make some notes for the first column in your electronic commerce series. You realize that Amazon.com's success provides a blueprint for any business that is thinking of ways to use the Web:

- Carefully analyze the characteristics of the markets into which you sell and from which you buy
- Consider the logistics of delivering your product or service to customers
- Identify ways the Web can help you capitalize on the opportunities that exist in your business

As important as the selling opportunities were to Amazon.com's success, the structure of the supply side of the book business was equally important. When the company started, there was a large number of book publishers, so it would be difficult for a single supplier to restrict Amazon.com's book purchases or enter its market as a competitor. The firm located in Seattle, close to a large pool of programming talent and near one of the largest book distribution warehouses in the world. Once again you see that a combination of business strategy and technology helped Amazon.com become successful.

Although the Web has made online shopping possible for many businesses and individuals, electronic commerce has existed for many years. For decades, banks have been using **electronic funds transfers** (**EFTs**, also called **wire transfers**) to exchange account information electronically over private communications networks. Businesses also have been engaging in a form of electronic commerce, known as electronic data interchange, for over 20 years. **Electronic data interchange** (**EDI**) occurs when one business transmits computer-readable data in an agreed-upon format to another business. Many large businesses have standardized the format of the paperwork they exchange with each other—such as invoices, purchase orders, and bills of lading—and transmit that information using EDI. Many firms also use EDI to authorize bank transfers instead of writing checks.

Traditional Commerce vs. Electronic Commerce

The origins of commerce occurred before recorded history, when our remote ancestors first decided to specialize their everyday activities. Instead of each family growing its own crops, hunting for its own meat, and making its own tools, families developed skills in one of these areas and traded for their other needs. For example, the tool-making family would exchange tools for grain from the crop-growing family. Services were bought and sold in these primitive economies, too. For example, the tribal spiritualist would cast spells or intercede with the deities in exchange for food and tools. Eventually, cattle and metal coins became accepted as currency, making transactions easier to settle. **Commerce**, or doing business, is a negotiated exchange of valuable objects or services between at least two parties (a buyer and a seller) and includes all activities that each of the parties undertakes to complete the transaction.

Buyer and Seller Roles in Electronic Commerce

Buyers begin the process of commerce by identifying a need. For example, an individual may decide that it is time for a new car, or a business manager may notice that a machine is wearing out. Once buyers have identified their specific needs, they must find products or services that will satisfy those needs. In traditional commerce, buyers use a variety of search techniques. They may consult catalogs, ask friends, read advertisements, or examine directories. The Yellow Pages is a good example of a directory that buyers often use to find products and services. Buyers may consult salespersons to gather information about specific features and capabilities of products they are considering for purchase. Business firms often have highly structured procedures for finding products and services that satisfy recurring needs of the business.

After buyers have selected a product or service that will meet the identified need, they must select a vendor that can supply the desired product or service. Buyers in traditional commerce contact vendors in a variety of ways, including by telephone, by mail, or at trade shows. Once the buyer chooses a vendor, the buyer negotiates a purchase transaction. This transaction may have many elements—such as a delivery date, method of shipment, price, warranty, and payment terms—and will often include detailed specifications the buyer can confirm by inspection when the product is delivered or the service is performed. This inspection process may be a very complicated step. For example, consider the complex ordering, delivery, and inspection logistics that must occur to provide the displays you see in a supermarket's produce section.

When the buyer is satisfied that the purchased product or service has met the terms and conditions agreed to by both buyer and seller, the buyer will pay for the purchase. After the sale is complete, the buyer may have further contact with the seller regarding warranty claims, upgrades, and regular maintenance.

Each action taken by a buyer engaging in commerce has a corresponding action that is taken by a seller. Sellers often undertake market research to identify potential customers' needs. Even businesses that have been selling the same product or service for many years are always looking for ways to improve and expand their offerings. Firms conduct surveys, employ salespersons to talk with customers, run focus groups, and hire outside consultants to help them make decisions during this identification process.

Once a seller identifies potential customer needs, it must then create products and services that can meet those needs. This creation activity includes design, testing, and production activities. Sellers then must make potential customers aware that the new product or service exists. Sellers engage in many different kinds of advertising and promotional activities to communicate information about their products and services to existing and potential customers.

When a customer responds to the seller's promotion activities, the two parties must negotiate the details of a purchase transaction. In some cases, this negotiation is simple. For example, many retail transactions involve nothing more than a buyer entering a seller's store, selecting items to purchase, and paying for them. In other cases, purchase transactions can require prolonged negotiations to settle the terms of delivery, inspection, testing, and acceptance.

After the seller and buyer resolve the logistics and delivery details of the purchase transaction, the seller ships the goods or provides the service and sends an invoice to the buyer. In some businesses, the seller will also provide a monthly billing statement to each customer that summarizes its invoicing and payment activities. In some cases, the seller will require payment before or at the time of shipment. However, most businesses sell to each other on credit, so the seller must keep a record of the sale and wait for the customer to pay. Most businesses maintain sophisticated systems for receiving and processing customer payments; they want to track the amounts they are owed and ensure that the payments they do receive are credited to the proper customer and invoice.

Following the conclusion of the sale transaction, the seller will often provide continuing after-sale support for the product or service. In many cases, the seller is bound by contract or statute to guarantee or warrant that the product or service sold will perform in a satisfactory manner. The seller provides support, maintenance, and warranty work to help ensure that the customer is satisfied and will return to buy again. Figure 1-2 summarizes the steps that buyers and sellers follow when they engage in commerce.

Figure 1-2   **BUYER AND SELLER ROLES IN COMMERCE**

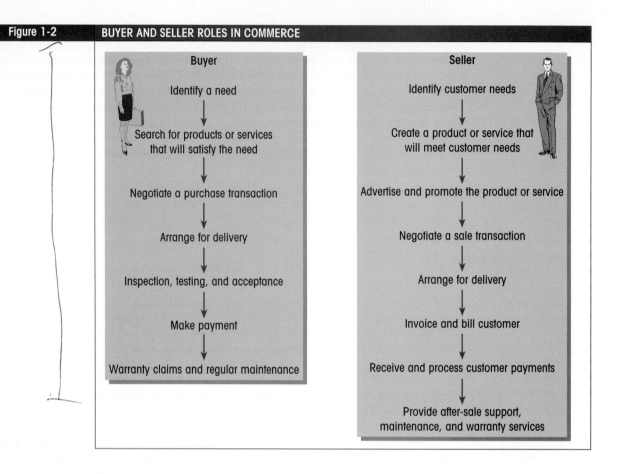

Evolution of Electronic Commerce

The goal of electronic commerce is to use electronic data transmission technologies, primarily those that are part of the Internet and the Web, to improve existing business processes, and to identify new business opportunities. Over the thousands of years that people have conducted business with each other, they have adopted new tools and technologies as they have become available. For example, the advent of sailing ships in ancient times opened new avenues of trade to buyers and sellers. The printing press, the steam engine, and the telephone each changed the way people conducted commerce activities.

The Internet was opened to commercial use during the early 1990s. That time period also saw the development of Web server and Web browser software. By 1995, the rapid growth of the Internet and the Web had combined with the proliferation of personal computers (PCs) in homes and businesses to create a new communications network that could support business transactions as nothing ever had before. These three factors—the commercialization of the Internet, the invention of the Web, and the proliferation of networked PCs—combined to make electronic commerce possible. The number of Web sites is currently estimated to be well over eight million and the number of Web documents over a billion. Each Web site can have hundreds or even thousands of individual Web pages. As more people obtain access to the Web, commercial interest in using the Web to conduct business will increase and the variety of nonbusiness uses will become even greater. Although the Web has already grown very rapidly, many experts believe that it will continue to grow at an increasing rate for the foreseeable future. The emergence of the Internet and the Web as new data communication tools is just another step in the increasing efficiency of business processes.

Reducing Transaction Costs

Many researchers and business managers argue that the main contribution of electronic commerce is to reduce transaction costs. **Transaction costs** are the total of all costs that a buyer and a seller incur as they gather information and negotiate a purchase-sale transaction. Transaction costs include brokerage fees, sales commissions, and the costs of information search and acquisition. Businesses and individuals can use the Web to reduce transaction costs that occur in virtually every step of commerce.

As you examine Figure 1-2, think about how buyers and sellers might use the Web to reduce the cost of each step. For example, buyers might use the Web to search for products more cheaply and efficiently than by making telephone calls, sending faxes, or driving from store to store in hopes of finding the right product at the right price. In fact, some enterprising firms have started services that help buyers find products. One of these firms is Price Watch. You want to upgrade the memory on your home computer, but you have been so busy working on the new series that you have not had time to shop for it. You decide to give Price Watch a try.

To use price comparison Web sites to search for a specific item:

1. Click your browser's **Back** button or use its history list to return to the Online Companion page for Session 1.1, and then click the **Price Watch** hyperlink and wait while your browser loads the Price Watch home page.

2. Click the **System** hyperlink under the Computer Hardware heading and the Memory subheading. Dell manufactured your computer, so you will search for Dell products.

3. Scroll down the list box on the right side of the Web page, click **Dell**, and then click the **...or by brand** button. The Price Watch site returns a list of memory chips for Dell computers that are offered for sale by a variety of vendors. See Figure 1-3. For each item, the search results page shows the brand, product name, description, price, shipping costs, and information about the dealer offering the item. The results page includes a hyperlink to each dealer's site that you can click to make your purchase. The Price Watch site includes information supplied voluntarily by vendors.

| Figure 1-3 | USING THE PRICE WATCH SITE |

BRAND	PRODUCT	DESCRIPTION	PRICE	DOMESTIC Ship/Handling	DATE/HR	DEALER	ST	PART#
Dell	87757MS	64MB DIMM 66MHZ FOR PENTIUM II 333MHZ	$ 64	Unknown??	2/28/00 12:07:13 PM CST	Firesale.com 877.firesale 719-593-1500	CO	87757MS
Dell	311-0688MS	64MB SDRAM NonECC DIMM MODULE	$ 90	Unknown??	12/2/99 1:23:00 PM CST	Firesale.com 877.firesale 719-593-1500	CO	311-0688MS
Dell	128MB PC100 SDRAM	for Dell Dimension XPS T450, T500,	$ 215	6	2/28/00 10:40:32 AM CST	Mohawk Memory Co., Inc. 800-986-6429 -- P.O.'s accepted Online Ordering	MA	DL1664P

Back To Category List   Back To System Memory List

Each row of information is an advertisement entered into the Price Watch database by the respective Dealer, on day and time indicated.

Price not honored? -- tell us

PRICE WATCH is a registered trademark of Price Watch Corporation

Other comparison shopping sites operate their own Web robots (bots) that search the Web and find price information from vendors' Web sites. MySimon is an example of another bot-based comparison shopping site.

4. Click your browser's **Back** button or use its history list to return to the Online Companion page for Session 1.1, and then click the **mySimon** hyperlink and wait while the mySimon home page loads in your Web browser.

5. Click the **Computers & Software** link, and then click the **Memory** link on the next Web page that loads.

6. Type **Dell** in the Model or Keyword text box, and then click the **Go Shop!** button.

7. Examine the search results page and compare these results to those you obtained using the Price Watch site. Depending on the available products at the time of your search, you might find many similar entries.

Within 10 minutes, you found several retailers from which to purchase your memory upgrade. You are happy to find that this part of electronic commerce is something that you can use easily.

You might again examine Figure 1-2 and think about how sellers can use the Web to reduce costs on their side of the purchase transaction. One of the most expensive parts of many sellers' transactions is the provision of after-sale support. After-sale support is especially high for complex technology products, such as computers and electronic equipment. For example, many computer printers use software drivers to translate the information a computer sends to them into printing instructions. As computers improve and new software becomes available, printer manufacturers can update their printer driver software to take advantage of new features and capabilities. The traditional method of providing this software on disk to customers who have purchased printers has always been difficult and expensive for printer manufacturers.

You remember that this morning Ben was complaining that he had just installed some new software on his computer that would not print correctly on his Hewlett-Packard printer. As the newspaper's technology expert, you suggest that he install an updated printer driver from Hewlett-Packard's Web site.

To find printer driver software for a Hewlett-Packard printer:

1. Click your browser's **Back** button or use its history list to return to the Online Companion page for Session 1.1, and then click the **Hewlett-Packard** hyperlink and wait while your browser loads the Hewlett-Packard home page.

2. Click the **HP Services & Support** button near the top of the Web page, and then click the **Drivers** link in the Printing & Digital Imaging section of the next Web page that loads.

3. In the text box under the QUICKFIND heading, type **LaserJet 4000** (the name of Ben's printer), and then click the **GO** button below the text box.

4. On the next Web page that loads, click the **Product Support** hyperlink to the right of the HP LaserJet 4000 link (alternatively, you could click the Software & Drivers hyperlink to go directly to the LaserJet 4000 printer software page). After a few moments, the page shown in Figure 1-4 opens. This page provides links to a number of helpful information resources that Hewlett-Packard customers can use to help themselves without needing to call a Hewlett-Packard representative during business hours or wait for a disk to arrive in the mail. Hewlett-Packard must provide people and resources for these activities to occur.

Figure 1-4	HEWLETT-PACKARD AFTER-SALE CUSTOMER SUPPORT

5. Close your browser and close your dial-up connection, if necessary.

You stop by Ben's office and show him how to use the Hewlett-Packard site to find the printer driver he needs. A short time later, Ben has downloaded and installed the updated printer driver, and his new software is working with the printer.

International Nature of Electronic Commerce

Many of the advantages that electronic commerce offers arise from its ability to reduce transaction costs. By making communication quick and inexpensive, technology makes commerce less expensive for both businesses and individuals. In addition to being inexpensive and easy to use, the Internet and the Web also offer people an unprecedented degree of geographic reach. The Internet brings people together from every country in the world because it reduces the distances between people in many ways. The predominant language on the Web is English, although sites in other languages and in multiple languages are appearing with increasing frequency. Once a business overcomes the language barrier, the technology exists for it to conduct electronic commerce with any other business or consumer, anywhere in the world.

Unfortunately, the political structures of the world have not kept up with Internet technology, so doing business internationally presents a number of challenges. Currency conversions, tariffs, import and export restrictions, local business customs, and the laws of each country in which a trading partner resides can all make international electronic commerce difficult. Many of the international issues that arise relate to legal, tax, and privacy concerns. Each country has the right to pass laws and levy taxes on businesses that operate within its jurisdiction. European countries, for example, have very strict laws that limit the collection and use of personal information that companies gather in the course of doing business with consumers. Even within the United States, individual states and counties have the power to levy sales and use taxes on goods and services. In other countries, national sales and value-added taxes are imposed on an even more comprehensive list of business activities. In Tutorial 6, you will learn more about the legal, tax, and privacy issues that can arise when conducting electronic commerce.

Value Chains in Electronic Commerce

As you interview businesspersons for your electronic commerce column, you find that electronic commerce includes so many activities that some managers find it difficult to decide where and how to use electronic commerce in their businesses. One way to focus on specific business processes as candidates for electronic commerce is to break the business down into a series of value-adding activities that combine to generate profits and meet other goals of the firm. Firms of all sizes conduct commerce. Smaller firms can focus on one product, distribution channel, or type of customer. Larger firms often sell many different products and services through a variety of distribution channels to several types of customers. In these larger firms, managers organize their work around the activities of strategic business units. A **strategic business unit**, or simply a **business unit**, is one particular combination of product, distribution channel, and customer type. A company can have many business units.

Strategic Business Unit Value Chains

In his 1985 book, *Competitive Advantage*, Michael Porter introduced the idea of value chains. A **value chain** is a way of organizing the activities that each strategic business unit undertakes. Although value chain analysts differ somewhat on how they classify activities, most break them into two categories—primary activities and supporting activities. A business unit's **primary activities** include designing, purchasing, producing, promoting, marketing, delivering, and providing after-sale support for its products or services. The unit's **supporting activities**, such as finance and accounting, human resource management, and technology development, are supplied to each of the primary activities. For example, people in the accounting department keep track of manufacturing costs, but they do not help build the product. Figure 1-5 shows the primary activities in a value chain for a strategic business unit.

Figure 1-5   PRIMARY ACTIVITIES IN A BUSINESS UNIT VALUE CHAIN

The left-to-right flow in Figure 1-5 does not imply a strict time sequence for these processes. For example, a business unit may engage in marketing activities before purchasing materials and supplies. For each business unit, the primary activities include:

■ *Identifying customers*: Activities that help the firm find new customers and new ways to serve old customers, including market research and customer satisfaction surveys.

- *Marketing and selling*: Activities that give buyers a way to purchase and provide inducements for them to do so, including advertising, promotion, managing salespersons, pricing, and identifying and monitoring sales and distribution channels.
- *Designing*: Activities that take a product from concept to manufacturing, including concept research, engineering, and test marketing.
- *Purchasing materials and supplies*: Vendor selection, qualification, negotiating long-term supply contracts, and monitoring quality and timeliness of delivery.
- *Manufacturing or providing service*: Activities that transform materials and labor into finished products, including fabrication, assembly, finishing, testing, and packaging. In a service business, these activities provide the service to the customer.
- *Delivering*: Activities that store, distribute, and ship the final product, including warehousing, materials handling, freight consolidation, selecting shippers, and monitoring timeliness of delivery.
- *Providing after-sale service and support*: Activities that provide a continuing relationship with the customer, including installation, testing, maintenance, repair, warranty replacement, and replacement parts.

Each business unit must also undertake activities that support the unit's primary activities. These support activities include:

- *Finance and administration*: Activities that provide the firm's basic infrastructure, including accounting, bill payment, borrowing funds, reporting to government regulators, and ensuring compliance with relevant laws.
- *Human resources*: Activities that coordinate the management of employees, including recruiting, hiring, training, compensation, and provision of benefits.
- *Developing technologies*: Activities that help improve the product or service the firm is selling and that help improve the business processes in every primary activity, including basic research, applied research and development, process improvement studies, and field tests of maintenance procedures.

Industry Value Chains

Porter's book also identified the importance of examining where the strategic business unit fits within its industry. Porter used the term **value system** to describe the larger stream of activities into which a particular business unit's value chain is embedded. However, many researchers and business consultants use the term **industry value chain** instead. When a business unit delivers a product to its customer, that customer may, for example, use the product as a part of its own value chain as purchased materials.

By becoming aware of how other business units in the industry value chain conduct their activities, managers can identify new opportunities for cost reductions or product improvements. Recall that Jeff Bezos carefully examined the book industry's value chain (shown in Figure 1-6) when he was planning the future of Amazon.com.

Figure 1-6 | **BOOK INDUSTRY VALUE CHAIN**

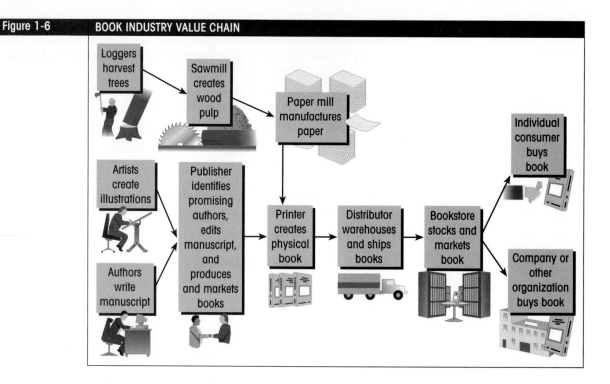

Bezos chose to use electronic commerce in a very specific part of the book industry value chain—the bookstore that sells books to consumers. His analysis showed that this part of the industry would be the easiest to improve with the technology that existed when he was making his plans in 1994.

As technology changed, new opportunities opened for other companies in the book industry. For example, **Fatbrain.com** began business (as CBooks Express) about one year after Amazon.com began selling books. Fatbrain.com originally targeted the same part of the industry value chain as Amazon.com; however, Fatbrain.com developed a reputation for having an excellent selection of computer, technical, and business books. Realizing that this book market segment was very attractive to businesses that purchased books for their employees, Fatbrain.com decided to focus on corporate customers. For example, one difference between Fatbrain.com and Amazon.com is that Fatbrain.com makes its books available at discounted prices on large companies' intranets.

More recently, Fatbrain.com has identified opportunities in the publisher, printer, and distributor elements of the book industry supply chain. Its eMatter electronic commerce initiative lets individuals and companies publish and sell their work in secure digital format via the Web. The Fatbrain.com home page site appears in Figure 1-7.

Figure 1-7	FATBRAIN.COM HOME PAGE

Disintermediation and Reintermediation

The strategies of both Amazon.com and Fatbrain.com are to remove and replace existing participants in the book industry value chain. Because most of the companies that participate in an industry value chain occupy an intermediate step between the manufacturer and the final consumer, they are called **intermediaries**. The process of one company removing another company from the industry value chain is called **disintermediation**. When a company enters the value chain with a new way of providing value to the other participants in the value chain, it is called **reintermediation**. For example, if Amazon.com displaces sales from neighborhood bookstores and forces the neighborhood bookstores to close, Amazon.com will have disintermediated those bookstores. By taking the place of the bookstores in the industry value chain, Amazon.com will have reintermediated itself into the book industry value chain.

Disintermediation can affect individual employees of companies as well as the companies themselves. For example, persons employed in the sale of autos, travel services, and securities are all facing the prospect of being laid off from their jobs as electronic commerce Web sites offer many of the same services they provide. Of course, these Web sites offer many new jobs for persons who have the necessary technical skills and business knowledge to create and build them.

Advantages and Disadvantages of Electronic Commerce

To be successful in electronic commerce, managers must identify the business processes that they can accomplish more effectively by using electronic commerce technologies. Some business processes use traditional commerce activities very effectively, and technology cannot improve them. Products that buyers prefer to touch, smell, or examine closely are difficult to sell using electronic commerce. For example, customers might not want to buy high-fashion clothing or perishable food products if they cannot examine the products closely before purchasing them.

Retail merchants have years of experience in store design, layout, and product display knowledge. This knowledge is called **merchandising**. Many salespeople have developed ways of identifying customer needs and matching products or services to those needs. Merchandising and personal selling can be difficult to practice over an electronic link.

Branded merchandise and products, such as books or CDs, can be sold easily using electronic commerce. Because one copy of a new book is identical to other copies, and because the customer is not concerned about fit, freshness, or other qualities, customers are willing to order a book without examining the specific copy they will receive. The advantages of electronic commerce, including the ability of one site to offer a wider selection of titles than even the largest physical bookstore, can outweigh the advantages of a traditional bookstore, such as the customer's ability to browse. In later tutorials, you will learn how to evaluate the advantages and disadvantages of using electronic commerce for specific business processes.

Figure 1-8 lists 12 examples of business processes. Four of these are well suited to electronic commerce, four are suited to a combination of electronic commerce and traditional commerce, and four are less suited to electronic commerce. Of course, these classifications depend on the current state of available technologies and thus may change as new tools for implementing electronic commerce emerge.

Figure 1-8	BUSINESS PROCESS SUITABILITY TO ELECTRONIC COMMERCE	
Well-Suited to Electronic Commerce	**Suited to a Combination of Electronic and Traditional Commerce Strategies**	**Less Suited to Electronic Commerce**
Sale/purchase of books and CDs	Sale/purchase of automobiles	Sale/purchase of high-fashion clothing
Online delivery of software	Online banking	Sale/purchase of perishable food products
Travel services	Roommate-matching services	Small-denomination transactions
Online shipment tracking	Sale/purchase of investment and insurance products	Sales of high-value jewelry and antiques

Advantages of Electronic Commerce

Your research and interviews with managers have convinced you that companies are interested in electronic commerce because, quite simply, it can help increase profits. You can summarize all of the advantages of electronic commerce for business entities in one statement: Electronic commerce can increase sales and decrease costs. For example, advertising on the Web can send a small firm's message to every country in the world. A firm can use electronic commerce to reach narrow market segments that are widely scattered geographically. The Internet and the Web are particularly useful in creating virtual communities that become ideal market targets.

A business can reduce the costs of handling sales inquiries, providing price quotes, and determining product availability by using electronic commerce in its sales support and order-taking processes. In 1998, **Cisco Systems** sold 72% of its computer equipment via the Web. Because no customer service representatives were involved in these sales, Cisco estimates that it avoided handling 500,000 calls per month for an annual savings of over $500 million.

Just as electronic commerce increases sales opportunities for the seller, it also increases purchasing opportunities for the buyer. Businesses can use electronic commerce in their purchasing processes to identify new suppliers and business partners. Negotiating price and delivery terms is easier because the Web can provide competitive bid information very efficiently. Electronic commerce increases the speed and accuracy with which businesses can exchange information, which reduces costs on both sides of transactions.

Electronic commerce provides consumers with a wider range of choices than traditional commerce because consumers can consider many different products and services from a wider variety of sellers. Consumers can evaluate their options 24 hours a day, every day. Some consumers prefer a great deal of information to use in deciding on a purchase; others prefer less. Electronic commerce provides consumers with an easy way to customize the level of detail in the information they obtain about a prospective purchase. Instead of waiting days for the mail to bring a catalog or product specification sheet, or even minutes for a fax transmission, consumers can have instant access to detailed information on the Web. Some products, such as software, audio clips, or images, can even be delivered via the Internet, which reduces the time customers must wait to begin enjoying their purchases.

The benefits of electronic commerce also extend to the general welfare of society. Electronic payments of tax refunds, public retirement, and welfare support cost less to issue and arrive securely and quickly when transmitted via the Internet. Furthermore, electronic payments can be easier to audit and monitor than payments made by check, helping protect against fraud and theft losses. To the extent that electronic commerce enables people to work from home, we all benefit from the reduction in commuter-caused traffic and pollution. Electronic commerce can make products and services available in remote areas. For example, distance education is making it possible for people to learn skills and earn degrees no matter where they live or which hours they have available to study.

Disadvantages of Electronic Commerce

As you begin to write your first column in the electronic commerce series, you realize that some business processes may never lend themselves to electronic commerce. For example, unique and high-cost items, such as jewelry or antiques, may continue to be difficult to inspect from a remote location. Most of the disadvantages of electronic commerce today, however, stem from the newness and rapidly developing pace of the underlying technologies. These disadvantages will disappear as electronic commerce matures and becomes more available to and accepted by the general population. Many products and services require that a critical mass of potential buyers be equipped and willing to buy via the Internet.

Another example of a technology problem on the Web today is that the color settings on computer monitors vary widely. Clothing retailers find it difficult to give customers an accurate idea of what a product's color will look like when it arrives. Most online clothing stores will send a fabric swatch on request, which also gives the customer a sense of the fabric's texture. As technology improves, this disadvantage will become less of an issue.

Businesses often calculate their potential profits before committing to any new technology. These calculations have been difficult to perform for investments in electronic commerce because the costs and benefits have been hard to quantify. Technology costs can change dramatically during electronic commerce implementation projects because the technologies can change so rapidly.

Many firms have trouble recruiting and retaining employees with the technological, design, and business process skills needed to create an effective electronic commerce presence. Another problem facing firms that want to do business on the Internet is the difficulty of integrating existing databases and transaction-processing software designed for traditional commerce into the software that enables electronic commerce.

In addition to the technology and software issues, many businesses face cultural and legal impediments to electronic commerce. Some consumers are still afraid to send their credit card numbers over the Internet. Other consumers are simply resistant to change and are uncomfortable viewing merchandise on a computer screen rather than in person. The legal environment in which electronic commerce is conducted is full of unclear and conflicting laws. In many cases, government regulators have not kept up with technologies. Laws that govern commerce were written when signed documents were a reasonable expectation in any business transaction. As more businesses and individuals find the benefits of electronic commerce to be compelling, many of these technology and culture-related disadvantages will disappear.

Session 1.1 QUICK CHECK

1. True or False: Businesses have been engaging in a form of electronic commerce called EDI for over 20 years.

2. What three factors combined to make electronic commerce possible?

3. How might using a price comparison site such as Price Watch or mySimon reduce a buyer's transaction costs?

4. Name three factors that might make international electronic commerce difficult.

5. What activities are included in the primary value chain category of "market and sell?"

6. True or False: Reintermediation occurs when a manufacturer stops selling through its distributors and begins selling directly to consumers through its Web site.

7. Name three ways in which electronic commerce can improve the general welfare of society.

SESSION 1.2

In this session, you will learn about some of the ways that companies conduct business using electronic commerce. Some firms have identified ways of adapting their existing selling and buying operations to the Web. Other firms have drastically changed the way they sell and buy. Some firms have created entirely new business models—businesses that would not have been possible just five or six years ago—using electronic commerce.

Selling on the Web

As you continue your research into businesses that sell on the Web, you decide to classify these companies into several different categories. Some sites sell goods and services, much like their retail counterparts. Other sites sell services of some kind, such as legal and business information or digital publications.

You also decide to classify e-commerce sites based on how they collect revenue. For example, some sites include advertisements. Often, these sites provide information or services to visitors at no charge. The revenues received from advertisers support the operation of the site. A variation of the advertising-supported site is one that runs some advertising to generate revenue but also charges visitors a subscription fee. The final category is where the site collects a fee for the product or service offered at the Web site. For example, online travel agencies collect fees from airlines, car rental companies, and hotels.

Selling Goods and Services

For many companies, selling goods and services on the Web is a logical extension of their mail order catalog businesses that predate the Web. Sellers establish brand images that convey quality, and then use the strength of those images to sell through catalogs mailed to prospective buyers. Buyers place orders by mail or by calling sellers' toll-free telephone numbers. Many firms that sell consumer goods such as apparel, computers, electronics, and gifts have used mail order catalogs in the past and now use the Web to sell in much the same way.

Many of the most successful Web catalog sales businesses are firms that were in the mail order business and have simply expanded their operations to the Web. One reason these firms have been successful is that they already have the order fulfillment activities—warehousing, purchasing, and delivery—up and running to service their mail order businesses. Leading PC manufacturers such as Dell and **Gateway** have had great success in adapting their mail and telephone ordering operations to selling on the Web.

To explore the Dell Web site:

1. Start your Web browser, and then go to the Online Companion page by entering the URL **http://www.course.com/NewPerspectives/EC** in the appropriate location of your Web browser. Click the **Tutorial 1** link, and then click the **Session 1.2** link. Click the **Dell** link and wait while your browser loads the Dell Computer home page shown in Figure 1-9. This page offers links to customized Web pages for several different types of customers, including individuals, small businesses, larger businesses, healthcare businesses, governmental agencies, and schools. Each of these customer types has specific needs that are different from the other customer types. Dell's Web site includes customized interfaces for each customer type.

Figure 1-9   DELL COMPUTER HOME PAGE

hyperlinks to customized Web pages

2. Click the **Medium & Large Business** hyperlink to open the Dell Business Center Web page. Note that this page offers links to pages that describe servers, workstations, and storage. These three links do not appear on the Home & Home Office page because they are primarily of interest to Dell's larger business customers.

3. Click the **What is Premier?** hyperlink on the left side of the page, and then browse the links on the page that opens to learn more about Dell's Premier Pages program. Dell uses this feature to create a customized page for each of its largest customers to make it easy for them to order computers, replacement parts, and upgrades. Dell has over 10,000 of these pages and makes over 40% of its sales—over $5 million per day—through these pages.

4. After you have examined the links and learned how the Premier Pages program works, click your browser's **Back** button twice to return to the Dell Computer home page.

5. Browse the other pages on the site to find out what other differences exist between the customized pages Dell offers its various customer groups. Dell has been a leader in allowing customers to specify exactly the configuration of computers they order via the Web. Dell has created value by designing its entire business around offering this high degree of configuration flexibility to its customers. As you can see, Dell's Web site emphasizes this flexibility.

Many apparel sellers have moved their catalog sales approaches to the Web, including **Lands' End** and **L.L. Bean**. In the fast-changing world of fashion, retailers have always had to deal with the problem of overstocks—products that did not sell as well as hoped. Many retailers use outlet stores to sell their overstocks. Lands' End has found that its online overstocks page has worked so well that it is closing many of its outlet stores.

Selling Information or Other Digital Content

Firms that own intellectual property or rights to that property have embraced the Web as a new and highly efficient distribution mechanism. LEXIS-NEXIS has been an important legal research tool that has been available as an online product for years. LEXIS-NEXIS provides full-text search of court cases, laws, patent databases, and tax regulations. To obtain access to this information in the past, law firms had to subscribe to this service and install expensive, dedicated computer systems. The Web has given LEXIS-NEXIS customers much more flexibility in how they purchase information. Through the **LEXIS-NEXIS Xchange** Web site, law firms can subscribe to one of several different versions of the service, which they can customize to match their firms' sizes and usage patterns. The site even offers a credit card charge option for infrequent users who do not want a subscription. LEXIS-NEXIS has used the Web to improve the delivery and variety of its existing product line and has been able to devise new products that take advantage of the Web's features.

ProQuest, a Web site that sells digital copies of published documents, has its roots in two businesses, the former Bell and Howell learning materials business and University Microfilms International (UMI). These firms had acquired reproduction rights to a variety of published and unpublished materials. For example, UMI had contracts with most North American universities to publish all doctoral dissertations and masters theses on demand. ProQuest sells digital versions of these documents, as well as documents from newspapers, journals, and other specialized academic publications. Many schools and libraries have subscriptions to ProQuest.

Dow Jones Interactive is a business-focused seller of subscriptions to digitized newspaper, magazine, and journal content. The Dow Jones Interactive site offers a customized digital clipping service that provides subscribers with daily e-mail messages with news on topics of interest to them.

To learn more about subscription-based Web sites:

1. Click your browser's **Back** button or use its history list to return to the Online Companion page for Session 1.2, and then click the **Dow Jones Interactive** hyperlink and wait while your Web browser loads the Dow Jones Interactive home page.

2. Click the **About Dow Jones Interactive** hyperlink to view the components of the Dow Jones services offered on this site.

3. Click the **CustomClips** hyperlink to open a page of information about that service. One useful service offered by Dow Jones is its CustomClips service. Businesspersons can have Dow Jones send them headlines and the full text of articles that are important to them.

4. To find out what this service costs, click your browser's **Back** button, click the **Quick Links** list arrow, click **Pricing Information**, and then click the **Single-User Pricing** link. The Single-User (Standard) Pricing page includes the prices for each service. Most people who use this service work for companies or schools that purchase a package of combined services for a fixed monthly fee.

As was the case for other technologies, such as VCRs and subscription cable television, many of the early commercial adopters of Web technology were dealers in adult-themed entertainment material. Many of the first profitable sites on the Web were sellers of adult digital content. These sites pioneered the processing of credit card payment transactions and many different types of digital video technologies that are now used by many types of businesses on the Web.

Encyclopædia Britannica is a company that has attempted to transfer an existing information business to the Web. Encyclopædia Britannica began in 1768 as a sort of pre-computer age frequently asked questions (FAQ) list. A group of professors collected notes they had made while conducting research and decided to publish them as a series of articles. Over 200 years later, the Encyclopædia Britannica opened for business on the Web. Originally, the firm had two Web-based offerings: the Britannica Internet Guide, a free Web navigation aid that classifies and rates thousands of information-laden Web sites, and the Encyclopædia Britannica Online, an online subscription. In 1999, disappointed by low subscription sales, the company converted to a free, advertiser-supported site. The first day the new site became available at no cost to the public, it had over 15 million visitors, forcing it to shut down for two weeks to upgrade its servers. The Britannica.com site now offers the full content of the print edition in searchable form, plus access to the *Merriam-Webster's Collegiate Dictionary* and the *Britannica Book of the Year*. One of the most successful aspects of the new site is the way it integrates the Web-rating service with its print content.

To examine the Britannica Web site's integration features:

1. Click your browser's **Back** button or use its history list to return to the Online Companion page for Session 1.2, and then click the **Britannica.com** hyperlink and wait while your browser loads the Britannica.com home page. If an advertiser's pop-up window opens, click its **Close** button to dismiss it.

2. Click the **History** subject heading, and then wait for the History page to open and display subject subheadings including People, Places, U.S. History, Women's History, and others.

3. Point to the **History** subject heading. When you point to a subject heading, a menu opens and displays hyperlinks to The Web's Best Sites, and for some of the subject headings, Encyclopædia Britannica and News & Features (see Figure 1-10). You can also point to a subject subheading to open similar menus that display hyperlinks to content related to each subheading. This interface element integrates the site's resources under common subject headings, aiding user access.

Figure 1-10   **BRITANNICA.COM HISTORY PAGE**

search expression text box

hyperlink to advanced search features

subject headings

menu opens and displays hyperlinks for each subject heading

subject subheadings for History

4. Follow some of the links to see how the Britannica content is organized on the site, and then click your browser's **Back** button to return to the Britannica.com home page. Many people who use Britannica.com are experienced researchers. These users can click the ADVANCED SEARCH button to open the Britannica.com Advanced Search page. Because advertising now supports the site, you will notice advertising banners on the pages and a STORE button, which opens Britannica's online sales outlet.

Advertising-Supported Web Sites

You are already familiar with a popular advertising-supported medium—network television broadcasters in the United States provide free programming to an audience along with advertising messages. The advertising revenue is sufficient to support network operations and the creation of the programs. Two major problems have hampered the success of Web advertising. First, no consensus has emerged on how to measure and charge for site visitor views. Newspapers and magazines have circulation numbers on which they can base their advertising charges. Television and radio stations are rated by outside agencies (Neilsen and Arbitron, respectively) that estimate the size of their audiences. The Web allows measurements of number of visitors, number of unique visitors, number of page loads, number of click-throughs, and other attributes of visitor behavior. Thus, Web sites and their advertisers have been unable to agree on a standard way of measuring and charging for audience size.

In addition to large numbers of visitors and page views, advertising-supported Web sites try to develop stickiness. The **stickiness** of a Web site is its ability to keep visitors at the site and to attract repeat visitors. People spend more time at a **sticky** Web site and are thus exposed to more advertising. In general, sticky Web sites can generate more advertising revenue than non-sticky Web sites.

The second problem is that very few Web sites have sufficient numbers of visitors to interest large advertisers. Most successful advertising on the Web is targeted to very specific groups. However, it can be difficult to determine whether a given Web site is attracting a specific market segment unless that site collects demographic information from its visitors—information that visitors are increasingly reluctant to provide because of privacy concerns.

Only a few general-interest sites have generated sufficient traffic to be profitable based on advertising revenue alone. One of these is **Yahoo!**, which was one of the first Web directories. Because so many people use Yahoo! as a starting point for searching the Web, Yahoo! has always attracted a large number of visitors. This large number of visitors made it possible for Yahoo! to take its directory and convert it to one of the first Web portal sites. A **Web portal** is a site that seeks to be the doorway to the Internet for its visitors. Web portals usually include search engines, directories, free e-mail, chat rooms, and other free features designed to attract a large number of visitors who begin their Web surfing at that site. Because the Yahoo! portal's search engine presents visitors' search results on separate pages, it can include advertising based on the terms in the search on each results page. For example, when the Yahoo! search engine detects that a visitor is searching using the phrase "new car deals," it can place a Ford ad at the top of the search results page. Ford might be willing to pay more for this ad because it is directed only at visitors who have expressed interest in new cars. Because this is one way of identifying a target market audience without collecting demographic information from site visitors, it is an attractive option. Unfortunately, only a few high-traffic sites are able to generate significant advertising revenues this way. Besides Yahoo!, the main portal sites in this market today are **Excite**, **Infoseek**, and **Lycos**. Smaller general-interest sites, such as Bob Drudge's **refdesk.com** site, have had much more difficulty attracting advertisers than the larger search engine sites. The lack of advertising support for smaller sites may change in the future as more people use the Web.

Newspaper publishers have experimented with various ways of establishing a profitable presence on the Web. It is unclear whether a newspaper's presence on the Web helps or hurts the newspaper business as a whole. Although it provides greater exposure for the newspaper brand and provides a larger audience for advertising than the paper carries, providing news content on the Web also can take away sales from the print edition in a process called **cannibalization**. Newspapers and other publishers worry about cannibalization because it is very difficult to measure. Some publishers have conducted surveys in which they ask people whether they have stopped buying the newspaper because the contents they want to see are available online, but the results of such surveys are not very reliable. Many leading newspapers, including **The Washington Post** and **The Los Angeles Times**, have established online presences in the hopes that they will generate enough revenue from advertising to cover the cost of creating and maintaining the Web site.

Although attempts to create general-interest Web sites that generate sufficient advertising revenue to be profitable have met with mixed results, sites that target niche markets have been more successful. For newspapers, classified advertising is very profitable, so Web sites that provide classified advertising have profit potential even if they reach only a narrow market.

Web employment advertising also shows potential for success. Web sites such as **CareerSite.com** and **JOBTRAK.COM** can advertise employment opportunities that are seen by people around the world—an advantage not offered by traditional classified ads. These sites can offer advertisers target markets, just as search engines do. For example, when a visitor specifies an interest in engineering jobs in Dallas, the results page can include a targeted banner ad for which an advertiser will pay more because it is directed at a specific audience segment. You decide that the business of advertising and finding jobs on the Web would be a nice addition to your electronic commerce column and decide to investigate one of the major job ad sites.

To learn how Monster.com attracts qualified job candidates to its site:

1. Click your browser's **Back** button or use its history list to return to the Online Companion page for Session 1.2, and then click the **Monster.com** hyperlink and wait while your browser loads the Monster.com home page. In addition to the content you would expect to see on an employment advertising Web site—

hyperlinks to job ads and resume storage—the Monster.com home page includes hyperlinks to information about companies that may be potential employers and hyperlinks to career resources that you might find worthwhile even if you are not looking for a job.

2. Click the **Career Center** link near the top of the page. The Career Center page opens with links to resources for creating a resume and for finding employment opportunities in different fields.

3. Click the drop-down list arrow near the top of the page, scroll down the list and click **Internships,** and then click the **Search** button. The page shown in Figure 1-11 includes hyperlinks to a number of articles on the Monster.com site that include information about internships.

Figure 1-11   **MONSTER.COM CAREER ADVICE SEARCH RESULTS PAGE**

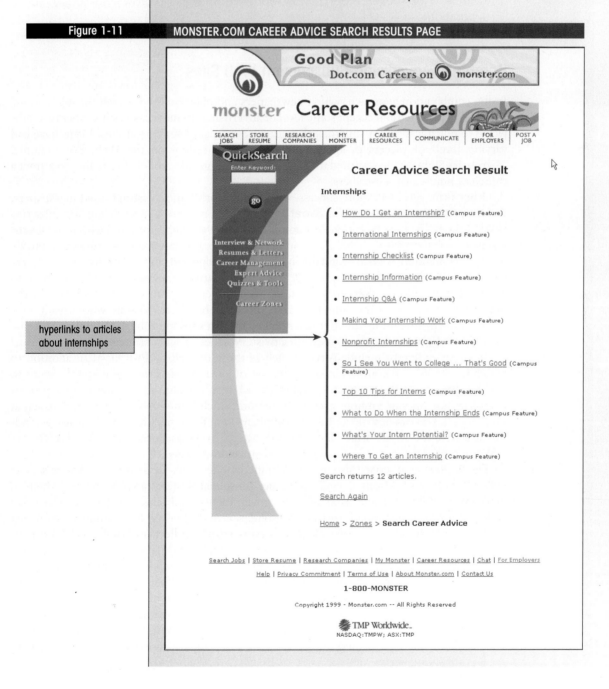

hyperlinks to articles about internships

4. Follow some of the links to see what kind of information Monster.com provides about internships, and then click your browser's **Back** button to return to the Monster.com home page.

5. Scroll to the bottom of the home page, and then click the **Research Companies** hyperlink. The Research Companies page opens and includes links to employers' Web sites.

6. In the Company Profiles by Alphabet section, click the **A** hyperlink to open a page of logos for companies whose names begin with the letter "A."

7. Click one of the logos to open that company's profile. Monster.com offers companies free space to display their logo and profile on the site. This added value to job seekers is part of how Monster.com works to draw high-quality job candidates to its site.

Combined Advertising-Subscription Web Sites

In the combination approach, which newspapers and magazines have used for many years, subscribers pay a fee and accept some level of advertising. In most cases, subscribers are subjected to much less advertising than they are on advertising-supported sites. Firms have had varying levels of success in applying this model to selling on the Web. For example, Microsoft's **Slate** e-zine returned to using an advertising-only model after failing to attract a sufficient number of subscribers.

Other firms have had more success. Two of the world's most distinguished newspapers, **The New York Times** and **The Wall Street Journal**, use a mixture of advertising and subscription revenue. *The New York Times* version is mostly advertising supported with a small subscription fee for visitors who want online access to the newspaper's crossword puzzle feature. Its premium service originally included the bridge and chess columns, but these services are now free to any site visitor. *The Wall Street Journal* relies more on subscription revenue. The site allows all visitors to view the classified ads and certain stories from the newspaper, but most of the content is reserved for subscribers. Visitors who already subscribe to the print edition are offered a reduced rate on subscriptions to the online edition.

Northern Light is a search engine with a twist. Northern Light's strategy extends the usual Web search engine to include services such as those offered by ProQuest. In addition to searching the Web, it searches its own database of journal articles and other publications to which it has acquired reproduction rights. Search results from the Northern Light proprietary database provide bibliographic information, which sometimes includes an abstract, at no charge. Users can download the full text of any item for a small fee, which varies depending on where the article originally appeared. Alternatively, users can subscribe though several different plans that offer free or reduced-price downloads.

The **Reuters** wire service also uses a combined model in its Web offerings. A wire service collects news reports from around the globe, consolidates these reports, and sells them to newspapers, radio and television stations, governments, and large companies. The value added by a wire service is information consolidation and filtering. For example, a company might want a wire service to provide it with every story it collects on itself and its competitors. Reuters provides some news headlines on its site, but it refers Web visitors to its subscribers, including Yahoo!, Lycos, Infoseek, and C-NET, through links on its headlines page.

Sports fans visit the **ESPN** site for all types of sports-related information. Leveraging its brand name from its cable television businesses, ESPN is one of the most-visited sites on the Web. ESPN sells advertising and offers a vast amount of free information, but die-hard fans can subscribe to its Insider service to obtain access to even more sports information. You decide to include a column in your series about sports because many of the newspaper's readers are sports fans.

To learn more about ESPN's Insider service:

1. Click your browser's **Back** button or use its history list to return to the Online Companion page for Session 1.2, and then click the **ESPN** hyperlink and wait while your browser loads the ESPN home page.

2. Click the **INSIDER** hyperlink located near the top of the Web page. The ESPN Insider page opens.

3. Click the **BENEFITS** hyperlink. Figure 1-12 shows the page that describes the features of the ESPN Insider service.

Figure 1-12	ESPN INSIDER SERVICE

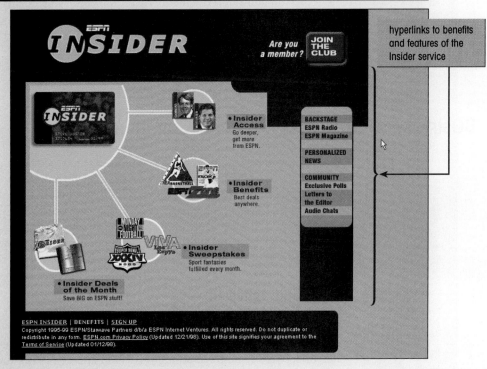

hyperlinks to benefits and features of the Insider service

Fee-for-Transaction Web Sites

Travel agents earn commissions on each airplane ticket, hotel reservation, auto rental, or cruise that they book. The transportation or lodging provider pays these commissions to the travel agent. The travel agency business model involves receiving a fee for facilitating a transaction. The value added by a travel agent is that of information consolidation and filtering. A good travel agent knows a lot about travel destinations and knows enough about the traveler to select the information elements that will be useful and valuable to the traveler. Computers, and particularly computers networked to large databases, are very good at information consolidation and filtering. In fact, travel agents have used networked computers, such as the **Sabre Group** systems, for many years to make reservations for their customers.

When the Internet emerged as a new way to network computers and then became available to commercial users, many online travel agencies began conducting business using the Web. Existing travel agencies did not, in general, rush to the new medium. They believed that a Web site could not replace the key value they added—personal customer service. Therefore, the first

Web-based travel agencies were new entrants. One of these sites, **Travelocity**, uses the same Sabre system that traditional travel agents use. Microsoft has entered the online travel agency business with its **Expedia** site. In addition to earning commissions from the transportation and lodging providers, these sites generate advertising revenue from ads placed on their travel information pages. These ads are similar to those on search engine results pages because they can be targeted without obtaining demographic details about the site visitor.

Auto dealers buy cars from the manufacturer and sell them to consumers. They provide showrooms and salespeople to help customers learn about product features, arrange financing, and make a purchase decision. **Autobytel.com** and other firms will locate dealers in the buyer's area that are willing to sell cars for a small premium over the dealer's cost. The buyer can purchase the car from the dealer without negotiating its price with a salesperson. Autobytel charges participating dealers a fee for this service. Autobytel is disintermediating the salesperson and reintermediating itself into the value chain. The consumer spends less time buying the car and often pays a lower price; the dealer pays a fee to Autobytel that is lower than the commission it would otherwise pay to its salesperson.

Stock brokerage firms also use a fee-for-transaction model. They charge their customers a commission for each trade executed. Online brokers are replacing traditional brokerage firms by offering trading over the Web.

Business-to-Business Electronic Commerce

You are going over your story ideas for another electronic commerce column with Ben and mention that businesses are increasingly using electronic commerce to improve their primary activities of purchasing and delivery, and all of their support activities. You explain to Ben that, at first glance, none of these business elements may seem as exciting as marketing and selling to customers on the Web; however, the potential for cost reduction in these business-to-business transactions is tremendous. You are convinced that a column on business-to-business electronic commerce would appeal to many of the newspaper's readers.

Purchasing Activities

Purchasing activities include identifying vendors, evaluating vendors, selecting specific products, placing orders, and resolving any issues that arise after receiving the ordered goods or services. These issues might include late deliveries, incorrect quantities shipped, incorrect items shipped, and defective items. By monitoring all relevant elements of purchase transactions, purchasing managers can play an important role in maintaining and improving product quality and reducing cost.

Many managers use the term *procurement* instead of purchasing to distinguish the broader range of responsibilities. **Procurement** generally includes all purchasing activities plus the monitoring of all elements of purchase transactions. It also includes the job of managing and developing relationships with key suppliers. In many cases, procurement department staff must have high levels of product knowledge. Specialized Web purchasing sites can be particularly useful in these situations.

A number of manufacturers dealing in general industrial merchandise and standard machine tools used in a variety of industries have created Web sites through which businesses can purchase to fulfill recurring needs. Many of the products that companies buy on a recurring basis are **commodities**; that is, standard items that buyers usually select using price as their main criterion. These products are often called **maintenance, repair, and operating (MRO)** supplies. By using a Web site to process orders, the vendors in this market can save the cost of printing and shipping catalogs, and the cost of handling telephone orders. Some industry analysts estimate that the cost to process an MRO order through a Web site can be less than one-tenth the cost of handling the same order by telephone.

One of the largest MRO suppliers in the world is W.W. Grainger. Its Web site, Grainger.com, offers over 500,000 products for sale. In 1999, Milacron opened its MILPRO Web site to sell MRO items such as cutting tools, grinding wheels, and manufacturing fluids. Milacron has experienced difficulty in effectively reaching one of its key markets—over 100,000 widely scattered machine and job shops—and hopes to reach that market through its Web presence. Milacron accepts credit card payments for purchases made using its Web site, which is very unusual for an industrial products vendor. You know that many readers of The Daily Metropolitan manage or work in businesses that use machine tools, so you decide to investigate the MILPRO site for a future column.

To examine Milacron's MILPRO MRO site:

1. Click your browser's **Back** button or use its history list to return to the Online Companion page for Session 1.2, and then click the **MILPRO** hyperlink and wait while your browser loads the MILPRO home page shown in Figure 1-13. The home page includes links to MRO-related sales, which is the main purpose of the site. However, the page also includes links to account and order status information, links to detailed technical specifications for the MRO products that Milacron sells, and links to pages that benefit the job shop community as a whole.

Figure 1-13	MILPRO HOME PAGE

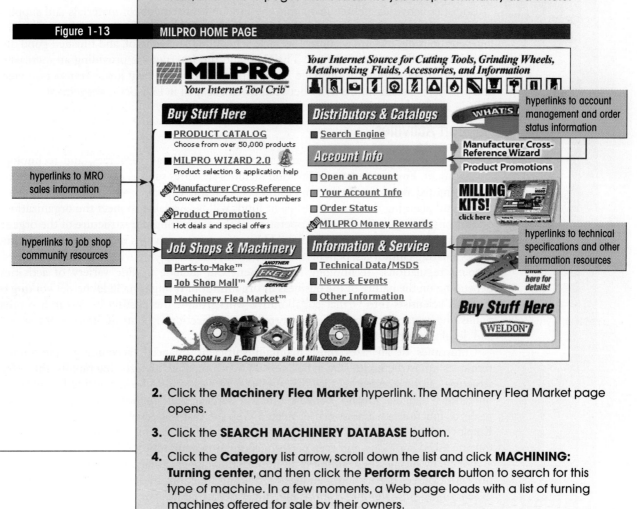

2. Click the **Machinery Flea Market** hyperlink. The Machinery Flea Market page opens.

3. Click the **SEARCH MACHINERY DATABASE** button.

4. Click the **Category** list arrow, scroll down the list and click **MACHINING: Turning center**, and then click the **Perform Search** button to search for this type of machine. In a few moments, a Web page loads with a list of turning machines offered for sale by their owners.

Office equipment and supplies are also items that are used by a wide variety of businesses. Market leaders **Office Depot** and **Staples** each have created Web sites devoted to helping business procurement departments buy routine office supplies and other office-related items as easily as possible.

Delivery Activities

The goal of delivery and warehousing activities, often called **logistics**, is to provide the right goods in the right quantities in the right place at the right time. Businesses have been increasing their use of information technology to achieve this objective. Indeed, major transportation companies such as **Schneider Logistics** and **J.B. Hunt Transport Services** now want their customers to see them as information management firms as well as freight carriers. For example, the recently introduced Schneider Track and Trace system delivers real-time shipment information to Web browsers on its customers' computers. This system uses a Java applet to show the customer which freight carrier is transporting a shipment, where the shipment is, and when it should arrive at its destination. **FedEx** and **UPS** also have freight tracking Web pages available to their customers. Firms that run their own trucking operations have also begun implementing tracking systems that use satellite global positioning technology to monitor vehicle movements.

Logistics activities include managing the inbound movements of materials and supplies and the outbound movements of finished goods and services. Thus, the activities of receiving, warehousing, inventory control, vehicle scheduling and control, and finished good distribution are all logistics activities. The Web and the Internet are providing an increasing number of opportunities to manage these activities better as they lower transaction costs and provide constant connectivity between firms engaged in logistics management.

Support Activities

Support activities include finance and administration, human resources, and technology development. Finance and administration includes activities such as payment of obligations, processing payments received from customers, planning capital expenditures, and the budgeting and planning that ensure sufficient funds will be available to meet the organization's obligations as they come due. The operation of the computing infrastructure of the organization is also an administration activity. Human resource activities include hiring, training, and evaluating employees; benefits administration; and complying with government record-keeping regulations. Technology development can include a wide variety of activities, depending on the nature of the business or organization. It might include the networking of research scientists into virtual collaborative workgroups, the posting of research results, publishing research papers online, or providing connections to outside sources of research and development services.

Companies of all sizes must maintain sufficient financial, accounting, and human resources infrastructure to stay in business. When companies are growing rapidly, this infrastructure can be stressed because the support activities tend to be last in line for increased operations budgets. **Online Benefits** offers a service that duplicates its clients' human resource functions on a password-protected Web site that is accessible to clients' employees. Employees can then access their employers' benefits information, find the answers to frequently asked questions, and even perform complex benefit option calculations.

For many businesses, training is an important support activity. In some companies, the human resources department handles the training function. In other companies, it may be decentralized and administered by individual departments. For example, insurance firms often invest heavily in sales training. This training is administered by the sales and marketing function in most insurance companies.

MicroAge is a technology and integration services company that invests considerable resources in training programs for its own sales force. MicroAge also trains the sales forces of its customers, who re-sell the computers and related technology items they buy from MicroAge. In 1997, MicroAge launched a series of Web-based sales training programs for its new Internet technology products. In addition to saving the costs of running classroom sessions in multiple locations, MicroAge found that training salespeople about specific product features increased its sales of those products.

MicroAge now tracks the courses that a salesperson has taken and assigns sales leads for specific products to the salespersons who have taken the course for that product. To keep salespersons updated after they have taken a course, MicroAge sends course graduates an e-mail notification whenever new information about a product becomes available.

New Businesses Made Possible by the Web

So far in this tutorial, you have learned how companies use the Internet and the Web to help them perform some of their primary and support activities faster, cheaper, and better. In this section you will learn how companies are using electronic commerce to create entirely new businesses on the Web. These new businesses include Web auctions (consumer and business-to-business), group purchasing sites, virtual communities, and Web portals.

Web auctions are one of the fastest growing segments of online business today. Business analysts and researchers predict that Web auctions will account for 30% of all electronic commerce by 2002. Although the online auction business is changing rapidly as it grows, three broad categories of auction Web sites are emerging: general consumer auctions, specialty consumer auctions, and business-to-business auctions.

Consumer Web Auctions

In many ways, online auctions provide a business opportunity that is perfect for the Web. An auction site can charge both buyers and sellers to participate and it can sell advertising on its pages. People interested in trading specific items can form a market segment that advertisers will pay extra to reach. Thus, the same kind of targeted advertising opportunities that search engine sites generate with their results pages are available to advertisers on auction sites. This combination of revenue-generating characteristics makes it relatively easy to develop Web auctions that yield profits early in the life of the project.

One of the Internet's strengths is that it can bring together people who share narrow interests but are geographically dispersed. Web auctions can capitalize on that ability by either catering to a narrow interest or by providing a general auction site that has sections devoted to specific interests.

In 1995, Pierre Omidyar was working as a software developer and, in his spare time, operating a small Web site that provided updates on the Ebola virus. His girlfriend collected Pez candy dispensers but had trouble finding other people who shared her interest. Omidyar decided to help her out by adding a small auction function to his Web site so that people could trade Pez dispensers and other items. Interest in the site's auctions grew so rapidly that, within a year, he had quit his job to devote his full energies to the Web auction business he had created. By the end of its second year in operation, Omidyar's Web site, which he called eBay, had auctioned over $95 million worth of goods.

Because eBay was one of the first auction Web sites and because it has pursued an aggressive promotion strategy, it has become the first choice for many people who want to participate in auctions. Both buyers and bidders benefit from the large marketplace that eBay has created. EBay's early advantage in the online auction business will be hard for competitors to overcome. You remember that your mother asked you for advice on selling a rare, antique clock that she inherited from a distant family member. You decide to check out eBay's auction site to gain experience for your column and to help your mother.

To search for an auction on the eBay auction site:

1. Click your browser's **Back** button or use its history list to return to the Online Companion page for Session 1.2, and then click the **eBay** hyperlink and wait while your browser loads the eBay home page shown in Figure 1-14. The home page includes hyperlinks to auction categories that each include thousands of ongoing auctions. The number of ongoing auctions appears in parentheses next to each hyperlink.

Figure 1-14	EBAY HOME PAGE

number of auctions currently underway in this category

hyperlinks to auction categories

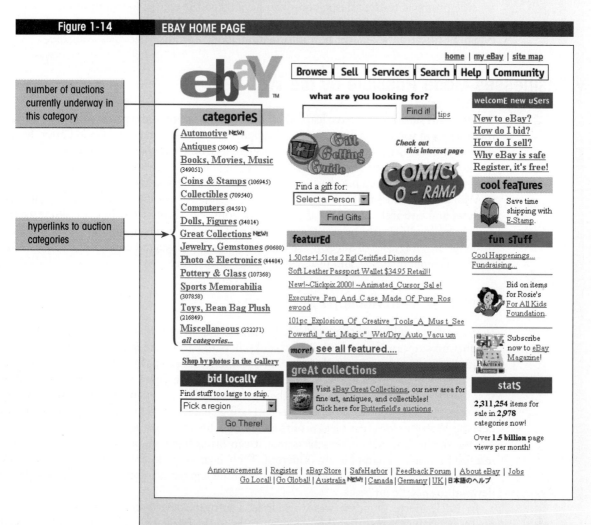

2. Click the **Antiques** hyperlink (or the **Antiques & Art** hyperlink) to open the page for that category. A page opens that includes hyperlinks to over a dozen antique categories, many of which contain their own subcategories.

3. Click the **Sell** hyperlink near the top of the page to open the eBay Sell Item Web page. Most of the interaction that buyers and sellers have with eBay is through Web forms. Examine the page and note that every bit of information eBay needs to obtain for an auction listing is included. Because eBay attracts sellers with varying degrees of computer expertise, it is careful to make the procedure easy, even for computer novices.

4. Click the **Help** hyperlink near the top of the page to examine the eBay Help page. Once again, notice how the hyperlinks are organized on the page in logical groups to make it easy for a person unfamiliar with computers, the Web, or auctions to find help on a specific topic. In case the hyperlinks do not provide sufficient assistance, the page includes a keyword search facility.

5. Close your Web browser and close your dial-up connection, if necessary.

Sellers and buyers must register with eBay and agree to the site's basic terms for doing business. Sellers pay a listing fee and a sliding percentage of the final selling price. Buyers pay nothing. In addition to the basic fees, sellers can choose from a variety of enhanced and extra-cost services, including having their auctions listed in bold type and included in preferred lists of auctions.

In an attempt to address buyer concerns about seller reliability, eBay has instituted a rating system. Buyers can submit ratings of sellers after doing business with them. These ratings are converted into graphics that appear with the seller's nickname on each auction in which that seller participates. Although this system is not without flaws, many eBay customers feel that it affords them some level of protection from unscrupulous sellers.

EBay has been successful because it was the first major Web auction site for consumers that did not cater to a specific audience and because it has advertised widely. In 1998, eBay spent almost $20 million to market and promote its Web site. A significant portion of this promotional budget was spent on traditional mass media, such as television advertising. For eBay, this advertising has been the best way to reach its main market—people who have a hobby or very specific interest in items that are not locally available. Whether those items are jewelry, antique furniture, coins, first-edition books, or stuffed animals, eBay has created a place where people can become collectors, dispose of their collections, or simply trade out of their collections.

Other firms have entered the general consumer auction market that eBay dominates. One of the best new entrants is **Auctions.com**. Newspaper companies started Auctions.com because they saw classified advertising on the Web as a threat. Newspaper classified advertising is one of the most profitable elements in the newspaper business. Classified Ventures, the group of newspaper companies that owns Auctions.com, sees the site as a key element in its strategy for moving classified advertising to the Web.

Auctions.com was modeled after eBay and offers similar types of auctions and services for buyers and sellers. Some critics have noted that the Auctions.com interface is more intuitive than eBay's and includes a better search engine; however, Auctions.com has thus far failed to mount a significant challenge to eBay's dominance. Even with major corporate sponsorship and a $10 million 1998 advertising campaign behind it, Auctions.com has been unable to displace the advantage eBay obtained as the first general consumer Web auction site.

Because one of the major determinants of Web auction site success is attracting enough buyers and sellers to create markets for enough items, some Web sites that already have a large number of visitors are entering this business. Sites such as **Yahoo! Auctions** have added auctions similar to those available on eBay. Yahoo! Auctions has had some success in attracting sellers, in part because it offers its auction service to sellers at no charge. However, Yahoo! Auctions has been less successful in attracting buyers, resulting in less bidding action in each auction than generally occurs on eBay. Because Yahoo! Auctions is still new, it is possible that Yahoo! Auctions will be able to convince its visitors to participate in its auctions with more success. The potential for success certainly exists because Yahoo! is one of the most-visited sites on the Web.

With its **Amazon.com Auctions** site, the pioneering Web bookseller has also recently expanded its business to include auctions. Although the number of auctions is still small, Amazon is aggressively marketing its new business. Some industry observers note that Amazon may earn more by charging a commission on the auction of a used book than it could earn by selling the same title as a new book! With over 14 million registered users of its existing book, music, video, and other sales pages, Amazon is well positioned to challenge eBay.

One of the aggressive marketing positions that Amazon has already taken is its "Auctions Guarantee." This guarantee directly addresses concerns raised in the media by eBay customers who had been cheated by unscrupulous sellers in the past. When Amazon opened its auctions site, it agreed to reimburse any buyer for merchandise purchased in an auction that was not delivered or that was "materially different" from the seller's representations. Amazon limited its guarantee to items costing $250 or less; however, buyers of more expensive items generally protect themselves by using a third party **escrow service**, which holds the buyer's payment until he or she receives and is satisfied with the purchased item. EBay responded immediately by offering its customers the same guarantee; however, this guarantee helped to establish Amazon as a serious competitor in the Web auction business.

Most general consumer Web auction sites have not been in business very long. The premier Web auction site in this category is still eBay. Although new entrants might be able to establish successful auction sites, they must overcome the strong advantage that eBay has built. One serious issue that any eBay challenger will face is that the economic structure of markets is biased against new entrants. Because markets become more efficient (yielding fairer prices both to buyers and sellers) as the number of buyers and sellers increases, new auction participants are inclined to patronize established marketplaces. Thus, existing auction sites, such as eBay, are inherently more valuable to customers than new auction sites. This basic economic fact will make the task of creating other successful general consumer Web auction sites even more difficult in the future.

Rather than struggle to compete in the general consumer auction market with a well-established rival such as eBay, many firms have decided to identify special interest market targets and create specialized Web auction sites that meet the needs of those market segments. Several of these early Web auction sites started by featuring technology items, such as computers, computer parts, photographic equipment, and consumer electronics.

Doug Salot started an auction site, **Haggle Online**, in September 1996. Salot had been buying and selling computer equipment on the Internet before the Web existed. He saw the potential for the Web's graphical user interface in creating auctions. Haggle has officially branched out to include noncomputer-related items; however, technology products continue to be its mainstay. The site even includes an online computer museum!

Another specialized auction site, **Onsale**, sells its own inventory of refurbished computers and computer-related items. Onsale offers warranties on some of its refurbished products and has established itself as a specialized Web auction site in its chosen market segment.

Creative Computers, a direct-mail catalog marketer of computer hardware and software, operates the **uBid** auction site, which targets the same technology markets as Onsale. Although Onsale and uBid have added other auction categories, their main appeal is to buyers in the computer and technology markets.

Although computers and technology were logical early choices for Web auctions, a number of other specialized Web auction sites have emerged recently. Golfers in search of bargains on new and used clubs can find them at the **Golf Club Exchange** Web auction. Collectors are attracted to auctions at sites such as **StampAuctions** or the **Coin Universe**, and wine enthusiasts can bid on their favorite vintages at **Winebid**.

Each of these sites gains an advantage by identifying a market of readily identifiable products that are desired by persons with relatively high levels of disposable income. Golf clubs, collectibles, wine, and technology products all meet these requirements very well. As other Web auction site developers identify similar market segments, these specialized consumer auctions may become profitable niches that can successfully coexist with large general consumer sites, such as eBay.

Business-to-Business Web Auctions

Unlike consumer Web auctions, business-to-business Web auctions evolved to meet a very specific need. Many manufacturing companies periodically need to dispose of unusable or excess inventory. Despite the best efforts of procurement and production management, businesses occasionally buy more raw materials than they need. Many times, unforeseen changes in customer demand for a product can saddle manufacturers with excess finished goods or spare parts.

Depending on its size, a firm will typically use one of two methods to distribute excess inventory. Large companies sometimes have liquidation specialists that find buyers for these unusable inventory items. Smaller businesses often sell their unusable and excess inventory to **liquidation brokers**, which are firms that find buyers for these items. Web auctions are the logical extension of these inventory liquidation activities to a new and more efficient channel—the Internet.

Two of the three main business-to-business Web auction models that are emerging are direct descendants of these two traditional methods for handling excess inventory. In the large company model, the business creates its own auction site that sells excess inventory. In the small company model, a third-party Web auction site takes the place of the liquidation broker and auctions excess inventory listed on the site by a number of smaller sellers. The third business-to-business Web auction model resembles a consumer Web auction. In this model, a new business entity enters a market that lacked efficiency and creates a site at which buyers and sellers who have not historically done business with each other can participate in auctions. An alternative implementation of this model occurs when a Web auction replaces an existing sales channel.

One major computer technology company that decided to build its own auction site to dispose of obsolete inventory is CompUSA. Although CompUSA sells to individuals, a significant portion of its sales is to corporate customers. Instead of selling through liquidation brokers, CompUSA decided to let mid-sized and smaller businesses bid directly on its technology inventory. CompUSA's Web auction site is **CompUSA Auctions**.

In the second business-to-business model, smaller firms sell their obsolete inventories through an independent third-party auction site. In some cases, the same liquidation brokers that have always handled the disposition of obsolete inventory conduct these Web auctions. These brokers have adapted to the changed environment and have implemented electronic commerce to avoid disintermediation. Other third-party auction sites have been started by newcomers or even by companies that want to liquidate their inventory and are willing to do the same for other companies in their industry.

Examples of completely new businesses that have created opportunities for business-to-business trade on Web auction sites include **NECX Online Exchange** for computer and electronics parts and **SciQuest** for laboratory instruments and supplies. The $1.6 trillion per year chemicals market has seen a number of new Web auction sites appear recently. Sites such as **CheMatch** for bulk petrochemicals and **Chemdex** for research chemicals are targeting specific parts of the industrial chemicals market, while the World Chemical Exchange is targeting the entire chemicals market with its **ChemConnect** auction site.

Established securities trading organizations such as the New York Stock Exchange (NYSE) and the Chicago Board of Trade (CBOT) are facing an electronic challenge to their time-honored ways of doing business. In 1998, electronic brokers E-Trade and Ameritrade Holdings funded a new venture with contributions from several other brokerage firms called the **International Securities Exchange (ISE)**. This new exchange will be the first to be registered in the United States in over 25 years.

Starting in 2000, the ISE plans to offer low-cost trading in a few hundred of the most actively traded stock options contracts. This new electronic securities exchange poses a threat to all existing securities exchanges because its lower fees might attract the most lucrative large trades of active issues from existing exchanges. Once the ISE becomes established and expands its list of securities traded, industry analysts question whether traditional exchanges such as the NYSE and the CBOT can continue to exist.

Seller-Bid Auctions and Group Purchasing Sites

An interesting variation on the traditional auction model, in which sellers bid the prices at which they are willing to sell, has come to the Web on sites such as **TravelBids**. These types of auctions are sometimes called **reverse auctions** because the role of the bidder as buyer is reversed to bidder as seller. For example, at the TravelBids site, a person who has booked an airline or cruise reservation can post a request for bids to write the ticket for that reservation. Travel agents, who receive a commission when they write tickets, then bid for the right to ticket the reservation. The travel agents' bids for the commissions they will accept to write the ticket decrease until no more travel agents bid or the buyer accepts the low bid.

Another new phenomenon on the Web is the group purchasing site. On a **group purchasing site**, an item is posted with a price. As individual buyers enter bids on an item (a **bid** is an agreement to buy one unit of that item), the site can negotiate a better price with the item's provider. The posted price ultimately goes down as the number of bids increases. **Mercata** was the first major group purchasing site on the Web. It offers group purchasing services, which it calls PowerBuys, on a variety of merchandise including electronics, appliances, luggage, and jewelry. The Mercata site encourages potential buyers to send e-mail messages to their friends who might be interested in the same item. When more people bid on a particular item, its price decreases.

Virtual Communities

A **virtual community**, also called a **Web community** or an **online community**, is a gathering place for people and businesses that does not have a physical existence. Virtual communities exist on the Internet today in various forms, including chat rooms and Web sites. These virtual communities help companies, their customers, and their suppliers to plan, collaborate, transact business, and otherwise interact in ways that benefit all of them.

One of the first Web communities was **The WELL**. Most original members of The WELL, which is an acronym for "whole earth 'lectronic link," were from the San Francisco Bay area. Members of The WELL pay a monthly fee to participate in its forums and conferences. The WELL has been home to many important researchers and participants in the growth of the Internet and the Web. Its membership also includes noted writers and artists. In 1999, the online magazine publisher **Salon.com** bought The WELL and promised to maintain the sense of community that has existed there for 15 years.

As the Web emerged in the mid-1990s, its potential for creating new virtual communities was quickly exploited. In 1995, Beverly Hills Internet opened a virtual community site that featured two Webcams aimed down Hollywood streets and links to entertainment information Web sites. The theme of this community was the formation of digital cities around the focus of the Webcams. The founders of Beverly Hills Internet wanted to create a sense of community and believed that the Webcams would help accomplish that goal. Their hope was that people would be attracted by the Webcam images and would want to add their own contributions, thus becoming members of a virtual neighborhood. Members were given free space on the Web site to create pages within these virtual cities to add their contributions. The first of these digital cities was created around Webcams in the Los Angles area and therefore was named for Los Angeles area communities. As the site grew to include more geographic areas, it changed its name to **GeoCities**. GeoCities earned revenue by selling advertising on members' Web pages and on pop-up pages that appeared when a visitor accessed a member's site. GeoCities grew rapidly and was purchased in 1999 by Yahoo! for $5 billion.

Other similar sites also became virtual communities. Tripod, now owned by the search engine site **Lycos**, was founded in 1995 in Massachusetts and offered its participants free Web page space, chat rooms, news and weather updates, and health information pages. Like GeoCities, Tripod sold advertising on its main pages and on participants' Web pages. Another virtual community site, **theglobe.com**, also started in 1995 as a class project at Cornell University. The students who created the site built in bulletin boards, chat rooms, discussion areas, and personal ads. They then sold advertising to support the site's operation.

Web Portal Strategies

By the late 1990s, virtual communities were selling advertising to generate revenue. Search engine sites and Web directories also were selling advertising to generate revenue. Beginning in 1998, a wave of purchases and mergers occurred among these sites. Still using an advertising-only revenue generation model, the new sites that emerged included all of the features offered by virtual community sites, search engine sites, Web directories, and other information-providing and entertainment sites. These sites are called Web portals, or simply portals, because their goal is to be every Web surfer's entryway to the Web.

Many Web observers believe that Web portal sites will be the great revenue-generating businesses of the future. They argue that incorporating the sense of belonging developed in Web communities with the handy tools of search engines and Web directory sites will yield high levels of stickiness that will be extremely attractive to advertisers.

Industry observers who are predicting success for Web portals may be correct. In 1998, the top 10 most-visited Web sites included seven Web portals. High visitor counts yield high advertising rates for these sites. More importantly, Web portals have been increasingly able to obtain up-front cash payments from advertisers. Excite, a search engine site, paid Netscape a $70 million advance fee for two-year rights to a prominent advertising location on its Netcenter Web portal site. Other portal sites are negotiating advertising deals that include a percentage of sales generated from sales leads on the portal site.

The companies that operate Web portals certainly believe in the power of portals. They have been aggressively adding sticky features such as chat rooms, e-mail, and calendar functions to their sites—often by purchasing the companies that create those features—to add to their portal sites.

Session 1.2 QUICK CHECK

1. True or False: Many firms that adapted their existing catalog-based mail order and telephone order operations to work on the Web have been successful in electronic commerce.

2. What is the main feature of Dell Computer's Premier Pages program?

3. What critical element must an advertising-supported Web site have to ensure that it will be attractive to advertisers?

4. Why is the ESPN Web site called a "combined model?"

5. Why has the success of eBay in the general consumer auction business been so hard for other auction sites to duplicate?

6. What specific need motivated many companies to create business-to-business Web auctions?

7. How do virtual community and Web portal sites generate revenue?

CASE PROBLEMS

Case 1. Flowers for Sale on the Web   Many firms sell flowers and related gift items on the Web. FTD.com started as the world's first "flowers-by-wire" service in 1910 and moved to the Web in 1994. The 1-800-flowers.com site is an outgrowth of that company's telephone order business. Newer entrants to the online flower industry, such as Proflowers.com, started their businesses on the Web and work with a very different business strategy.

1. Start your Web browser, and then go to the Online Companion page by entering the URL http://www.course.com/NewPerspectives/EC in the appropriate location of your Web browser. Click the Tutorial 1 link, and then click the Case Problems link. Click the FTD.com link and wait while your browser loads the FTD.com home page.

2. Click the About FTD hyperlink near the bottom of the page to open the About FTD page in your browser. This page includes a history of the company and describes many of the details of its operations. Read this page carefully so you understand what FTD.com is, who its customers are, and how it accepts and delivers orders. You might want to explore other pages on the site to learn more about how FTD.com does business.

3. When you have finished exploring the FTD.com site, click your browser's Back button until you have returned to the Case Problems section of the Online Companion for Tutorial 1.

4. Click the 1-800-flowers.com hyperlink. When the 1-800-flowers.com home page opens, click the About Us hyperlink near the bottom of the page. When the About 1-800-flowers.com page opens, read it carefully. This page includes a company overview, information about the company's access channels, and a description of the flower shop network that fulfills the company's orders. You might want to explore other pages on the site to learn more about 1-800-flowers.com.

5. When you have finished exploring the 1-800-flowers.com site, click your browser's Back button until you have returned to the Case Problems section of the Online Companion for Tutorial 1.

6. Click the Proflowers.com hyperlink. When the Proflowers.com home page opens, click the About Us hyperlink on the left side of the page. When the About Us page opens, read it carefully. This page includes a mission statement, information about how the company does business, and a section on how they ship and package the flowers. You might want to explore other pages on the site to learn more about Proflowers.com.

7. When you have finished examining the Proflowers.com site, close your browser and your dial-up connection, if necessary.

8. Each of these three companies uses a different business strategy to sell flowers and related gift items to consumers. Based on your examination of the three Web sites, write one paragraph for each company that describes the key elements in its business strategy, and then write one paragraph in which you compare and contrast the three different business strategies.

Case 2. Finding a New VCR on the Web   Your VCR has started randomly ejecting the video-tape while you are watching your favorite movies, so you decide it is time to buy a new VCR. You want to buy your new VCR on the Web and would like to start by doing some comparison shopping.

1. Start your Web browser, and then go to the Online Companion page by entering the URL http://www.course.com/NewPerspectives/EC in the appropriate location of your Web browser. Click the Tutorial 1 link, and then click the Case Problems link. Click the buy.com link and wait while your browser loads the buy.com home page.

2. Click the Electronics hyperlink near the top of the buy.com home page to open the BuyElectronics.com page.

3. When the BuyElectronics page has loaded in your browser, type VCR in the Electronic Store Search text box, and then click the Search button.

4. The search results page appears, listing over a dozen VCRs with their part numbers, prices, and information about their current availability for shipment. Some buyers may make their selection using the brief descriptions that appear on this page. However, other buyers may want more information. To provide a customized level of product information on this site, buy.com formatted the name of each VCR as a hyperlink that you can click to learn more about that particular model. Click some of these hyperlinks to learn more about at least three VCRs that are currently for sale. Print one page of information about a particular VCR at the site.

5. When you have finished examining information about VCRs for sale at the buy.com site, click your browser's Back button until you have returned to the Case Problems section of the Online Companion for Tutorial 1.

6. Click the Amazon.com link and wait while your browser loads the Amazon.com home page.

7. Click the ELECTRONICS hyperlink near the top of the Amazon.com home page to open the Electronics page. When the page has loaded in your browser, type VCR in the Search text box, and then click the Go! button.

8. The first page of search results appears, listing 20 VCRs with their part numbers, prices, and current availability for shipment. Each listing has a hyperlink named "Click here for more information" that you can follow to obtain more details about each VCR. The additional information includes customer reviews of the product and even includes ratings of the reviews (each review has an indicator that states how many people found that review to be helpful). Click some of these hyperlinks to learn more about at least three VCRs that are currently for sale. Print one page of information about a particular VCR at the site.

9. When you have finished examining information about VCRs for sale at Amazon.com, close your browser and your dial-up connection, if necessary.

10. For each site, answer the following questions: Was the site easy to use? Why or why not? Did the site offer VCRs in which you would be interested? Did the site display product information that was easy to understand? Why or why not? Would you use these sites to purchase items online? Why or why not? On each page that you printed, indicate one helpful design feature.

Case 3. Comparing Auction Sites   You have an antique clock that you inherited from your grandmother several years ago. You never really liked the clock and you need to raise some down-payment money to buy a new car, so you have decided to sell it. You asked several local antique dealers to make you an offer, but you were disappointed in the amounts they were willing to pay. You believe the clock is worth about $600 and are considering selling the clock in a Web auction.

1. Start your Web browser, and then go to the Online Companion page by entering the URL http://www.course.com/NewPerspectives/EC in the appropriate location of your Web browser. Click the Tutorial 1 link, and then click the Case Problems link. Click the eBay link and wait while your browser loads the eBay home page.

2. Type Clock in the "what are you looking for?" text box near the top of the eBay home page, and then click the Find it! button. The search results page loads, showing the first 50 of several thousand auctions. You decide to narrow your search by sorting the auctions by bid price.

3. Click the Sort drop-down list arrow, click Highest prices first, and then click the Go! button next to the text box containing your search expression.

4. When the new search results page has loaded, scroll down to find auctions that have a bid price of between $400 and $800. If necessary, click the Next button at the bottom of the page to open a page with additional search results (you may need to do this several times, depending on how many auctions are underway).

5. Note the number of auctions that are similar to the auction you would like to hold. Click the hyperlinks to specific auctions to see how sellers present the clocks they hope to sell in this price range. For example, you may note that many of the auctions in this price range include multiple photographs of the clock and detailed descriptions of the clock's condition.

6. When you have finished examining the auctions, click your browser's Back button until you have returned to the Case Problems section of the Online Companion for Tutorial 1.

7. Click the Auctions.com link and wait while your browser loads the Auctions.com home page.

8. When the page has loaded, type Clock in the Keyword Item Search text box, and then click the SEARCH button.

9. The search results page loads, showing the first 50 of several hundred auctions. You can also narrow your search by sorting the auctions by bid price on this site. Scroll to the bottom of the search results page, click the Sort results by list arrow and click Start Bid, click the Descending option button, and then click the Search button below the text box containing your search expression.

10. As you did on the eBay site, note the number of auctions in your price range and click their hyperlinks to see how sellers present their clocks on the Auctions.com site.

11. When you have finished examining the auctions at this site, close your browser and your dial-up connection, if necessary.

12. Write a 100-word report that summarizes what you learned about auctions for antique clocks on these two sites. Choose the site at which you prefer to hold your auction. Provide the reasons for your choice.

Case 4. Shopping for a Baby Stroller at Mercata   You have a new member of the family. Your niece was born last week, and you would like to buy a stroller for her. You are concerned that the specialty stores that sell baby products might not offer the best prices, but you worry that a large discount store might not have a wide selection of strollers. You decide to explore the Mercata group purchasing Web site.

1. Start your Web browser, and then go to the Online Companion page by entering the URL http://www.course.com/NewPerspectives/EC in the appropriate location of your Web browser. Click the Tutorial 1 link, and then click the Case Problems link. Click the Mercata link and wait while your browser loads the Mercata home page.

2. Click the PowerBuy Center hyperlink near the top of the page, type Stroller in the Quick search text box near the top of the page that opens, and then click the GO button.

3. The search results page loads, showing the first of several dozen items. Each item description begins with a hyperlink to a detailed description of the item. Scroll down the list until you see an item that is designated a PowerBuy item (if necessary, click the Next hyperlink at the bottom of the page to open more search results pages to find a PowerBuy item). The PowerBuy items include information about the time remaining. As more Mercata customers agree to buy an item, the price drops. Mercata passes along to the customer a portion of the quantity discount it receives from the vendor for buying in greater volume.

4. Click the hyperlink that appears at the beginning of the description of a PowerBuy item. A page opens that includes detailed descriptive information about the product and a PowerBuy summary. This summary includes the original price, the current price, and information about shipping charges.

5. When you have finished examining the stroller's description, close your browser and your dial-up connection, if necessary.

6. Write a 100-word report that summarizes the advantages and disadvantages of using a group purchasing site such as Mercata to shop for a baby stroller, compared to shopping at either a specialty baby store or a large discount store.

QUICK | CHECK ANSWERS

Session 1.1

1. True
2. Commercialization of the Internet, invention of the Web, and the wide availability of networked personal computers
3. Saves the time and cost of making telephone calls, sending faxes, or driving from store to store
4. Currency conversions, tariffs, import and export restrictions, local business customs, and the laws of each country in which a trading partner resides
5. Advertising, promotion, managing salespersons, pricing, and identifying and monitoring sales and distribution channels
6. False
7. Electronic payments of tax refunds, public retirement, and welfare support cost less to issue, arrive securely and quickly, and are easier to protect from fraud and theft losses. Telecommuting can reduce commuter-caused traffic and pollution. Electronic commerce can make products and services available in remote areas.

Session 1.2

1. True

2. Provides a customized interface for each type of customer that gives customers a high degree of configuration flexibility

3. Stickiness

4. Some of the information on the site is supported by advertising, and thus available at no cost to visitors; other information on the site is available only to those visitors who pay a subscription fee.

5. Auction markets become more efficient (yield fairer prices both to buyers and sellers) as the number of buyers and sellers increase. New auction participants will more likely patronize an established marketplace such as eBay rather than new Web auction sites because eBay already has a large number of buyers and sellers.

6. The need to dispose periodically of unusable or excess inventory

7. Most rely on advertising revenue; however, a few virtual community sites (such as The WELL) obtain all or part of their revenue from membership fees.

In this tutorial you will:

- Explore Web sites that have an effective business presence

- Learn about Web promotion techniques used by businesses

- Understand how to meet the needs of Web site visitors

- Explore usability testing in Web site design

- Identify and reach customers on the Web

- View marketing approaches that work on the Web

- Understand elements of branding

- Understand branding strategies and costs

CREATING A SUCCESSFUL WEB PRESENCE

Designing the User Interface and Promoting the Electronic Commerce Web Site

CASE

Treasure Trove Antiques and Gifts

Jean Mischel is the owner of Treasure Trove, a large antique and gift store located in a small town outside of San Francisco. Treasure Trove is a popular weekend drive destination from several nearby cities. Jean has been operating Treasure Trove for many years. She left San Francisco to find a less hectic life in a smaller town and started Treasure Trove as a way to earn a living while working only weekends. As the store became more popular, she expanded its hours and opened the store six days a week, closing it only on Mondays. Jean hires high school and college students to work with her in the store on the weekends because weekends are still the store's busiest days. Although the weekend traffic is very good and sales have been increasing, Jean is always exploring ways to increase the store's profits.

During the slower business days in the middle of the week, Jean started using the Internet to stay in contact with her San Francisco customers. She found several e-mail lists devoted to antiques and has learned a great deal about finding good buys and negotiating better prices with customers. Soon, she was surfing the Web and finding sites that offered even more information about antiques and gifts. As Jean explored the Web, it occurred to her that she might be able to use the Web to expand her business. She wasn't exactly sure how she could do this, however. While in high school and college, you worked for Jean on weekends and during the summers, and now you have a successful career working for a large corporation's internal Web group. Jean called and asked if you could help her use the Internet and the Web to expand Treasure Trove's market beyond the limits of its physical location. Jean has read about some other antique shops that have opened storefronts on the Web. She hopes that reaching more customers on the Web will allow her to expand Treasure Trove's inventory, so sales in the store will increase, too. You told Jean that you would explore ways she might take Treasure Trove onto the Web. You also agreed to help Jean learn more about how she might take her business onto the Internet.

SESSION 2.1

In this session, you will learn about business presences on the Web. You will visit successful e-commerce Web sites to see how companies establish effective business presences on the Web, promote their businesses on the Web, and design Web sites that meet the needs of their visitors. You will also study ways of testing Web sites to determine their overall effectiveness.

Creating an Effective Web Presence

A business creates a presence in the physical world by building stores, factories, warehouses, and office buildings. An organization's **presence** or **reputation** is the public image it conveys. Individual persons create a presence every time they meet another person. This first impression is enhanced by every subsequent contact, whether that contact is a face-to-face meeting, a phone call, a letter, or an e-mail message.

In smaller businesses, the individual employees of the firm create much of a firm's presence by making personal impressions on the company's customers and suppliers. For example, much of Treasure Trove's presence is the result of Jean's long-standing relationships with regular customers and suppliers. Jean is always very careful when hiring new store employees—she knows that one bad impression can damage years of building Treasure Trove's reputation.

Jean is also very careful to properly maintain her store's appearance. She makes sure that the exterior is clean and well maintained, with trees trimmed and sidewalks kept clear. Jean uses her business's name to stay active in the local community and in charitable organizations, as well. She wants to make sure that her store makes a positive impression, even on people who are not customers or suppliers.

As companies grow, they tend not to worry much about the image they project. Managers of growing companies are often completely occupied with the day-to-day tasks of managing growth. Although the growing company's salespersons work to maintain a good reputation with customers and its purchasing agents do the same with suppliers, very few growing firms make a concerted, centrally organized effort to build the reputation of the company as a whole. When companies reach a significant size, they again turn their attentions and resources to building and maintaining a presence as a means of maintaining their market share and customer base. Most large companies have a well-staffed public relations department to communicate with customers and the media. However, very few rapidly growing firms will put the same emphasis on public relations because they are focused primarily on growth.

On the Web, presence can be much more important for businesses of all sizes, instead of just for large businesses. Often, the only contact that customers and suppliers have with a firm on the Web is through its presence on the Internet. Creating an effective Web presence is equally critical for the smallest companies, the most rapidly growing companies, and the largest companies when those companies are operating on the Web. Thus, every business operating on the Web must identify its Web presence goals.

Identifying Web Presence Goals

When a business creates a physical space in which to conduct its activities, its managers focus on very specific objectives. Unless the business is a retail store, such as Treasure Trove, few of these objectives are driven by a desire to create a particular image. Managers are more concerned with finding a convenient location for customers that will have sufficient floor space and features to allow selling activities to occur, and that will balance the need for room to store inventory and provide space to conduct business with the costs of obtaining that space. The presence of a physical business location results from satisfying these and many other objectives, and is rarely a main goal of designing the space.

On the Web, however, businesses and other organizations can intentionally build a space that creates a distinctive presence. A firm's physical location must satisfy so many other business needs that it often fails to convey a recognizable presence. A Web site can perform many image-creation and image-enhancement tasks very effectively; it can serve as a sales brochure, a product showroom, a financial report, an employment ad, or a customer contact point. Each entity that establishes a Web presence must decide which tasks the Web site must accomplish and which tasks are the most important to include. Different companies—even those in the same industry—might establish very different Web presence goals. For example, Coca Cola and Pepsi are two companies in the same business that have established very strong brand images, but have developed very different Web presences. You decide to show Jean these two sites as examples of how a Web site can convey a brand image.

To compare the Web presences of Coca-Cola and Pepsi:

1. Start your Web browser, and then go to the Online Companion page by entering the URL **http://www.course.com/NewPerspectives/EC** in the appropriate location of your Web browser. Click the **Tutorial 2** link, and then click the **Session 2.1** link. Click the **Coca-Cola** link and wait while your browser loads the Coca-Cola home page shown in Figure 2-1. (Your home page might look different.) The most prominent feature of the Coca-Cola home page shown in Figure 2-1 is the glistening bottle of Coke. The "story" of how the home page came to be is set in a font designed to look like informal hand printing. The Coke bottle is one of the most recognized objects in the world. Coca-Cola capitalizes on this recognition and uses it to extend its presence. The theme of the home page "story" is that the best minds at Coca-Cola considered many interesting ideas, but in the end decided that nothing represented the company as well as a reliable, trustworthy bottle of Coke. In fact, to proceed into the company's Web site, you must click the bottle of Coke, an action that further emphasizes the importance of the bottle as a corporate symbol.

| Figure 2-1 | COCA-COLA HOME PAGE |

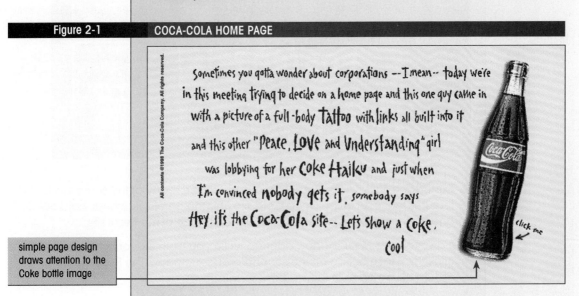

simple page design draws attention to the Coke bottle image

TROUBLE? Your Coca-Cola home page and other pages that you visit might look different because companies change their Web sites regularly.

2. Click the **Coke bottle** image to enter the Coca-Cola Web site. (If your home page looks different, click the **About the Company** hyperlink.) The Web page that opens contains hyperlinks to company financial information, a trading post for Coca-Cola memorabilia and collector's items, and several entertainment pages. Coca-Cola does not sell its products on this Web site; the site is devoted to promoting the company's reputation and image.

3. Click your browser's **Back** button or use its history list to return to the Online Companion page for Session 2.1, and then click the **Pepsi** hyperlink and wait while your browser loads the Pepsi home page shown in Figure 2-2. (Your home page might look different.) Note how the Pepsi page differs from the Coca-Cola page. The Pepsi page shown in Figure 2-2 has a very busy design and includes many hyperlinks—a stark contrast to the Coca-Cola page's simple design and single hyperlink. Pepsi has pursued a reputation for many years of being the action-oriented, aggressive drink for younger people and those of the older generation who want to feel like younger people. This consistent theme, featured in Pepsi advertising for decades, is reflected in the bold colors and design of the Pepsi home page.

Figure 2-2	PEPSI HOME PAGE

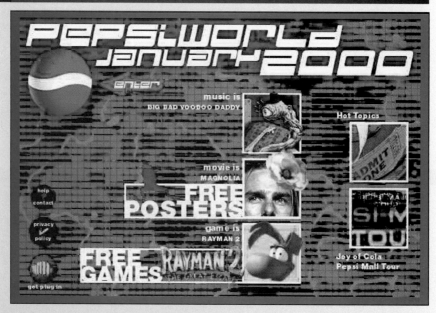

4. Explore the links on the Pepsi home page to see many of the same kinds of site features that exist in the Coca-Cola site. This theme of brightness, bold colors, and busy activities is consistent throughout much of the Pepsi site.

5. If a second browser window opened while you were exploring the Pepsi site, click the **Close** button on the second browser window. The Pepsi home page should still be open in the first browser window.

After seeing these two Web sites, Jean agrees that it would be difficult to argue that one of these sites is better than the other. Both companies are in the same industry, and each site offers similar opportunities to obtain information, but Jean and most other visitors would agree that these companies have established Web presences that are very different from each other. As you talk with Jean about what kind of Web presence might work best for

Treasure Trove, she begins to identify key elements of a good online presence. Jean notes that the popularity of the small town in which the store is located might be an important presence element. She also mentions that many of the figurines sold in the gift section have well-known brand names. You agree that the name of the town and the figurine brand names should be incorporated into the presence objectives for the Treasure Trove Web site.

Achieving Web Presence Goals

An effective Web site creates an attractive presence that meets the objectives of the business or other organization. These objectives include:

- Attracting visitors to the Web site
- Making the site interesting so that visitors stay and explore it
- Encouraging visitors to follow the site's links to obtain information
- Creating an impression consistent with the organization's desired image
- Reinforcing positive images about the organization that the visitor might already have

In the Coca-Cola Web site, you saw how that company used its recognizable trademarked Coke bottle to attract visitors into the site. Both the Coca-Cola and Pepsi sites include games and entertainment designed to make their sites interesting so visitors will stay and perhaps return to the site. Although the impressions created by the Coca-Cola and Pepsi sites are quite different, each is consistent with its organization's desired image and both sites are intended to reinforce the positive images that visitors are likely to already have.

Two other companies that have Web sites featuring their well-known brands are Toyota and Quaker Oats. Jean is interested in learning more about how brands can become part of a Web presence, so you decide to examine these two sites.

To examine the Toyota and Quaker Oats Web sites:

1. Click your browser's **Back** button or use its history list to return to the Online Companion page for Session 2.1, and then click the **Toyota** hyperlink and wait while your browser loads the Toyota home page shown in Figure 2-3. The Toyota site is a good example of an effective Web presence. The site provides a product showroom feature, links to detailed information about each product line, links to dealers, and links to information about the company and the ancillary services it offers, such as financing and insurance. The page offers a link for help and information about how to contact the company; it also has a site search feature. The owners' community link allows registered Toyota car owners to obtain answers to questions about maintenance and estimates of their auto's current value. Toyota has created a presence with this page that is consistent with its corporate philosophy. The statement that appears on the page, "We've built a Web site that illustrates why Toyota's Cars and Trucks are ideal for your life," illustrates the consistency of the message that Toyota is trying to convey. To the extent that the Web site fulfills that promise, it is an effective extension of Toyota's corporate presence through the Internet to customers and potential customers.

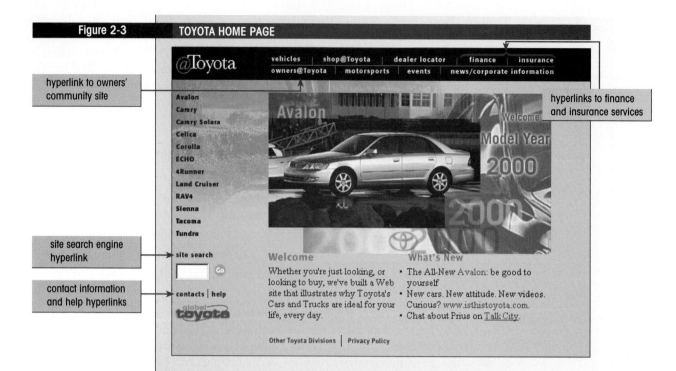

Figure 2-3   **TOYOTA HOME PAGE**

hyperlink to owners' community site

hyperlinks to finance and insurance services

site search engine hyperlink

contact information and help hyperlinks

2. Click your browser's **Back** button or use its history list to return to the Online Companion page for Session 2.1, and then click the **Quaker Oats** hyperlink and wait while your browser loads the Quaker Oats home page shown in Figure 2-4. The Quaker Oats site offers far fewer hyperlinks than the Toyota site and provides a more subtle sense of corporate presence. The page includes pictures of popular consumer products made by Quaker Oats—including the smiling Quaker figure—although it does not focus its page on that image as Coca-Cola does with its Coke bottle. The page provides hyperlinks to a good selection of information about the company. The site is a very straightforward presentation of these information links. The Quaker Oats home page includes links to many of the same topics as the Toyota site, including financial information, employment opportunities, and other information about the company. Yet, the Quaker Oats site offers the visitor a completely different experience and impression than the Toyota site offers its visitors.

Figure 2-4	QUAKER OATS HOME PAGE

stock price and trading volume information

images from easily recognized consumer brands

These examples illustrate that the Web can integrate an opportunity for enhancing the image of a business with the provision of information. For some organizations, this integrated image-enhancement capability is a key goal of their Web presence efforts. Many not-for-profit organizations use their Web sites effectively to enhance their images. You explain to Jean that businesses like hers can learn many things about creating a Web presence from these organizations.

Exploring the Web Presences of Not-for-Profit Organizations

Businesses are organized to generate revenue that is greater than their expenses, resulting in a profit. A **not-for-profit organization** is an organization that is devoted to some other goal, such as promoting science, the arts, humanitarian causes, education, political interests, or the general welfare. Not-for-profit organizations can use their Web sites as a central resource for integrated communications with their varied and often geographically dispersed constituencies.

An important part of many not-for-profit organizations' missions is information dissemination. The Web allows them to integrate information dissemination with fund raising while providing a two-way contact channel with persons engaged in the organization's work. This combination of information dissemination with a two-way contact channel can be a key element in any successful electronic commerce Web site. Interestingly, many not-for-profit organizations have been far ahead of most businesses in combining these two elements in their Web presences. The Web site of the American Civil Liberties Union (ACLU), which is devoted to the advocacy of individual rights in the United States, is one excellent example of a site with this combined thrust.

To examine the ACLU Web site:

1. Click your browser's **Back** button or use its history list to return to the Online Companion page for Session 2.1, and then click the **ACLU** hyperlink and wait while your browser loads the ACLU home page shown in Figure 2-5. This page allows interested visitors to learn more about the ACLU and to join the organization if their interest is piqued by what they see. The right side of the page contains hyperlinks to ACLU pages organized by issue. Many visitors to this site are seeking information about a particular issue and find this way of organizing ACLU resources to be very helpful. The center section of the page highlights current controversies or important issues in which the ACLU is playing a major role. Because these issues change frequently, the Web page you see will contain different issues.

Figure 2-5	ACLU HOME PAGE

2. Click one of the center section links and read enough text on the page that loads in your browser to learn what the issue or controversy is and what position the ACLU is taking. Consider whether you would be encouraged by the ACLU position if it were similar to your own feelings about the issue. This is one way the ACLU provides information and attracts like-minded people to join.

3. Click your browser's **Back** button to return to the ACLU home page.

4. Click the **FEEDBACK** hyperlink at the bottom of the page. Your browser will load a form that you can use to report a civil liberties violation, obtain assistance with legal research, ask questions about ACLU membership, or request permission to reprint ACLU publications. This is an example of how the ACLU uses their Web site as a communication tool. Through this link, the ACLU makes many first contacts with people who later become members of the organization.

Not-for-profit organizations can use the Web to stay in touch with existing members and identify new opportunities for serving them. Organizations such as **Amnesty International** and the **United Nations** also use the Web to create international communities of interested persons. Similarly, political parties use the Web to offer information about party positions on issues, to recruit members, to keep existing members informed, and to provide communication links to visitors who have questions about the party. All of the major U.S. political parties have Web sites. In addition, political organizations that are not affiliated with a specific party also accomplish similar goals with their Web presences. Jean asks if her business can use a Web presence to stay in touch with customers and help her identify new items and services that customers might want. You point out that Treasure Trove has much in common with museums. For example, many customers come to the Treasure Trove to admire antiques that they could never afford to buy. In many cases, these customers become store patrons when they purchase a less expensive item or a book about the antiques they came to see.

Museums have found that the Web helps them introduce interested visitors to their collections and create a presence that matches their image. The Museum of Modern Art (MoMA) in New York City was one of the first museums in the world to use the Web this way.

To examine the MoMA Web site:

1. Click your browser's **Back** button or use its history list to return to the Online Companion page for Session 2.1, and then click the **MoMA** hyperlink and wait while your browser loads the MoMA home page shown in Figure 2-6. The museum has created a page that features a clean and functional design—two tenets of the modern art movement to which it is devoted. Each image represents a category of information about the museum. As you move your pointer over the descriptive text below each image, you will see a list of related hyperlinks.

Figure 2-6	MOMA HOME PAGE

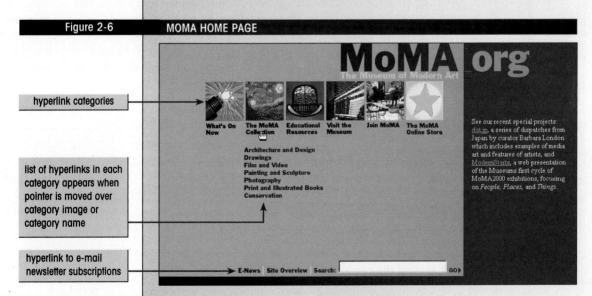

hyperlink categories

list of hyperlinks in each category appears when pointer is moved over category image or category name

hyperlink to e-mail newsletter subscriptions

TROUBLE? If a MoMA Online Survey window opens, click the Close button on its title bar. If you do not see the hyperlink list for a category, ask your instructor or technical support person for help.

2. Click the **E-News** hyperlink at the bottom of the page. Your browser will load a form that you can use to subscribe to e-mail newsletters about the museum and its activities. For example, one of the subscriptions provides an annotated listing of special exhibitions appearing each month at the museum.

You tell Jean that the MoMA Web site is interesting while providing clear paths to museum resources for visitors who know what they are seeking when they access the Web site. More importantly, its e-mail newsletters offers site visitors a way of communicating with the museum. You suggest to Jean that an e-mail newsletter might be a good idea for the Treasure Trove Web site. Such a newsletter would help Jean communicate with customers who visit infrequently or make small purchases. A newsletter can be a very inexpensive way of building positive feelings and even loyalty in customers who may someday return to purchase more expensive items.

How the Web Is Different

When firms first started creating Web sites in the mid-1990s, they often built simple sites that conveyed basic information about their businesses. Few firms conducted any market research to see what potential visitors might want to obtain from these Web sites, and even fewer considered what business infrastructure adjustments would be needed to service the site. For example, few firms had an e-mail address link on their sites. Those firms that did include an e-mail link often understaffed the department responsible for answering visitors' e-mail messages. Thus, many site visitors sent e-mail messages that were never answered. This failure to understand how the Web is different from other presence-building media is one reason that so many businesses fail to achieve their objectives. Dr. Jakob Nielsen, a noted Web site usability researcher, has written widely on this subject and on other general Web site design issues. You may wish to follow the hyperlink in the Online Companion to his **Failure of Corporate Websites** article to learn more about his views.

Most Web sites that are designed to create an organization's presence on the Web include links to a fairly standard collection of information about the organization. Such sites often give their visitors easy access to a history of the organization, a statement of objectives or mission statement, information about products or services, financial information, and ways to communicate with the organization. Sites achieve varying levels of success based largely on how they offer this information. Web site designers need to know that visual presentation qualities are important, but it is even more important that they understand the Web as an interactive medium.

Meeting the Needs of Web Site Visitors

Businesses realize that every visitor to their Web sites is a potential customer. Thus, an important concern for businesses crafting a Web presence is the variation in important visitor characteristics. People who visit a Web site seldom arrive by accident; they are there for a reason. Unfortunately, for the Web designer trying to make a site that will be useful for everyone, those visitors arrive for many different reasons, such as:

- Learning about products or services that the company offers
- Buying the products or services that the company offers
- Obtaining information about warranties or service and repair policies for products they have purchased
- Obtaining general information about the company or organization
- Obtaining financial information for making an investment or credit-granting decision
- Identifying the people who manage the company or organization
- Obtaining telephone or other contact information for a person or department in the organization

Creating a Web site that meets the needs of visitors with such a wide range of motivations can be challenging. Not only do Web site visitors arrive with different needs that they hope to meet, they arrive with different experience levels. Technology issues can also arise. Web site visitors can be connected to the Internet through a variety of communication channels that provide different bandwidths and data transmission speeds. They also will be using several different Web browsers. Even those visitors who are using the same browsers can have a variety of configurations and might include different browser add-in or plug-in software. Web sites that consider and accommodate these many visitor characteristics and technology variations can better convert visitors into customers by Web sites that cater to as many people as possible.

Creating Flexible Web Site Interfaces

One of the best ways to accommodate a broad range of visitor needs is to build flexibility into the Web site's interface. The **interface** of a Web site is the view it offers to visitors and includes its layout, colors, hyperlinks, images, and controls (such as buttons). Many sites offer separate versions with and without frames and give visitors the option of choosing either one. Some sites offer a text-only version of the site. A text-only version can be an especially important feature for blind or visually impaired visitors who use software such as the **IBM Home Page Reader** to access Web site content. This software "speaks" the content of a Web page as it appears in a browser window. It reads the text of a Web page and describes the graphics objects of the page if they have been marked with alternative tags. An **alternative tag** is an HTML tag that includes a text description of a graphic object. The alternative tag is ALT and is an optional component of an image source HTML tag. For example, the HTML code

    <IMG SRC="Virginia300.gif" WIDTH=302 HEIGHT=114 ALT="Virginia's Antiques">

is used in the Web page for Virginia's Antiques that appears in Figure 2-7.

| Figure 2-7 | VIRGINIA'S ANTIQUES HOME PAGE |

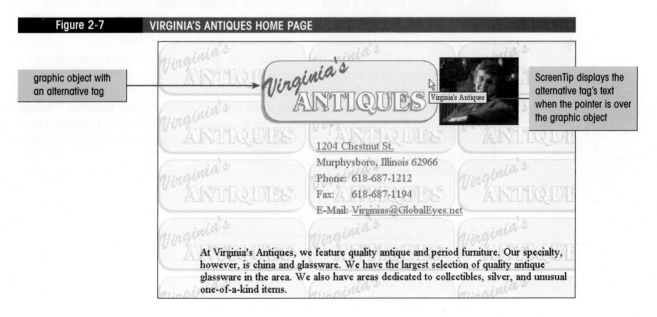

graphic object with an alternative tag

ScreenTip displays the alternative tag's text when the pointer is over the graphic object

1204 Chestnut St.
Murphysboro, Illinois 62966
Phone: 618-687-1212
Fax: 618-687-1194
E-Mail: Virginias@GlobalEyes.net

At Virginia's Antiques, we feature quality antique and period furniture. Our specialty, however, is china and glassware. We have the largest selection of quality antique glassware in the area. We also have areas dedicated to collectibles, silver, and unusual one-of-a-kind items.

Most browsers display a ScreenTip, such as the one shown in Figure 2-7, when the pointer moves over a graphic object that includes an alternative tag. The browser also displays the alternative tag's text as the images load or when a browser cannot load the images. The **W3C Web Accessibility Initiative** site includes many useful links to information about making Web pages easier to use for people with disabilities.

Jean wants the Treasure Trove site to include photos of antiques that are currently for sale. You explain that a site design with many graphics can be very slow to load in visitors' browsers. You suggest providing Web site visitors with the option of selecting smaller versions of the images so the page will load on low bandwidth connections in a reasonable time. Visitors who wish to examine an item more closely can select a larger version of just that item. One popular way to implement this feature is to provide small images (or **thumbnails**) for all items that are hyperlinks to larger images of those items. A visitor clicks the small image to open a larger version. By taking advantage of a user's intuition (most people will instinctively try clicking an image to learn more about it), you can create more effective Web interfaces.

Some antiques, such as clocks, have intricate mechanisms and movements that are interesting to potential customers. You suggest including streaming video clips of these items in the Web site and offering visitors the option of specifying a connection type so the streaming media adjusts itself to the bandwidth for that visitor's connection. These design features will ensure that all Web site visitors will download images in the fastest possible manner for their connection speeds.

A good site design lets visitors choose among information attributes, such as level of detail, ways of grouping or selecting items to display, viewing format, and downloading format. Many sites give visitors a selectable level of detail by organizing product information by product line, with hyperlinks to pages containing pictures of each item in that product line and brief descriptions. By using hyperlinked graphics for the product pictures, the site offers visitors the option of clicking the product picture, which then opens a page of detailed specifications for that product. This approach might work well for the Treasure Trove Web site, so you decide to show Jean an example of selectable level of detail at the Alice's Antiques of SoHo Web site.

To examine the Alice's Antiques of SoHo Web site:

1. Click your browser's **Back** button or use its history list to return to the Online Companion page for Session 2.1, and then click the **Alice's Antiques of SoHo** hyperlink and wait while your browser loads the home page.

2. Click the **Go Directly To My Inventory** link to open the current version of the page shown in Figure 2-8 (this store's inventory changes regularly; your page will look different). Because this page (and the other pages on this site) contain large image files, the pages may load slowly in your browser. Note the "Please be patient" message at the top of the page shown in Figure 2-8. It explains to site visitors that the page might be slow to load, so they do not become overly concerned.

Figure 2-8   **ALICE'S ANTIQUES OF SOHO INVENTORY PAGE**

message that informs visitors of possible page-loading delay

click these photos to open larger, more detailed photos

hyperlinks to query form

Alice's Antiques of SoHo

Click on a picture to bring up a larger, more detailed image of the catalog item. There are 65 items in the catalog. Listing items 1 to 10. Please be patient.

Room setting.

For more information, or to purchase this item

Antique aquarium.

For more information, or to purchase this item

Room setting.

For more information, or to purchase this item

3. Click one of the photos that appears on the inventory page to see a larger, more detailed version of the item. The larger picture shows more detail about the item; loading a page full of such large images would take a long time. By offering the smaller photos, Alice's Antiques gives visitors a way to browse the inventory and select only those items they want to view in more detail.

4. Click your browser's **Back** button to return to the inventory page, and then click one of the text hyperlinks that appears to the right of the photos. A query form opens that you can use to request more information about the item or make an offer to purchase the item.

Web sites can also offer visitors multiple information formats by including links to files in those formats. For example, a company's site might include a Web page with financial information. This page could include links to an HTML file, an Adobe PDF file, and an Excel workbook file. Each of these files would contain the same financial information; however, the use of multiple file types lets visitors choose the format that best suits their immediate needs. Visitors looking for a specific financial fact might choose to scan the HTML files displayed in their Web browsers. Other visitors might want a copy of the entire annual report as it was printed. These visitors could select the PDF file and either view it in their browser or download and print the file. Visitors who want to conduct analyses on the financial data could download the Excel workbook file and perform calculations with the data using their own Excel software. One of the world's largest manufacturers of computer processor chips, Intel, offers these options for its financial reports.

To examine the Intel Web site:

1. Click your browser's **Back** button or use its history list to return to the Online Companion page for Session 2.1, and then click the **Intel** hyperlink and wait while your browser loads the Intel home page.

2. After the home page has been loaded, move your pointer over the **company info** link on the left side of the Web page. As you move the pointer over this heading, a menu will appear.

   TROUBLE? If the menu does not appear and you cannot see the Investor Relations link, then the home page is still loading in your browser. Wait a moment, and then repeat Step 2. If the page has loaded and you still cannot see the menu, ask your instructor or technical support person for help.

3. Click the **Investor Relations** link that appears in the company info menu to open the Investor Relations page. The left side of the Investor Relations page includes several subheadings, including one titled "financials".

4. Click the **Annual Reports** link under the financials subheading to open the Annual Reports page, and then click the link to the most recent Intel annual report in the page that opens. Explore the pages of the annual report. You will find that Intel provides ways to read each page of the report in your Web browser, print each page from your Web browser, read the entire report using the Adobe PDF reader software, and download the entire report in Adobe PDF format. If you follow the facts and figures or financial information links, you will find that Intel has also provided downloadable Excel files containing a variety of information about the company, including its complete set of financial statements.

Another way to increase the flexibility of user interaction with a Web site is to provide multiple ways to find information on the site. Companies that organize their products, services, or information offerings in more than one way on their Web sites make it easier for different visitors to find exactly what they want. Many Treasure Trove customers collect specific items, such as porcelain figures. When these customers visit the Treasure Trove site, they might want to look for figures made by a certain manufacturer such as Lladro or Wedgewood. Other customers might not collect a particular manufacturer's figures but instead might collect types of figures, such as ballet dancers or animals. You explain to Jean that Web sites often provide different ways for customers to search their inventories for specific items. You decide to show Jean this type of Web site organization by visiting a vitamin and health food site that lets you easily locate certain brands of products, particular categories of products, or products with a specific name. The VitaminShoppe.com site is a good example of how a firm in this industry gives its site visitors a variety of ways to obtain information about its products.

To examine the VitaminShoppe.com Web site:

1. Click your browser's **Back** button or use its history list to return to the Online Companion page for Session 2.1, and then click the **VitaminShoppe.com** hyperlink and wait while your browser loads the home page shown in Figure 2-9. The VitaminShoppe.com home page includes several ways to browse or search its product offerings. The top of the page includes links to two broad categories of products. The home page displays the Vitamins & Supplements page by default.

Figure 2-9	VITAMINSHOPPE.COM HOME PAGE

links to two broad categories of products

browse or search using five different product classification schemes

links to products grouped by customer category

2. Click the **Health Care Products** link at the top of the page to see a list of the items the company offers in this category, such as back supports, ankle supports, and similar products.

3. Click your browser's **Back** button to return to the VitaminShoppe.com home page, and then click the **By Brand** link to open the Shop by Brand page. VitaminShoppe.com carries a large number of brands, so it has organized this section alphabetically.

4. Click the **S** link, and then click the **Solaray** link on the page that opens. The Solaray page includes an alphabetical list of all Solaray products that VitaminShoppe.com carries.

5. Click the **By Category** link to browse within product categories. For example, if you click the link for Herbal Products, you would find lists of herbs that VitaminShoppe.com carries. You could use this feature to find a particular type of herb packaged by different manufacturers. The A to Z Index performs a similar function; however, it includes all products in an alphabetized list, not just a particular category of products.

The VitaminShoppe.com site offers many other ways to search for products. For example, the links on the right side of the home page take site visitors to products grouped by customer category. After reviewing the VitaminShoppe.com site, Jean tells you that she is beginning to think of many different ways for categorizing Treasure Trove's inventory on the new Web site.

Usability Testing

Research indicates that few businesses meet their visitors' needs with their current Web presences. Even sites that succeed in achieving most of their goals often fail to provide sufficient interactive contact opportunities for site visitors. Many firms' Web sites still give the general impression that the firm is too important and its employees are too busy to respond to inquiries. This is no way to encourage visitors to become customers! In response to criticisms that their Web sites are not meeting users' needs, some organizations have started performing usability tests on their Web sites. A **usability test** is an observation or monitoring of persons' actions as they use a Web site.

A growing number of consulting firms offer usability testing services; however, many companies are creating their own testing facilities. In its simplest form, a usability test will ask the Web site users to talk aloud as they use the site in a testing facility. The testers record the Web site user's comments as they navigate the site in search of information. More sophisticated usability tests use cameras that track users' eye movements, mouse clicks, and keyboard activity. The recordings of Web user activities are then analyzed to determine which parts of the Web site work well and which do not.

Companies that have done usability tests have found that they can learn a great deal about meeting visitor needs by conducting focus groups and watching how different customers navigate through a series of Web site test designs. Most Web design experts agree that the cost of usability testing is so low compared to the total cost of a Web site design project that it should almost always be included in such projects.

Although some common themes appear repeatedly in usability testing results, each company will find that some characteristics of its Web site should be designed to match how its visitors use the site. Thus, companies that do usability testing often create sites that look quite different from one another even though they might all be doing usability testing.

Jean is interested in learning more about how companies have improved their Web sites based on the results of usability testing. You tell Jean about two firms that have undertaken major redesign efforts after examining how visitors were navigating and obtaining information from their sites.

T. Rowe Price built its first Web site in 1996. Within two years, there was so much information on the site that visitors had a difficult time getting to the data they were seeking. For example, users had to click through five or six pages to get to investor reports. The company rolled out a redesigned Web site in late 1998. One of the design team's goals was to ensure that customers would never need to click through more than two pages to get the information they were seeking. The new design was focused on function rather than visual appeal and included a greater number of links on the home page. Eastman Kodak also redesigned its site in response to user feedback. Kodak's redesign resulted in a Web site structure similar to that of the T. Rowe Price design, with a large number of links on the home page.

To compare the T. Rowe Price and Eastman Kodak Web site redesigns:

1. Click your browser's **Back** button or use its history list to return to the Online Companion page for Session 2.1, and then click the **T. Rowe Price** hyperlink and wait while your browser loads the home page. The home page includes many links, but they are well organized. Links to current financial news items appear in a column in the center of the page. It is easy for site visitors to narrow their visual search of the page if they are seeking a particular type of information. The drop-down lists of links on the right side of the page (titled "I Want To..." and "I Want Fund Info On...") give visitors access to frequently used services, such as accessing their accounts or requesting information about a particular investment. These lists are a good way to provide many links without using a lot of space on the Web page.

2. Use the home page links to explore the T. Rowe Price site. Note that links to similar information are grouped together. For example, the links to information about retirement planning, saving for college, and tax strategies are all in the same section of the page's left column.

3. Click your browser's **Back** button to return to the Online Companion page for Session 2.1, and then click the **Eastman Kodak** hyperlink and wait while your browser loads the home page shown in Figure 2-10. The Eastman Kodak page is similar to the T. Rowe Price page because it includes many links. The page has three important elements at the top of the page: the Products link, the Service & Support link, and a search text box for the site. Kodak's usability studies indicated that these were the three features visitors expected to find on the site and would use most frequently. Some site visitors were seeking advice on taking better pictures or had general questions about photography. The remaining links on the home page provide information for these visitors.

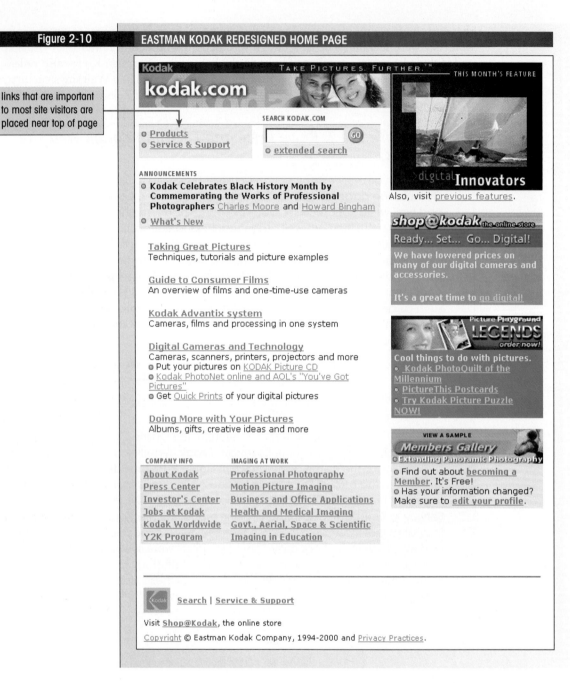

Figure 2-10   EASTMAN KODAK REDESIGNED HOME PAGE

links that are important to most site visitors are placed near top of page

In contrast to the experience of Kodak and T. Rowe Price, usability research conducted by **Maytag** found that its customers wanted fewer links on the home page. Both Kodak and T. Rowe Price sell products that have a large intangible element. The benefits of high-quality photographs and sound investment plans are complex and can be hard for consumers to evaluate. Thus, both the Kodak and T. Rowe Price Web sites offer customers and potential customers a large number of links on their home pages so each customer can explore and identify benefits in a different way. The tangible nature of Maytag's main product line is different from T. Rowe Price's intangible financial products and the intangible benefits of Kodak's cameras and photofinishing products. Thus, the Maytag home page includes a single graphic link to one featured product, a drop-down list of links to information about other products, and only a few other links at the top of the home page. The links at the top of the page take the visitor to important information, such as dealer locations and customer service pages. The Maytag home page appears in Figure 2-11.

Figure 2-11	MAYTAG HOME PAGE

drop-down list of hyperlinks to information about specific appliances

hyperlink to featured product

Although the resulting Web sites were different, all three of these redesigned sites are notable for the attention the design team paid to the needs of potential site visitors. Web site usability experts have identified the following important factors that Web site designers should consider as they create or update Web sites:

- Design the site around how visitors will navigate the links, not around the company's organizational structure
- Use small graphics and keep file sizes small so pages load quickly
- Place frequently used links at the top of the page
- Clearly show the company name and contact information on the home page
- Ensure that all pages include a link back to the home page for visitors who do not enter the site through the home page
- Avoid using business jargon and terms that visitors might not understand
- Build the site to work for visitors using the oldest Web browser software on the oldest computer with the smallest monitor connected through the lowest bandwidth connection still likely to be in use—even if you must create multiple versions of Web pages
- Be consistent with the use of design features and colors on all Web pages within a site
- Make sure that navigation controls and links are clearly labeled or otherwise recognizable
- Check that text and background color combinations are visible to color-blind visitors
- Conduct usability testing on several versions of the Web site design, and update the site as necessary to implement user suggestions

Using these guidelines can help make visitors' Web experiences more efficient, effective, and memorable in a positive way. Usability is an important element of creating an effective Web presence. For an interesting look at Web design issues, you can visit the **Webby Awards** site. The Webby Awards are given to sites that "exemplify the kinds of sites that Internet users should visit every day for information and entertainment" as judged by a panel of Web designers, journalists, and industry leaders. Of course, not all Web sites are up to the standards set by the Webby Awards judging panel. The Spinfrenzy.com Mud Brick Awards, also known as the "Muddies," are awarded tongue-in-cheek to sites that are, according to the Spinfrenzy.com page, "the world's ugliest Web sites."

To examine some Web sites "before" and "after" their redesigns:

1. Click your browser's **Back** button or use its history list to return to the Online Companion page for Session 2.1, and then click the **Spinfrenzy.com Mud Brick Awards** hyperlink and wait while your browser loads the home page.

2. Scroll down to the **For more dirt** heading, and then click the **Click here** hyperlink to before and after shots of past Muddies winners. Examine some of the sites that have taken their Mud Brick Award statuses seriously enough to redesign their sites.

3. Click your browser's **Back** button to return to the Mud Brick Awards main page. From here you can follow hyperlinks to learn more about the Mud Brick Awards and even submit a site you think is a bad example of Web site design.

4. Close your Web browser and close your dial-up connection, if necessary.

Although individual perceptions vary, the Webby Awards site and the Mud Brick Awards site provide links to examples of some of the best and the worst in Web page design. Jean thanks you for taking her on a tour of these sites. She agrees that they can provide guidance as you both work on the Web site design for Treasure Trove.

Web Site Advertising Effectiveness and Cost

As more companies rely on their Web sites to create favorable impressions on potential customers, the issue of measuring Web site effectiveness has become important. Mass media efforts are measured by estimates of audience size, circulation, or number of addressees. When a company purchases mass media advertising, it pays a dollar amount for each thousand persons in the estimated audience. This pricing metric is called **cost per thousand** and is often abbreviated **CPM**.

Measuring Web audiences is more complicated because of the Web's interactivity and because the value of a visitor to an advertiser depends on how much information the site gathers from the visitor (such as the visitor's name, address, e-mail address, telephone number, and other demographic data). Because each visitor volunteers or declines to provide this kind of information, all visitors are not of equal value. Internet advertisers have developed some Web-specific metrics for site activity; however, these metrics are not generally accepted and are currently the subject of debate.

A **visit** occurs when a visitor loads a page from the Web site. Further page loads from the same site are included in the visit for a set period of time. The period of time chosen depends on the type of site. A site that features stock quotes might use a short time period because visitors may load the page to check the price of one stock and reload the page 15 minutes later to check the stock's price again. A museum site would expect a visitor to load multiple pages over a longer time period during a visit and would use a longer visit time window. The first time that a particular visitor loads a Web site page is called a **trial visit**; subsequent page loads are called **repeat visits**. Each page loaded by a visitor counts as a **page view**. If the page contains an ad, the page load is called an **ad view**. Some Web pages have banner ads that continue to load and reload as long as the page is open in the visitor's Web browser. Each time the banner ad loads an ad it is called an **impression**, and if the visitor clicks the banner ad to open the advertiser's page, that action is called a **click** or a **click-through**.

Banner ads are often sold on a CPM basis where the "thousand" is 1,000 impressions. Rates vary greatly and depend on how much demographic information the Web site obtains about its visitors, but most are within the range of $1 to $100 CPM. The percentage of site visitors that click banner ads, called the **click-through rate**, has steadily declined as the Web has matured. Once over 2%, the click-through rate is currently under 1% and is continuing to drop. Decreasing click-through rates have made it difficult for sellers of banner ad space on the Web to maintain their CPM rates for that space. Advertising researchers and consultants continue to search for ways to make banner ads more effective and to identify better ways of attracting visitors to Web sites. You will learn about some of these newer techniques for attracting Web site visitors in Session 2.2.

Session 2.1 QUICK CHECK

1. True or False: Companies that are in the same industry will usually develop similar Web presences.

2. What are three important things that an effective Web site should encourage site visitors to do?

3. Having a Web site that integrates image enhancement with communications capabilities is especially important for _____ organizations.

4. In Web site design, creating an attractive presentation is important, but even more important is understanding the Web as an _____ medium.

5. True or False: Web site visitors will be connected to the Internet in many different ways.

6. Offering a(n) _____ version of a Web site can be important for users who are visually impaired or blind.

7. Because different Web site visitors often seek different kinds of information, what key elements should a good Web site design include?

8. What is a Web site usability test?

SESSION 2.2

In this session, you will learn how to identify and reach customers on the Web by using marketing approaches designed specifically to work on the Web, such as technology-enabled relationship management and permission marketing. Because the Web is a new way to communicate with customers, companies face challenges when measuring the effectiveness of that communication. You will learn about these challenges and how businesses are trying to overcome them. You will also learn about branding, how businesses develop brands, and the costs of branding strategies. You will learn how some branding strategies, such as affiliate marketing, have became feasible for the first time on the Web.

Identifying and Reaching Customers

An important element of success in doing business on the Web is identifying your customers and connecting with them. The people who visit electronic commerce Web sites are either customers or potential customers. In this section, you will learn how a Web site can help firms identify potential customers, encourage existing customers to visit the site, and reach out to new customers.

The Nature of Communication on the Web

As you talk with Jean to get a better idea of how she and her employees interact with their customers, you explain that businesses use two general ways of identifying and reaching customers: personal contact and mass media. In **personal contact**, the firm's employees individually search, qualify, and contact potential customers. This personal contact approach to identifying and reaching customers is sometimes called **prospecting**. Companies that use the **mass media** approach prepare advertising and promotional materials about the company and its products or services. They then deliver these messages to potential customers by broadcasting them on television or radio, printing them in newspapers or magazines, posting them on highway billboards, or mailing them.

Some experts divide mass media approaches into two categories: broadcast media and addressable media. **Broadcast media** are directed toward the general public—the company does not know which specific customers or potential customers will receive the advertising. Television, radio, and newspaper advertising fall into this category. **Addressable media** are sent to a known addressee and include direct mail, telephone calls, and e-mail.

Many businesses use a combination of mass media and personal contact to identify and reach customers. For example, an insurance company might use mass media to create and maintain the public's general awareness of its insurance products and reputation, while its salespersons might use prospecting techniques to identify specific potential customers. Once an individual becomes a customer, the insurance company maintains contact through a combination of personal contact and mailings.

Even though a large number of people now use the Internet and many companies seem to view their Web sites as billboards or broadcasts, the Internet is not a mass medium. Nor is the Internet a personal contact tool, although it can provide individuals with the convenience of making personal contacts through e-mail and newsgroups. Jeff Bezos, founder of Amazon.com, has described the Web as the ideal tool for reaching what he calls "the middle," markets that are too small to justify a mass media campaign, yet too large to cover using personal contact. Figure 2-12 illustrates the position of the Web as a customer-contact medium, between the broad markets addressed by mass media and the highly focused markets addressed by personal contact selling and promotion techniques.

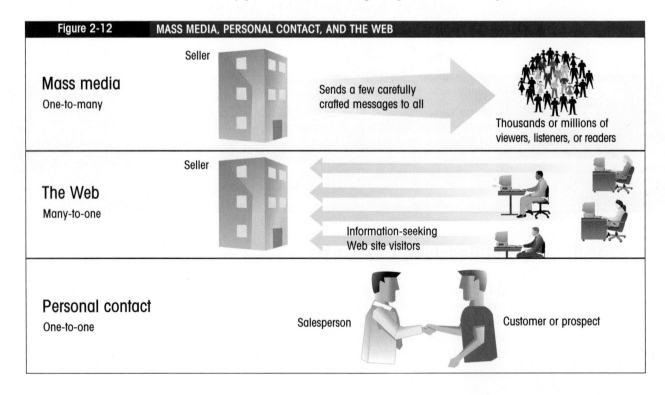

Figure 2-12   MASS MEDIA, PERSONAL CONTACT, AND THE WEB

Mass media
One-to-many

Seller

Sends a few carefully crafted messages to all

Thousands or millions of viewers, listeners, or readers

The Web
Many-to-one

Seller

Information-seeking Web site visitors

Personal contact
One-to-one

Salesperson

Customer or prospect

To help Jean better understand the three approaches to selling that appear in Figure 2-12, you present an example of a Treasure Trove customer who has heard about a new Waterford crystal vase design but would like to know more about it before making a purchase. You explain how the customer's information acquisition process would vary depending on the medium that the customer used to gather information about the vase design, as follows:

- *Mass media:* The customer was exposed to general promotional messages from Waterford that created impressions about the level of quality associated with the Waterford brand. Any existing impressions of Waterford quality will influence the customer's expectations and perceptions of the quality and attractiveness of the new vase design. The Waterford advertising may have appeared on television, radio, or in print. For example, the customer may have heard the designer interviewed on a radio program or might have read a review of the new design in a collectors' magazine. Most of the elements in this process involve the customer as a passive recipient of information. This communication channel is labeled "Mass media" and appears at the top of Figure 2-12. Communication in this model flows from one advertiser to many potential customers and thus is called a **one-to-many communication model**. The defining characteristic of mass media promotion is that the seller is active and the buyer is passive.

- *Personal contact:* Most items sold using personal contact are high-dollar value items such as houses, cars, boats, or furniture. The cost of devoting a salesperson's efforts to smaller dollar value sales can be prohibitive. However, in the case of gift items such as crystal vases, gift store owners and employees often devote considerable time and resources to developing a close relationship with their customers. Although each individual gift item sale may not be a large-value transaction, people who frequent local gift stores tend to buy many items over time. Thus, the gift store's investment in developing personal contacts is often rewarded. A customer may visit a local gift store and strike up a conversation with the owner or a knowledgeable employee. In the personal contact model, this person would most likely be someone with whom the customer has already established a relationship. The owner or employee would offer the customer an opinion on the new vase design based on having seen many vases and perhaps by having studied art or having done glassmaking. This opinion would be expressed as part of a two-way conversational interchange. This interchange would usually include several conversational elements, such as discussions about the weather, local sports, or politics, which are not directly related to the transaction. These other interchanges are part of the trust-building and trust-maintaining activities that gift store owners and employees undertake to maintain the relationship element of the personal contact model. The underlying **one-to-one communications model** appears at the bottom of Figure 2-12 and is labeled "Personal contact." The defining characteristic of information gathering in the personal contact model is the wide-ranging interchange that occurs within the framework of an existing trust relationship. Both the buyer and the seller (or the seller's representative) actively participate in this exchange of information.

- *The Web:* To obtain information about the new Waterford crystal vase design on the Web, the customer could search for Web site references to the new design. The customer might identify several Web sites that offer such information. These sites might include the manufacturer's **Waterford Crystal** site, the sites of gift shops that sell Waterford crystal, sites operated by collectors or dealers of crystal glassware, or discussion groups focused on the subject of collectible crystal glassware. The customer might encounter some advertising material created by the manufacturer while searching the Web;

however, customers can choose not to view the manufacturer's ads. The Web affords its users many communication channels. Figure 2-12 shows only one of the communication models that can occur when using the Web to search for product information. The model labeled "The Web" in Figure 2-12 is the **many-to-one communications model**. The Web gives buyers and sellers the flexibility of using a one-to-one model (as in the personal contact model) in which buyers communicate via the Web with individuals working for the seller, or even to engage in **many-to-many communications** with other potential buyers. The defining characteristic of product information searches on the Web is that the buyer actively participates in the search and controls the length, depth, and scope of the search.

Jean is very interested in these different communication models. Treasure Trove uses the mass media approach for many of its branded gift items and supplies. Branded gift items include figurines, books, miniatures, and greeting cards. Supply items include polishes, furniture restoration kits, and storage bags for silverware. The manufacturers of these items often advertise in mass media outlets, such as television and collectors' magazines.

Jean tells you that Treasure Trove uses the personal contact model to sell the more expensive items in the store, such as antique furniture and paintings. However, Jean notes that personal contact is also necessary to sell many lower-priced items, such as the handmade craft items made by local townspeople. Because no manufacturer uses mass media to advertise or promote these smaller-valued items, Treasure Trove must use personal contact to provide customers with product awareness and information.

You both agree that Treasure Trove may be able to use the Web to help sell all of its products in some way. Using the Web site to advertise the items currently sold through personal contact should make it easier to sell those items. Some of the smaller-valued gift items and many of the supplies are good candidates for direct sales through the Web site.

Using the Web's Interactive Nature Effectively

After reviewing these communication models, Jean wonders if there might be even more creative ways to use the Web to promote Treasure Trove and its products. You explain that many Web designers and consultants have criticized firms for their uninspired use of the Web's interactive nature. Some of these criticisms appear in the print media, but many appear in online newsletters or Web sites. The **Cluetrain Manifesto** Web site is a good example. On this site, four experienced Web design consultants present 95 statements directed at major businesses and other organizations that use the Web. These statements include many short phrases such as "Markets are conversations" and "Hyperlinks subvert hierarchy," but also include more lengthy bits of advice for Web presence creators. The Cluetrain Manifesto has generated considerable discussion and has been electronically "signed" by hundreds of visitors to the site, many of whom have added their own comments.

The main point of the Cluetrain Manifesto is that large firms must acknowledge and use the Web's capability for meaningful two-way communication between firms and their customers. They further argue that use of this communication process is not optional; companies that fail to communicate effectively through this channel will lose customers to competitors who do recognize that the Web is indeed different from traditional marketing channels.

New Marketing Approaches for the Web

Jean realizes that the Web is somewhere between mass media and personal contact, but that it covers a wide range of activities that lie between those two ways of interacting with customers. Using the Web to communicate with potential customers offers many of the advantages of personal contact selling and many of the cost savings of mass media. Figure 2-13 shows how these three information dissemination models compare on another important dimension—trust.

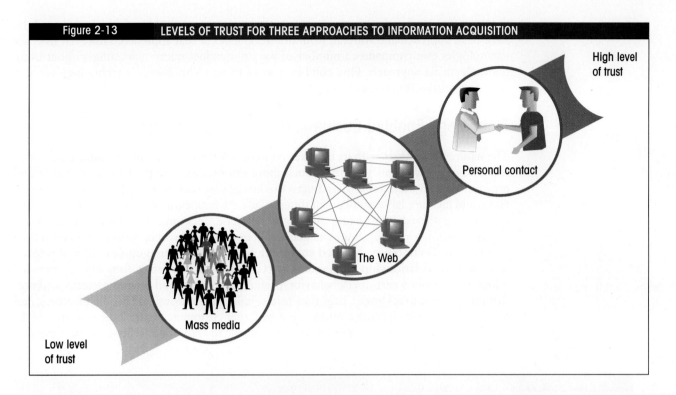

Figure 2-13   LEVELS OF TRUST FOR THREE APPROACHES TO INFORMATION ACQUISITION

After years of being barraged by television and radio commercials, most people have developed a resistance to the messages conveyed in the mass media. For example, in most cases, the audience impact of the shouted expression "New and improved!" has diminished to almost nothing. The overuse of superlatives has caused most people to distrust or ignore the messages contained in mass media. Television remote controls have a mute button and make channel surfing easy for a reason. As passive recipients of mass media messages that have no specific interesting content for us personally, many people have become advertising resistant. Attempts to re-create mass media advertising on the Web are doomed to fail for the same reasons.

Companies can use the Web to capture some of the benefits of personal contact and yet avoid some of the costs inherent in that approach. Most experts agree that it is better to scale up the trust-based model of personal contact selling to the Web than to scale down the mass marketing approach. Early in the life of the Web, researchers and business analysts began to see that customer-centered marketing strategies would be an excellent fit for the Internet marketplace that was then emerging. Increased consumer expectations and reduced product differentiation had led to increased competition and a splintering of mass markets. Both of these factors reduced the effectiveness of mass media advertising.

The main advertiser response to this decrease in effectiveness had been to identify specific portions of their markets and to target them with specific advertising messages. This practice, called **market segmentation**, divides the pool of potential customers into segments. **Segments** are usually defined in terms of demographic characteristics, such as age, gender, marital status, income level, and geographic location. For example, single women between the ages of 19 and 25 might be one market segment.

In the early 1990s, firms began identifying smaller and smaller market segments for specific advertising and promotion efforts. This practice of targeting very small market segments is called **micro marketing**. However, the low per-customer costs of traditional mass media advertising campaigns were not available when those media were targeted at very small market segments. This hampered the success of micro marketing strategies. Even though micro marketing was an improvement over mass media advertising, it still used the same basic approach and suffered from the weaknesses of that approach. However, Internet technologies give companies a number of ways to conduct micro marketing without using the mass media approach. One combination of these technologies is technology-enabled customer relationship management.

Technology-Enabled Customer Relationship Management

The nature of the Web, with its two-way communication features and traceable connection technology, allows firms to gather much more information about customer behavior and preferences than they could using micro marketing approaches. For the first time, companies could measure large numbers of things that were happening as customers and potential customers gathered information and made purchase decisions. The idea of technology-enabled customer relationship management became possible when promoting and selling via the Web. **Technology-enabled customer relationship management**, often shortened to **customer relationship management (CRM)**, occurs when a firm obtains detailed information about a customer's behavior, preferences, needs, and buying patterns, *and* uses that information to set prices, negotiate terms, tailor promotions, add product features, and otherwise customize its entire relationship with that customer. Figure 2-14 compares technology-enabled customer relationship management to traditional seller-customer interactions on seven dimensions.

Figure 2-14	CUSTOMER RELATIONSHIPS	
DIMENSIONS	TECHNOLOGY-ENABLED CUSTOMER RELATIONSHIP MANAGEMENT	TRADITIONAL RELATIONSHIPS WITH CUSTOMERS
Advertising	Information provided in response to specific customer inquiries	Deliver a uniform message to all customers
Targeting	Identifying and responding to specific customer behaviors and preferences	Market segmentation
Promotions and discounts offered	Individually tailored to customer	Same for all customers
Distribution channels	Direct or through intermediaries; customer's choice	Through intermediaries chosen by seller
Pricing of products or services	Negotiated with each customer	Set by seller for all customers
New product features	Respond to customer demands	Seller-determined based on its own research and development
Measurements used to manage the customer relationship	Customer retention, total value of the individual customer relationship	Market share, profit

Many business researchers distinguish between commerce in the physical world, or marketplace, and commerce in the information world, which they termed the **marketspace**. In the information world's marketspace, digital products and services are delivered through electronic communication channels, such as the Internet.

For years, businesses have valued information as a way of increasing sales, controlling costs, or both. However, few companies have considered how information itself might be a source of value. In the marketspace, firms can use information to create new value for customers. For example, CDnow, an online seller of music CDs, provides many valuable customer services that are derived purely from activities in the information world. CDnow will, if a customer so chooses, store an order history, provide recommendations based on previous purchases, and show current information on performing artists in which the customer is interested. You decide to show Jean some of the technology-enabled customer relationship management features of the CDnow Web site.

To examine the CDnow Web site:

1. Start your Web browser, and then go to the Online Companion by entering the URL **http://www.course.com/NewPerspectives/EC** in the appropriate location of your Web browser. Click the **Tutorial 2** link, and then click the **Session 2.2** link. Click the **CDnow link** and wait while your browser loads the CDnow home page.

2. Click the **MY CDNOW** tab, and then click the **Create Account** button in the New Customers area of the page.

   TROUBLE? If you do not wish to create an account with CDnow by providing your name, address, telephone number, and e-mail address, read the remaining steps without performing them at the computer.

3. Type your first name, your last name, and a password in the appropriate boxes in the Login Information section of the page.

4. If necessary, click the **Always login automatically** check box to clear it.

5. Type your name, address, telephone, and e-mail information in the appropriate boxes in the Shipping Address and Contact Information section of the page.

6. Scroll to the bottom of the page, click the **I do not wish to enroll in either program at this time** option button, and then click the **Create Account** button. A My CDnow page, customized with your name, appears in your browser.

7. Click the **Preferences** link on the left side of the page (you might need to scroll down to see this link). In the Email Subscriptions section of the page that opens, click any check boxes that contain check marks to clear them. Note in the Music Interests section of the page that, as a new customer, CDnow has already selected Rock as the default music interest for you. Most music buyers purchase CDs in that category, however, CDnow gives its customers the ability to specify which types of music they prefer. Even if you do not select a music preference on this page, CDnow will use technology-enabled customer relationship management techniques to provide suggestions as it learns more about your music preferences.

8. Scroll to the bottom of the page, click the **Update Preferences** button, click the **Search Classical** link that appears near the top of the page, type **Mozart** in the Composer box, and then click the **Find It** button. A search results page opens with a list of CDs that includes recordings of music written by Mozart. CDnow uses a different search engine for classical music. In most other types of music, the artist performing the music is usually more important to listeners than the composer (or the artist and composer are the same person). Classical music is also different because an orchestra and a conductor often perform it. Listeners may want to search these items separately. CDnow's classical search engine allows users to search by composer, conductor, and orchestra.

9. Click one of the links to open a page about the selected CD, and then click the **Save to Wish List** hyperlink. A page similar to the one shown in Figure 2-15 opens. (Your page will include the CD you selected in Step 8.) CDnow's customer relationship management software has tracked your selection and added that information to what it knows about your music preferences (the default check for rock music).

Figure 2-15	CDNOW WISH LIST PAGE

10. To see how CDnow incorporated this new information, click the **CDNOW Recommends** hyperlink. CDnow's recommendations for Ct Student, a customer who followed the preceding steps, appears in the Web page shown in Figure 2-16. Your page should list some rock music CDs, and at least one classical CD. CDnow selects CDs to show you based on what you have purchased or placed in your Wish List. CDnow has categorized you as a person who likes rock music but occasionally buys a classical CD. If you add more classical CDs to your Wish List, CDnow will include more classical CDs in the recommendations it makes to you. It will also select different rock CDs based on its profiling of other customers who buy both rock and classical CDs because those customers prefer different rock CDs than customers who never buy classical CDs.

Figure 2-16 — CDNOW RECOMMENDATIONS FOR CT STUDENT

In addition to recommending CDs to its customers based on their expressed preferences and buying behavior, CDnow offers other customer relationship management features. Teenagers and young adults—people who often want more CDs than they can afford to buy right away—are important CDnow customers. The CDnow Wish List feature that you used in the preceding steps is designed to meet the needs of those customers. Many CDnow customers order CDs as gifts for others, so the Web site provides a way to store gift recipient names and addresses to make repeat shopping easier. The CDnow site also has a Gift Registry in which customers can list CDs they would like to receive as gifts. Gift-givers can then use the Gift Registry to look up CD preferences for persons in the registry and order just the right CD. Finally, there is a way for parents to buy CDs for their teen-aged children!

All of the features that CDnow has built into its site add value for its customers. None of the features mentioned here occur in the physical marketplace; they all occur in the virtual information world of the marketspace. CDnow can only provide these features to customers who are willing to interact with the site or allow it to track their behaviors. Note that all of these marketspace site features are optional and can be selected by the individual customer. CDnow is implementing technology-enabled customer relationship management on five (advertising, targeting, promotions, distribution, and measurement) of the seven dimensions listed in Figure 2-14.

Jean asks if these CDnow features are unusual for a Web site. You explain that many electronic commerce sites are trying to accomplish the same goals as CDnow; however, there are many different ways of accomplishing those goals. For example, people who enjoy movies are often interested in finding movies that are about the same subject, feature the same actors or director, appeal to the same audience, or provide an entertainment experience similar to their old favorites. You tell Jean that Reel.com, a company that sells movie videos online, has developed a very successful marketing technique called Movie Matches that helps customers find movies like the ones they already know and love.

To use the Reel.com Movie Matches feature:

1. Click your browser's **Back** button or use its history list to return to the Online Companion page for Session 2.2, and then click the **Reel.com** hyperlink and wait while your browser opens the home page.

2. Type **Casablanca** in the Search our Database text box, and then click the **MATCH IT!** button. The results page that opens includes hyperlinks to information about two movies that each have "Casablanca" in the title. *Casablanca* is a classic 1940s film about romance and politics during World War II. It stars Humphrey Bogart and Ingrid Bergman, both of whom went on to appear in many other films.

3. Click the **Casablanca** hyperlink to load the information page for that film. This page includes information about videotapes, DVDs, and other media on which the movie and related items are available, such as the soundtrack CD. The page includes some information about the film and hyperlinks to even more information.

4. Scroll down the information page to the section titled MOVIE MATCHES, which appears in Figure 2-17. The Reel.com site sorts the Movie Matches search results for Casablanca into two categories: Close Movie Matches and Creative Movie Matches. The first category includes films that have similar plots, star the same actors, or occur in similar settings. These films were also all made about the same time as *Casablanca* (during the 1940s and 1950s). The second category includes films from a wider range of dates that Reel.com believes people who liked *Casablanca* might also enjoy. These films have a less direct or less objective connection to *Casablanca*, but Reel.com's movie experts who liked *Casablanca* also liked these films. This personal touch is much like the subjective evaluations that salespeople provide in the one-to-one communication model described earlier in this tutorial.

TROUBLE? Depending on which browser you are using, your steps might work differently than those provided.

Figure 2-17	REEL.COM MOVIE MATCHES RESULTS FOR CASABLANCA

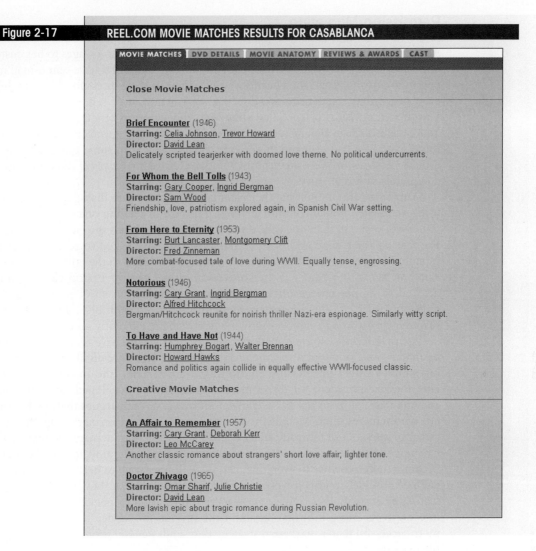

Jean is very impressed with this matching technique and would like to include something similar in the Treasure Trove Web site. She tells you that she has many customers who come to Treasure Trove looking for items similar to items they already own, such as antique furniture from a particular period or porcelain figures of angels. You explain to Jean that successful new Web marketing approaches all involve enabling the potential customer to find information easily and to customize the depth and nature of that information, and should encourage the customer to buy. Firms should track and examine the behaviors of their Web site visitors, and then use that information to provide customized, value-added digital products and services in the marketspace.

Jean agrees with you that technology-enabled customer relationship management tools could improve Treasure Trove's contact with customers and help it be more successful on the Web than it would be if it merely adapted the advertising and promotion strategies that have been successful for the store's physical location. Jean is particularly impressed with the ways in which CDnow interacts with its online customers and how CDnow uses e-mail to communicate with customers. You tell Jean that the key to using e-mail effectively to maintain contact with customers is making sure that you send them e-mail messages they will find interesting.

Permission Marketing

Although Jean is interested in exploring ways to send e-mail messages to her customers, she does have some concerns. She has heard about companies that have sent e-mail messages to potential customers and then been severely criticized in the press for doing so. Jean said she even heard that some firms were facing legal action after sending out mass e-mailings. Unsolicited e-mail is often called **spam** and the action of sending it is called **spamming**. You explain to Jean that sending unsolicited e-mail messages to potential or existing customers can be a bad idea and might even violate the law in some states. However, sending e-mail messages to Web site visitors who have expressly *requested* the e-mail messages is a completely different story.

Many firms are finding that they can maintain an effective dialog with their customers by using automated e-mail communications. The cost of sending one e-mail message to a customer can cost less than one cent if the company already has the customer's e-mail address. Purchasing the e-mail addresses of persons who have asked to receive specific kinds of e-mail messages will add between a few cents and a dollar to the cost of each message sent. Another factor to consider is the conversion rate. The **conversion rate** of an advertising method is the percentage of recipients who respond to an ad or promotion. Conversion rates on requested e-mail messages range from 10% to over 30%. These are much higher than the click-through rates on banner ads, which are currently under 1% and decreasing.

The practice of sending e-mail messages to people who have requested information on a particular topic or about a specific product is called **opt-in e-mail** and is part of a marketing strategy called **permission marketing**. Seth Grodin, the founder of YoYoDyne and later the vice-president for direct marketing at Yahoo!, developed this marketing strategy and publicized it in his book, *Permission Marketing*. Grodin argues that, as the pace of modern life increases, time becomes a valuable commodity. Most marketing efforts that traditional businesses use to promote their products or services depend on potential customers having enough time to listen to sales pitches and pay attention to the best ones. As time becomes more precious to everyone, people no longer wish to hear and evaluate advertising and promotional appeals for products and services in which they have no interest. Thus, a marketing strategy that only sends specific information to persons who have indicated an interest in receiving information about the product or service being promoted should be more successful than a marketing strategy that sends general promotional messages through the mass media.

To induce potential customers to accept, or opt in to, advertising information sent via e-mail messages, the seller must provide some incentive. This incentive could be entertainment, a chance to win a prize, or even a direct cash payment. The incentive may even be in the form of information; this is the incentive that CDnow offers. When you created an account with CDnow, you were offered the chance to sign up for several e-mail subscriptions. The portion of the CDnow Preferences page showing these e-mail subscription options appears in Figure 2-18.

Figure 2-18 **CDNOW EMAIL SUBSCRIPTIONS PAGE**

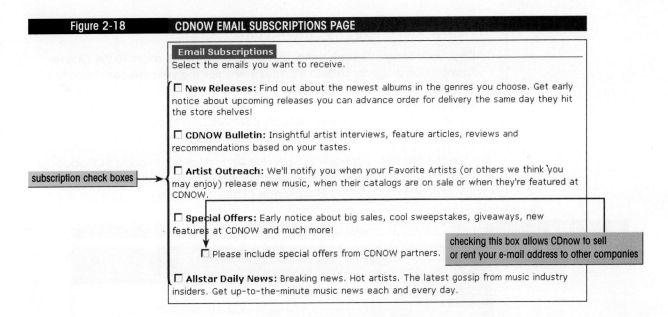

When you completed the CDnow steps, you cleared the check boxes on this page. CDnow customers who leave the boxes checked will receive regular e-mail messages from CDnow. The first check box opts a customer in to e-mail messages that announce upcoming album releases. Although these e-mail messages are sales promotions, a music enthusiast who wants to be among the first persons to get new releases will find that this subscription offers a valuable incentive to subscribe.

The other subscriptions offer interviews with performers, music industry gossip, and information about sweepstakes and giveaways. Each of these options might be a sufficient incentive for a particular customer to opt in. By providing value to subscribers, CDnow builds a continuing communication channel that promotes its products. This page also includes a check box that lets subscribers opt in to "special offers from CDnow partners" and gives CDnow permission to sell or rent those subscribers' e-mail addresses to other companies.

Many firms currently offer e-mail technologies and services to companies that want to begin permission marketing efforts but do not have a substantial customer base of e-mail addresses. These firms buy or rent lists of e-mail addresses, names, subscription preferences, and other demographic information from companies such as CDnow to create a large database. The firms then rent or sell e-mail addresses to other companies. By collecting large numbers of potential subscribers into one database, these firms can offer specialized lists of subscribers that meet the specific needs of permission marketers. Jean is intrigued by this idea, especially when you tell her that she can probably rent or purchase lists of e-mail addresses and names of persons who have requested information about antiques and who live within 100 miles of Treasure Trove.

One company that offers permission marketing e-mail services to other companies is yesmail.com. This firm collects e-mail addresses, identities, and permissions from its own Web site and from its partners (other firms that collect this information from their customers), and then sells the rights to send e-mail messages to portions of its subscriber database. One advantage that yesmail.com offers to subscribers is that it never sells or rents its subscriber lists to other companies. It only contracts with companies to send their e-mail permission marketing messages for them.

To learn more about yesmail.com:

1. Click your browser's **Back** button or use its history list to return to the Online Companion page for Session 2.2, and then click the **yesmail.com** hyperlink and wait while your browser loads the home page. The company uses the same Web site to advertise its services to permission marketers, to solicit subscriber lists from potential network partners, and to accept subscription requests from individuals, whom it calls members.

2. Click the **Member** hyperlink to open the MyYesMail Login page that appears in Figure 2-19. This page allows new members to sign up and existing members to log in and manage various aspects of their accounts.

Figure 2-19	MYYESMAIL LOGIN PAGE

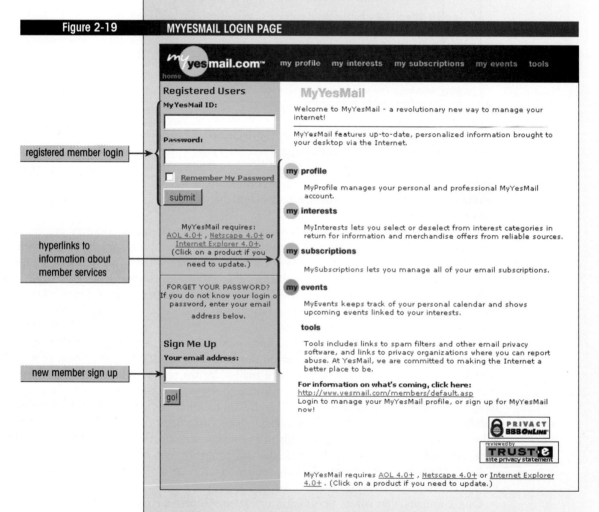

registered member login

hyperlinks to information about member services

new member sign up

3. Click the **my profile** hyperlink to open a page with information about the MyProfile function. If you are a yesmail.com member, you could make changes to the demographic information that you provided when you registered. You can also use the e-mail account that yesmail.com provides to its members.

4. Click your browser's **Back** button, and then click the **my interests** hyperlink to open a page of information about how you specify the categories to which you would like to subscribe. You can click the other links on the MyYesMail Login page to learn more about yesmail.com. You can also use your browser's Back button to return to the yesmail.com home page and, from there, explore the information yesmail.com provides to its customers and network partners.

You explain to Jean that companies such as yesmail.com will send your e-mail message to its members who have subscribed with requests for information that matches what Treasure Trove offers. Jean tells you that she has been thinking about writing a quarterly newsletter about the care of antique furniture. The cost of sending the newsletter by e-mail to potential customers identified by a company such as yesmail.com is very attractive. For less than a dollar each, Jean can send the newsletter to people who have specifically requested information about antique furniture care. If Jean can provide useful information to these potential customers, a level of trust will build over time. Eventually, some of these potential customers will visit the Treasure Trove Web site and become customers of the antique furniture care products that Jean sells. Right now, these products are not a major revenue source for the store, but Jean thinks that with a permission marketing campaign, they may grow into one!

You have identified many techniques and approaches for marketing strategy that Jean can use. She asks you about ways to capitalize on brand names. Treasure Trove sells many items that are not branded (the antique furniture, for example); however, most of the gift items are nationally recognized brands.

Creating and Maintaining Brands on the Web

A known and respected brand name can present to potential customers a powerful representation of quality, value, and other desirable qualities in one recognizable element. Branded products are easier to advertise and promote than nonbranded products because each branded product carries the reputation of the brand name. Companies have developed and nurtured their branding programs in the physical marketplace for many years. Consumer brands such as Ivory soap, Walt Disney entertainment, Maytag appliances, and Ford automobiles have been developed over many years with the expenditure of tremendous amounts of money. However, the value of these and other trusted major brands far exceeds the cost of creating them.

Elements of Branding

The key elements of a brand are differentiation, relevance, and perceived value. Product differentiation is the first condition that must be met to create a product or service brand. The company must clearly distinguish its product from all others in the market. This differentiation makes branding difficult for commodity products such as salt, nails, or plywood—difficult, but not impossible.

The classic case of branding a near-commodity product is Procter & Gamble's creation of the Ivory brand over 100 years ago. The company was experimenting with manufacturing processes and had accidentally created a bar soap that contained a high percentage of air. When one of the workers noted that the soap floated in water, the company decided to sell the soap using the differentiating characteristic in packaging and advertising by claiming "it floats." Thus, the Ivory soap brand was born.

The second element of branding—relevance—is the degree to which the product offers utility to a potential customer. The brand will only have meaning to customers if they can visualize its place in their lives. For example, many people understand that Tiffany & Co. creates a highly differentiated line of jewelry and gift products, but very few people can see themselves purchasing and using such goods.

Perceived value is a key element in creating a brand that has value. Even if your product is different from others on the market and potential customers can see themselves using the product, they will not buy it unless they perceive value. Some large fast food outlets have well-established brands that actually work against them. People recognize their brands and avoid eating at their restaurants because of negative associations, such as low overall quality and high fat content menu items.

If a brand has established that it is different from competing brands and is relevant to and inspires a perception of value in potential purchasers, those purchasers will buy the product and become familiar with how it provides value. Brands only become established when they reach this level of purchaser understanding.

Emotional Branding vs. Rational Branding

Unfortunately, brands can lose their value if the environment in which they have become successful changes. A dramatic example is Digital Equipment Corporation (DEC). DEC was a leading manufacturer of midrange computers for years. When the computing market shifted to personal computers, DEC found that its branding did not transfer to the personal computers that it produced. The consumers in that market did not see the same perceived value or differentiation in DEC's personal computers that the buyers of midrange systems had seen for years. Web-based firms must remember this important element of branding because the Web is still evolving and changing at a rapid pace.

Companies have traditionally used emotional appeals in their advertising and promotion efforts to establish and maintain brands. One branding expert, Ted Leonhardt, has defined "brand" as "an emotional shortcut between a company and its customer." These emotional appeals work well on television, radio, billboards, and in print media because the ad targets are in a passive mode of information acceptance. However, emotional appeals are difficult to convey on the Web because it is an active media controlled to a great extent by the customer. Many Web users are actively engaged in such activities as finding information, buying airline tickets, making hotel reservations, and obtaining weather forecasts. These are busy people who will happily click away from emotional appeals.

Marketers are attempting to create and maintain brands on the Web by using rational branding. **Rational branding** substitutes an offer to help Web users in some way in exchange for their viewing an ad. The emotional appeal of a television ad is replaced with the cognitive appeal of providing functional assistance. For example, Web e-mail services such as **Yahoo! Mail** give users a valuable service—an e-mail account and storage space for messages. In exchange for this service, users see an ad on each page that provides this e-mail service.

To examine the difference between emotional branding and rational branding:

1. Click your browser's **Back** button or use its history list to return to the Online Companion page for Session 2.2, and then click the **Procter & Gamble** hyperlink and wait while your browser loads the home page.

2. Click the **P & G Products** hyperlink. On the page that loads, click the **Laundry/Cleaning** hyperlink.

3. Scroll down the page to find the part of the world in which you live (for example, North America), and then read the list of laundry and cleaning products that Procter & Gamble offers for sale where you live.

Most people recognize more than half of Procter & Gamble's brands. For most of these brands, people recall television commercials that have conveyed a specific emotional sense of the product. These ads have been carefully crafted to convey that emotional sense. Think about how this type of branding is different from your experience at the yesmail.com site. That site offered you specific benefits (such as free e-mail) in exchange for your providing information about yourself that yesmail.com could sell.

Other Web Branding Strategies

Rational branding is not the only way to build brands on the Web. One method that is working for well-established Web sites is to take their dominant positions and extend them to other products and services. Yahoo! is an excellent example of this strategy. Yahoo! was one of the first directories on the Web. It added a search engine function early in its development and has continued to parlay its leading position by acquiring other Web businesses and expanding its existing offerings. Recently, Yahoo! acquired GeoCities and Broadcast.com, and entered into an extensive cross-promotion partnership with several Fox entertainment and media companies. Yahoo! continues to lead its two nearest competitors in ad revenue, Excite and Infoseek, by adding features that Web users find useful and that increase its value to advertisers. Amazon.com's expansion from its original book business into CDs, videos, and auctions is another example of a Web site taking its dominant position and leveraging it by adding features useful to existing customers.

Of course, this leveraging approach only works for firms that already have Web sites that dominate a particular market. As the Web matures, it will be increasingly difficult for new entrants to identify unserved market segments and attain dominance.

Affiliate Marketing

At Amazon.com, founder Jeff Bezos encouraged early customers to submit reviews of books, which he posted with the publisher's information about the book. By encouraging this participation, he provided a substitute for the corner bookshop staff's friendly advice and recommendations. Bezos saw the power of the Internet in reaching small, highly focused market segments, but he realized that his comprehensive bookstore could not be all things to all people. Therefore, he created a sales associate program in which Web sites devoted to a particular topic, such as model railroading, could provide links to Amazon.com books that related to that topic. In return, Amazon.com would remit a percentage of sales to the referring site. This sales associate program became the prototype of a tool called affiliate marketing that many new, low-budget Web sites are using to generate revenue. In **affiliate marketing**, one firm's Web site—the affiliate firm's—includes descriptions, reviews, ratings, or other information about a product that are linked to another firm's site that offers the item for sale. For every visitor that follows a link from the affiliate's site to the seller's site, the affiliate site receives a commission. The affiliate site also obtains the benefit of the selling site's brand in exchange for the referral.

The affiliate saves the expense of handling inventory, advertising and promoting the product, and processing the transaction—in fact, the affiliate risks no funds whatever. Amazon.com created one of the first and most successful affiliate programs on the Web. The Amazon.com program has over 100,000 affiliate sites. Most of these sites are devoted to a specific issue, hobby, or other interest. These affiliate sites choose books that are related to their visitors' interests and include links to Amazon.com on their Web pages. Books are a natural product for this type of shared promotional activity, but sellers of other products and services also have affiliate marketing programs. **B & D Gourmet Coffee**, **eToys**, and **Proflowers.com** all offer programs to affiliate Web sites.

Another way to leverage the established brands of existing Web sites was devised by **Della Weddings**, an online bridal registry whose home page appears in Figure 2-20.

Figure 2-20   **DELLA WEDDINGS HOME PAGE**

Although a number of national department store chains, such as Macy's, have established online registries for their own stores, Della Weddings offer a single registry that connects to several local and national department and gift stores, including Crate & Barrel, Dillard's, Gump's, Neiman Marcus, and Williams-Sonoma. The logo and branding of each participating store is featured prominently on the Della Weddings site. The founders of Della Weddings identified an opening for a market intermediary when they found that the average engaged couple registers at three different stores. Thus, they are providing a valuable consolidating activity for registering couples and their wedding guests that no store operating alone could provide. Della Weddings does sell incidental wedding items that do not compete with the offerings of their online branding partners.

Costs of Branding

Transferring existing brands to the Web or using the Web to maintain an existing brand is much easier and less expensive than creating an entirely new brand on the Web. According to studies by the Intermarket Group, the top 100 electronic commerce sites spent an average of $8 million each to create and build their online brands in 1998. Two of the top spenders included the battling book Web sites Amazon.com, which spent $133 million, and BarnesandNoble.com, which spent $70 million. Most of this spending was for television, radio, and print media—not for online advertising. Online brokerages E*Trade and Ameritrade Holding were also among the top five, spending $71 million and $44 million, respectively.

Promoting the company's Web presence should be an integral part of brand development and maintenance. The company's URL should always be included on product packaging and in mass media advertising on radio, television, and in print. Ensuring that the site is included in search engine databases and that the site includes appropriate META tags are both important elements in developing site awareness among the visitors the firm wants to attract. (**META tags** are HTML tags you insert in a Web page that contain information to describe its contents for Web search engines.) Integrating the URL with the company logo on brochures can also be helpful in getting the word out about the Web site.

Web Site Naming Issues

Firms that have a major investment in branding a product or service must protect that investment. Although a variety of state and federal laws protect trademarks, the procedure for creating and using Web site names that are not trademarks can present some challenging issues. Obtaining identifiable names to use for branded products on the Web can be just as important as ensuring legal trademark protection in protecting a branding investment.

Many Web users use simple approaches to finding useful sites. Often, they will simply type a reasonable-sounding name in their browser's address field and hope for the best. Many times, this works well because many companies have obtained the rights to use URLs (also known as domain names) that match their corporate names. In other cases, someone else already owns the "obvious" URL. Other Web users will type a reasonable-sounding name in the search field of their favorite search engine, which leads to results that are similar to using the Web browser's address field. In addition to registering URLs that match their corporate names, many firms try to identify URLs that are related to their products. For example, Jean might want to find out if www.antiques.com is available.

In 1998, a poster art and framing company named Artuframe opened for business on the Web. With quality products and an appealing site design, the company was doing well, but it was concerned about its URL, which was www.artuframe.com. After searching for a more appropriate URL, the company's president found the Web site of Advanced Rotocraft Technology, an aerospace firm, at the URL www.art.com. After learning that its site was drawing 150,000 visitors each month that were looking for something art-related, Artuframe offered to buy the URL. The aerospace firm agreed to sell the URL to Artuframe, which immediately changed its name to **Art.com**. The newly named company did not rely on the name change alone, however. It entered a joint marketing agreement with Yahoo! that places an ad for Art.com on art-related search results pages. Art.com has also created an affiliate program with businesses that sell art-related products and other organizations that have Web sites devoted to art-related topics.

Another company that invested in an appropriate URL was **Cars.com**. The firm paid $100,000 to the speculator who had originally purchased the rights to the URL. Cars.com is a themed-portal site that displays ads for new and used cars, financing, leasing, and other car-related products and services. The major investors in this firm are newspaper publishers that wanted to retain an interest in automobile-related advertising as it moved online. Classified automobile ads are an important revenue source for many newspapers.

Jean is interested in domain names that are similar to the name of her store, Treasure Trove, or that relate to the items she sells there. You explain that, until 1999, Network Solutions, Inc. handled domain registrations for .com, .net, .edu, and .org URLs under an exclusive contract with the U.S. government agencies that created the Internet. In 1999, the domain registration business was opened up to other companies. Currently, over a dozen companies have entered this business, with many more awaiting approval to begin doing business. You decide to perform some searches for URLs that might be suitable for Treasure Trove.

To search for available domain names:

1. Click your browser's **Back** button or use its history list to return to the Online Companion page for Session 2.1, and then click the **Network Solutions** hyperlink and wait while your browser loads the home page.

   TROUBLE? If a pop-up window containing an advertisement opens, click the Close button on its title bar.

2. Type **TreasureTrove** in the Search for a domain name text box, and then click the **Go!** button. A search results page appears that includes information on whether the domain name you entered is available. Try several variations of the name to see if one is available.

3. Click your browser's **Back** button to return to the Online Companion page for Session 2.2, and then click the **BetterWhois.com** hyperlink to load the page shown in Figure 2-21. This site provides more information about failed searches than the Network Solutions site. Note the list of domain registrars in the right column of the page.

Figure 2-21	BETTERWHOIS.COM HOME PAGE

4. Type **TreasureTrove.com** in the Search text box, and then click the **Search** button. A search results page appears and lets you know whether the domain name you entered is available. This site also provides information about the current owner of the domain name. Try several variations of the name to see if one is available. You suggest to Jean that she might want to contact the owners of one or more of the domain names in which she is interested to see if any of them are willing to sell them or assign their rights.

5. Close your Web browser and your dial-up connection, if necessary.

Jean is now convinced that developing an online version of Treasure Trove will add to her business considerably. She truly appreciates your advice regarding the importance of Web presence, Web site design, and branding.

Session 2.2 QUICK | CHECK

1. True or False: Radio and television are examples of addressable media.

2. The underlying communications model for personal contact sales is
   _____ to _____.

3. Describe the defining characteristic of product information searches on the Web.

4. What danger is faced by large firms that do not acknowledge and use the Web's capability for meaningful two-way communication with their customers?

5. What term(s) define the process when an online music store such as CDnow gathers information about its customer's purchase patterns and preferences, and then uses that information to improve the customer's shopping experience?

6. The practice of sending e-mail messages to people who have requested information on a particular topic is part of what marketing strategy?

7. True or False: An offer to help Web users in some way or offer value in exchange for those users viewing an ad is called rational branding.

CASE PROBLEMS

Case 1. Smash Hits Recording Studio Janice Yamimori, the manager of Smash Hits Recording Studio, has hired you to help her create a Web presence for the studio. Smash Hits wants to build a reputation as the studio of choice for new bands that are recording their first demonstration CDs in hopes of landing major recording contracts.

1. Start your Web browser, and then go to the Online Companion page by entering the URL http://www.course.com/NewPerspectives/EC in the appropriate location of your Web browser. Click the Tutorial 2 link, and then click the Case Problems link. Click the Unique Recording Studios link and wait while your browser loads that firm's home page.

2. Explore the links on this site and identify the Web presence goals that the site has achieved.

3. Use your browser's Back button to return to the Online Companion page for this case problem, and then click the DogHouse Recording & Production hyperlink. When that firm's home page loads, click the Studio Entrance hyperlink.

4. Explore the links on this site and identify the Web presence goals that the site has achieved.

5. Identify two Web presence goals from each site that Janice might use in designing the Smash Hits site. Write a report that includes a paragraph for each goal in which you describe the goal, explain how Unique or Doghouse achieved that goal, and explain why Janice should consider including that goal in the Smash Hits site.

6. When you are finished, close your browser and your dial-up connection, if necessary.

Case 2. Charitable Organizations Most business Web sites can focus on the needs of their customers when they design their Web sites. Charitable organizations face a more difficult task. Many different types of visitors access the Web sites of charitable organizations.

1. Start your Web browser, and then go to the Online Companion page by entering the URL http://www.course.com/NewPerspectives/EC in the appropriate location of your Web browser. Click the Tutorial 2 link, and then click the Case Problems link. The Case Problem 2 section of the Online Companion includes links to three different charitable organizations. Click the link of the organization your instructor has assigned to you to open that organization's home page. (If your instructor has not assigned a specific organization, choose one.)

2. Follow the links on the home page to learn more about the organization and its mission. Identify three different needs that Web visitors might expect to have met through the site.

3. Write a report that includes three paragraphs. In each paragraph, describe one need that a visitor to this Web site might expect to have met and explain how the site meets or fails to meet that need.

4. When you are finished, close your browser and your dial-up connection, if necessary.

Case 3. Sears.com Sears is one of the oldest and most respected retailers in the United States. Its Web site provides information about its products and store locations and also offers online shopping. Sears has hired you, as a typical college student, to help with its usability study. To complete this case problem, assume that you wish to buy a new microwave oven for your dorm room.

1. Start your Web browser, and then go to the Online Companion page by entering the URL http://www.course.com/NewPerspectives/EC in the appropriate location of your Web browser. Click the Tutorial 2 link, and then click the Case Problems link. Click the Sears.com link to open that company's home page.

2. Follow the links on the home page to shop for and purchase your microwave oven. Identify three elements of the Web site that could be improved.

3. Write a report that includes three paragraphs. In each paragraph, describe one element of the site design that could be improved and suggest a way to make the improvement.

4. When you are finished, close your browser and your dial-up connection, if necessary.

Case 4. *Technology-Enabled Customer Relationship Management at Crutchfield*

Crutchfield is a retailer of auto and home stereo equipment that has been sold through mail order catalogs for many years. Crutchfield now has a Web site that offers online shopping and support for its catalog sales. In the past, Crutchfield kept records of customer purchases and used them to provide customized solicitations. For example, customers who purchased a car stereo would receive a flyer with their purchase that featured discounts on car speakers included with the stereo. Crutchfield also tracked customer purchases by type of product. Because the company sells a wide range of audio products, it was interested in knowing whether a particular customer tended to purchase top-of-the-line products or made more modest purchases. Now that Crutchfield is selling on the Web, it is interested in the more precise tracking available in that environment.

1. Start your Web browser, and then go to the Online Companion page by entering the URL http://www.course.com/NewPerspectives/EC in the appropriate location of your Web browser. Click the Tutorial 2 link, and then click the Case Problems link. Click the Crutchfield link to open that company's home page.

2. Follow the links on the home page to shop for a car audio system and a home CD player. Identify two opportunities that Crutchfield has for gathering and using information to manage its customer relationships.

3. Write a report of approximately 200 words that outlines these two opportunities. Describe the elements of a customer's activity on the Web site that Crutchfield would need to track if it takes advantage of these opportunities.

4. When you are finished, close your browser and your dial-up connection, if necessary.

Case 5. *Holiday Toys*

You and your classmates often volunteer at a nearby homeless shelter. For the past two years, you have been collecting toys that the shelter distributes to children who are staying in the shelter during the holidays. In the past, you have used flyers and made announcements in classes to ask for toy donations. Now you have formalized your group and would like to create a centralized location where potential donors can visit to learn more about what you do.

Note: To complete this case problem you must know how to create Web pages using HTML, Microsoft FrontPage, Netscape Composer, or some other tool. You must also have access to that tool.

1. Create a home page that describes your efforts and provides links to other pages that include more detailed information.

2. Design the other pages so they include at least the following: The name of the homeless shelter to which you donate the toys, ways to contact your group, locations at which you collect the toys, and guidelines for types of toys that you can accept as donations. Be sure to incorporate the Web site design guidelines you learned in this tutorial as you create your pages.

3. When you are finished, save your Web site on a floppy disk or on a server specified by your instructor.

QUICK | CHECK ANSWERS

Session 2.1

1. False
2. To visit the site, to stay and explore the site, and to follow the site's links to obtain additional information
3. not-for-profit
4. interactive
5. True
6. text-only version
7. The Web site design should include multiple ways to access information or information with a selectable level of detail.
8. An observation or monitoring of person's actions as they use a Web site

Session 2.2

1. False
2. one [-to-] one
3. The buyer actively participates in the search and controls the length, depth, and scope of the search.
4. They will lose those customers to competitors that do understand the Web's capability for meaningful two-way communication with customers.
5. Technology-enabled relationship management
6. Permission marketing
7. True

OBJECTIVES

In this tutorial you will:

- Explore the client/server infrastructure that supports electronic commerce

- Investigate the costs of building an online store

- Learn about some basic electronic commerce software functions

- Promote your store using advertisements, banner exchange programs, and search engines

- Build a Yahoo! Store

- Build a Bigstep store

BUILDING AN ONLINE STORE

Commerce Infrastructure and Software Choices

CASE

The Coffee and Tea Merchant

The Coffee and Tea Merchant is a small, privately owned coffee bean and tea wholesale and retail store. Known locally as the best gourmet coffee and tea store that sells difficult-to-find coffees and teas, the Coffee and Tea Merchant has been modestly successful. Franklin Toadvine, the store's owner, started the business in 1978 in San Diego. Nearly all of Franklin's customers were from the local area. Soon, tourists attracted to San Diego's mild climate discovered Franklin's store. Many customers commented that Franklin's coffee was especially fresh and that he offered the widest selections of coffee beans they had ever seen.

Although Franklin's store is thriving in the San Diego area, he wants to expand his coffee and tea business beyond San Diego's borders. Franklin has many loyal customers outside California who would like to purchase his coffee. However, Franklin and his employees are not able to handle the telephone call volume they have been receiving lately. Several customers have written letters to Franklin asking how they might order coffee and tea products from his store, because the store's phone is always busy.

To respond to his customers' needs, Franklin wants to investigate building an online store to market and sell coffee and tea products using an Internet storefront. Besides widening his store's customer base in the United States, an online store would reduce or eliminate the telephone traffic his customers have experienced.

Franklin has hired you to perform a preliminary study about various electronic commerce options and their costs. If your preliminary study looks promising, Franklin will hire you to create the online store.

SESSION 3.1

In this session, you will learn about the basic infrastructure that supports electronic commerce. You will then learn about the fundamental components of an electronic store and how to promote your store using advertising and search engines.

Infrastructure Support

Several technologies must be in place for electronic commerce to exist. The most obvious technology needed for electronic commerce is the Internet. Beyond that system of inter-connected networks, many other sophisticated software and hardware components—including database software, network switches and hubs, encryption hardware and software, multimedia support, and the World Wide Web—provide the required support structure to maintain an electronic commerce site. To compete in the constantly changing realm of the Internet, businesses that conduct electronic commerce must be able to adapt their sites to use new technology as it becomes available, or risk losing existing and potential customers to better sites. More online shoppers and the increasing traffic between businesses will force companies to find faster and more efficient ways to conduct business electronically. For companies that plan their electronic commerce strategies well, the payoff can be huge—with online business volumes sometimes doubling in less than a year.

Packet-switched Networks

The early models (dating back to the 1950s) for networked computers were the local and long-distance telephone companies. Most early computer networks used leased telephone company lines for their connections. In those days, a telephone call established a single connection between caller and receiver. Once a connection was established, data traveled along that single path. Telephone company switching equipment (both mechanical and computerized) selected specific telephone lines, or **circuits**, that were connected to create a single path between caller and receiver. This centrally controlled, single connection model is known as **circuit switching**.

While circuit switching works well for telephone calls, using the same technique for sending data across a large network, or a network of networks like the Internet, does not work well. Establishing point-to-point connections for each pair of senders and receivers is both expensive and difficult to manage. The Internet uses a more efficient and less expensive technique to move data between two points. This method is called packet switching. In a **packet-switching network**, files and messages are broken down into packets that are labeled electronically with codes indicating both their origins and destinations. Packets travel from computer to computer along the network until they reach their destinations. The destination computer collects the packets and reassembles the original data from the pieces in each packet. Each computer that an individual packet encounters on its trip from its origin to its destination determines the best way to move the packet forward to its destination. Computers performing this determination are often called **routers**, and the programs that determine the best path to follow are called **routing algorithms**. Packet switching is the method used to move data on the Internet.

Packet switching has several benefits. First, long streams of data can be broken down into small manageable data chunks, allowing the small packets to be distributed over a wide number of possible paths to balance the traffic across the network. Another advantage is that it is relatively inexpensive to replace damaged data packets after they arrive. If a data packet is altered in transit, then only a single packet is retransmitted.

The set of protocols that underlie the basic operation of the Internet are **Transmission Control Protocol (TCP)** and the **Internet Protocol (IP)**. Developed by two Internet pioneers named Vincent Cerf and Robert Kahn, these two protocols establish fundamental rules about how the data is moved across networks and how network connections are established and broken. The common acronym **TCP/IP** refers to the two protocols.

TCP/IP is a two-layered program. The TCP protocol includes rules that computers on a network use to establish and break connections. TCP controls the assembly of a message into smaller packets before it is transmitted over the Internet and the reassembly of packets when they reach their destination. The IP protocol includes rules for routing individual data packets from their sources to their destinations. IP handles all the addressing details for each packet, ensuring that each is labeled with the correct destination address.

Intranets and Extranets

For larger companies, creating an intranet usually follows the creation of the company's Internet Web presence. An **intranet** is a Web-based private network that hosts Internet applications on a local area network. (A **local area network (LAN)** is a computer network that spans a geographically small area.) Technically, intranets are not much different from the Internet, except that only selected individuals are allowed to access an intranet. Often an intranet facilitates dissemination of company information within the confines of the company and its departments. Intranets are an extremely popular and low-cost way to distribute corporate information. An intranet uses Internet-based protocols, including TCP/IP, FTP, Telnet, HTML, HTTP, and Web browsers. Because corporate intranets are compatible with the Internet, selected information from intranets can be readily shared with external consumers. One other benefit of using an intranet is that different departments of a company having different computer hardware can interact with one another on an intranet.

Not long after a company creates an intranet, it is extended to an extranet. An **extranet** extends the intranet concept to provide a network connecting a company's network to the networks of its business partners, selected customers, or suppliers. Traditionally, an extranet connects companies with suppliers or other business partners by using facsimile, phone, electronic mail technologies, and express carriers. An extranet can be any of the following types: a virtual private network, a public network, or a secure (private) network. A **virtual private network (VPN)** extranet is a network that uses public networks and their protocols to send sensitive data to partners, customers, suppliers, and employees by using a system called **tunneling** or **encapsulation**, in which a message is secured from eavesdroppers. A **public network** extranet exists when an organization allows the public to access its intranet from any public network, such as the Internet, or when two or more companies agree to link their intranets using a public network. A **private network** is a private, leased-line connection between two companies that physically connects their intranets to one another. Each company has the same capability of sharing information with each other. Information on extranets is secured to prevent security breaches from intruders not authorized to access it. Authorized users connect transparently to another company's network via the extranet. Extranets provide the private infrastructure for companies to coordinate their purchases, exchange business documents (using EDI), and communicate with one another.

Web Clients and Servers

When you use your Internet connection to become part of the Web, your computer becomes a **Web client** in a worldwide client/server network. Your Web browser software, such as Microsoft Internet Explorer or Netscape Navigator, is the software that makes your computer work as a Web client. The Internet connects many different types of computers running different operating system software. Because Web software is platform-neutral, it lets your computer communicate with different types of computers easily and effectively, which is a critical ingredient in the widespread use of the Web.

The advantage of this client/server architecture in electronic commerce is that a customer's browser works only to display the information it receives from the server that hosts an online store. Nearly always, the client does very little work. While the client's workload is light, the server's workload is not. Besides receiving and interpreting requests from the client, the server must locate information, reprocess it, and request computer resources found on the server. This workload-sharing arrangement is why servers generally must be powerful computers with enormous disk capacity, speedy and robust processors, and ample memory. On the other hand, clients require no more capability than what is found on any ordinary PC. For electronic commerce applications, this translates to low-cost computers (client machines) for people wanting to purchase goods and services from a Web-hosted business. In this case, a Web business must shoulder larger costs to purchase and run robust computers and software (servers) to serve a potentially large customer base.

Web server program features can range from basic to extensive, depending on the software package chosen. Web server software features fall into natural groups based on their purpose. All Web server programs provide a certain core feature set without which the program wouldn't be a Web server at all. **O'Reilly Software**, producer of WebSite Professional, classifies its Web server's features into these categories: core capabilities, site management, application building, commerce, and dynamic content. One core capability of a Web server is to locate a client-requested Web page and send it to the client. Another core server capability is to translate the Web address, or Uniform Resource Locator (URL), that you supply through your Web browser into a physical file address. The translated address points directly to a page requested by a client browser and is returned to it. For example, the Web server might translate the URL www.mywebsite.com/infosheet.html into the filename C:\Home\Web\Info.html.

Web Server Software Choices

There isn't one best Web server package for all businesses. Several factors affect your choices, not the least of which are the hardware and operating system that are installed and the Web server features that are the most important to a particular company. Apache HTTP Server, Microsoft Internet Information Server (IIS), and Netscape Enterprise Server (NES) are three popular Web servers that are widely in use on the Web. Apache HTTP Server dominates the Web in numbers partly because it is free, performs very efficiently, and runs on most operating systems. As part of your fact-finding mission for Franklin, you decide to learn more about Apache HTTP Server, as it might be a good Web server on which to operate his Web site.

To visit the Apache Web server home page:

1. Start your Web browser, and then go to the Online Companion by entering the URL **http://www.course.com/NewPerspectives/EC** in the appropriate location of your Web browser. Click the **Tutorial 3** link, and then click the **Session 3.1** link. Click the **Apache HTTP Server** link and wait while your browser loads the Apache Software Foundation home page shown in Figure 3-1.

| Figure 3-1 | APACHE SOFTWARE FOUNDATION HOME PAGE |

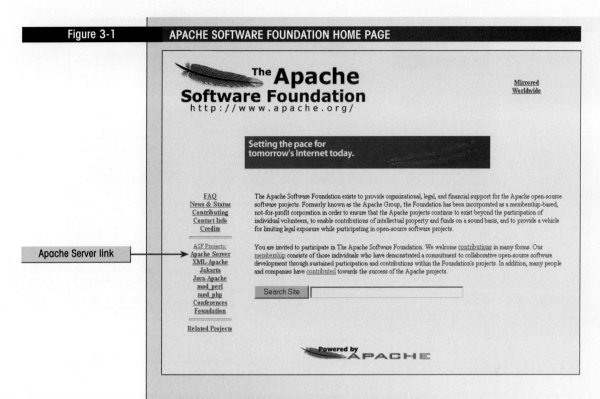

Apache Server link

2. Click the **Apache Server** link on the left side of the home page.

3. Click the **About the Apache Project** link and read about the history of the group effort.

Microsoft's Internet Information Server (IIS) comes bundled (free) with Microsoft's Windows NT Server operating system. IIS serves equally well as an intranet Web server or a public Web server. IIS is the second-most popular installed Web server software for total (public and intranet) Web sites. A robust and capable Web server program, IIS is suitable for a wide range of business needs. Currently, IIS runs only on the Windows NT and Windows 2000 operating systems. Figure 3-2 shows an IIS feature comparison page. By reviewing this page, you can compare the setup and administrative features of IIS to other servers.

Figure 3-2   MICROSOFT INTERNET INFORMATION SERVER FEATURE COMPARISON PAGE

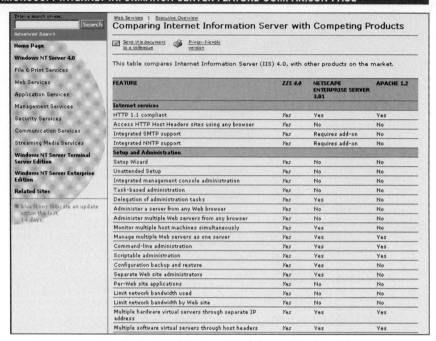

Another very popular Web server is **Netscape Enterprise Server** (**NES**), which is available in several versions. The licensing fee for NES ranges from $1,300 to $2,000, and it provides a free 60-day trial. The NES software runs on most operating systems, making it easy for businesses to use it. Some of the busiest and best-known sites on the Internet, including E*Trade, Schwab, Digex, Excite, and Lycos, are running, or have run, NES. Figure 3-3 shows the NES information page.

| Figure 3-3 | NETSCAPE ENTERPRISE SERVER INFORMATION PAGE |

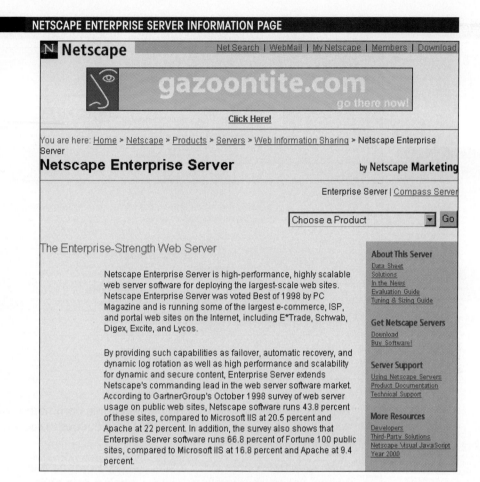

You give Franklin a preliminary report about Web servers and software, but he is concerned about which server he should use, either by installing it for his business or searching for an Internet service provider that uses it. He asks if you can learn which Web server software is in use by other electronic commerce sites. You tell Franklin that you can use a special Netcraft site feature that allows you to determine the software running on a specific site. Franklin just purchased a new computer from Dell Computer's Web site, and he is curious to learn which Web server software Dell.com is using.

To determine which Web server software is in use on a Web site:

1. Click your browser's **Back** button or use its history list to return to the Online Companion page for Session 3.1, and then click the **What Web software is running on a site?** link and wait while your browser loads the Netcraft What's that site running? Web page.

2. Type **www.dell.com** in the Hostname text box, and then click the **Examine** button. The Netcraft site gathers information from www.dell.com and opens the page shown in Figure 3-4, which indicates both the name of the computer operating system and the Web server software name. Examine the results to learn which server and operating system is running on Dell.com.

| Figure 3-4 | NETCRAFT INFORMATION ABOUT SOFTWARE RUNNING ON THE DELL.COM WEB SITE |

Web server software running Dell.com

operating system information

other sites using the same Web server software

enter URL in the Hostname text box

Franklin asks you to choose another electronic commerce site and determine which Web server software is in use. You are curious to see what Web server software FedEx uses.

3. Type **www.fedex.com** in the Hostname text box, and then click the **Examine** button. Notice what software FedEx is running. Also notice which other companies run the same Web server software.

This information will be helpful to Franklin as he considers which Web server to use for his store's site. Regardless of which Web server Franklin chooses to deliver Web pages to users' browsers, he must ensure that the electronic commerce software—the software that allows customers to browse a store, purchase items, view a catalog, and pay for their purchases—is compatible with the Web server software.

Basic Electronic Commerce Software Functions

Regardless of how an electronic commerce site is created, most electronic commerce sites have the following common features and functions:

- **Catalog**: Contains detailed information about each product sold by the company, including the item's name, description, price, shipping cost, size, color, and sometimes even a picture. Most sites include a search feature that lets customers search for an item and determine its availability.

- **Shopping cart**: Keeps track of the items a customer has selected to purchase and lets the customer view and update the contents of the cart, add new items to it, or remove items from it. When a customer adds an item to a shopping cart, all of the product's details, including its item code, description, and price, are stored automatically. Some Web commerce sites let customers use a shopping cart to add items for purchase, put the cart in "virtual storage," and then return to the site later to confirm and pay for the purchases.

- **Transaction and payment processing**: Occurs when the shopper proceeds to the virtual checkout. The electronic commerce software calculates volume discounts, sales tax, shipping cost, and the order's total cost, and then processes the customer's payment (credit or debit card, or other form of payment), including any verification process.

- **Automated fulfillment system**: Notifies customers that their orders were received and then ships the orders to the correct locations.

Most sites also provide a return policy page, which includes information about how to return a purchase or instructions for returning damaged or defective items. After a user submits payment and the system secures authorization for that payment, the system opens a Web page with an order number and other order information, and informs the user that it has accepted the order. Finally, the system forwards the user's order to the processing network for payment processing and order shipment (called **fulfillment**). These steps are common to both online and physical stores.

In addition, the electronic commerce site should provide the following convenient features for the site developer/entrepreneur, as well as for the shopper:

- Tools for creating the store catalog of products
- Tools for populating the store catalog
- Tools for building or modifying the site and its pages
- A mechanism to register and track shoppers—both for other businesses and consumers
- Security measures to secure transactions to prevent fraud and theft

Transaction Processing

At checkout, the customer's Web browser normally switches into a secure state of communication. Unless the customer has disabled it, a dialog box opens and indicates that the browser is entering or leaving a secure state. Transaction processing is the most complicated part of an electronic sale. Computing taxes and shipping costs is an important part of this process; commerce administrators must continually check the tax and shipping tables to ensure their accuracy. Some programs simplify shipping calculations by connecting directly to shipping companies such as UPS, FedEx, and Airborne Express to retrieve shipping costs. One site, **SmartShip**, will calculate the lowest-price shipper for a package.

There are other details that the software must handle, such as tax-exempt sales. Many business-to-business (B2B) transactions involve tax-free sales when items are purchased for resale and under certain other conditions. Some business-to-consumer (B2C) sales are also tax-exempt. Many retailers are not required to charge sales tax when the sale originates outside the state in which those retailers are doing business. Other calculation complications include provisions for coupons, special promotions, and time-sensitive offers (for example, purchasing a round-trip airline ticket before a specified date to receive a 50% discount off the regular fare).

Merchant Account

To accept and process payments from customers, both conventional and online businesses should have a **merchant account**, which allows businesses to accept credit card payments and receive authorization to process those payments by the bank that issued the credit card. Without a merchant account, a store is limited to accepting CODs (cash on delivery), money orders, or personal checks paid in advance as payment for goods and services. By far, the most widely used forms of payment are credit and debit cards. Customers everywhere expect merchants to accept major credit cards and debit cards. Not having a merchant account is a major disadvantage. Of course, Franklin has already established a merchant account with a bank that accepts cards from around the world because he has accepted them for a number of years at his traditional store. You will learn more about merchant accounts in Tutorial 5.

Making Host or Build Decisions

There are many software options for conducting electronic commerce. Large businesses, such as Amazon.com, use high-end choices such as Netscape's CommerceXpert, which can cost more than $100,000 and can handle high traffic volumes using a rich assortment of facilities and tools. CommerceXpert and similar software choices require significant hardware resources and considerable expertise to create an online commerce site. Between these two extremes is a wide variety of computer and software choices—ranging in price from $1,000 to over $25,000—which require skilled system analysts to install, fine-tune, and maintain. If you are not Amazon.com with a large investment already made in one or more in-house Web sites, then you might not want to spend a lot of money to acquire the hardware and software needed to start an online business. The total costs of setting up your own in-house Web commerce site can easily exceed $50,000 because you have to purchase hardware, Web server software, electronic commerce software, and a high-speed Internet connection.

If you do not have the necessary infrastructure to host your own Web site, you can choose one of several inexpensive Web hosting services to create storefronts, such as Yahoo! Store or Bigstep. **Web hosting services** (also known as **commerce service providers**, or **CSPs**) allow businesses to jump into electronic commerce easily and affordably by providing the necessary hardware, Web server software, and electronic commerce software to create a site quickly. Targeted at smaller stores, Web hosting services offer complete electronic commerce services and software that let entrepreneurs quickly create storefronts that include all of the necessary items to run the store.

Using a Web Hosting Service

Web hosting services provide the same services as an ISP, plus electronic commerce software, store space, and electronic commerce expertise. Web hosting services have many advantages, including spreading the fixed and variable Web site costs over several "renters" hosted by the service. Web hosting services provide expertise, register and supply your domain name, maintain the Web service 24 hours a day, process payments, authorize credit cards, and take care of calculating shipping costs and taxes. Of course, the biggest single advantage—low cost—occurs because the Web hosting service has already purchased and configured the server. The best Web hosting services offer reliability, good security, system simplicity, and widespread acceptability. When you use a Web hosting service to host an electronic commerce site, you will get a variety of services for a low monthly fee; this fee includes the necessary hardware and software to run the site as well as the technical support to sustain it.

Along with hardware, software, and people services, some Web hosting services can also provide you with your own domain name for an additional monthly fee of approximately $25 to $200. When you use your own domain name, you receive disk storage space on which to store your site's Web pages. Usually, 25 to 60 megabytes of space are allocated to a small store, and more space is available for larger stores at higher fees. You can create Web pages using any Web page creation software program, and then upload the pages to your site. If you don't have or know how to use a Web page creation software program, some Web hosting services will provide templates on which to base your own pages. Your research so far has revealed that both Yahoo! Store and Bigstep provide templates and a button-driven interface that simplifies the creation of Web pages, without the need to learn a Web page creation program or a Web programming language. These advantages will be important to the Coffee and Tea Merchant, because Franklin does not have the skills required to prepare his store's pages from scratch.

When you sign up for monthly service, there is usually no fixed-length contract, so you can terminate the contract at any time. Setup fees range from free to a few hundred dollars and can include your officially registered domain name. Most Web hosting services will register your domain name with **Network Solutions**, a designated domain name provider in the United States. Registering your domain name costs $35 per year for one to 10 years. In addition, the Web hosting service might charge a monthly fee to allow you to use your domain name instead of its domain name. For example, you might use the domain *http://www.bigshot.com*, instead of the domain name supplied by Yahoo! Store, such as *http://stores.yahoo.com/bigshot*. Customers appreciate shorter, easy-to-remember domain names, and having your own domain name adds a high level of professionalism and credibility to your business.

Your research has convinced you that using a Web hosting service such as Yahoo! Store or Bigstep is the best choice for Franklin's first online coffee store. After viewing his server options, Franklin decides that the Coffee and Tea Merchant's online sales volume will be small initially, and that the proposed online store will not require either elaborate hardware or expensive commerce software. You decide to examine some online stores on two Web hosting services, Yahoo! Store and Bigstep.

To open a Yahoo! Store commerce site:

1. Click your browser's **Back** button or use its history list to return to the Online Companion page for Session 3.1, and then click the **Yahoo! Store Listings** link and wait while your browser loads the Yahoo! Stores page. This page lists categories of stores built using Yahoo! Store software.

2. Click the **Apparel** link in the Fashion category. The page that opens contains links to stores that sell apparel items using a Yahoo! Store.

3. Type **Collegiate Outfitters** in the Search Merchants text box, and then click the **Search Merchants** button. Click the **CollegiateOutfitters.com** link and wait while your browser opens the CollegiateOutfitters.com home page shown in Figure 3-5.

| Figure 3-5 | COLLEGIATEOUTFITTERS.COM HOME PAGE |

hyperlinks to products for different universities

Index link

sale items are highlighted on the home page (your home page might display different sale items)

TROUBLE? If you cannot locate the Collegiate Outfitters store, open any other store.

4. Click the **Index** link located on the left side of the page (you might need to scroll down the page to find it). An alphabetical listing of products and product categories appears.

5. Click the **Kentucky Athletic Department T-Shirt** link. A page opens and displays detailed product and pricing information about the T-shirt.

   TROUBLE? If the Kentucky Athletic Department T-Shirt link is not available, click another link to open a detailed product page.

6. Click the **Size** list arrow, and then click **L**.

7. Click the **Order** button. After a moment, a shopping cart page opens and shows what you have selected to purchase so far. (You will not actually purchase anything from this site.) After selecting an item for purchase, you can use the shopping cart to change some of your purchase's details, such as the quantity ordered for a specific item. Also notice that the Web site changes to a secure connection, as indicated by the padlock icon on your browser's status bar.

   TROUBLE? If your browser opens a Security Alert dialog box, click the OK button to continue.

8. Select the value **1** in the Quantity text box, type **5**, and then click the **Update Quantities** button to recalculate your subtotal. The new subtotal appears in the right column. See Figure 3-6.

| Figure 3-6 | SHOPPING CART CONTENTS |

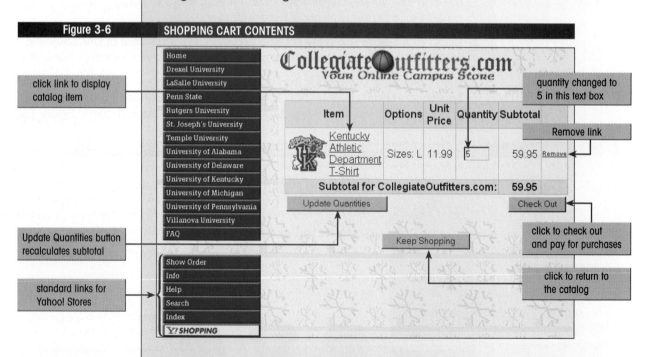

Clicking the Remove link removes the item(s) from your shopping cart. In this case, you would empty your shopping cart of all five T-shirts. You won't actually make a purchase, but you would like to go to the virtual checkout and see how this store lets customers pay for their purchases.

9. Click the **Check Out** button. The Order Form page opens and displays your purchase details. Scroll down the Order Form page to examine the information required by this seller in order to complete the transaction. If you were a real customer, you would provide the seller with your mailing address and payment information. (*Do not* enter any information into the Order Form.)

10. Scroll to the bottom of the Order Form page. Notice that two buttons appear, providing an option to continue and an option to cancel. This seller has provided two very clear options that allow the customer to continue with the transaction or cancel it. You will cancel the sale.

11. Click the **No: Do Not Order** button, click the **Remove** link on the Shopping Cart page, wait for a page to open that displays the message "Your shopping cart is empty," and then click the **Home** link to return to the CollegiateOutfitters.com home page. The Web page displays a message indicating that your shopping cart is empty, and your browser returns to an unsecured state.

TROUBLE? If a Security Alert dialog box opens and warns that you are about to leave a secure Internet connection, click the Yes button to continue.

The CollegiateOutfitters.com home page contains links—the buttons appearing along the left edge of the page—that divide the online store into departments, or sections, of related items. In Figure 3-5, for example, each university defines its own section. Clicking any of the college links opens the section containing items for that college. A section contains one or more items for sale. The last six links in the column of links shown in Figure 3-6 are standard on Yahoo! stores. The Show Order link displays the contents of your shopping cart, and the Info link opens a page containing information about the online store. The Help link opens a page that provides helpful suggestions about navigating the store. Clicking the Search link displays a simple text box and search button, allowing you to type the name of any item you want to locate in the store. The Index link opens a page displaying links to each item available in the online store. Clicking the Y!SHOPPING link returns to the main Yahoo! Stores page, so you can click a link to open a store for another merchant.

The layout of the previous Yahoo! Store is clean, and selecting merchandise and ordering seems simple enough. A Yahoo! Store is certainly a candidate for the Coffee and Tea Merchant's online store. Just to make sure you are on the right track, you decide to investigate another Web hosting service, Bigstep, so Franklin has more than one option to select from for building his own store. You have heard that Bigstep stores are easy to build and maintain, so you want to show Franklin a typical store.

To open a Bigstep commerce site:

1. Click your browser's **Back** button or use its history list to return to the Online Companion page for Session 3.1, and then click the **Bigstep home page** link and wait while your browser loads the Bigstep.com home page shown in Figure 3-7. Online storeowners can enter their e-mail address and password into the text boxes under the "Already a member?" heading to change their existing stores. If you were not a current storeowner, you would click the Sign up! link to enter the site.

Figure 3-7   **BIGSTEP.COM HOME PAGE**

current online store
owners sign in here

click here to take a test
drive before you decide

first time users click
this link

Bigstep.com.
Where ebusiness is everybody's business℠

Member Sign In   Register

Main
① Get info
② Quick tour
③ Example sites
④ Test drive
⑤ Register

Sweepstake$
Register now to enter our
$5000 Business Builder
Sweepstakes!

Build your business on the Web.
Use Bigstep.com to create and manage a Web site, market your business online, sell products with secure ecommerce, promote events, display a portfolio, send email newsletters, and more. Most services are free.

Work-at-home mom Ragan Hughs wrote the book "The Complete Guide to Making Money At Home." Then she started her own Web site -- an online community for moms in business at home.

Tom Pattavina and his mother Frances **took their bakery business to the Internet** -- now they're shipping pastries nationwide. Find out how they expanded their market online.

See the list of awards we've won!

BUSINESS TIPS

Six Tips for Building a Successful Homepage
In the online world, there's only one place your customers get their first impression of your business: your homepage.

Ecommerce Essentials
With so many businesses flooding the online marketplace, how can you make a painless entry into the ecommerce arena?

Privacy Policy | About Bigstep.com | Jobs | Member Agreement
© 2000 Bigstep.com. All rights reserved. Please read our privacy policy and our terms of service.

2. Click your browser's **Back** button or use its history list to return to the Online Companion page for Session 3.1, and then click the **SeattleGallery.com** link and wait while your browser opens the SeattleGallery.com store, which was created using Bigstep software. Several black and white photographs appear on the page. Each photograph has a link below it that opens a larger version of the photograph so customers can examine the photograph more closely.

3. Scroll down the home page and locate the photograph named *Perfection*, and then click the **Perfection** link located below it. A larger version of the photograph opens.

   TROUBLE? If you cannot locate the Perfection link, click any other link for a photograph.

4. Scroll to the bottom of the page and click the **11" x 14"** link in the Matted Only column. A page containing more details about the photograph opens.

5. Click the **Add to Shopping Cart** button at the bottom of the page. A summary page named "Your shopping cart" displays the item, its cost, and the quantity you have ordered. See Figure 3-8. Notice again that your browser changes to a secure state.

| Figure 3-8 | **BIGSTEP SHOPPING CART CONTAINING ONE ITEM** |

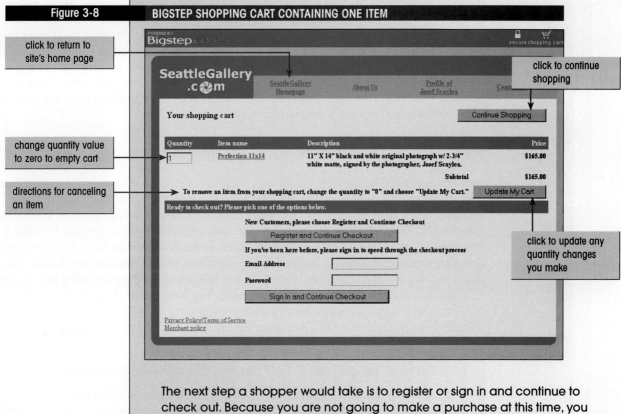

The next step a shopper would take is to register or sign in and continue to check out. Because you are not going to make a purchase at this time, you will follow the directions provided on the Your shopping cart page and cancel the order.

6. Select the value **1** in the Quantity text box, type **0**, and then click the **Update My Cart** button to empty your shopping cart.

7. Click the **SeattleGallery Homepage** link located near the top of the page. Your browser returns to an unsecured state and the home page reopens.

You are satisfied that the Seattle Gallery commerce site, hosted by Bigstep and built using Bigstep software, is both easy to navigate and visually appealing. Bigstep seems to be another good choice. Of course, you want to investigate more about the cost of creating a store and try building a store before you make any recommendations to Franklin.

Promoting Your Store

Imagine for a moment that you have built Franklin's Coffee and Tea Merchant online store. It sports a clean design, is easy to navigate and select products, has a shopping cart, and accepts various forms of payment. You fling open the virtual doors of the store and wait. You wait some more. For the first 24 hours the store is open, the Coffee and Tea Merchant has no online business. What is going on? Where are your customers? Where are the mobs of people who want to purchase your products? This situation is similar to a physical store located on a back street of a small town in any country in the world. If you rented physical space for a store in an obscure location and tried to sell goods and services at market prices, very few customers would stumble into your store accidentally. Both online and offline (physical) stores must attract customers through marketing, which consists of advertisements and promotions. Online stores benefit from the same types of advertising and promotions as their physical counterparts, such as using newspaper advertisements, radio promotions, and similar channels where people are likely to visit.

For online stores, there are at least two distinct ways to make potential customers aware of your electronic commerce site: strategic advertisements directed at your target market, and by using search engines to your advantage. When your site attracts visitors and customers based on your advertising, its satisfied customers will spread the word to potential customers for you. However, you must continue to actively promoting your site to attract new customers and maintain the interest of existing customers.

Promoting an Online Store Using Advertisements

Just like any other business, Franklin uses advertisements in newspapers, magazines, and, sometimes, radio promotions to promote his store's location, inventory, and specials. He also uses direct mail to send his customers bimonthly newsletters to provide information about new coffee and tea products and to advertise periodic specials. You tell Franklin that he will need to change his advertising goals when he starts his online store. He wants you to investigate online advertising channels and report back to him. He has seen banner advertisements on various competitors' Web sites, but he wonders if there are other places where he could find low-cost, online advertising space. You have heard about **banner exchange** services in which members post banner advertisements on each other's sites. This exchange of banners provides a low-cost investment and a highly visible form of advertising.

To examine an online advertisement exchange service:

1. Click your browser's **Back** button or use its history list to return to the Online Companion page for Session 3.1, and then click the **HitExchange** link and wait while your browser loads the HitExchange home page shown in Figure 3-9.

Figure 3-9	HITEXCHANGE HOME PAGE

banner exchange link

what's the catch? link

2. Click the **banner exchange** link. A page opens that describes the HitExchange banner exchange system. Read the page to understand more about banner exchanges, and consider which businesses would be a candidate for a banner exchange with the Coffee and Tea Merchant. The banner exchange service provided by HitExchange is free. You can click the "what's the catch" link on the home page to learn about the site's requirements.

3. Click your browser's **Back** button to return to the HitExchange home page, and then click the **what's the catch?** link to learn about the advertising costs of using HitExchange as compared to other banner exchange systems.

Visiting just one example of an advertising banner exchange service has provided you with some valuable information. HitExchange has members whose banners run on each other's sites. A central server stores and displays the banners so the individual Web site owners do not have the added burden of updating or refreshing banner ads on their sites.

There are several other banner exchange services, including **BannerExchange, European Banner Exchange, Exchange-it, Microsoft bCentral,** and **SmartClicks.** Each of these banner exchange services has members. The policies of each banner exchange service varies in the way it charges and whether it allows nonmember advertisements on member sites. You can use the links provided on the Online Companion page for Session 3.1 to investigate these other banner exchange sites.

Another approach—one that is more costly than banner exchange advertisements—is to pay for your Web site's advertisement on another site. You want to choose the site on which your advertisement is placed carefully. You probably do not want to advertise the Coffee and Tea Merchant on a site whose main product is imported wine. Similarly, an auto parts Web site is a poor place to advertise a bicycle Web site. There are many smaller sites whose products reach narrow-interest audiences. When selecting a Web site on which to advertise an online store, choose one that reaches the largest audience that will be interested in your related product. Ads on sites with small hit rates can cost as little as $50 to $100 per 1,000 visitors. If you purchase space for a banner ad on a related Web site, check the site periodically to make sure that your ad is actually there, correct, and in a location where it is easily seen.

Banner exchange advertising intrigues Franklin. He is very interested in joining one of the banner exchanges so that he can obtain free or low-cost advertisements to promote the Coffee and Tea Merchant's Web site. He wants to know more about promoting his Web store using search engines. You decide to examine that option next.

Promoting an Online Store Using a Search Engine

Another great opportunity to market your Web site is to have it listed by popular search engines such as AltaVista, Excite, HotBot, Lycos, Northern Light, Yahoo!, and many others. While the details of how search engines work are interesting, Franklin asks you to research *how* to submit the Coffee and Tea Merchant's Web site to the various search engines. He wants you to research what steps he can take to ensure that his Web site is ranked high in any searches for keywords such as "coffee" or "coffee and tea." One approach you could take to have an online store's Web site retrieved in a user search is to build a site and let the various search engines find your store. Taking that passive approach might mean your store is not listed in search engine **indexes**—the search engine's database of Web pages—for a long time. Some search engines have **spiders**, or information retrievers, that crawl through the Web and index your entire Web site beginning with your home page. They do this for pages all over the Internet. Some sites create an index only for a site's home page. Other search engines traverse all links in a Web site and index everything they encounter.

On the other hand, you can be proactive and submit your Web site's address to individual search engines, or use a specialized Web site to submit your information to multiple search engines simultaneously. Submitting your Web page to various search engines shortens to almost zero the number of days it takes for search engines to list your Web page(s). If you do not want to submit your Web site's home page to many different search engines, there are several Web sites that automatically submit your Web pages to several search engines simultaneously. To use such a service, you fill out a form and the search engine submission service does the rest of the work. The disadvantage of this shotgun submission approach is that different search engines rank Web pages using different techniques. If you want to maximize your chances of a high ranking (your site is listed near the top of a particular search request), then you are better off tailoring your submissions individually to each search engine. Of course, you can do both if you have some time to fine-tune your submissions.

You inform Franklin about search engine submission Web sites. He's very interested and asks you to investigate them more. Your brief research indicates that Submit It! is one of the premiere search engine submission Web sites. Reading more about Submit It! will help you to determine how the submission service works, how much it costs, and whether it would be a good option for the Coffee and Tea Merchant.

To examine the Submit It! Web site submission service:

1. Click your browser's **Back** button or use its history list to return to the Online Companion page for Session 3.1, and then click the **Submit It!** link and wait while your browser loads the Submit It! home page shown in Figure 3-10.

Figure 3-10   SUBMIT IT! HOME PAGE

2. Click the **Price** link near the top of the page. A page opens containing the service's key features, benefits, and prices.

3. Click your browser's **Back** button to return to the Submit It! home page.

4. Click the **monthly reports** link near the bottom of the page. Figure 3-11 shows a sample report created using Submit It!

| Figure 3-11 | SUBMIT IT! SAMPLE REPORT |

clicking the Re-Schedule Now button refreshes the report with current results

You can also submit your Web site to a specific search engine so that your site will be included in its search results, as you will see next. You will submit the URL of your school to simulate how a business might submit its own URL to the search engine for indexing.

To submit a Web page to a search engine to be indexed:

1. Click your browser's **Back** button or use its history list to return to the Online Companion page for Session 3.1, and then click the **AltaVista Help** link and wait while your browser loads the AltaVista Help page shown in Figure 3-12.

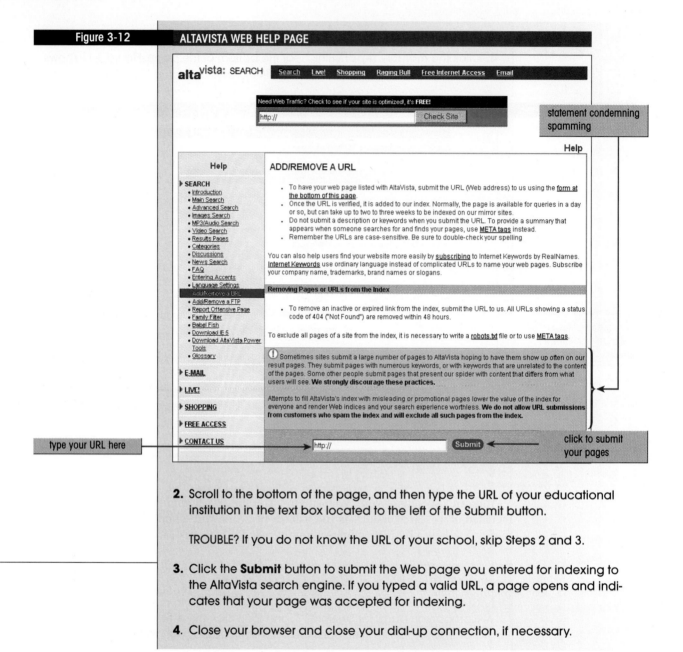

Figure 3-12 | **ALTAVISTA WEB HELP PAGE**

2. Scroll to the bottom of the page, and then type the URL of your educational institution in the text box located to the left of the Submit button.

   TROUBLE? If you do not know the URL of your school, skip Steps 2 and 3.

3. Click the **Submit** button to submit the Web page you entered for indexing to the AltaVista search engine. If you typed a valid URL, a page opens and indicates that your page was accepted for indexing.

4. Close your browser and close your dial-up connection, if necessary.

Other search engines have similar pages that you use to submit the URL for a Web site or Web page to the search engine's index. Most search engines have safeguards that prevent **search engine spamming**, which is the activity of submitting the same Web page an excessive number of times to the same search engine.

You wonder what factors affect where your Web page is ranked by a search engine when a user specifies a search question that should return your page as one of the search results. Search engines continually refine how they index Web pages. Be aware that search engines have idiosyncrasies. Your Web page might be the authoritative source on some topic but end up with a low ranking in response to a user's search request. The following general guidelines will help you to fine-tune your Web pages and maximize your Web page rankings:

- Several search engines index Web pages based on the content of META tags. **META tags** are pieces of information you place in a Web page that describe the page's content using keywords and descriptions. Including accurate information in the META tags increases your Web page rankings when searchers use keywords that match those in your META tags.

- Create accurate keywords in the META tags for each Web page. Your keywords should match the potential keywords that users will use to search for your Web site.

- Some search engines scour all the Web pages leading from a home page when you submit a home page for indexing, and other search engines examine only one page (usually, this page is the home page). Determine how the search engine works to maximize your subsequent ranking. You should submit the URL for each Web page in your Web site if the search engine does not crawl the entire Web site, beginning with a home page.

- Create a descriptive and relevant title for each Web page. Most search engines place heavy weight on the words in the text of the title HTML tag (the text between the <title> and </title> tags in the Web page).

- Search engines index Web pages on words appearing in the Web pages. In the past, people used particular keywords repeatedly in a Web page to increase its rank based on a few repeated words. Today, most search engines either ignore excessive repetitions of words or penalize Web pages by demoting them.

Now that you understand how to build, market, and index your online store, you are ready to build it. In Session 3.2, you will build an online store using Yahoo! Store. In Session 3.3, you will build an online store using Bigstep.

Session 3.1 QUICK | CHECK

1. What protocol includes rules that computers on a network use to establish and break connections?

2. Why might a private network be a more expensive extranet than a virtual private network?

3. What is the name of the Web server software that was developed by a group of webmasters and is available free of charge?

4. List three features electronic commerce software should provide.

5. What are META tags and why are they useful?

6. What can you do to make your store's home page show up in a search engine's index as quickly as possible?

SESSION 3.2

In this session, you will learn how to design and create an online store. You will use the commerce service provider, Yahoo! Store, to build an online store that sells coffee and tea. Creating a Yahoo! Store requires you to first obtain a free Yahoo! account. You will then build your store using your Web browser and the Yahoo! Store tools. After you have finished building your store, you will publish it, log into your site, modify its design, and add a few more products.

Note: You can create and save a Yahoo! Store for 10 days without incurring a fee. After that, you must either pay a monthly rental fee for your store or Yahoo! will remove it from the site. Therefore, you must complete this session within the 10-day limit. If your instructor also assigns Case Problem 3, make sure that you complete Session 3.2 and Case Problem 3 within 10 days so your site will still be on the Yahoo! server.

Building a Yahoo! Store

After completing your research and submitting your online store plan to Franklin, he approved it and authorized you to begin work. Based on your recommendation, Franklin decided to use Yahoo! Store to host the site. After securing Franklin's approval, you contacted Yahoo! Store and discovered that it charges a monthly fee of $100 for a small store selling up to 50 different products, or $300 for a store selling up to 1,000 products, with an additional monthly fee of $100 for each additional 1,000 products. You learn that you can build a store and try it out for 10 days at no charge, which will be enough time for Franklin and you to decide if the online store is going to meet your customers' needs.

Obtaining a Yahoo! ID

In order to build a Yahoo! store, you need two IDs. First, you need a Yahoo! ID so the software can identify you as the owner of one or more stores. Second, you need a store ID to identify your store. You can use your Yahoo! ID to create one or more stores—each store's store ID identifies it. Because you want to build a store to demonstrate to Franklin a prototype he can critique, you obtain a Yahoo! ID.

To obtain a Yahoo! ID:

1. Start your Web browser, and then go to the Online Companion by entering the URL **http://www.course.com/NewPerspectives/EC** in the appropriate location of your Web browser. Click the **Tutorial 3** link, and then click the **Session 3.2** link. Click the **Obtain a Yahoo! ID** link and wait while your browser loads the Yahoo! Store member sign-in page shown in Figure 3-13. When you want to create a new store, add products to an existing store, or edit an existing store, you begin with this page. On subsequent visits to this page, you sign into this page using your Yahoo! account information to gain access to your store.

   TROUBLE? If you already have a Yahoo! e-mail address, your Yahoo! logon serves as your Yahoo! ID. You can skip Steps 2 through 7, or use the steps to create a new Yahoo! account.

Figure 3-13   **YAHOO! STORE MEMBER SIGN-IN PAGE**

existing users fill in
these text boxes and
click the Sign in button

new users click here to
obtain a Yahoo! account

2. Click the **Sign Up Here** link to open the Welcome to Yahoo! sign up page.

3. Enter a Yahoo! ID in the Yahoo ID text box. Choose a Yahoo! ID by typing your first and last names followed by your birthday in the form ddmmyy, with no spaces (for example, John Smith, born on November 24, 1982, would have the Yahoo! ID johnsmith241182).

4. Enter a password in the Password text box, and then enter the same password in the Retype Password text box. Make sure that you select a password that you can remember easily.

5. Enter the requested information in the In case you forget your password section.

6. Enter the requested information in the Personal Account Information section, but do not enter any information in the optional Tell Us About Your Interests section.

7. Click the **Submit This Form** button at the bottom of the page to send your registration to Yahoo! for verification. If your Yahoo! ID is not already taken, then a Welcome to Yahoo! page opens. Otherwise, you are warned that the name exists. In this case, change your Yahoo! ID and resubmit the form until you obtain a Yahoo! ID.

Yahoo! remembers your Yahoo! ID by placing a file on your computer called a cookie that contains your Yahoo! ID. If you are using a public computer, such as a university computer in a public laboratory, make sure to sign out so someone else cannot use your ID.

To sign out of your Yahoo! ID:

1. Click the **Continue to Yahoo! Store** link at the bottom of the page.

2. Click the **Sign Out** link near the top of the page that opens. A "Thank you for using Yahoo! Store" page opens, indicating that your account is signed off.

Now you have a Yahoo ID! or an e-mail account that you can use to log in and create a Yahoo! Store. You are excited about creating the new Yahoo! Store.

Logging into Yahoo!

With your new Yahoo! ID you are ready to log in and begin building a store. Your 10-day store duration does not start until you first log in and begin building a store.

To log in with your Yahoo! ID:

1. Click the **Return to Yahoo! Store** link, click in the Yahoo! ID text box and type your Yahoo! ID, press the **Tab** key to move to the Password text box, type your password, and then click the **Sign in** button.

TROUBLE? If an AutoComplete dialog box opens and asks if you want Windows to remember your password, click the No button.

The "Welcome" greeting at the top of the page that includes your Yahoo! ID indicates that you have successfully logged in using your Yahoo! ID. Now that you are logged in, you can begin creating a store. Always remember to sign out before you close your browser so that the next person to go to the Yahoo! Store page does not have access to your ID.

Creating a Yahoo! Store ID

You have thought a lot about the design of the Coffee and Tea Merchant's online store, and you are eager to build a small prototype to show Franklin. You are already logged into Yahoo! with your Yahoo! ID. Next, you will obtain a store ID and then open your new store.

To create a store ID and log into your new store:

1. Click the **Create a Store** link that appears below the Manage My Stores heading on the left side of the page. The Create Your Own Yahoo! Store Account page opens. Your store ID identifies the store associated with your Yahoo! ID. You can create more than one store ID using the same Yahoo! ID; however, each store must have its own store ID. The ID does not appear anywhere in the store, but it is part of the URL—the address that anyone uses to browse your Web site. For example, if you choose *gourmetfoods* as your store ID, then your store's URL would be http://store.yahoo.com/gourmetfoods.

2. Enter a store ID that you make up into the first text box. You must select a store ID that is a single word containing numbers, letters, or dashes. Once you create a store ID, you cannot change it.

3. Press the **Tab** key to move to the second text box, and then type **The Coffee and Tea Merchant** to establish the full text name for your store. See Figure 3-14. The full text name you enter appears on your store's home page and other pages you create. You can change the title any time you want as you design your store.

| Figure 3-14 | CREATING A STORE ID |

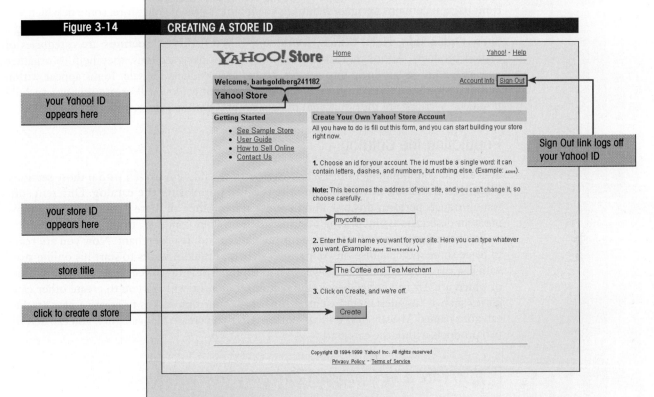

your Yahoo! ID appears here	
your store ID appears here	
store title	
click to create a store	

4. Click the **Create** button to create your store. A page opens acknowledging that Yahoo! has created your store account (store ID). Read the page, noting your store ID for future reference.

TROUBLE? If an error page opens indicating the store ID is in use, then create any other name and click the Create button again. If you have difficulty settling on a meaningful store ID, use your own name and some random digits, which should yield a unique store name. Be sure to note the ID (your store name) that you create. You will need it to visit your store as a customer later in this session.

5. Read the agreement on the page that opens, and then click the **I Accept** button at the bottom of the page to acknowledge that you have read and understood the agreement, which activates your store for 10 days. The next Web page offers you a chance to take a guided tour. Instead of taking the tour, you will sign out of your Yahoo! account to skip the tour, and then you will sign back in later to create your store.

6. Click the **Sign Out** link to sign out of your Yahoo! ID, and then click the **Close** button to close your browser. You must sign out of your Yahoo! account *and* close your browser to cancel the tour.

Creating a Store

There are three types of pages you will use to create your Yahoo! Store: the front page, sections, and items. The **front page** is the first page of your store—the one you see when you or your customers go to your store. In addition to content that you create and add to the front page, it contains navigation buttons to all other parts of your store, some of which you must create. Yahoo! creates the following standard buttons for you on your front page: Show Order, Info, Help, Search, Index, and Y!SHOPPING. **Sections** are categories of related products. Although a store does not need to have sections, they help to organize your store and its products into groups. **Items** are products for sale. Items appear within one of a store's sections. In the illustrations that follow, you will create sections to hold products. Sections are the equivalent of departments within a store.

Populating the Catalog

Your first task in building a store is to create sections and items to sell within those sections. Placing items for sale in your online store is called **populating the catalog**. Different software products perform this task in different ways, but they all share a common goal—moving item descriptions and pricing information from your computer to the online store.

You have created a shell of a store for the Coffee and Tea Merchant. Now you are ready to place some merchandise on your store's shelves. Franklin wants to start his online store with just two coffee products: Kenya AA and Ethiopia Sidamo coffee beans (the items), both of which are African coffee beans (the section). Later, he will ask you to create other categories such as Indonesian and Central American. Your first task is to create a new product category named African and Arabian Coffee. After you create that category, you can add the two products within the category.

To create a new product category in your store:

1. Start your Web browser, and then go to the Online Companion by entering the URL **http://www.course.com/NewPerspectives/EC** in the appropriate location of your Web browser. Click the **Tutorial 3** link, and then click the **Session 3.2** link. Click the **Yahoo! log in** link and wait while your browser loads the Yahoo! Store home page.

2. Enter your Yahoo! ID and password in the correct text boxes, and then click the **Sign in** button.

3. Click the link for your store ID under the Manage Your Store heading to open your store. The Yahoo! Store Management page opens. See Figure 3-15.

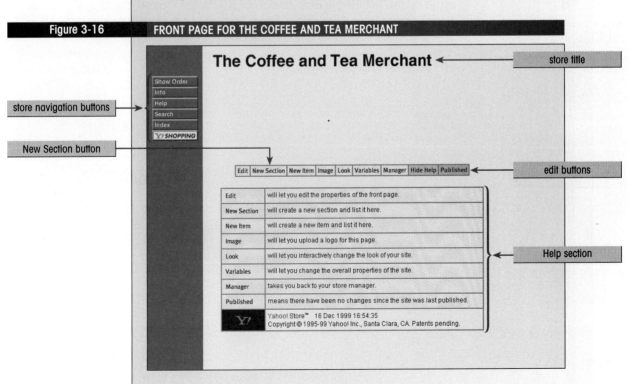

Figure 3-15	YAHOO! STORE MANAGEMENT PAGE

YAHOO! Store   mycoffee

store interface choices →

Edit
Simple
Regular
Advanced

Process
Orders
Requests

Statistics
Per Page
References
Searches
Shopping Searches
Graphs
Click Trails
Reports
Repeats

Order Settings
Order Form
Fax/Email
Shipment Status
Pay Methods
Ship Methods
Ship Rates
Tax Rates
Foreign Orders
Test
Auctions Checkout
Published

Site Settings
Access
Preferences
Domain Names
Email
Customer Access
Registration
Ratings

Promote
Create Links
Track Links
Mailing Lists
Search Engines
Yahoo! Directory
Yahoo! Shopping NEW!

Statistics at a Glance (last 120 days)

Page Views   0.00 Revenue

Customer Ratings
No ratings yet. [Info]

total revenue generated by the store so far

number of pages viewed by all customers to date

Your demo account will expire after 10 days. Open your account soon.

Help User Guide
Go Feedback | Published Site | Yahoo! Store | Sign out

Note: This procedure is called **logging into a store**. Because you will log into a store frequently, the steps that follow will ask you to "log into your store," which means going to http://store.yahoo.com and repeating Steps 2 and 3.

4. Click the **Simple** link under the Edit heading. Your store's front page opens (see Figure 3-16), with your store's name at the top of the page. This page includes edit and store navigation buttons to help you build your store, along with a Help section in the main part of the page.

Figure 3-16	FRONT PAGE FOR THE COFFEE AND TEA MERCHANT

The Coffee and Tea Merchant ← store title

store navigation buttons →

Show Order
Info
Help
Search
Index
Y! SHOPPING

New Section button

Edit | New Section | New Item | Image | Look | Variables | Manager | Hide Help | Published ← edit buttons

Edit	will let you edit the properties of the front page.
New Section	will create a new section and list it here.
New Item	will create a new item and list it here.
Image	will let you upload a logo for this page.
Look	will let you interactively change the look of your site.
Variables	will let you change the overall properties of the site.
Manager	takes you back to your store manager.
Published	means there have been no changes since the site was last published.

Help section

Y!   Yahoo! Store™   16 Dec 1999 16:54:35
Copyright © 1995-99 Yahoo! Inc., Santa Clara, CA. Patents pending.

The simple interface provides the best interface for new online store builders and owners. The Regular and Advanced options provide more commands and capabilities to edit your store than the Simple option. When you need more features to modify your store, then you can choose the Regular or Advanced options.

5. Click the **New Section** button to open the page shown in Figure 3-17. This page lets you add new items and sections to your site. The specific fields supplied in the form depend on what you are creating. You will create a coffee category (section).

Figure 3-17	CREATING A NEW SECTION

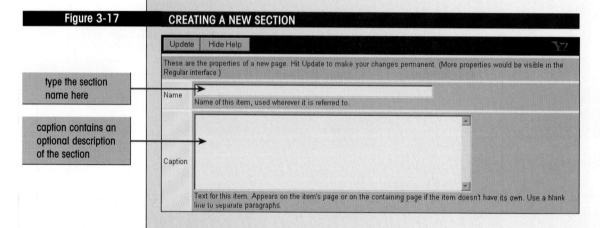

type the section name here

caption contains an optional description of the section

6. Click in the Name text box, and then type **African and Arabian Coffee**. You will not enter anything in the Caption scrolling text box. The caption is a description of the section that appears just below the section name when the section is open.

7. Click the **Update** button near the top of the page to open the page that you just created. See Figure 3-18. Notice the two new buttons in the navigation pane on the left: Home and African and Arabian Coffee. Clicking the Home button opens your store's front page. Also notice that your browser's title bar now displays this page's title, African and Arabian Coffee.

Figure 3-18 NEW SECTION CREATED

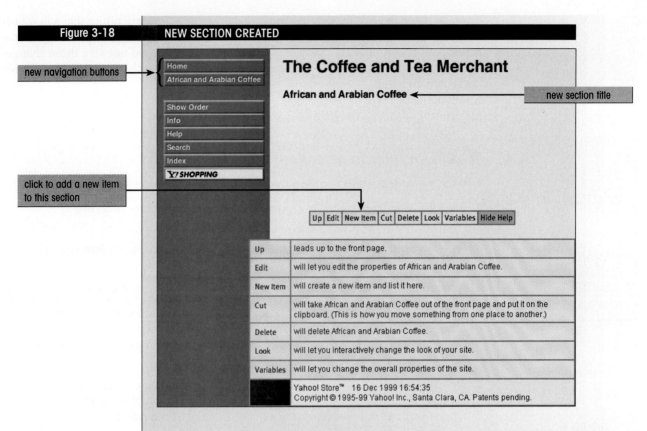

new navigation buttons

new section title

click to add a new item
to this section

8. Click the **Home** button to open the store's front page, which does not contain a "Home" link to itself. See Figure 3-19. Notice the new African and Arabian Coffee navigation button, which when clicked will open the page containing this store section.

Figure 3-19 HOME PAGE AFTER CREATING A SECTION

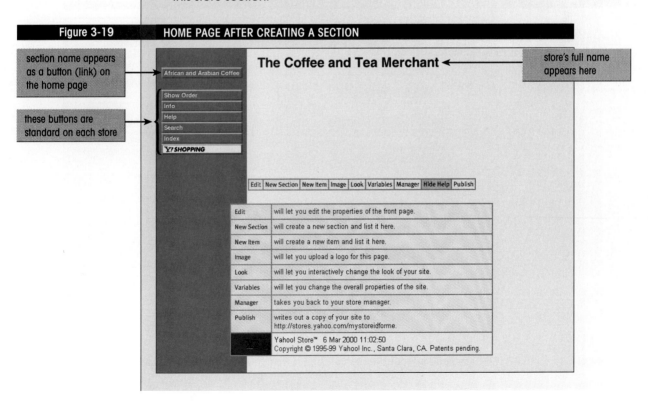

section name appears
as a button (link) on
the home page

store's full name
appears here

these buttons are
standard on each store

If you compare the edit buttons in Figures 3-18 and 3-19, you will notice that a new button named Publish was added to the front page. When the Publish button appears on one of your store's pages, it indicates that you changed your store but did not save those changes permanently. A Published button in this same position indicates that your store's contents are saved and up to date.

Now you have a section into which you can place items that Franklin sells. With the front page still open, you can populate your catalog.

To add an item to a section:

1. Click the **African and Arabian Coffee** button to open that section.

2. Click the **New Item** button. A page opens with fields that you can use to describe the new item.

3. Type **Ethiopia Sidamo** in the Name text box, and then press the **Tab** key to move to the Code text box.

4. Type **ethio** and then press the **Tab** key to move to the Price text box.

5. Type **14 2 26.50** in the Price text box. This value is the price per pound you will charge your customers. The first number—14—is the price in dollars for one pound. The second two numbers—2 and 26.50—indicate a volume discount where two pounds cost $26.50.

6. Press the **Tab** key to move to the Caption scrolling text box. You use the Caption scrolling text box to enter a detailed description of the item. What you type will appear on the screen when the user opens this page.

7. Type **It has a floral aroma and lively acidity. Ethiopia is where coffee originated.** in the Caption scrolling text box, as shown in Figure 3-20.

Figure 3-20	ENTERING INFORMATION ABOUT A NEW ITEM

Update button

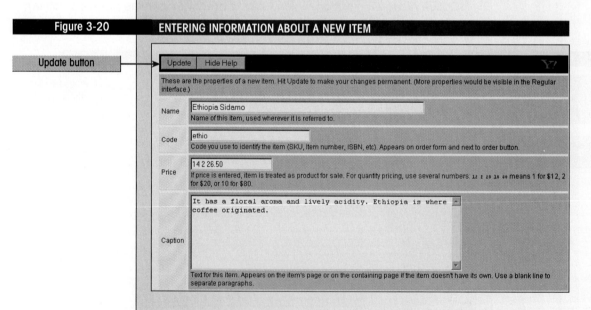

8. Click the **Update** button to finish creating this item. The item's description and price information appears on the new page.

Next, add a second item to The Coffee and Tea Merchant's catalog.

To add another item to a section:

1. Click the **Up** button to return to the African and Arabian Coffee section. The section now contains one item.

2. Click the **New Item** button. An empty item description page opens.

3. Type **Kenya AA** in the Name text box, and then press the **Tab** key to move to the Code text box.

4. Type **kenya** in the Code text box, and then press the **Tab** key to move to the Price text box.

5. Type **10 2 18** in the Price text box, and then press the **Tab** key to move to the Caption scrolling text box.

6. Type **Kenya is popular, tangy, and has medium body.** in the Caption scrolling text box.

7. Click the **Update** button to complete the process. The item's description and price information appears on the new item page.

8. Click the **Up** button to return to the African and Arabian Coffee section shown in Figure 3-21. The two new items appear on the section page. The item names are actually links—clicking the item name opens the item's page.

| Figure 3-21 | TWO ITEMS IN THIS SECTION |

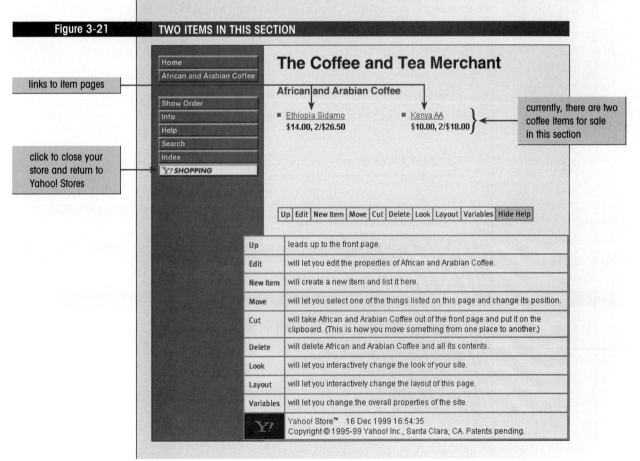

links to item pages

click to close your store and return to Yahoo! Stores

currently, there are two coffee items for sale in this section

9. Click the **Home** button to open your store's front page. So far, none of the changes you have made appear in your Yahoo! Store site. Now is a good time to save all your work. You always save your changes from your store's front page.

10. Click the **Publish** button to save your store. The Publish button changes to a Published button, indicating that the store has been saved on the Yahoo! Store server.

11. Click the **Y! SHOPPING** link (see Figure 3-21) to return to the Yahoo! Store page.

12. Click the **Sign Out** link near the top of the page to sign out of your Yahoo! account.

Visiting Your Store

Now you can visit your store as a customer and examine the site, click its links, and really see how the store operates. This is a terrific way to discover any site navigation difficulties and experience the site as a customer would. You will need your store's ID to access it. Suppose you choose the store ID *myfinecoffee*. The URL to access your store would be http://store.yahoo.com/myfinecoffee. Anyone entering that URL in a Web browser would see your store's front page. Open your own store and click the links you created.

To open your Yahoo! Store:

1. Click in the address bar for your Web browser, and then type **http://store.yahoo.com/** plus your Yahoo! store ID.

2. Press the **Enter** key to open your store's front page. Your store opens in the browser.

   TROUBLE? If your store does not open, repeat Steps 1 and 2 and make sure that you entered your store ID, and not your Yahoo! ID.

3. Click the **African and Arabian Coffee** link. That section of your store opens and displays two coffee links.

4. Click the **Ethiopia Sidamo** link. A page containing a description of the coffee, its price, and an Order button opens. See Figure 3-22.

| Figure 3-22 | ETHIOPIA SIDAMO ITEM PAGE |

Home
African and Arabian Coffee

Show Order
Info
Help
Search
Index
Y! SHOPPING

The Coffee and Tea Merchant

Ethiopia Sidamo

It has a floral aroma and lively acidity. Ethiopia is where coffee originated.

ethio $14.00, 2/$26.50   Order

5. Click the **Order** button. The Shopping Cart page opens and displays your order of one pound of Ethiopia Sidamo coffee.

6. Select the value **1** in the Quantity text box, type **2**, and then click the **Update Quantities** button to recalculate your subtotal. Notice that the new price is $26.50, not $28.00, which is two times the unit price. When you created the Ethiopia Sidamo item, you specified that two pounds sell for a discounted price of $26.50.

7. Click the **Keep Shopping** button to purchase another item.

8. Click the **African and Arabian Coffee** link to return to that store section.

9. Click the **Kenya AA** link. When the Kenya AA page opens, click the **Order** button. The Shopping Cart page opens again.

10. Select the value **1** in the Quantity text box, type **4**, and then click the **Update Quantities** button to recalculate your subtotal. Notice that the Kenya AA is priced at $9.00 per pound. See Figure 3-23.

| Figure 3-23 | YAHOO! SHOPPING CART PAGE WITH TWO ITEMS |

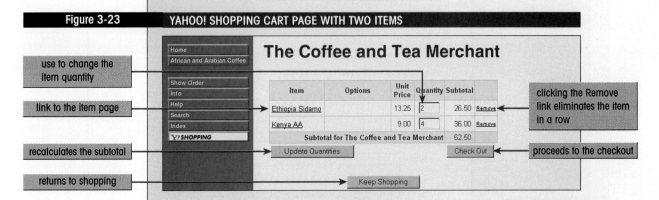

use to change the item quantity

link to the item page

recalculates the subtotal

returns to shopping

clicking the Remove link eliminates the item in a row

proceeds to the checkout

The Coffee and Tea Merchant

Item	Options	Unit Price	Quantity	Subtotal	
Ethiopia Sidamo		13.25	2	26.50	Remove
Kenya AA		9.00	4	36.00	Remove
Subtotal for The Coffee and Tea Merchant				62.50	

Update Quantities   Check Out

Keep Shopping

11. Click the **Check Out** button. The Order Form page opens and displays your completed order and several text boxes for your name, address, and other shipping information. See Figure 3-24. At the top of the Order Form page are two sentences that indicate your store is not yet functional and ordering is allowed for testing purposes only. Scroll down to the bottom of the page, examining the form as you scroll.

Figure 3-24	ORDER FORM PAGE

The Coffee and Tea Merchant

message indicating that this store is not yet functional →

The Coffee and Tea Merchant is not open for business. Ordering is allowed for testing purposes only.

1. Review your order from The Coffee and Tea Merchant

order information →

Item	Options	Unit Price	Quantity	Subtotal
Ethiopia Sidamo		13.25	2	26.50
Kenya AA		9.00	4	- 36.00
		Subtotal for The Coffee and Tea Merchant		62.50

Shipping and tax may be added to your order. For terms, see the Info page.

2. Choose the shipping address

shipping address information →

Name:
Address:

City: State:
Zip: Phone:
Country: US United States

3. Choose shipping options for The Coffee and Tea Merchant

Air

4. Choose the billing address

○ Same: (Use shipping address)

◉ Other: Name:
Address:

City: State:
Zip: Phone:
Country: US United States

billing information →

5. Enter billing info

Email Address:

☐ Your opinion counts! Check this box, and we will send you an email giving you a chance to rate this merchant.
Comments:

6. Choose a payment method for The Coffee and Tea Merchant

make payment choices here →

Payment method: Visa
Card or account number:
Expiration date: — —

click to place your order →   [Yes: Place Order]   [No: Do Not Order]   ← click to cancel your order

Copyright © 2000 Yahoo! Inc. Disclaimer

12. Click the **No: Do Not Order** button at the bottom of the page to cancel your order. The Shopping Cart page opens again. You can abandon your shopping cart in the virtual parking lot by going to another Web site, or you can empty the cart before leaving your store. Either way, you will not have to check out or pay for anything. You can empty your cart before leaving the store by clicking the Remove link on every item in your shopping cart.

13. Click the **Remove** link on the Ethiopia Sidamo order line. Yahoo! removes this item from your shopping cart. Click the **Remove** link on the Kenya AA row to remove that item. Your shopping cart is empty, and the confirming message "Your shopping cart is empty" appears.

Whenever you want to review what is in your shopping cart, you can click the Show Order button. The buttons appearing in the left panel are always visible, so you can look in your shopping cart from any page in your store and at any time.

After creating a store, you can return to the Yahoo! Store page and make changes to your store. For example, you might need to change an item to reflect a price increase or to correct a typographical error.

Changing an Item

You show Franklin your Web pages. He takes a tour of the African and Arabian Coffee section and notices a mistake in one of the prices for Ethiopia Sidamo coffee beans. The discounted price for two pounds should be $27.00, not $26.50. You must edit that catalog item to reflect the correct price.

To edit an item within a section:

1. Log into your store.

TROUBLE? If you cannot remember how to log into your store, return to the steps titled "To create a new product category in your store" for help.

2. Click the **Simple** link under the Edit heading.

3. Click the **African and Arabian Coffee** button to open the page containing this section.

4. Click the **Ethiopia Sidamo** link to open the page containing this item.

5. Click the **Edit** button.

6. Select the value **26.5** in the Price text box, and then type **27**.

7. Click the **Update** button to make the change. The revised Ethiopia Sidamo page opens, showing the new discount price of $27.00.

You also can add a comment to the African and Arabian Coffee section.

To edit an item within a section:

1. Click the **Up** button to open the African and Arabian Coffee section page.

2. Click the **Edit** button. The Simple interface displays two section text boxes— Name and Caption.

3. Click in the Caption scrolling text box, and then type **African and Arabian coffees have robust body and taste. We believe that one of the best in this category is Kenya AA.**

4. Click the **Update** button to finish updating the page. The caption that you just added appears below the section heading on the revised page. Next, you will publish your changes to save them. Remember, you must open your front page to publish your changes.

5. Click the **Home** link to open the front page.

6. Click the **Publish** button to save your changes. The Publish button changes to a Published button and your changes now appear in your Yahoo! Store.

Creating Your Information Page

Almost every online store has an information page that contains the company's name, address, e-mail address, telephone number, shipping rates, return policy, and privacy statement. You talk to Franklin about the history of the company and you gather contact information including Franklin's preferred e-mail address. You are now ready to create an information page that customers can open to obtain this important information.

To create an information page:

1. Click the **Info** button. A blank information page opens. Notice that the options in the Help panel and the buttons above it change to reflect that you are working on an Info page. See Figure 3-25.

Figure 3-25	EDITING THE INFO PAGE

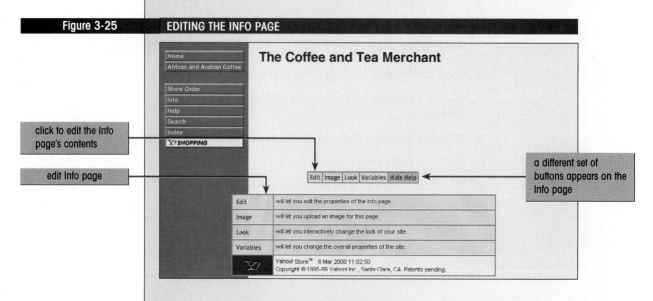

2. Click the **Edit** button. A page opens with blank fields that you will use to create the information requested by Franklin.

3. Click in the Greeting scrolling text box, type **Welcome to the Coffee and Tea Merchant. We can ship any product the same day for all orders received before 4:00 PM, U.S. Pacific Time.**, and then press the **Tab** key to move to the Address-phone scrolling text box.

4. Type the following information in the Address-phone scrolling text box, pressing the **Enter** key to end each line:

The Coffee and Tea Merchant
2234 Roasting Lane
San Diego, CA 90000-1234
(619) 555-8500
OTToadvine@yahoo.com

5. Press the **Tab** key to move to the Info text box, and then type **The first Coffee and Tea Merchant was established in 1978 in Setubal, Portugal.**

6. Click the **Update** button to post your changes to the Info page. See Figure 3-26.

| Figure 3-26 | COMPLETED INFO PAGE |

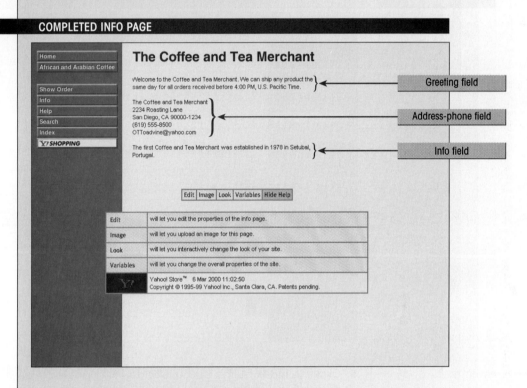

7. Click the **Home** button to return to the front page.

8. Click the **Publish** button to save the changes you made to the store.

Creating Product Specials

Successful online stores often have one or more items featured as specials on the front page. Because the front page is the first one that a customer sees, the specials listed there immediately grab a customer's attention. Periodically, the Coffee and Tea Merchant runs specials. Franklin wants you to show him how to create a special using one of your existing pages.

To edit an item within a section:

1. Click the **African and Arabian Coffee** button to move to that section.

2. Click the **Ethiopia Sidamo** link to open that item's page.

3. Click the **Special** button. The Ethiopia Sidamo product is now featured on the front page. Clicking the Special button creates a link to the item on your front page and automatically opens your store's front page.

4. Click the **Ethiopia Sidamo** link on the front page to open the item's page. See Figure 3-27. Notice that a Not Special button is added to the edit buttons. Clicking the Not Special button removes a special item from the specials list. It is a good idea to change specials regularly, to keep your customers interested in returning to your store.

Figure 3-27	SPECIALS ITEM

removes an item from the specials list

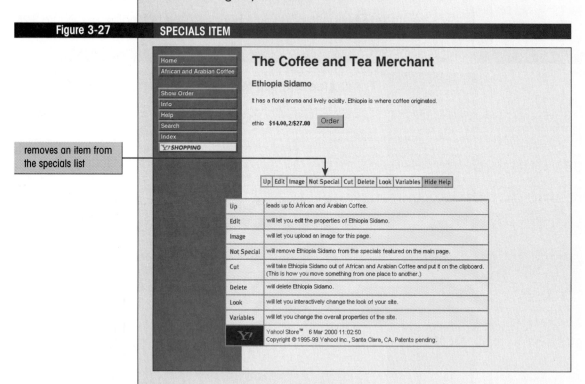

5. Click the **Index** button on the left side of the page to view the list of links (mostly products) on your site. See Figure 3-28.

Figure 3-28	INDEX PAGE SHOWING STORE LINKS

online store links to sections, items, and a search engine

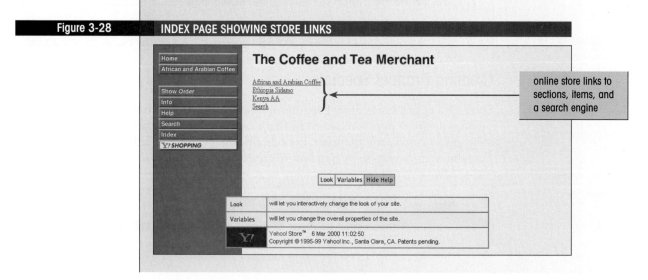

6. Click the **Home** button to return to the front page, and then click the **Publish** button to save your changes.

Finally, you can view your store from the Internet as a customer would to see how your changes are taking shape.

To view your store:

1. Click the **Y!SHOPPING** button to return to the Yahoo! Shopping page, and then click the **Sign Out** link near the top of the page to sign out of your Yahoo! account.

2. Select the URL in your browser's address bar, and then type the URL for your store (**http://store.yahoo.com/** plus your store ID). You might need to refresh or reload your store's front page to see the special that you added.

3. Click the links to move around your site, observing the changes that you made.

4. When you are finished, close your browser and close your dial-up connection, if necessary.

Franklin is very pleased with the appearance of the new Yahoo! Store. He wants you to add several more categories of coffee and tea. You can do that later, though—after you get some rest and perhaps a cappuccino.

Session 3.2 QUICK CHECK

1. Name three types of pages you can use in a Yahoo! Store.

2. When you place items for sale in your online store, you are completing a task known as _____.

3. To save all the changes you have made to your Yahoo! Store, open the _____ page, and then click the _____ button.

4. What is the name of the Yahoo! page on which you post information such as your street address and shipping policy?

5. Related items (products) are normally grouped together by category and placed into a(n)_____.

6. You can feature one or more items on the front page of your store; these featured front page items are called product _____.

SESSION 3.3

In this session, you will learn how to design and create an online store. You will use the commerce service provider, Bigstep, to build an online store that sells coffee and tea. Creating a Bigstep store requires you to first obtain a free Bigstep account. You will then build your store using your Web browser and the Bigstep tools. After you have finished building your store, you will visit it on the Web.

Building a Bigstep Store

Franklin wants you to build another store for him using the Bigstep software and site. Bigstep's interface is much more involved than what you experienced while building your Yahoo! Store. Franklin wants you to create a basic store shell so you can report back to him about building an online store using Bigstep. Franklin might decide to create two online stores so he can examine the number of visitors to each one and then decide if one store attracts a larger number of online shoppers. Building a second online store hosted by Bigstep costs Franklin nothing beyond the fee charged by Bigstep on any sales the store makes. Therefore, Franklin authorizes you to begin work on the second store. You will obtain a Bigstep ID first, and then create the basic structure for the store. However, you should note that because Bigstep offers many more options for creating your site, it takes longer to create a fully functional store. In this session, you will create a store that uses a preset design and color scheme, and includes one section and two items. If you wish to do so, you can follow the help links on each page to enhance your site further. Bigstep provides online help for every task required to finish your site.

Obtaining a Bigstep ID

In order to build a Bigstep store, you need a Bigstep ID so that the software can identify you as the owner of your store. With your Bigstep ID, you can create a store, create a catalog of items for sale, and have all the privileges of a store owner. A Bigstep store costs you nothing to design and create. Your store will remain on the Bigstep site indefinitely and free of charge because Bigstep does not begin charging store owners until they obtain a merchant account and actually begin selling merchandise online. Bigstep provides you with 12 megabytes of storage space, so you can build an extensive store—as long as you avoid using too many large graphics files.

To obtain a Bigstep ID:

1. Start your Web browser, and then go to the Online Companion by entering the URL **http://www.course.com/NewPerspectives/EC** in the appropriate location of your Web browser. Click the **Tutorial 3** link, and then click the **Session 3.3** link. Click the **Obtain a Bigstep ID** link and wait while your browser loads the Bigstep home page. When you want to modify your store, you begin with this page. On subsequent visits to this page, you sign into this page using your Bigstep ID to gain access to your store.

2. Click the **Sign up!** link to open the Bigstep.com Join now page. See Figure 3-29.

Figure 3-29 | BIGSTEP MEMBERSHIP APPLICATION FORM

3. Click in the Email text box, type your full e-mail address, press the **Tab** key to move to the Confirm your email text box, and then type your full e-mail address again. Bigstep uses your e-mail address to identify you. You can only create one Bigstep store using your e-mail address. If you want to create additional stores, you must use a different e-mail address for each one.

4. Press the **Tab** key to move to the Password text box, type a password, press the **Tab** key to move to the Confirm your password text box, and then type the same password again. Make sure that you select a password that you can remember easily.

5. Press the **Tab** key to move to the Password hint text box, and then type a brief hint to help you remember your password should you forget it.

6. Click the **Title** list arrow, and then click the appropriate response.

7. Enter the requested information in the First name and Last name text boxes.

8. In the Business name text box, type **The Coffee and Tea Merchant**. The business name that you enter will be the name of your store.

9. Enter the requested information in the Zip/Postal code text box, and then, if necessary, click the **Country** list arrow and then click your country.

10. Click the **How did you hear about Bigstep.com?** list arrow, and then click **Referral from friend or colleague**.

11. Click the **Pick the category that best describes your business** list arrow, and then scroll down the list and click **Not a business**.

12. Click the **What is your role?** list arrow, and then click **Founder/Owner**.

13. Click the **How many people work in your business?** list arrow, and then click **1**.

14. Click the **Member Agreement** link, read the agreement, click the **Return to Registration** link at the bottom of the agreement, and then click the check box at the bottom of the form indicating you accept the Bigstep.com Member Agreement.

15. Click the **I have read and agree to the Member Agreement** button located near the bottom of the form to send your registration to Bigstep for verification. Bigstep displays a message indicating you have successfully joined Bigstep.

16. Click the **Enter Bigstep.com to start building your online business** button.

   TROUBLE? If you do not see the button to enter Bigstep.com, then you may have made a typing error. Scroll the form to locate and correct any errors, and then repeat Step 16.

Bigstep remembers your Bigstep ID by placing a file on your computer called a cookie, which contains your Bigstep ID. If you are using a public computer, such as a university computer in a public laboratory, make sure to sign out so someone else cannot use your Bigstep ID.

To sign out of your Bigstep ID:

1. Click the **Sign out** link near the top of the page. A page opens and indicates that your have signed out of your account. Bigstep will sign out your account if it is inactive for more than 30 minutes, so you should make sure that you have sufficient time to complete this session without taking any breaks.

Now you have a Bigstep ID that you can use to log in and create a Bigstep store. You are excited about moving on to create your store.

Logging into Bigstep

With your new Bigstep ID, you are ready to log in and begin building a store. Your first task is to log into Bigstep using your e-mail address and password.

To log in with your Bigstep ID:

1. With the Bigstep home page open in your browser, click in the Email address text box, type your Bigstep ID (your e-mail address), press the **Tab** key to move to the Password text box, and then type your password.

2. Click the **Sign In** button. Your Bigstep store building home page opens. See Figure 3-30.

Figure 3-30	BIGSTEP STORE BUILDING HOME PAGE

click the Site Building link to begin building your store

your name appears here

Sign out link

Bigstep store building tasks

TROUBLE? If an AutoComplete dialog box opens and asks if you want Windows to remember your password, click the No button.

The to-do list with your first name displayed indicates that you have successfully logged in using your Bigstep ID. Now that you are logged in, you can begin creating a store. Always remember to sign out before you close your browser so that the next person to go to a Bigstep page does not have access to your ID.

Creating a Bigstep Store Web Address

You have thought a lot about the design of the Coffee and Tea Merchant's online store, and you are eager to build a store to demonstrate to Franklin how Bigstep's store will work. You are already logged into Bigstep with your Bigstep ID. Next, you will obtain a unique Bigstep store Web address—the URL by which your customers will locate your store.

To create a Bigstep store Web address:

1. Click the **Site Building** link that appears at the top or bottom of the home page. The Site Building page opens. Next you will select and enter your store name, which will become part of your store's URL, or your Web address. Your store name identifies the store associated with your Bigstep ID. The store name is part of the URL—the address that anyone uses to browse your Web site. For example, if you choose *reallyfinecoffee* as your store name, then your store's URL would be http://www.reallyfinecoffee.bigstep.com.

2. Click the **Web address** link in the Getting started section. The Web address - Work with your Web address page opens.

3. Click in the Pick a Web Address text box, and then type a store name that you make up. See Figure 3-31. You must select a store ID that is a single word containing numbers, letters, or dashes. Be sure to write down the URL of your new store as you will need it later in this session to open your site from the Web.

| Figure 3-31 | CREATING A STORE WEB ADDRESS |

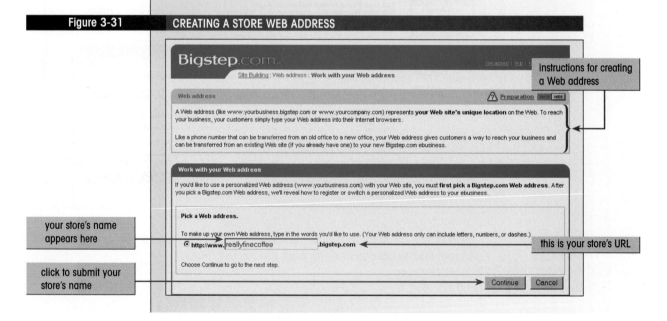

4. Click the **Continue** button to submit your store name to Bigstep. The Web address - Approve your Bigstep.com Web address page opens.

TROUBLE? If an error page opens indicating the store name you entered is in use, create any other name and click the Continue button again. If you have difficulty selecting a store name, use your own name and some random digits, which should yield a unique store name. Be sure to note the ID (your store name) that you create. You will need it to visit your store later in this session.

5. Click the **Finish** button to confirm your store's Web address. The Site Building page reopens. This time, the Appearance task appears below the Getting started banner. This task is the next one that you must complete.

Creating a Store

There are three types of pages you will use to create your Bigstep store: the home page, front page, and item pages. The **home page** is the first page of your store—the one you see when you or your customers go to your store. It contains links to other parts of your store. The **front page** is the main entrance to your catalog or portfolio of goods. An **item page** is an individual product, service, or piece of artwork that you sell or display in your catalog or portfolio. An item page shows the name, description, picture, and other information about a single item in your catalog.

Now that you have a Web address, you can continue building your store. The next task is to pick an overall store color scheme. If you decide later that you do not like your color scheme, you can always go back and change it. With the exception of your store's name, every store design choice you make can be changed later.

Selecting a Store-wide Appearance

Selecting your store's overall color scheme and appearance is the next task. You will notice that as you complete each site building task, Bigstep suggests the next logical task to complete. Completed tasks are noted with a solid green button to the left of their names.

To set the site-wide colors of your store:

1. Click the **Appearance** link in the Getting started section of the Site Building page. The Appearance - About your site's appearance page opens.

2. Click the **Basic** button to choose from a selection of page styles. (The Advanced button provides more Web page styles from which to choose.) The Appearance - Pick a design page opens. See Figure 3-32. You use this page to select a design for your store. You decide that the Basic sidebar design best suits your store's needs.

Figure 3-32	PICKING A SITE-WIDE PAGE DESIGN

instructions for selecting a design

click to select the Basic sidebar design

click to continue

preset design options

3. Click the **Basic sidebar** option button, and then click the **Continue** button at the bottom of the page. The Appearance - Set your color scheme page opens. See Figure 3-33.

Figure 3-33	PICKING A SITE-WIDE COLOR SCHEME

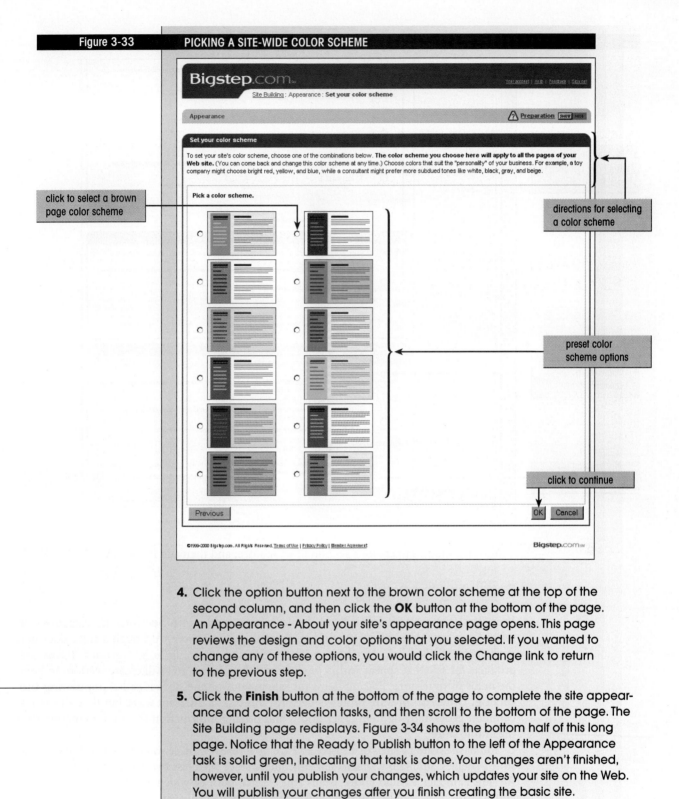

click to select a brown page color scheme

directions for selecting a color scheme

preset color scheme options

click to continue

4. Click the option button next to the brown color scheme at the top of the second column, and then click the **OK** button at the bottom of the page. An Appearance - About your site's appearance page opens. This page reviews the design and color options that you selected. If you wanted to change any of these options, you would click the Change link to return to the previous step.

5. Click the **Finish** button at the bottom of the page to complete the site appearance and color selection tasks, and then scroll to the bottom of the page. The Site Building page redisplays. Figure 3-34 shows the bottom half of this long page. Notice that the Ready to Publish button to the left of the Appearance task is solid green, indicating that task is done. Your changes aren't finished, however, until you publish your changes, which updates your site on the Web. You will publish your changes after you finish creating the basic site.

| Figure 3-34 | SITE BUILDING PAGE WITH TASK LIST |

store building tasks that have not been started

solid green circle indicates a completed task

Site Building is the active activity

Catalog link

Your next task is to create a section in your store, and then add items to it.

Populating the Catalog

Your Bigstep store's catalog is divided into sections and items. **Sections** are categories of related products, like you might find in departments in a store. Although a store does not need sections, they help to organize your store and its products into groups. **Items** are products for sale that appear within one of a store's sections. You will create sections to hold the items in your store. Placing items for sale in your online store is called **populating the catalog**. Different software products perform this task in different ways, but they all share a common goal—moving item descriptions and pricing information from your computer to the online store.

You have created a shell of a store. You are now ready to place some merchandise on your store's shelves. Franklin wants to start his online store with just two coffee products: Kenya AA and Ethiopia Sidamo coffee beans (the items), both of which are African and Arabian coffee beans (the section). Later, he will ask you to create other categories such as Indonesian and Central American. Your first task is to create a new product category named African and Arabian Coffee. After you create that category, you can add two products in the section.

To create a new section in your store:

1. Click the **Catalog** link either at the bottom or top of the page. The Catalog page opens. See Figure 3-35. Notice that the Catalog page contains a list of tasks to complete in order to build a catalog of products. Scroll down the page until you see the section titled "Work with your catalog."

Figure 3-35 CATALOG PAGE

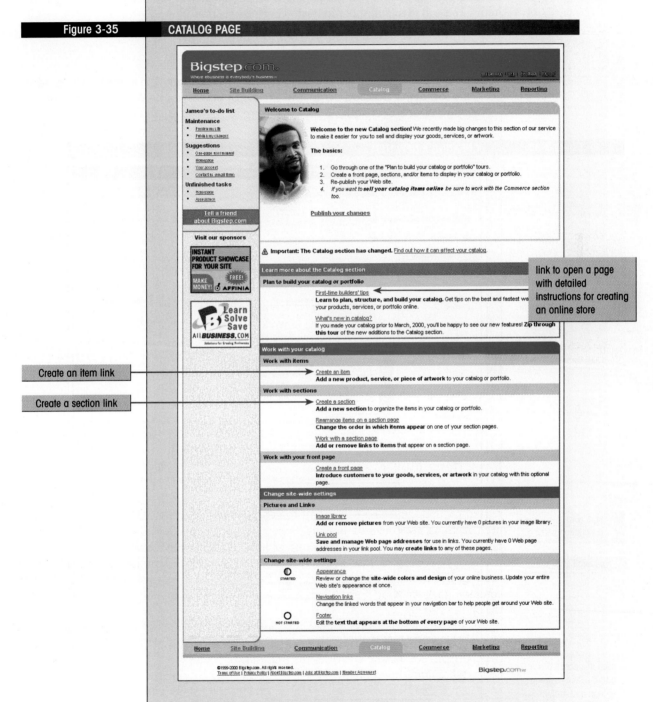

Create an item link

Create a section link

link to open a page with detailed instructions for creating an online store

2. Click the **Create a section** link located below the Work with sections heading. The Create or edit a section - Work with a section page opens.

3. Click in the Section name text box, and then type **African and Arabian Coffee**.

4. Scroll to the bottom of the page, and then click the **Finish** button to create the new section.

Now you have a section into which you can place items that Franklin sells. With the Catalog page displayed, you can populate your catalog. You will begin by creating two new items. You will then add those items to your new section.

To create a new item:

1. Click the **Create an item** link located below the Work with items heading near the top of the Catalog page. The Create or edit an item - Work with an item page opens. See Figure 3-36.

Figure 3-36	CREATING A NEW ITEM

type item name here

type item description here

type retail price here

click this check box to add the item to the African and Arabian Coffee section

2. Click in the Item name text box, and then type **Ethiopia Sidamo**.

3. Scroll down the page as necessary, click in the Item description scrolling text box, and then type **It has a floral aroma and lively acidity. Ethiopia is where coffee originated.**

4. Click in the Retail price text box, and then type **14.00**.

5. Scroll down the page, and then click the **African and Arabian Coffee** check box (see Figure 3-36) to add this item to that section. When your site contains other sections, they will appear in this list so you can add items to them.

6. Scroll to the bottom of the page, and then click the **Add Another Item** button to add another item to your store. The Create or edit an item - Work with an item page opens again.

7. Click in the Item name text box, and then type **Kenya AA**.

8. Scroll down the page as necessary, click in the Item description scrolling text box, and then type **Kenya is popular, tangy, and has medium body.**

9. Click in the Retail price text box, and then type **10.00**.

10. Scroll down the page, and then click the **African and Arabian Coffee** check box (see Figure 3-36) to add this item to that section.

11. Scroll to the bottom of the page, click the **Finish** button, and then click the **Edit an item** link to open the Catalog: View Items and Sections page. See Figure 3-37. The two items you added appear on the Your items tab with the item names and prices. Notice the DELETE button on right side of each item line. You can click the DELETE button to remove an item. You can click the Your sections tab to display the names of the sections you have created.

| Figure 3-37 | VIEWING YOUR CATALOG |

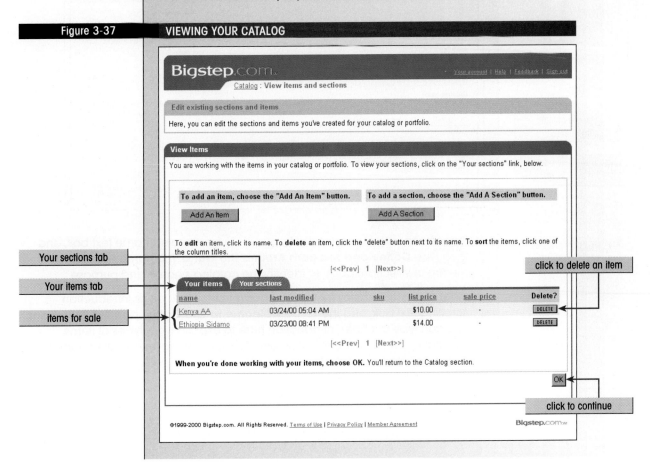

12. Click the **OK** button at the bottom of the page. The Catalog page redisplays.

Creating Your Catalog's Front Page

Next, you will create your front page, which is similar to the home page for your Web site. This optional page can list and link to some or all of the sections and/or items in your catalog. Although the page is optional, it provides an electronic welcome mat and is a place where you can prominently display sections or any special items for sale.

To create your store's front page:

1. From the Catalog page, scroll down to the section titled "Work with your front page," and then click the **Create a front page** link. The Create or edit your front page - Work with your front page page opens. See Figure 3-38.

Figure 3-38	CREATING A FRONT PAGE

type the catalog name here

type a short introduction to your store here

2. If necessary, select any text that appears in the Catalog name text box, and then type **Coffee and Tea from Around the World**. This name will appear at the top of your front page to identify the catalog's name and purpose.

3. If necessary, select any text that appears in the Front page introduction scrolling text box, and then type **Welcome to The Coffee and Tea Merchant**. You can type a longer introduction here to explain what types of items appear in your catalog. You can also provide general information, such as announcing new or sale items.

4. Scroll to the bottom of the page, and then click the **Finish** button. The Catalog page redisplays. Notice that the Edit your front page task has a solid green circle to its left labeled "Ready to publish," indicating you have completed building the front page but you have not yet published your changes. When you publish your store's pages, any new or updated pages are uploaded to your online store from their temporary location where you work on them. If you do not publish your store after making changes to it, then the changes are not visible to store browsers.

Placing Sections on Your Catalog's Front Page

The catalog's front page is a convenient page on which you can place links to sections. A section contains links to groups of related items in the catalog. Placing links to sections on your catalog's front page makes it easy for users to locate related items. You will place the African and Arabian Coffee section on the front page so your store's visitors can quickly link to its items.

To add a link to your catalog's front page:

1. Scroll down to the Work with your front page heading, and then click the **Change links on your front page** link. The Work with your front page - Add or remove sections or items page opens. See Figure 3-39.

Figure 3-39	PLACING A SECTION LINK ON THE CATALOG'S FRONT PAGE

click the section name

click to add a section link to the front page

directions for adding and removing sections and items

2. Click **African and Arabian Coffee** in the All list box, and then click the **Add** button to move the section link to the Current list box. You create a link named "African and Arabian Coffee" on the catalog's front page.

3. Scroll to the bottom of the page. Notice that you can also create a link to an item on your front page.

4. Click the **Finish** button at the bottom of the page. The Catalog page redisplays.

Creating Site-wide Navigation Links

Placing a link to the sections in your catalog on your site's pages makes it easier for customers to go directly to items for sale. The home page is a logical place to locate catalog links because it is the first page customers see when they visit your store. You can also place site-wide links on your site's page. Site-wide links appear on every page in your store.

Next, you will place a site-wide link to the African and Arabian Coffee section.

To add a site-wide link:

1. Click the **Site Building** tab at the top of the catalog page. The Site Building page opens.

2. Scroll to the bottom of the page, and then click the **Navigation links** link below the Change site-wide settings heading. The Navigation links - Work with your site-wide navigation links page opens. You use this page to create links that appear on *all* of your Web pages.

3. Click the **Add Link** button. The Navigation links - Add a navigation link page opens.

4. Click in the Name your navigation link text box, and then type **African and Arabian Coffee**.

5. Click the **Choose a destination page from inside your site** list arrow to display a list of pages to which you can link (see Figure 3-40), and then click the **African and Arabian Coffee** link.

| Figure 3-40 | CREATING A SITE-WIDE LINK |

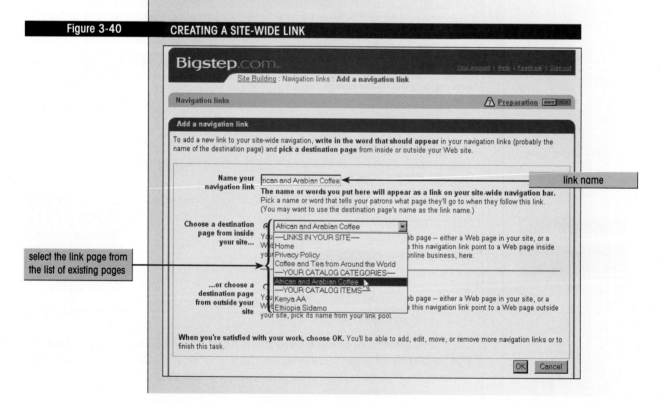

6. Click the **OK** button to finish creating the link. The Navigation links - Work with your site-wide navigation links page redisplays.

7. Click the **Finish** button. The Site Building page redisplays.

Creating Your Information Page

Almost every online store has an information page that contains the company's name, address, e-mail address, telephone number, shipping rates, and return policy. You talk to Franklin about the history of the company and you gather contact information including Franklin's preferred e-mail address. Franklin will also provide you with a return policy, which you can add to the site later. You are now ready to create an information page that customers can open to obtain this important information.

To create an information page:

1. Click the **About us** link located below the Create pages heading on the Site Building page. The About us page - About this page page opens.

2. Click the **Continue** button. The About us page - Pick a layout page opens. You can select an information page layout by clicking an option button next to the page layout you want to use.

3. Click the **Bottom left** option button, scroll to the bottom of the page, and then click the **Continue** button. The About us page - Add content to your "About us" page page opens, containing several fields into which you can enter various types of company information. Your store's business name appears in the first text box. Bigstep added your business name using the one that you entered into the Business name text box in your membership application form (see Figure 3-29).

4. Click in the Business slogan scrolling text box, and then type **Not a robusta bean anywhere**. (Robusta coffee beans are an inferior class of coffee beans. The finest beans are called arabica beans.)

5. Scroll down the page as necessary, click in the What does your business do? scrolling text box, and then type **Welcome to the Coffee and Tea Merchant. We can ship any product the same day for all orders received before 4:00 PM, U.S. Pacific Time.**

6. Scroll down the page as necessary, click in the Business history scrolling text box, and then type **The first Coffee and Tea Merchant was established in 1978 in Setubal, Portugal.**

7. Scroll down the page as necessary, click in the Who runs the business? scrolling text box, and then type the following information, pressing the **Enter** key to end each line *except* the last line:

The Coffee and Tea Merchant
2234 Roasting Lane
San Diego, CA 90000-1234
(619) 555-8500
OTToadvine@yahoo.com

The completed form appears in Figure 3-41.

Figure 3-41	CREATING THE ABOUT US PAGE

8. Scroll to the bottom of the page, and then click the **Continue** button. The About us page - Name your page page opens.

9. Click the **OK** button to save the About us page changes, and then click the **Finish** button on the next page that opens. The Site Building page redisplays. The About us task has a solid green button next to it, indicating you have completed that store building task.

Publishing Your Store

Publishing the changes you have made to your store makes them available to your customers. Changed pages that are not yet published are unavailable to customers. When you are ready to release new items or sections that you have added to your store, you publish the changes. The time between when you request your new and changed pages to be published and when they appear in your store can range from a few seconds to several hours.

You do not have to publish your store's pages in the same session as when you make changes to them. For example, you can make extensive changes to your store, sign out of Bigstep, close your browser, and then log into your store at another time or on another day. When you return, all of your changes are safely stored in a temporary area waiting for publishing. Normally, you will want to publish your pages soon after you alter them so online customers can see the new features. If you make changes to your site but do not publish them, Bigstep displays a Publish my changes link on its site building pages to remind you to publish your changes.

To publish the changes to your store:

1. Click the **Publish your changes** link located near the top of the page. The Publish - Publish your finished pages page opens. See Figure 3-42. Notice the list of changed or new pages to be published.

Figure 3-42	PREPARING TO PUBLISH YOUR PAGES

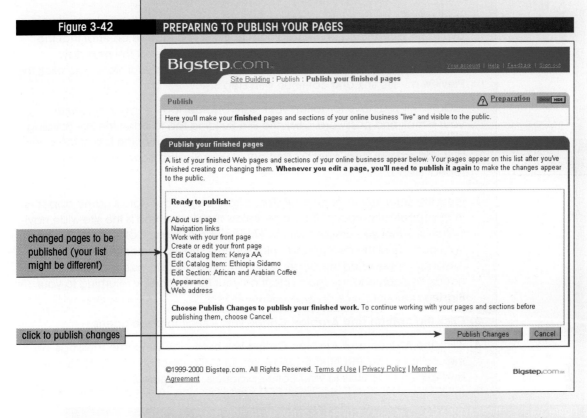

changed pages to be published (your list might be different)

click to publish changes

2. Click the **Publish Changes** button. The Publish - Announce your changes page opens. Read the message that appears on this page to learn why it might take up to several hours for your store to appear on the Web.

3. Click the **Finish** button at the bottom of the page. You return to the home page. Notice that your to-do list no longer shows a Publish my changes link. Now, a Preview my site link appears. You could click this link to see a preview of your store; however, if you want to view your store as a Internet visitor would, you must sign out of your Bigstep account, and then enter your store's URL in your browser's address bar.

4. Click the **Sign out** link located near the top of the page to sign out of your Bigstep account.

Visiting Your Store

Now you can visit your store as a customer and examine the site, click any links, and really see how the store operates. This is a terrific way to discover any site navigation difficulties and experience the site as a customer would. Remember your store name to access it.

Suppose you choose the store name *myfinecoffee*. The URL to access your Bigstep store would be http://www.myfinecoffee.bigstep.com. Anyone entering that URL in a Web browser would see your store's home page. Franklin asks you to open your Bigstep store so he can evaluate the site's design, colors, and other elements that you have added.

To open your Bigstep store:

1. Click in the address bar of your Web browser, and then type **http://www.[*insert your Bigstep store name here*].bigstep.com**.

   TROUBLE? It might take up to 24 hours before your new store is published and available, depending on Bigstep.com traffic. If you receive an error that the page cannot be displayed, try opening your store later or the next day. Alternatively, you can go to www.bigstep.com, log into your store, and click the Preview my site link and continue with Step 3.

   TROUBLE? If you have forgotten your store's name, log into your store with your e-mail and password. Click the Site Building tab to open the Site Building page. The URL, including your store's name, appears near the top of the page. Write down your store's name, sign out of your Bigstep account, and then repeat Step 1.

2. Press the **Enter** key to open your store's front page. Your store's name appears in the upper-left corner of the page. Below the store name is the site-wide navigation link that you created for the African and Arabian Coffee section. Your front page uses the design and color scheme that you selected. Notice that a message appears on this page, reminding you to customize it for your store's needs. You can change the content on your front page by returning to your Bigstep account.

3. Click the **African and Arabian Coffee** link. A section page opens.

4. Click the **African and Arabian Coffee** link below the welcome message on the section page. The African and Arabian Coffee section of your store opens and displays two links to your coffee products. See Figure 3-43.

| Figure 3-43 | AFRICAN AND ARABIAN COFFEE SECTION WITH TWO ITEMS |

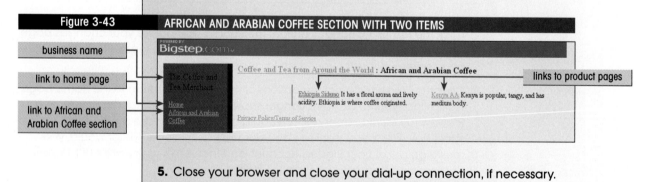

5. Close your browser and close your dial-up connection, if necessary.

Franklin likes your basic Bigstep store. He will provide you with the content for the front page, information page, and additional coffee sections and products so you can continue updating the store in preparation of using it to accept online orders.

Session 3.3 QUICK CHECK

1. Name three types of pages you can use in a Bigstep store.

2. A(n) _____ is a category or group of related products for sale.

3. An individual product appears on what type of page in your catalog?

4. The first page of a Bigstep catalog is called the _____ page.

5. When you make changes to your Bigstep store, you should update your store's changed pages by _____ them.

6. If your Bigstep store's name is exoticfruit, what URL will customers use to open your store?

CASE PROBLEMS

Case 1. Summit Trails Galleries   Allison Drake is the owner of Summit Trails Galleries in Sedona, Arizona. Summit Trails Galleries specializes in fine contemporary Western art. Allison's small gallery sells art from mostly local artists. Because Sedona comprises several artist colonies and houses many established artists, the city attracts many art customers. However, Allison knows that a significant number of art collectors and dealers don't have the time to visit Sedona. She wants to increase her sales volume by displaying her artists' works in a tastefully designed online store. Several gallery owners in the area have mentioned that the Internet is a good way to promote her Sedona store. The larger galleries and art show production houses have Web pages that they use to post event information, but few of them actually sell art through their Web sites. Allison believes that she can capture new sales from an online store without stealing sales from her Sedona gallery and store. Allison wants you to design and create an online store to showcase a representative sampling of her art for sale. She knows that Yahoo! is popular, and she would like you to build her store using that software. You offer to create a prototype store for her to examine. Once she approves the overall design, you will then populate the store with a few artists' works.

1. Start your Web browser, and then go to the Online Companion by entering the URL http://www.course.com/NewPerspectives/EC in the appropriate location of your Web browser. Click the Tutorial 3 link, and then click the Case Problems link. Click the Yahoo! log in link and wait while your browser loads the Yahoo! Store home page.

2. Log into Yahoo! Store using your Yahoo! ID and password. (If you do not have a Yahoo! ID, follow the instructions in Session 3.2 to create one.)

3. Click the Create a store link in the Getting Started section to create a new store.

4. Enter a unique store name in the first text box.

5. Enter the title "Summit Trials Galleries" in the second text box.

6. Click the Create button to submit your store name. If your store name is taken already, change your store name and then resubmit the form.

7. Read and then accept the terms of the Yahoo! agreement.

8. Click the Home button near the top of the page to avoid taking the Yahoo! tour.

9. Click the new store's link in the My Stores section to open the new store.

10. Choose the Regular interface.

11. Add a section named "Western Art."

12. Add two items to the Western Art section named "Ground Tied" and "Western Roundup." Create a short description for each item. Price the Ground Tied piece at $3,500 and the Western Roundup piece at $6,500.

13. Create an Info page that includes a greeting and contact information. Type a name and address for the store's contact information.

14. Publish your pages to save them, and then log out of your Yahoo! account.

15. Visit your store by typing the URL for your store (http://store.yahoo.com/[*insert your store ID here*]).

16. Use your browser's Print button to print the Western Art Web page showing the two items and their costs, and then print the information page.

17. Order an item and proceed to the checkout. Print the checkout page, and then cancel the order and empty your shopping cart.

18. Close your browser and close your dial-up connection, if necessary.

Case 2. WestArk Community College Bookstore   WestArk Community College is feeling the pressure from successful Web sites such as Amazon.com. WestArk wants to increase its bookstore's overall sales by selling t-shirts, coffee mugs, and other nonbook items on a Web site. You work at the bookstore part-time in the stock room, but Alice Hayes, your supervisor, knows you have a lot of Web experience. She wants you to create a small store with a few items for sale. If that goes well, then you can add more items to the store in several different departments.

1. Start your Web browser, and then go to the Online Companion by entering the URL http://www.course.com/NewPerspectives/EC in the appropriate location of your Web browser. Click the Tutorial 3 link, and then click the Case Problems link. Click the Yahoo! log in link and wait while your browser loads the Yahoo! Store home page.

2. Log into Yahoo! using your Yahoo! ID and password, and then create a new Yahoo! store using an appropriate store name. (If you do not have a Yahoo! ID, follow the instructions in Session 3.2 to create one.)

3. Separate the items for sale into three departments: Paper Supplies and Notebooks, Novelty Items, and Memorabilia.

4. Stock three appropriate items in each section. For example, in the Paper Supplies and Notebooks section you might add, "Loose Leaf, three-ring punched paper." Price items using prices you might find at your school's bookstore.

5. Publish your pages to save them.

6. Log out of your Yahoo! account.

7. Visit your store as a customer, and then print the page for each section in your Web site.

8. Close your Web browser and close your dial-up connection, if necessary.

Case 3. The Coffee and Tea Merchant   Franklin wants you to enhance the Coffee and Tea Merchant site you created in Session 3.2 (using Yahoo! Store) by adding a picture to the site. To complete this case problem, you might need to use Yahoo! Store's online Help system to learn more about each task.

Note: You must complete this case problem within 10 days of finishing Session 3.2 so your Yahoo! Store will still exist on the Yahoo! server.

1. Start your Web browser, and then go to the Online Companion by entering the URL http://www.course.com/NewPerspectives/EC in the appropriate location of your Web browser. Click the Tutorial 3 link, and then click the Case Problems link.

2. Click the Coffee cup logo link to open a Web page that contains a picture of a coffee cup. Right-click the logo to open the shortcut menu, and then click the Save As command to save the logo file on a blank floppy disk or on your hard drive.

3. Return to the Online Companion page for Case Problem 3, and then click the Yahoo! log in link and wait while your browser opens the Yahoo! Store home page. Log into the Yahoo! Store that you created in Session 3.2.

4. Select the Simple interface on the management page.

5. With the front page open, upload the coffee cup picture to your Web site. Start the process by clicking the Image button in the list of edit buttons.

6. Click the Browse button, browse to the drive and folder that contains the image file (cup.jpg) that you downloaded in Step 2, and then click the Open button.

7. Click the Send button to upload the image to your Web site. Depending on the speed of your Internet connection, it might take a few minutes to upload the file to your site.

8. Publish your Web pages.

9. Log out your Yahoo! account, and then open your store using its URL.

10. Use your browser's Print button to print the front page of your store.

11. Close your browser and close your dial-up connection, if necessary.

Case 4. Pet Pleasin' People   Pet Pleasin' People is a pet-sitting service. For a small daily fee, a Pet Pleasin' employee will visit your pet in your home three times a day. During each of these 15-minute visits, the employee plays with your pet or takes it for a walk. Carmen Lighspeed, the owner, wants to branch out and offer pet supplies and gourmet dog and cat food in an online store. Create a Bigstep store for her business.

1. Start your Web browser, and then go to the Online Companion by entering the URL http://www.course.com/NewPerspectives/EC in the appropriate location of your Web browser. Click the Tutorial 3 link, and then click the Case Problems link. Click the Bigstep log in link and wait while your browser loads the Bigstep home page.

2. Create a new store using your e-mail address and password. If you already have created a store using your e-mail address, then obtain another e-mail address at Yahoo! or Excite.com. Complete the registration form and select an appropriate store name.

3. Create a unique Web address for your Bigstep store.

4. Select a basic design and color scheme for your Bigstep store.

5. Create some appropriate content on your home page.

6. Click the Catalog link to open a page that contains options for creating a catalog, and then create two sections named Dog Treats and Cat Treats. Include a short description for each section.

7. Add two items to the Dog Treats section: Liver Snack Delights ($15.00 per 16 oz. bag) and Chewy Dog Bone ($2.30 per bone).

8. Add one item to the Cat Treats section: Fussy Feline Catnip ($4.50).

9. Create site-wide navigation links to the Dog Treats and Cat Treats sections.

10. Create the content for your front page, including links to your sections.

11. Publish your pages to save them.

12. Use the Preview my site link to preview your site. If necessary, make any changes and then republish your site.

13. Log out of your Bigstep account, and then visit your store by typing its URL in your browser's address bar.

14. Use your browser to print your front page, the Dog Treats section page, and the Fussy Feline Catnip page.

15. Close you browser and close your dial-up connection, if necessary.

QUICK | CHECK ANSWERS

Session 3.1

1. TCP

2. A VPN requires no extra hardware—it requires only the Internet to function. A private network requires a physical, direct connection between two parties and costs much more.

3. Apache

4. Any three of: catalog or catalog display, shopping cart, transaction processing, fulfillment, tools to populate the store catalog, software to modify the site and its pages, registration of shoppers

5. META tags are pieces of information you place in a Web page that describe the page's content using keywords and descriptions. Including accurate information in the META tags increases your Web page rankings when searchers use keywords that match those in your META tags.

6. You can submit your Web page to one of the many search engines to be indexed.

Session 3.2

1. front page, sections, items

2. populating the catalog

3. front, Publish

4. Info (Information) page

5. section

6. specials

Session 3.3

1. home page, front page, item page

2. section

3. item page

4. front

5. publishing

6. www.exoticfruit.bigstep.com

OBJECTIVES

In this tutorial you will:

- Explore the threats to electronic commerce

- Learn how privacy threats can affect your electronic commerce business and your customers' perception of your storefront

- Uncover typical sources of secrecy, integrity, and delay/denial threats

- Discover security protection techniques that will maintain customer privacy, keep transactions confidential, thwart eavesdropping, and ensure customer identification and authentication

- Investigate the role of encryption in maintaining confidentiality

- Use message digests to provide integrity assurance

- Examine intellectual property protection issues

ELECTRONIC COMMERCE SECURITY

Creating a Secure Commerce Environment

CASE

e-Clip Services, Inc.

Marcia Cogburn is the founder and Chief Executive Officer of e-Clip Services. Her company of 25 employees provides an electronic news clipping service for business executives in different fields. E-Clip Services might provide general financial and economic news or detailed reports of news reports about a company's competition. This service helps executives stay informed about the business and economic climates in their areas without needing to subscribe to multiple newspapers, journals, and business magazines. For a fixed monthly fee and a per-item transaction fee, members receive summaries of important business articles by e-mail. The articles are carefully selected each day from many paper and electronic news sources, and each member only receives summaries in his or her selected areas of interest. For example, a member might request summaries of all articles that discuss electronic payment systems, local area network technologies, and Java programming. E-Clip Services summarizes articles from computer-centered newspapers, computer science newsletters, and computer trade magazines. Recently, several members have requested an e-clip service for articles that are unrelated to computers. Marcia realizes that growing her business too quickly can be difficult at best, and she wants her company to remain focused on computer-related news and general interest articles.

Most members pay their subscription and per-article fees by submitting a credit card number to e-Clip Services via its Web site. Because of the high demand for summaries, Marcia is concerned about the security of the company's Web site. She is particularly concerned about protecting members' credit card numbers and personal information, such as their mailing addresses, as well as the ability of the Web server to send the requested articles to the member who requests them.

Marcia has hired you to investigate computer security issues for her business. She wants to know what security threats exist for online commerce businesses and how to eliminate or reduce the risks posed by these security threats. You realize that investigating security threats and protecting a Web server against these threats is a huge task, because new security threats arise each day as businesses conduct electronic commerce. Marcia asks you to begin by investigating threats to electronic commerce. After you identify the specific security threats to e-Clip Services and its customers, she wants you to explore methods for protecting her business from commerce threats.

SESSION 4.1	In this session, you will learn about the different kinds of threats that businesses and individuals face when conducting electronic commerce. You will learn about the different methods that a Web server can use to gather information about you, and how that information can be used to both benefit and harm your Web browsing experience. You will examine the privacy policies of different Web sites to understand how businesses strive to protect their customers' privacy. Finally, you will examine the different places in the communication channel where threats can occur.

Introduction to Security

Not long ago, when the Internet was young, e-mail was one of its most popular uses. A common worry people had then and that persists today is that an unknown party might intercept their e-mail messages and exploit them for commercial gain. Another fear is that the boss might read an employee's Monday morning analysis of the weekend social scene. At one time, these concerns were both significant and realistic. But today, the stakes are much higher. The Internet has matured, and so have its users. The consequences of an unknown party having unauthorized access to others' messages and digital property are far more serious than in the past. Electronic commerce brings to the forefront long-held information security concerns.

Web shoppers contemplating first-time Internet purchases often fear that their credit card numbers will be exposed to everyone in cyberspace as they travel from their computers across the Internet to their final destinations. Of course, this echoes the same concern shoppers have expressed for the last 30 years about using a credit card to pay for purchases over the phone: "Can I trust the person on the other end of the phone who is writing down my credit card number?" These days, consumers give their credit card numbers and other information over the phone to strangers without thinking twice, but many of those same people hesitate when asked to enter their credit card numbers on a keyboard for transmission over the Internet.

Computer security, and specifically computer security for electronic commerce, is a complex and broad issue and the subject of ongoing research. **Computer security** is the protection of assets from unauthorized access, use, alteration, or destruction. There are two general types of security: physical and logical. **Physical security** includes tangible protection devices, such as alarms, guards, fireproof doors, security fences, safes or vaults, and bombproof buildings. Protecting assets using nonphysical mechanisms, such as antivirus software and passwords, is called **logical security**. An example of antivirus software is VirusScan from Network Associates, which scans your disks in search of viruses. A password is another protective measure that denies access to unauthorized persons. Any act or object that poses a danger to computer assets is known as a **threat**.

Countermeasure is the general name for a procedure, either physical or logical, that recognizes, reduces, or eliminates a threat. The countermeasures can vary, depending on the importance of the asset at risk. Countermeasures can recognize and manage threats, or they can eliminate them. A business can choose to ignore other threats that are deemed low-risk and unlikely to occur when the cost to protect against the threat exceeds the value of the protected asset. For example, it would make sense to protect an electronic commerce server from tornadoes in Oklahoma City, where there is a lot of tornado activity, but not to protect one in Los Angeles, where tornadoes are rare.

Protecting Internet and electronic commerce assets from both physical and nonphysical threats is important. Examples of threats to the Internet and its traffic include impostors, eavesdroppers, and thieves. An **eavesdropper**, in this context, is a person or device that is able to listen to and copy Internet transmissions. To implement a security scheme, you must identify the risk, determine how to protect the asset, and calculate how much you can afford to spend to protect it. Marcia has identified several key areas that she feels are threats to the electronic commerce server for e-Clip Services. She wants you to focus on the central issues of identifying threats and determining ways to protect the company's assets from those threats. In response to Marcia's request, you decide that it will be necessary to visit Web sites that contain information to help you identify security problem areas and learn about solutions to these problems.

One of your first tasks is to identify where electronic commerce security threats arise from and where attackers can enter the system. First, an attacker may assail a PC connected to the Internet—a client machine. More commonly, security is compromised along the path between a client and an electronic commerce site—the Internet and networks that comprise the Internet. Or, an attacker may gain access through an electronic commerce server computer.

Security attacks take many forms, including theft or fraud, data alteration and contamination, eavesdropping, misappropriation, loss of valuable transaction data, or degrading service. **Theft** or **fraud** is the unauthorized appropriation or use of goods or services. Theft is usually the result when the client or server does not have adequate authentication, allowing an attacker to impersonate a legitimate user successfully. **Data alteration**, or **contamination**, can be extremely destructive and occurs when an unauthorized user changes data as it passes over a network from a user to a commerce site, for example. When payments from customers are misrouted to an unauthorized person, then **misappropriation** occurs. Misappropriated goods are shipped to a third party who did not pay for them; misappropriated credit card numbers are used to pay for goods and services not authorized by the credit card's owner. In many cases, electronic thieves misappropriate equipment and stockpile it in warehouses and garages for later sale. **Data loss**, also called a **denial attack**, occurs when a thief removes electronic information while it is in transit. Data loss also can occur when a thief copies and then subsequently erases data files from a destination computer. In either case, the data files' intended receivers often do not realize that they did not receive the data. **Degrading service**, also called a **delay**, disrupts service and can cause critical, time-sensitive transactions to falter. For example, a delay occurs when a thief prohibits an emergency medical record needed by a hospital treating a critically ill patient from reaching its destination by two hours. Critical information, such as the patient's intolerance to antibiotics, could drastically affect the success of the hospital's treatment.

Many sources use the terms *privacy* and *secrecy* interchangeably, but a closer evaluation reveals that these terms are different. **Privacy** is the protection of individual rights to nondisclosure. In the United States, local and national laws govern privacy. For example, the Privacy Act of 1974 ensures that information you provide to a government agency will not be disclosed to anyone outside of that agency. **Secrecy**, however, provides protection from inadvertent information disclosure without regard to existing legislation. For example, the failure of the same government agency to protect your Social Security number from unauthorized access is a secrecy risk. Marcia is concerned with both privacy and secrecy for her company. On one hand, she wants to protect each customer's privacy by not disclosing the customer's name and address to anyone outside of the company. Simultaneously, her biggest worry is protecting credit card information from unauthorized access, which is a secrecy concern.

Intellectual property rights govern when and how someone other than the original creator of the intellectual property can use the property. Music, art, and newspaper articles are familiar examples to you and Marcia. The main threat to intellectual property is unauthorized use, or theft. E-Clip Services must be careful not to pose a threat inadvertently when it transmits material to its customers.

You begin your security quest by examining privacy threats, and then you will look at intellectual property threats. Finally, you will study security threats. With this background firmly in place, you can probe deeper into each of the preceding areas and identify the location of different threats to e-Clip Services and its customers.

Privacy **Threats**

Marcia is particularly worried about privacy threats and electronic commerce. Newspapers have featured a number of hacker attacks against high-profile electronic commerce sites—sites that should have provided adequate protections. If hackers can attack big companies, Marcia realizes that threats to her company are just as real. She wants to make sure that her commerce site provides assurances, both written and in software, and collects only minimal information from its customers. She knows that most Web sites collect information from people who visit their sites, whether they purchase something or not. For example, a Web server can determine the last Web site you visited before coming to the current one. Web servers also can overtly collect information from you by requesting your name and other identifying information before entering the site. Frequently, businesses gather demographic information from their Web site's visitors to identify their audience more precisely. For example, a business might collect customers' credit card numbers and information about the links within the site that they use.

Some, but not all, Web sites sell the information that they gather about their visitors to other businesses, or use the information in an inappropriate manner. Not long ago, a prominent commerce site confessed to collecting information about music preferences of people who used its electronic music player. Soon after the public discovered that the Web site was gathering data, a court decision forced the company to stop the covert information collection practice. In addition, the court ruled that the software publisher must make available to the public a software fix that users could apply to their systems to disable the data collection mechanism.

Not protecting consumers' privacy can be costly for businesses. Individuals regularly sue firms for not abiding by their published Internet privacy policies. Privacy policies form the cornerstone of thwarting privacy attacks. Information technology experts should not be solely responsible for formulating a company's privacy policy; the policy must be formulated from a wide corporate community consisting of people from various functional units of the organization and from all levels of the corporate hierarchy. At a minimum, a company's **privacy policy** must clearly state what information the company is collecting, how the company will use that information, and with whom (if anyone) the company will share that information. Electronic commerce consumers must be able to exercise control over how much, if any, information they divulge to a Web commerce site. Lastly, consumers should be able to review and correct any information about themselves—similar to options extended for their personal credit reports—when information about them is collected by a Web site.

Two other prominent sources of information—both potential privacy threats—are cookies and Web site registrations.

Cookies

Because the Internet is a stateless machine and cannot remember a response from one Web page view to another, Web sites often rely on cookies to solve the problem of remembering customer order information or user names and passwords. A **cookie** is a small data file that some Web sites write to your hard drive when you view the Web site. Sites that create cookies do it transparently by recording information about Web browsing choices that you make, or by storing your user name and password for a particular Web site that you visited.

Your computer might store thousands of cookies—one for each Web site that wishes to record them—without your knowledge. Frequently, cookies make access to selected areas of a Web site more efficient. Many Web sites recover critical user identification information from cookies that they have stored previously on your computer. Storing a cookie on your computer eliminates requiring you to log in to a Web site with a user name and password each time you access the Web site that originally wrote the cookie to your computer. Because cookies contain specific information about you, they are similar to photo identification. Browsers support cookies, and they provide various protection mechanisms to partially block or completely disallow cookie storage. Cookies are a privacy threat because they usually contain accurate information—such as your name, address, and credit card number—unless you falsify this information when providing it to the Web site. Falsified information that is stored in a cookie poses no privacy threat because it is inaccurate.

Cookies are widely used to aid the Web-browsing public. Excite.com uses cookies to personalize browsers' experiences at the Excite Web site. Expedia.com, an online travel agent, uses cookies to maintain data about you and your accounts so that it can retrieve previous or pending itineraries from its Web server. Amazon.com stores information about your book preferences. Airlines record your seating and meal preferences in cookies. Cookies are convenient and helpful for enhancing your Web experience. However, even with these advantages, collected personal information poses a privacy threat because the collecting Web site might sell this information about you to others without your permission. Once out of the original collector's control, there is very little you can do to curb abusive practices, such as e-mail marketing campaigns or unsolicited sales calls.

Because collecting information from e-Clip customers could pose a privacy threat, you want to learn more by exploring some Web sites that provide information about cookies. You decide to begin your cookie investigation by looking at the All About Cookies page maintained by **CNET**, one of the world's leading news-media companies providing information about computers, the Internet, and digital technologies via print, television, and the Web.

To explore adding cookies to your Web site:

1. Start your Web browser, and then go to the Online Companion page by entering the URL **http://www.course.com/NewPerspectives/EC** in the appropriate location in your Web browser. Click the **Tutorial 4** link, and then click the **Session 4.1** link. Click the **Adding cookies to your site** link and wait while your browser loads the page shown in Figure 4-1.

| Figure 4-1 | ALL ABOUT COOKIES HOME PAGE |

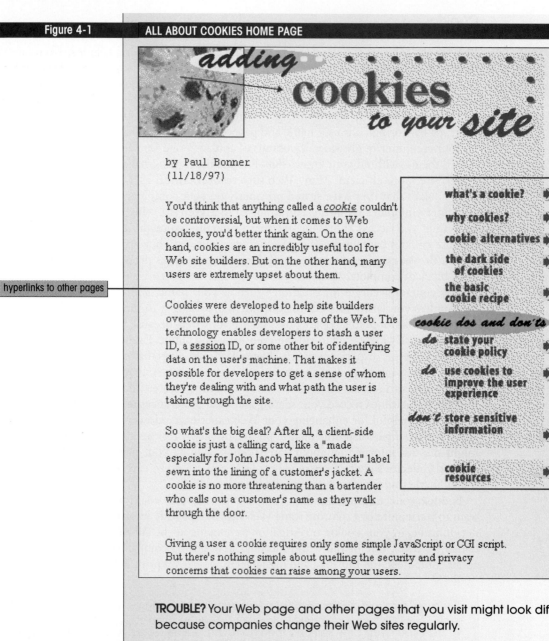

hyperlinks to other pages

TROUBLE? Your Web page and other pages that you visit might look different because companies change their Web sites regularly.

2. Read the All About Cookies page, which contains good information about cookies.

3. Click the ***don't* store sensitive information** link located on the right side of the page, and then read the page that opens to learn more about what a Web site should and should not store in a cookie.

4. Click your browser's **Back** button to return to the cookie home page, click **the dark side of cookies** link, and then read the page that opens. This page provides information to dispel some rumors about how cookies are used and what information they collect.

Another site that is loaded with cookie information is Cookie Central, which is a Web site devoted to Internet cookies and everything about them. You decide to learn about cookie information from another source before reporting back to Marcia.

To explore the Cookie Central Web site:

1. Click your browser's **Back** button or use its history list to return to the Online Companion page for Session 4.1, and then click the **Cookie Central** link and wait while your browser loads the page shown in Figure 4-2.

Figure 4-2	COOKIE CENTRAL HOME PAGE

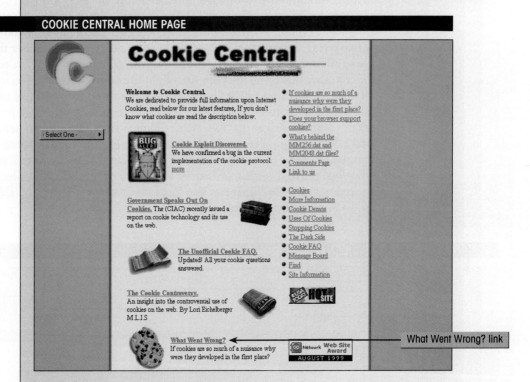

2. Read the Cookie Central page, which contains cookie information from many different sources.

3. Click the **What Went Wrong?** link, and then read the page that opens to learn about the misuse of cookies.

You have learned just enough about cookies to understand situations in which they could be misused. Further, you realize that cookies are not inherently bad. However, some people dislike the idea of storing cookies on their computers. Over time, it is possible for you to accumulate large numbers of cookies as you browse the Internet, and some cookies could contain sensitive, personal information. Several Web sites have clearly stated policies that describe when and where the Web sites will collect information and store it in cookies. DoubleClick, once accused of collecting information and providing it to other businesses without obtaining consent from the site's users, provides a clear statement of its cookie policy and privacy statement. (You can view the privacy statement by clicking the **DoubleClick privacy statement** link in the Session 4.1 section of the Online Companion.) In Session 4.2, you will learn how to manage and eliminate cookies.

Next, you want to learn what privacy risks are inherent in Web site registration. You continue your privacy threat Web research.

Software and Web Site Registration

Customer information is relatively easy to gather, and many Web sites take advantage of this by asking you to supply them with personal information. Shareware sites, which contain software you can download and try for a specific period before paying for it, often require anyone who downloads software to register with the site. **Registering** with a Web site usually consists of creating a user ID and entering your name, address, phone number, and e-mail address into a form. The registration form might also ask you for some demographic or marketing information, such as your age or the type of computer that you own. The Web site stores this information as a cookie on your computer. After you register with a Web site, the company that owns the Web site might use your information to inform you about newer software versions in which you might be interested, or to assess information about your shopping experience. Qualcomm, the firm that publishes the Eudora Pro e-mail client program, requires users at its Web site to fill out a registration form before letting them download a demonstration version of Eudora Pro or Eudora Light, its free e-mail client program. Figure 4-3 shows the software registration form that users must complete before they can download the trial version of Eudora Pro. Notice that the form collects the user's first name, last name, and e-mail address. The form also asks for information about the user's Web site use and online shopping habits.

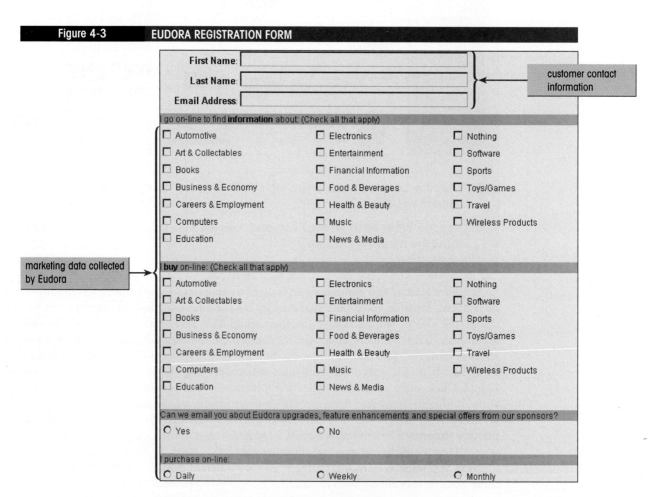

Figure 4-3   EUDORA REGISTRATION FORM

Although it does not pose a privacy threat, Eudora's registration form is an example of the information that companies collect from their customers. Clearly, several of the questions help the company identify its target customers by analyzing the answers customers supply in the registration form. The Eudora division of Qualcomm prominently posts its privacy policy, which states in part that "Eudora will never share information about you without your permission (unless required by law)," on its Web site.

Electronic Privacy Information Center (EPIC)

One of the searches you performed with a Web search engine turned up the name Electronic Privacy Information Center (EPIC), which is a public-interest research center in Washington, D.C., whose mission is to spotlight civil liberties issues and to protect privacy. This organization interests you because you learned that it has proposed regulations to restrict the use of cookies. One direct result of that effort is the cookie-restricting function built into browsers, which you will learn about in Session 4.2. What interests you about the organization is that it produces reports about electronic privacy, and then publishes these reports online. You want to view one of the online reports before completing this part of your research for Marcia.

To explore the EPIC Web site:

1. Click your browser's **Back** button or use its history list to return to the Online Companion page for Session 4.1, and then click the **EPIC Report on Privacy** link and wait while your browser loads the Web page shown in Figure 4-4.

Figure 4-4 | EPIC PRIVACY POLICIES REPORT

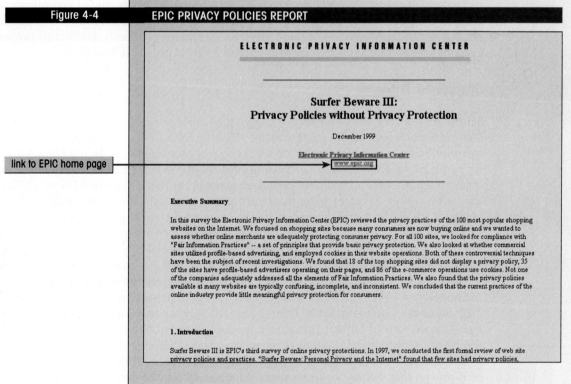

link to EPIC home page

2. Read the Web page, which describes an EPIC survey of 100 Web sites that allow shopping activities. According to the report, 18 of the 100 sites surveyed did not display a privacy policy, and 86 of them used cookies. The first paragraph is critical of how little privacy protection is apparently provided for consumers.

3. Click the **www.epic.org** link located near the top of the Web page to open EPIC's home page.

TROUBLE? If the EPIC Report on Privacy Web page does not display the www.epic.org link, type the URL in Step 3 in the correct location in your Web browser to open it.

4. Click the **About EPIC** link located near the top of the EPIC home page, and then read the first paragraph. This page describes the EPIC organization and its purpose.

5. Click the **Internet Privacy Coalition** link in the paragraph below the "About EPIC" heading. A new browser window opens and displays several interesting news items about the Internet and privacy. Review the page to become familiar with its contents.

6. Close the browser window that contains the Internet Privacy Coalition document, but leave the remaining browser window open.

Intellectual Property Threats

Copyright and intellectual property rights can be threatened also. **Copyright** is the protection of expression—someone or some entity's intellectual property—and it typically covers items such as literary and musical works; pantomimes and choreographic works; pictorial, graphic, and sculptural works; motion pictures and other audiovisual works; sound recordings; and architectural works. **Intellectual property** is the ownership of ideas and control over the tangible or virtual representation of those ideas. As mentioned previously, intellectual property does not need to have an explicit copyright for U.S. law to protect it from theft.

Copyright Threats

Similar to violating computer security, copyright infringement causes damage. However, unlike computer security breaches, damage resulting from a copyright violation is typically narrower and has a smaller impact on an organization or individual. In the United States, for example, the Copyright Act of 1976 protects items, including those in any of the preceding categories, for a fixed time period. In general, for items published before 1978, the copyright expires 75 years from the item's publication date. For items published after January 1, 1978, the copyright expires 50 years beyond the life of the author for an individual holder or 75 years after the date of the publication for employers of the author. Every work is protected when it is created—even those works that do not include a copyright notice, such as *Copyright © 2001 Whimsey Company*—and this fact is the most misunderstood part of U.S. copyright law. In other words, if you reproduce or alter a picture or text that appears on a Web site without the express written permission from the site's owner, you may violate the Copyright Act by reproducing the same or adapted item on your Web site. For example, fans of Dilbert cartoons unwittingly violate copyright laws when they post Scott Adams' cartoons without his permission on fan club Web sites and Web storefronts.

You can enter the search term *copyright* into any Web search engine and locate hundreds of Web sites that discuss copyright issues. One example is the very informative Copyright Clearance Center (CCC), which is an excellent source of copyright information. Because e-Clip Services is in the business of summarizing information gleaned from publications whose contents are protected by U.S. copyright law, you know that being on top of the latest copyright information makes good business sense. Of course, Marcia will pay fees to copyright holders when necessary to reproduce copyrighted material for her e-Clip Services customers. You decide to investigate the CCC.

To explore the Copyright Clearance Center Web site:

1. Click your browser's **Back** button or use its history list to return to the Online Companion page for Session 4.1, and then click the **Copyright Clearance Center** link and wait while your browser loads the CCC home page shown in Figure 4-5.

Figure 4-5	COPYRIGHT CLEARANCE CENTER HOME PAGE

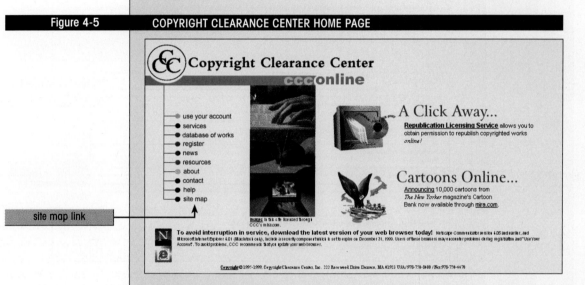

site map link

2. Click the **site map** link to open a page with an overview of the entire site and its contents, grouped by category. The Help category contains many links to FAQs, or frequently asked questions, which are a good source of information.

3. Locate and click the **Copyright FAQs** link under the Help category. The Frequently Asked Questions about Copyright page opens. Read the FAQs and their answers.

4. Click the **http://www.loc.gov/copyright/circs/index.html** link in the first FAQ to open the U.S. Copyright Office home page shown in Figure 4-6. This page contains links to PDF and text files that you can download and read for topics related to copyright law, maintaining a copyright, and other copyright-related materials. (**PDF**, or **Portable Document Format**, is a file format that provides a convenient, self-contained package for delivering and displaying documents containing text, graphics, charts, and other objects. You must have Adobe Acrobat Reader installed on your computer to read a PDF file. Clicking a Text link usually opens a document in Notepad, WordPad, or another text editor on your computer, or opens the page's contents in the browser window.)

| Figure 4-6 | U.S. COPYRIGHT OFFICE HOME PAGE |

U.S. Copyright Office   Library of Congress

Home · Forms · Records · Registration · Law · Comments · Library of Congress

**Copyright Information Circulars
and Form Letters**

The Copyright Office information circulars are available in the Adobe Acrobat PDF format. You must have the Adobe Acrobat Reader installed on your computer to view and print the circulars. The Adobe Acrobat Reader is available for free from Adobe Systems Incorporated. Note: If you are experiencing difficulty viewing or printing these files, please ensure that you have the latest Acrobat Reader version installed.

Circulars

1 - Copyright Basics
Version: PDF, Text ← Text format opens in a Web browser

1b - Limitations on Information Furnished by the Copyright Office
Version: PDF

1c - Make Sure Your Application Will Be Acceptable
Version: PDF

2 - Publications on Copyright
Version: PDF

3 - Copyright Notice
Version: PDF ← PDF format requires Adobe Acrobat to display it

4 - Copyright Fees
Version: PDF

5 - How to Open and Maintain a Deposit Account in the U.S. Copyright Office
Version: PDF

6 - Access to and Copies of Copyright Records and Deposit
Version: PDF

TROUBLE? If the link specified in Step 4 does not appear in the first paragraph, click the U.S. Copyright Office link in the Session 4.1 section of the Online Companion.

5. Scroll down the page and locate item 22, "How to Investigate the Copyright Status of a Work," and then click the **Text** link below it. A lengthy Web page opens that contains information on determining whether an item is protected by copyright.

6. Click the **In General** link, and then scan the page that opens. This page provides general information about copyrights and copyright protection.

The sites you visited will be very helpful to Marcia so she can determine how to use copyrighted material, including paying for reprints and summarizing articles from various sources. Marcia can use the CCC to access a wide variety of copyrighted material, and the CCC makes it convenient to pay permission fees for using those materials.

Protecting Intellectual Property

Because of your extensive research, Marcia now knows that U.S. copyright laws protect intellectual property as well as published works. Summaries and condensations that e-Clip creates and distributes to its clients are original works belonging to e-Clip and therefore are entitled to protection. Marcia wants to ensure that these summaries and condensations—e-Clip's intellectual property—are owned by e-Clip and protected by the same laws as the original published documents on which they are based.

The goal of protecting intellectual property from unauthorized use is to promote the creation of knowledge and to ensure a competitive marketplace. Without intellectual property protection, authors, artists, and composers would have less incentive to create manuscripts, art, or music if someone other than the works' creators could claim credit for and profit from them. Often there are conflicting claims over who owns new developments. In the United States, ownership disputes are resolved using intellectual property laws and court decisions. For example, a dispute arose over the use of windowing to solve the Y2K problem. (**Windowing** is a technique in which some two-digit years—88 for example—are considered to be in the 20th century, whereas others, such as 19, are considered to be in the 21st century.) McDonnell Douglas Corporation, owner of the windowing patent, transferred the patent to its inventor, Bruce Dickens. Shortly after the transfer, Dickens declared that he would seek royalty payments from any firm using windowing to make its software Y2K compliant. (You might want to use the **Windowing Inventor Seeks Payback** and **Windowing Patent Holder Seeks Fees** links in the Session 4.1 section of the Online Companion to learn more about the dispute.) In other words, Dickens felt that his intellectual property was being used without his permission when another company used it for profit.

Intellectual property threats are now a larger problem than they were prior to the widespread use of the Internet, because it is relatively easy to use existing material found on the Internet without the owner's permission. Actual monetary damage resulting from a copyright violation is more difficult to measure than damage from secrecy, integrity, or necessity computer security violations. However, the harm can be just as damaging. The Internet presents a particularly tempting target for at least two reasons. First, it is very simple to reproduce an exact copy of anything you find on the Internet, even if it is subject to copyright restrictions. Second, many people are simply naïve or unaware of copyright restrictions that protect intellectual property. Unwitting and willful copyright infringements occur daily on the Internet. Although copyright laws were enacted before the creation of the Internet, the Internet itself has complicated publishers' enforcement of copyrights. While recognizing unauthorized reprinting of written material is relatively easy, perceiving when a photograph has been borrowed, cropped, or illegally used on a Web page is a more difficult task. Some organizations are working toward educating people about cyberspace theft. For example, the **Berkman Center for Internet and Society** at the Harvard Law School recently introduced a course entitled "Intellectual Property in Cyberspace." **The Copyright Website** tackles the issues of copyright and newsgroup postings, and fair use. **Fair use** allows limited use of copyrighted material when certain conditions are met. Figure 4-7 shows The Copyright Website's home page, which includes links to copyright violations for different categories and links to news stories.

Figure 4-7   THE COPYRIGHT WEBSITE HOME PAGE

Most experts agree that copyright infringements on the Web occur as a result of ignorance about copyright law. Most people do not maliciously copy a protected work and post it on the Web; they just don't understand that works without specific copyright notices are still protected by copyright law. Quite a bit of controversy has sprung up in the last couple of years about intellectual property rights and Internet domain names. The courts have a growing number of cases swirling around the controversy of cybersquatting. **Cybersquatting** is the practice of registering a domain name that is the trademark of another person or company with the hope that the owner will pay huge dollar amounts to acquire the URL. You can find the latest happenings surrounding cybersquatting by clicking the **Cybersquatting and the law** link in the Session 4.1 section of the Online Companion. The law firm of Oppendahl & Larson maintains the site. Other resources about cybersquatting include the links to **Cybersquatting Article**, **Cybersquatting and the Law**, and **Cybersquatting Law**.

Commerce Security Threats

Computer security experts generally agree that you can classify computer security into three categories. The names of these categories sometimes vary, but the widely accepted ones are secrecy, integrity, and necessity. **Secrecy** refers to protecting against unauthorized data disclosure and ensuring the authenticity of the data's source. **Integrity** refers to preventing unauthorized data modification. **Necessity** refers to preventing data delays or denials (removal). Secrecy and threats to secrecy are the best known of the computer security categories. Every day, newspapers report accounts of illegal break-ins to governmental computers or unauthorized uses of stolen credit card numbers that thieves use to order goods and services. Integrity threats tend to be reported less frequently and thus may be less familiar to the public. An integrity violation occurs, for example, when an Internet e-mail message's contents are changed, possibly to negate the message's original meaning. There are several instances of necessity violations, and they occur relatively frequently. Delaying a message or completely destroying it can have huge consequences. For example, suppose you send an e-mail message at 10:00 A.M. to E*Trade, an online stock trading company, and request a purchase of 500 shares of IBM stock at market price. If a thief delays the message and prevents E*Trade from receiving it until 2:30 P.M, and during the delay the stock's price increases by 12%, then this delay will cost you 12% of the value of the trade.

Creating a Security Policy

An organization concerned about protecting its electronic commerce assets should have a security team that creates, updates, and maintains a security policy. A **security policy** is a written statement that describes what assets a company wants to protect, why the company wants to protect these assets, who is responsible for that protection, and acceptable and unacceptable employee behaviors. The main goal of a security policy is to address physical security, network security, access authorization, virus protection, and disaster recovery. A company must develop its security policy over time and review and update it at regular intervals.

The first step in creating a security policy is to determine what to protect. For example, an electronic commerce site needs to protect its customers' credit card numbers from eavesdroppers, or protect the network from hackers bent on disrupting service at an online store. Second, the security team must determine who should have access to various parts of the system. Third, the security team must determine what resources are available to protect the identified assets. At this point, the security team uses the information garnered in the three previous steps and develops a written security policy. Finally, the company must commit resources to building or buying software, hardware, and physical barriers that implement its security policy. For example, if the security policy states that "...no unauthorized access to customer information is allowed, including access to credit card numbers and credit histories," then the security team must either develop software that guarantees end-to-end secrecy for electronic commerce customers or purchase software (programs or protocols) to enforce that security policy. Absolute security is difficult—if not impossible—to achieve, but a company can create enough barriers to deter violations. If the cost to an electronic thief of an unauthorized activity exceeds the value of accomplishing the illegal action, then the security team protects the company's assets by significantly lowering the probability of a security breach.

The concept of **integrated security** ensures that all security measures work together to prevent unauthorized disclosure, destruction, or modification of assets. A security policy addresses many security concerns, all of which must be addressed by a comprehensive and integrated security "blanket." Some elements that a security policy must address include the following:

- **Access control**: Who is allowed to log on to the electronic commerce site and access it and other resources?
- **Audit**: What, when, and who caused selected events to occur?
- **Authentication**: Who or what is trying to access the electronic commerce site and how can its identity be verified?
- **Data integrity**: Who is allowed to change data at the electronic commerce site?
- **Secrecy**: Who is permitted to view selected information?

After meeting with Marcia to review the information you have found about secrecy, Marcia now understands that transactions between a customer and the commerce site must be protected—and kept secret—so valuable information is not disclosed. The electronic chain between a customer and an electronic commerce site consists of a client computer, a communication channel, and a commerce server. You can study electronic commerce security requirements by examining the overall process beginning at the consumer's end and proceeding to the commerce server. Considering each logical piece of the "commerce chain," the assets that must be protected to ensure secure electronic commerce include client computers, the messages traveling on the communication channel, and the Web and commerce servers, including any hardware attached to the servers. Many movies portray the business of espionage as activities that focus on wiretapping and listening in on various communications devices, such as telephone lines and satellite communication links. While telecommunications are certainly one of the major assets to be protected, the telecommunications links are not the only concern in computer and electronic commerce security. If a client computer contains a virus, for example, then it could securely deliver contaminated information to a Web or commerce server. In this case, the commerce transactions would be only as secure as the least secure element—the client machine.

Client Computer Threats

Although Marcia must consider client computers in e-Clip's security plan, she knows that protecting client computers—computers belonging to her customers—is the duty of individual customers. Although Marcia and her staff can only protect communications and the commerce server, she also wants to provide consumers with information about client computer threats. With your research help, she can educate consumers by posting information about client computer threats and, ultimately, about ways to protect client computers.

Active Content Threats

Until the debut of executable Web content, Web pages displayed mostly static information. A **static Web page** displays content and provides links to related pages containing additional information. Today, Web pages often contain active content. **Active content** refers to programs that are embedded transparently in Web pages and cause some action to occur. Active content can display moving graphics, download and play audio files, or open Web-based spreadsheet programs. For example, active content places items you wish to purchase into your shopping cart and computes the invoice total, including the sales tax, handling, and shipping costs. Developers embrace active content because it extends the functionality of HTML and adds spark and excitement to Web pages. The best-known active content forms are Java applets, ActiveX controls, JavaScript, and VBScript. Similar to ordinary programs, some of the active content implementations do not always work correctly and consistently on all Web browsers. ActiveX controls, for example, normally run on your computer when you use Internet Explorer. Java applets run best in Netscape Navigator.

You don't need to do anything special to view active content in a Web page—any Web browser that supports it displays the active content automatically. For example, a Java applet might automatically download with the page you are viewing and run on your computer. An **applet** is a program written in the Java™ programming language that is embedded in a Web page that you download and display. Therein lies the potential threat. Because applets, which drive active content modules, are embedded in Web pages, they can be completely transparent to users browsing a page that contains them. Anyone intent on doing mischief to client computers can embed malicious active content in a seemingly innocuous Web page. This delivery technique, called a Trojan horse, immediately begins executing and taking actions that cause harm in some way. A **Trojan horse** is a program hidden inside another program or Web page that masks its true purpose. The Trojan horse could snoop around your computer and send information that is private to a cooperating Web server—a secrecy violation. Worse yet, the program could alter or erase information on a client computer—an integrity violation.

Intrigued and concerned by active content and the programs that provide the active content, you decide to visit a Web site that includes information about these issues.

To learn more about security and Java:

1. Click your browser's **Back** button or use its history list to return to the Online Companion page for Session 4.1, and then click the **Java Security** link and wait while your browser loads the Frequently Asked Questions page at Sun Microsystems.

2. In the text box near the Search button at the top of the page, type **java security**.

3. Click the **Search** button to search the Sun Microsystems site for information about Java security. The search engine returns several thousand links, ranked in relevance order from high to low.

4. Scroll down the list, and then locate and click the **Fundamentals of Java Security** link. A page from a like-named Java training course opens. See Figure 4-8.

| Figure 4-8 | FUNDAMENTALS OF JAVA SECURITY PAGE |

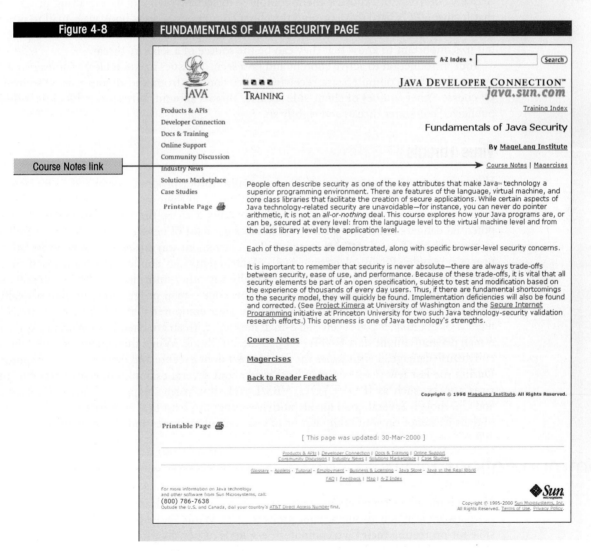

Course Notes link

TROUBLE? If you cannot find the link described in Step 4, click the Fundamentals of Java Security link in the Session 4.1 section of the Online Companion.

5. Click the **Course Notes** link located near the top of the page. A detailed outline of Java security topics appears. Scan the page and read a few topics of interest.

Another source of client computer threats that are closely related to Java applets are ActiveX controls. An **ActiveX control** is an object that contains programs and properties that Web designers place in their Web pages to perform particular tasks. When a Web browser downloads a Web page containing an embedded ActiveX control, the Web browser on the client computer executes the control. Shockwave, an animation and entertainment plug-in for your Web browser, is available as an ActiveX control, for example. Other examples of ActiveX controls include Web-enabled calendar controls and a nearly infinite number of Web games. (You may wish to follow the **ActiveX Controls Library** link in the Session 4.1 section of the Online Companion to obtain a comprehensive list of ActiveX controls by category.)

Unlike Java code, which any Web browser can run, ActiveX controls run only on computers running the Windows operating system. But similar to Java applets, renegade ActiveX controls can expose a client computer to security dangers by executing programs that format a PC's hard drive or send the client computer's address book via e-mail to other users. Most ActiveX controls are not malevolent and provide active content in Web pages, but it is important to know that they can be the source of a security threat.

Your introduction to active content and Java security issues makes it clear that users must ensure that their computers are receiving active content from known and trusted sources. Of course, other sources of client-side security threats abound. Viruses are the most widely publicized computer threat, and rightly so.

Virus Threats

Viruses are malevolent programs that hide within other programs or in e-mail messages. Viruses are incapable of traveling to other computers on their own. When a user executes a program or opens an e-mail message that contains a virus, the virus also executes. The potential dangers lurking in e-mail attachments get a lot of news coverage and are familiar to most people. E-mail attachments provide a convenient way to send nontext information over a text-only system (electronic mail). Attachments can contain word-processed files, spreadsheets, databases, picture files, or virtually any other information. When you receive an e-mail message that contains an attachment, your e-mail program might automatically open the attachment by starting a program on your computer that can display the attachment. For example, if you receive an e-mail message with an attached Excel workbook, your e-mail program might start Excel and open the workbook. While this activity doesn't inherently cause damage, a virus *inside* the workbook might execute and damage your computer. During the last few years you may have read about several examples of e-mail attachment virus attacks, such as ILOVEYOU, VBS/LoveLetter.worm, Happy99 Worm, Triplicate, and Chernobyl. Several good quality antivirus programs exist that eliminate viruses or warn of their existence on your computer or in your e-mail messages and attachments.

Communications Threats

Marcia is most concerned about security threats to her network and to the Internet to which her network is attached—communications threats. While individual customers are responsible for protecting their own computers, e-Clip is responsible for the secure delivery of its information via the Internet to and from customers' computers. Today, the Internet is a reliable public network, but it is not a *secure* public network. Messages on the Internet travel a random path from a source node to a destination node. The message passes through a number of intermediate computers on the network before reaching its final destination, and the path can vary each time a message is sent between the same source and destination points. It is impossible to guarantee that every computer on the Internet through which messages pass is safe, secure, and nonhostile. For example, a message you send from London, England, to a merchant in Cairo, Egypt, might pass through a competitor's computer located in Beirut, Lebanon. Because you cannot control your message's path and do not know where your message's packets have been, it is possible that some intermediary can read your message, alter your message, or even completely eliminate your message from the Internet.

You decide to investigate communication channel (Internet) security threats by examining secrecy, integrity, and necessity threats.

Secrecy Threats

Secrecy is the prevention of unauthorized information disclosure. Privacy is the protection of individual rights to nondisclosure. Protecting one's secrecy focuses on keeping unauthorized users from reading information they should not be reading, which is different from protecting one's privacy. Marcia's privacy policy states that any transactions coming into or out of the e-Clip offices are the property of e-Clip; therefore, these transactions are not private. In addition, all information flowing out of e-Clip's server or out of the office cannot be exposed to anyone outside the office; this is a secrecy issue.

A significant danger when conducting electronic commerce is theft of sensitive or personal information, including credit card numbers, names, addresses, and other personal information. As you learned earlier, this type of theft can occur when someone uses a form to register with a Web site or submits credit card information to the site. It is not difficult for an ill-intentioned person to record information packets (violating secrecy) from the Internet for later examination. The same problems can occur in e-mail transmissions. Special software called **sniffer programs** provides the means to tap into the Internet and record information that passes through a particular computer (router) from its source to its destination. A sniffer program is analogous to tapping a telephone line and recording a conversation. Sniffer programs can read e-mail messages as well as electronic commerce information. Credit card number theft is an obvious problem, but proprietary corporate product information or prerelease data sheets mailed to corporate branches can be intercepted and passed along easily, too. Often, corporate confidential information is even more valuable than a few credit cards, which usually have spending limits. Purloined corporate information can be worth millions of dollars.

Breaching secrecy on the Internet is not difficult. For example, you can inadvertently leak information that an eavesdropper can pick up by simply filling out a Web form. Suppose you visit a Web site—call it *www.anybiz.com* for this illustration—that contains a form with text boxes for your name, address, and e-mail address. After you complete the form and submit it to the Web site, the information is sent to the Web server for processing. One popular way to transmit the form data to a Web server is to place a compact form of the information that a user enters at the end of the target server's URL. The Web page address and the captured data go to the server. Suppose you decide not to wait for the anybiz.com server to respond. Instead, you type the URL of another site—*www.somecompany.com*, for example—in your browser's address field. The new destination can grab the URL from anybiz.com—including your completed form—and process that information. This problem is not uncommon, because Web sites like to know the address of the site you visited previously before opening the current site. By recording the previous anybiz.com URL, somecompany.com has breached secrecy by innocently recording the confidential information you entered for the anybiz.com site. This problem doesn't always occur, but the point is that it *can* occur. You want to see this for yourself.

To see your responses in a site's URL:

1. Click your browser's **Back** button or use its history list to return to the Online Companion page for Session 4.1, and then click the **American Greetings** link and wait while your browser loads the American Greetings home page shown in Figure 4-9.

Figure 4-9	AMERICAN GREETINGS HOME PAGE

free card of the day (yours might look different)

2. Click the **Card of the Day** link located on the left side of the page. (Depending on the holiday season during which you open the American Greetings site, your link might contain a different slogan or icon.) Depending on the season, one or several customized (and sometimes animated) cards appear. You can click a card to send it to anyone with an e-mail address. Figure 4-10 shows the Internet Explorer Address bar. The data that follows the question mark indicates choices you have made or will make to create the card.

Figure 4-10	PERSONAL INFORMATION IN A URL

personal information about your selection appears in the URL (your information might be different)

americangreetings.com - Order A Card - Microsoft Internet Explorer

File   Edit   View   Favorites   Tools   Help

Back | Forward | Stop | Refresh | Home | Search | Favorites | History | Mail | Print | Edit

Address ://www.americangreetings.com/greetingcard/pd/porder.pd?L0=25&L1=101&L2=24&L3=10900&L4=0&L5=0&product=2028821

TROUBLE? If a dialog box opens and displays a message about Quick Time, close the dialog box to continue.

TROUBLE? If the Address bar in Internet Explorer is not visible, click View on the menu bar, point to Toolbars, and then click Address Bar to display it.

TROUBLE? If the Location Toolbar in Netscape Navigator is not visible, click View on the menu bar, point to Show, and then click Location Toolbar to display it.

3. Close your Web browser and close your dial-up connection, if necessary.

Just by selecting a card, some of the data you entered appears in the address field of your Web browser. Interesting! Of course, you did not reveal anything very interesting to anyone. However, you see how anyone interested in doing so can extract unprotected information.

Secrecy is obviously a very important concern to any commerce site. In order to process online orders securely, software or hardware must be in place to protect information so that an interloper cannot grab information off the Internet as it travels between a client's computer and the commerce site's server. In Session 4.2, you will learn how to protect transactions from secrecy threats.

Integrity Threats

Because of recent news coverage of integrity threats, Marcia wants to make sure that her customer's transactions are not intercepted, altered, or destroyed before they reach the e-Clip commerce site. High on her security priority list is protection of the e-Clip Web site itself. More than a few articles have crossed her desk describing attacks on Web sites in which hackers spread electronic graffiti over a Web site. She wants to minimize or eliminate that threat, if possible. She asks you to continue exploring security threats involving message and transaction alterations, as well as Web site hacking, so she can better understand these problems and plan appropriately to prevent them. Later, she will ask your help to locate tools that prevent integrity threats.

An **integrity threat**, also known as active wiretapping, exists when an unauthorized party could alter a message stream of information. Unprotected banking transactions, such as deposit amounts transmitted over the Internet, are subject to integrity violations. Of course, an integrity violation implies a secrecy violation, because an intruder who alters information can read and interpret that information. Unlike secrecy threats, where a viewer could see information he or she should not see, integrity threats can change the actions a person or corporation takes because the transmission has been altered.

Cyber vandalism is another example of an integrity threat. **Cyber vandalism** is the electronic defacing of an existing Web site's pages—the electronic equivalent of destroying property or placing graffiti on objects. Cyber vandalism occurs when someone is able to replace a Web site's regular content with his or her own content. Recently, there have been several reports of Web page defacing in which vandals replace business content with pornographic material and other offensive content. Unsuspecting Web surfers are shocked when they go to their favorite site and find the offensive graphics and text. Figure 4-11 shows an example of a Web site that lists attacks.

Figure 4-11   **ARCHIVE OF HACKED WEBSITES**

The cost of Web site security breaches is great. Besides spending money reconstructing damaged Web pages and restoring databases, a defaced Web site can be expensive both in investigative time and negative publicity. For example, imagine how hard it would be to convince your customers that it is safe to purchase goods and services from your Web site following a Web site attack. Your brief tour convinces you that protecting a Web site is a tough task. There are thousands of ways to violate a Web site. Hackers often start by looking for well-known Web server weak points and flaws that are not patched with the latest security fixes.

Integrity threats can alter vital financial, medical, or military information. You can imagine the impact if an unauthorized person captures a message that credits a bank account for $5,000 and then changes the message to credit his or her own account instead. Similarly, an integrity violation that alters a résumé that is attached to an e-mail message can affect the applicant's chances of being hired by the company that receives it. Information alteration can have very serious financial and physical consequences, as well. Not long ago, a thief broke into an online music retailer's Web site and stole credit card numbers. He subsequently attempted to extort a $100,000 ransom from the music company. When the company refused, the cyber extortionist released thousands of credit card numbers on a Web site. *The New York Times* reported that the hacker claimed to have extracted over 300,000 CD customers' credit card numbers. After the attack, the music company quickly hired security experts to fortify the site's security system. (You might wish to click the **CYBER EXTORTION** link in the Session 4.1 section of the Online Companion to read more about the attack.)

Necessity Threats

Necessity threats, also know as **delay** or **denial** threats, disrupt or deny normal computer processing. A program that has experienced a necessity threat retards processing to an intolerably slow speed. For example, if the normal processing speed of a single transaction on Dell.com takes 12 minutes instead of the usual 15 seconds, users will abandon the purchase transaction or cease browsing the Dell.com site entirely—a lost sale of several thousands of dollars or more. In general, slowing down any Internet service will drive customers to competitors' Web or commerce sites, possibly causing them to never return to the original commerce site.

Denial attacks remove information altogether or delete information from a transmission or file. One documented denial attack caused selected PCs that have Quicken, an accounting program, to divert money to a hacker's bank account. The denial attack denied money from its rightful owners. Arguably the most infamous Internet (necessity) attack is the Internet Worm. Created in 1988 by a 23-year-old Cornell graduate student named Robert Morris Jr., the worm caused thousands of computers around the country to slow down or cease production altogether. Called a **worm** because it automatically propagated versions of itself to other machines, the worm worked its way through thousands of computers on the Internet within a few hours.

Understanding and preventing denial attacks is high on your priority list. Marcia wants to ensure that e-Clip Services has a strong protection mechanism in place to thwart necessity attacks. She doesn't want to lose consumers due to delays beyond those inherent on the Internet.

In the next session, you will explore some of the countermeasures available to prevent electronic commerce threats.

Session 4.1 QUICK CHECK

1. Why do cookies pose a slightly more serious privacy threat than Web site registration information?

2. Do you think copyright laws prevent you from using information in a published report (such as a newspaper) and rewriting and republishing ideas from that report in a different form?

3. Why do you think that intellectual property is protected? For example, what loss does Scott Adams experience if someone uses a Dilbert cartoon without his written permission?

4. Suppose an eavesdropper intercepts an Internet transaction and records the titles of books that you ordered from Amazon.com. What category of security breach is that? Is it a secrecy, integrity, or necessity violation?

5. How is a worm different from a virus?

6. Is the threat of a hacker intercepting and then changing a message a secrecy threat, an integrity threat, or a delay/denial attack?

SESSION 4.2

In this session, you will learn how to combat electronic commerce security threats by using countermeasures, including antivirus software, encryption, message digests, digital certificates, authentication challenges and responses, and physical protection procedures.

Protecting Your Privacy

As a consumer, you can protect your privacy by withholding private information from businesses and individuals that might misuse it. You cannot withhold personal information if you are purchasing an item—you must disclose your mailing address and provide payment information. However, sometimes you can limit the amount of personal information that you want to reveal. For example, if you are purchasing a software product from an electronic commerce site, the registration form might contain questions with text boxes and option buttons to gather marketing information, such as your age, income, and occupation, which isn't relevant to your purchase. The answers to marketing questions help companies understand their target audiences better so they can focus their advertising campaigns on the correct market segment. However, often this information reveals something that you probably would not reveal under other circumstances. In most cases, the "less is more" rule is the best one to follow—reveal what you must but nothing more.

When you surf the Web and use it to purchase goods and services, these Web sites are gathering more marketing information about your browsing and purchasing habits than you might realize. The collection of marketing information about visitors to a Web site is called **Web profiling**. Web profiling reveals important information about Web consumer shopping trends and consumer needs. Because there is no standard for Web profiling, a group of companies is working together to create a unifying standard called **Customer Profile Exchange** (**CPEX**). This evolving standard governs the way companies collect customer information and share it with others. CPEX differs from other customer and surfer information collection efforts because CPEX is being designed so that consumers have more control over what personal information they allow to be circulated. In other words, CPEX provides consumers with some control over the circulation of their personal data. While the main business of the CPEX backers, in part, is to collect and share information about shoppers and their shopping habits, the member companies are sensitive to the consumers' desires to control what information is released.

After sharing the information you found about the CPEX initiative with Marcia, she decides that she is interested in collecting some information about her online customers, but she also wants her online customers and visitors to the e-Clip Services Web site to know that e-Clip Services respects their privacy. Her goal is to provide online assurances about privacy protection for e-Clip's customers. Marcia asks you to see what other respected Web sites do to protect their customers' privacy. Marcia knows that the seal of the Better Business Bureau (BBB) conveys a message of trust when its logo appears in a merchant's store window. She asks you to continue your research to discover if a similar seal of credibility exists for electronic commerce sites.

During your research, you noticed that many Web sites display a TRUSTe icon on their home pages, like the one shown in Figure 4-12.

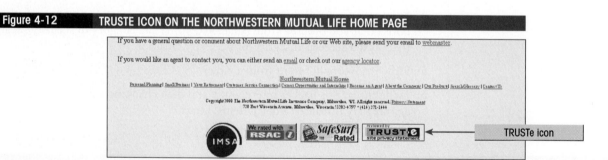

Figure 4-12   **TRUSTE ICON ON THE NORTHWESTERN MUTUAL LIFE HOME PAGE**

This icon indicates that Northwestern Mutual Life Insurance Company, for example, is a member of the TRUSTe organization. TRUSTe is a not-for-profit, independent organization whose mission is to build users' trust and confidence of the Internet. To verify that a site is a current TRUSTe member, you can click the icon, which searches the TRUSTe site for the member's identification information and then displays the site's membership confirmation. Because Marcia wants to show her customers that her site is safe and trustworthy, you decide to investigate further.

To learn more about TRUSTe:

1. Start your Web browser, and then go to the Online Companion by entering the URL **http://www.course.com/NewPerspectives/EC** in the appropriate location of your Web browser. Click the **Tutorial 4** link, and then click the **Session 4.2** link.

   Click the **TRUSTe** link and wait while your browser loads the TRUSTe home page shown in Figure 4-13.

Figure 4-13 TRUSTE HOME PAGE

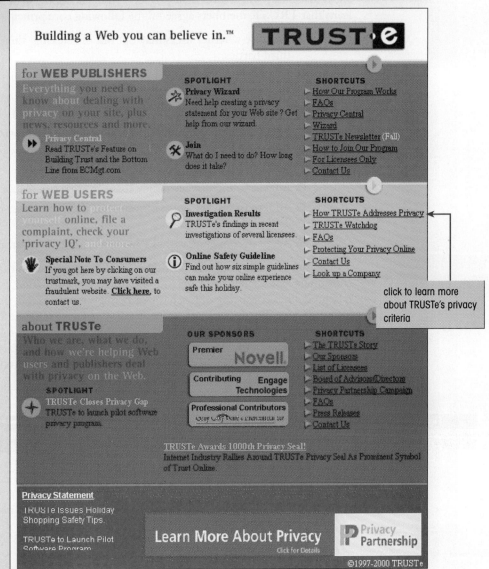

2. Click the **How TRUSTe Addresses Privacy** link located in the Shortcuts column in the "for WEB USERS" section. The TRUSTe: for WEB USERS page opens. Read the page, which describes what Web browsers and shoppers can expect from a Web site bearing the TRUSTe trustmark.

3. Click the arrow to the right of the **for WEB PUBLISHERS** link located on the left side of the page near the top. The TRUSTe: for WEB PUBLISHERS page opens. Read the page, which describes the benefits of obtaining and adhering to the TRUSTe principles. The How To Join link describes the procedure e-Clip must follow to submit its Web site to TRUSTe for consideration.

You are convinced that the TRUSTe trustmark will provide customers with additional assurances that e-Clip will protect their privacy. From reading the material on the TRUSTe site, you learn that TRUSTe members agree on the following core principles. The Web site must:

■ Disclose whether users may opt out of releasing their information for use by third parties

■ Display the trustmark on its home page, or the same page that discloses the site's general privacy policy

■ Explain exactly what data the Web site is gathering

■ Summarize the Web site's general data gathering practices

■ Refrain from monitoring personal communications to third parties except as required by law

■ Adhere to the privacy policy that the Web site places on its home page

■ Adhere to privacy policies even after the Web site chooses to halt its TRUSTe membership

■ Agree to cooperate with TRUSTe Web site monitoring and auditing activities

The Better Business Bureau (BBB) is another organization that is very active in boosting consumers' confidence by protecting their private information. The BBB has drafted voluntary guidelines consisting of five basic principles, ranging from disclosing to customers what information is being collected to protecting children online. It has reviewed more than 5,000 commerce Web sites to determine if they qualify for the BBB Reliability Seal or the BBB Privacy Seal. You might wish to click the **Better Business Bureau** link in the Session 4.2 section of the Online Companion to review the BBB site and to learn about its Privacy Seal and Reliability Seal. Figure 4-14 shows the BBB home page.

Figure 4-14	BETTER BUSINESS BUREAU HOME PAGE

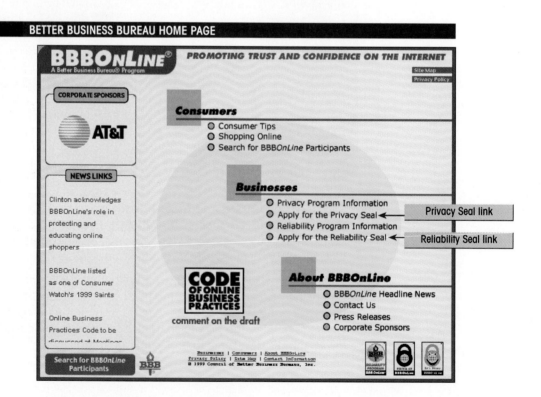

Marcia is pleased with the information you found, which will help to assure consumers that e-Clip Services will protect their privacy. She is enthusiastic about applying for the

TRUSTe trustmark for the e-Clip site because she knows that the trustmark conveys to customers that her site maintains a high level of credibility. Now that you have found ways to protect e-Clip's customers, Marcia wants you to research ways to protect e-Clip's intellectual property.

Protecting Intellectual Property

Protecting digital intellectual property poses problems that are different in many ways from protecting traditional intellectual property. Traditional intellectual property, such as written works, art, and music, is protected by national and, in some cases, international laws. National and international laws also protect digital intellectual property, such as art, logos, and music posted on Web sites. While these laws act as a theft deterrent, they do not prevent violations, nor do they provide a means to reliably trace the path taken by the violators to acquire the intellectual property. The real dilemma for companies that post their digital property on a Web site is determining how to display it and secure it against theft. While absolute intellectual property protection so far has proven elusive, there are measures e-Clip can take to provide some level of protection and accountability for its copyrights for digital works.

The U.S. Congress has been trying to deal legislatively with digital copyright issues. An international body known as the **World Intellectual Property Organization** (**WIPO**) has been trying to promote and oversee digital copyright issues internationally. Meanwhile, a few companies are providing the first and second generation of products that provide a measure of protection for digital copyright holders. While the case law dealing with copyright issues is still limited in this young field, some experts believe that U.S. copyright laws do apply to the Internet and other digital media. The **Information Technology Association of America** (**ITAA**), a trade organization representing U.S. information technology companies, is a rich source of information about intellectual property protection, especially for digital intellectual property.

Due to intensive efforts of the U.S. Congress, the WIPO, and the ITAA, new technology is being developed to protect digital works from theft. Several methods show promise in the battle to protect digital works. For example, digital copyright holders can now use software metering, digital watermarks, and digital envelopes to protect their works. **Software metering** tracks the number of times someone uses a digital item. A **digital watermark** is a pattern of bits inserted into a digital image, audio, or video file that identifies the file's copyright information. A **digital envelope** is a type of security that uses two layers of encryption to protect a message. The first layer encrypts the message itself, and the second layer encrypts the newly encrypted message and the user's public key. The protection provided by each method varies widely, and none of these methods is foolproof. However, they do provide some protection now as better methods are being developed.

Now and in the future, digital copyright holders might use steganography to protect their works. **Steganography** is the art and science of hiding information by embedding messages within other messages or graphics. Steganography appears to be both an interesting technology and a promising way to protect e-Clip proprietary information. **Verance Corporation** is a company that provides digital audio watermarking systems to protect audio files on the Internet. Its systems identify, authenticate, and protect intellectual property. Typically, the embedded, hidden information, which is called a **digital watermark**, uniquely identifies the intellectual property's owner. The primary advantage of using steganography is that it is undetectable. The watermark is a digital code that is embedded undetectably in a digital image or audio file. A watermark can be encrypted to protect its contents, or it can simply be hidden among the bits—or digital information—that comprise the image or recording. Verance's Musicode® system allows recording artists to monitor, identify, and control the use of their digital recordings. The audio watermarks do not alter the audio fidelity of the recordings in which they are embedded—the watermark just ensures that the owners of those recordings have control over their reproduction. Figure 4-15 shows the Verance Corporation home page.

Figure 4-15   **VERANCE CORPORATION HOME PAGE**

Digimarc Corporation is another company providing watermark protection systems and software. Its products embed a watermark that allows any work protected by the Digimarc system to be tracked across the Web. In addition, the watermark can link viewers to commerce sites and databases, and control software and playback devices. Finally, the imperceptible watermark contains copyright information and electronic links to the work's creator. The watermark identifies the work's creator and facilitates electronic purchase and licensing of the work.

E-Clip could use Digimarc technology to protect original articles it creates and provides to selected subscribers. Should an unauthorized copy of an e-Clip article ever appear on a Web site, it would be a simple task to reveal the hidden watermark to establish the intellectual property's true owner.

SoftLock.com produces a technology that lets authors and publishers lock files containing digital information for sale on the Web. Using the SoftLock, authors and other copyright holders can allow purchasers to unlock the files they purchased. This system provides a secure way to post downloadable files on a Web site, because the downloaded files will not function without the purchase of a key to unlock them.

Securing a Client

Providing security for commerce transactions means establishing security both on a client computer and on the network and Internet—the communication channel. Securing a client computer includes protecting it to ensure message secrecy, integrity, and on-time delivery (necessity). You can use antivirus software, set your browser to restrict the use of cookies, and use different technologies to ensure a client's security.

Running Antivirus Software

No client computer defense would be complete without antivirus software. While it isn't the purpose of this textbook to endorse one product over another, it is important that you include this valuable class of protection in any security plan. Antivirus software only protects your computer from viruses that your antivirus software recognizes. Therefore, using antivirus software is a defense strategy. Regardless of which vendor's software you choose, it is only effective if you download and install the program's virus updates on a regular basis to keep the antivirus data files current. Antivirus data files contain information about recognized viruses, such as the virus name and its identifying information, and are used to detect viruses on your computer. Because people generate hundreds of new viruses every month, you must be vigilant and update your antivirus data files regularly so your antivirus software recognizes and eliminates the newest viruses.

Although e-Clip does not supply antivirus software to its customers, Marcia wants online shoppers to know that viruses are an Internet problem. She wants her customers to know that a good way to protect their computers against viruses is to install an antivirus program. To emphasize her support for using the latest antivirus software and updating any virus information files the software uses, Marcia asks you to look at two popular antivirus sites. The first product Marcia wants to examine is McAfee VirusScan.

To find information about McAfee VirusScan:

1. Click your browser's **Back** button or use its history list to return to the Online Companion page for Session 4.2, and then click the **McAfee** link and wait while your browser loads the McAfee home page shown in Figure 4-16.

Figure 4-16   MCAFEE'S HOME PAGE

Anti-Virus tab

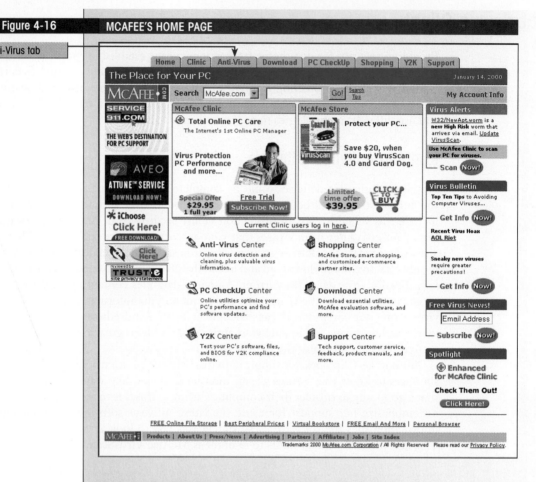

2. Click the **Anti-Virus** tab located at the top of the page. The Anti-Virus Center page opens.

3. Click the **Virus Info** link located near the top of the Anti-Virus Center page. The Virus Information Library page opens. This page contains information about viruses that McAfee software identifies and eliminates. The database also contains information about virus hoaxes, the top virus threats, and a link to explain how McAfee assesses a virus's risk. To get more information about a specific virus, click a letter in the Virus Information Library panel, and then search for the virus. To get more information about a recently discovered, recently updated, or a top reported virus, click the appropriate link in the Information Center panel.

4. Click the **Recently Discovered Viruses** link in the Information Center panel, and then click the first link in the Virus Name column on the page that opens. Read the page that opens, which includes detailed information about the virus, including its name, characteristics, and how to recognize and eliminate the virus.

5. Click your browser's **Back** button until you return to the Anti-Virus Center page.

6. Click the **Shopping** tab located at the top of the page. The Shopping Center page opens. You can use this page to purchase McAfee products.

7. Click the **Enter McAfee Store** icon (see Figure 4-17) to open a page that lists McAfee products for sale. VirusScan, McAfee's flagship product, is sold using this Web page. Note the retail price of the VirusScan for Windows 95/98.

Figure 4-17	MCAFEE SHOPPING CENTER PAGE

click either link to enter the McAfee store

TROUBLE? If you do not see the Enter McAfee Store icon on the Shopping Center page, click the McAfee Store tab located near the top of the page to enter the store.

8. Click the **More Info** link to the right of the VirusScan for Windows product listing to open a page with detailed information about the latest version of VirusScan. Read the information. This product seems very affordable and provides excellent client protection against Internet viruses. In addition, McAfee provides free product updates to ensure that the software will recognize and eliminate current and future viruses.

Marcia also wants you to find information about another popular antivirus software program from Symantec called Norton AntiVirus.

To find information about Norton AntiVirus:

1. Click your browser's **Back** button or use its history list to return to the Online Companion page for Session 4.2, and then click the **Norton** link and wait while your browser loads the Norton AntiVirus information page shown in Figure 4-18. This page contains links to retail antivirus software products, including Norton AntiVirus, for several computer operating systems.

Figure 4-18   NORTON ANTIVIRUS PRODUCT INFORMATION PAGE

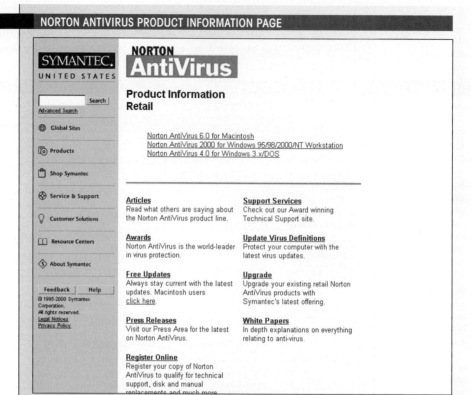

2. Click the **Norton AntiVirus 2000 for Windows 95/98/2000/NT Workstation**
   link. A product information page opens and highlights the Windows version of
   the Norton AntiVirus software. Note the list price for the software and the link to
   a page that you can use to purchase the software.

Marcia will use the information that you found to add links on e-Clip's home page to the
home pages of the antivirus software publishers, so consumers can visit the publishers' Web
sites to get more information about protecting their computers from virus threats.

Restricting Cookies

In Session 4.1, you learned that many Web sites use cookies to enhance your Web browsing
experiences. A Web site might store one or more cookies on your computer, or a Web site
might create, use, and then destroy one or more cookies during the course of a single Web
browsing session. While browsing the Web, you may have noticed that advertisement banners on sites you visit often cater to your interests. Your interests often are encoded in cookies on your computer. Two popular Web browsers, Microsoft Internet Explorer and
Netscape Navigator, both provide options to deal with cookies. Your choices range from
allowing cookies to be stored on your computer unconditionally to disallowing cookie storage altogether. Although the latter choice is the safest, it precludes you from enjoying some
of the benefits of cookies. For example, e-Clip stores cookies on client computers, with
their customers' permission, to save login and password information. If e-Clip clients disallow cookie storage on their computers, then they will experience the slight inconvenience of
needing to log in to the e-Clip site to enjoy the special member services. Marcia wants to see
how to change a browser's cookie settings so she can communicate the procedure to customers who do not want e-Clip Services to store cookies on their computers. You will see
how to change your cookies settings in Internet Explorer and Navigator next.

To change cookie settings in Internet Explorer:

1. Click **Tools** on the menu bar, and then click **Internet Options**. The Internet Options dialog box opens.

2. Click the **Security** tab. You can set the security level for the Internet content zone or for a content zone defined by your connection to an intranet.

3. If necessary, click the **Internet** content zone, and then click the **Custom Level** button. The Security Settings dialog box opens. Scroll down the Settings list until the Cookies group appears at the top of the list box, as shown in Figure 4-19. You can click the Disable, Enable, or Prompt option buttons under the Allow cookies that are stored on your computer heading to prevent a Web site from storing a cookie on your computer, to allow a Web site to store cookies on your computer automatically, or to ask for your permission before allowing a Web site to store a cookie on your computer, respectively. These same settings apply to the Allow per-session cookies (not stored) heading, which lets you control how to store cookies during a visit to a single Web site. By changing these options, you can control how to use cookies on your computer.

| Figure 4-19 | INTERNET EXPLORER COOKIE SECURITY SETTINGS |

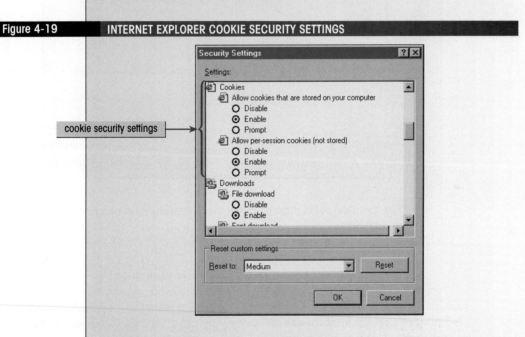

cookie security settings

4. Click the **Cancel** button to close the Security Settings dialog box, and then click the **Cancel** button again to close the Internet Options dialog box without making any changes.

Navigator provides similar cookie protection.

To change cookie settings in Navigator:

1. Click **Edit** on the menu bar, and then click **Preferences**. The Preferences dialog box opens.

2. Click **Advanced** in the Category list. The Advanced settings for your browser are displayed. See Figure 4-20. You can select one of three option buttons for dealing with cookies: Accept all cookies, which lets a Web site store a cookie

on your computer automatically; Accept only cookies that get sent back to the originating server, which ensures that a cookie will be used only by the Web site that issued it; or Disable cookies, which prevents a Web site from storing a cookie on your computer. In addition to selecting one of these three option buttons, you can select or clear the Warn me before accepting a cookie check box, which asks for your permission before a Web site can store a cookie on your computer.

| Figure 4-20 | NAVIGATOR COOKIE SECURITY SETTINGS |

3. Click the **Cancel** button to close the Preferences dialog box without making any changes.

In either browser, when you select the option to prompt you before a Web site stores a cookie on your computer, a dialog box similar to the one shown in Figure 4-21 will open. This dialog box shows the Netscape Navigator warning that opens when Amazon.com tries to store a cookie on the user's computer. You can click the OK button to store the cookie, or click the Cancel button to prevent Amazon.com from storing the cookie on your computer.

| Figure 4-21 | NETSCAPE NAVIGATOR COOKIE WARNING |

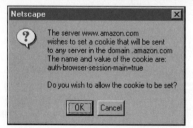

Because she realizes that some users do not want cookies stored on their computers, Marcia plans to include a help page in the e-Clip Web site that explains what e-Clip is storing in cookies and how the cookies help customers use the e-Clip site. By providing more information about how e-Clip uses cookies, Marcia believes that users will have more information about making decisions for storing cookies from the e-Clip Web site.

Protecting Communication Channels

Protecting the electronic commerce channels—the network and Internet—is by far the most visible segment of computer security. Hardly a day passes without a newspaper or magazine article describing attacks on the Internet or reporting about hackers gaining entrance to a computer system by way of an insecure communication channel. Consequently, security experts have invested a great deal of time and research into protecting assets while they are in transit between client computers and remote servers. Providing commerce channel security means providing channel secrecy, guaranteeing message integrity, and ensuring channel availability. In addition, a complete security plan includes authentication, or ensuring that those using computers are who they say they are.

Because it is impossible to prevent eavesdroppers from snooping on the Internet, businesses must use techniques that prevent them from *reading* Internet messages that they intercept. Sending a message over the Internet is like sending a postcard through the mail: The postcard will probably reach its destination, but everyone involved with delivering it can read its details on the face of the card. Without protecting your Internet transmissions, they are as vulnerable as the postcard for anyone who intercepts them. The only way to prevent snoopers from copying down your credit card number, for example, is to encrypt it and other sensitive information before you send it over the Internet. Encrypting e-mail messages or Internet commerce transactions is like writing a message on the postcard in a language that only you and the recipient understand. No one else in the entire world understands that language, so even though another person might intercept and read the message, it will make no sense to the interceptor.

Providing Secrecy with Encryption

Marcia wants you to focus your attention on secrecy. Her biggest fear is that a customer's credit card number could be compromised. She wants to know what e-Clip must do to protect both payment information and transaction details. In other words, she wants only the customer and the e-Clip Web site to be able to process the information sent between them. If an intruder taps into the data line, she doesn't want the intruder to be able to obtain any useful information. Finally, she has read many news stories about intruders gaining access to customer credit card information stored in Web site databases. She wants a protection mechanism in place that either prevents database break-ins or at least stores the information in a way that makes it unintelligible and thus useless to an intruder.

You have heard a lot in the press about encrypting information so that unauthorized parties cannot make sense of the encrypted information, even if they can access it. You think encryption is a good place to start your research. **Encryption** is the process of encoding information using a secret key to produce a string of unintelligible characters. The science that studies encryption is called **cryptography**, which comes from a combination of the two Greek words *krupto* and *grafh*, which mean *secret* and *writing*. Cryptography is not related to steganography, which makes text invisible to the naked eye. Cryptography doesn't attempt to hide text; it converts text to strings that are visible but do not appear to have any meaning. A string of these unintelligible characters is made up of combinations of bits, many of which correspond to alphabetic or numeric characters forming a message that seems to be a random assemblage. When someone or some program receives an encrypted message, the message is decoded, or **decrypted**, using a decryption program. A **decryption program** is a program that reverses the encryption procedure. For example, before you use your Web browser to send your credit card number or other sensitive data to a commerce site such as

Amazon.com, your browser encrypts the data. The information that is sent from your PC across the Internet to Amazon.com is an apparently random, jumbled message with no intelligible information. When the transaction arrives at the **secure commerce site**—a commerce site that uses encryption techniques to protect transactions—the data is decrypted back into its original, intelligible form. Encryption is similar to using an armored car to deliver money securely from the bank to a store. Although the armored car travels over regular streets and highways, the contents are protected while in transit.

Your preliminary research indicates that there are two main encryption groups or methods: asymmetric encryption and symmetric encryption. You are eager to look at both techniques to determine the better choice for e-Clip.

Symmetric Encryption

Symmetric encryption, also known as **private-key encryption**, encodes a message by using a single key—which is usually a large integer number—to encode and decode data. Because the same key is used for encryption and decryption, both the message's sender and receiver must know the key. Encoding and decoding messages using symmetric encryption is very fast and efficient. However, the sender and receiver must guard the key. If the key is made public, then all previous messages are vulnerable, and both the sender and receiver must use new keys for future communications.

The problem with symmetric encryption is that it is difficult to distribute new keys securely to authorized parties. To transmit *anything* privately—including the new, secret key—it must be encrypted. Shared secret keys do not work well on the Internet, because there must be a private key for *each pair* of users on the Internet who want to share information privately. This potentially huge number of key-pair combinations is analogous to connecting every pair of people in the world with their own private telephone line.

The U.S. government uses a well-publicized example of a symmetric encryption system called the Data Encryption Standard. The **Data Encryption Standard (DES)** is an encryption standard adopted by the U.S. government for encrypting sensitive or commercial information. DES is the most widely used private-key encryption system on the Internet.

Asymmetric Encryption

Asymmetric encryption, also called **public-key encryption**, encodes messages by using two mathematically related numeric keys. In 1977, Ronald Rivest, Adi Shamir, and Len Adleman invented the RSA Public Key Cryptosystem while they were professors at MIT. Their invention revolutionized the way people and organizations exchange sensitive information. In their system, one key of the pair, called a **public key**, is freely distributed to the public at large and to anyone interested in communicating securely with the holder of both keys. An e-Clip customer who wants to send a message to Marcia, for example, would encrypt the message using Marcia's public key, which the customer can easily obtain. The second key, called a **private key**, belongs to the key owner, who carefully keeps the key secret. The owner uses the private key to decrypt messages sent to him or her. For example, when Bill wants to send a message to e-Clip, he obtains e-Clip's public key from any of several well-known public places. Then Bill encrypts the message he is sending to e-Clip using e-Clip's public key. After Bill encrypts the message, only e-Clip employees who have e-Clip's private key can use the key to decrypt and read the message. Because the key pairs are unique, only one secret key can open the message encrypted with a corresponding public key, and vice versa. Reversing the process, e-Clip can send a private message to Bill using Bill's public key to encrypt the message. When Bill receives e-Clip's message, he uses his private key to decrypt and read the message. Figure 4-22 shows a graphical representation of private-key and public-key encryption methods.

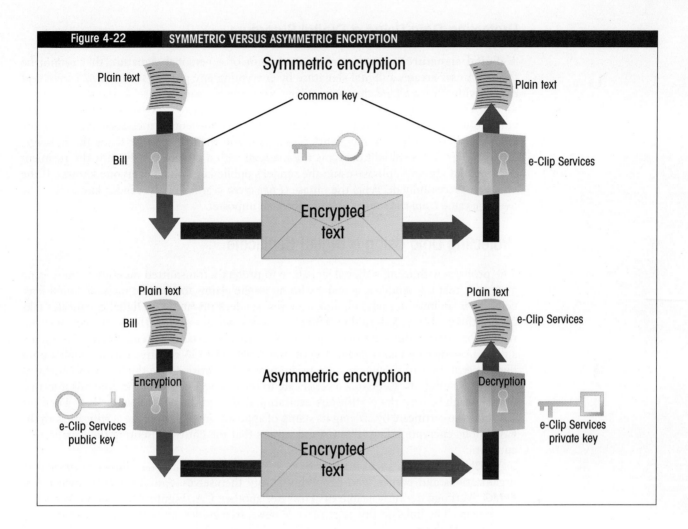

Figure 4-22 | **SYMMETRIC VERSUS ASYMMETRIC ENCRYPTION**

Using **Digital Signatures and Certificates**

Occasionally, an e-Clip customer service representative takes a customer order over the phone in which the customer uses a third party's credit card as payment, such as when an assistant uses the boss's credit card. When a representative does not properly verify that the customer's shipping address and the credit card's billing address are identical, e-Clip might inadvertently allow a customer to use a credit card number to pay for services without the credit card holder's permission. To complicate the problem of accepting payment further, some countries cannot validate credit cards properly. Keenly aware that her company has to absorb fraudulent credit card transactions, Marcia wants to do all that she can to avoid the problem online.

One potential security problem unique to online commerce is the identification of both customers and commerce sites. Customers who download e-Clip news items or browse e-Clip's premium content areas must be reliably identified before they can use the service. The reverse is also true: Customers want to know they are communicating with an authentic site, and not an imposter or knock-off Web site. In either case, the way to identify an individual or a company is to use a digital signature.

Protecting Data Using a Digital Signature

A **digital signature** is the electronic equivalent of a personal signature that cannot be forged. A user creates a digital signature by encrypting any phrase, such as *I like green vegetables*, with a private (and thus secret) key. Next, the encoded phrase is attached to a message before it is sent to another person or Web site, similar to how you would sign a letter you are about to mail. Finally, the sender encrypts the entire message—including the encoded phrase—with the recipient's public key, and then the sender sends the message. Upon receipt, the recipient decrypts the message with a private key. Finally, the recipient decrypts the signature phrase using the sender's public key (which everyone knows). If the recipient successfully decrypts the phrase (*I like green vegetables*), the sender knows that the message came from the sender and not from an imposter.

Protecting Data Using a Digital Certificate

The problem with using a digital signature to protect a transmitted message is there is no guarantee that the sender is actually who he or she claims to be. The message could have come from an imposter who obtained the real sender's private key. Digital certificates take care of this problem. A **digital certificate**, also known as a **digital ID**, is an electronic signature that verifies the identity of a user or Web site. A **certification authority (CA)** issues a digital certificate to an organization or individual. The CA requires entities applying for digital certificates to supply an appropriate proof of identity. Once the CA is satisfied that the entity is valid, the CA issues a certificate to the entity. The certificate contains information about the entity, the certificate's expiration date, and the entity's public key. Then the CA signs the certificate by affixing its stamp of approval and encrypts the certificate with the CA's public encryption key. The CA guarantees that the entity presenting the certificate is authentic.

    VeriSign is one of a small number of trusted companies that issues digital certificates to organizations and parties who properly identify themselves. Another well-known CA is **KPMG**. VeriSign recently acquired Thwarte, another CA. Figure 4-23 shows VeriSign's home page. The links on this page provide news, free guides, and other information about securing a Web site.

Figure 4-23   **VERISIGN'S HOME PAGE**

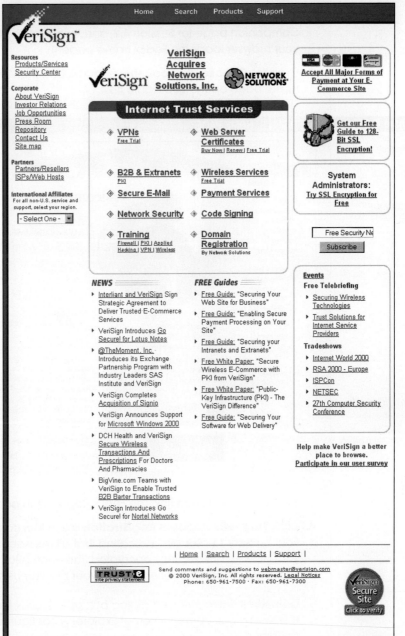

Certificates are classified as low, medium, or high assurance based largely on the identification requirements they impose on certificate seekers. VeriSign, for instance, offers several classes of certificates using the notations Class 1 through Class 4. Class 1 certificates are the lowest level and bind e-mail addresses and associated public keys. Class 4 certificates apply to servers and their organizations. Requirements for Class 4 certificates are significantly greater than those for Class 1. VeriSign's Class 4 certificate, for example, offers assurance of the individual's identity and of that person's relationship to the specified company or organization. Certificates exist for individuals (**personal certificates**), software publishers (**software publisher certificates**), and Web site servers (**site certificates**). When you browse to a Web site, you can view the Web site's certificate, if it has one, with your Web browser. FedEx has a digital certificate to demonstrate that the Web site at the URL www.fedex.com is really FedEx's Web site.

To view FedEx's digital certificate:

1. Click your browser's **Back** button or use its history list to return to the Online Companion page for Session 4.2, and then click the **FedEx** link and wait while your browser loads the FedEx home page.

2. Click the **Choose your country** list arrow, and then click **U.S.A.** The FedEx U.S. Home page opens. See Figure 4-24.

Figure 4-24	FEDEX U.S. HOME PAGE

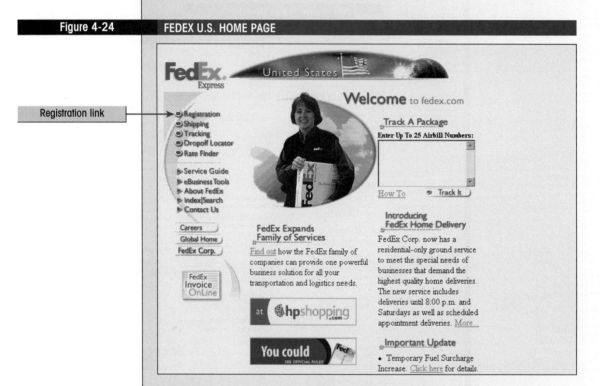

Registration link

3. Click the **Registration** link. The FedEx Registration page opens.

4. Click the **FedEx Account Registration** link. A locked padlock icon appears in your browser's status bar, indicating that all messages between the server and your browser are securely encrypted. This encryption is possible because FedEx has reliably identified itself to your browser using a site certificate.

   TROUBLE? If a Security Alert dialog box opens, click the OK button to continue. This dialog box opens if Internet Explorer is configured to alert you when you change security zones.

   TROUBLE? If a Security Information dialog box opens, click the Continue button to continue. This dialog box opens if Navigator is configured to alert you when you change security zones.

When a site includes a certificate, as indicated by a padlock icon on the browser's status bar, you can obtain more information about the site's certificate using your browser. If you are using Internet Explorer, complete the first set of steps. Navigator users should complete the second set of steps.

To examine a certificate using Internet Explorer:

1. Double-click the **padlock icon** on the status bar. The Certificate dialog box opens and reveals the FedEx certificate shown in Figure 4-25. Notice that the certificate guarantees the identity of the remote server named www.fedex.com. The certificate also shows the valid dates for this certificate, which is approximately one year.

Figure 4-25   INTERNET EXPLORER CERTIFICATE DISPLAY

2. Click the **Details** tab to reveal more information about the certificate and its issuer.

3. Click the **OK** button to close the Certificate dialog box.

4. Close your Web browser and close your dial-up connection, if necessary.

To examine a certificate using Navigator:

1. Click the **padlock icon** on the left side of the status bar. The Netscape Security Info window opens.

2. Click the **View Certificate** button. The View A Certificate - Netscape window opens and displays FedEx's certificate. See Figure 4-26. The certificate shows the company's name, issuer, and valid dates. **RSA Data Security, Inc.** issued the site certificate for FedEx.

Figure 4-26   NETSCAPE NAVIGATOR CERTIFICATE DISPLAY

3. Click the **OK** button to close the View A Certificate - Netscape window, and then click the **OK** button to close the Netscape Security Info window.

4. Close your Web browser and close your dial-up connection, if necessary.

Digital certificates are valid for approximately one year. Near the end of a certificate's validity period, the company or individual must renew the certificate. Creating digital certificates with short life spans decreases the danger that a company's certificate will be valid after the company ceases to exist. However, by forcing companies to renew their certificates, customers are reassured that the company's Web site is valid.

You've learned a great deal about certificates. It is clear that e-Clip will need to apply for a site certificate from a CA in order to conduct secure transactions. Marcia is worried that she will have to hire someone to figure out how to use encryption, digital certificates, and digital signatures in order to provide secure online transactions. You have anticipated her angst and believe that the technology exists to handle security automatically. With a little more research, you believe that e-Clip Services can provide security that is simple to use and transparent to e-Clip customers. Secure protocols are the final piece of the security puzzle.

Secure Protocols: SSL and S-HTTP

If users had to encrypt transmissions and obtain digital certificates just to be able to order a book from Amazon.com, then electronic commerce would be an unrealized dream. Instead, Web browsers and Web servers automatically and invisibly handle all the work of encryption and digital signature exchanges when required. The main secure protocols that provide automatic encryption between browsers and Web sites are **Secure Sockets Layer (SSL)** and, to a lesser degree, **Secure HTTP (S-HTTP) protocols**. SSL has become the *de facto* standard secure protocol; both Netscape Navigator and Internet Explorer support it.

When a consumer enters a secure Web server, the Web browser and server send commands between them to decide on the best encryption method to use. This communication, called **negotiation**, results in the browser and server agreeing on the highest level of protection that both have in common—that both can handle—to secure subsequent information exchanges between them. Using your Web browser, the negotiation process occurs—and the SSL protocol takes over—when you click a link for a URL beginning with *https*. For example, in the URL *https://www.fedex.com/us/registration/account.html*, the *s* following *http* stands for secure. Negotiations between a consumer's browser and a commerce site are complete when the security indicator (a padlock icon) appears on the browser's status bar.

You make your final report on SSL to Marcia, who is relieved that security—both encryption of sensitive information and digital certificate exchange—occurs automatically with SSL.

Providing Integrity and Guaranteeing Delivery

Besides keeping selected commerce transactions secret from prying electronic eyes, security must address integrity and delay/denial threats. Recall that an integrity threat attempts to alter a message before it arrives to the recipient. Delay or denial threats slow processing time or erase transactions. If an online request is either altered or eliminated, heavy damage can result. There are ways to eliminate or reduce both threats. Marcia wants to know about these preventive measures to protect e-Clip's server and its customers.

Providing Transaction Integrity and Authentication

Although it is difficult and expensive to *prevent* a perpetrator from altering a message, there are security techniques that allow the receiver to *detect* when someone has altered a message. When the receiver—a commerce server for example—receives an altered message, the receiver can ask the sender to retransmit the message. Apart from being annoying, no one is harmed by a damaged message as long as both parties are aware of the alteration. The only time real damage occurs is when unauthorized message changes go undetected.

Authentication is establishing the validity of one's claimed identity, and it is vital in establishing that transactions come from an established and known system user. Authentication eliminates the possibility of an imposter gaining access to a system by claiming to be someone else. **Authorization,** which is the process of giving individuals access to information based on their identity, occurs *after* a person's true identity is established. Authentication and transaction integrity go hand-in-hand because techniques that create tamperproof messages also require identifying the message's true sender.

A combination of techniques creates messages that are tamperproof and authenticated. To eliminate fraud and abuse caused by the alteration of commerce messages, two separate procedures are applied to a message. First, the message passes through a hash function. A **hash function** creates a fixed length number—often 128 bits (16 characters) long—that summarizes a message's contents. A message's computed number is called a **message digest**, because it is a summary, or digest, of the entire message. After the hash function computes a message digest, the message digest is appended to the message. For example, suppose the message to be sent is a purchase order containing a customer's address and payment information. When the commerce Web site receives the purchase order and attached message digest, Web site software strips off the received message digest and recalculates the message digest for the message. If the message digest value that the commerce site calculates matches the message digest attached to the message, then the message is unaltered. Matching message digests means that no one altered the amount or the shipping address information. If someone altered the information, then the two message digests would be different. In that case, the Web site simply requests the Web browser to retransmit the purchase order. After confirming that the message digests match, another procedure attaches the sender's digital signature to the message to authenticate it.

There is another problem, however. Because the hash function is public and (by design) widely known, anyone could intercept the purchase order, alter the shipping address and quantity ordered, re-create the message digest, and send the message and new message digest to the commerce site. Upon receipt, the commerce site would calculate the message digest and confirm that the two message digests match. The commerce site is fooled into the apparent conclusion that the message is unaltered and genuine. To prevent this type of fraud, the sender encrypts the message digest using his or her private key. The encryption message digest, called a digital signature, accompanies the purchase order to provide the commerce site with positive identification of the sender and to assure the commerce site that the message was not altered. The digital signature provides **nonrepudiation**, which ensures that a message sender's digital signature is proof the sender was the true author of the message. SSL handles all of the details of computing message digests and signatures, so neither the consumer nor the commerce site need to worry about implementing that security feature. Figure 4-27 illustrates how a message, its message digest, and a digital signature are sent.

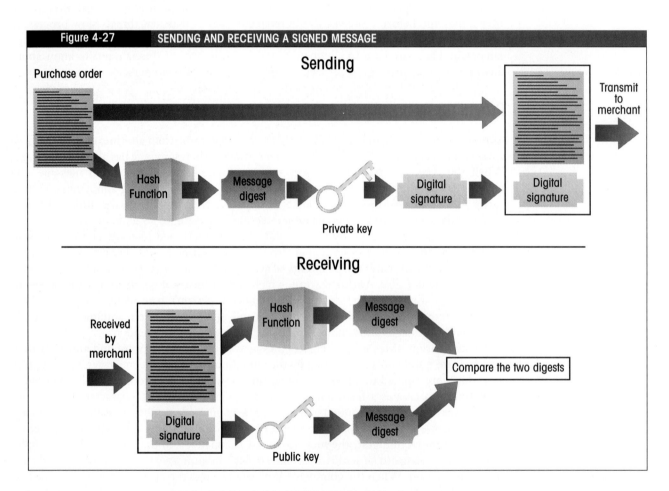

Figure 4-27   SENDING AND RECEIVING A SIGNED MESSAGE

Marcia is pleased to know that e-Clip will have a method to detect altered messages. However, after ensuring that messages are not altered, e-Clip still needs to ensure the delivery of messages back to its customers.

Guaranteeing Delivery

Denial of service removes or absorbs resources. One way to deny service to many people is to flood the Internet with a large number of messages in order to crash a specific server or slow down a specific server to levels of service that are unacceptable to people attempting to conduct business. One defense—and perhaps the most effective one—for that type of irrational behavior is the threat of punishment. Denial attacks also can mean removal of Internet packets, causing them to disappear altogether. If this happens frequently to a particular commerce site, then browsers and buyers will start to avoid that site. Neither encryption nor digital signatures protect information packets from theft or slowdown. However, the Transmission Control Protocol (TCP) half of the TCP/IP pair is responsible for end-to-end control of packets. When TCP reassembles packets at the destination in the correct order, it handles all the details when packets do not appear. TCP requests that the client computer resend data when packets seem to be missing. That is, there is no special computer security protocol beyond TCP/IP that is required as a countermeasure against denial attacks. The TCP/IP protocol builds checks into the data so that it can tell when data packets are inadvertently or otherwise altered.

You find it reassuring that TCP/IP guarantees delivery of packets, including commerce information sent to the e-Clip site. That means one less security issue for Marcia and e-Clip. Your security research and report to Marcia are complete. You feel confident that e-Clip's online transactions will be secure. Using secure computing practices, such as encouraging users to protect their client computers and using secure protocols, go a long way toward providing secure commerce. No online enterprise is immune from all security violations, but you know that e-Clip will be protected from security threats as well as any other online organization.

Session 4.2 QUICK CHECK

1. List one principle by which TRUSTe members must abide.

2. What is the general name of the process that provides embedded and hidden author information inside a digital document or graphic?

3. What type of encryption uses a private key and a public key to unlock a secure message?

4. VeriSign and RSA are examples of companies that are called _____.

5. What is the name of the protocol that automatically encrypts information flowing between a browser and a secure Web site?

6. Software known as a(n) _____ creates a short summary of a message, called a message _____, that the receiver can use to determine if the message has been altered and whether the message is truly from the sender.

CASE PROBLEMS

Case 1. Branded Software Products   Branded Software Products sells a variety of software products on its Web commerce site. Mario Picconi, the company's CEO, wants customers to feel comfortable shopping at his company's Web site. Some customers have sent e-mail messages to him asking what the company does with the information it collects from customers when they make a purchase. Mario wants his online customers to know that no information he collects about them is sold to another company or used by anyone outside of Branded Software Products. Mario asks you to help him draft a privacy policy that will serve as a "safe shopping" guarantee for Branded Software Products' customers. Mario wants the policy to comply with the BBB guidelines for commerce sites. Mario wants you to gather some information from the BBB site to help him get started.

1. Start your Web browser, and then go to the Online Companion page by entering the URL http://www.course.com/NewPerspectives/EC in the appropriate location of your Web browser. Click the Tutorial 4 link, and then click the Case Problems link.

Click the Beyond.com link and wait while your browser loads the Beyond.com home page.

2. If necessary, click the Individual Customers tab. Click the Help tab located near the top of the page.

3. Click the Safe Shopping Guarantee link located near the top of the page, and then click the Privacy Policy link.

4. Use your browser's Print button to print the Privacy Policy page.

5. Return to the Online Companion page, and then click the Better Business Bureau link in the Case Problem 1 section.

6. Locate the BBB link to its privacy program information and click it.

7. Locate and click a link that describes the cost of the BBB Privacy Program, and then print the page that opens.

8. Locate and click a link to open a page that contains a sample privacy policy link, and then print the page.

9. The Better Business Bureau provides a privacy seal that assures customers that their privacy is protected. Locate the BBB's step-by-step guide for applying for a privacy seal. Click the link to that application guide.

10. Write down the major steps a merchant must follow to apply for the BBB privacy seal.

11. To be eligible for the BBB privacy seal, businesses must complete a Compliance Assessment Questionnaire. Summarize the questions a business must answer about information collection in the Compliance Assessment Questionnaire.

12. Mario's Web site will contain a hyperlink to a page belonging to another Web site. Write a short summary of the questions he must answer about the external links in the Compliance Assessment Questionnaire.

13. Click your browser's Back button twice to return to the step-by-step guide to applying for a privacy seal. How much is the application fee? Upon what value does the BBB base its annual assessment fees? How much is the annual assessment fee for a company with 300 employees located in Chicago whose *monthly* online and offline sales are $500,000?

14. Close your browser and close your dial-up connection, if necessary.

Case 2. Pampered Paws   Pampered Paws is a small, privately owned pet-sitting service that caters to small pet owners, usually with cats and dogs. Its clients typically want to leave their pets at home while they are out of town. A designated Pampered Paws employee visits a client's pet in the client's home up to three times a day. The employee spends 30 minutes on each visit playing with the pet, checking the food and water containers, and occasionally taking the pet for a walk. All of the Pampered Paws employees, except the owner, are college students who work irregular, part-time schedules. Pampered Paws owner Barbara Frockmeister sends an e-mail message to each employee that contains the next week's client pet-sitting schedule. She wants to make sure that her competitors are not able to read each week's e-mail messages because they contain clients' names, addresses, and other confidential information. Barbara has asked each employee to obtain a Class 1 Digital ID from VeriSign so that messages between employees and Barbara are encrypted and contain a digital signature. She has agreed to pay the annual VeriSign fee for the license. After you obtain the ID, she wants you to send her a simple e-mail message acknowledging that you received and installed the Digital ID. *Note*: You must have an e-mail program and an e-mail address to complete this case problem.

1. Start your Web browser, and then go to the Online Companion page by entering the URL http://www.course.com/NewPerspectives/EC in the appropriate location of your Web browser. Click the Tutorial 4 link, and then click the Case Problems link. Click the VeriSign link. After the VeriSign home page opens, locate and click the Products link located near the top of the page.

2. Scroll down the page, and then click the Individual Digital Certificates for E-Mail link.

3. On the next page that opens, click the Get your VeriSign Digital ID now! link. (There might be two, similarly named links on the page. Click either one.)

4. Click the Enroll Now button that appears below the Class 1 Digital ID description. *Note*: You are applying for a free, 60-day trial digital ID, which will not cost you anything. At the end of the 60-day trial period, VeriSign will automatically cancel your Digital ID. You will receive a second e-mail message near the end of the trial period asking you if you want to create a permanent Digital ID. You can ignore that message.

5. If necessary, select a browser preference, and then enter your first name, last name, and e-mail address into the correct text boxes. Then, if necessary, click the Yes option button to include additional information.

6. Select your country from the list box. Then enter your five-digit Zip code if appropriate, and your birthday (in the format mmddyy) into the correct text boxes. (*Note*: Double-check your entries to make sure they are in the correct format. If you made a mistake, correct it. Otherwise, a dialog box that you cannot close might open. If this happens, close your browser to continue, and then repeat the steps. If you cannot close the browser, reboot your computer.) Click the appropriate gender option button.

7. Scroll down the form and then read the instructions for creating a challenge phrase. Enter an appropriate phrase into the Enter Challenge Phrase text box.

8. Click the "I'd like to test drive a 60-day trial Digital ID for free" option button to select it.

9. Do *not* enter any billing information. (Ignore the Encryption Strength text box.)

10. Scroll down the page and read the subscriber agreement, and then click the Accept button to submit your application to VeriSign. Click the OK button to accept your e-mail ID or click the Cancel button to change it.

    Note: If you are using Navigator, a Generate A Private Key dialog box opens. Click the OK button to continue. Next, a Setting Up Your Communicator Password dialog box opens. Type a password of eight characters or more in the Password text box. Type the same password in the Try it again to confirm text box, and then click the OK button.

    Note: If you are using Internet Explorer, click the OK button to confirm your e-mail address or click the Cancel button to reenter it, if necessary.

11. Within 20 minutes, you will receive an e-mail response from VeriSign. Use your e-mail program to open the message. Follow the instructions in VeriSign's e-mail message to copy your Digital ID PIN and paste it into a Web page to which you are directed at VeriSign's site. Do this very carefully. It is best to copy/paste the Digital ID PIN rather than trying to retype it.

12. Follow the instructions to enter and install your new Digital ID. (Use the Securing your e-mail link on the Online Companion page for Case Problem 2 for more information about installing your new Digital ID, if necessary.)

    Note: If you are using Navigator, a Password Entry dialog box opens. Type the same password you typed in Step 10 into the text box, and then click the OK button.

13. Print the What Do You Do Next? page, and then follow its instructions to associate your digital ID with your e-mail address. The processes differ depending on which e-mail program you are using.

14. View your digital ID. (*Hint*: If you are using Outlook Express, click Tools on the menu bar, click Accounts, click the Mail tab, select your mail account, click the Properties button, click the Security tab, click the Select button, select your certificate, and then click the View Certificate button. If you are using Netscape Messenger, click the Security icon on the toolbar. In the Security Info window, click the Yours link in the left frame. Select your name in the These are your certificates list box, and then click the View button.)

15. With your certificate displayed, press the Print Screen key to capture a screen shot of your certificate in the active window. Click the Start button on the taskbar, point to Programs, point to Accessories, and then click WordPad. Click Edit on the menu bar, and then click Paste to paste your screen shot in the WordPad document. Click the Print button on the WordPad toolbar to print the document. Close WordPad without saving your document.

16. Send your instructor an e-mail message with your new digital ID. Enter your e-mail address in the CC text box to send a copy of the message to yourself. Type a short message, such as "I got my VeriSign digital ID," and then send the message.

17. Retrieve your new messages. Examine the message that you sent and open its certificate.

18. Close your browser, e-mail program, and your dial-up connection, if necessary.

Case 3. Grundies' Flowers   Sherri Grundies opened a flower store seven years ago in a local mall. Now she wants to expand her business to the Internet. Similar to most online stores, she will accept money orders, checks, and major credit cards as payment for goods and services. Sherri also wants to use the commerce site to collect information about the site's browsers and customers. Sherri wants to create and post a privacy policy on the Web site that tells its visitors what information the site is collecting and how Grundies' Flowers will use it. She will place a prominent link on her home page the privacy policy so that customers who are concerned about how the store will use their personal information can read the privacy statement. She has hired you to advise her about how to phrase her Web site's privacy statement. Your first task is to view the policy statements on other Web sites and to use these statements as samples before drafting the privacy statement for Sherri's approval.

1. Start your Web browser, and then go to the Online Companion page by entering the URL http://www.course.com/NewPerspectives/EC in the appropriate location of your Web browser. Click the Tutorial 4 link, and then click the Case Problems link. Click the Proflowers.com link for Case Problem 3 and wait while your browser loads the Proflowers home page.

2. Locate and click the About Us link in the left panel of the home page. Scroll to the bottom of the About Proflowers.com page, locate the Privacy Policy heading and read its contents, and then click the privacy policy link in the Privacy Policy paragraph to view the full privacy policy.

3. Read the Proflowers.com privacy policy, and then use your browser's Print button to print the page.

4. Write a short answer to each of these questions:

   ■ What information does Proflowers collect?

   ■ Does Proflowers collect information from customers? How does Proflowers define a customer?

■ How does Proflowers respond to a flower recipient's request to know who sent them flowers?

5. Return to the Online Companion, right-click the Dell.com link to open the shortcut menu, click Open in New Window, and then wait while your browser loads the Dell Computer home page.

6. Scroll to the bottom of Dell's home page, and then click the Online Privacy Practices link (it appears in very small type).

7. Read the Dell's Online Policies page, and then use your browser's Print button to print the page.

8. Write the answers to these questions about Dell's site:

   ■ Is Dell a member of the BBB Online Privacy Program? Can you tell if it is a member by looking at the Dell.com home page?

   ■ Does Dell collect information from kids at its DellKids Web site?

   ■ In a few areas of the Dell Web site, Dell asks users to provide additional information. List four examples of when Dell might request additional information.

9. Locate the hyperlink to an e-mail address on the Privacy and Data Security page and click it. (If a dialog box opens and displays a message that your e-mail address has not been specified, ask your instructor or technical support person for help.) When your e-mail program opens, type *privacy* on the Subject line and send the message. Dell will respond with information about its privacy and information usage guidelines. Print the e-mail message you receive from Dell.

10. Close the Dell browser window.

11. Return to the Online Companion, click the Cisco.com link, and then wait while your browser loads the Cisco home page.

12. Scroll to the bottom of the home page, and then click the Privacy Statement link.

13. Read the Cisco Online Privacy Statement page, and then use your browser's Print button to print the page.

14. Write the answers to these questions about Cisco's site:

   ■ Is Cisco a member of the BBB Online Privacy Program?

   ■ List the types of information that Cisco collects from its Web visitors.

   ■ Do you have to allow cookies to be stored on your computer in order to view Cisco Web pages?

15. Close your browser and close your dial-up connection, if necessary.

Case 4. Radical Surfboard Designs   Jon Sandy is Radical Surfboard Designs' chief board designer and shaper. He is also an accomplished artist who has designed some very popular surfing logos for shirts and surfboards. Among his most treasured designs is one he designed for a board owned by a surfer who was a scientist with an advanced degree in biology. For that client, Jon designed a colorful chain that resembled a strand of DNA. The idea caught on and surfers from all over the western United States began asking Jon to create custom surfboard designs for their boards. Seeing an opportunity to open his business to a larger market, Jon opened an online store containing samples of his logos and designs. He scanned some of his popular designs and saved them in JPEG formats in both thumbnail and full-screen sizes. Jon is concerned that visitors to his Web site could download his graphics and then use them in their own surf shop designs without giving Jon credit, or royalties, for licensing his work. Help Jon learn more about how to protect his intellectual property.

1. Start your Web browser, and then go to the Online Companion page by entering the URL http://www.course.com/NewPerspectives/EC in the appropriate location of your Web browser. Click the Tutorial 4 link, and then click the Case Problems link. Click the Stealthencrypt.com link and wait while your browser opens the Stealthencrypt home page.

2. Click the About button on the left side of the page. Read the page that opens, and then use your browser's Print button to print the page.

3. Review the page and answer these questions:

   - What is the name of the encryption algorithm that Stealthencrypt.com uses to protect information?
   - Is software available that can remove some watermarks?
   - Where in a graphic or other digital property does Stealthencrypt.com place its encrypted watermark information?

4. Click the Free button on the left side of the page. The Stealth Encryption FREE Page opens. Use your browser's Print button to print the page.

5. Close any open dialog boxes, return to the Online Companion for Case Problem 4, and then click the About.com link.

6. Click the Techniques For Data Hiding link. An article from the IBM Systems Journal opens.

7. Right-click the ASCII link on the line that begins "This article" to open the shortcut menu, and then click Open in New Window to display the article in text format in a separate browser window.

8. Read the article, and then print the first three pages of the article.

9. Close your browser and close your dial-up connection, if necessary.

10. Write 250 words about steganography and how it can identify copyrighted digital information for Jon's designs.

QUICK CHECK ANSWERS

Session 4.1

1. Cookie information is usually accurate because it is collected by software. An individual can falsify Web site registration information and thus obtaining this information poses no particular privacy threat.

2. No, U.S. copyright laws protect the expression but not the information. In other words, the wording that an author uses in a copyrighted document is protected, but the facts that the wording conveys are not protected. For example, if you write "…protecting credit card transactions is the low-hanging fruit of electronic commerce security," someone else could not use your exact words without risking copyright violation. However, someone could rephrase your expression as "…securing credit card transactions from prying eyes is relatively simple and profitable…" without risk of copyright violation.

3. Using someone's intellectual property, such as a Dilbert cartoon, without permission of the copyright holder denies the copyright holder of royalties and his right to determine when and where his intellectual property (his cartoons) will appear.

4. secrecy violation

5. While a worm is a type of virus, it has the additional ability to automatically spread from host to host using the Internet. In other words, worms can travel on their own. Viruses can only travel when someone sends a program containing a virus to another person or manually places the program containing the virus on a disk or computer.

6. integrity threat

Session 4.2

1. Any one of the following: disclose whether users may opt out of releasing their information for use by third parties, display the trustmark on its home page (or the same page that discloses the site's general privacy policy), explain exactly what data the Web site is gathering, summarize the site's general data gathering practices, refrain from monitoring personal communications to third parties except as required by law, adhere to its stated privacy policy as stated on its home page, adhere to its privacy policies even after the Web site chooses to halt its TRUSTe membership, and agree to cooperate with TRUSTe Web site monitoring and auditing activities

2. digital watermark

3. public-key encryption (asymmetric encryption)

4. certification authorities (CAs)

5. Secure Sockets Layer (SSL)

6. hash function; digest

OBJECTIVES

In this tutorial you will:

- Learn about the different types of online payment options

- Investigate the use of online gift certificates for consumers and merchants

- Examine how some merchants use rewards to encourage people to visit and purchase items from their Web sites

- Examine how online credit cards are processed and identify the parties involved in these transactions

- Identify different types of electronic cash systems

- Explore the differences between smart cards and stored-value cards, and investigate how to use them

- Install and use an electronic wallet

ELECTRONIC PAYMENT SYSTEMS

Accepting and Processing Customer Payments

CASE

The Glass Gallery

The Glass Gallery is a small, stained glass arts and crafts center located in Lincoln, Nebraska. Owned by Mike King, the Glass Gallery employs Mike's wife, Charlotte, and two part-time professionals. Last year, the store had annual gross sales of approximately $400,000, and sales have been climbing slowly since the store opened in 1997. The Glass Gallery sells to trade and retail customers, but most of its sales are to retail customers. It sells whole and half sheets of stained glass, solder, glass-working tools, stained glass books, lamp parts, copper foil, lead came (the lead between the glass in many leaded glass panels), beveled glass pieces of various shapes, and other glass craft items. Besides selling stained glass products, the Glass Gallery also conducts inexpensive stained glass classes. The average cost of a class is $200 per person for five hours of instruction. Mike offers classes in introductory stained glass, intermediate stained glass, advanced Tiffany glass panel techniques, and glass beveling.

By far, the Glass Gallery's largest income source is the many stained glass panels that customers commission Mike to design and create. Mike and his artisans have produced some wonderful stained glass panels for churches, restaurants, and shopping malls in Nebraska and as far away as California. Panels of moderate complexity cost as little as $100 per square foot, and more complex, intricate panels can cost up to $300 per square foot.

Mike recognizes that business has been good and that the cost of doing business in Lincoln is low compared to larger U.S. cities; however, although Lincoln is near the center of the United States, it certainly is not the center of the art and stained glass "world." Almost no one from outside the Lincoln area calls or visits Mike's store. Worse yet, few potential customers realize that Mike's store produces some of the finest glass panels in the United States. To expand business, Mike needs to expand his reach to markets beyond Lincoln. He believes that the time is right to create a wider presence by launching a Web site.

A Web site, he reasons, will provide his store with the larger presence it needs to grow. At first, he wants to sell only a few items. His primary goals are to advertise his custom glass panels and to promote his monthly newsletter, which provides information about his work and topics of interest to people who enjoy stained glass.

Mike's two major concerns about the Web site that he has asked you to develop for him are issues related to security and accepting payment. He wants you to learn more about accepting electronic payments and to see what is needed to connect the payment acceptance mechanism to his forthcoming Web site.

SESSION 5.1

In this session, you will study the different types of electronic payments that merchants might accept at online stores. An increasing number of merchants are accepting electronic gift certificates and electronic checks. In addition, some merchants are giving rewards, which are redeemable for merchandise, to customers who visit their Web sites. Almost all online merchants accept credit cards. You will learn about the advantages and disadvantages of credit cards, and investigate the process of authorizing and settling credit card transactions. Finally, you will learn about merchant accounts and their role in online transactions.

Introduction to Electronic Payment Systems

Huge amounts of money are tendered every hour on the Internet. Money is deposited and managed electronically by the many online brokerages managing assets worth more than $900 billion. This number will swell to more than $3 trillion by 2003, according to **Jupiter Communications,** a firm that conducts market research and analysis on the consumer online industry. For example, each day, Dell Computer takes in more than $10 million on its Web site. Americans alone will spend more than $41 billion online in 2002, according to a *PC Magazine* article. Analysts predict that 183 million people are expected to shop online by 2003, and they will likely demand a rich variety of payment options to satisfy their diverse needs and life styles. Existing systems are being improved to handle these huge and growing transaction volumes.

Currently, the most popular way to pay for online purchases is to use credit cards, followed by electronic cash, checking account withdrawal, and ATM or debit cards. (**Online purchases** occur on the Internet. **Offline purchases** do not occur on the Internet—these purchases occur in physical stores.) In a recent survey, Jupiter Communications noted that 65% of online shoppers prefer to use credit cards, 13% prefer to have money withdrawn from their checking accounts, another 13% prefer to use electronic cash, and 8% use an ATM or debit card for online purchases.

Contrast these online preference percentages to the offline payment preferences of shoppers in physical stores: cash payments account for 55%, check payments account for 29%, and credit cards account for only 15%. Of all offline purchases, 12% are for less that $10, which may account for some of the popularity of cash. Typically, shoppers prefer to pay cash for small purchases instead of writing a check. Furthermore, few merchants will accept a credit card as payment for purchases totaling less than $10 because the cost of processing small credit card transactions is a high percentage of the total transaction cost, which therefore reduces or eliminates the merchant's profit for small purchases.

One thing is clear to everyone considering or using electronic payments systems: Electronic payments are far cheaper than mailing out paper invoices and later processing received payments. David Samuel, vice president of customer care at BEC Energy's Boston Edison (with more than 640,000 customers), says that using electronic billing and payment systems is a win-win situation: They are convenient for customers and save the company a lot of money. Estimates indicate that the cost of billing one person varies between $1 and $1.50. Sending bills and receiving payments over the Internet promises to drop the billing/paying cost to an average of 50 cents per bill. The total saved is huge when you multiply the unit cost by the number of customers that could use electronic payment methods. In the case of BEC Energy, the company could save over 50 cents per customer, or $325,000 for every billing cycle. In addition, electronic payments eliminate cutting trees for paper and reduce pollution from paper mills. In one illustration, John Dodge, a columnist for the Wall Street Journal Interactive edition, wrote "GTE sends out 53.5 million bills annually, consuming 1.6 million pounds of paper. That's 2,073 trees."

An online merchant might accept a credit or charge card, debit card, ATM card, certified check, money order, or COD (collect on delivery) as payment for purchases made at its Web site. Each of these payment types has advantages and disadvantages. In most cases, the advantage of each payment type is that payment is guaranteed for the merchant; in other words, there is little risk of not receiving funds when a consumer uses a credit card or a certified check as payment. On the other hand, online merchants also lose a small percentage (usually 1 to 3%, or a minimum of 20 cents) for every credit card transaction that they accept; this processing fee erodes the merchants' profits. Because of these disadvantages, online merchants are starting to use alternate forms of payment that lower their processing fees and risks of nonpayment. Consumers also view using these forms of payment on the Web with advantages and disadvantages. Some consumers worry about sending their credit card numbers and other personal information to online merchants. Fortunately, some new alternate forms of payment, such as scrip and electronic checks, which are described in the following sections, address some of these merchant and consumer concerns.

Using Scrip for Online Purchases

Scrip, also known as **server scrip**, is a form of electronic cash that is stored on your computer and that you obtain by depositing money at a scrip vendor's server. Scrip is the equivalent of a paper gift certificate. You can spend scrip just like cash to purchase an item at any merchant that accepts your particular brand of scrip. Currently, the number of online stores that accepts various types of scrip is small but increasing. Flooz and Beenz are two popular brands of scrip.

Flooz

Flooz is scrip that you purchase using a credit card and either use yourself or send to a recipient. Flooz is redeemable for purchases at any merchant that accepts it. The Flooz exchange rate is one Flooz equals one dollar, and Flooz.com does not charge a service fee to purchase it. You mail the scrip, along with an electronic greeting card (an **e-card**), to the recipient, who can spend his or her Flooz at online stores such as Proflowers.com, Nirvana Chocolates, Books.com, and Starbucks. Flooz earns a commission, which is paid by the merchant, when a consumer spends scrip at an online store. A merchant installs software that communicates with the Flooz.com servers and pays Flooz.com a commission. Consumers cannot exchange Flooz for cash; however, they can use it to pay for goods and services at participating merchants.

Because many of the Glass Gallery's customers are glassmakers by hobby, Mike wants you to investigate whether Flooz might be a way of providing his customers with gift ideas or a way of purchasing small-valued goods for themselves. Mike is intrigued by Flooz and wants to consider offering it as one of the ways to purchase some items at the Glass Gallery's online store. He wants you to investigate how consumers purchase and use Flooz, and where Flooz is accepted.

To learn how Flooz works:

1. Start your Web browser, and then go to the Online Companion by entering the URL **http://www.course.com/NewPerspectives/EC** in the appropriate location of your Web browser. Click the **Tutorial 5** link, and then click the **Session 5.1** link. Click the **Flooz** link and wait while your browser loads the Flooz home page shown in Figure 5-1. The Flooz home page contains links for sending Flooz, identifying merchants that accept it, and managing your Flooz account.

Figure 5-1	FLOOZ HOME PAGE

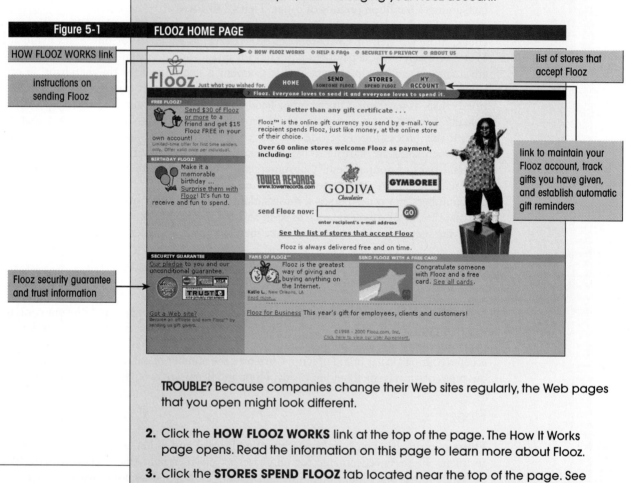

HOW FLOOZ WORKS link

instructions on sending Flooz

list of stores that accept Flooz

link to maintain your Flooz account, track gifts you have given, and establish automatic gift reminders

Flooz security guarantee and trust information

TROUBLE? Because companies change their Web sites regularly, the Web pages that you open might look different.

2. Click the **HOW FLOOZ WORKS** link at the top of the page. The How It Works page opens. Read the information on this page to learn more about Flooz.

3. Click the **STORES SPEND FLOOZ** tab located near the top of the page. See Figure 5-2. Scroll down the page, noting which merchants accept Flooz. Notice that the name of each merchant that accepts Flooz is formatted as a hyperlink, which opens a page with detailed information about what you can purchase from the merchant. You note for Mike that the Art & Culture category might be a good place to advertise the Glass Gallery.

Figure 5-2

ONLINE STORES THAT ACCEPT FLOOZ

STORES SPEND
FLOOZ link

SECURITY & PRIVACY
link

click a store's links to
open a page about the
merchant

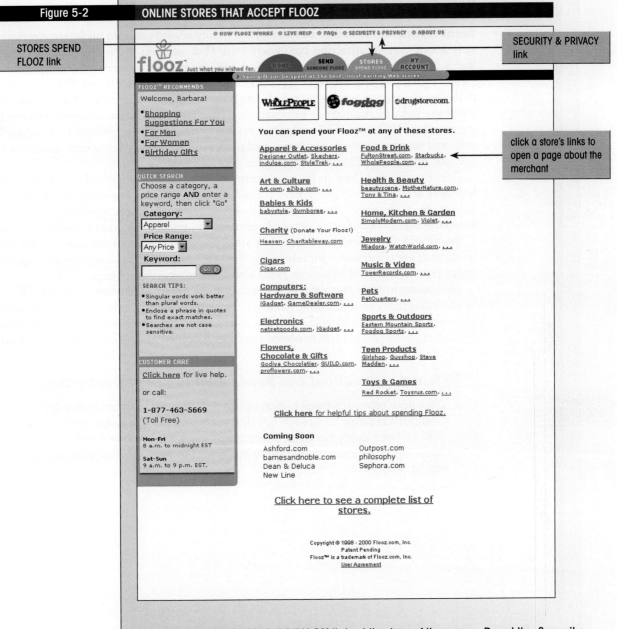

4. Click the **SECURITY & PRIVACY** link at the top of the page. Read the Security Guarantee/Privacy page that opens. Notice that when you sign up for a Flooz account, you must provide some information about yourself.

The Flooz account procedure seems simple enough. Any Glass Gallery customer who wants either to send or receive Flooz should not have any trouble signing up for a new account. Mike thinks this might be a fun and interesting way to attract customers with items on special sale if they use Flooz scrip.

Beenz

Beenz is a brand of scrip that is marketed as a loyalty reward program for Internet consumers. It is a new way of attracting consumers to a Web site and rewarding them for visiting. Beenz.com has partnered with over 100 Web sites to offer its beenz reward points, which consumers earn for visiting and making purchases at Web sites that offer beenz. Web site members of the beenz program pay browsers in beenz scrip for visiting their sites or for clicking designated site links. Consumers collect beenz and later redeem it for merchandise at participating merchant Web sites. The program is relatively young, yet over 400,000 consumers have collected beenz, and beenz.com has issued more than 90 million beenz scrip units. On average, one beenz is worth approximately one cent.

Beenz.com is not alone in the marketing loyalty program. Other industry giants such as **MyPoints** and **America Online** have started similar consumer reward programs to attract visitors to their sites. There are so many rewards programs springing up that the **RewardsPrograms.com** site is devoted exclusively to tracking Internet rewards programs.

Beenz and Flooz both have a goal of attracting customers to Web sites. Unlike Flooz, beenz units are not available for purchase—they are rewards for consumers to use to purchase items. However, anyone who owns Flooz scrip can exchange it for beenz.

Mike wants to see if beenz might be another good way to attract customers to his Web site by rewarding them for visiting. He has heard from other online merchants that beenz uses banner advertising to promote stores that give and redeem beenz scrip and thinks providing beenz rewards might be another way to obtain some much needed advertising for his online store.

To learn more about the beenz loyalty reward program:

1. Click your browser's **Back** button or use its history list to return to the Online Companion page for Session 5.1, and then click the **Beenz** link and wait while your browser loads the initial Beenz page. Click the Choose Your Country list arrow, and then click your country in the list. The Beenz home page shown in Figure 5-3 opens.

Figure 5-3	BEENZ HOME PAGE

join beenz by clicking this link

TELL ME MORE link

existing members sign in here

earn beenz rewards at these sites (your list might be different)

check your beenz account balance

spend beenz at these merchants' sites

2. Click the **TELL ME MORE** link in the Welcome to beenz box located near the top of the page.

3. Click the **sign me up** link to open the registration page. See Figure 5-4. Note the information required to open a beenz account. (*Note:* You will not actually sign up for a beenz account.)

Figure 5-4	BEENZ REGISTRATION PAGE

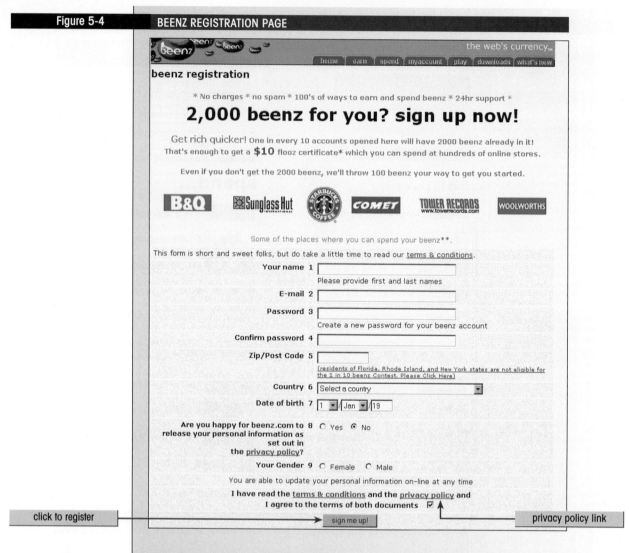

4. Click the **privacy policy** link at the bottom of the page. Scan the page to see how beenz.com collects information about its account holders and what beenz.com does with that information. You will need to give this information to Mike, as it will be an important factor as he considers using beenz at the Glass Gallery Web site.

Using **Electronic Checks for Online Purchases**

An **electronic check** is the digital equivalent of a conventional paper check. An electronic check works like any paper check or wire transfer drawn against a conventional checking account. Like conventional checking accounts, electronic checks are backed by money on deposit in an existing bank account. If you have a conventional checking account, you do not need to open another checking account to write an electronic check. Electronic checks clear through an electronic maze in the same way as conventional checks. All checks eventually pass through the **Automated Clearing House (ACH) Network**, where checks from consumers are credited to merchant accounts and deducted from consumer checking accounts. **NACHA**, a not-for-profit trade association, develops operating rules and business practices for the ACH Network and for other forms of electronic payments, including the electronic check issuers **CheckFree Corporation** and **NetCheque**.

Because banks shoulder most of the costs to issue paper checks, consumers have no real incentive to switch to electronic checks. However, electronic checks are fast becoming a popular payment mechanism in the business-to-business electronic commerce segment. Because Mike uses paper checks to pay for supplies from other businesses, he is very interested in learning how to use the Internet to send electronic checks. He asks you to find more information about some electronic check issuers.

CheckFree

One of the major electronic check issuers is CheckFree. CheckFree offers a receipt system for electronic bills and provides consumers with the capability to use electronic checks at merchant sites. CheckFree earns a profit by collecting interest on the money deposited by consumers and merchants into its accounts, and by charging a transaction fee for each electronic check it processes. CheckFree supplies software to its users that lets them pay their bills with electronic checks. Figure 5-5 shows a Web page from a demonstration available on the CheckFree Web site. The figure shows a check in the process of being constructed and paid by an online consumer. The CheckFree bill payment demonstration walks you through the process, but your browser must have the Macromedia Flash plug-in to work properly. (You can download this plug-in from the Online Companion by clicking the **Macromedia Flash** link.) If your browser has Macromedia Flash installed, you can click the "see a demo" link on the CheckFree home page to view a five-minute animated demonstration of CheckFree.

Figure 5-5	CHECKFREE ELECTRONIC CHECK DEMONSTRATION PAGE

Clickshare

Clickshare is an electronic cash system aimed at magazine and newspaper publishers. Clickshare's technology has occasionally been miscast as a micropayment-only system. A **micropayment** is a payment of less than one dollar that you might use to purchase a single track on a music album, a newspaper article, or a complicated literature search. The ability to make micropayments is only one of Clickshare's features. Users with an Internet service provider (ISP) that supports Clickshare are automatically registered with Clickshare. When users click links leading to other sites that are registered with Clickshare, they can make purchases on those other sites without having to register with Clickshare again. Clickshare keeps track of transactions and bills the user's ISP. The ISP, which already has an account relationship with the user, then bills the user for his purchases. Another feature of Clickshare is that it tracks where a user travels on the Internet. This feature has significant value to advertisers and marketers that want to measure audience preferences. The micro-payment capability is, according to the company, a byproduct of the core functionality of tracking identified users. Clickshare tracks users without relying on cookies or other code stored on a user's computer. Clickshare claims to be the only company that can provide information about user preferences. Figure 5-6 shows Clickshare's home page.

Figure 5-6   **CLICKSHARE'S HOME PAGE**

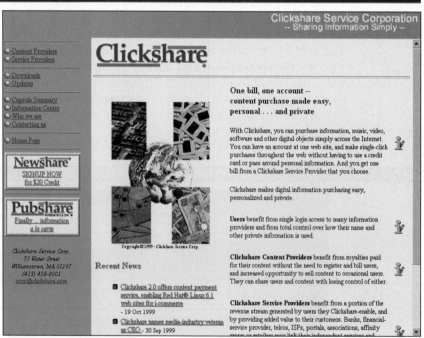

CyberCash

CyberCash combines features from cash and checks. CyberCash offers Internet payment options, including credit card, micropayment, and check payment services. Since 1995, CyberCash has been securely servicing credit cards over the Internet by linking a merchant's commerce site to credit card processors providing authorization for credit purchases in real time. (**Real time** refers to processing immediately. Transactions not occurring in real time incur delays and may be too late to reject a transaction if there are insufficient funds to pay for it.) CyberCash provides micropayment services through its CyberCoin service. Customers store their CyberCoins in a CyberCash wallet, which is a software storage mechanism located on the consumer's computer. PayNow is the electronic check service available from CyberCash. With PayNow, customers can make payments to CyberCash directly from their checking accounts. Both businesses and consumers can use the PayNow service for their online purchases.

A key to wide acceptance of any electronic payment system is that it must be cost-effective, securely implemented, and easy for consumers to use. Consumers are familiar with fulfilling monthly payment obligations using paper checks. Merchants, particularly offline ones, have preferred checks to other payment forms because checks are the least expensive way to receive payment.

Electronic checks fulfill the same function as paper checks, but they are used on the Internet. Subscribing to an electronic check service, such as CyberCash's PayNow, allows merchants to accept and process electronic checks on their own Web sites. Another CyberCash software product, called CashRegister, provides a connection to a merchant's bank. That software implements depositing electronic checks and provides information needed by the merchant to update its own accounts receivable system. (**Accounts receivable** contains information about money owed to the merchant or company, which is money that should flow into the merchant's account.) You decide to take a closer look at this well-known Internet electronic payment service organization. You are particularly interested in the PayNow system. Mike might change his site after one year to accept electronic checks, so you want to be ready when Mike decides to take another look at electronic checks.

To learn more about CyberCash:

1. Click your browser's **Back** button or use its history list to return to the Online Companion page for Session 5.1, and then click the **CyberCash** link and wait while your browser loads the CyberCash home page.

2. Click the **Billers** link in the upper-right corner of the earth picture. A CyberCash Billers information page opens.

3. Click the **6 Step Diagram** link in the Related Links section. The CyberCash, 6 Steps page opens. This page explains how a consumer submits an electronic check and how CyberCash processes it. See Figure 5-7. Read the information on this page to understand how electronic checks are processed.

Figure 5-7 **CYBERCASH ELECTRONIC CHECK PROCESSING DIAGRAM**

Example Billers link

6 Steps of a PayNow transaction:

1. Bill is presented to user - After verification of user (user name and password), the biller's Web server gathers the bill detail and presents the customer the bill.

2. Bill payment - Customers review and analyze their bill. When finished and ready to pay, they fill in the amount he or she would like to pay and presses the "Pay" button. Transaction detail is transparently sent via the Merchant Connection Kit (at the biller's Web server) to the CyberCash CashRegister.

3. Posting transaction to ACH file - At the CashRegister, the transaction detail is unwrapped and decrypted. Then the routing number is verified using a modulus 10 checksum logarithm and the information is posted to the biller's ACH flat file.

4. Response returned to MCK - Success or failure response of the verification and posting of the transaction information is sent by the CashRegister back to the biller's MCK.

5. Customer receipt - Based on the response back from the CashRegister, the MCK will spawn a receipt or failure message to the customer. These messages can be customized and altered with specific messages the biller would like the consumer to view.

6. Transmission of ACH file - A few minutes before the biller's determined ACH window, the transaction file is formatted into NACHA format specifications. The information is then sent to the biller's ODFI via the ACH network for account settlement.

CyberCash, CyberCoin, PayNow and the CyberCash logo are trademarks of CyberCash, Inc. ©1998 CyberCash, Inc. All rights reserved.
Legal Information -- Contact: info@cybercash.com.

4. Click the **Example Billers** link on the left side of the page. A page opens with links to several companies that use the CyberCash direct billing system, PayNow.

Using **Credit Cards for Online Purchases**

Credit cards are by far the most popular form of online payments for consumers. Credit cards are widely accepted by merchants around the world and provide assurances for both the consumer and the merchant. A consumer is protected by an automatic 30-day period in which he can dispute an online credit card purchase. A merchant has a high degree of confidence that a credit card can be safely accepted from an unseen purchaser. Paying for online purchases with a credit card is just as easy as in an offline store. Merchants that already accept credit cards in an offline store can accept them immediately for online payment because they have a merchant account. Online purchases require an extra degree of security not required in offline purchases. Because online transactions pass from the consumer to the merchant over the Internet, which is an open and highly vulnerable network, merchants must work to protect sensitive information, such as credit card numbers. Additional software, such as the Secure Sockets Layer (SSL) protocol, protects transactions in transit from being viewed by unauthorized parties.

Anyone who has made a purchase on the Web knows that using a credit card to pay for purchases is easy. Most people have concluded that conducting credit card transactions over the Internet, when accompanied by built-in safeguards such as secure servers, is as safe as presenting a credit card to a merchant in person. Most online shoppers are fairly comfortable that merchants are doing their best to protect consumers' credit card information.

Mike also has purchased goods and services on the Web using his personal credit card. He is certain that he wants to offer to his online customers the convenience of paying for purchases at the Glass Gallery with their credit cards. However, he is uncertain what processes, if any, are different for handling credit card transactions over the Internet. Furthermore, his store in Lincoln accepts only cash and checks written on local banks. The Glass Gallery does not have a merchant account yet, so it is not able to accept credit cards. Mike hopes that he can set up credit card processing capabilities simultaneously for his online and offline stores. He asks you to determine what is needed so the Glass Gallery can accept credit cards at both of his stores.

Currently, online shoppers use credit and charge cards for a majority of their Internet purchases. A **credit card** is a card that has a preset spending limit based on the user's credit limit. A user can pay the balance of the credit card or a minimum amount for each billing period. Credit card issuers charge interest on any unpaid balances. A **charge card**, such as American Express, carries no preset spending limit, and the entire amount charged to the card is due at the end of the month. Charge cards do not involve lines of credit and do not accumulate interest charges. Because the distinction between credit cards and charge cards is unimportant in the discussion of processing credit and charge cards in this tutorial, the term *credit card* will refer to both types of cards.

To process credit card orders, a merchant first must set up a merchant account. For an online merchant, accepting credit cards avoids the additional expense and trouble of paper, which is part of invoicing systems, unless it uses a business-to-business electronic system of invoicing and payment. The elaborate series of actions associated with using a credit card are often transparent to the consumer. Several groups are involved: the merchant, the merchant's bank, the customer, the customer's bank, and the credit card company that issued the customer's credit card. All of these people and organizations must work together in order for customers' charges to be credited to merchants' accounts (and vice versa when a customer receives a credit for returned goods).

Advantages and Disadvantages of Credit Cards

Credit cards have several features that make them an attractive and popular choice both with consumers and merchants in online and offline transactions. For merchants, credit cards provide fraud protection. When a merchant accepts credit cards for online payment—called **card not present** because the merchant's location and the purchaser's location are different—they can authenticate and authorize purchases using a credit card processing network. For consumers, credit cards are advantageous because the Consumer Credit Protection Act limits the cardholder's liability to $50 if the card is used fraudulently. Once the cardholder notifies the card's issuer of the card theft, the cardholder's liability ends. Frequently, the credit card's issuer waives the $50 consumer payment when a stolen card is used to purchase goods online or offline. Perhaps the biggest advantage of using credit cards is their worldwide acceptance. You can pay for goods with credit cards anywhere in the world, and the currency conversion, if needed, is automatic. For online transactions, credit cards are particularly advantageous. When a consumer reaches the electronic checkout, she enters the credit card's number and her shipping and billing information in the appropriate fields to complete the transaction. The consumer does not need any special hardware or software to complete the transaction.

Credit cards have very few disadvantages, but they do have one when compared to cash. Credit card service companies charge merchants per-transaction fees and monthly processing fees. These fees can add up, but online and offline merchants view them as a cost of doing business. Any merchant that does not accept credit cards for purchases is probably losing significant sales because of it; a huge percentage of online sales today are paid by credit cards. The consumer pays no direct fees for using credit cards, but the prices of goods and services are slightly higher than they would be in an environment free of credit cards altogether.

Applying for a Merchant Account

A **merchant bank** or **acquiring bank** is a bank that does business with online and offline merchants that accept credit cards. To process credit cards for Internet transactions, an online merchant must set up a merchant account. A **merchant account** is a numbered account into which accumulated credit card sales' totals are deposited. When the merchant's bank acquires the sales records, it credits their value to the merchant's account. A business must provide a potential merchant bank certain business information before a merchant bank will provide an account through which the business can process credit card transactions. Because online merchants cannot check a credit card holder's photo identification when accepting a credit card for an online transaction, online businesses face a slightly higher fraud risk than offline merchants. Classified as **MOTO (Mail Order/Telephone Order)** by acquiring banks, as a consequence, online-only merchants usually pay higher credit card processing fees than offline merchants. Typically, a new business owner must supply a business plan, details about existing bank accounts, and a business and personal credit history when applying for a merchant account. The merchant bank must be confident that the merchant has a good prospect of staying in business, as it wants to minimize its risk by working with a well-focused store with a bright future. An online business that appears disorganized is less attractive to a merchant bank than a well-organized online business.

Mike wants to apply for a merchant account for the Glass Gallery. He wants you to find out how to apply for a merchant account using the Web. In addition, he wants to know what fees his store will incur for accepting credit cards. You begin your research for Mike. Because Mike is considering using a commerce service provider for his Web site, you decide to investigate how a commerce service provider processes applications for its members' online stores.

To learn about applying for a merchant account to process credit cards:

1. Click your browser's **Back** button or use its history list to return to the Online Companion page for Session 5.1, and then click the **Yahoo! Store** link and wait while your browser loads the Yahoo! Store home page.

2. Click the **How it Works** link in the Getting Started section.

3. Click the **Merchant Account** link in the Related Links section on the left side of the page. The Online Processing page opens. See Figure 5-8.

Figure 5-8	YAHOO! STORE ONLINE PROCESSING PAGE

How it Works link

Merchant Account link

click to apply for a merchant account

4. Click the **apply** link in the second paragraph of the Online Processing section. The Merchant Account Application page opens. Scroll down the page to the section titled "How much does it cost?" Notice that Yahoo! Store charges a one-time setup fee, a monthly service fee, a per-transaction fee, and a percentage of each transaction's total.

Note: To continue, you must have a Yahoo! Store. If you do not have a 10-day temporary Yahoo! Store, read the remaining steps without completing them at the computer. If you do have a Yahoo! Store, which you created in Tutorial 3, then continue with Step 5.

5. Log in to your Yahoo! Store by clicking the **Sign In** link at the top of the page, and then enter your Yahoo! ID and password into the appropriate text boxes. Click the **Sign In** button to open your store. The Yahoo! Store: Create your own secure online store page opens.

6. Click your store name link in the Manage My Store section on the left side of the page. Your Yahoo! Store Management page opens. See Figure 5-9.

Figure 5-9	YAHOO! STORE MANAGEMENT PAGE

YAHOO! Store

Edit
Simple
Regular
Advanced

Process
Orders
Requests

Statistics
Per Page
References
Searches
Shopping Searches
Graphs
Click Trails
Reports
Repeats

Order Settings
Order Form
Fax/Email
Shipment Status
Pay Methods
Ship Methods
Ship Rates
Tax Rates
Foreign Orders
Test
Auctions Checkout
Publish Order Settings+

Site Settings
Account Info
Open for Business
Access
Preferences
Domain Names
Email
Customer Access
Registration
Ratings

your store name appears here

Promote
Create Links
Track Links
Mailing Lists
Search Engines
Yahoo! Directory
Yahoo! Shopping(NEW!)

Statistics at a Glance (last 120 days)

1,112 Page Views   31.50 Revenue

Customer Ratings
No ratings yet. [Info]

Pay Methods link

consumer page viewing activity—your store's activity levels will be different

Help   User Guide
Go   Feedback | Published Site | Yahoo! Store | Sign out

7. Click the **Pay Methods** link below the Order Settings heading. The Verify your Yahoo! Security page opens.

8. Type your Yahoo! Security Key, and then click the **Enter Secure Area** button to continue. The Payment Methods page opens. See Figure 5-10.

TROUBLE? If you do not have a Security Key, read the remaining steps without completing them at the computer.

Figure 5-10   **YAHOO! STORE PAYMENT METHODS PAGE**

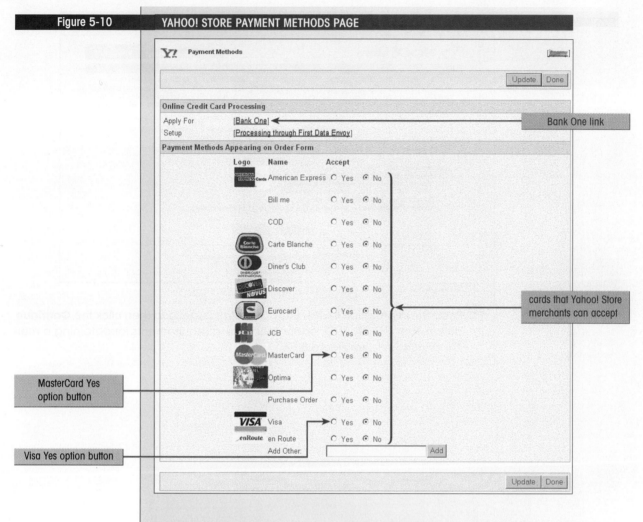

9. Click the **Visa** option button, click the **MasterCard** option button, and then click the **Update** button to update your store's payment choices. The Payment Methods page redisplays and confirms the new choices.

10. Continue the application process by clicking the **Bank One** link in the Online Credit Card Processing section near the top of the page. The Bank One Start Page opens. See Figure 5-11.

Figure 5-11   BANK ONE START PAGE

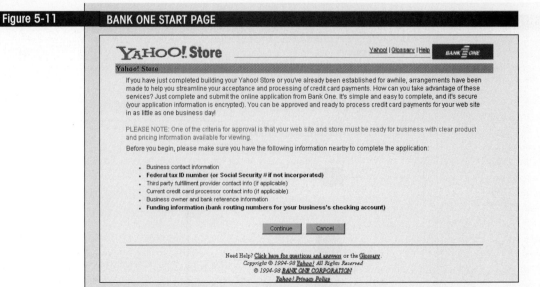

YAHOO! Store   Yahoo! | Glossary | Help   BANK ONE

Yahoo! Store

If you have just completed building your Yahoo! Store or you've already been established for awhile, arrangements have been made to help you streamline your acceptance and processing of credit card payments. How can you take advantage of these services? Just complete and submit the online application from Bank One. It's simple and easy to complete, and it's secure (your application information is encrypted). You can be approved and ready to process credit card payments for your web site in as little as one business day!

PLEASE NOTE: One of the criteria for approval is that your web site and store must be ready for business with clear product and pricing information available for viewing.

Before you begin, please make sure you have the following information nearby to complete the application:

- Business contact information
- **Federal tax ID number (or Social Security # if not incorporated)**
- Third party fulfillment provider contact info (if applicable)
- Current credit card processor contact info (if applicable)
- Business owner and bank reference information
- **Funding information (bank routing numbers for your business's checking account)**

[Continue]   [Cancel]

Need Help? Click here for questions and answers or the Glossary.
Copyright © 1994-98 Yahoo! All Rights Reserved
© 1994-98 BANK ONE CORPORATION
Yahoo! Privacy Policy

11. Read the information on the Bank One Start Page, and then click the **Continue** button. The LOGON PAGE opens, containing requirements for obtaining a merchant account. See Figure 5-12.

Figure 5-12   **BANK ONE REQUIREMENTS**

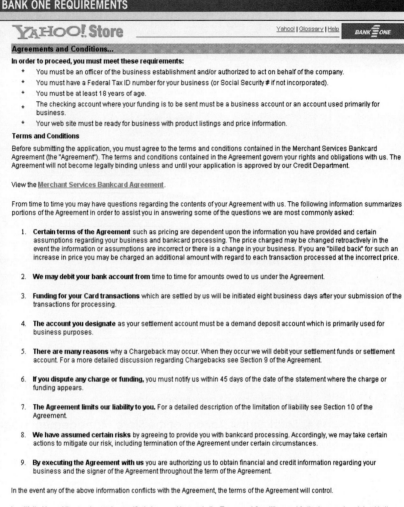

YAHOO! Store   Yahoo! | Glossary | Help   BANK ONE

Agreements and Conditions...

In order to proceed, you must meet these requirements:

* You must be an officer of the business establishment and/or authorized to act on behalf of the company.
* You must have a Federal Tax ID number for your business (or Social Security # if not incorporated).
* You must be at least 18 years of age.
* The checking account where your funding is to be sent must be a business account or an account used primarily for business.
* Your web site must be ready for business with product listings and price information.

Terms and Conditions

Before submitting the application, you must agree to the terms and conditions contained in the Merchant Services Bankcard Agreement (the "Agreement"). The terms and conditions contained in the Agreement govern your rights and obligations with us. The Agreement will not become legally binding unless and until your application is approved by our Credit Department.

View the Merchant Services Bankcard Agreement.

From time to time you may have questions regarding the contents of your Agreement with us. The following information summarizes portions of the Agreement in order to assist you in answering some of the questions we are most commonly asked:

1. **Certain terms of the Agreement** such as pricing are dependent upon the information you have provided and certain assumptions regarding your business and bankcard processing. The price charged may be changed retroactively in the event the information or assumptions are incorrect or there is a change in your business. If you are "billed back" for such an increase in price you may be charged an additional amount with regard to each transaction processed at the incorrect price.

2. **We may debit your bank account from** time to time for amounts owed to us under the Agreement.

3. **Funding for your Card transactions** which are settled by us will be initiated eight business days after your submission of the transactions for processing.

4. **The account you designate** as your settlement account must be a demand deposit account which is primarily used for business purposes.

5. **There are many reasons** why a Chargeback may occur. When they occur we will debit your settlement funds or settlement account. For a more detailed discussion regarding Chargebacks see Section 9 of the Agreement.

6. **If you dispute any charge or funding,** you must notify us within 45 days of the date of the statement where the charge or funding appears.

7. **The Agreement limits our liability to you.** For a detailed description of the limitation of liability see Section 10 of the Agreement.

8. **We have assumed certain risks** by agreeing to provide you with bankcard processing. Accordingly, we may take certain actions to mitigate our risk, including termination of the Agreement under certain circumstances.

9. **By executing the Agreement with us** you are authorizing us to obtain financial and credit information regarding your business and the signer of the Agreement throughout the term of the Agreement.

In the event any of the above information conflicts with the Agreement, the terms of the Agreement will control.

I certify that I meet the requirements specified above and I agree to the Terms and Conditions set forth above and contained in the Merchant Services Bankcard Agreement.

Review what you will need to complete the application in more detail.

I Agree   I Disagree

12. Read the information on the LOGON PAGE, and then click the **I Agree** button to continue the application process. The FDMS LINEAR – GENERAL PAGE opens. See Figure 5-13. This very long page of the form is only one of five pages that you must complete to obtain a merchant account. If you were applying for a merchant account, you would continue by submitting your application. You will not submit an application, so you will click the Cancel button.

Figure 5-13   **BANK ONE MERCHANT APPLICATION PAGE (1 OF 5)**

13. Scroll down the page, and then click the **Cancel** button. The Yahoo! Store Management page redisplays.

14. Scroll to the bottom of the Store Management page, and then click the **Sign out** link to sign out of your store.

15. Close your browser and close your dial-up connection, if necessary.

Bank One is just one of many banks that offers credit card processing services. Before approving a merchant account, Bank One will want to ensure that the Glass Gallery is a good risk. If Bank One approves Mike's application, his store can begin accepting credit card payments immediately.

Payment Acceptance and Processing

Most people are familiar with the use of credit cards in offline stores: When you purchase one or more items, the clerk runs your card through the online payment card terminal and your card account is charged immediately. The process is slightly different on the Internet, but the purchase and charge processes follow the same rules.

Merchants often cannot accept credit card payments to their merchant accounts until the merchants pack and ship the products to the cardholder. In an offline store, you walk out of the store with the purchase in your possession, so charging and shipment occur nearly simultaneously. The steps in a typical online credit card transaction are as follows:

1. Using a secure transmission protocol (Secure Sockets Layer, for example), the cardholder sends his credit card number to the merchant along with his shipping and billing information.

2. The online merchant sends to his merchant's bank an authorization request, which requests that the amount be reserved against the purchaser's credit.

3. The merchant bank sends the request along a network to the bank that issued the cardholder's credit card, called an **issuing bank**.

4. If the cardholder has available credit, then the issuing bank sends back an approval message through the network, thereby authorizing the transaction. However, if the transaction will exceed the cardholder's credit limit, then the issuing bank denies the authorization request. An authorization usually expires after a few days—three days is the usual time limit.

5. The merchant can check with the cardholder's card issuer to ensure that funds are available and put a hold on the funds needed to satisfy the current charge.

Usually, online transactions are settled after they are authorized, when the merchant ships the goods or supplies the service. When a transaction is **settled**, the merchant's account receives a deposit equal to the transaction amount (minus any credit card processing fees) and, simultaneously, the cardholder's credit card is charged the transaction amount. If an Internet consumer is downloading soft goods, such as digital files for programs or data files, the merchant can request authorization and settle immediately. Merchants must consider more complicated credit card transactions, including handling partial orders (orders in which some items are available for shipment and others are backordered). Merchants must be able to handle returns and issue RMA (return materials authorization) numbers for defective goods or incorrect shipments.

Often, the merchant's computer system that processes credit card payments connects directly to merchant banks. Sometimes, merchant banks turn over the entire authorization and settlement services to other organizations, which are known by the generic name of card processors. **Card processors** handle all the details of processing credit cards and charge a fee for their services. Examples of card processors include **Authorize.Net**, **ICVERIFY**, and **InternetSecure**.

Payment **Risks**

No electronic payment system is free of risk. Elaborate computer security mechanisms are in place to reduce the risk of information theft or alteration. In addition to computer security threats, both merchants and shoppers have distinct risks they must consider when either offering merchandise for sale or purchasing merchandise and services online.

Internet consumers also face many risks, such as the threat that someone could steal payment credentials (electronic checks, credit card numbers, and so on) and associated passwords. Because Internet transactions rarely involve the purchaser and seller meeting each other, customers run the risk of dealing with dishonest merchants. On the eBay auction site, for example, eBay management has several merchant reporting mechanisms in place that allow consumers to report dishonest merchants or shady deals. A subtle but widespread practice among a small number of merchants is the unwitting or intentional, inappropriate use of customer information and transaction details. For example, suppose a site decides to reveal your preferences to an outside source without your permission. Marketing mavens could learn a lot about you and subsequently bombard you with unsolicited e-mails about their products. A dispute over the quality of merchandise is also a risk that the online consumer, similar to the offline consumer, must assume and resolve. For example, if you order a handcrafted Peruvian vase from an online merchant but later actually receive a machine-made imitation, then you must spend time returning the item or requesting a substitute.

Online merchants also bear many risks that mirror those faced by consumers. A user who logs in to a merchant site and registers with the site can supply forged, false, or stolen information, including his name, address, and payment information. A risk that is particularly insidious in the business of online digital content distribution is the unauthorized redistribution of purchased software, music, and other digital products. Current estimates indicate that 50% of existing microcomputer software programs have been illegally redistributed or sold to others. Most software, for example, is licensed and cannot be sold by the software's purchaser, who only purchases a license to use the software. Merchants must be wary of dishonest commerce service providers that appear to provide online Web space or store creation software, but actually sign up merchants and supply little or no service at all. Cash flow is always a critical factor, especially for small start-up online stores. Slow paying **merchant service providers**—providers that process credit card accounts and with whom you have a merchant account—can be at least disruptive to a business by damaging an online company's cash flow. In the worst case, slow-paying vendors can cause online and offline stores to fail completely. The best defense in this case is word of mouth and recommendations from other online businesses.

Mike is pleased with the information that you gathered for him about accepting scrip, electronic checks, and credit cards at the Glass Gallery. In the next session, you will continue your investigation of Mike's online payment options by examining electronic cash and electronic wallets.

Session 5.1 QUICK CHECK

1. What is the term used to describe a small-valued purchase made on the Web?

2. The network that processes electronic checks is called the _____ Network.

3. The term used to describe an online credit card holder who presents a credit card number as payment for purchases is _____.

4. Why is there more risk of nonpayment when a merchant accepts a credit card as payment for an online transaction?

5. A bank that provides consumers with credit cards is called a(n) _____ bank.

6. What happens when an electronic transaction involving a credit card is settled?

7. Organizations providing authorization and settlement services for merchants are called _____.

SESSION 5.2

In this session, you will learn about different kinds of electronic cash and the advantages and disadvantages of using and accepting it. You will investigate smart cards and stored-value cards. Finally, you will see how consumers can use electronic wallets to store personal information and automatically supply that information to Web sites.

Introduction to Electronic Cash, Smart Cards, and Electronic Wallets

After considering the information you gathered, Mike decides to create a commerce site that accepts credit cards and scrip. For now, he wants to use electronic checks for his own company's business-to-business transactions, but he will consider expanding his site to accept electronic checks from customers within the next year. He is also interested in accepting electronic cash as an alternative payment method for small-valued purchases. He believes that by offering a variety of payment programs, more customers will be attracted to the Glass Gallery's Web site.

The Glass Gallery also mails a monthly newsletter containing tips and articles about working with glass to interested subscribers. Included in each newsletter are items for sale and one or two pictures of noncommissioned, salable glass panels that Mike produces. Mike plans to include a subscription form on the Web site to let customers subscribe to the newsletter. Many parts of the form, such as the person's name, address, and payment type fields, also will appear on the online order form when the Web site begins accepting online orders. Mike wants to eliminate the need for returning customers to fill out a form each time they visit the Glass Gallery site to order items. He thinks that electronic wallets might eliminate the repetitive and time-consuming activity of providing customer information. An **electronic wallet** is an electronic storage device that stores electronic currency and information about the wallet's owner, such as the owner's name, address, phone number, and credit card numbers. One of your duties will be to investigate electronic wallets and their hardware counterpart, smart cards. A **smart card** is a plastic card that contains a computer chip, which stores electronic currency and information about the card's owner.

Electronic payment systems on several online merchants' sites may require you to use an electronic wallet or a smart card when you choose to pay for items with electronic currency. Both types of electronic storage commonly protect their contents through public-key encryption and provide user authentication with stored digital certificates issued through trusted certificate authorities. An electronic wallet resides either on the user's computer or on the server of the wallet's vendor, and its contents are available for release whenever a user completes a purchase transaction or encounters a Web page that contains a form. To use a smart card to pay for online purchases, a user must insert the smart card into a special device that reads the card's contents to release the information or currency to the online merchant.

Using Electronic Cash for Online Purchases

The Glass Gallery sells many glass tools that cost less than $10. When the Glass Gallery accepts a credit card as payment for the purchase of a $5 glasscutter, for example, most of its profit is eliminated by the card's processing fee—in fact, sometimes the Glass Gallery actually *loses* money on the transaction. **Electronic cash** is similar to currency you carry in your wallet. Typically, you purchase electronic cash with a credit card and then download the currency to your computer or smart card. Just like with real cash, you do not need any additional permission or authorization to use electronic cash. The only restriction is that the merchant must accept the particular brand of electronic cash you offer. When you pay for online purchases using electronic cash, a merchant can deposit your payment into an account or spend it on the Internet. For example, if you buy a $5 glasscutter from the Glass Gallery, it might deposit your payment into an account from which it purchases supplies for the art classes.

A consumer benefit of electronic cash transactions is that they can be entirely anonymous, and the worry of revealing personal information is eliminated. Electronic cash is frequently used to make micropayments—or payments of less than one dollar—for small-valued items. From a merchant's point of view, accepting electronic cash is attractive because electronic cash does not have a processing fee.

With very low fixed costs, electronic cash provides the promise of allowing users to spend 50 cents for an online Sunday newspaper or $1.55 to send an electronic greeting card. Using electronic cash, online users can buy low-cost goods and services that aren't normally chargeable on the Internet. Electronic cash also opens online purchasing to children. Children are not normally given access to credit cards, but electronic cash allows them to pay for access to online games and e-zines. Adults can use electronic cash to purchase commuter train schedules, newspaper articles, or restaurant menus.

To use electronic cash, a consumer opens a bank account in person. After showing the bank proper identification, a consumer can withdraw electronic cash up to some limit. Some systems make consumers transfer funds into an account or use a credit card upon which electronic cash is drawn. The consumer can then operate from her PC to obtain and spend the electronic cash. If the consumer wants cash, she presents proof of identity electronically— a consumer certificate from VeriSign would be sufficient, for example—and requests a withdrawal. The bank sends to the user via the Internet—using e-mail for example—the requested amount in electronic cash. Once received and validated, the electronic cash resides on the consumer's personal computer in a software wallet stored on the user's disk or on a smart card that resides on a special reader connected to the consumer's computer. Later, when the consumer wants to spend the electronic cash, she visits a site that accepts that brand of electronic cash. The merchant receives and validates the electronic cash using cryptographic public-key methods for the bank from which the user drew the electronic cash. After the merchant validates the electronic cash, the bank deposits it in the merchant's account. When the merchant needs real cash, it can write and cash a check drawn against the bank's electronic cash account. Figure 5-14 shows how electronic cash flows from a consumer to a merchant.

Figure 5-14   **TYPICAL ELECTRONIC CASH TRANSACTION FLOW**

The steps noted in Figure 5-14 are as follows:

1. The consumer acquires electronic cash from the electronic cash broker's server.

2. The consumer purchases goods and services from a merchant.

3. The merchant sends a specially coded invoice to the consumer's browser.

4. The consumer's electronic wallet interprets the invoice and sends it and the electronic cash amount to the broker.

5. The electronic cash broker interprets the invoice and validates the electronic cash.

6. The broker notifies the merchant that the transaction is valid and deposits the transaction amount in the merchant's account.

7. The merchant ships the goods or performs the service after receiving confirmation from the broker that the transaction is valid. The merchant can use the electronic cash to purchase goods and services for its business.

Because there are different electronic cash payment systems in place on the Internet, electronic cash has been slow to emerge as an accepted and widely used technology. Part of the reason for this slow reception is because the technology is young and there are several competing electronic cash payment schemes available. In addition, consumer concerns about the safety of electronic cash transactions are genuine. Electronic cash has unique security problems in common with real currency: It must be impossible to spend electronic cash more than once, and electronic cash should be anonymous in a transaction. That is, security procedures should be in place to guarantee that the entire electronic cash transaction occurs between two parties so that the merchant knows the electronic currency it is receiving is not counterfeited and that the consumer has not used the same currency in two *different* transactions. In addition, the consumer (and sometimes the seller) might use electronic cash to avoid revealing his identity, for a variety of completely legitimate reasons. Anonymity also prevents the seller from collecting information about individual or group spending habits. Credit card users, on the other hand, realize that they are giving up some measure of privacy by using a credit card.

To be widely accepted, electronic cash must be able to pass transparently across international borders and be automatically converted to the recipient country's currency; in other words, it must be **portable**. Electronic cash portability means that it must be freely transferable between any two parties. In contrast, credit cards have the same degree of portability or transferability between every combination of two parties. For example, credit card transactions require that the receiver already have a merchant account established with a bank—a condition that is not required with electronic cash.

Divisibility is a property that distinguishes electronic cash from real currency and determines the size of payment units. Both the number of different electronic cash units and their values can be defined independently of real currency. For example, parties to electronic cash transactions in the United States might decide that the smallest electronic cash unit they want to accept is $1, with increasing increments of 20 cents, up to a set amount. The denominations are up to the definers and are not limited to the typical breakdowns of a real cash system.

Perhaps the most important characteristic of cash is **convenience**. If electronic cash requires special hardware, software, or requires the user to have a finely honed expertise, customers will cast a virtual no confidence vote for it. Any difficult-to-use electronic cash system will quickly cease to exist.

The research you have conducted recently using search engines and talking to online merchants has lead you to a few key vendors that supply electronic cash systems for merchants. Three of these vendors have attracted your attention because they seem to crop up more frequently than other electronic cash names in your research. In addition, you have noticed that there are several proposed or theoretically possible electronic cash systems that are not yet available. You would rather look at systems that are in place, even though all electronic cash systems are quite new. The three systems you want to investigate for the Glass Gallery are eCash, PayPal, and Mondex, which all appear to have different and interesting ways of providing electronic cash to customers.

eCash

ECash Technologies owns, develops, markets, and supports the eCash software suite, which is one of the few secure and private electronic cash systems on the Internet. Not long ago, eCash Technologies purchased DigiCash, a company that originally developed an early, secure electronic cash system called DigiCash. ECash owns and uses a patented blind signature encryption technology. A **blind signature** is a cryptographic modification of an owner's digital money to validate the electronic cash without revealing the payer's identity. **Blind** means that electronic money remains anonymous and thus cannot be traced back to the original spender. **Signature** means that the cash is not counterfeit, because it has the issuing institution's signature and the purchaser's signature. ECash software uses digital signature technology based on public-key encryption to provide authentication, nonrepudiation, data integrity, and confidentiality. Nonrepudiation ensures that a message sender's digital signature is proof the sender was the true author of the message.

ECash products and services are provided to consumers and merchants through financial institutions. ECash is an open, nonexclusive system that is available for implementation by any bank and usable by any bank customer or merchant. Consumers and merchants around the world use eCash to purchase goods and services.

Although you are not sure if Mike will want to accept electronic cash as a payment option from his customers, it is important for Mike to understand more about electronic cash and how typical systems work. You decide to visit the eCash Web site and investigate several pages within that site to learn more about this electronic payment option.

To learn more about eCash:

1. Start your Web browser, and then go to the Online Companion by entering the URL **http://www.course.com/NewPerspectives/EC** in the appropriate location of your Web browser. Click the **Tutorial 5** link, and then click the **Session 5.2** link. Click the **eCash** link and wait while your browser loads the eCash home page shown in Figure 5-15.

Figure 5-15   ECASH HOME PAGE

2. Click the **Merchants** link located near the top of the page. A page opens and describes the benefits of using eCash for the merchant. Read these benefits to understand more about how the Glass Gallery could benefit from accepting eCash.

3. Click the **eCash Basics** link on the left side of the page to open more detailed information about eCash from a merchant's perspective. See Figure 5-16. Read about the benefits on this page before going to the next step.

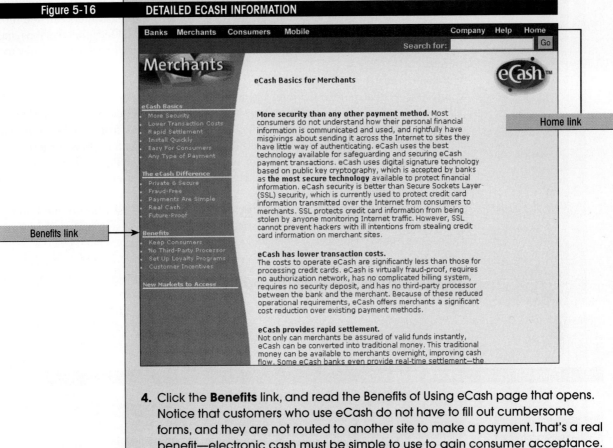

| Figure 5-16 | DETAILED ECASH INFORMATION |

4. Click the **Benefits** link, and read the Benefits of Using eCash page that opens. Notice that customers who use eCash do not have to fill out cumbersome forms, and they are not routed to another site to make a payment. That's a real benefit—electronic cash must be simple to use to gain consumer acceptance.

5. Click the **New Markets to Access** link, and then read the Accessing New Markets with eCash page that opens. Notice that eCash does not have international boundaries. Foreign currencies are converted transparently to a common currency. ECash also provides a convenient way for children to shop online; minors cannot use credit cards, so eCash solves that problem. There are people who could not otherwise shop online for other reasons outlined on the page; the eCash system opens your online store to those additional people.

PayPal

PayPal is an electronic cash payment system that is a popular way for consumers to pay for online purchases. Touted as the world's first e-mail payment service, PayPal.com is a free service that earns a profit on the **float**, which is money that is deposited in PayPal accounts. PayPal eliminates the need to pay for online purchases by writing and mailing checks or using credit cards. PayPal allows consumers to send money instantly and securely to anyone with an e-mail address, including an online merchant. PayPal is a convenient way for auction bidders to pay for their purchases, and sellers like it because it eliminates the risks associated with accepting other types of online payments. PayPal transactions clear instantly so that the sender's account is reduced and the receiver's account is credited when the transaction occurs. Anyone with a PayPal account—online merchants or auction participants alike—can withdraw cash from their PayPal accounts at any time.

To use PayPal, merchants and consumers first must register for a PayPal account. There is no minimum amount that a PayPal account must contain, and customers can add money to their PayPal accounts by sending a check or using a credit card. Once members' payments are approved and deposited into their PayPal accounts, they can use their PayPal money to pay for purchases.

Merchants must have PayPal accounts to accept PayPal payments, but consumer-to-consumer markets are more flexible. Using PayPal to pay for auction purchases is very popular. A consumer can use PayPal to pay a seller for purchases even if the seller does not have a PayPal account. When you use PayPal to pay for purchases from a seller or merchant that does not have a PayPal account, the PayPal service sends the seller or merchant an e-mail message indicating that a payment is waiting at the PayPal Web site. To collect PayPal cash, the seller or merchant that received the e-mail message must register and provide PayPal with payment instructions.

Mike is very interested in PayPal because it costs nothing to use, has no minimum payment amount, and appears to be a secure method. He asks you to sign up for an account so that the Glass Gallery can accept PayPal payments.

To sign up for a PayPal account:

1. Click your browser's **Back** button or use its history list to return to the Online Companion page for Session 5.2, and then click the **PayPal** link and wait while your browser loads the PayPal home page shown in Figure 5-17.

Figure 5-17	PAYPAL HOME PAGE

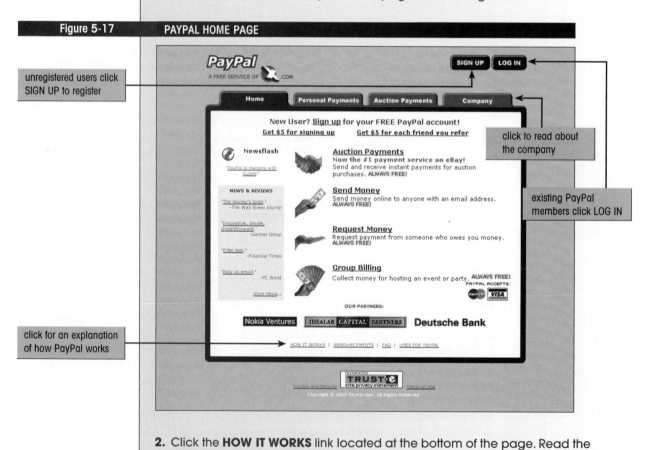

2. Click the **HOW IT WORKS** link located at the bottom of the page. Read the information provided on the How it works page to learn more about this electronic payment system.

3. Click the **SIGN UP** button located at the top of the page. The PayPal.com - Quick 1-Page Registration page opens. See Figure 5-18.

Figure 5-18 | **PAYPAL REGISTRATION FORM**

fill in all required fields

terms of use link

click to submit your completed form

4. Use the text boxes in the registration page to enter your first and last names, address, city, state, Zip code, day (or evening) phone, e-mail address (twice), and a password (twice). Follow the directions to create a question and an answer to use in case you forget your password.

5. Click the **terms of use** link to open the PayPal.com - Terms of Use page in a separate browser window. Read the agreement. Notice that the PayPal.com site allows transactions of one cent or greater, which makes this service perfect for small-valued items. When you are finished reading the terms page, close the browser window that contains it.

6. Click the **Check here to indicate that you have read and agree to the terms of use** check box to select it, and then click the **submit** button to send your completed application form to PayPal for processing. The PayPal.com - Thank You! page opens and instructs you to check your e-mail for a PayPal message, which contains a secure link that you must click to return to the PayPal site.

7. Click the **continue** button. The PayPal Overview page opens and indicates that you have an account with a balance of $0.00. See Figure 5-19. Account registrants who confirm their e-mail addresses and register their credit cards with PayPal receive a $5 bonus. (For this exercise, you will *not* register a credit card.)

| Figure 5-19 | PAYPAL ACCOUNT CONFIRMATION |

8. Click the **LOG OUT** button at the top of the page to log out of your account. A page opens and confirms that you have logged out of your PayPal account.

9. Click the **here** link ("Click **here** to return to the home page.") to return to the PayPal home page.

10. Use your e-mail program to retrieve the message sent by PayPal, and then follow the on-screen instructions to complete your account registration. Following the steps in the e-mail message confirms your e-mail address.

11. Click the **continue** link on the Email Confirmed page, and then scroll down the referral page and click the **Skip** button to skip this step. The Overview page opens and displays your PayPal account information.

12. Click the **LOG OUT** button at the top of the page to log out of your account.

Your research shows that PayPal is easy to use, secure, and free. In addition to recommending that the Glass Gallery accept this form of payment from customers, you also will suggest that Mike include an icon on his site's home page to indicate that the Glass Gallery accepts PayPal payments. This option will work especially well for transactions involving payments for small-valued items.

Two other well-known companies that provide electronic cash systems are **IBM Micro Payments** and **MilliCent** (available from Compaq). IBM's Micro Payments is available and installed at a number of merchants' sites. MilliCent has been deployed after several years of research and customer data gathering. Figure 5-20 shows the IBM Micro Payments home page.

Figure 5-20	IBM MICRO PAYMENTS HOME PAGE

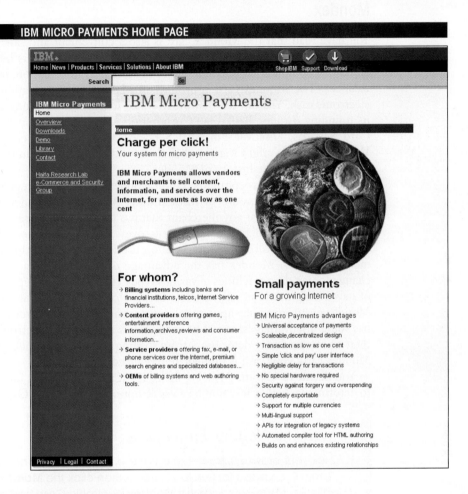

ECash, PayPal, IBM Micro Payments, and MilliCent are all examples of electronic cash systems in which the electronic cash is stored on the user's computer or on a remote server. There is no special electronic hardware device needed to hold or spend these types of electronic cash. Another type of electronic cash is one in which a special reader holds it. In this case, when you wish to spend your electronic cash, you must use a special hardware reader. Mondex is an example of this type of electronic cash. Both types of systems have distinct advantages and disadvantages.

Using Stored-Value Cards for Online Purchases

Consumers can store electronic cash on their computer's hard drive, or they can use stored-value cards or electronic wallets to hold their cash. **Stored-value cards** can be elaborate smart cards or simple plastic cards with magnetic strips to record the currency balance. A stored-value card that you might be familiar with is a prepaid phone, copy, subway, or bus card. The Internet equivalent and more complicated stored-value card is called a smart card. A **smart card** stores much more information than a plastic card with a magnetic strip. A smart card can also do limited processing—it can store electronic currency, personal information, credit card information, and a cardholder's encrypted identification. **Electronic wallets** are the software equivalent of smart cards. They reside on your computer and also can complete Internet forms with your name and address.

Mondex

You have read that the Mondex card is also a convenient and safe way to store electronic cash. **Mondex** is an electronic cash system in which money is held in a smart card that contains a computer chip with memory to store user information, including electronic cash balances. The Mondex card, a product of MasterCard International, holds and dispenses electronic cash. You can tell that the Mondex USA card has strong backing by the names of its founding owners: Bank One Corporation, Chase Manhattan Bank, Citibank Universal Card Services, Discover Financial Services, MasterCard, Michigan National Bank, and Wells Fargo. You might want to click the **Mondex history** link in the Online Companion to learn more about the history of Mondex.

Containing a microcomputer chip, Mondex cards can accept electronic cash directly from a user's bank account or from another Mondex cardholder. Cardholders can spend their electronic cash at any merchant that has a Mondex card reader. Two cardholders can even transfer cash between their cards over a telephone line. That is an advantage of Mondex: A single card will work both on the Internet and in the offline world of physical merchant stores. Mondex has the advantage of the cardholder always having the correct change for vending machines of various types. (Coca Cola has reported that as much as 25% of its vending machine sales are lost because consumers do not have the correct change.) Mondex electronic cash supports micropayments as small as three cents. However, Mondex has some disadvantages, too. The card carries real cash in electronic form, and the risk of theft of the card may deter users from loading it with very much money. When you use a Mondex card, your cash is immediately reduced.

You decide to visit the Mondex site to learn more about this form of electronic payment to determine whether it would be a viable option for the Glass Gallery.

To visit the Mondex home page:

1. Click your browser's **Back** button or use its history list to return to the Online Companion page for Session 5.2, and then click the **Mondex** link and wait while your browser loads the Mondex Electronic Cash home page.

2. Move your pointer over each of the eight circles outside the main circle bearing the Mondex image. Notice that names such as Mondex International, Internet, and Technology appear as the pointer passes over each circle.

3. Click the circle that displays **Technology** when you move the pointer over it. The Mondex Technology page opens.

4. Click the **intro** link in the Mondex menu bar at the top of the page. The What is Mondex? page opens. See Figure 5-21.

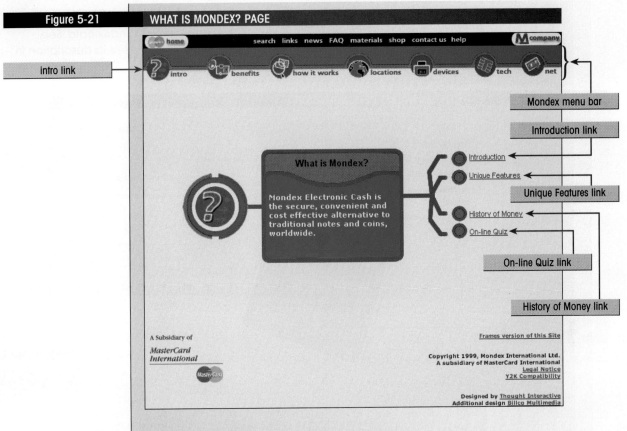

Figure 5-21   WHAT IS MONDEX? PAGE

intro link

Mondex menu bar

Introduction link

Unique Features link

On-line Quiz link

History of Money link

5. Click the **Introduction** link, and then read the information on the page that opens. One paragraph in the introduction explains that the Mondex "purse" contains five separate pockets to hold five different currencies simultaneously. This feature would be advantageous to international customers of the Glass Gallery.

Next, you decide to go to the Mondex USA site to see what Mondex is doing in the U.S. market.

To visit the Mondex USA home page:

1. Click your browser's **Back** button or use its history list to return to the Online Companion page for Session 5.2, and then click the **Mondex USA** link and wait while your browser loads the Mondex USA Web page. The page contains mostly marketing information for U.S. consumers and merchants.

2. Click the **How Mondex Works** link located on the left side of the page, and then read the Mondex USA - Take it With You page that opens. This page describes how the Mondex chip works and provides a description of the behind-the-scenes actions that take place during a Mondex transaction.

3. Click the **Consumer Benefits** link on the left side of the page, and then read the Consumer Benefits page that opens. Depending on when you view the page, you may see a small, key ring card-reading device displayed on the page. This device accepts a Mondex card and reads its electronic cash balance.

4. Click the **Mondex Wallet** link at the bottom of the page to start an animated display of how a special, pocket-sized device reads a Mondex card. See Figure 5-22. Click a button on the picture of the device to see its description in the scrolling text box on the page.

Figure 5-22   MONDEX WALLET DEMONSTRATION

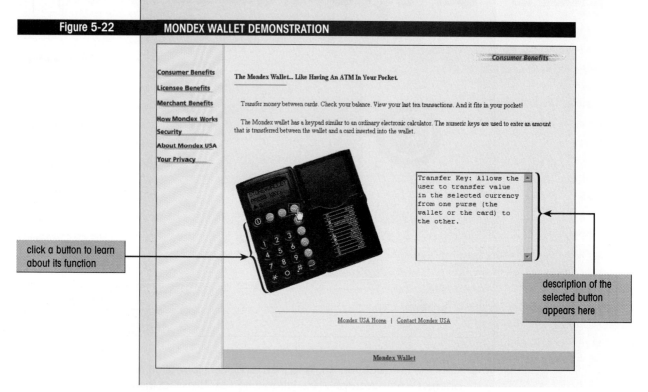

click a button to learn about its function

description of the selected button appears here

Electronic cash has disadvantages that vendors must address before consumers and merchants will embrace it. Unscrupulous or unwitting consumers can double spend their electronic cash if safeguards are not in place to prevent that deliberate or accidental act. **Double spending** occurs when the same electronic cash is paid to two different merchants. Unlike real cash that you remove from your wallet and give to a merchant, it is possible in poorly designed electronic cash systems to send the same payment twice. There are security mechanisms available to prevent double spending, but not every electronic cash system protects against the problem. Another problem that consumers consider to be a shortcoming of some electronic cash systems is that the cash is not anonymous. Many electronic cash systems associate the cash with a consumer until after the purchase, allowing the merchant bank to deduct the electronic cash tendered by a merchant from the purchasing consumer's account; however, this eliminates an important advantage of real cash—anonymity.

Naturally, consumers whose electronic cash is stored on their computer's hard drive face other potential problems. What if their hard drive fails and they lose their cash? Can they recover the cash? Is the issuing institution responsible? How portable is a consumer's electronic cash? If a consumer has cash stored on his computer in Portland, Maine, can he make purchases with that type of electronic cash from a public computer in Indianapolis, Indiana? Storing electronic cash on a consumer's computer—called **client-side storage**—reduces electronic cash's portability. Some electronic cash vendors will provide credit for electronic cash that is destroyed or unavailable on a consumer's computer system. Replacing lost electronic cash requires that the electronic cash be uniquely identifiable so that destroyed cash cannot be spent along with the replacement cash.

The Glass Gallery must consider these disadvantages when considering whether to accept electronic cash. Consumers must also be cautious. Do they want the convenience of electronic cash for small purchases, considering some of its disadvantages? Mike is certainly faced with some tough questions.

Storing Information in an Electronic Wallet

Mike wants to collect information from his Web site's visitors and potential purchasers even before they buy anything from his online store. He would like to capture the names and addresses of anyone who visits the site and expresses an interest in his monthly newsletter. Mike would gather information from interested consumers with a short, online form that contains text boxes for a visitor's name, address, telephone number, and e-mail address. In addition, he wants the form to contain a dozen check boxes that site visitors use to indicate their interest in future newsletter articles on specialized topics, such as creating three-dimensional glass objects and cleaning a finished glass panel. However, Mike realizes that many Web surfers do not like to complete multiple forms at the same Web site because doing so is both time-consuming and tedious. Mike has completed his share of forms on various online sites prior to completing purchase transactions, and he would like to shorten the process, or eliminate it altogether, for his customers. He thinks that using electronic wallets will shorten the time it takes for his customers to complete online forms.

Filling out forms to complete an online transaction ranks high on Web shoppers' lists of frustrating activities. The forms are a necessary part of any online transaction because they contain the shipping and billing addresses and other customer information needed to complete the transaction and ship ordered goods. Figure 5-23 shows a typical form that a shopper must fill out to complete a transaction. For every Web site that you visit to make purchases, you will find a similar form that requests the same basic information.

| Figure 5-23 | TYPICAL ONLINE FORM |

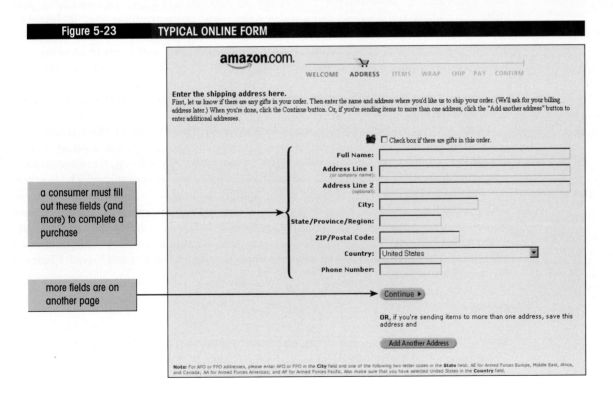

An electronic wallet is a secure virtual container that holds an owner's personal data and extracts that data to a merchant site at the time of purchase. By using an electronic wallet, consumers won't need to complete online forms—the data stored in the electronic wallet is extracted automatically and inserted in the appropriate places in online forms. Electronic wallets are hardware or software. Hardware electronic wallets, or smart cards, contain an embedded computer chip that stores the card owner's purchase and identification information. Software versions of electronic wallets currently are more prevalent. Their information storage technology is implemented with software. (In this book, the term *electronic wallet* will mean the software wallet.)

What do electronic wallets store? Minimally, electronic wallets store shipping and billing information, including a consumer's first and last names, street address, city, state, country, and postal code. Most electronic wallets also can hold one or more credit card names and numbers, affording the consumer a choice of credit cards at the online checkout. Some electronic wallets also hold electronic cash from one or more suppliers, such as CyberCash. Finally, some wallets contain an encrypted digital certificate, which securely identifies the wallet's owner. Wallets that store digital certificates are particularly handy when you shop at a site that requests user authentication information because the wallet can supply the certificate automatically.

Electronic wallets fall into two categories based on where they are stored. **Server-side electronic wallets** store consumer information on a remote server belonging to a particular merchant or (better yet) belonging to the wallet's publisher. **Client-side electronic wallets** store a consumer's information on the consumer's own computer. Many of the early electronic wallets were client-side wallets and required lengthy downloads, which remains one of their chief disadvantages. Server-side wallets, on the other hand, remain on a server and therefore require no download time or installation on a user's computer. Another disadvantage of client-side wallets is that they are not portable. For example, a client-side wallet is not available when you make a purchase at a location other than the computer on which your wallet resides. Most Internet consumers are nomadic and enjoy the freedom of purchasing anywhere and anytime. For a wallet to be useful at many online sites, it should be able to populate the data fields in any merchants' forms at any site the consumer visits. This accessibility means that the electronic wallet manufacturer and merchants from many sites must coordinate their efforts so that a wallet can "recognize" what consumer information goes into each of a given merchant's forms. This task can be daunting, but wallet manufacturers are making huge strides in achieving a universal wallet; however, that dream has not yet been achieved.

There are many different electronic wallets available, in part because there is no established standard for them. Examples of electronic wallets include **Brodia**, **eWallet**, Gator, **InstaBuy**, Passport, Qpass PowerWallet, and **Yahoo! Wallet**. In addition, there are no clear front-runners in the race to become the favored electronic wallet technology. The best you can do is to investigate some of these wallet options, and then watch for developments in wallet technology and look for emerging wallet standards. Standards will emerge because consumers cannot tolerate using multiple electronic wallets in order to shop at the many different online stores they frequent. Currently, the situation is similar to shopping at an international food store and having to spend Rupees at the tea counter and French Francs in the French wine section.

Gator

You decide to investigate some of the electronic wallets that seem to be very popular and whose names pop up frequently in search engine queries. First, you look at one with an unforgettable name, Gator.

To learn more about the Gator electronic wallet:

1. Click your browser's **Back** button or use its history list to return to the Online Companion page for Session 5.2, and then click the **Gator** link and wait while your browser loads the Gator home page shown in Figure 5-24.

Figure 5-24	GATOR HOME PAGE

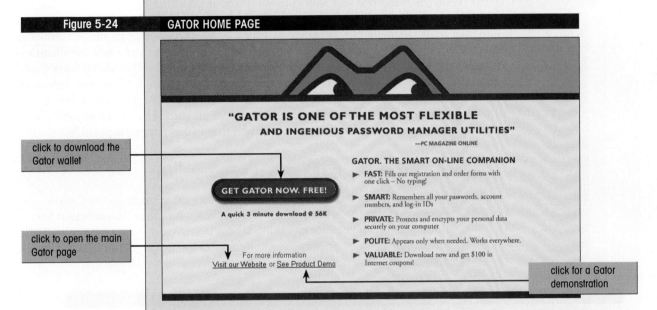

click to download the Gator wallet

click to open the main Gator page

click for a Gator demonstration

"GATOR IS ONE OF THE MOST FLEXIBLE AND INGENIOUS PASSWORD MANAGER UTILITIES"
—PC MAGAZINE ONLINE

GET GATOR NOW. FREE!

A quick 3 minute download @ 56K

For more information
Visit our Website or See Product Demo

GATOR. THE SMART ON-LINE COMPANION

▶ **FAST:** Fills out registration and order forms with one click – No typing!

▶ **SMART:** Remembers all your passwords, account numbers, and log-in IDs

▶ **PRIVATE:** Protects and encrypts your personal data securely on your computer

▶ **POLITE:** Appears only when needed. Works everywhere.

▶ **VALUABLE:** Download now and get $100 in Internet coupons!

2. Click the **See Product Demo** link. A new browser window opens and starts a three-minute demonstration of how Gator works. View the demo by clicking the **Next** button when you are ready to move to the next step in the demonstration. When you are finished, click the **Close** button on the title bar of the browser window that contains the demo.

3. On the Gator home page, click the **Visit our Website** link to open the main page, and then click the **Support Center** link located near the top of the page that opens.

4. Click the **Frequently Asked Questions** link to view some common questions and their answers. The Help and FAQ page opens. Scan this page to learn more about Gator.

5. Click the **Installing and Uninstall Questions** link. Scroll down the page that opens until you reach the question "**Q.** How do you uninstall Gator?" Read the response, which indicates that Gator is a client-side wallet residing on the user's computer.

Gator seems like a good choice for a client-side wallet. If Mike seems interested in Gator, you can evaluate it further. Another electronic wallet that you want to investigate is the Qpass PowerWallet.

Qpass PowerWallet

Because Qpass is a server-side wallet, a consumer can invoke his personal wallet at purchase time from any browser in the world. Qpass is an intelligent wallet that provides benefits to both consumers and online merchants. Unlike many other electronic wallets, Qpass PowerWallet is useable at any Web site—not just at sites that have a special relationship with Qpass. The accessibility of the Qpass PowerWallet is possible because of specially designed artificial intelligence technology, which enables Qpass to learn and remember site-specific information. When Qpass encounters an unfamiliar form at a new merchant's site, it learns the association between the consumer's information and the related form fields by observing where the consumer places each piece of information. The new information Qpass learns from a particular site is uploaded to the Qpass site and shared with all other Qpass customers. This community learning benefits all parties to an online sale: the merchant, the consumer, and the financial institution that makes payments possible.

To learn more about the Qpass PowerWallet:

1. Click your browser's **Back** button or use its history list to return to the Online Companion page for Session 5.2, and then click the **Qpass PowerWallet** link and wait while your browser loads the Qpass home page shown in Figure 5-25. The large number that appears in the middle of the page is the approximate number of digital services and products currently enabled by Qpass.

Figure 5-25	QPASS HOME PAGE

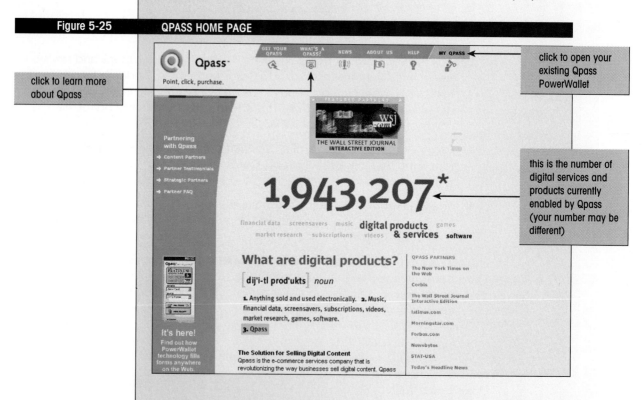

click to learn more about Qpass

click to open your existing Qpass PowerWallet

this is the number of digital services and products currently enabled by Qpass (your number may be different)

2. Click the **WHAT'S A QPASS?** link at the top of the page. The What's a Qpass? page opens.

3. Click the **SEE HOW QPASS WORKS** link on the left side of the page. The Tutorials & Trial Sites page opens. This page includes a link to a tutorial that you can view to learn more about Qpass.

4. Click the **Start tutorial now** link below the first paragraph to start the Qpass tutorial. Read each page that opens, and then click the **next** link at the top of each Qpass tutorial page to open the next page. When you click the "next" link on the last page of the demonstration, the Tutorials & Trial Sites page reappears.

5. Click the **WHERE CAN I USE MY QPASS?** link on the left side of the page, and then click the **other merchants** link in the first paragraph to view a list of sites that accept Qpass. Review the merchants listed on the page. This list is not comprehensive; however, as the page indicates that you can use Qpass features at *any* commerce site.

6. Click the **Qpass logo** in the upper-left corner of the page to return to the Qpass home page.

7. Review the Qpass privacy policy by clicking the **Privacy Policy** link at the bottom of the page. (It appears in small type.) Part of the privacy policy states that Qpass stores a cookie on your computer so that your user name and password are available the next time you visit Qpass. The statement also indicates that Qpass is careful with your data and that some information is optional. Qpass is a certified participant of the BBBOnline Privacy Program, and it subscribes to TRUSTe.

Qpass appears to be an excellent choice for both consumers and merchants. It is convenient for consumers because they do not have to download software and go through a lengthy wallet installation process. Furthermore, the wallet is portable because the server stores critical information, not the client machine. Finally, a feature unique to Qpass is its ability to learn the structure of new purchase forms it encounters on the Internet.

Microsoft Passport

As part of your investigation of electronic wallets, you decide to install an electronic wallet. You have heard that Microsoft's Passport wallet, a server-side wallet, is both simple to use and widely recognized. Like other wallets, Passport supplies identification and payment information at many Web sites. The Passport wallet is free to consumers; however, merchants pay a fee for using the Passport service. Merchant fees currently range from $1,000 per year for small online shops to over $100,000 for very large sites. Unique to Microsoft is its very strong privacy policy guidelines that merchants agree to abide by in order to join the Passport program. Some privacy advocates are expressing concern for online shoppers because Microsoft requests demographic information from subscribing shoppers before they are issued a free Passport. Every time a shopper uses the Passport wallet, details about the consumer, including the consumer's e-mail address, are sent to the vendor along with registration information. For this reason, Microsoft insists that merchants abide by strict security guidelines.

Passport consists of two integrated services: Passport single sign-in service (SSI) and Passport Wallet Service. The sign-in service allows a user to sign in at a participating Web site using her user name and password. The Passport wallet service provides standard electronic wallet functions, such as secure storage and form completion of credit card and address information. When requested by a participating merchant, a consumer's secure information is released to the merchant so that the consumer does not need to enter data into a form. You decide to review Microsoft's Passport service and look at the agreement form.

To learn more about Microsoft Passport:

1. Click your browser's **Back** button or use its history list to return to the Online Companion page for Session 5.2, and then click the **Passport Wallet** link and wait while your browser loads the Microsoft Passport home page shown in Figure 5-26.

Figure 5-26   MICROSOFT PASSPORT HOME PAGE

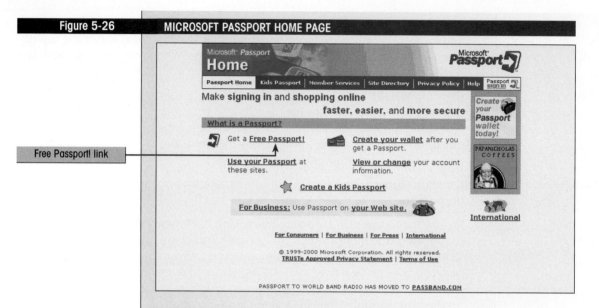

Free Passport! link

2. Click the **Free Passport!** link on the left side of the page. The Get a Passport page opens and displays a form with several text boxes.

   TROUBLE? If you have a hotmail.com e-mail address, then you already have an account. Enter your user name and password, click the Sign In button, and then skip to Step 5.

3. Enter the following information into the appropriate fields: E-mail address, Password, Retype password, Secret question for password reset, Answer to secret question, Country/Region, State, and Zip code. Click the two check boxes to clear them and to prevent disclosure of your information.

4. Click the **Sign Up** button at the bottom of the page to process your passport. The Member Services page opens with a congratulatory message and your chosen sign-in name.

   TROUBLE? If you choose a sign-in name that is already taken, a page will open and suggest some other possible sign-in names. Either select one of those suggested names, or click the "or another name" option button and then enter another name in the text box. Click the Sign Up button to resubmit your form until you select an available sign-in name.

5. Log in to your e-mail account using your e-mail program. Open the Microsoft Passport e-mail message with the subject line "Please Verify Your Microsoft Passport E-Mail address." Do *not* reply to the message. Instead, click the verification link in the message. A Web page opens indicating your e-mail address is verified. Close your e-mail program and return to your Web browser to continue the sign-up process.

6. Click the **Click here to create your Passport wallet now** link. The Microsoft Passport Wallet: Enter payment information page opens. See Figure 5-27. Notice that your browser changes to a secure state by placing a padlock icon on the status bar. You use this page to enter your secure information into the Passport wallet. The E-mail and Zip code entries are already entered for you because you entered this information into your Passport application form.

| Figure 5-27 | PASSPORT WALLET DATA ENTRY FORM |

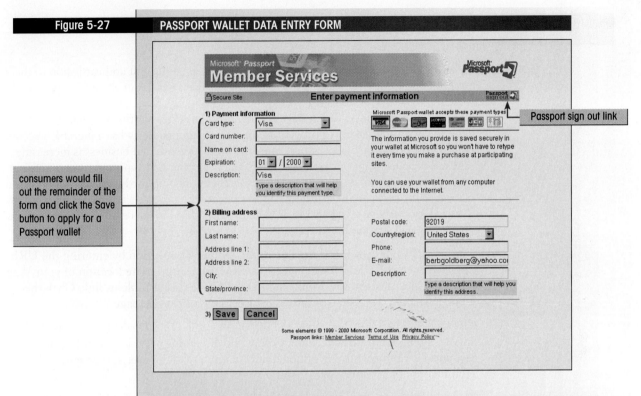

consumers would fill out the remainder of the form and click the Save button to apply for a Passport wallet

Passport sign out link

7. Because you do not need to supply a credit card and other personal information at this time, click the **Passport sign out** link near the top of the page to log out of your Passport account and to stop creating your Passport wallet. The Passport home page opens. If you return to this page, you can re-establish yourself by clicking the Passport sign in link located near the top of the page.

8. Close your browser and close your dial-up connection, if necessary.

Mike is very impressed with the information that you have collected about electronic cash and electronic wallet options. He will consider one of several server-side wallets to make it more convenient for his customers to complete online forms and to make purchases at the Glass Gallery commerce site.

Session 5.2 QUICK CHECK

1. List three properties that electronic cash must have in order to be widely accepted.

2. What is a blind signature?

3. What is double spending?

4. What is the difference between a smart card and a stored-value card?

5. Describe the two types of electronic wallets that use software.

6. What kind of data can a consumer store in an electronic wallet?

CASE PROBLEMS

Case 1. Betty's Gift Shop Betty Carroll has owned and managed her gift and card shop in the Central Shopping Mall for three years. Business has been good, but she'd like to expand her reach. Last year, Betty hired a Web designer who built a Web site that is hosted by a national Internet service provider. Part of the monthly ISP fee for the merchant site includes the software needed to process credit card payments. Betty has a merchant account with a national credit card processing company. Betty's Web-based business is increasing, and she has received requests from customers who want the site to provide more payment options. Betty has hired you to find out how merchants sign up for Flooz and how much it costs to offer the service. She also asks you to evaluate the process a consumer must follow to create a Flooz account. If your research determines that Flooz is easy and inexpensive to process, Betty will sign up for the service.

1. Start your Web browser, and then go to the Online Companion by entering the URL http://www.course.com/NewPerspectives/EC in the appropriate location of your Web browser. Click the Tutorial 5 link, and then click the Case Problems link. Click the Flooz link and wait while your browser loads the Flooz home page.

2. Click the MY ACCOUNT tab at the top of the page. On the page that opens, click the link to sign up for a Flooz account. Follow the directions provided to create the account. Do not provide any optional information, read the user agreement, and then submit your application.

3. Use the Reminders page to enter your birthday information. Set the reminder for 30 days prior to your birthday.

4. Scroll to the bottom of the Reminders page, and then click the SAVE THESE REMINDERS button. Click the PRINT THIS PAGE button to print the Reminders page.

5. Click the ADD FLOOZ TO ACCOUNT button on the left side of the page. The Account: Add Flooz To Your Account page opens. Use your browser's Print button to print this page.

6. Click the HOME tab at the top of the page, and then click the Flooz for Business link in the left panel.

7. Click the Learn more about Flooz for Business link. In a memo addressed to Betty, identify three ways that she can use Flooz as a business incentive.

8. Click the Features and Benefits: Printable Fact Sheet link. Print the Flooz: Business-to-Business page that opens.

9. Click the Back to Flooz for Business Home Page link at the bottom of the page.

10. Click the Go to Flooz.com link at the bottom of the Flooz for Business page. The Flooz home page redisplays.

11. Click the HOW FLOOZ WORKS link located at the top of the page. Scroll to the bottom of the page and click the link labeled Click here for a demo.

12. Click the Spending button and follow the demonstration, clicking the forward link to open the next demonstration page. Continue your memo to Betty by summarizing the ways in which you think that accepting Flooz at her online store might help her business. Close the demonstration window.

13. Click the MY ACCOUNT tab, click the Flooz icon in the top-left corner of the page, and then click the LOG OUT button to log out of your account. Close your Web browser and close your dial-up connection, if necessary.

14. Finish your memo to Betty by recommending whether she should offer and redeem Flooz at her online store. Defend your recommendation using information you learned while visiting the Flooz Web site.

Case 2. Exotic Woods Bill Word owns a North Carolina wood supply store that imports and sells exotic hardwoods from all around the world. His store has been a fixture at the corner of Broadway and Walnut Streets in downtown Asheville for more than 20 years. Two years ago, Bill enlisted the help of two community college students and built a "brochureware" store hosted by Yahoo! Store. Now Bill wants to go beyond simply displaying advertising about his store on the Web site. He would like to create a catalog and set up a complete shopping cart system to accept orders and customer payments. He would like you to compare the benefits and costs of selected credit card processing services that authorize and settle customers' credit card transactions.

1. Start your Web browser, and then go to the Online Companion by entering the URL http://www.course.com/NewPerspectives/EC in the appropriate location of your Web browser. Click the Tutorial 5 link, and then click the Case Problems link. Click the Charge Solutions link and wait while your browser loads the Charge Solutions home page.

2. Click the Merchant Services link at the top of the page, and then read the page that opens.

3. Click your browser's Back button, click the Features and Rates link at the top of the page, and then use the page that opens to answer the following questions: For Plan 2 subscribers, what are the costs to set up a merchant account? How much is the monthly service fee? How much is the fee for each transaction?

4. Return to the Online Companion page for Case Problem 2, and then click the CREDITNET.COM link and wait while your browser loads the CREDITNET.COM home page.

5. Click the Merchant Services link on the left side of the page.

6. Locate and click a link that describes the company's rates. A form opens. *Do not* fill out or submit the form. Use your browser's Print button to print the form.

7. Click your browser's Back button to return to the home page, click the Features at a Glance link, and then read the page that opens to understand the features provided by CREDITNET.COM.

8. Return to the Online Companion for Case Problem 2, and then click the CyberSource Payment Services link.

9. Click the Credit Card Services link on the right side of the page.

10. Click the How It Works link that appears in the Related Links section on the right side of the page. Print the page that opens, which contains a diagram of how the service works.

11. Close your Web browser and close your dial-up connection, if necessary.

12. Write a brief report that compares and contrasts the services offered by Charge Solutions, CREDITNET.COM, and CyberSource. What steps occur after a shopper submits a credit card number for processing? What institutions are involved in authorizing a credit card purchase and authorizing fulfillment? What role does each processor have in the process? Which processor should Bill use for his online store? Defend your selection.

Case 3. Great! Newsletters Great! Newsletters has formed a small business and has just completed building an electronic commerce Web site that sells subscriptions for special interest newsletters, such as *Apple Growers Digest and Newsletter* and *Wilderness Backpacking Newsletter*. Many organizations and individuals produce the newsletters, and your role is to raise the visibility of these sometimes obscure publications produced in out-of-the-way places. Each newsletter is published either biweekly or monthly. Unlike traditional subscription services, you have an agreement from the newsletter publishers that lets you sell subscriptions for single issues or subscriptions of up to three years. Your policy is to accept a credit card as payment for subscriptions lasting for one or more years. J.D. Bentworth, the founder of Great! Newsletters, wants you to investigate accepting eCoin scrip for newsletter subscriptions of less than one year, including single issues. He wants to know what charges are associated with eCoin and how he can start accepting it.

1. Start your Web browser, and then go to the Online Companion by entering the URL http://www.course.com/NewPerspectives/EC in the appropriate location of your Web browser. Click the Tutorial 5 link, and then click the Case Problems link. Click the eCoin link and wait while your browser loads the eCoin home page.

2. Click the Sign Up button on the eCoin home page. (*Note*: If a dialog box opens with a security alert indicating that the name on the certificate does not match the name of the site, click the Yes button to proceed. The certificate is genuine; eCoin changed the site's name but the eCoin managers have not yet updated the certificate.)

3. Read the page that opens, enter your e-mail address into the appropriate text box, and then click the Send Me Signup ID button. The sign up page closes, eCoin sends an e-mail address to your mailbox with a link to a special eCoin Web location, and the Create Account Response page opens.

4. Use your e-mail program to download and read the message sent by eCoin. The message's subject line is "ecoin." There are two URLs in the message. Either click the first URL listed (the longer one) or copy and paste the second URL into your browser's address field, and then press the Enter key to go to the eCoin Web site. In either case, the Create Account (on Server) page opens. Type your e-mail address and new signup ID as provided in the eCoin e-mail message. Then click the Continue -> Sign Me Up button.

5. Type a password in the Enter password and Re-Type password text boxes, and then click the Create My Account button. The Enter Contact Info page opens.

6. Read the page that opens, and then complete the form. Leave the Phone text box empty. Click the Continue-> Update My Contact Info button. The Contact Info Updated page opens.

7. Click the Free VIRC eCoin link located in the colored table in the middle of the page.

8. Read the page that opens, and then click the Next -> Download Free eCoins button. (Notice that coins have a lifetime of 180 days.) The Download Response page opens. (*Note*: A dialog box might open and indicate that you need a missing browser plug-in. If this dialog box opens, click the Cancel button and then ask your instructor or technical support person for assistance. You might not be allowed to download the eCoin wallet at your installation.)

9. If more than one browser window is open on your desktop, close all but one of them. (It doesn't matter which browser windows you close.)

10. Click the Log Out button to log out of your account. The eCoin home page reappears.

11. Click the Login button, and then enter your user name and password in the appropriate text boxes. Click the Next -> Login button to log in.

12. On the page that opens, click the Wallet Balance button located on the left side of the page to check your VIRC coin balance. (If a dialog box opens and asks if you want to display secure and nonsecure items, click the Yes button.) You should have 1000.00 VIRC coins in your server account. Use your browser's Print button to print this page. (*Note*: If you could not download the eCoin wallet in Step 8, the wallet feature will not work.)

13. Click other links, such as the Surfing History and Transaction History links. What appears on each of these pages?

14. Scroll to the bottom of the page, and then click the Log Out link.

15. Click the Become A Merchant link, and read the information on the page that opens. In a memo addressed to J.D., briefly explain the steps he would need to take to establish Great! Newsletters as an eCoin merchant. Click your browser's Back button to return to the eCoin home page.

16. Click the Walletless Payment Interface link in the Merchant's corner part of the page. Continue your report to J.D. by briefly describing the advantages of using the Wallet method instead of storing eCoins.

17. Click the Samples link located near the top of the page, and then click the VD#3 WLP version link. This page provides an example of implementing a Walletless eCoin interface. Click the Vol II SQL Specification link to open a Walletless Payment Interface example.

18. Log in by typing your eCoin user name and password in the text boxes. Click the Next -> Verification button to purchase a document with your free VIRC coins. (If a Security Alert dialog box opens, click the Yes button to continue.)

19. Use your browser's Print command on the File menu to print only the first page of the SQL manual that opens to verify that you purchased the document.

20. Return to the Online Companion for Case Problem 3, click the eCoin link, click the Login button, type your eCoin user name and password, and then click the Next -> Login button to log back into your eCoin account.

21. Click the Wallet Balance link on the left side of the page. Use your browser's Print button to print the page that shows your VIRC coin balance. Close your Web browser and close your dial-up connection, if necessary.

22. Finish your report to J.D. by evaluating your experience using eCoin. Should Great! Newsletters become an eCoin merchant? Why or why not?

Case 4. Teach-U-Comp Learning Center Evan Moskowitz and you have formed an Internet company called Teach-U-Comp Learning Center, which markets and sells online computer courses. The first online courses you will offer are for computer programming languages, such as Visual Basic, Java, and C++. Students can sign up for as many courses as they would like. Each four-week course costs $55 and students receive continuing education units (CEUs) based on the duration of the course and its difficulty. Evan is busy creating the online content and installing the course delivery software. He has asked you to investigate and report back to him about the feasibility of implementing electronic wallet payment systems, in addition to the existing credit card payment system. Students could download an electronic wallet that Teach-U-Comp supports, install it on their own computer, and then use the wallet to pay for their courses as well as to shop at other electronic commerce sites that support the selected electronic wallet software. Evan asks you to investigate electronic wallet software, sign up for a server-side electronic wallet, and print a few pages from the wallet's vendor. You will then report to Evan on the utility of using a wallet for Teach-U-Comp.

1. Start your Web browser, and then go to the Online Companion by entering the URL http://www.course.com/NewPerspectives/EC in the appropriate location of your Web browser. Click the Tutorial 5 link, and then click the Case Problems link. Click the Brodia link and wait while your browser loads the Brodia home page.

2. Click the Get Brodia. It's Free! button at the top of the page to create a new Brodia account.

3. Enter your information into the form. Click the Brodia Terms of Use link, read the page that opens, click the Accept button at the bottom of the page, click the I accept check box to select it, and then clear the Please send me check box.

4. Click the NEXT button to continue the sign up process. A page opens explaining that a security warning dialog box will probably appear and what to do if it does. Read the information on this page, and then click the Yes button. There is a noticeable delay while Brodia processes your information. The Your Account Information page opens.

5. *Do not* enter any credit card information. Fill in your billing address information in the middle section of the form. Leave the Daytime Phone and Evening Phone fields empty. Use your browser's Print command to print the page, and then click the DONE button to continue.

6. Click the Get Started link on the page that opens. A new browser window should open and display your Brodia wallet. (If a new window does not open, click the START WALLET button at the top of the Brodia home page.) Click the new window's Minimize button. Brodia's home page should still appear in the first browser window.

7. Return to the Online Companion page for Case Problem 4, and then click the Coffee and Tea Merchant link. (This demonstration site will not charge you for anything you might order—this is a safe site.)

8. Use the Web site to order some coffee beans, click the Order button, and then click the Check Out button. Your Brodia wallet should wake up and appear on top of the Coffee and Tea Merchant order form. If your wallet does not automatically open, maximize the Brodia wallet window.

9. Drag the Brodia wallet window to the right so you can see the empty form fields.

10. Click the FILL button in the Brodia wallet window. Brodia wallet fills in many of the name and address fields on the shopping form.

11. Use your browser's Print button to print the completed Coffee and Tea Merchant order form.

12. Scroll to the bottom of the page and click the No: Do Not Order button.

13. Click the Brodia Shopping Service program button on the taskbar to open the Brodia wallet.

14. Click the Sign Off link in the wallet window, and then click the OK button to sign out.

15. Close your Web browser and close your dial-up connection, if necessary.

16. Write a paragraph on your observations about using the wallet. What are the advantage(s) of using Brodia? What are the disadvantages? Should Teach-U-Comp Learning Center consider using Brodia at its Web site? Why or why not?

QUICK | CHECK ANSWERS

Session 5.1

1. micropayment
2. Automated Clearing House (ACH)
3. card not present
4. Because it is difficult to verify that the person electronically presenting the card is the card's owner, there is a greater risk of fraud.
5. merchant (acquiring)
6. The merchant's account receives a deposit equal to the transaction amount (minus any credit card processing fees) and, simultaneously, the cardholder's credit card is charged the transaction amount.
7. card processors

Session 5.2

1. Any three of: portable, divisible, convenient, and anonymity
2. A cryptographic modification of an owner's digital money to validate the electronic cash without revealing the payer's identity
3. The act of paying the same electronic cash to two different merchants
4. A stored-value card is a plastic card containing a magnetic strip or computer chip that records a currency balance. A smart card can do limited processing, and it can store electronic currency, personal information, credit card information, and a cardholder's encrypted identification.
5. Server-side electronic wallets store consumer information on a remote server belonging to a particular merchant or the wallet's publisher. Client-side electronic wallets store a consumer's information on the consumer's own computer.
6. Electronic currency, name and address information, and credit card information

In this tutorial you will:

- View examples of Web sites that conduct international electronic commerce

- Examine some of the cultural issues that affect businesses conducting electronic commerce

- Examine laws that govern electronic commerce activities

- Explore contracts and contractual issues in electronic commerce

- Examine the issues of trademark infringement, deceptive trade practices, and the regulation of advertising and solicitation activities

- Consider ethics issues that arise for companies conducting electronic commerce

- Discover the taxes that are levied on businesses conducting electronic commerce

INTERNATIONAL, LEGAL, AND ETHICS ISSUES

Conducting Electronic Commerce in a Global Business Environment

CASE

Cinematique

Amy Baker is the owner of Cinematique, a store that sells classic movie posters and related memorabilia. Some of the posters that Amy sells in her store are original prints of posters used in movie theaters in the 1930s and 1940s, but most are reproductions. Amy sells framed and unframed posters. The memorabilia items include movie props and costumes that Amy has acquired at estate sales and auctions. She keeps many of these items on permanent display in the store, but she does occasionally sell them. In addition, she sells reproductions of some of these items, many of which are very popular with customers. However, Amy has found it difficult at times to obtain reproduction rights from the copyright or trademark holders for these items; and consequently, part of her business has not grown as much as she had hoped it might.

Cinematique has one retail location in a suburban shopping mall in Upstate New York. Amy is considering opening other stores to expand her business. She has read about the great successes of online stores such as Amazon.com and CDnow and is thinking about opening her next store online. Amy is a good merchandiser and a good buyer, but she is not a computer whiz. She has asked you to help her plan her new online store. She is especially excited about selling posters in international markets because the trade journals she reads have noted an increasing interest in classic films in Europe, Asia, and Latin America. However, Amy is concerned about the many issues that she will face in advertising and selling her products, often copyrighted or trademarked, to a wider market through the Internet. You agree to help Amy research the international, legal, ethics, and tax issues that she will face as she moves her business online.

SESSION 6.1

In this session, you will learn about some issues that arise when a business opens its doors to the world on the Internet. These include language issues, culture issues, and technical infrastructure issues.

Electronic Commerce: International by Nature

Because the Internet is a worldwide network of networked computers, any business that moves its operations to the Web becomes an international business. Once the Cinematique Web site is launched, anyone in the world with an Internet connection will be able to visit it. The Web does not reveal very much about a business. When a person visits the Cinematique site, that person will not know if Cinematique is a small store with five employees or an international chain of stores with thousands of employees. A now-famous cartoon that appeared in *The New Yorker* magazine shows two dogs sitting at a computer. The caption indicates that one dog is saying to the other, "On the Internet, nobody knows you're a dog." This kind of anonymity extends to all aspects of a Web presence. For example, a U.S. bank can establish a Web site that offers services throughout the world. No potential customer visiting the site will know by browsing through the site's pages just how large or well established the bank is.

Trust on the Web

Because Web site visitors will not become customers unless they can trust the company behind the site, a plan for establishing credibility is essential. Sellers on the Web cannot assume that visitors will know that a trustworthy business operates the site. You explain to Amy that establishing trustworthiness will be one of the first challenges that Cinematique will face as it creates and promotes its online business, both in the United States and in international markets.

Customers' lack of inherent trust in "strangers" on the Web is logical; after all, people have been doing business with their neighbors—not strangers—for thousands of years. As businesses expanded to become large corporations with multinational operations, their reputations grew commensurately. Before a company could do business in dozens of countries, it had to prove its trustworthiness by satisfying customers for many years as it was growing. Businesses on the Web must find ways to overcome this well-founded tradition of distrusting strangers because today a company can incorporate one day and, through the Web, be doing business the next day with persons in almost every country in the world.

Customers can only trust a company if they know how that company will act in specific circumstances. For example, a buyer who is unhappy with the quality of goods delivered must know how the seller will react to a claim that the quality of the goods has been misrepresented. Part of this knowledge derives from the buyer and seller sharing a common language and similar customs. Another part derives from having a common legal structure for resolving disputes.

Importance of Culture in Electronic Commerce

The combination of language and customs is often called **culture**; however, many experts agree that language and customs are just the observable manifestations of culture. Thus, it is helpful to think of language and customs as being the *result* of culture. Most researchers agree that culture varies across national boundaries and, in many cases, across regions within nations. Businesses engaging in electronic commerce must be aware of the differences in language and customs that are part of the culture for any region in which they intend to do business. **Business policies** are the elements of a country's culture that have become ingrained in the everyday business practices of a particular country. The **technology infrastructure** of a country includes the business and government telecommunications networks that carry and route computer data traffic in that country.

The potential cultural barriers to international electronic commerce include differences in language, customs, business policies, and technology infrastructures. Figure 6-1 shows how these four factors relate to culture.

| Figure 6-1 | FOUR CULTURE-DRIVEN FACTORS THAT CAN AFFECT INTERNATIONAL ELECTRONIC COMMERCE |

Figure 6-1 shows culture as the driving force behind language, customs, and business policies. In turn, a combination of customs and business policies determines what kind of technology infrastructure a given country will have. Many researchers believe that culture, language, and customs are so deeply intertwined that it is difficult to discuss them separately. However, because language issues require that Web developers include specific design elements in Web sites intended for electronic commerce, you will examine language issues first.

Language Issues in Electronic Commerce

Most companies have realized that the only way to do business effectively in other cultures is to adapt their business policies to those cultures. The phrase "think globally, act locally" is often used to describe this approach. The first step that a Web business usually takes to reach potential customers in other countries, and thus in other cultures, is to provide local language versions of its Web site. Often, providing local language versions of a Web site includes translating the Web site into another language or regional dialect. Researchers have found that customers are far more likely to buy products and services from Web sites created in their own language, even if they can read English well. Although the proportion of electronic commerce that occurs in international markets today is relatively small, experts predict that by 2001, 60% of Web use and 40% of electronic commerce sales will involve at least one party located outside the United States.

Other than English, U.S. companies' most-used languages are Spanish, German, Japanese, French, and Chinese. Following closely behind these languages is a second tier of languages that includes Italian, Korean, Portuguese, Russian, and Swedish. Some languages require multiple translations for separate dialects. For example, the Spanish spoken in Spain is different from that spoken in Mexico, which is different from that spoken in the rest of Latin America. People in parts of Argentina use yet a fourth dialect of Spanish.

Many of these dialect differences are spoken inflections, which are not important for Web site designers (unless, of course, the sites include audio or video elements); however, a significant number of differences do occur in word meanings and spellings. You may be familiar with these types of differences because they occur in the U.S. and British dialects of English. The U.S. spelling of *gray* becomes *grey* in Great Britain, and the meaning of *bonnet* changes from a type of hat in the United States to an automobile hood in Great Britain. Chinese has two main systems of writing: one is used in mainland China and another is used in Hong Kong and Taiwan. Furthermore, the writing language used in mainland China is pronounced differently in various parts of that country.

Although most Web sites that include foreign language elements will translate all of their pages, some sites have thousands of pages, many of which are devoted to targeted content. The cost of translating all of these pages might be prohibitive for some firms. The decision to translate a particular page should be made by the corporate department responsible for each page's content. The home page should have versions in all supported languages, as should all first-level links to the home page. Beyond that, pages devoted to marketing, product information, and establishing brand should be given a high translation priority. Some pages, especially those devoted to local interests or issues, might be maintained only in the relevant language. For example, a weekly update on local news and employment opportunities at a U.S. company's plant in Frankfurt probably only needs to be maintained in German.

When Web browsers and Web servers communicate with each other, the message that a Web browser (client) sends to the Web server when it establishes a connection can include a request header. The **request header** contains information about the browser software, including the browser's default language setting. The Web server can detect the default language setting of the browser and automatically redirect the browser to the set of Web pages created in that language.

An alternative approach is to include links to multiple language versions on the Web site's home page. The Web site visitor must select one of the languages by clicking the appropriate link. Web sites using this approach must make sure that the links are identifiable to visitors who only read those languages. Thus, the links should show the name of each language in that language. Many Web sites use country flags to indicate language. This practice can lead to errors and unintentional ill will. For example, a Bolivian visitor who must click Spain's flag to navigate to the Spanish language pages might have difficulty identifying the Spanish flag, and might resent that Bolivia's flag was not presented as a choice. The **Europages** home page shown in Figure 6-2 includes identifiable links to pages in German, English, Spanish, French, Italian, and Dutch. Clicking any of these language hyperlinks opens the equivalent home page in that language.

Figure 6-2   EUROPAGES HOME PAGE

Many firms provide Web page translation services for companies. These firms will translate Web pages and maintain them for a fee that is usually between 25 and 50 cents per word. Languages that are complex or spoken by relatively few people are generally more expensive to translate than other languages. These language translation service firms use a variety of approaches when they translate material for use in electronic commerce. For key marketing messages, the touch of a human translator is essential to capture subtle meanings. For more routine functions, such as processing transactions or handling customer inquiries, automated software translation may be an acceptable alternative. Software translation can reach speeds of 400,000 words per hour, so even if the translation is not perfect, businesses might find it preferable to a human, who can translate between 400 and 600 words per hour.

Translation service firms and translation software manufacturers that work with electronic commerce sites do not generally use the term "translation" to describe what they do. They prefer the term **localization**, which means a translation that considers multiple elements of the local environment, such as business and cultural practices, in addition to local dialect variations in the language. The cultural element is very important because it can affect—and sometimes completely change—intended meanings. Amy is interested in learning more about the firms that offer localization services, so you offer to take her on a Web tour of a few major firms.

To learn more about language translation service firms:

1. Start your Web browser, and then go to the Student Online Companion page by entering the URL **http://www.course.com/NewPerspectives/EC** in the appropriate location of your Web browser. Click the **Tutorial 6** link, and then click the **Session 6.1** link. Click the **Transparent Language** link and wait while your browser loads the Transparent Language home page. Transparent Language is a firm that sells a variety of services. Like most Web businesses, it offers some free features to attract customers. These features include newsletters, games, a "Word of the Day," and even a Web site that performs free translations.

2. Click the link to **FreeTranslation.com** on the right side of the page to open the free translation site. The FreeTranslation.com page that loads in your browser lets you translate text that you type in the Text Translator box. The page also offers a Web Page Translator. You can type the URL of a Web page in this box and the site will translate the Web page. The page also includes a list of frequently asked questions about machine translation.

3. Use the FreeTranslation.com page to try out a few translations, and then click your browser's **Back** button to return to the Transparent Software home page.

4. Click the **Language & Culture** link on the left side of the page to open the Language and Culture Pages. This page contains links that are devoted to a more detailed description of over a dozen frequently used languages on the Web.

5. Follow a few of the links and learn more about the languages these pages describe. When you are finished exploring these links, click your browser's **Back** button to return to the Transparent Software home page.

6. Click the **PlusTranslation.com** link on the left side of the page to open the Web page shown in Figure 6-3. This page provides links to four levels of translation services that range from the free service on the FreeTranslation.com site to professional translators who are familiar with particular industry terminology. A business such as Cinematique that needs a precise localized translation to use on its Web site would most likely select the Personal Plus or the Premium Plus service levels. You can click these links to find out more about what each of these services offers and how each service is priced.

| Figure 6-3 | PLUSTRANSLATION.COM TRANSLATION SERVICES LINKS |

TROUBLE? Because companies change their Web sites regularly, the pages you open might be different.

7. When you are finished examining the Transparent Language translation services, click your browser's **Back** button or use its history list to return to the firm's home page. You can explore the other links on the site, including the link to Enterprise Solutions, which includes ways of incorporating Transparent Language's translation software into your Web site to do automatic translations of communications to and from Web site visitors.

Amy sees how the PlusTranslation.com site can help her to ensure that her Web site is accessible to people around the world. You want to show her another site that performs translation services, Lernout & Hauspie.

To visit the Lernout & Hauspie Web translation service firm:

1. Click your browser's **Back** button to return to the Online Companion page for Session 6.1, and then click the **Lernout & Hauspie** link and wait while your browser loads the Lernout & Hauspie home page.

2. Click the **Services** hyperlink near the top of the page to open the page shown in Figure 6-4. This page includes a brief description of Lernout & Hauspie's services. It also provides links to more detailed information about the firm's localization, translation, Web building, and other services that Amy might find useful as she creates an international sales Web site for Cinematique.

Figure 6-4	LERNOUT & HAUSPIE TRANSLATION AND DOCUMENTATION SERVICES

hyperlinks to translation and documentation services

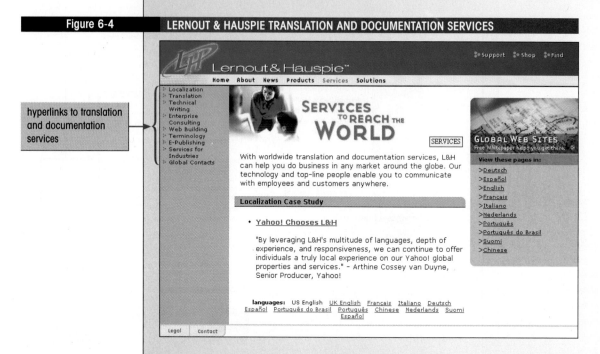

3. Click some of the links on the left side of the page to explore these services. When you have finished examining the Lernout & Hauspie translation and documentation services, click the **Products** hyperlink near the top of the page to open a page of links to Lernout & Hauspie products. Notice that this firm sells products that synthesize speech and understand speech in addition to their language translation products.

Amy is very pleased to find that these services are available and that the rates seem affordable. She explains that she wants her Web site to have more pictures than words because of the nature of the product she is selling. You explain that these two sites are not the only language translation product and service firms, and that a number of other firms, such as **Berlitz**, also offer these products and services.

As the Cinematique site grows, Amy can use software to help maintain a larger number of Web pages in multiple languages. For example, **Idiom** sells software that helps maintain Web pages in multiple language versions. Idiom's WorldServer software tracks text that needs to be translated and inserts the translations into all sites that include that language. A human translator still must perform the translation, but automating the update process helps companies reduce the cost of maintaining multiple-language Web sites. On each translated Web page, WorldServer places tags in the text that identify each text element as being the translation of a corresponding text element at the company's main Web site. When the text in a page at the main Web site changes, the software sends out a notification of the change to the translation team. The notification shows which pages need to be updated and tracks the exact location of the change in every page that needs updating. When the human translation is complete, the software inserts the translated text in the correct locations automatically.

Of course, the language itself is only part of making a Web site international. Although the translation and localization services try to include cultural issues when they perform Web site translations, you explain to Amy that she will need to understand and deal with these cultural issues as she designs her online store and decides in which countries she will do business.

Customs and Business Policy Issues in Electronic Commerce

To give Amy an example of the subtle culture issues that can arise in international electronic commerce, you tell her about Virtual Vineyards, which now does business under the name Wine.com. This company sells wine and specialty food items on the Web. Soon after it began doing business internationally, Wine.com noticed that it was getting an unusually large number of customer complaints about "short" shipments. The customer service representatives noticed that most of these complaints were coming from customers in Japan. Wine.com sold much of its wine in case (12 bottles) or half-case quantities; however, it did sell one or two bottles at a time to some customers. To save on operating costs, Wine.com only stocked shipping materials in case, half-case, and two-bottle sizes. After investigating the short-shipment complaints further, the company determined that many of its Japanese customers ordered only one bottle of wine, which was shipped in a two-bottle container. The cultural expectations of Japanese customers, who consider packaging to be an important element of a high-quality product, made it inconceivable that anyone would ship one bottle of wine in a two-bottle container. Customers from Japan sent e-mail messages to Wine.com asking where the other bottle was, even though they had ordered only one bottle!

The Wine.com example is just one of many classic situations that arise from subtle language and cultural standards that are regularly used to train international businesspersons. Some other examples of mistranslations and misunderstandings of cultural standards include the following:

- General Motors could not understand why its Chevrolet Nova model was not selling well in Latin America until someone pointed out that *no va* means "it will not go" in Spanish.
- Pepsi's "come alive" advertising campaign fizzled in China because its message came across as "Pepsi brings your ancestors back from their graves."
- Baby food in jars adorned with the picture of a very cute baby had sold well everywhere it had been introduced. When the company began selling the baby food in African markets, however, it found sales to be disappointing. Many African countries do not have a single language. In fact, the large number of African languages and dialects creates a labeling problem for products sold in those countries. Low literacy levels add to the problem. The solution to the labeling problem is that product packages carry a picture of their contents instead of a written description. When the baby food manufacturer became aware of this cultural issue, it removed the baby picture from the baby food jars and sales increased dramatically.

The cultural overtones of simple design decisions can be dramatic. In India, for example, it is inappropriate to use the image of a cow in a cartoon or other comical setting. An image that shows persons' arms or legs uncovered on products sold in Muslim countries can offend potential customers. Even colors or Web page design elements can be troublesome. A Web page that is divided into four segments or includes large white elements can be offensive to a Japanese visitor. Both the number four and the color white are symbols of death in that culture.

Softbank, a major Japanese firm that invests in Internet companies, has devised a way to introduce electronic commerce to a reluctant Japanese population. Japanese people have resisted the U.S. version of electronic commerce because they prefer to pay in cash instead of by credit card. They also have a high level of apprehension about doing business online. In 1999, Softbank created a joint venture with 7-Eleven, Yahoo! Japan, and a major Japanese book distributor, Tohan, to sell books and CDs on the Web. This new venture, called eS-Books, allows customers to order items on the Internet, and then pick them up and pay for them in cash at the local 7-Eleven convenience store. By adding an intermediary—the exact opposite of the disintermediation strategy used so often by U.S. firms—that satisfies the needs of the Japanese customer, Softbank plans to bring electronic commerce to Japan.

Some parts of the world have cultural environments that are extremely inhospitable to electronic commerce initiatives. For example, many Middle Eastern and North African countries do not allow their citizens free access to the Internet. Governments in these countries regularly prevent free expression and have taken specific steps to prevent the exchange of information via the Internet. Saudi Arabia, Yemen, and the United Arab Emirates all use proxy servers to filter content. A **proxy server** is a computer that is inserted into a network between Web clients in a specific domain and Web servers outside of that domain. The owner of the domain can set up a proxy server to block traffic from Web servers at particular IP addresses or within particular domains. Jordan has imposed taxes that limit access to the Internet by making its cost very high. Jordan also passed a law in 1998 prohibiting publications in any media, including the Web, that conflict with the values of an Islamic nation. In many of these countries, Internet technology is so at odds with existing traditions, cultures, and laws that electronic commerce is unlikely to exist there at any significant level in the near future. Exceptions to this do exist, however. Algeria, Morocco, and the Palestinian Authority have not limited Internet access or censored content.

Although they do not ban electronic commerce entirely, some countries have strong cultural requirements that have found their way into the legal codes that govern business conduct. In France, an advertisement for a product or service must be in French. Thus, a U.S. business that advertises its products on the Web and is willing to ship goods to France must provide a French version of its pages. Many U.S. electronic commerce sites provide a Web page with a list of the countries from which they will accept orders through their Web sites.

The official language of the Canadian province of Quebec is French. Quebec provincial law requires street signs, billboards, directories, and advertising created by Quebec businesses to be in French. In 1999, the government of Quebec fined photographer Michael Calomiris and ordered him to either remove his English-language Web site or add a French translation of the pages to the site. Located in Quebec, Calomiris had been advertising his photographs for sale on the Web site and had targeted his ads to the U.S. market.

You explain to Amy that these culture issues will be important as she decides from which countries Cinematique will accept orders. She agrees that, in some cases, it might be best to forego sales in some countries to avoid some of these issues. You suggest to Amy that by carefully comparing the costs and benefits of doing business in a particular country, she can make good decisions. Many companies find that the costs of doing business in certain countries outweigh the benefits of potential sales in those countries.

Infrastructure Issues in Electronic Commerce

Even if Cinematique successfully meets the challenges posed by language and culture issues, it will still face the challenge posed by inadequacies in the infrastructure that supports the Internet throughout the world. **Internet infrastructure** includes the computers and software connected to the Internet and the communications networks over which the message packets travel. The capacity and quality of this electronic equipment varies tremendously from country to country throughout the world. Two sites that allow you to see this variability are the Internet Traffic Report and the Matrix Information and Directory Services Web sites.

To learn more about the variability in international Internet infrastructure:

1. Click your browser's **Back** button or use its history list to return to the Online Companion page for Session 6.1, and then click the **Internet Traffic Report** hyperlink and wait while your browser loads the home page shown in Figure 6-5. This site provides continuous and historical statistics on response times and packet loss rates. (Your statistics will be different.) It also provides graphs of the **traffic index**, which is a measure of the speed at which packets travel through the Internet (the traffic index graphs do not appear in Figure 6-5). The Internet Traffic Report obtains these statistics from cooperating operators of router computers on the Internet at multiple sites in each continent. As you can see, there are dramatic differences among the five reporting continents in these two measures of Internet transmission quality. Note that Africa is not included in these reports. If it were, the differences would be even larger.

| Figure 6-5 | INTERNET TRAFFIC REPORT HOME PAGE |

Internet response time and packet loss statistics by continent (your statistics will be different)

2. Click your browser's **Back** button or use its history list to return to the Online Companion page for Session 6.1, and then click the **Matrix Information and Directory Services (MIDS)** hyperlink and wait while your browser loads the MIDS home page.

3. Scroll down the page to examine the links in the Traditional Products area, and then click the **World Map** link to load the page shown in Figure 6-6. This map shows that the number of Internet hosts varies widely by continent.

| Figure 6-6 | MIDS WORLD MAP OF THE INTERNET |

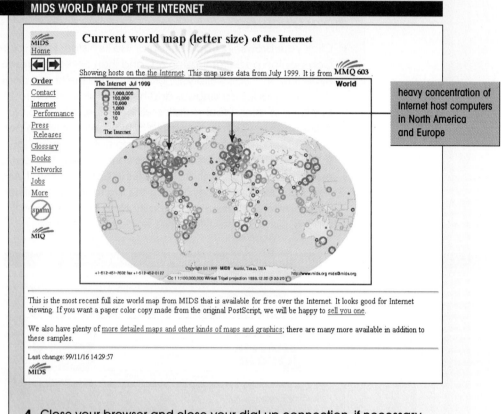

This is the most recent full size world map from MIDS that is available for free over the Internet. It looks good for Internet viewing. If you want a paper color copy made from the original PostScript, we will be happy to sell you one.

We also have plenty of more detailed maps and other kinds of maps and graphics; there are many more available in addition to these samples.

Last change: 99/11/16 14:29:57

4. Close your browser and close your dial-up connection, if necessary.

In many countries other than the United States, the telecommunications industry is either government owned or heavily regulated by the government. In many cases, regulations in these countries have inhibited the development of the telecommunications infrastructure, or limited the expansion of that infrastructure to a size that can support Internet data packet traffic reliably.

Local connection costs through the existing telephone networks in many countries are very high relative to U.S. costs for similar access. This difference can have a profound effect on the behavior of electronic commerce participants. For example, in Europe, where Internet connection costs can be quite high, few people would spend time surfing the Web to shop for a product. They will only use a Web browser to navigate to a specific site that they know will offer the product they want to buy. You explain to Amy that to be successful in selling to European customers, she will need to advertise Cinematique's Web presence in television, radio, and print media instead of relying on high placement on search engine results pages. In Europe, search engine result placements will not drive traffic to her site as long as access charges are high.

There are signs that this high access charge problem in Europe might change in the near future. In 1998, business and government leaders in several European countries began pushing for flat-rate telephone line Internet access charges. Europeans pay for the time they are using the telephone line—even for local calls—despite recent moves to deregulate the telecommunications industries in those countries. In a **flat-rate access** system, the consumer or business pays one monthly fee for unlimited telephone line usage. Activists in Germany, Ireland, and Spain have all argued that flat-rate access has been the key to the success of electronic commerce in the United States.

The paperwork that accompanies international commerce is another target for technology. Most businesses that conduct business internationally rely on a complex array of freight forwarding companies, customs brokers, international freight carriers, and importers to navigate the maze of paper they must complete at every step of the transaction to satisfy government and insurance requirements.

Domestic transactions usually include only the seller, the buyer, their respective banks, and one freight carrier. International transactions require physical handling by several carriers that government customs offices must monitor, in addition to the seller and buyer monitoring required by domestic transactions. International transactions often require the coordinated efforts of brokers and freight forwarders because they are so complex; however, including them in the information flows adds even more complexity.

The United Nations estimated that the cost of handling all of this paperwork amounted to $420 billion in 1998, or approximately 6% of the total $7 trillion in world international trade for that year. Many firms sell software-based systems designed to automate this process; however, automating trade procedures is a difficult task because each country has its own paper-based forms and procedures with which international shippers must comply. Even countries that have automated some procedures use computer systems that are incompatible with those of other countries. In 1999, a consortium of 120 banks and freight-handling firms founded **bolero.net**, an association dedicated to replacing the paper maze with a set of interoperable electronic commerce applications.

Amy thanks you for the information you have provided about the challenges of doing online business internationally. She still wants Cinematique to offer its posters and memorabilia to foreign customers, but she now understands that it will take a variety of strategies and a considerable financial investment to do this effectively. She also realizes that Cinematique should restrict overseas sales and place a list of the countries in which she is willing to make sales on the Web site.

Session 6.1 QUICK CHECK

1. True or False: When a company opens an online store, it becomes an international business immediately.

2. What are two things that most customers and companies must share in order for customers to trust the companies with which they conduct business?

3. Culture is the driving force behind _____, _____, and _____.

4. Why are images of flags *not* a good way to denote links to Web pages in alternative languages?

5. Software translation is approximately _____ times faster than human translation.

6. Firms that provide language translation services for Web sites usually use the term _____ instead of "translation" to describe what they do.

7. True or False: The speed and quality of transmission is fairly constant on the Internet throughout the world.

SESSION 6.2

In this session, you will learn about the legal and ethical environment of electronic commerce. Businesses that operate on the Internet are subject to the same laws and ethical standards as other businesses; however, the broad reach and lack of paper records for many transactions completed on the Web present new challenges for these laws. You will also learn how various governmental entities tax electronic commerce transactions and about related public policy issues.

The Legal Environment of Electronic Commerce

When operating Cinematique on the Web, Amy will face two complicating factors as she tries to follow the law and abide by ethical standards. The first factor is that the Web will extend her company's reach beyond its current geographical boundaries. As you learned in Session 6.1, any business that uses the Web immediately becomes an international business. Thus, a company can become subject to many more laws more quickly than it would if it was a traditional brick-and-mortar business tied to one specific physical location. The second factor is the speed and efficiency of communications on the Web. Customers often have much more interactive and complex relationships with Web-based companies than they do with traditional merchants. Further, customers using electronic commerce often have significant levels of interaction with other customers of the company. Web businesses that violate the law or breach ethical standards can face rapid and intense reactions from their customers and other interested parties that become aware of their activities.

The Web banner advertising firm DoubleClick learned this lesson. It had been accumulating information as to which Internet users were clicking on which ads for several years, and then storing this information in an anonymous format by placing cookies on the users' computers and recording when a browser with that cookie accessed particular banner ads. In early 2000, DoubleClick announced that it would begin identifying people with these anonymous cookie records so it could build a large database of consumer behavior. By buying DoubleClick's services, companies could know who was visiting their Web sites. The outrage was swift and massive. Online news services and computer industry magazines carried dozens of stories criticizing the new policy. Online privacy advocates took strong positions against the policy. Government agencies and DoubleClick's competitors outlined publicly their criticisms of the policy. DoubleClick's stock price plunged as investors sold their shares in protest. The U.S. Federal Trade Commission initiated a probe of the company's practices and several states threatened lawsuits.

Eventually, DoubleClick modified its policy, stating that it would only place ads on Web sites that notify consumers of the data collection practices and that give those consumers a choice to opt out of the data collection. DoubleClick hired a chief privacy officer and an accounting firm to conduct privacy audits. It also set up an advisory board of consumer, security, and privacy experts.

Compliance with Laws and Regulations

Businesses operating on the Web must comply with the same laws and regulations that govern the operations of all businesses. If they do not, they face the same set of penalties that any business faces, including fines, reparation payments, and even jail sentences for officers and owners. Companies using Web sites to conduct electronic commerce should also adhere to the same ethical standards that other businesses follow. If they do not, they will suffer the same consequences that all companies suffer—the long-term loss of trust that can result in loss of business.

As companies expand their markets on the Web, they encounter different laws and different ethical frameworks, especially when they begin doing business in other countries.

Even when operating within the United States, the extended reach of an online business can create problems. In the U.S., the **Federal Trade Commission (FTC)** is the main federal agency responsible for enforcing a variety of consumer protection laws. These laws ensure the smooth operation of markets by investigating and prosecuting unfair or deceptive practices. Such practices threaten consumers' opportunities to exercise informed choice when buying products or services.

One recent FTC case that points out how the extended reach of an online business can create problems is the agency's investigation of Dell Computer and Micron Electronics, two companies that sell personal computers through their Web sites. In 1999, Dell and Micron agreed to settle FTC charges that they had disseminated misleading advertising to their customers and potential customers. The advertising in question was for computer leasing plans that both companies had offered on Web pages at their sites. The ads stated the price of the computer along with a monthly payment.

Unfortunately for Dell and Micron, stating the monthly payment without disclosing full details of the lease plan is a violation of the Consumer Leasing Act of 1976. This law is implemented through a federal regulation that was written and is updated periodically by the Federal Reserve Board. This regulation, called Regulation M, was designed to require banks and other lenders to fully disclose the terms of leases so that consumers would have enough information to make informed financing choices when leasing cars, boats, furniture, and other goods.

Both Dell and Micron had included the required information on their Web pages, but FTC investigators noted that important details, such as the number of payments and fees due at the signing of the lease, were placed in a small typeface at the bottom of a long Web page. A consumer who wanted to determine the full cost of leasing a computer would need to scroll through a number of densely filled screens to obtain enough information to make the necessary calculations. In the settlement, both companies agreed to provide consumers with clear, readable, and understandable information in their lease advertising. The companies also agreed to record keeping and federal monitoring activities designed to ensure their compliance with the terms of the settlement. Dell and Micron are computer manufacturers, not banks. Thus, it probably did not occur to them that they needed to become experts in Regulation M, which is generally considered to be a banking regulation.

Companies doing business on the Web can expose themselves to liabilities—often unintentionally—that arise from the environment of business today. That environment includes laws and ethical considerations that may be different from those with which the business is familiar. In the case of Dell and Micron, they were unfamiliar with the laws and ethics of the banking industry. That industry has a different culture; it is unlikely that a bank manager would have made such a mistake. Another online business, Wine.com, has gone to great lengths to comply with the laws it faces as it sells alcoholic beverages across state lines. Complex state laws control the sale of alcoholic beverages. These laws are different in each state and many of them are quite restrictive. Wine.com is located in California, but whenever it ships wine to a customer in another state, it becomes subject to the liquor control laws of that state.

To see how Wine.com complies with state liquor control laws:

1. Start your Web browser, and then go to the Student Online Companion page by entering the URL **http://www.course.com/NewPerspectives/EC** in the appropriate location of your Web browser. Click the **Tutorial 6** link, and then click the **Session 6.2** link. Click the **Wine.com** link and wait while your browser loads the Wine.com home page.

2. Click the **Wine Shop** hyperlink located near the top of the page. After the Wine Shop page loads, find a product for an alcoholic beverage and click its hyperlink.

3. When the description page for the product you have selected appears in your Web browser, examine it to make sure that it includes an item with alcohol content, such as a bottle of wine. Click the **Add to Cart** button to open the page shown in Figure 6-7. Wine.com opens this page when you buy an alcoholic beverage. The page includes a description of shipping restrictions and delays that might be caused by various state laws. Some states prohibit direct shipment of alcoholic beverages to consumers. Other states require that the shipment be routed through a state-licensed wholesaler. These shipment routings can cause the delays explained in the right column of the page. This page is an example of good Web site design because it lets customers know that there might be problems or delays with their orders as soon as possible. Many Web sites allow a customer to enter a large amount of ordering information and select a number of products before explaining that shipments might be delayed or not possible. Note that some states (in the example shown in Figure 6-7, the states are Texas and Arizona) have local alcoholic beverage laws in addition to the state laws. Thus, the page asks for the Zip code of customers in those states.

Figure 6-7	WINE.COM DESTINATION SELECTION PAGE

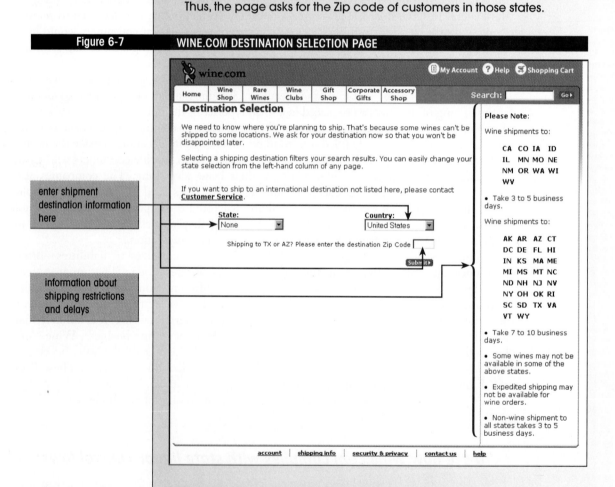

TROUBLE? Because states occasionally change their laws, the list of states you see might differ from that shown in the figure.

4. Click the **State** list arrow, scroll down the list and click **Tennessee**, and then click the **Submit** button. You should see a message similar to the one that appears in Figure 6-8. Again, Wine.com provides an example of good Web site design. The site quickly gives the customer a reason for Wine.com's inability to

ship and offers the customer several alternatives, including the option to ship to a different address. If desired, a customer can click the Destination Selection list arrow on the left side of the page to select another shipping destination.

| Figure 6-8 | WINE.COM SHIPMENT APOLOGY NOTICE |

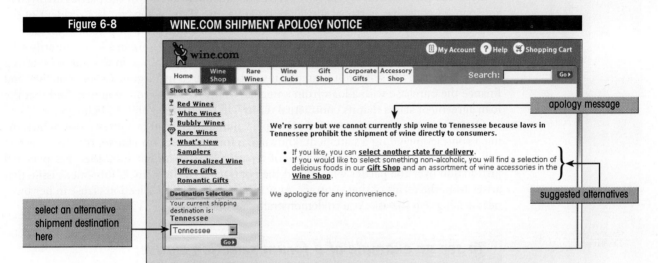

TROUBLE? You may not see the message shown in Figure 6-8 because Tennessee could change its laws to allow the shipment of alcoholic beverages into the state.

You explain to Amy that Wine.com is an unusual case because it sells a product that is highly regulated. However, the Wine.com Web site includes many customer-friendly features that any electronic commerce site should consider using to warn customers of potential problems with their orders. A key point is that Wine.com lets its customers know that a problem might exist at the earliest point possible. Even customers who find that they cannot purchase wine through the site will be pleased with the way Wine.com has handled the situation.

Jurisdiction

The ability of a government to exert control over a person or corporation is called **jurisdiction**. Governments that want to enforce laws regarding business conduct on the Internet must establish jurisdiction over that conduct. Two common types of business conduct that give rise to legal actions are conduct pursuant to a contract and conduct that causes harm. A **contract** is an agreement between two or more legal entities—persons or corporations— that provides for an exchange of value—goods, services, or money—between or among them. A **tort** is an action taken by one legal entity that causes harm to another legal entity. For example, a company that hires a burglar to break into a competitor's offices to steal its customer list would be committing a tort against its competitor, in addition to violating the criminal laws that prohibit breaking and entering and hiring the burglar to commit the crime. A tort is sometimes also called a **tortious action**. Persons or corporations that want to use the legal system to enforce their rights under contracts or to be compensated for tort damages must find courts that have sufficient jurisdiction to hear their cases.

A court has sufficient jurisdiction in a matter if it has both subject-matter jurisdiction and personal jurisdiction. **Subject-matter jurisdiction** is a court's authority to decide the type of dispute. For example, in the United States, federal courts have subject-matter jurisdiction over issues governed by federal law (for example, bankruptcy, copyright, patent, and federal tax matters), and state courts have subject-matter jurisdiction over issues governed by state laws (for example, professional licensing and state tax matters). If the parties to a contract are both located in the same state, a state court would have subject-matter jurisdiction. The rules for determining whether a court has subject-matter jurisdiction are very clear and easy to apply. Thus, very few disputes arise over subject-matter jurisdiction.

Personal jurisdiction is generally determined by the residence of the parties involved in a dispute. A court has personal jurisdiction over a case if the defendant is a resident of the state in which the court is located. In such cases, the determination of personal jurisdiction is straightforward. However, an out-of-state person or corporation can also voluntarily submit to the jurisdiction of a particular state court by agreeing to do so in writing or by taking certain actions in the state. For example, if you buy a stereo in Virginia (where you live) and finance the purchase with a loan from a finance company in Detroit, you may find that the loan agreement states that its contractual terms will be enforced under Michigan law.

One of the most common ways that people voluntarily submit to a jurisdiction is by signing a contract including a statement, known as a **forum selection clause**, that the contract will be enforced according to the laws of a particular state. That state then has personal jurisdiction over the parties who signed the contract regarding any enforcement issue that arises from the terms of that contract. Amy hasn't seen a forum selection clause in her business dealings, so she asks you to demonstrate one on an existing Web site.

To see an example of a forum selection clause:

1. Click your browser's **Back** button or use its history list to return to the Online Companion page for Session 6.2, and then click the **X:drive** link and wait while your browser loads the X:drive home page.

2. Click the **X:drive Affiliate** hyperlink on the right side of the page to open the Affiliate Program page. X:drive is a company that offers free Web space to its customers. One way it attracts new customers is through an affiliate program. This page provides information to prospective affiliate site owners.

3. Click the **agreement** link to view the terms of the contract between X:drive and its affiliates.

4. Scroll down the agreement to item 13, titled "Miscellaneous." The second to last paragraph in this item is a forum selection clause. See Figure 6-9.

| Figure 6-9 | FORUM SELECTION CLAUSE IN X:DRIVE AFFILIATE AGREEMENT |

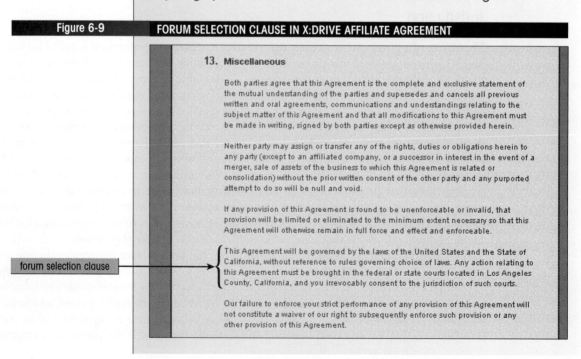

Individual states also have laws that can create personal jurisdiction for their courts. The details of these laws, called **long-arm statutes**, vary from state to state, but generally they create personal jurisdiction over nonresidents who transact business or commit tortious acts in the state. Businesses should be aware of the terms of these laws when conducting electronic commerce. In most states, the extent to which these laws apply to companies doing business over the Internet is very unclear. The laws were written before electronic commerce existed, thus the application of these laws to Internet transactions is evolving as courts make decisions in cases regarding such transactions. The trend in this evolving law is that the more business activities a company conducts in a state, the more likely it is that a court will assert personal jurisdiction over that company through a long-arm statute.

One important exception to this trend occurs in cases involving tortious acts. A business can commit a tortious act by selling a product that causes harm to a buyer. The tortious act can be negligence, in which the seller unintentionally provides a harmful product, or it can be an intentional tort, in which the seller knowingly causes injury to the buyer. The most common examples of intentional torts are defamation, fraud, and theft of trade secrets. Courts tend to invoke their state's long-arm statutes much more readily in the case of tortious acts than in other business cases. If the case involves an intentional tort or a criminal act, courts will almost always assert jurisdiction. Consider an example in which a computer hacker in New Jersey breaks into a company's Web site in Indiana. If the hacker copies files containing trade secrets (an intentional tort), an Indiana court would be more likely to assert jurisdiction than if the hacker just leaves a harmless file on the computer.

You explain to Amy that jurisdictional issues are complex and change rapidly. Any business that intends to conduct electronic commerce should consult an experienced lawyer. Some online resources for learning more about the law in this area do exist, however.

To learn more about jurisdiction issues:

1. Click your browser's **Back** button or use its history list to return to the Online Companion page for Session 6.2, and then click the **John Marshall Law School Cyberspace Law Index** link and wait while your browser loads the page shown in Figure 6-10.

| Figure 6-10 | THE JOHN MARSHALL LAW SCHOOL CYBERSPACE LAW INDEX PAGE |

Cyberspace Law Subject Index

THE JOHN MARSHALL LAW SCHOOL
CHICAGO
CENTER FOR INFORMATION TECHNOLOGY & PRIVACY LAW
Cyberspace Law

- Advertising
- Anonymity
- Antitrust and unfair competition
- Child pornography
- Constitutional law
- Consumer protection
- Contracts
- Copyright
- Crime
- Diversity, discrimination, and harassment
- Domain name disputes
- Domain name system
- Education
- Electronic commerce
- Employment
- Encryption
- Filtering and rating systems
- Free speech
- Freeware and shareware
- Gambling

- Governance
- Hacking/cracking, viruses, and security
- Health care
- Information access and control
- Internet background
- Jurisdiction ← *link to information about jurisdiction issues*
- Keyword registration systems
- Linking and framing
- Lobbying and net activism
- Mergers and acquisitions
- Meta-tagging and "spamdexing"
- Microsoft Corporation
- Privacy
- Professional regulation
- Protection of children
- Taxation
- Telecom regulation
- Tort liability
- Trademarks
- Universal service
- Unsolicited e-mail

Subject Index | FAQ | Update service | Submit an item | Broken links | Comments

2. Click the **Jurisdiction** hyperlink to open a page of links to current cases, law review articles, and other resources on jurisdictional issues that arise for companies engaging in electronic commerce.

3. Click the **Other Materials** link near the top of the page and find the entry for the Minnesota Attorney General's Office, Memorandum on Internet Jurisdiction (July 1995). Click the **WWW** link to open the Web page containing this memorandum and read it. The memorandum describes the State of Minnesota's position on its jurisdiction over information transmitted via the Internet that is disseminated in Minnesota.

4 Click your browser's **Back** button to return to the Cyberspace Law Index page. You can explore the links on other pages within the Cyberspace Law site to learn more about legal issues that affect businesses conducting commerce on the Internet.

Borders and Jurisdiction

Borders between countries in the physical world serve a useful purpose for people and businesses—they mark the range of culture and law very clearly. When persons travel across international borders, they are made aware of the transition in many ways. For example, most border crossings have a formal procedure for exiting one country and entering the other that requires an examination of documents. Businesses that transport products across an international border will find that the products are subject to inspection. The language and the currency usually change when a person crosses a border. Figure 6-11 shows four elements of business culture that change when a person crosses the U.S.-Mexico border: currency, language, the legal system, and the predominant form of business ownership.

Figure 6-11	FOUR ELEMENTS OF BUSINESS CULTURE THAT DIFFER BETWEEN THE UNITED STATES AND MEXICO

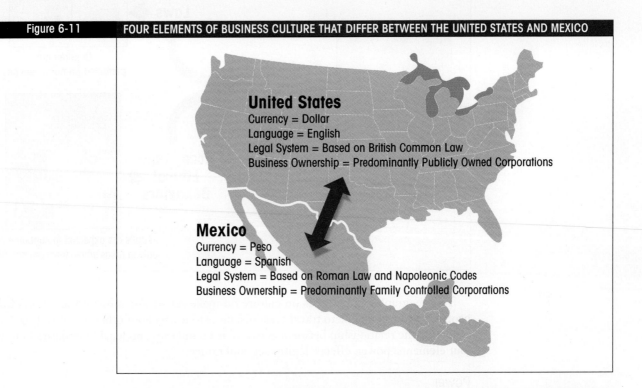

United States
Currency = Dollar
Language = English
Legal System = Based on British Common Law
Business Ownership = Predominantly Publicly Owned Corporations

Mexico
Currency = Peso
Language = Spanish
Legal System = Based on Roman Law and Napoleonic Codes
Business Ownership = Predominantly Family Controlled Corporations

The four elements shown in Figure 6-11 are manifestations of the differences in legal rules and cultural customs in the two countries. In the physical world, geographic boundaries almost always coincide with legal and cultural boundaries. The limits of acceptable ethical behavior and the laws that are adopted in a geographic area are the result of the influences of the area's dominant culture. This relationship between a society's culture, laws, and ethical behaviors appears in Figure 6-12.

Figure 6-12   CULTURE AFFECTS LAWS AND ETHICAL BEHAVIOR

The geographic boundaries on culture do make sense. For most of the world's history, people have been unable to travel great distances to learn about other cultures. Legal scholars define the relationship between geographic boundaries and legal boundaries in terms of four elements: power, effects, legitimacy, and notice.

Power

Power is the control of a government over physical space and the people, businesses, and objects that reside in that space. To have effective laws, a government must be able to enforce them by exercising physical control over its residents and imposing sanctions on those who violate the law.

Laws in the physical world do not apply to people who are not located or do not own assets that are located in the geographic area that created those particular laws. For example, the United States cannot enforce its copyright laws on a citizen of Japan who is doing business in Japan and who owns no assets in the United States. Any U.S. assertion of power over such a Japanese citizen would conflict with the Japanese government's recognized monopoly on using force with its citizens. The level of power asserted by a government is limited to that accepted by the culture that exists within its geographic boundaries. Ideally, geographic boundaries, cultural groupings, and legal structures all coincide. When they do not, internal strife and civil wars often erupt.

Effects *Customs dictate*

Effects in the physical world occur because a person's behavior occurs within physical proximity of another. Personal or corporate actions have a stronger influence on people and things that are close than on those that are far away. Government-provided trademark protection is a good example of an effect. The Italian government, for instance, can provide and enforce trademark protection for a business named Caruso's Ristorante that is located in Rome. The effects of another restaurant using the same name are strongest in geographic areas in Rome, close to Rome, and in other parts of Italy. If a restaurant named Caruso's Ristorante opens in Kansas City, the restaurant in Rome would experience few, if any, negative effects from having this restaurant use its trademarked name. Thus, the law in Italy adequately controls the impact of the trademark violation because of the limited geographic area within which that violation has effects.

A local culture's acceptance or reluctance to accept various kinds of effects will determine its laws. For example, certain communities in the United States require houses to be built on lots of at least five acres. Other communities prohibit outdoor advertising of various kinds. As you learned earlier in this session, some states control alcoholic beverage sales in a more restrictive way than others. In all of these cases, the local cultures make the effects of such restrictions acceptable.

Legitimacy

Most people agree that those who are subject to laws should have some role in formulating them. In 1970, the United Nations passed a resolution that a government's **legitimacy** derives from the mandate of the people who will be subject to that government's laws. The resolution made clear that the persons who live within a set of recognized geographic boundaries are the ultimate source of legitimate legal authority over persons and actions within those boundaries.

People in different cultures do, however, have different ideas about how much authority their government should have. Some cultures allow their governments to operate with a high degree of autonomy and unquestioned authority. China and Singapore, for example, are two countries in which cultural permission for a high-authority government exists. Other cultures, such as those of the Scandinavian countries, place strict limits on governmental authority over the rights of individuals.

Notice

Physical boundaries are a convenient and effective way to announce the ending of one legal or cultural system and the beginning of another. The physical boundary, when crossed, provides **notice** that one set of rules has been replaced by a different set of rules.

People cannot be expected to obey laws or follow cultural norms unless they are notified of their existence. Borders provide this notice in the physical world. Figure 6-13 shows how power, effects, legitimacy, and notice flow from geographic boundaries to provide the basis for legal boundaries.

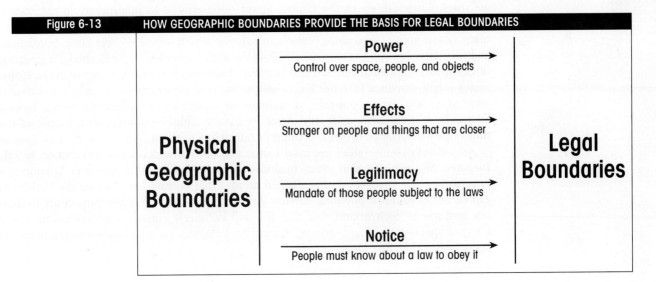

| Figure 6-13 | HOW GEOGRAPHIC BOUNDARIES PROVIDE THE BASIS FOR LEGAL BOUNDARIES |

Power
Control over space, people, and objects

Effects
Stronger on people and things that are closer

Legitimacy
Mandate of those people subject to the laws

Notice
People must know about a law to obey it

Physical Geographic Boundaries → **Legal Boundaries**

Jurisdiction on the Internet

Establishing jurisdiction is much more difficult on the Internet than it is in the physical world because geographic boundaries do not exist in any meaningful sense. For example, a Swedish company that sells on the Internet may have a Web site in English and a URL that ends in ".com," thus not indicating to customers that it is a Swedish firm. The server that hosts this company's Web page might be in Canada, and the people who maintain the Web site might work from their homes in Australia.

A Turkish citizen who buys a product from the firm described above might be unhappy with the purchase and want to file a lawsuit. The world's geographic borders-based system of laws does not provide much help for this Turkish citizen, who must try to figure out where to file the lawsuit. The Internet does not provide anything like the obvious boundaries that rivers, mountains, and oceans provide in the physical world. The four factors that work so well in the physical world—power, effects, legitimacy, and notice—do not translate very well to the virtual world of electronic commerce.

Guidelines for determining jurisdiction are still developing for cases in which the contract violation or tortious action occurred on the Internet. Some courts have taken the position that a person who, in the course of business, posts something on the Internet is "doing business" everywhere. Thus, a court anywhere would have jurisdiction over a legal action arising from such a posting. Other courts require a person to take other specific business action within the geographic boundaries of the state or country before exercising jurisdiction in a case.

International Jurisdiction

Jurisdiction issues that arise in international business are even more complex than the rules governing personal jurisdiction across state lines within the United States. Treaties between the countries involved govern the exercise of jurisdiction across international borders.

In general, U.S. courts determine personal jurisdiction for foreign companies and persons in much the same way that those courts interpret U.S. long-arm statutes. Non-U.S. corporations and individuals can be sued in U.S. courts if they conduct business or commit tortious acts in the United States. Similarly, U.S. courts can enforce foreign court decisions against U.S. corporations or individuals if personal jurisdiction can be established.

A foreign court will find it difficult to exercise jurisdiction over a person or company that is located elsewhere. One trend that may grow in the future is for companies to find countries with laws and regulations that are especially friendly regarding electronic commerce activities. Corporations in the United States often choose to incorporate in the state of Delaware because its corporate statutes are less restrictive than in other states. Similarly, many ocean-going cargo ships register in Liberia, which imposes fewer taxes, regulations, and restrictive laws on the ship owners than do other countries. In 2000, the U.S. Chamber of Commerce expressed concern that over-regulation of electronic commerce in the United States might convince Internet businesses to move to other countries and should thus be avoided to the extent possible. A number of countries, including Bermuda, Ireland, Switzerland, the Netherlands, and Australia have established low-regulation policies that they hope will attract electronic commerce businesses to them.

Amy thanks you for all of the information you have provided about jurisdiction and the Internet. She explains that every business owner worries about customer lawsuits and government regulations, but that she had no idea that putting her store on the Web could expose her to so much potential liability. Amy tells you that she is not quite ready to move her business to Switzerland, but that she will definitely consult a lawyer before taking Cinematique online. Thanks to you, she will have a number of good questions ready for that lawyer when they first meet.

Contracting and Contract Enforcement

You tell Amy that another important area of law is contracts. Amy responds by saying that Cinematique does not enter into contracts very often. You explain that every sale or purchase that Cinematique makes is a contract, so Amy is entering into contracts far more often than she thinks.

A contract includes two elements: an offer and an acceptance. The contract is formed when one party accepts the offer of another party. An **offer** is a declaration of willingness to buy or sell a product or service that includes sufficient details to be firm, precise, and unambiguous. An offer can be revoked as long as no payment or other consideration has been accepted. An **acceptance** is the expression of willingness to take an offer, including all of its stated terms. When one party makes an offer that is accepted, a contract is created. A contract can also be implied by actions that recognize the existence of a contract.

Contracts are a key element of traditional business practice and they are equally important on the Internet. Offers and acceptances can occur when parties exchange e-mail messages, engage in electronic data interchange (EDI), or fill out forms on Web pages. These Internet communications can be combined with traditional methods of forming contracts, including the exchange of paper documents, faxes, and verbal agreements made over the telephone or in person. The Uniform Commercial Code includes many of the laws that govern business contracts, especially for transactions within the jurisdiction of U.S. courts.

To learn more about the Uniform Commercial Code:

1. Click your browser's **Back** button or use its history list to return to the Online Companion page for Session 6.2, and then click the **Legal Information Institute** hyperlink and wait while your browser loads the home page of that Institute at Cornell Law School.

2. Move your pointer over the **Constitutions & codes** area, and then click the **Uniform Commercial Code** hyperlink that appears in the menu shown in Figure 6-14. The Uniform Commercial Code page provides links to most of the current sections of the Uniform Commercial Code. Most states have adopted this code, however, each state has the option of modifying sections of the code when adopting it. The Legal Information Institute site provides links to many of these state laws. You can explore this site to learn more about the Uniform Commercial Code and how it affects business transactions.

Figure 6-14	SELECTING THE UNIFORM COMMERCIAL CODE PAGE LINK

You explain to Amy that when Cinematique advertises goods for sale on its Web site, it will not be making an offer, but it is merely inviting offers from potential buyers. If a Web ad were a legal offer to contract, a seller could easily become liable for delivering more goods than it had available to ship. When a buyer submits an order, which *is* an offer, the seller can accept that offer and create a contract. If the seller does not have the ordered items in stock, the seller then has the option of refusing the buyer's order.

In most cases, making a legal acceptance of an offer is easy to do. When enforcing contracts, courts tend to view offers and acceptances as actions that occur within a particular context. So, if the actions are reasonable in the circumstances, courts tend to interpret those actions as offers and acceptances. For example, courts have held that actions such as mailing a check, shipping goods, shaking hands, nodding one's head, taking an item off a shelf, or opening a wrapped package, are all, in some circumstances, legally binding acceptances of offers. Although the case law is limited regarding acceptances on the Internet, most businesses assume that courts would view clicking a button on a Web page, entering information in a Web form, or downloading a file to be legally binding acceptances.

Written Contracts on the Web

Contracts can be enforceable even if they are not written or signed. However, certain categories of contracts—for example, contracts for the sale of goods worth over $500 or contracts that require actions that cannot be completed within one year—are not enforceable unless the parties create a signed writing. Fortunately for businesses and persons that want to form contracts using electronic commerce, a writing does not require either pen or paper.

Most courts will hold that a **writing** exists when the terms of a contract have been reduced to some tangible form. An early court decision in the 1800s held that a telegraph transmission was a writing. Later courts have held that tape recordings of spoken words, computer files on disks, and faxes are also writings. Thus, the parties to an electronic commerce contract should find it relatively easy to satisfy the writing requirement. Courts have been similarly generous in determining what constitutes a signature. A **signature** is any symbol executed or adopted for the purpose of authenticating a writing. Courts have held names on telegrams, telexes, faxes, and Western Union Mailgrams to be signatures. Even typed names or names printed as part of a letterhead have served as signatures. It is reasonable to assume that a symbol or code included in an electronic file would constitute a signature. For example, most courts would hold that digital signatures are signatures for contract purposes.

In many cases, firms conducting international electronic commerce do not need to worry about the signed writing contract requirement. The main treaty that governs international sales of goods, Article 11 of the United Nations Convention on Contracts for the International Sale of Goods, requires neither a writing nor a signature to create a legally binding acceptance. However, international contracts do raise other issues. A valid contract can only occur when both parties understand the agreement.

As you learned from reading about the FTC investigation of Dell and Micron, it is also important that sellers inform customers of certain issues in a way that ensures that customers understand those issues. You explain to Amy that if a German customer buys something from a Cinematique site that is written in English, a court may hold that the customer did not understand some or all elements of the transaction. Amy has already agreed that she will have Web sites in multiple languages, but she now understands that there are legal reasons to do this in addition to the customer service reasons she already had.

Warranties

You explain to Amy that Cinematique will probably have little trouble fulfilling the requirements it needs to create enforceable contracts as it buys and sells products on the Web. One issue that she will need to consider carefully, however, is the issue of warranties. A **warranty** is a promise about how a product will perform or that it is suitable for a particular purpose. Any contract for the sale of goods includes implied warranties. An **implied warranty** is a promise that is not expressly stated but that a buyer may infer from the seller's advertising or from a generally existing understanding of the product's use.

In most selling situations, a seller implicitly warrants that the goods it sells are fit for the purposes in which they are normally used and would be accepted by another merchant in the same trade. If the seller knows specific information about the buyer's requirements, acceptance of an offer from that buyer may imply an additional warranty that the goods are suitable for the specific uses of that buyer. Sellers can also create an **explicit warranty** by providing a specific description of additional warranty terms. Sellers can also create explicit warranties, often unintentionally, by making general statements in brochures or other advertising materials about product performance or suitability for particular tasks.

You explain to Amy that Cinematique can avoid some implied warranty liability by making a warranty disclaimer. A **warranty disclaimer** is a statement that the seller will not honor some or all implied warranties. Any warranty disclaimer must be stated conspicuously, which means it must be easily noticed. On a Web page, sellers can meet this requirement by putting the warranty disclaimer in larger type, a bold font, or in a contrasting color. To be legally effective, the warranty disclaimer must be stated obviously and must be easy for a buyer to find on the Web site.

Amy thanks you for the information about warranties. She tells you that she will be especially careful to make it clear which posters are original and which posters are reproductions, for example. Amy is also thinking about ways to describe the condition of the original posters. Some of these posters were actually used outside movie theaters and have sun-faded colors. Others have marks from being folded in storage. These defects are not easy to see on a photograph of the item that is small enough to fit in a Web browser window. To avoid implied warranty problems with these items, she will make sure to describe the condition of each of these posters in individual warranty disclaimer statements.

Web Site Content Issues

Many other legal issues can arise regarding the Web page content of electronic commerce sites. These issues include trademark infringement, deceptive trade practices, and the regulation of advertising and solicitation activities.

Trademark Infringement

You explain to Amy that trademarks, such as Cinematique, the name of her store, are a form of intellectual property that protect the consumer and protect the seller. Trademark laws protect the consumer by helping prevent fraud caused by confusion over brand names and identities of goods. These same laws protect sellers that have invested in developing, improving, and marketing their products. To create trademark rights in a name, a company must advertise, promote, and use the name as a brand name or description of an actual product or service. In the United States, companies can register their trademarks with the U.S. Patent and Trademark Office.

The owners of registered trademarks often have invested considerable amounts of money in the development and promotion of their products and their products' trademarks. Web site designers must be very careful not to use any trademarked name, logo, or other identifying mark without the express permission of the trademark owner. For example, a company Web site that includes a photograph of its president, who happens to be holding a can of Pepsi, could violate Pepsi's trademark rights. Pepsi can argue that the appearance of its trademarked product on the Web site implies an unauthorized endorsement of the president or the company by Pepsi.

On the Internet, the issue of domain names as trademarks and the issue of trademarks that are used by others as domain names often arises. Although having a domain name, by itself, does not give a company trademark rights, using another company's trademark as a domain name can be a violation of the other company's trademark rights. For example, Avon was able to stop another company from using the domain "avon.com" and Hasbro Toys was successful in preventing another company from using "candyland.com" because it infringed on the trademark it held on its board game product "Candyland."

When several companies have an element of a domain name included in one of their registered trademarks, the general rule courts follow is that the first company to register the domain may continue using that domain. Thus, the domain "delta.com," which might be a good name for the Web sites of Delta Airlines, the Delta Steamboat Company, or Delta Dental Plans Association, was first registered by the Delta Financial Corporation, the company that currently uses that domain name.

Amy agrees that she should investigate other companies' potential trademark rights to "Cinematique." You explain to her that there is a way to search for U.S. trademark registrations online.

To search for existing U.S. trademark registrations:

1. Click your browser's **Back** button or use its history list to return to the Online Companion page for Session 6.2, and then click the **U.S. Patent and Trademark Office** hyperlink and wait while your browser loads that site's home page.

2. Click the **Trademarks** hyperlink on the left side of the page to open the Trademark information page. This page includes links to a wide variety of information about trademarks and trademark registration.

3. Click the **New Trademark Electronic Search System (TESS)**. When the search system's main page loads, click the **Structured Form Search** hyperlink to open the page shown in Figure 6-15.

| Figure 6-15 | U.S. PATENT AND TRADEMARK OFFICE TRADEMARK ELECTRONIC SEARCH SYSTEM PAGE |

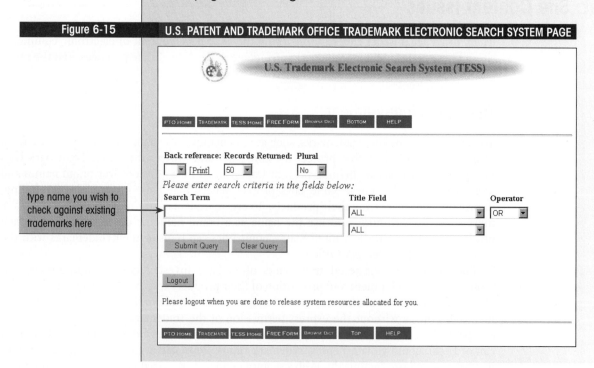

type name you wish to check against existing trademarks here

4. Type **Cinematique** in the Search Term text box, and then click the **Submit Query** button. You can review the results to see if Amy might have an issue with a company that has a similar trademark. If your search results include companies that still appear to be operating, you would advise Amy to discuss with her attorney whether or not the businesses might have a legitimate claim to exclusive use of the name on the Internet.

Computer graphics, audio, and video technology allow Web site designers to do many creative and interesting things. Manipulations of existing pictures, sounds, and video clips can be very entertaining. If the objects being manipulated are trademarked, however, these manipulations can violate the trademark holder's rights. Fictional characters can be trademarked or otherwise protected. Many personal Web pages include unauthorized pictures of cartoon characters and scanned photographs of celebrities; often, these images are altered in some way. A Web site that uses an altered image of Mickey Mouse speaking in a modified voice is issuing an electronic invitation to the Disney legal team!

Web sites that include links to other sites must be careful not to imply a relationship with the companies sponsoring the other sites, unless such a relationship actually exists. For example, a Web design studio's Web page might include links to company Web sites that show good design principles. If the design studio did not create those Web sites, the studio must be very careful to state that fact clearly. Otherwise, it would be easy for a visitor to assume that the linked sites were the work of the design studio.

In general, trademark protection prevents another firm from using the same or a similar name, logo, or other identifying characteristic in a way that would cause confusion in the minds of potential buyers of the trademark holder's products or services. For example, one company uses the trademarked name *VISA* for its credit card and another company uses *VISA* for its brand of synthetic fiber. This duplication of trademarked names is acceptable because the two products are very different. However, the use of very well known trademarks can be protected for all products if there is a danger that the trademark might be diluted. Various state laws define **trademark dilution** as the reduction of the distinctive quality of a trademark by alternative uses. Trademarks such as *Hyatt, Trivial Pursuit, Tiffany*, and the shape of the Coca-Cola bottle have all been protected from dilution by court rulings. For example, a Web site that sells gift-packaged seafood and claims to be the "Tiffany's of the Sea" would risk a lawsuit claiming trademark dilution by the famous jeweler.

Regulation of Advertising

As you learned earlier in this session, the FTC is the agency charged with investigating false and misleading advertising in the United States. You tell Amy that the FTC publishes its regulations and helpful guidelines for businesses that want to comply with the law. Many of these publications appear on the **U.S. Federal Trade Commission** Web site, which appears in Figure 6-16.

Figure 6-16	U.S. FEDERAL TRADE COMMISSION HOME PAGE

Any advertising claim that can mislead a substantial number of consumers in a material way is illegal under U.S. law. In addition to its own investigations, the FTC accepts referred investigations from organizations such as the Better Business Bureau. The FTC provides policy statements that can be helpful guides for designers creating electronic commerce Web sites. These policies include information on what is permitted when advertising and cover specific areas such as:

- Bait-and-switch advertising
- Consumer lending and leasing
- Endorsements and testimonials
- Energy consumption statements for home appliances
- Guarantees and warranties
- Prices

Unlike newspaper or television advertising, Web sites allow customers to control their points of entry and exit to the shopping experience. One danger that this control raises is that a customer might only see a small portion of the full information about a product or a company's selling terms that exists on a site. You tell Amy that one good way to make sure that her customers see all of the necessary disclosures, statements, and disclaimers is to put every one of them in a prominent position and in a large type face on each page that contains ordering information.

Other federal agencies have the power to regulate online advertising in the United States. These agencies include the Food and Drug Administration (FDA), the Bureau of Alcohol, Tobacco, and Firearms (ATF), and the Department of Transportation (DOT). The FDA regulates information disclosures for food and drug products. In particular, any Web site that is planning to advertise pharmaceutical products will be subject to the FDA's drug labeling and advertising regulations. The ATF works with the FDA to monitor and enforce federal laws regarding advertising for alcoholic beverages and tobacco products. These laws require that very specific statements be included in every ad for such products. Many states also have laws that regulate advertising for alcoholic beverages and tobacco products. The state and federal laws governing advertising and sale of firearms are even more restrictive. Any Web site that plans to deal in these products should consult with an attorney who is familiar with the relevant laws before posting any advertising for them. The DOT works with the FTC to monitor the advertising of companies over which it has jurisdiction, such as bus lines, freight companies, and airlines.

Regulation of E-Mail Solicitations

You explain to Amy that the FTC also has rules that regulate the details of how Cinematique must fulfill orders it receives. The FTC's Mail or Telephone Order Merchandise Trade Regulation requires that a seller soliciting mail or telephone orders must have a reasonable basis for stating shipment terms. The law defines "mail or telephone orders" to include orders received via fax or the Internet. Sellers may state the time within which they will ship an order in their solicitation, if they wish. If no such statement is included in the solicitation, the law requires the seller to ship within 30 days. If the seller cannot ship within the stated time (or within 30 days, if no time is stated), the seller must give the buyer a choice between accepting an additional shipment delay or canceling the order and getting a prompt refund. Many online companies go further than the law requires and do not charge a customer's credit card (an action which finalizes the order) until the customer's order is ready to ship.

Internet e-mail allows companies to send messages to thousands of potential customers inexpensively and easily. The potential for abuse is as great as the potential for opening new markets. The electronic equivalent of junk mail, these mass mailings are sometimes called **spam** and the companies that issue them are called **spammers**. (The name "spammers" comes from a Monty Python comedy routine in which everyone is eventually drowned out by a chorus that repeatedly sings the word "spam.")

The use of mass e-mailings to promote various products and services has caused recipients of these messages to ask their state and federal representatives to create laws to control this problem. A Nevada law gives the recipient of commercial e-mail messages a right to sue the message sender unless they have an existing business relationship. Virginia's Computer Crimes Act outlaws the use of false return address information in unsolicited bulk e-mail messages. A Washington law prohibits the transmission of commercial e-mail that includes false or misleading information in its subject header. A proposed Colorado law would require e-mail advertisers to include "ADV:" as the first four characters in a message's subject header. Most legal experts believe that these and other laws that have been passed to date are susceptible to constitutional challenges because they overly restrict free speech; however, the public is demanding that they be protected from unsolicited junk e-mail, so lawmakers will likely continue creating legislation until they succeed.

Amy appreciates your telling her about this issue. She now understands that she will need to investigate a variety of state laws before sending any unsolicited e-mail advertising to potential Cinematique customers.

Ethics Issues in Electronic Commerce

You explain to Amy that there are a number of online business practices that, although they may be technically legal, can violate commonly held ethical standards. For example, the law does require that Web sites include only true statements. However, the law does not necessarily prohibit the omission of information that could affect a potential purchaser's impression of a product or service in a material way. Even true statements have been held to be misleading when important related facts have been omitted from the ad. Any comparisons to other products should be supported by factual information.

From a very practical standpoint, ethical considerations are important in operating a business on the Web. Remember that buyers on the Web often communicate with each other, and an ethical lapse that is rapidly passed among customers can have serious effects on a company's reputation. In 1999, *The New York Times* ran a story that disclosed Amazon.com's arrangements with publishers for book promotions. Amazon.com was accepting payments of up to $10,000 from publishers to give their books editorial reviews and placement on lists of recommended books as part of a cooperative advertising program. When this news broke, Amazon.com issued a statement that it had done nothing wrong and that such advertising programs were a standard part of publisher-bookstore relationships. The outcry on the Internet in newsgroups and mailing lists was overwhelming. Two days later—before most mass media outlets had even reported on the story—Amazon.com announced that it would end the practice and offer unconditional refunds to any customers who had purchased a promoted book. Amazon.com had done nothing illegal, but the practice appeared to be unethical to many of its customers and potential customers.

A similar outrage occurred when Yahoo! purchased GeoCities, a virtual community site that provided free Web space to customers. Many of these customers had made large investments of time and money in their Web sites. When Yahoo! took over the operation of GeoCities, it made a change in the terms governing the free Web sites. Yahoo! claimed a copyright ownership interest in every Web site in the GeoCities community. The backlash from thousands of angry Web site owners was enough to make Yahoo! reconsider its position and rewrite the terms of the agreement in a way that satisfied most of the community members. Yahoo! had not violated any laws, but it realized that it needed to respect the ethical standards of its community members.

Defamation

Defamation is a violation of ethical standards that can rise to the level of a violation of the law or an infringement on the rights of another person or company. A **defamatory** statement is a statement that is false and injures the reputation of another person or company. If the statement injures the reputation of a product or service instead of a person, it is called **product disparagement**. In some countries, a true and honest comparison of products can lead to product disparagement. It may be best for commercial Web sites to avoid making negative evaluative statements about other persons or products, given the highly subjective nature of defamation and product disparagement. The line between justifiable criticism and defamation can be hard to determine.

Web site designers should be especially careful to avoid potential defamation liability by altering a photo or image of a person in a way that depicts the person unfavorably. In most cases, a person must establish that the defamatory statement caused injury; however, most state laws recognize that some types of statements are so negative that injury can be assumed. One category of such statements alleges conduct that would be injurious to a person's business, trade, profession, or office. Thus, online statements about competitors should always be reviewed carefully before posting to determine if they contain the elements of defamation. A good general rule is to abide by the old saying, "If you can't say something good about a person, don't say anything at all."

Privacy Rights and Obligations

The issue of online privacy continues to evolve as the Internet and the Web grow in importance as tools of communication and commerce. Many legal and privacy issues remain unsettled and are hotly debated in many forums. The Electronic Communications Privacy Act of 1986 is the main law governing privacy on the Internet today. Of course, this law was enacted before the general public began its wide use of the Internet. A more recent law, the Children's Online Privacy Protection Act of 1998, provides restrictions on data collection that must be followed by electronic commerce sites aimed at children.

Many legislative proposals have been advanced in recent years that address online privacy issues, but none has thus far withstood constitutional challenges. In July, 1999, the FTC issued a report that examined how well Web sites were respecting visitors' privacy rights. Although it found a significant number of sites that did not have posted privacy policies, the report concluded that companies operating Web sites were developing privacy practices with sufficient speed and that no federal laws regarding privacy were required at that time.

Privacy advocacy groups responded to the FTC report with outrage and calls for legislation. Thus, the near-term future of privacy regulation in the United States is unclear. The Direct Marketing Association (DMA), a trade association of businesses that advertises its products and services directly to consumers by mail, telephone, the Internet, and through mass media outlets, has established a set of privacy standards for its members; however, critics note that past efforts by the DMA to regulate its members' activities have been less than successful.

Ethics issues are significant in the area of online privacy because laws have not kept pace with the growth of the Internet and the Web. The privacy of personal behavior that may be revealed by Web sites collecting information about visitors' page-viewing habits, product selections, and demographic information is significant. Differences in cultures throughout the world have resulted in different expectations about privacy in electronic commerce. In Europe, most persons expect that information they provide to a commercial Web site will be used only for the purpose it was collected. Many European countries have laws that prohibit companies from exchanging consumer data without the express consent of the consumer. In 1998, the European Union adopted a Directive on the Protection of Personal Data. This directive codifies the constitutional rights to privacy that exist in most European countries and applies it to all Internet activities. In addition, it prevents businesses from exporting personal data outside the European Union unless the data will continue to be protected in accordance with the directive.

Until the legal environment of privacy regulation becomes clearer, electronic commerce sites should be conservative in their collection and use of customer data. Mark Van Name and Bill Catchings, writing in *PC Week* in 1998, outlined four principles for handling customer data that provide a good set of guidelines for Web site administrators. These principles include:

- Use the data collected to provide improved customer service
- Avoid sharing customers' data with others outside your company without their permission
- Tell customers what data you are collecting and what you are doing with it
- Give customers the right to have you delete any of the data you have collected about them

Amy is very interested in protecting the privacy of her customers. She asks you if there are any guidelines for writing a privacy statement other than the four principles listed above. You tell Amy that a number of companies have done a good job of writing comprehensive privacy statements and that she can examine them on their Web sites. **Backflip** is a company that provides a free service to people who use more than one Web browser or use more than one computer for Web browsing. Such people need a common place to store their bookmarks or favorites in a way that will work with either Netscape Navigator or Microsoft Internet Explorer on any computer they happen to be using. Because information about which sites a person uses can be very personal and private information, Backflip has designed a strong and clear statement of its privacy policy.

To examine Backflip's privacy policy statement:

1. Click your browser's **Back** button or use its history list to return to the Online Companion page for Session 6.2, and then click the **Backflip** hyperlink and wait while your browser loads the Backflip home page.

2. Click the **privacy** hyperlink to open the Backflip Privacy Policy statement in a new browser window. The Privacy Policy is a rather long document, so Backflip has included links that allow you to navigate from one section of the statement to another. The policy begins with a clear statement of the things that Backflip will *not* do with its customers' personal information, and then it describes its membership in the TRUSTe program. The rest of the statement includes detailed information about how the company protects the information its customers entrust to it.

3. Close all browser windows and close your dial-up connection, if necessary.

Amy thanks you for the information you have provided about ethics and online privacy issues. She agrees that operating Cinematique in a way that goes beyond the minimum legal requirements and respects the rights of her customers is the best way to do business in the long run.

Taxation of Electronic Commerce

You explain to Amy that when Cinematique begins doing business online, it will be subject to the same taxes as any other company; however, Cinematique might instantly become subject to taxes in many states and countries because of the Internet's worldwide scope. Right now, Cinematique operates in one location and has been subject just to one set of tax laws since it began operations. If Amy had chosen a traditional growth pattern of opening more retail stores in multiple states or countries, Cinematique would have developed the internal staff and the record-keeping infrastructure needed to comply with multiple sets of tax laws. By engaging in electronic commerce, Cinematique will need to comply with multiple sets of tax laws from its first day of online operation. Most companies engage the services of an accounting firm to advise them on tax matters when they first begin operations. For online businesses, it is even more important to have good professional tax advice. Amy tells you that Cinematique has had its tax returns prepared by an accounting firm for several years, but notes that she would like to learn more about what tax burdens Cinematique will face as it moves to the Web.

A government acquires the power to tax a business when that business establishes a connection with the area controlled by the government. For example, a business that is located in Kansas has a connection with the state of Kansas and is subject to Kansas taxes. If that company opens a branch office in Arizona, it forms a connection with Arizona and becomes subject to Arizona taxes on the portion of its business that occurs in Arizona. This connection between a taxpaying entity and a government with taxing authority is called **nexus**.

The concept of nexus is similar in many ways to the concept of jurisdiction that you learned about earlier in this session. The activities that create nexus vary from state to state. Nexus issues have been frequently litigated and the case law is fairly complex. Determining nexus can be difficult when a company conducts only a few activities in or has minimal contact with the state. In such cases, it is advisable for the company to obtain the services of a professional tax advisor.

An online business is potentially subject to several types of taxes, including income taxes, transaction taxes, and property taxes. **Income taxes** are levied by national, state, and local governments on the net income generated by business activities. **Transaction taxes**, which include sales taxes, use taxes, and excise taxes, are levied on the products or services that the company sells or uses. **Customs duties** are taxes levied by the United States on certain commodities when they are imported into the country. **Property taxes** are levied by states and local governments on the personal property and real estate used in the business. In general, the taxes that cause the greatest concern for Web businesses are income taxes and sales taxes.

Income Taxes

The **Internal Revenue Service** is the U.S. government agency charged with administering the country's tax laws. Any Web site that is located in the United States and generates income will be subject to U.S. federal income tax. In addition, persons and corporations that are residents of the United States must pay federal income tax on income earned regardless of where it is earned. The U.S. tax law provides a credit for taxes paid to foreign countries, so the incidence of double taxation of foreign earnings is reduced.

Most states levy an income tax on business earnings. If a company conducts activities in several states, it must file tax returns in all of those states and apportion its earnings in accordance with each state's tax laws. In some states, the individual cities, counties, and other political subdivisions within the state also have the power to levy income taxes on business earnings. Companies that do business in multiple local jurisdictions must apportion their income and file tax returns in each locality that levies an income tax. There are more than 30,000 individual taxing authorities in the United States alone, so large companies must employ many tax accountants to manage the records and file the required forms on time.

Companies that sell through their Web sites do not, in general, establish nexus everywhere their goods are delivered to customers. Usually, a company can accept orders and ship from one state to many other states and avoid nexus by using a contract carrier such as FedEx or United Parcel Service to deliver goods to customers.

Sales and Use Taxes

Most states levy a sales tax on goods sold to consumers. Businesses that establish nexus with a state must file sales tax returns and remit the sales tax they collect from their customers. If a business ships goods to customers in other states, it is not required to collect sales tax from those customers unless the business has established nexus with the customer's state. However, the customer in this situation is required to file a use tax return and pay the amount that the business would have collected as sales tax had it been a local business. Few consumers file use tax returns and few states enforce their use tax laws with any regularity.

Amy thanks you for your help in identifying the legal, ethics, and tax issues that might arise as she takes Cinematique online. She plans to meet soon with her lawyer and her accountant to go over her business plans and to make sure that Cinematique's online store will be in compliance with all applicable laws and tax-filing requirements. Amy is convinced that she can bring the same personal touch to her online business that has made Cinematique's mall store such a success.

Session 6.2 QUICK CHECK

1. How can you ensure that the laws of a particular state govern a contract?

2. A state's long-arm statute creates _____ over nonresidents who transact business or commit tortious acts within the state.

3. True or False: Every contract must be in the form of a signed writing or it is not enforceable.

4. A seller can avoid some implied warranty liabilities by making a clear statement of a(n) _____ on its Web page.

5. What is trademark dilution?

6. True or False: The FTC's regulations for mail and telephone orders apply to orders placed through the Internet.

7. Because U.S. regulators have allowed online businesses to set their own privacy policies, the obligation to protect customers' privacy is more of a(n) _____ obligation than a legal obligation in the United States at the present time.

8. What is nexus, as it is used in tax law?

CASE PROBLEMS

Case 1. Swenson Machine Tools Phil Swenson, president of Swenson Machine Tools, has asked for your help in evaluating the feasibility of creating multiple language versions of the Swenson Machine Tools Web site. The company sells replacement parts for industrial machinery, including cutting tools, grinding wheels, and gears. Swenson sells many of these items on the company's Web site. The Web site has been instrumental in reducing customer service costs at Swenson Machine Tools by allowing customers to log in and check prices, an order's status, and shipping information. Phil would like you to help him determine whether a simple language translator will work well enough for the site, or if he will need to use a translation and localization service. Because much of Swenson's inventory is for German-engineered machinery, Phil interacts with many German businesses. Phil has created three sample messages that he believes are representative of the types of messages his German customers might see when they log in to their accounts. One is an order status message, the second is a technical information follow-up request, and the third is a sales promotion message. Phil wants you to perform a test backtranslation using these sample messages. In a backtranslation, you translate from one language to another, and then translate the result back into the original language.

1. Start your Web browser, and then go to the Online Companion page by entering the URL http://www.course.com/NewPerspectives/EC in the appropriate location of your Web browser. Click the Tutorial 6 link, and then click the Case Problems link. Click the FreeTranslation.com link and wait while your browser loads the Free Translation home page.

2. Select the text that appears in the Text Translator scrolling text box, and then type "The flight has been delayed for three hours and your shipment will not arrive at its scheduled time." (Do not type the quotation marks.)

3. Click the Text Translator list arrow, click English to German, and then click the Translate! button.

4. Use your mouse to select the German language translation, and then press Ctrl + C to copy the text to the Windows Clipboard.

5. Click your browser's Back button, use your mouse to select the text in the Text Translator scrolling text box, and then press Ctrl + V to paste the German text.

6. Click the Text Translator list arrow, click German to English, and then click the Translate! button.

7. Use your browser's Print button to print the page.

8. Click your browser's Back button. Select the text that appears in the Text Translator scrolling text box, and then type "We have received your order for a #5899 beveled gear. Please send us the engineering drawings for the subassembly in which you plan to use this gear. Also specify the metal composition tolerances you require." (Do not type the quotation marks.)

9. Translate the text into German. Use your mouse to select the German language translation, copy the translation to the Windows Clipboard, click your browser's Back button, and then translate the text you selected back into English. Print the page that contains the English backtranslation.

10. Translate the text, "Special! Hot deal for this week only! We are offering two-for-one pricing on all grinding wheels. Stock up now while the price is right!" into German, and then translate the German results back into English. Print the page that contains the English backtranslation.

11. Close your browser and close your dial-up connection, if necessary.

12. Review each of the three translations that you performed. Write a 200-word report to Phil describing how well the general translation software worked for each message. Conclude your report with a recommendation about whether Phil should use this free service, or investigate other options.

Case 2. AllergiesNet   You work as a Web consultant for Barbara Steiner, the founder of

Explore

AllergiesNet. AllergiesNet offers information to the general public about seasonal allergies and potential treatments. In addition to articles written by physicians and other health-care professionals, the site displays banner ads for over-the-counter drugs and other non-prescription items often used by seasonal allergy sufferers. Barbara has been careful not to provide specific medical advice to individuals anywhere on the site. The site also offers chat rooms in which visitors can join in discussions about their allergies. To participate in a chat session, a visitor must register and provide a name, password, and e-mail address. The following privacy statement appears on the AllergiesNet registration page:

> AllergiesNet stores your name and e-mail address when you register with the site. We also place a cookie on your computer to make subsequent logins easier for you. We promise that we will never sell your e-mail address or name to any other company. We will use your e-mail address only to contact you and to provide services you request.

For visitors who have requested more information from the Web site, AllergiesNet sends monthly newsletters focusing on specific allergies to their e-mail addresses. The chat rooms often fill with visitors discussing the content of the newsletters soon after the newsletters are sent. A major pharmaceutical company is preparing a drug that it believes will reduce the symptoms of hay fever. This company has approached Barbara because it would like to include information about its drug research in an upcoming AllergiesNet newsletter directed at hay fever sufferers. The company is especially interested in possible consumer acceptance of the drug's side effects, which it plans to disclose with the research. The company is willing to pay AllergiesNet a large fee if it will include the research report in its newsletter and then provide a transcript of all chat room sessions for the two weeks following the newsletter's release.

1. The disclosures that the pharmaceutical company is willing to pay AllergiesNet to make are not specifically prohibited by the terms of the AllergiesNet privacy statement. Consider whether the pharmaceutical company's proposal would violate the spirit of the privacy statement and write a 100-word essay supporting your position.

2. Assume that Barbara decides to go ahead with the pharmaceutical company's proposal. Write a paragraph that describes the disclosures that you would recommend AllergiesNet provide to its chat room participants during the two-week period.

Case 3. Huggable Joys You are the assistant to Cathy Zhu, president of Huggable Joys, a company that manufactures and sells small stuffed animal toys. Cathy has been selling these stuffed animals through local retail toy stores and gift shops, but would like to begin selling the toys directly to customers using the Web. Because most of her products are sold to parents of young children, Cathy has worked very hard to create a company image that projects a high level of trust and caring. She wants to make sure that the Huggable Joys Web site reflects that same level of trust and concern for her customers. Cathy expects that many visitors to the Web site will be young children who are either using the computer with their parents or by themselves. She has asked you to learn more about what guidelines exist for Web sites that appeal to young children.

Explore

1. Start your Web browser, and then go to the Online Companion page by entering the URL http://www.course.com/NewPerspectives/EC in the appropriate location of your Web browser. Click the Tutorial 6 link, and then click the Case Problems link. Click the FTC Consumer Protection link and wait while your browser loads the FTC Consumer Protection page.

2. Click the E-Commerce & the Internet link, and then explore the TEXT links on the page that might help you to identify guidelines for creating and designing Web pages that appeal to young children.

3. Prepare a two-page report that includes two lists: a list of features that the Huggable Joys Web site should include to comply with the law and a list of features that would help project a high level of trust and concern for Huggable Joys' customers.

4. Close your Web browser and close your dial-up connection, if necessary.

Case 4. Soccer CDs Vijay Singh, owner of Soccer CDs, has hired you to help him use a Web site to promote his store's products. Soccer CDs obtains the reproduction rights to film footage of famous soccer players, and then creates CDs that include film clips from important tournaments and player profiles and statistics. Vijay would like to sell these CDs on the Internet. He asks you to design a Web page for the site that will advertise and promote the store's products effectively.

Explore

Note: To complete this case problem you must know how to create Web pages using HTML, Microsoft FrontPage, Netscape Composer, or some other tool. You must also have access to that tool. If you do not have access to a Web page creation program, skip Steps 3 and 5.

1. Start your Web browser, and then go to the Online Companion page by entering the URL http://www.course.com/NewPerspectives/EC in the appropriate location of your Web browser. Click the Tutorial 6 link, and then click the Case Problems link. Click the Yahoo! Web Page Design and Layout link and wait while your browser loads the Yahoo! directory page for this topic. You can use the links on this page as a reference resource as you complete the next two steps.

2. Prepare a sketch of a Web page that would be effective for selling Soccer CDs to the U.S. market. Your sketch should specify the page's content and should indicate the placements of text and graphics. Use the links on the Yahoo! Web site and the material presented in this tutorial when designing the page's layout and content.

3. Use a Web page creation program or HTML to create the Web page you designed in Step 2, save it as Soccer.htm, and then print it.

4. Prepare a sketch of a Web page that would be appropriate for selling Soccer CDs to Japanese customers. Your sketch should specify the page's content (in English) and should indicate the placements of text and graphics. Use the links on the Yahoo! Web site and the material presented in this tutorial when designing the page's layout and content. Make sure that you consider Japanese customs when creating the page.

5. Use a Web page creation program or HTML to create the Web page you designed in Step 4, save it as JapanSoccer.htm, and then print it.

6. Close your browser, your Web page creation program, and your dial-up connection, if necessary.

QUICK | CHECK ANSWERS

Session 6.1

1. True
2. Share a common language and similar customs, and have a common legal structure for resolving disputes
3. language, customs, and business policy
4. Many languages are spoken in several different countries, which can cause confusion for a Web visitor.
5. 1,000
6. localization
7. False

Session 6.2

1. Add a forum selection clause to the contract specifying the state of the contract's governing law.
2. personal jurisdiction
3. False
4. warranty disclaimer
5. The reduction in a trademark's value that can occur if other companies use it for other products
6. True
7. ethical
8. The connection between a taxpaying entity and a government with taxing authority

New Perspectives on

E-COMMERCE

TUTORIAL 7   EC 7.03

Creating a Web Page
Web Fundamentals and HTML

TUTORIAL 8   EC 8.01

Marketing for the Online Business
Strategies for Marketing, Promoting, and Advertising an Electronic Commerce Initiative

TUTORIAL 9   EC 9.01

Planning for the Online Business
Developing Ideas and Creating Business Plans for Web Enterprises

Read This Before You Begin

To the Student

Data Disks

To complete the exercises and Case Problems in Tutorial 7, you need one Data Disk. Your instructor will either provide you with the Data Disk or ask you to make your own.

If you are making your own Data Disk, you will need one blank, formatted high-density disk. You will need to copy a set of files and/or folders from a file server, standalone computer, or the Web onto your disk. Your instructor will tell you which computer, drive letter, and folders contain the files you need. You can also download the files by going to www.course.com and following the instructions on the screen.

The information below shows you the folder that goes on your disk:

Data Disk

Write this on the disk label:
Data Disk 1: E-Commerce Tutorial 7

Put this folder on the disk:
Tutorial.07

See the inside front or inside back cover of this book for more information on Data Disk files, or ask your instructor or technical support person for assistance.

Using Your Own Computer

If you are going to work through this book using your own computer, you need:

■ **Computer System** Microsoft Internet Explorer version 5.0 or higher or Netscape Navigator version 4.7 or higher must be installed on your computer. If you use lower versions of these browsers, some Web pages might look slightly different from what you see in the figures. This book assumes a complete installation of the browser. You can download current browser versions from **www.microsoft.com** or **www.netscape.com**.

■ **Data Disk** You will not be able to complete the exercises in Tutorial 7 using your own computer until you have your Data Disk.

■ **Internet Connection** You must connect to the Internet to complete the tutorials in this book. For some tutorials, you must have an e-mail address. If you do not have an e-mail address, you can obtain one for free at **www.hotmail.com**, **www.altavista.com**, **www.email.com**, **mail.yahoo.com**, or any other Internet site that provides free a-mail accounts.

What to Do if a Web Site Looks Different from What Is Printed in the Book

Because companies change their Web sites occasionally, the Web sites that you visit in the tutorials might look different from the Web pages that appear in the figures in this book. Important content is pointed out in the tutorial or in the figure's callouts. If you cannot find a hyperlink on the page, try scrolling the page to see if the link appears in a different location, or look for a link with a similar name.

Using the Student Online Companion

The Student Online Companion for this book contains the links that you need to complete the tutorial steps and case problems. The URL is www.course.com/NewPerspectives/EC. The Student Online Companion also contains links to site that ser set in the tutorial in bold, blue, sans serif type. Although you are not directed to visit these sites in the tutorial steps, you can link to them using the Student Online Companion page to broaden your experiences while learning about electronic commerce. These links might include resources for important topics or different examples of electronic commerce sites. The Student Online Companion pages also include updated tutorial material to keep the tutorials current in a constantly changing Web environment.

Visit Our World Wide Web Site

Additional materials designed especially for you are available on the World Wide Web. Go to www.course.com/NewPerspectives.

To the Instructor

The Data Disk Files are available on the Instructor's Resource Kit for this title. Follow the instructions in the Help file on the CD-ROM to install the programs to your network or standalone computer. For information on creating Data Disks, see the "To the Student" section above.

You are granted a license to copy the Data Files to any computer or computer network used by students who have purchased this book.

CREATING A WEB PAGE

Web Fundamentals and HTML

CASE

The Coffee and Tea Merchant

In Tutorial 3, you were introduced to Franklin Toadvine, the owner of The Coffee and Tea Merchant, a coffee store in San Diego, California. You helped Franklin create a small online store. Both stores sell a variety of coffee beans and bulk tea to wholesale and retail customers. The San Diego also store sells coffee and tea drinks to consumers.

Like other retail and hospitality businesses, The Coffee and Tea Merchant frequently has job openings. In the past, Franklin or his manager placed job listings in print publications, such as the local newspaper and the coffee trade publication *Bean News*. Franklin wants to explore as many employment avenues as possible, and with the success of the online store, Franklin wants to place a copy of a current job listing on the World Wide Web. Creating an online job listing will provide Franklin several advantages. The Web's skyrocketing popularity gives Franklin the potential of reaching a large and varied audience. He will be able to continually update an online job listing, offering details on his latest projects and jobs. An online job listing will also gives a prospective employee the chance to look at employment opportunities in more detail than is normal with a paper advertisement, because Franklin can include links to other relevant documents. Franklin asks you to create an online job listing.

SESSION 7.1

In this session, you will enter the text that will form the basis of the online job listing Web page. You will insert the appropriate HTML code, creating a simple Web page that outlines the responsibilities and qualifications an applicant must possess.

Creating an HTML Document

It's always a good idea to plan the appearance of your Web page before you start writing it. Recently, Franklin wrote a description for a coffee store manager position and distributed copies at college campus job fairs. Half his work is already done because he can use the paper version of the job description as a model for his job listing Web page. Figure 7-1 shows a copy of the job description that Franklin wrote.

Figure 7-1	PAPER VERSION OF FRANKLIN'S JOB LISTING

Coffee Store Manager

The Coffee and Tea Merchant · 2234 Roasting Lane, San Diego, CA 90000-1234

Responsibilities

Responsible for profitable and efficient operation of The Coffee and Tea Merchant store. Critical contributor to the company's success. Monitor and maintain quality store operations, provide quality customer service experience, lead and empower store employees in a positive manner, and maximize the store's financial performance.

Qualifications

Education

- High school diploma required
- College degree preferred

Experience

- Three to five years' experience in the restaurant or hospitality industry
- Minimum two years' management experience
- Time management and organizational experience

Knowledge and Ability

People Skills Ability to motivate employees. Demonstrate strong independent discretion and judgment to accomplish day-to-day objectives. Maintain employee communication. Provide assistance to customers in a courteous and professional manner.

Financial Operation Proven store banking and bookkeeping skills. Use the automated payroll system. Produce employee schedules. Generate weekly financial status reports. Order bulk coffee and tea.

Coffee Knowledge Barista experience including preparing a wide variety of espresso beverages. Knowledge of coffee beans, including country of origin.

How to Apply

Please e-mail your resume to Otis Toadvine: otistoadvine@hotmail.com

Franklin's paper job listing includes several features that he wants you to implement in the online version. The Coffee and Tea Merchant position, or job title, appears at the top formatted in a large font. Beneath the job title is a picture of a coffee cup. Below the image, there is a job description that is divided into four sections: Responsibilities, Qualifications, Knowledge and Ability, and How to Apply. Within the Responsibilities section, a paragraph describes the job requirements and goals. Within the Qualifications section, two smaller headings subdivide the job qualifications into education and experience. Under each of these headings, a bulleted list details the qualifications. The Knowledge and Ability section describes different categories of abilities a successful candidate should possess, with the knowledge or ability category name in boldface and italics. Franklin's paper job description has three heading levels, bulleted lists, formatted characters, and graphics. When you create the online job listing with HTML, Franklin wants you to include these features. As you create this document for the World Wide Web, you will probably want to refer to Figure 7-1 frequently.

HTML Syntax

An HTML document is a simple text document that includes two elements: document content and tags. **Document content** includes those parts of the document that you want the user to see, such as text and graphics. **Tags** are the HTML codes that control the appearance of the document content.

The HTML syntax for creating the kinds of features that Franklin wants in his page follows a very basic structure. You apply a tag to document content using the syntax:

<Tag Name Properties>Document Content</Tag Name>

You can always identify a tag by the brackets (<>) that enclose the tag name. Some tags can include **properties**, or additional information placed within the brackets that controls how the tag is used. Tags usually come in pairs: the **opening tag** is the first tag, which tells the browser to turn on the feature and apply it to the document content that follows. The browser applies the feature until the browser encounters the **closing tag**, which turns off the feature. Note that closing tags are identified by a slash (/) that precedes the tag name. Not every type of tag has an opening and closing tag. Some tags are known as **one-sided** tags because they require only the opening tag. **Two-sided** tags require both opening and closing tags.

For example, look at the first line of Franklin's job description, the job title Coffee Store Manager, in Figure 7-1. You could format this line with the two-sided HTML tag as follows:

<H1 ALIGN=CENTER>Coffee Store Manager</H1>

Here the <H1 ALIGN=CENTER> opening tag tells the browser that the text that follows, Coffee Store Manager, should be formatted with the H1 style (H1 stands for Heading 1; you'll learn what this means later). This tag also includes a property, the **alignment property** (ALIGN), which tells the browser how to align the text, and in the example above, the text should be centered. After the opening tag comes the content, Coffee Store Manager. The </H1> tag signals the browser to turn off the H1 style. Remember that each browser determines the exact effect of the H1 tag. One browser might apply a 14-point Times Roman bold font to the job title text, whereas another browser might use 18-point Arial italic—but in each case, the font would be appropriately larger than the normal font of the document. Figure 7-2 shows how three different browsers might interpret this line of HTML code.

Figure 7-2	INTERPRETATIONS OF THE HTML <H1> TAG BY DIFFERENT BROWSERS

BROWSER	APPEARANCE OF THE DOCUMENT CONTENT
Browser A	Mary Taylor
Browser B	**Mary Taylor**
Browser C	*Mary Taylor*

Tags are not case sensitive. That means that typing "<H1>" has the same effect as typing "<h1>". Many Web authors like to use only uppercase for tags, to distinguish tags from document content. This book follows that convention.

Creating Basic Tags

When you create a Web page, you first enter tags that indicate the markup language used in the document, identify the document's key sections, and assign the page a title.

In the steps that follow, type the text exactly as you see it. The text after the steps explains each line. To start entering code, you need a basic text editor such as Notepad or WordPad.

To start creating an HTML file:

1. Start your computer and then place your Data Disk in the appropriate drive.

   TROUBLE? If you don't have a Data Disk, you need to get one before you can proceed. Your instructor or technical support person will either give you one or ask you to make your own. See the Read This Before You Begin page at the beginning of the tutorials for instructions.

2. Open a text editor on your computer, and then open a new document.

   TROUBLE? The text editor used to create this book is the Windows Notepad editor. If you are not sure which text editor you should use, ask your instructor or technical support person for help.

3. Type the following lines of code into your document. Press the **Enter** key after each line (twice for a blank line).

   <HTML>

   <HEAD>

   <TITLE>Coffee Store Manager Job Posting</TITLE>

   </HEAD>

   <BODY>

   </BODY>

   </HTML>

4. Save the file as **Joblisting.htm** in the Tutorial.07\Tutorial folder on your Data Disk, but do not close your text editor. See Figure 7-3.

Figure 7-3	INITIAL HTML TAGS

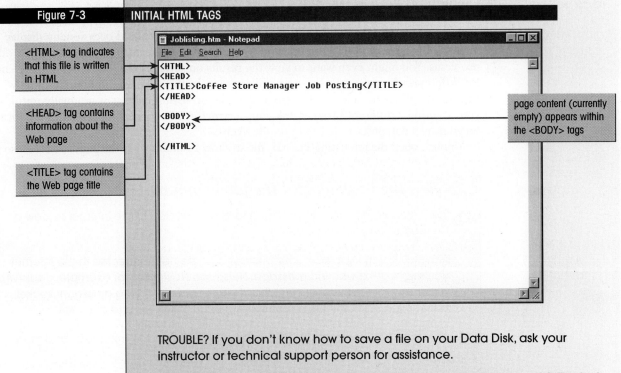

<HTML> tag indicates that this file is written in HTML

<HEAD> tag contains information about the Web page

<TITLE> tag contains the Web page title

page content (currently empty) appears within the <BODY> tags

```
Joblisting.htm - Notepad
File  Edit  Search  Help
<HTML>
<HEAD>
<TITLE>Coffee Store Manager Job Posting</TITLE>
</HEAD>

<BODY>
</BODY>

</HTML>
```

TROUBLE? If you don't know how to save a file on your Data Disk, ask your instructor or technical support person for assistance.

TROUBLE? Don't worry if your screen doesn't look exactly like Figure 7-3. The text editor shown in the figure is the Windows Notepad editor. Your text editor might look very different. Just make sure you entered the text correctly.

TROUBLE? If you are using the Windows Notepad text editor to create your HTML file, make sure you type the .htm or .html extension when you type the filename, and make sure you save the file using the All Files (*.*) option, which you must select from the Save as type list box. Do not save the file using the Text Document type (.txt), which Notepad automatically adds to the filename. This renders the file unreadable to the Netscape Navigator browser, which requires an .htm or .html file extension. Most browsers can read files with either file extension.

The opening and closing HTML tags bracket all the remaining code you'll enter in the document. These tags indicate to a browser that the page is written in HTML. Although you don't have to include these tags, they are used by applications.

The <HEAD> tag is used where you enter information about the Web page itself. One such piece of information is the title of the page, which appears in the title bar of the Web browser. This information is entered using the <TITLE> tag. The title in this example is "Coffee Store Manager Job Posting."

Finally, the portion of the document that Web users will see is contained between the <BODY> tags. At this point, the page is blank (no text or graphics). You will add those later. The <HEAD> and <BODY> tags are not strictly required, but you should include them to better organize your document and make its code more readable to others. The extra space before and after the BODY tags is also not required, but using spaces will make your code easier to view as you add more features to your document.

Displaying Your HTML Files

As you continue adding to the job listing HTML file, you should occasionally display the formatted page with your Web browser to verify that there are no syntax errors or other problems. You might even want to view the results on several browsers, if possible, to check for differences between one browser and another. In the steps and figures that follow, the Internet Explorer browser is used to display the job listing page as it gradually unfolds. If you are using a different browser, ask your instructor how to view local files (those located on your own computer rather than on the Web).

You will open the job listing HTML file to show Franklin what the page looks like so far.

To view the beginning of the job listing page:

1. Start your browser. You do not need to be connected to the Internet to view a file loaded on your computer.

   TROUBLE? If you try to start your browser and are not connected to the Internet, you might get a warning message. Netscape Navigator, for example, displays a warning message telling you that it was unable to create a network socket connection. Click the OK button to ignore the message and continue.

2. After your browser loads its home page, click **File** on the menu bar, and then click **Open**.

   TROUBLE? If you're using Netscape Navigator, you will have to use a different command to open the file from your Data Disk. Ask your instructor or technical support person for specific steps to open the file.

3. Locate the **Joblisting.htm** file that you saved in the Tutorial.07\Tutorial folder on your Data Disk, and then click the **OK** button. Your browser displays the job listing page, as shown in Figure 7-4. Note that the page title, which you typed earlier between the <TITLE> tags, appears in the browser's title bar. Also note that there is no text in the window because you have not typed the content of the body.

Figure 7-4	THE INITIAL HTML FILE IN INTERNET EXPLORER

the text you entered between the <TITLE> tags

the address box indicates the name of the HTML file and its path

TROUBLE? If your browser displays something different, compare the code in your file to the code shown in Figure 7-3, and correct any errors.

4. Return to your text editor. You can leave your browser open.

Creating **Headers, Paragraphs, and Lists**

Now that the basic structure of Franklin's job listing page is set, you can start filling in the page content. One place to start is the headers for the various sections of the document. The document needs a header for the entire page and headers for each of the four sections: Responsibilities, Qualifications, Knowledge and Ability, and How to Apply. The Qualifications section has two additional headers that list education and experience requirements. You can create these headers using HTML header tags.

Creating Header Tags

HTML supports six levels of headers, numbered <H1> through <H6>, with <H1> being the largest and most prominent and <H6> being the smallest. Headers (even the smallest) appear in a larger font than normal text, and some headers are boldface. The general syntax for a header tag is *<H#>Heading Text</H#>* where # is a header numbered 1 through 6. Figure 7-5 illustrates the general appearance of the six header styles. Your browser might use slightly different fonts and sizes.

Figure 7-5	SIX HEADER LEVELS

This is an H1 Header

This is an H2 Header

This is an H3 Header

This is an H4 Header

This is an H5 Header

This is an H6 Header

REFERENCE WINDOW   RW

Creating a Header Tag
- Open the HTML file with your text editor.
- Type <H#> where # is the header number you want to use.
- If you want to use special alignment, specify the alignment property setting after the header number and before the closing symbol (>).
- Type the text that you want to appear in the header.
- Type </H#> to turn off the header tag.

Starting with HTML 3.2, the header tag can contain additional properties, one of which is the alignment property. Franklin wants some of the section titles centered on the page, so you use the alignment property to position the titles in the middle of a line. Although the coffee store address is not really header text, you decide to format it with an <H5> tag, because you want the address to stand out a little from normal text.

To add headings to the job listing file:

1. Make sure the **Joblisting** file is displayed in your text editor.

2. Position the insertion point at the end of the <BODY> tag, and then press the **Enter** key to insert a blank line.

3. Type the following text between the <BODY> and </BODY> tags, making sure that the company name, address, and phone number appear on one line as shown in Figure 7-6:

    <H1 ALIGN=CENTER>Coffee Store Manager</H1>

    <H5 ALIGN=CENTER>The Coffee and Tea Merchant 2234 Roasting Lane, San Diego, CA 90000-1234</H5>

    <H2 ALIGN=CENTER>Responsibilities</H2>

    <H2 ALIGN=CENTER>Qualifications</H2>

    <H3>Education</H3>

    <H3>Experience</H3>

    <H2 ALIGN=CENTER>Knowledge and Ability</H2>

    <H2 ALIGN=CENTER>How to Apply</H2>

    Figure 7-6 shows the revised code. Note: To make it easier to follow the changes to the HTML file, new and altered text will be highlighted in red in the figures throughout the tutorial. Text in your HTML file will not appear in red.

Figure 7-6   ENTERING HEADER TAGS

```
<BODY>
<H1 ALIGN=CENTER>Coffee Store Manager</H1>
<H5 ALIGN=CENTER>The Coffee and Tea Merchant 2234 Roasting Lane, San Diego, CA 90000-1234</H5>
<H2 ALIGN=CENTER>Responsibilities</H2>
<H2 ALIGN=CENTER>Qualifications</H2>
<H3>Education</H3>
<H3>Experience</H3>
<H2 ALIGN=CENTER>Knowledge and Ability</H2>
<H2 ALIGN=CENTER>How to Apply</H2>
</BODY>
```

> **TROUBLE?** Depending on the size of your screen, the address line might wrap to a second line. Wrapping to a second line is okay.
>
> **4.** Save your changes to the file. You can leave your text editor open.

The section headers all use the ALIGN=CENTER property to center the text on the page. The <H#> tags used for the two qualifications headers, however, do not include that property and will be left-justified because that is the default alignment setting. If a browser that displays the job listing page does not support HTML 3.2 (or above) or does not support the alignment property through an extension, the headers will appear, but all of them will be left-justified.

You will preview the job listing page that now includes the section headers.

> ### To display the revised job listing page:
>
> **1.** Return to your Web browser.
>
> **2.** If the previous version of the page still appears in the browser window, click **View** on the menu bar, and then click **Refresh**. See Figure 7-7.

Figure 7-7	HEADERS AS THEY APPEAR IN THE BROWSER

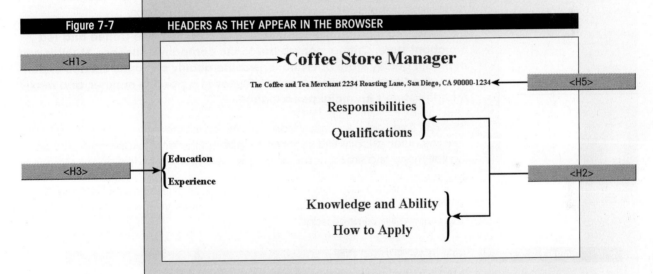

> **TROUBLE?** If you are using Netscape Navigator, you must click **View** on its menu bar and then click **Reload**. Some browsers include a Refresh button on their toolbars, which you can click to refresh the view of the current page displayed in the browser window.

Entering Paragraph Text

The next thing that you have to do is enter information for each section. If your paragraph does not require any formatting, you can enter the text without tags.

REFERENCE	WINDOW

Creating a Paragraph
- Open the HTML file with your text editor.
- Move to the place in the document where you want the paragraph to start.
- Type <P> to indicate the beginning of the paragraph.
- Enter the text for the paragraph.
- Type </P> to indicate the ending of the paragraph.

Note that if the paragraph text does not require any formatting, you can enter the text without tags. The paragraph just below the Responsibilities heading does not require formatting, so you will enter the text without including the paragraph tags.

To enter the paragraph text:

1. Return to the **Joblisting** file in your text editor.

2. Position the insertion point at the end of the code for the Responsibilities header, press the **Enter** key, and then type the following text:

   Responsible for profitable and efficient operation of The Coffee and Tea Merchant store. Critical contributor to the company's success. Monitor and maintain quality store operations, provide quality customer service experience, lead and empower store employees in a positive manner, and maximize the store's financial performance.

   TROUBLE? If you are using a text editor like Notepad, the text might not wrap to the next line automatically. You might need to select the Word Wrap command on the Edit menu or a similar command, so you can see all the text on your screen.

   Make sure the text appears between the Responsibilities header and the Qualifications header, as shown in Figure 7-8. Check your work for mistakes, and edit the file as necessary.

Figure 7-8	ENTERING PARAGRAPH TEXT

```
<BODY>
<H1 ALIGN=CENTER>Coffee Store Manager</H1>
<H5 ALIGN=CENTER>The Coffee and Tea Merchant 2234 Roasting Lane, San Diego, CA 90000-1234</H5>
<H2 ALIGN=CENTER>Responsibilities</H2>
Responsible for profitable and efficient operation of The Coffee and Tea Merchant store. Critical
contributor to the company's success. Monitor and maintain quality store operations, provide
quality customer service experience, lead and empower store employees in a positive manner, and
maximize the store's financial performance.
<H2 ALIGN=CENTER>Qualifications</H2>
<H3>Education</H3>
<H3>Experience</H3>
<H2 ALIGN=CENTER>Knowledge and Ability</H2>
<H2 ALIGN=CENTER>How to Apply</H2>
</BODY>
```

3. Save the changes you made to the file.

4. Return to your Web browser, and then refresh your view of the job listing page. See Figure 7-9.

Figure 7-9	PARAGRAPH TEXT DISPLAYED BY THE BROWSER

Coffee Store Manager

The Coffee and Tea Merchant 2234 Roasting Lane, San Diego, CA 90000-1234

Responsibilities

Responsible for profitable and efficient operation of The Coffee and Tea Merchant store. Critical contributor to the company's success. Monitor and maintain quality store operations, provide quality customer service experience, lead and empower store employees in a positive manner, and maximize the store's financial performance.

Qualifications

Now you will enter the Education paragraph text.

5. Return to your text editor, position the insertion point at the end of the code for the Knowledge and Ability header, press the **Enter** key, and then type the following text (pressing the Enter key after the first and second paragraphs of text):

People Skills Ability to motivate employees. Demonstrate strong independent discretion and judgment to accomplish day-to-day objectives. Maintain employee communication. Provide assistance to customers in a courteous and professional manner.

Financial Operation Proven store banking and bookkeeping skills. Use the automated payroll system. Produce employee schedules. Generate weekly financial status reports. Order bulk coffee and tea.

Coffee Knowledge Barista experience including preparing a wide variety of espresso beverages. Knowledge of coffee beans, including country of origin.

Figure 7-10 shows the new code in the Joblisting file.

Figure 7-10	ENTERING SKILLS TEXT

```
<H3>Education</H3>
<H3>Experience</H3>
<H2 ALIGN=CENTER>Knowledge and Ability</H2>
People Skills Ability to motivate employees. Demonstrate strong independent discretion and
judgment to accomplish day-to-day objectives. Maintain employee communication. Provide assistance
to customers in a courteous and professional manner.

Financial Operation Proven store banking and bookkeeping skills. Use the automated payroll
system. Produce employee schedules. Generate weekly financial status reports. Order bulk coffee
and tea.

Coffee Knowledge Barista experience including preparing a wide variety of espresso beverages.
Knowledge of coffee beans, including country of origin.
<H2 ALIGN=CENTER>How to Apply</H2>
</BODY>
```

6. Save the changes you have made to the file.

7. Return to your Web browser, refresh your view of the job listing page, and then scroll down to see how the new text looks. See Figure 7-11.

Figure 7-11

KNOWLEDGE AND ABILITY PARAGRAPHS DISPLAYED BY THE BROWSER

text is not displayed in separate paragraphs

To your surprise, the text you typed into the HTML file looks quite a bit different from the way it appeared in the browser, as you can see from Figure 7-11. Instead of being separated by blank lines, the three paragraphs are running together. What went wrong?

The problem here is that HTML formats text only through the use of tags. HTML ignores such things as extra blank spaces, blank lines, or tabs. As far as HTML is concerned, the following three lines of code are identical, so a browser interprets and displays each line just like the others, ignoring the extra spaces and lines:

<H1>To be or not to be. That is the question.</H1>

<H1>To be or not to be.   That is the question.</H1>

<H1>To be or not to be.

            That is the question.</H1>

At first glance, the Knowledge and Ability section seemed not to need any formatting; however, each paragraph needs to be separated by a blank line. To add this space between paragraphs, you need to use the **paragraph tag**, **<P>**, which adds a blank paragraph (the extra line you need) before text to separate it from any text that precedes it.

You will add the tags to insert the blank lines needed between the paragraphs in the Knowledge and Ability section.

To add the paragraph tags to insert blank lines:

1. Return to the **Joblisting** file in your text editor.

2. Position the insertion point at the beginning of the People Skills paragraph, and then type **</P>**.

3. Position the insertion point at the end of the People Skills paragraph, and then type **</P>**.

4. Insert the **<P>** and the **</P>** paragraph tags at the beginning and at the end of the Financial Operation and the Coffee Knowledge paragraphs.

5. Save the revised file, return to your Web browser, and then refresh your view of the job listing page. The text in the Knowledge and Ability section is properly separated into distinct paragraphs. See Figure 7-12.

Figure 7-12	TEXT APPEARS IN SEPARATE PARAGRAPHS

Qualifications

Education

Experience

Knowledge and Ability

People Skills Ability to motivate employees. Demonstrate strong independent discretion and judgment to accomplish day-to-day objectives. Maintain employee communication. Provide assistance to customers in a courteous and professional manner.

Financial Operation Proven store banking and bookkeeping skills. Use the automated payroll system. Produce employee schedules. Generate weekly financial status reports. Order bulk coffee and tea.

Coffee KnowledgeBarista experience including preparing a wide variety of espresso beverages. Knowledge of coffee beans, including country of origin.

How to Apply

If you start examining the HTML code for pages that you encounter on the Web, you might notice that the <P> tag is used in different ways on other pages. In an earlier version of HTML, the <P> tag inserted a blank line into the page. In HTML 1.0, <P> was placed at the end of each paragraph; no </P> tag was required. In versions 2.0 and 3.2, the paragraph tag is two-sided: both the <P> and the </P> tags are used. Moreover, the <P> tag is placed at the beginning of the paragraph, not the end. Starting with HTML 3.2, you can specify the alignment property in a paragraph tag, but in HTML 1.0 and 2.0, you cannot; paragraphs are always assumed to be left-justified. For the Web documents you are creating in this book, you should use the style convention shown in the above example.

Creating Lists

You still need to enter the lists describing the educational and experience qualifications that appear below the Education and Experience headings. HTML provides tags for such lists. HTML supports three kinds of lists: ordered, unordered, and definition.

An **ordered list** is a list in numeric order. HTML automatically adds the numbers once you display your Web page in a browser. If you remove an item from the list, HTML automatically updates the numbers to reflect the new order. For example, Franklin might want to list the experience requirements for the coffee store manager job in order from most important to the least important. To do so, you could enter the following code into the HTML document:

<H3>Experience</H3>

<OL>

<LI>Three to five years' experience in the restaurant or hospitality industry

<LI>Minimum two years' management experience

<LI>Time management and organizational experience

</OL>

This example shows the basic structure of an HTML list. The list text is bracketed between the <OL> and </OL> tags, where OL stands for *ordered list*. This code tells the browser to present the text between the tags as an ordered list. A single <LI> tag identifies each list item, where LI stands for *list item*. There is no closing tag for list items.

A Web browser might display this code as:

Experience

1. Three to five years' experience in the restaurant or hospitality industry

2. Minimum two years' management experience

3. Time management and organizational experience

You can also specify the symbol used for the ordered list using the **TYPE** property. The default is a number. By setting the TYPE property to "a", you can use letters instead of numbers. For example, the code:

<OL TYPE=a>

<LI>Three to five years' experience in the restaurant or hospitality industry

<LI>Minimum two years' management experience

<LI>Time management and organizational experience

</OL>

Including the TYPE property yields the following list:

a. Three to five years' experience in the restaurant or hospitality industry

b. Minimum two years' management experience

c. Time management and organizational experience

Other values of the TYPE property are "A" for uppercase letters, "i" for lowercase Roman numerals, and "I" for uppercase Roman numerals. Be aware that not all browsers support the TYPE property. It was not part of the HTML standards prior to HTML 3.0.

You can also create an **unordered list**, in which list items have no particular order. Browsers usually format unordered lists by inserting a bullet symbol before each list item. The entire list is bracketed between the <UL> and </UL> tags, where UL stands for *unordered list*. If Franklin wanted to display the experience qualifications without regard to their importance, you could enter the following code:

<H3>Experience</H3>

<UL>

<LI>Three to five years' experience in the restaurant or hospitality industry

<LI>Minimum two years' management experience

<LI>Time management and organizational experience

</UL>

A Web browser might display this code as:

Experience

■ Three to five years' experience in the restaurant or hospitality industry
■ Minimum two years' management experience
■ Time management and organizational experience

Note that the items appear in the order in which they were entered in the list.

As with the ordered list, you can use the TYPE property to specify the type of symbol to use in the list. The default symbol is the bullet or "disc." Other values for the TYPE property are SQUARE for square bullets and CIRCLE for circles. HTML 3.0 introduced this property, although Netscape has supported it since version 1.0. Internet Explorer does not support this property, although this may change with new versions. If symbol type is an important part of your document, you will probably want to test this feature on several different browsers.

A third type of list that HTML can display is a definition list. A **definition list** is a list of terms, each followed by a definition line, usually indented slightly to the right. The <LI> tag used in ordered and unordered lists for individual items is replaced by two tags: the <DT> tag used for each term in the list and the <DD> tag used for each term's definition. As with the <LI> tag, both of these tags are one-sided. The entire list is bracketed by the <DL> and </DL> tags, indicating to the browser that the list is a definition list. Here's an example of the code to create a definition list of coffee drinks served by The Coffee and Tea Merchant:

<H3>Espresso Drinks</H3>

<DL>

<DT>Espresso Shot<DD>A fresh shot forms three layers: the aromatic crema, the billowing body, and the dark, intense heart

<DT>Caffe Latte<DD>Steamed milk with a rich, full-bodied shot of espresso topped with a delicate crown of foamed milk

<DT>Caffe Mocha<DD>Intensely flavored mocha syrup mixed with espresso and steamed milk and finished with a cloud of whipped cream

</DL>

A Web browser might display the code as:

Espresso Drinks

Espresso Shot

A fresh shot forms three layers: the aromatic crema, the billowing body, and the dark, intense heart

Caffe Latte

Steamed milk with a rich, full-bodied shot of espresso topped with a delicate crown of foamed milk

Caffe Mocha

Intensely flavored mocha syrup mixed with espresso and steamed milk and finished with a cloud of whipped cream

As indicated on the paper version of the job listing (Figure 7-1), there are bulleted lists under the Education and Experience headings of the Qualifications section. You will add the bulleted items to the text by using the <OL> and <LI> tags.

To add unordered lists:

1. Return to the **Joblisting.htm** file in your text editor.

2. Position the insertion point at the end of the code for the Education header, press the **Enter** key, and then type the following code:

   <UL>

   <LI>High school diploma required

   <LI>College degree preferred

   </UL>

3. Position the insertion point at the end of the code for the Experience header, press the **Enter** key, and then type of the following code:

   <UL>

   <LI>Three to five years' experience in the restaurant or hospitality industry

   <LI>Minimum two years' management experience

   <LI>Time management and organizational experience

   </UL>

   See Figure 7-13.

Figure 7-13	ENTERING UNORDERED LISTS

```
<H2 ALIGN=CENTER>Qualifications</H2>
<H3>Education</H3>
<UL>
<LI>High school diploma required
<LI>College degree preferred
</UL>
<H3>Experience</H3>
<UL>
<LI>Three to five years' experience in the restaurant or hospitality industry
<LI>Minimum two years' management experience
<LI>Time management and organizational experience
</UL>
<H2 ALIGN=CENTER>Knowledge and Ability</H2>
```

4. Save the changes to the file.

5. Switch to your Web browser and refresh your view of the job listing page. See Figure 7-14. The job listing page now includes lists formatted much like those on the page version of Franklin's job listing.

| Figure 7-14 | THE UNORDERED LIST DISPLAYED IN THE BROWSER |

Qualifications

Education

- High school diploma required
- College degree preferred

Experience

- Three to five years' experience in the restaurant or hospitality industry
- Minimum two years' management experience
- Time management and organizational experience

TROUBLE? If your browser does not create a page that looks like the page in Figure 7-14, return to the HTML file and check for inconsistencies.

Creating Character Tags

Until now, you've worked with tags that affect either the entire document or individual lines. HTML also lets you modify the characteristics of individual characters. A tag that you apply to an individual character is called a **character tag**. You can use two kinds of character tags: logical and physical. **Logical character tags** indicate how you want to use text, not necessarily how you want to display it. Figure 7-15 lists some common logical character tags.

Figure 7-15	COMMON LOGICAL CHARACTER TAGS
TAG	**DESCRIPTION**
<EM>	Indicates that characters should be emphasized in some way. Usually displayed with italics.
<STRONG>	Emphasizes characters more strongly than <EM>. Usually displayed in a bold font.
<CODE>	Indicates a sample of code. Usually displayed in a Courier font or a similar font that allots the same width to each character.
<KBD>	Used to offset text that the user should enter. Often displayed in a Courier font or a similar font that allots the same width to each character.
<VAR>	Indicates a variable. Often displayed in italics or underlined.
<CITE>	Indicates short quotes or citations. Often italicized by browsers.

Figure 7-16 shows examples of how these tags might appear in a browser. Note that you can combine tags, allowing you to create text that is both bold and italicized by using both the <EM> and the <STRONG> tags.

Figure 7-16	LOGICAL CHARACTER TAGS AS THEY APPEAR IN THE BROWSER

examples of individual logical character tags →

This is an example of the *EM tag*

This is an example of the **STRONG tag**

This is an example of the `CODE` tag

This is an example of the KBD tag

This is an example of the *VAR tag*

This is an example of the *CITE tag*

combined logical character tags →

This is an example of a combination of the ***EM and STRONG tags***

HTML authors can also use **physical character tags** to indicate exactly how characters are to be formatted. Figure 7-17 shows common examples of physical character tags.

Figure 7-17	COMMON PHYSICAL CHARACTER TAGS

TAG	DESCRIPTION
<B>	Indicates that the text should be bold.
<I>	Indicates that the text should be italic.
<TT>	Indicates that the text should be used with a font such as Courier that allots the same width to each character.
<BIG>	Indicates that the text should be displayed in a big font. Available only in HTML 3.0.
<SMALL>	Indicates that the text should be displayed in a small font. Available only in HTML 3.0.
<SUB>	The text should be displayed as a subscript, in a smaller font if possible. Available only in HTML 3.0.
<SUP>	The text should be displayed as a superscript, in a smaller font if possible. Available only in HTML 3.0.

Figure 7-18 shows examples of how these tags might appear in a browser. Some browsers also support the <U> tag for underlining text, but other browsers might not show underlining, so use it sparingly.

Figure 7-18   PHYSICAL CHARACTER TAGS AS THEY APPEAR IN THE BROWSER

This is an example of the **B tag**

This is an example of the *I tag*

This is an example of the `TT` tag

This is an example of the **BIG tag**

This is an example of the SMALL tag

This is an example of the SUB tag

This is an example of the SUP tag

Given the presence of both logical and physical character tags, which should you use to display some text in an italicized font: <EM> or <I>? Some older versions of browsers are text-based and cannot display italics. These older browsers ignore the <I> tag, so the emphasis you want to place on a certain piece of text is lost. If this is a concern, you should use a logical tag. On the other hand, the physical character tags are more commonly used today and are easier to interpret. Some Web page authors believe that the use of logical character tags, such as <EM> and <STRONG>, is archaic and confusing; therefore, using these tags should be avoided.

Only one part of Franklin's online job listing requires character tags: the Knowledge and Ability section, where he wants to emphasize the title of each ability or skill. You will use a combination of the <B> and <I> tags to display the titles in boldface and italics.

To add character tags:

1. Return to the **Joblisting.htm** file in your text editor.

2. Type the **<I>** and **<B>** tags around the titles in the Knowledge and Ability section (just after the <P> tags), so that the text reads:

<I><B>People Skills**</B></I>**

<I><B>Financial Operation**</B></I>**

<I><B>Coffee Knowledge**</B></I>**

See Figure 7-19. Whenever you use two or more tags to surround text, the tags must be properly nested. Avoid overlapping tags. For example, **<I><B>***Coffee Knowledge***</I></B>** is not nested properly. Improperly nested tags can cause the browser to misinterpret your intended meaning.

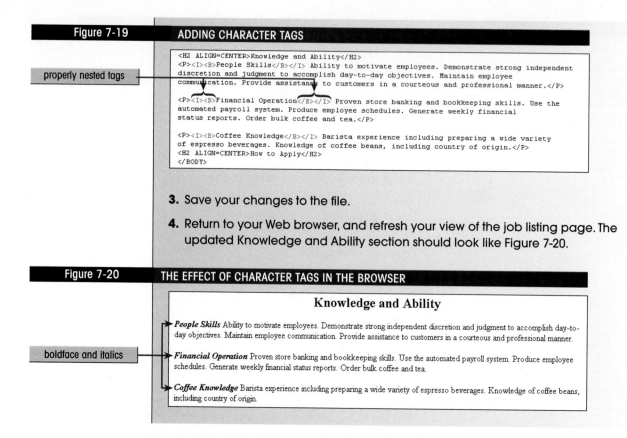

| Figure 7-19 | ADDING CHARACTER TAGS |

properly nested tags

```
<H2 ALIGN=CENTER>Knowledge and Ability</H2>
<P><I><B>People Skills</B></I> Ability to motivate employees. Demonstrate strong independent
discretion and judgment to accomplish day-to-day objectives. Maintain employee
communication. Provide assistance to customers in a courteous and professional manner.</P>

<P><I><B>Financial Operation</B></I> Proven store banking and bookkeeping skills. Use the
automated payroll system. Produce employee schedules. Generate weekly financial
status reports. Order bulk coffee and tea.</P>

<P><I><B>Coffee Knowledge</B></I> Barista experience including preparing a wide variety
of espresso beverages. Knowledge of coffee beans, including country of origin.</P>
<H2 ALIGN=CENTER>How to Apply</H2>
</BODY>
```

3. Save your changes to the file.

4. Return to your Web browser, and refresh your view of the job listing page. The updated Knowledge and Ability section should look like Figure 7-20.

| Figure 7-20 | THE EFFECT OF CHARACTER TAGS IN THE BROWSER |

Knowledge and Ability

boldface and italics

People Skills Ability to motivate employees. Demonstrate strong independent discretion and judgment to accomplish day-to-day objectives. Maintain employee communication. Provide assistance to customers in a courteous and professional manner.

Financial Operation Proven store banking and bookkeeping skills. Use the automated payroll system. Produce employee schedules. Generate weekly financial status reports. Order bulk coffee and tea.

Coffee Knowledge Barista experience including preparing a wide variety of espresso beverages. Knowledge of coffee beans, including country of origin.

Adding Special Characters

Occasionally you will want to include special characters in your Web page that do not appear on your keyboard. For example, a math page might require mathematical symbols such as Π or λ. As Franklin reviews the job listing file, he notices a place where he would like to add a special symbol. In the address information under the title at the top of the page, Franklin does not like the way the store name and address flow together. He wants to use special character to separate the two pieces of information.

HTML supports several character symbols that you can insert into your page. The **World Wide Web Consortium (W3C)** has several examples of special character symbols and the way they are coded. **Webmonkey**, a reference about all things related to the Internet and to the development of Web pages, contains several good tutorials about special HTML symbols. A code number or name identifies each character symbol. To create a special character, type an ampersand (&) followed either by the code name or the code number and then a semi-colon. Code numbers must be preceded by a pound sign (#). Figure 7-21 shows some HTML symbols and the corresponding code numbers or names.

Figure 7-21   **SPECIAL CHARACTERS AND CODES**

SYMBOL	CODE	CODE NAME	DESCRIPTION
©	&#169;	&copy;	Copyright symbol
®	&#174;	&reg;	Registered trademark
•	&#183;	&middot;	Middle dot
º	&#186;	&ordm;	Masculine ordinal
™	&#153;	&trade;	Trademark symbol
			Nonbreaking space, useful when you want to insert several blank spaces, one after another
<	&#60;	&lt;	Less than sign
>	&#62;	&gt;	Greater than sign
&	&#39;	&amp;	Ampersand

One way to separate the store name and address is to insert several nonbreaking spaces using the   character code. However, Franklin thinks that it would look better to insert a bullet (•) between the store name and the address. You will insert inserting the code for a middle dot, &#183.

To add a character code in the address line:

1. Return to the **Joblisting** file in your text editor.

2. Revise the address line at the beginning of the file by typing **·** between the company name and the street address, so that the line reads "The Coffee and Tea Merchant · 2234 Roasting Lane, San Diego, CA 90000-1234."

   TROUBLE? In your text editor this line probably appears as a single line.

3. Save the changes to the file.

4. Return to your Web browser, and refresh your view of the job listing page. Figure 7-22 shows the updated job listing page with the bullet separating the store name from the street address.

Figure 7-22   **SPECIAL CHARACTER DISPLAYED IN THE BROWSER**

bullet character now appears in the address line

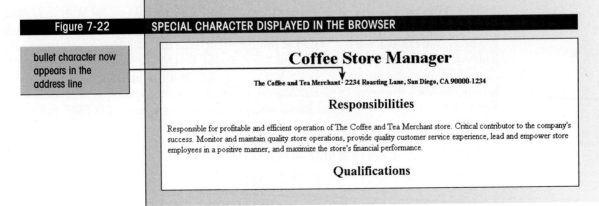

The next thing that Franklin wants in the job listing page is a horizontal line separating the store name and address information from the rest of the job information.

Inserting **Horizontal Lines**

The horizontal line after the business name and address in Figure 7-1 lends shape to the appearance on the job listing. Franklin would like you to duplicate that in the online version. You use the **<HR>** tag to create a horizontal line, where HR stands for horizontal rule. The <HR> tag is one-sided, so you do not terminate it with </HR>, a nonexistent tag. When a text-based browser encounters the <HR> tag, this browser inserts a line by repeating an underline symbol across the width of the page. A graphical browser inserts a graphical line. You will insert a horizontal line so it will appear under the address line.

To add a horizontal line under the address line:

1. Return to the **Joblisting** file in your text editor.

2. At the end of The Coffee and Tea Merchant's address line, press the **Enter** key to insert a new blank line.

3. In the new line, type **<HR>**.

4. Save the changes to the file.

5. Return to your Web browser, and refresh your view of the job listing page. Figure 7-23 shows the updated job listing page with the horizontal line inserted near the top of the page.

Figure 7-23	HORIZONTAL LINE AS IT APPEARS IN THE BROWSER

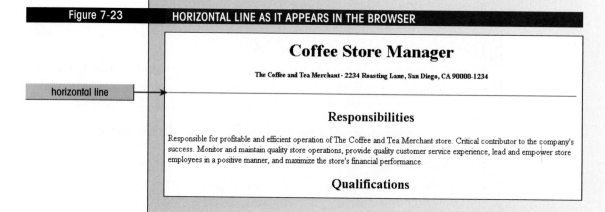

horizontal line

Coffee Store Manager

The Coffee and Tea Merchant · 2234 Roasting Lane, San Diego, CA 90000-1234

Responsibilities

Responsible for profitable and efficient operation of The Coffee and Tea Merchant store. Critical contributor to the company's success. Monitor and maintain quality store operations, provide quality customer service experience, lead and empower store employees in a positive manner, and maximize the store's financial performance.

Qualifications

The <HR> tag has several properties that you may want to use in your Web page. The ALIGN property can be set to left, right, or center to place the line on the page (the default is center). You can also use the WIDTH property to tell the browser what percentage of the width of the page the line should occupy. For example, WIDTH= 50% tells the browser to place the line so that its length covers half of the page. You can use the SIZE property to specify the line's thickness in pixels. A pixel, short for picture element, is 1/72-inch wide. Figure 7-24 shows how a browser would interpret the following lines of HTML code:

<HR> ALIGN=CENTER SIZE=12 WIDTH=100%>

<HR> ALIGN=CENTER SIZE=6 WIDTH=50%>

<HR> ALIGN=CENTER SIZE=3 WIDTH=25%>

<HR> ALIGN=CENTER SIZE=1 WIDTH=10%>

Figure 7-24 DIFFERENT LINE STYLES

Netscape Navigator and Internet Explorer also support properties specific to those browsers. As always, you should remember that using browser-specific extensions might produce wildly different results on browsers that do not support the extensions.

Inserting a Graphic

One feature of Web pages that has made the World Wide Web so popular is the ease of displaying a graphic image. The Web supports two methods for displaying a graphic: as an inline image and as an external image.

An **inline image** appears directly on the Web page and is loaded when the page is loaded. Two of the more commonly supported image types are GIF (Graphics Interchange Format) and JPEG (Joint Photographic Experts Group). Before you display a graphic image, you should convert it to one of these two types.

An **external image** is not displayed with the Web page. Instead, the browser must have a **file viewer**—a program that the browser loads automatically—whenever the browser encounters the image file and uses the program to display the image. You can find file viewers at several Internet Web sites. Most browsers make it easy to set up viewers for use with the Web. External images have one disadvantage: You cannot actually display them on the Web page. Instead, an external image appears as an icon that a user clicks to view the image. However, external images are not limited to GIF or JPEG formats. You can set up virtually any image format as an external image on the Web page, including video clips and sound files.

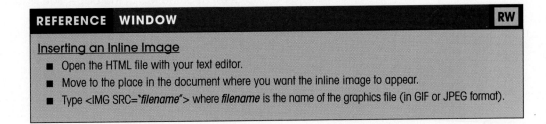

REFERENCE   WINDOW   RW

Inserting an Inline Image
- Open the HTML file with your text editor.
- Move to the place in the document where you want the inline image to appear.
- Type <IMG SRC="*filename*"> where *filename* is the name of the graphics file (in GIF or JPEG format).

Franklin is more interested in using an inline image than an external image; therefore, you will use the <IMG> tag to display an inline image. You can place inline images on a separate line in your document, or you can place the image within a line of text (hence the term "inline"). To access the image file, you need to include the filename within the tag. You do this using the SRC property, short for "source." The general syntax for an inline image is:

<IMG SRC="filename">

If the image file is located in the same folder as the HTML file referencing it, you do not need to include any folder or path information. However, if the image file is located in another folder on another computer, you need to include the full path with the SRC property. Try, if at all possible, to keep the files in the same folder, which will keep things simple. Note that the filename must appear in quotation marks. For now, assume that Franklin's image file is placed in the same folder as the HTML file. The image file that Franklin has created is a picture of a coffee cup in JPEG format. The name of the file is Cup.jpg.

Franklin also wants you to center the image on the page. There is no property in the <IMG> tag that would allow you to center it on a page. But you can nest the <IMG> tag within a paragraph tag, <P>, and then center the paragraph on the page using the ALIGN=CENTER property for the <P> tag. Nesting these tags has the effect of centering all of the text (and inline images) in the paragraph. Note that the ALIGN property was introduced in HTML 3.2; in browsers that do not support this convention, the image may be left-justified.

To add an image to the Joblisting.htm file:

1. Look in the Tutorial .07\Tutorial folder on your Data Disk and verify that both the Joblisting.htm and Cup.jpg files are there.

2. Return to the **Joblisting.htm** file in your text editor.

3. At the end of the line with the <HR> tag that you just typed, press the **Enter** key to create a new blank line.

4. In the new line, type **<P ALIGN=CENTER><IMG SRC="Cup.jpg"></P>** and then save the changes to the file.

5. Print a copy of your completed job listing HTML file, and then close your text editor.

6. Return to your Web browser, and refresh your view of the job listing page. The inline image is displayed near the top of the page. See Figure 7-25 for a view of the entire page.

Figure 7-25	JOB LISTING PAGE WITH INLINE IMAGE

Coffee Store Manager

The Coffee and Tea Merchant · 2234 Roasting Lane, San Diego, CA 90000-1234

Responsibilities

Responsible for profitable and efficient operation of The Coffee and Tea Merchant store. Critical contributor to the company's success. Monitor and maintain quality store operations, provide quality customer service experience, lead and empower store employees in a positive manner, and maximize the store's financial performance.

Qualifications

Education

- High school diploma required
- College degree preferred

Experience

- Three to five years' experience in the restaurant or hospitality industry
- Minimum two years' management experience
- Time management and organizational experience

Knowledge and Ability

People Skills Ability to motivate employees. Demonstrate strong independent discretion and judgment to accomplish day-to-day objectives. Maintain employee communication. Provide assistance to customers in a courteous and professional manner.

Financial Operation Proven store banking and bookkeeping skills. Use the automated payroll system. Produce employee schedules. Generate weekly financial status reports. Order bulk coffee and tea.

Coffee Knowledge Barista experience including preparing a wide variety of espresso beverages. Knowledge of coffee beans, including country of origin.

How to Apply

7. Use your browser to print a copy of The Coffee and Tea Merchant's job listing. Compare the printout of the code with the online job listing displayed by your browser.

8. Close all open files and close your browser.

Leave your browser open to continue with the next section.

Session 7.1 QUICK CHECK

1. Why should you include the <HTML> tag in your Web document?

2. If you want to display several paragraphs, why can't you simply type an extra blank line in the HTML file?

3. Describe the syntax for creating an ordered list, an unordered list, and a definition list.

4. How would you insert a copyright symbol © into your Web page?

5. What is the syntax for inserting a horizontal line into a page?

6. What is an inline image?

7. What are two graphic file formats you can use for inline images?

SESSION 7.2

In this session, you will create anchors on a Web page that let you jump to specific points in the document. After creating those anchors, you will create and then test a hypertext link to another document.

Creating a Hypertext Document

A hypertext document contains **hypertext links**, which are items that you can select, usually by clicking a mouse, to instantly view another topic or document, often called the **destination** of the link. These hypertext links (also called **hyperlinks** or just **links**) can point to another section in the same document, to an entirely different document, to a different Web page, or to a variety of other Web objects, which you will learn about later in this lesson. In addition to making access to other documents easy, hypertext links provide some important organizational benefits. They indicate what points or concepts that you think merit special attention or further reading. You can take advantage of these features by adding hypertext links to the online job listing.

At this point, the job listing has four main sections: Responsibilities, Qualifications, Knowledge and Ability, and How to Apply. Because of the document window's limited size, the opening screen does not show many of the main sections. The browser shown in Figure 7-26 shows half of the job listing, omitting from the display the Knowledge and Ability section and the How to Apply section (which is currently empty). Readers will have to scroll through the document to see the additional information.

| Figure 7-26 | OPENING SCREEN OF THE COFFEE AND TEA MERCHANT'S JOB LISTING PAGE |

> **Coffee Store Manager Job Posting - Microsoft Internet Explorer**
>
> File   Edit   View   Favorites   Tools   Help
>
> Back   Forward   Stop   Refresh   Home   Search   Favorites   History   Mail   Print   Edit   Discuss
>
> Address   A:\Tutorial.07\Tutorial\Joblisting.htm   Go   Links »
>
> # Coffee Store Manager
>
> The Coffee and Tea Merchant · 2234 Roasting Lane, San Diego, CA 90000-1234
>
> ## Responsibilities
>
> Responsible for profitable and efficient operation of The Coffee and Tea Merchant store. Critical contributor to the company's success. Monitor and maintain quality store operations, provide quality customer service experience, lead and empower store employees in a positive manner, and maximize the store's financial performance.
>
> Qualifications
>
> Done   My Computer

Without using hypertext links, you can do little to show more of the job listing page in the browser except remove the image file or move it to the end of the job listing. However, you can insert text for all four headings (Responsibilities, Qualifications, Knowledge and Ability, and How to Apply) at the top of the document and then turn these headings into hypertext links. When readers open the job listing, they will see not only the business address and graphic, but also links to the main parts of the Web page. Interested job applicants can then click any of the headings and immediately see that section of the job listing. The hypertext links that you create at the top of the document point to sections within the same document. You will create such hypertext links in the job listing by following three steps:

1. Type the headings into the HTML file.

2. Mark each section in the HTML file using an anchor. (You'll learn what this is shortly.)

3. Link the text you added in Step 1 to the anchors you added in Step 2.

You can accomplish the first step using techniques you learned in Session 7.1. You need to open the Joblisting.htm file in your text editor (Notepad, for example) and then enter the text. You want the section headings to appear on the same line as the graphic image in the browser, as shown in Figure 7-27.

| Figure 7-27 | NEW TEXT ON SAME LINE AS THE GRAPHIC IMAGE IN THE BROWSER |

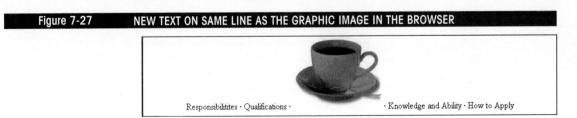

Responsibilitites · Qualifications ·   · Knowledge and Ability · How to Apply

To achieve this, you place the text within the paragraph tags that already encompass the Cup.jpg graphic file. You could type all the text into the HTML file on the same line, but to keep the HTML file as legible as possible, add the text in two lines instead. This way, when you add more tags to the text later, it will still be easy to read. Remember that because you format with markup tags in HTML, putting the text on different lines does not affect its appearance in the browser.

To add text that indicates the different sections of the job listing:

1. Open your text editor, and then open the file **Joblisting.htm** located in the Tutorial.07\Tutorial folder on your Data Disk.

   TROUBLE? If you cannot locate the Joblisting.htm file in your text editor's Open dialog box, you might need to set the Files of type to All Files (*.*).

2. Position the insertion point before the <IMG SRC="Cup.jpg"> line of code, press the **Enter** key, type **Responsibilities · Qualifications ·** (be sure to include the semicolons), and then press the **Enter** key so this new entry is on its own line.

3. Position the insertion point before the <P/> tag in the <IMG SRC="Cup.jpg"> line of code, press the **Enter** key again to create another new line, type **· Knowledge and Ability · How to Apply**, and press the **Enter** key so this new entry is on its own line. See Figure 7-28. The new lines include the special character code · which inserts a small bullet into the text to separate section headings crisply.

Figure 7-28	ENTERING NEW TEXT THAT WILL BE ALIGNED WITH GRAPHIC

```
<BODY>
<H1 ALIGN=CENTER>Coffee Store Manager</H1>
<H5 ALIGN=CENTER>The Coffee and Tea Merchant &#183;  2234 Roasting Lane, San Diego, CA
90000-1234</H5>
<HR>
<P ALIGN=CENTER>
Responsibilities &#183; Qualifications &#183;
<IMG SRC="Cup.jpg">
&#183; Knowledge and Ability &#183; How to Apply
</P>
<H2 ALIGN=CENTER>Responsibilities</H2>
```

4. Save your changes.

5. Start your Web browser (you do not have to connect to the Internet), and open the **Joblisting.htm** file located in the Tutorial.07\Tutorial folder on your Data Disk to see the revised page. See Figure 7-29.

Figure 7-29	JOB LISTING PAGE WITH NEW TEXT

Coffee Store Manager

The Coffee and Tea Merchant · 2234 Roasting Lane, San Diego, CA 90000-1234

Responsibilities · Qualifications ·   · Knowledge and Ability · How to Apply

Creating **Anchors**

Now that you have created the text describing the listing's different sections, you need to locate each header and mark it in the document, using the <A> tag. The <A> tag creates an **anchor**, which is text that is specially marked so that you can link *to* it from other points in the document. Text that is anchored will become the *destination* of a link; it is *not* the text you click. You assign each anchor its own anchor name, using the NAME property. Anchor names typically are abbreviations that have significance. For example, if you want the text "Knowledge and Ability" to be an anchor, you could assign it the anchor name "KA":

<A NAME="KA">Knowledge and Ability</A>

Later, when you create a link to this anchor from the headings you just inserted at the beginning of the job listing page, the link will point to this particular place in the document, using the anchor name KA. Figure 7-30 illustrates how the anchor you create will work as a reference point to a link.

Figure 7-30	ANCHORING TEXT

An anchor does not have to be just text. You can also mark an inline image using the same syntax:

<A NAME="PHOTO"><IMG SRC="Cup.jpg"></A>

You can create a link to a graphic from other points in the document by using the anchor name PHOTO. As you will see, adding an anchor does not change your document's appearance in any way.

REFERENCE   WINDOW   **RW**

<u>Creating Anchors</u>
- Locate the text or graphic you want to anchor.
- Before the text or graphic, place the tag <A NAME="*anchor_name*"> where *anchor_name* is the name you choose for your anchor.
- After the text or graphic, place a closing </A> anchor tag to turn off the anchor.

For the job listing document, you will create four anchors using the names RES, QUAL, KA, and HOW for the Responsibilities, Qualifications, Knowledge and Ability, and How to Apply sections.

To add anchors to the section headings:

1. Return to the **Joblisting.htm** file in your text editor.

2. Locate the H2 header for the Responsibilities section in the line that reads: *<H2 ALIGN=CENTER>Responsibilities</H2>*.

3. Add an anchor tag around the Responsibilities heading so that it reads: <H2 ALIGN=CENTER>**<A NAME= "RES">**Responsibilities**</A>**</H2>.

4. Locate the H2 header for the Qualifications section in the line that reads: *<H2 ALIGN=CENTER>Qualifications</H2>*.

5. Add an anchor tag around the Qualifications heading so that the line reads: <H2 ALIGN=CENTER>**<A NAME= "QUAL">**Qualifications**</A>**</H2>.

6. Locate the H2 header for the Knowledge and Ability section in the line that reads: *<H2 ALIGN=CENTER>Knowledge and Ability</H2>*.

7. Add an anchor tag around the Knowledge and Ability heading so that the line reads: <H2 ALIGN=CENTER>**<A NAME= "KA">**Knowledge and Ability**</A>**</H2>.

8. Locate the H2 header for the How to Apply section, in the line that reads: *<H2 ALIGN=CENTER>How to Apply</H2>*.

9. Add an anchor tag around the How to Apply heading so that the line reads: <H2 ALIGN=CENTER>**<A NAME= "HOW">**How to Apply **</A>**</H2>.

10. Save your changes.

11. Return to your Web browser, and refresh your view of the job listing page. Scroll through the page to confirm that the file appears unchanged. Remember that the marks you placed in the document are reference points and should not change the appearance of the job listing page in your browser.

TROUBLE? If you see a change in the document, check to make sure that you used the NAME property of the <A> tag.

Creating Links

After you anchor the text that will be the destination for your links, you create the links themselves. For The Coffee and Tea Merchant's job listing, you want to link the text you entered around the graphic to the four sections in the document. Figure 7-31 shows the four links you want to create.

Figure 7-31	LINKS YOU WILL NEED TO CREATE

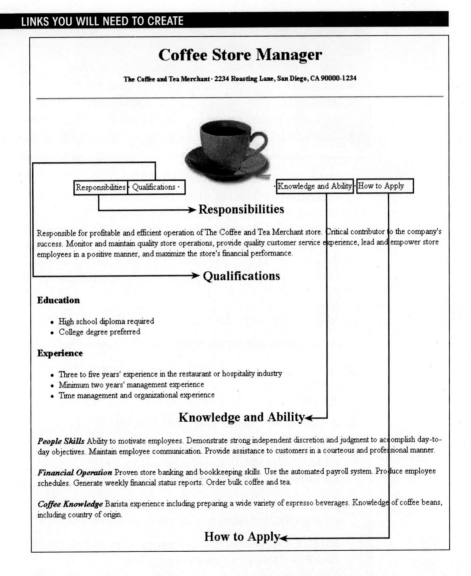

To create a link to an anchor, you use the same <A> tag you used to create the anchor. The difference is that instead of using the NAME property to define the anchor, you use the **HREF** property, short for Hypertext Reference, to indicate the location to jump to. HREF can refer to an anchor that you place in the document, or, as you will see later, to a different Web page or a resource on the Internet. The <A> tags that create links are called **link tags**.

You link to an anchor using the anchor name preceded by a pound (#) symbol. For example, to create a link to the Responsibilities heading in the job listing, you use the anchor name RES and this HTML tag:

<A HREF="#RES">Responsibilities</A>

In this example, the entire word "Responsibilities" becomes a hypertext link. When you open the job listing in your Web browser and click any part of that word, you jump to the location of the RES anchor.

You can also designate an inline image as a hypertext link. To turn an inline image into a hypertext link, place it within link tags, as in:

<A HREF="#IMAGELINK"><IMG SRC="Cup.jpg"></A>

REFERENCE WINDOW   **RW**

Linking to Text Within a Document
- Mark the destination text with an anchor.
- Locate the text or graphic you want to designate as the link.
- Before the text or graphic, place the tag <A HREF="*anchor_name*"> where *anchor_name* is the name of the anchor.
- Close the link tag with the </A> closing tag after the text or graphic you designated as the link.

Sometimes a link does not work as you expect. One common source of trouble is the case of the anchor. The HREF property is case-sensitive. The anchor name "RES" is not the same as "res". You should also remember to make each anchor name unique within a document. If you use the same anchor name for different text, your links won't go where you expect.

In the current HTML document, you have created four anchors to which you can link. You're ready to place the link tags around the appropriate text in the HTML file.

To add link tags to the four sections in the job listing:

1. Return to the **Joblisting.htm** file in your text editor.

2. Locate the paragraph containing the four section headings and the coffee cup graphic at the top of the page. Within that paragraph you need to bracket each section heading with a link tag and the HREF property.

3. In the line that reads "Responsibilities · Qualifications ·", change the text (keeping all the text on one line) to:

   <A HREF="#RES">Responsibilities**</A>** ·
   <A HREF="#QUAL">Qualifications**</A>** ·

4. In the line that reads "· Knowledge and Ability · How to Apply", change the text (keeping all the text on one line) to:

   · **<A HREF="#KA">**Knowledge and Ability**</A>** ·
   <A HREF="#HOW">How to Apply**</A>**

5. Compare your HTML file to Figure 7-32.

Figure 7-32   **ADDING LINK TAGS**

```
<BODY>
<H1 ALIGN=CENTER>Coffee Store Manager</H1>
<H5 ALIGN=CENTER>The Coffee and Tea Merchant &#183;  2234 Roasting Lane, San Diego, CA
90000-1234</H5>
<HR>
<P ALIGN=CENTER>
<A HREF="#RES">Responsibilities</A> &#183; <A HREF="#QUAL">Qualifications</A> &#183;
<IMG SRC="Cup.jpg">
&#183; <A HREF="#KA">Knowledge and Ability</A> &#183; <A HREF="#HOW">How to Apply</A>
</P>
<H2 ALIGN=CENTER>Responsibilities</H2>
```

6. Save the changes you made to the Joblisting.htm file.

7. Return to your Web browser, and refresh your view of the job listing page. The headings should now be a different color and be underlined—the standard formatting for links in most browsers. See Figure 7-33.

| Figure 7-33 | TEXT LINKS AS THEY APPEAR IN THE BROWSER |

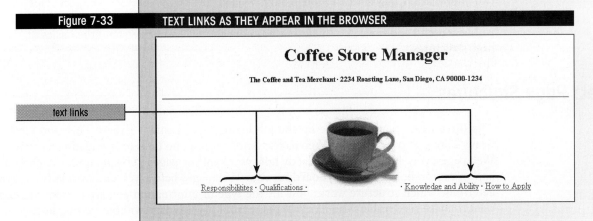

text links

Coffee Store Manager

The Coffee and Tea Merchant · 2234 Roasting Lane, San Diego, CA 90000-1234

Responsibilitites · Qualifications ·   · Knowledge and Ability · How to Apply

TROUBLE? If the headings do not appear as text links, check your code and make sure that you are using the <A> tag around the text and the HREF property within the tag.

Before continuing, you should verify that the links work properly. To test a link, you click it and observe the part of the page at the top of the screen.

To test your links:

1. Click one of the links. You should jump to the section of the document indicated by the link. If this doesn't happen, check your code for errors by comparing it with Figure 7-32.

2. Scroll to the top of the page (or click the Back button on your browser's toolbar).

3. Click each of the other links, scrolling back to the top of the page each time.

4. Leave your text editor and browser open.

If you still have problems, make sure you used the correct case and that you coded the anchor and link tags correctly. When you add an anchor to a large section of text, such as a section heading, make sure to place the anchor within the header tags. For example, you should write your tag as:

<H2><A NAME="QUAL">Qualifications</A></H2>

not as:

<A NAME="QUAL"><H2>Qualifications</H2></A>

The latter could confuse some browsers. The general rule is to always place anchors within other tag elements. Do not insert any tag elements within an anchor, except for tags that create document objects such as inline graphics.

You show the new links to Franklin. He is very pleased to see how they work. He thinks they will quickly inform interested potential employees about the work requirements and qualifications at The Coffee and Tea Merchant and help future employees find the information they want. Next, you will create links that jump to other HTML documents.

Franklin wants to add two more pages to his online job listing—information pages. One page contains information about storage, grinding, and brewing coffee. The other page is the description of the coffee beans produced by four countries. Franklin wants to link the two information pages to the job listing Web page—pages he calls "Expert Tips" and "Coffee Beans." Although you agree with Franklin that adding the two information pages will be a useful addition, you think that Franklin should first understand the basics of Web page structures.

Web Page Structures

The three pages that will make up the job listing—Job Listing, Expert Tips, and Coffee Beans—are part of a system of Web pages. Before you set up links for navigating a group of Web pages, you should map out exactly how you want the pages to relate, using a technique known as storyboarding. **Storyboarding** your Web pages before you create links helps you determine which structure works best for the type of information you are presenting. You want to make sure readers can navigate easily from page to page without getting lost.

Linear Structures

You'll encounter several Web structures as you navigate the Web. Examining these structures can help you decide how to design your own system of Web pages. Figure 7-34 shows one common structure, the **linear structure**, in which each page is linked to the next and the previous pages, in an ordered chain of pages.

| Figure 7-34 | LINEAR STRUCTURE |

link to previous page

in this structure you can jump only from one page to the next or previous page

link to next page

You could use this type of structure in Web pages that have a defined order. Suppose that a Web site of Shakespeare's *Hamlet* has a single page for each scene. If you use a linear structure for these pages, you assume that user wants to progress through the scenes in order.

You might, however, want to make it easier for users to return immediately to the opening scene, rather than backtrack through several scenes. Figure 7-35 shows an **augmented linear structure**, in which you include a link in each page that jumps directly back to the first page, while keeping the links that allow you to move to the next and previous pages. This kind of storyboarding can reveal approaches to organizing the Web site that otherwise might not be noticed.

Figure 7-35 | AUGMENTED LINEAR STRUCTURE

first link jumps to
previous page

second link jumps back
to beginning

Act I
Scene I

Act I
Scene II

Act I
Scene III

Act I
Scene IV

third page has three links

third link jumps to
next page

Hierarchical Structures

Another popular structure is the hierarchical structure of Web pages shown in Figure 7-36. A **hierarchical structure** starts with a general topic that includes links to more specific topics. Each specific topic includes links to yet more specialized topics, and so on. In a hierarchical structure, users can move easily from general to specific and back, but not from specific to specific. As with the linear structure, including a link to the top of the structure on each page gives users an easy path back to the beginning. Subject catalogs such as the Yahoo! directory of Web pages often use this structure.

Figure 7-36 | HIERARCHICAL STRUCTURE

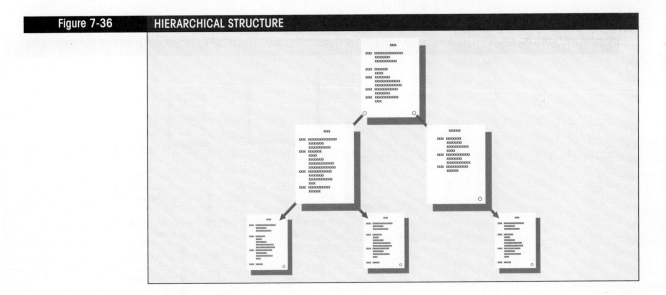

Mixed Structures

You can also combine structures. Figure 7-37 shows a hierarchical structure in which each level of pages is related in a linear structure. You might use this system for the *Hamlet* Web site to let the user move from scene to scene linearly, or from a specific scene to the general act to the overall play.

Figure 7-37	COMBINATION OF LINEAR AND HIERARCHICAL STRUCTURES

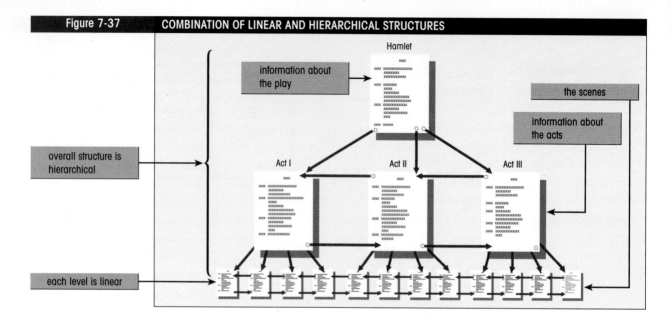

As these examples show, a little foresight can go a long way toward making your Web pages easier to use. The best time to organize a structure is when you first start creating multiple pages and those pages are small and easy to manage. If you are not careful, your structure might look like Figure 7-38. This structure is confusing, and it makes it difficult for readers to grasp the contents of the entire Web site. Moreover, a user who enters this structure at a certain page might not even be aware of the presence of other pages at the far end of the page chain.

Figure 7-38	MULTIPAGE DOCUMENT WITH NO COHERENT STRUCTURE

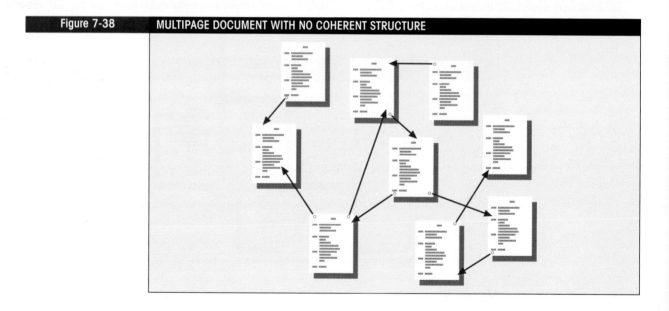

Creating **Links Between Documents**

Franklin and you discuss the type of structure that will work best for the job listing page. He wants viewers to move effortlessly among the pages. Because there are only three Web pages, all focused on the same topic, you decide to include links within each document to the other two. If Franklin later adds other pages, he will need to create a more formal structure. The two additional pages that you will link to the original job listing are in the Tutorial.07\Tutorial folder on your Data Disk. They are called Tiptext.htm and Beantext.htm. You should save these files with new names, Tip.htm and Bean.htm, to keep the originals intact.

> ### To rename the two additional pages in your Web structure:
>
> 1. Using your text editor, open the **Tiptext.htm** file located in the Tutorial.07\Tutorial folder on your Data Disk, and save it as **Tip.htm** in the same folder.
>
> 2. With your text editor, open the file **Beantext.htm** from the Tutorial.07\Tutorial folder on your Data Disk, and save it as **Bean.htm** in the same folder.

To link the job listing page to the tip and bean pages, you use the same <A> tag that you used earlier. For example, if you wanted a user to be able to click the phrase "All about coffee beans" to jump to the Bean.htm file, you could enter this HTML command in your document to accomplish that:

<A HREF="Bean.htm">All about coffee beans</A>

In this example, the entire text "All about coffee beans" is linked to the HTML file, Bean.htm. For the browser to be able to locate and open the Bean.htm file, this file must be in the same folder as the Joblisting.htm file, the document containing the links.

REFERENCE WINDOW **RW**

Linking to a Document Located on Your Computer
- Locate the link text or graphic (that is, the text or image you want to click to jump to the destination of the link).
- Before the text or graphic, place the tag <A HREF="*filename*"> where *filename* is the name of the destination document.
- After the link text or graphic, place the tag </A>.

Unlike creating hypertext links between elements on the same page, this process does not require you to set an anchor in a file to link to it—the filename serves as the anchor.

To add links in the job listing page to the tip and bean pages:

1. Return to the **Joblisting.htm** file in your text editor.

2. Scroll down to the Coffee Knowledge paragraph within the Knowledge and Ability section near the bottom of the page.

   You will link the phrase "Barista experience" to the Tip.htm file and link the "coffee beans" phrase to the Bean.htm file. Both of these phrases are in the paragraph describing Coffee Knowledge.

3. Add a link tag and the terminating </A> tag to the text that begins "Barista experience including" so that it reads:

   <A HREF="Tip.htm">Barista experience**</A>** including preparing a wide variety of espresso beverages.

4. Add a link tag and the terminating </A> tag to the text that begins "Knowledge of coffee beans, including" so that it reads:

   Knowledge of **<A HREF="Bean.htm">**coffee beans**</A>**, including country of origin. (Make sure the closing tag is placed before the comma.) See Figure 7-39.

Figure 7-39	TEXT LINKED TO OTHER FILES

```
<P><I><B>Coffee Knowledge</B></I> <A HREF="Tip.htm">Barista experience</A> including preparing a
wide variety of espresso beverages. Knowledge of <A HREF="Bean.htm">coffee beans</A>, including
country of origin.</P>
<H2 ALIGN=CENTER>How to Apply</H2>
</BODY>

</HTML>
```

5. Save the changes to the file.

6. Return to your Web browser, and refresh your view of the job listing page. Scroll down to the bottom of the page to see the links for the tip and bean pages. The items in the Coffee Knowledge paragraph contain two text links as shown in Figure 7-40.

Figure 7-40	NEW LINKS

Knowledge and Ability

People Skills Ability to motivate employees. Demonstrate strong independent discretion and judgment to accomplish day-to-day objectives. Maintain employee communication. Provide assistance to customers in a courteous and professional manner.

Financial Operation Proven store banking and bookkeeping skills. Use the automated payroll system. Produce employee schedules. Generate weekly financial status reports. Order bulk coffee and tea.

Coffee Knowledge Barista experience including preparing a wide variety of espresso beverages. Knowledge of coffee beans, including country of origin.

links to related files

7. Click the **Barista experience** link to verify that you jump to a Web page called "Expert Tips" shown in Figure 7-41.

Figure 7-41 | **EXPERT TIPS PAGE**

Expert Tips

View Job Listing · View Coffee Beans

Storage

For the freshest coffee, purchase only about a week's worth of coffee beans. Keep the beans whole until you are ready to brew them. When you bring your coffee home, store the unused beans in an airtight container. Store only whole beans in the freezer. Ground coffee can be stored in the refrigerator, but never store unsealed beans near other food, because the beans will absorb odors quickly.

Grinding

There's one rule to remember: match the grind to the brew pot. Common grinds include espresso, automatic drip, or press pot. This ensures the proper extraction of solids from the bean. If the grind is too fine, your coffee may taste bitter. If the grind is too coarse, the brew will be weak. Pulse the grind every three seconds so that the beans don't overheat.

Brewing

Coffee is slightly over 98% water, so always use fresh, cold, tap water or bottled water. Make sure that your coffee pot is clean. If you use an automatic drip machine, clean the machine with a weak vinegar solution followed by several gallons of fresh water. For the best results, use one rounded tablespoon per cup of coffee and later adjust to your taste. If necessary. Some coffee drinkers may prefer up to two tablespoons of coffee per cup. (A cup of coffee is approximately six ounces of liquid.) Once the brew is done, remove it from the heat immediately. If you let the coffee sit on a burner, it will start to deteriorate in about 20 minutes. If you need to store brewed coffee longer, then keep it in a thermos or vacuum container.

TROUBLE? If the link doesn't work, check to see that Tip.htm and Bean.htm are in the same folder on your Data Disk.

8. Go back to the job listing page by clicking your browser's **Back** button (found on the toolbar), and then click the **coffee beans** link to verify that the jump to the page describing various countries' coffee beans works. See Figure 7-42.

Figure 7-42 | **COFFEE BEANS PAGE**

Coffee Beans

View Job Listing · View Expert Tips

Costa Rica

Interestingly, it is illegal to grow robusta coffee in Costa Rica. (Robusta beans are inferior to arabica beans, which are typically grown at higher altitudes throughout the world.) Some of the best Costa Rican coffee is grown in Tarrazu, which is located near San Jose. The Tarrazu beans are consistently rich in body. Not wanting to tarnish its reputation, Costa Rica exports only the best of the best coffee beans.

Guatemala

Guatemala has pockets of different climates. Climate strongly influences a coffee's characteristics. Coffees grown in moister regions tend to produce a fruitier flavor. A favorite of many is the bluish bean produced in the Antigua region. Because of the region's rich, volcanic soil, a cup of coffee from Antigua-grown beans produces a wonderful balance of acidity and body.

Jamaican Blue Mountain (Wallenford Estate)

Jamaican Blue Mountain is the undisputed king of coffees. For over 250 years ranchers have grown this coffee in the mountains above Kingston in a particular region where the rainfall, the topography, and the mist collectively create a perfect growing environment for this fine coffee. The Wallenford Estate, one of very few estates that produce Jamaica Blue Mountain coffee, produces the best of the Jamaican Blue Mountain coffees. Certified tasters working for the Coffee Industry Board test every exported bag of coffee. This guarantees a uniform and wonderfully predictable coffee bean--a bean that is perfectly balanced, full bodied, and possessing a vibrancy and a smoothness that are unsurpassed by any other coffee bean.

Kenya

Kenya AA coffee beans produce a cup of coffee with a bright, acidy snap. This type of coffee is fragrant with a hint of a wine scent. Kenya truly is a world-class coffee.

Next, you want to add similar links to the Tip.htm and Bean.htm files that point to the other two pages. Specifically, in Tip.htm, you need to add one link to Joblisting.htm and another to Bean.htm. Similarly, in Bean.htm you need to add one link to Joblisting.htm and another to Tip.htm. This way, each page will have two links on it that point to the other two pages.

To add links in the tip page to the job listing and bean pages:

1. Return to your text editor and then open the **Tip.htm** file located in the Tutorial.07\Tutorial folder on your Data Disk.

2. Locate the H4 header at the top of the page.

3. Change the text "View Job Listing" to:

   <A HREF="Joblisting.htm">View Job Listing**</A>**

4. Press the **Enter** key immediately following the closing anchor tag </A> to move the remainder of the line to a new line.

5. Locate the text "View Coffee Beans" on the new line you created, and change the "View Coffee Beans</H4>" line of code to:

   <A HREF="Bean.htm">View Coffee Beans**</A>**</H4>

6. Compare your code with Figure 7-43.

Figure 7-43	ADDING LINKS TO THE TIP PAGE

```
</HEAD>
<BODY>
<H1 ALIGN=CENTER>Expert Tips</H1>

<H4 ALIGN=CENTER><A HREF="Joblisting.htm">View Job Listing</A>
&#183; <A HREF="Bean.htm">View Coffee Beans</A></H4>
<HR>
```

7. Save the changes to the file.

8. Return to your Web browser and open the **Tip.htm** file located in the Tutorial.07\Tutorial folder on your Data Disk to view the tip page. The links in the tip page should now look like those in Figure 7-44.

Figure 7-44	LINKS ON THE TIP PAGE

Expert Tips

View Job Listing · View Coffee Beans

links to other pages

Storage

For the freshest coffee, purchase only about a week's worth of coffee beans. Keep the beans whole until you are ready to brew them. When you bring your coffee home, store the unused beans in an airtight container. Store only whole beans in the freezer. Ground coffee can be stored in the refrigerator, but never store unsealed beans near other food, because the beans will absorb odors quickly.

9. Test the two links to verify that you jump to the job listing and bean pages.

   TROUBLE? If the links do not work, check the spelling of the filenames in the HREF property of the <A> tag. For some Web servers, the case (upper or lower) is also important, so you should make sure that the case matches the filenames as well.

Because The Coffee and Tea Merchant is hosted by Hotmail.com, all the managers use this Web-based e-mail program to send and receive their e-mail. When you click the text "Otis Toadvine" and you have Microsoft Outlook or Outlook Express installed as your default e-mail program, then the Outlook or Outlook Express window appears.

Franklin wants a final addition to his job listing page: a link to the e-mail address of his human resources manager, Otis. With this link, an interested reader can quickly send Otis a message through the Internet. Otis placed his e-mail address at the bottom of the job listing page, following the "How to Apply" heading. Now you need to add a sentence containing a hypertext link that launches an e-mail program when someone clicks the link.

To add an e-mail link to the job listing page:

1. Scroll to the bottom of the **Joblisting.htm** file in your text editor.

2. Position the insertion point at the end of the line of code "<H2 ALIGN=CENTER> <A NAME="HOW">How to Apply</A></H2>", and then press the **Enter** key to create a new line.

3. Type **Please e-mail your resume to Otis Toadvine:** and then press the **Enter** key to create another line.

4. Type **<A HREF="mailto:otistoadvine@hotmail.com"> otistoadvine@hotmail.com</A>** (which includes the hypertext link).

5. Save your changes.

6. Return to your Web browser, refresh the file **Joblisting.htm**, and scroll to the bottom of the page. The e-mail link should look like the hypertext link shown at the bottom of Figure 7-51.

Figure 7-51   COMPLETED JOB LISTING PAGE WITH E-MAIL LINK

Knowledge and Ability

People Skills Ability to motivate employees. Demonstrate strong independent discretion and judgment to accomplish day-to-day objectives. Maintain employee communication. Provide assistance to customers in a courteous and professional manner.

Financial Operation Proven store banking and bookkeeping skills. Use the automated payroll system. Produce employee schedules. Generate weekly financial status reports. Order bulk coffee and tea.

Coffee Knowledge Barista experience including preparing a wide variety of espresso beverages. Knowledge of coffee beans, including country of origin.

How to Apply

Please e-mail your resume to Otis Toadvine: otistoadvine@hotmail.com ← e-mail link

7. Click the hypertext link to Otis's e-mail address. Your default e-mail program opens. Figure 7-52 shows an example of the Microsoft Outlook Express e-mail program, but your e-mail program may be different.

6. Click the **Coffee Store** link. The Coffee Universe home page appears. See Figure 7-50 for the address.

TROUBLE? If the Coffee Universe home page does not appear, make sure the changes you made to the Joblisting.htm file are correct and that you saved the changes before opening the file in your browser.

TROUBLE? If you are not connected to the Internet, you will not be able to display the Coffee Universe home page. If you have Internet access, connect to the Internet and then click the Coffee Store link.

| Figure 7-50 | THE COFFEE UNIVERSE HOME PAGE |

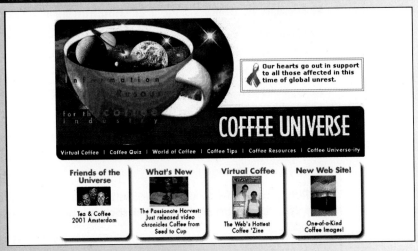

7. Click the **Back** button in your browser to return to the Joblisting.htm file in your text editor.

Linking to E-Mail

Many Web authors include their e-mail addresses on their Web pages so that users who access these pages can easily send feedback. You can set up these e-mail addresses to act as hypertext links. When a user clicks the e-mail address, the browser starts a mail program and automatically inserts the author's e-mail address into the outgoing message. The user then types the body of the message and mails it. The URL for an e-mail address is mailto:*e-mail address*. For example, to create a link to e-mail address to Otis Toadvine, Franklin's son and manager of human resources for The Coffee and Tea Merchant, you enter the following into your Web document:

<A HREF="mailto:otistoadvine@hotmail.com">Otis Toadvine</A>

If you know a document's URL, you can add the code that creates the link—that is, you can use the <A> code with the HREF property. For example, to create a link on the Internet with the URL http://www.coffeeuniverse.com/tips.html, you would enter the following:

<A HREF="http://www.coffeeuniverse.com/tips.html">More Coffee Tips</A>

This example links the text "More Coffee Tips" to the Internet document located at http://www.coffeeuniverse.com/tips.html. If your computer is connected to the Internet, clicking the text within the tag should make your browser jump to that document.

REFERENCE WINDOW   **RW**

Linking to a Document Located on the Internet
- Locate the text or graphic you want to designate as the link.
- Before the text or graphic, place the tag <A HREF="*URL*"> where *URL* is the URL of the Web page to which you want to link.
- After the text or graphic, insert the </A> closing tag.

You will create a link to the Coffee Universe home page using the text "coffee store," which is part of the H1 header of the job listing.

To add a link to the Coffee Universe home page from the job listing page:

1. Return to your text editor, and reopen the **Joblisting.htm** file.

2. Locate the H1 header at the top of the page.

3. Change the "<H1 ALIGN=CENTER>Coffee Store Manager</H1>" line of code to:

   <H1 ALIGN=CENTER>**<A HREF="http://www.coffeeuniverse.com/">**Coffee Store**</A>** Manager</H1>

4. Save the changes to the file.

5. Return to your Web browser and open the file **Joblisting.htm**. The Coffee Store Manager entry should look like the text link shown in Figure 7-49.

Figure 7-49	LINK TO A PAGE ON THE WEB

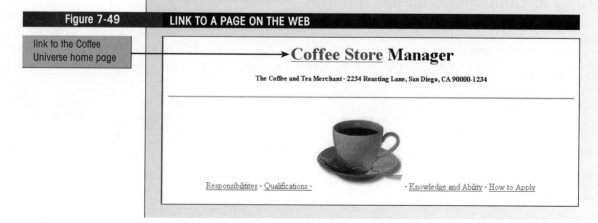

link to the Coffee Universe home page

Even the absolute pathnames of files located on different hard disks begin with a slash. To differentiate these files, HTML requires you to include the drive letter followed by a vertical bar (|). For example, a file named Joblisting.htm in the student folder on drive A of your computer has the absolute pathname "/A|/student/Joblisting.htm".

Relative Pathnames

If a computer has many folders and subfolders, absolute pathnames can be long, cumbersome, and confusing. For that reason, most Web authors use relative pathnames in their hypertext links. A **relative path** gives a file's location in relation to the current Web document. As with absolute pathnames, folder names are separated by slashes. Unlike absolute pathnames, a relative pathname does not begin with a slash. To reference a file in a folder above the current folder in the folder hierarchy, relative pathnames use two periods (..).

For example, if the current file is resume.htm, located in the /student/tutorial2 folder shown in Figure 7-46, the relative pathnames and their interpretations for the other four files in the folder tree appear in Figure 7-48.

Figure 7-48	RELATIVE PATHNAMES
RELATIVE PATHNAME	**INTERPRETATION**
../home.htm	The home.htm file in the folder one level up in the folder tree from the current file
../tutorial1/chester.htm	The chester.htm file in the tutorial1 subfolder of the folder one level up from the current file
refer.htm	The refer.htm file in the same folder as the current file
cases/ludwig.htm	The ludwig.htm file in the cases subfolder, one level down from the current folder

A second reason to use relative pathnames is that they make your hypertext links portable. If you have to move your files to a different computer or server, you can move the entire folder structure and still use the relative pathnames in the hypertext links. If you use absolute pathnames, you need to painstakingly revise each and every link. Ouch! That's a painful process.

Linking to Documents on the Internet

Now you can turn your attention to creating a link on the Joblisting.htm file to the Coffee Universe. To create a hypertext link to a document on the Internet, you need to know its URL. A **URL**, or **Uniform Resource Locator**, gives a file's location on the Web.

When referencing files in different folders in the link tag, you must include each file's location, called its **path**. HTML supports two kinds of paths: absolute paths and relative paths.

Absolute Pathnames

The **absolute path** shows exactly where the file is on the computer. In HTML you start every absolute pathname with a slash (/). Then you type the folder names on the computer starting with the topmost folder in the folder hierarchy and progressing through the different levels of subfolders. You separate each folder name from the next with a slash. The pathname, from left to right, leads down through the folder hierarchy to the folder that contains the file. After you type the name of the folder that contains the file, you type a final slash and then the filename. For example, consider the folder structure shown in Figure 7-46.

Figure 7-46	FOLDER TREE

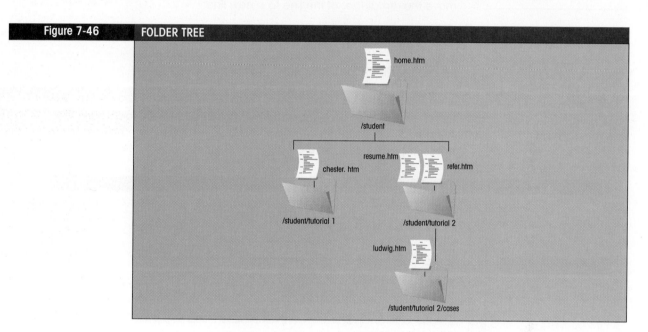

Figure 7-46 shows five HTML files contained in four different folders. The topmost folder is the student folder. Within the student folder are the tutorial1 and tutorial2 folders, and within the tutorial2 folder is the cases folder. Figure 7-47 shows absolute pathnames for the five files.

Figure 7-47	ABSOLUTE PATHNAMES

ABSOLUTE PATHNAME	INTERPRETATION
/student/home.htm	The home.htm file in the student folder
/student/tutorial1/chester.htm	The chester.htm file in the tutorial1 folder, a subfolder of the student folder
/student/tutorial2/resume.htm	The resume.htm file in the tutorial2 folder, another subfolder of the student folder
/student/tutorial2/refer.htm	The refer.htm file in the same folder as the resume.htm folder
/student/tutorial2/cases/ludwig.htm	The ludwig.htm file in the cases folder, a subfolder of the /student/tutorial2 folder

Now you need to follow similar steps so that the bean page links to the two other pages.

To add links in the bean page to the job listing and tip pages:

1. Return to your text editor and then open the file **Bean.htm** located in the Tutorial.07\Tutorial folder on your Data Disk.

2. Locate the H4 header at the top of the page.

3. Change the text "View Job Listing" to:

   <A HREF="Joblisting.htm">View Job Listing**</A>**

4. Press the **Enter** key immediately following the terminating anchor tag </A> to move the remainder of the line to a new line.

5. Locate the text "View Expert Tips" on the new line you created, and change the "View Expert Tips <H1>" line of code to:

   <A HREF="Tip.htm">View Expert Tips**</A></H4>**

6. Save the changes to the file.

7. Return to your Web browser, and open the **Bean.htm** file located in the Tutorial.07\Tutorial folder on your Data Disk. The links in the bean page should now look like those in Figure 7-45.

| Figure 7-45 | LINKS ON THE COFFEE BEANS PAGE |

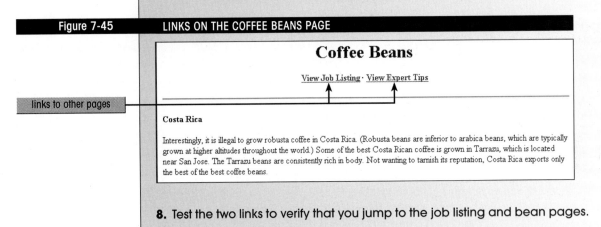

links to other pages

8. Test the two links to verify that you jump to the job listing and bean pages.

Linking to Documents in Other Folders

Franklin wants to add a link to his online coffee store, which is on a different Web site from where the job listing is placed. The link gives potential employees a chance to learn more about the online coffee store in general and The Coffee and Tea Merchant's products specifically. Before creating this link for Franklin, you need to review the way HTML references files in different folders and computers.

Until now you have worked with documents that were all in the same folder. When you created links to other files in that folder, you specified the filename in the link tag, but not its location. Browsers assume that if no folder information is given, the file is in the same folder as the current document. In some situations you might want to place different files in different folders, particularly when working with large multidocument systems that span several topics, each topic with its own folder.

Figure 7-52	MAIL MESSAGE WITH OTIS TOADVINE'S E-MAIL ADDRESS

e-mail address inserted automatically

TROUBLE? Some browsers do not support the mailto URL. If you use a browser other than Netscape Navigator or Internet Explorer, check to see if it supports this feature.

8. In the e-mail window subject line, type **Testing the mailto link**.

9. In the message body, write a one-sentence message that includes your first and last names. Send a copy of the letter to your e-mail address. Send the message to Otis by clicking your e-mail program's send button. (Don't worry. Although that is Otis's e-mail address, he will not review the messages that he receives, and he will not contact you.)

10. Close your Web browser and text editor.

You show Franklin the completed job listing page. He is very pleased with the result. You tell him that he can post the job listing page on any of the several popular sites that specialize in job postings—such as **Monster.com**.

For more opportunities to learn about creating Web pages using HTML, you can go to the **Maricopa** center for free online tutorials on HTML, or visit **World Wide Learn**, a Web site that provided access to Webmaster certificate programs, Web design courses, free online HTML tutorials, and Web authoring guides. You can also visit the National Center for Supercomputing Applications **NCSA**, which provides a comprehensive list of HTML codes and descriptions of their functionality.

Session 7.2 QUICK CHECK

1. What is the HTML code for marking the text "Cuyamaca Community College" with the anchor name CCC?

2. What is wrong with the following statement?

   <A NAME="INFO"><H3>For more information</H3></A>

3. True or False: Anchor names are case insensitive.

4. What code would you enter to link the text "Sports info" to the HTML file Sports.htm if both files are in the same folder?

5. What is the difference between an absolute path and a relative path?

6. What tag would you enter to link the text "President" to the e-mail address president@whitehouse.gov?

CASE PROBLEMS

Case 1. Creating a Web Page Listing Internet Resources You are the assistant to Jodi Ragsdale, an instructor at Cuyamaca Community College, who is trying to create a Web page that her students can use to locate important Web resources. Jodi wants to create a page showing information about two types of Internet resources: **search engines** and **domain name registrars**. When completed, the Web page should appear as shown in Figure 7-53.

Figure 7-53

Internet Resources

Search Engines

- Hotbot
- Google
- Alta Vista

Domain Name Registrars

1. Registrars.com
2. Network Solutions
3. List of domain name registrars

The page includes three headings, a bulleted list of links to search engines, and a numbered list of domain name registrars.

1. Open your text editor program.

2. Type the <HTML>, <HEAD>, and <BODY> tags to identify the different section of the page.

3. With the HEAD section, insert a <TITLE> tag with the text "Internet Resources".

4. With the BODY section, create an H1 header with the text "Internet Resources" and center the heading on the page with the ALIGN property.

5. Below the H1 header, create an H2 header with the text "Search Engines".

6. Create an unordered list using the <UL> tag with the list items "Hotbot", "Google", and "Alta Vista".

7. Change the text "Hotbot" into a hypertext link with the URL http://hotbot.lycos.com/.

8. Change the text "Google" into a hypertext link with the URL http://www.google.com/.

9. Change the text "Alta Vista" into a hypertext link with the URL http://www.altavista.com/.

10. Below the bulleted list, create an H2 header with the text "Domain Name Registrars".

11 Create an ordered list using the <OL> tag with the list items "Registrars.com", "Network Solutions", and "List of domain name registrars".

12. Change the text Registrars.com" into a hypertext link with the URL http://registrars.com/.

13. Change the text "Network Solutions" into a hypertext link with the URL http://networksolutions.com/.

14. Change the text "List of domain name registrars" into a hypertext link with the URL http://internic.net/alpha.html.

15. After the H2 header Domain Name Registrar, insert a horizontal line that extends the width of the page.

16. Save the file as **Internet.html** in the Tutorial.07\Cases folder on your Data Disk, and then print the file.

17. View the file with your Web browser, and then print the page.

18. If you have an Internet connection, test the links, and then close your Web browser.

19. Close your text editor.

Case 2. Modifying a Pet Gourmet Bakery Web Page Geraldine Flaggler owns the Pet Pleasing Bakery, a gourmet bakery for cats and dogs. Pet Pleasing Bakery bakes pet cookies and other treats twice a day. Geraldine has three stores in southern California. She wants to sue the Internet to attract more customers to her stores. Although she is not yet ready to open an electronic commerce storefront, she had found a Web host and is ready to create a Web site advertising her stores. Geraldine has created a simple Web page that lists the addresses of her stores, features some of the items that they bake, and lists her e-mail address. She wants you to take the Web page called Bakery.htm and enhance it. When you are through, the enhanced Web Page should resemble the one in Figure 7-54.

Figure 7-54

Pet Pleasing Bakery

(619) 555-1234 · 2141 Avocado Avenue

We bake our pet treats in our bakery once a day. Here are some of our treats and clearance items:

- Dog Treats
- Cat Treats
- Clearance

We have three Pet Pleasing Bakeries conveniently located throughout San Diego County. They are:

1. Pet Pleasing Bakery, 3324 Pacific Beach Drive, La Jolla (858) 555-2231
2. Pet Pleasing Bakery, 2141 Avocado Avenue, La Mesa (619) 555-1234
3. Pet Pleasing Bakery, 451 Cliff View, Encinitas (858) 555-3344

Dog Treats

- Carob Dipped Peanut Butter Treat $12.95
- Bacon Snaps $3.50
- Chicken Amore $5.65

Cat Treats

- Hearty Crunchies $3.50
- Vegi Bisgetti (5 lb. bag) $25.50
- Animal Krackers $4.95

Clearance

- Jumbo size dog bones
- Catnip

E-mail us at petpleasing@doggie.com

---

1. Open your text editor program and then open the **Bakery.htm** file located in the Tutorial.07\Cases folder on your Data Disk.

2. Within the HEAD section, insert a <TITLE> tag with the text "Pet Pleasing Bakery".

3. In the BODY section, surround the "Pet Pleasing Bakery" text with <H1> tags and center the text.

4. Add <H2> tags to the text line containing the telephone number and address, and add a bullet character (·) between the last digit of the telephone number and the first digit of the address.

5. Change the three items Dog Treats, Cat Treats, and Clearance into a bulleted list. (*Hint*: These items no longer need paragraph tags.)

6. Change the text "Dog Treats" into a hypertext link to an anchor called "dog", Cat Treats into a hypertext link to an anchor called "cat", and Clearance into a hypertext link to an anchor called "clearance". (*Hint*: Remember to precede each anchor name with the pound sign (#).

7. Select the three paragraphs that describe the locations of the stores, and change the paragraphs into a numbered list.

8. Alter the text "Dog Treats" found below the address line for the third store by enclosing the text in <H2> tags, and place an anchor called "dog" after the <H2> tag.

9. Change the three paragraphs following the Dog Treats heading into a bulleted list.

10. Repeat Step 8 for the text "Cat Treats" found below the Chicken Amore line, and place an anchor called "cats" after the <H2> tag.

11. Change the three paragraphs following the Cat Treats heading into a bulleted list.

12. Add <H2> tags to the text "Clearance" found below the Animal Krackers line.

13. Change the two paragraphs following the Clearance heading into a bulleted list.

14. Change the text "petpleasing@doggie.com" into an e-mail link.

15. Save your changes to the file.

16. Open your Web browser and open the Barkery.htm file, and then print the page.

17. Close your browser and then close your text editor.

Case 3. Creating and Linking Web Pages for Lincoln Beveling Company You work for Lincoln Beveling Company, which produces beveled art glass for wholesale and retail customers. Your supervisor has asked you to enhance the company's Web site, which describes the company's products and the machinery that bevels the glass. There are three Web pages in the site: a product Web page, a beveling machinery description Web page, and a frequently asked questions (FAQs) Web page. Your task is to add the links to the connect the pages together, format the headings, add titles to some of the pages, and insert a graphic object in the home page. Figure 7-55 shows the completed Lincoln Beveling Company home page.

Figure 7-55

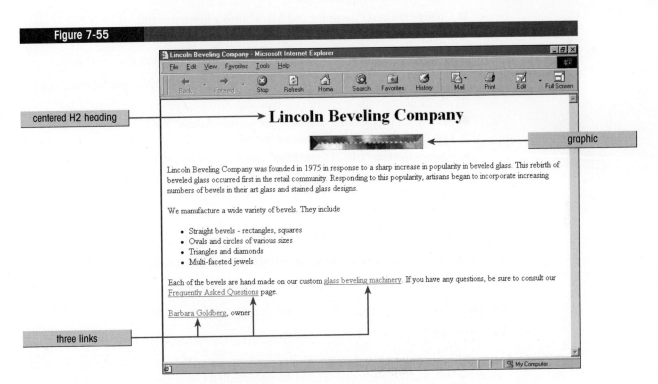

1. Open your text editor and then open the LBCmain.html file located in the Tutorial.07\Cases folder on your Data Disk.

2. Add <H2> tags around the text "Lincoln Beveling Company" located near the top of the page, and center the text.

3. Insert the graphic **LBCbevel.jpg** using the <IMG> tag so the graphic appears just below the Lincoln Beveling Company heading you formatted in Step 2.

4. Change the text "glass beveling machinery", located in the line near the bottom of the page, into a hypertext link to the Web page called **LBCmachinery.html**.

5. Change the text "Frequently Asked Questions", located near the bottom of the page, into a hypertext link to the Web page called **LBCglassFAQ.html**.

6. Change the text "Barbara Goldberg" into an e-mail hyperlink with the address **barbgoldberg@yahoo.com**.

7. Save the changes to the LBCmain.html file, and then close your text editor.

8. Open the **LBCmachinery.html** file in your text editor, and make the following changes to the file.

   ■ Add <H2> tags around the text "Beveling Machinery" in the first line of text, and center the heading.

   ■ Change the text "LBC Home Page" into a hypertext link to the LBCmain.html file.

   ■ Change the text "Frequently Asked Questions" into a hypertext link to the LBCmain.html file.

   ■ Change the text "Denver Glass Machinery" into a hypertext link to http://www.denverglass.com/.

   ■ Change the text "Sommer and Maca" into a hypertext link to http://www.somaca.com/.

9. Save the change to the LBCmachinery.html file, and then close your text editor.

10. Open the **LBCglassFAQ.html** file in your text editor, and make the following changes to the file.

    ■ Add <H2> tags around the text "Frequently Asked Questions (FAQs)" in the first line of text, and center the heading.

    ■ Change the text "LBC Home Page" into a hypertext link to the LBCmain.html file.

    ■ Change the text "Beveling Machinery", located in the second line of text, into a hypertext link to the LBCmachinery.html file.

    ■ Select each question line and make the text bold.

11. Save the change to the LBCglassFAQ.html file, and then close your text editor.

12. Open the LBCmain.html file in your Web browser and then print the page.

13. Test all the links that you created to ensure that they work.

14. Open the other two pages in your Web browser and print them.

15. Close your browser.

Case 4. Create Your Own Home Page You create your own Web page. Imagine that you are creating two pages for a home grocery business called Great Grocers Online. Create a home page called Index.htm and another page called Privacy.htm. The home page should contain the following features:

   ■ A heading formatted with the text "Great Grocers Online" and formatted with <H2> tags

   ■ Two main sections labeled "Products" and "Privacy Policy"

   ■ Bold and italic font styles in the text

   ■ Paragraphs

   ■ An ordered list and an unordered list

- An inline graphic image
- A link from the "Privacy Policy" heading to your second Web page that contains your privacy policy

The privacy page called Privacy.htm contains a simple privacy policy, and near the bottom of the privacy policy, there is a link back to the home page. If you are having trouble formulating a privacy policy, visit the **Electronic Privacy Information Center (EPIC)** and **Truste** for more information about setting privacy policies. Or visit Web sites such as **Amazon.com** or **eBay** to read the privacy policies for these online organizations.

QUICK CHECK ANSWERS

Session 7.1

1. The <HTML> tag identifies the language of the file as HTML to packages that support more than one kind of generalized markup language.

2. HTML does not recognize the blank lines as a format element. A Web browser will ignore blank lines and run the paragraphs together on a page.

3. Unordered list:

   <UL>
       <LI> *List item*
       <LI> *List item*
   </UL>

   Ordered list:

   <OL>
       <LI> *List item*
       <LI> *List item*
   </OL>

   Definition list:

   <DL>
       <DT> *List term* <DD> *Term definition*
       <DT> *List term* <DD> *Term definition*
   </DL>

4. ©

5. <HR>

6. An inline image is a GIF or JPEG that appears on a Web document. A browser can display it without a file viewer.

7. GIFs and JPEGs (or .gif and .jpg)

Session 7.2

1. <A NAME="CCC">Cuyamaca Community College</A>

2. Anchor tags should be placed within style tags such as the <H3> header tag.

3. False

4. <A HREF="Sports.htm">Sports info</A>

5. An absolute path gives the location of a file on the computer's hard disk. A relative path gives the location of a file relative to the active Web page.

6. <A HREF="mailto:president@whitehouse.gov">President</A>

In this tutorial you will:

- Identify market segments for Web marketing and advertising efforts

- Divide customers into market segment categories

- Identify key characteristics of customers in each market segment

- Design Web site features that appeal to different types of visitors

- Design marketing tactics that will reach customers in each market segment

- Learn how advertising works on the Web

- Develop effective e-mail promotions

- Select marketing affiliates that can deliver the right visitors to your site

MARKETING FOR THE ONLINE BUSINESS

Strategies for Marketing, Promoting, and Advertising an Electronic Commerce Initiative

CASE

Personal Touch Gifts and Awards

Amanda Gridley started Personal Touch Gifts and Awards 20 years ago in a corner of her living room. She began by engraving trophies and other types of awards for local schools and sports teams. Gradually, she added other personalized awards and several gift product lines. Ten years ago, she opened her first retail store in a local shopping mall. More recently, the company started selling engraved awards and holiday gift packages to businesses.

Today, Personal Touch has five retail locations and sells via mail order to a wide range of individual and business customers in several states. Amanda sends out five catalogs a year, one for each season plus an extra holiday edition. Each catalog is printed in a consumer version and a business version. The catalogs for each season are different because they each feature the sports for which customers want awards and trophies for each particular time of the year. Amanda relies on a three-person sales team to call on Personal Touch's larger clients. Although this team is called "Corporate Sales," it is responsible for serving larger schools and sports-sponsoring organizations along with the larger corporate customers.

In the past two years, Amanda has become increasingly interested in the potential of doing business on the Web. So many of her mail-order customers had asked for Personal Touch's URL that she finally had a small Web site created. The site included the locations of Personal Touch retail stores and some general information about the products that Personal Touch sells. Response to the Web site has been good, but many customers have asked about buying items through the site. Amanda has decided to create a full-fledged electronic commerce site for Personal Touch.

Amanda was happy with the work of the design firm she hired to create the current Personal Touch Web site, so she plans to have the same company create the new electronic commerce site. She has discussed the expected number of visitors that the new site might draw with the Internet service provider (ISP) that is hosting the current site. Based on those discussions, Amanda believes that her current ISP will be able to handle the increased traffic.

Amanda is concerned about creating a successful marketing campaign to launch the site. She is also concerned about how Personal Touch can make sure the new site is successful once it is launched. Amanda has established a very good track record in building her retail, mail-order, and direct corporate businesses, but she wonders whether she will face new challenges and opportunities with this new online selling presence. Amanda has hired you to advise her on marketing approaches, advertising, and customer service issues for the new Personal Touch electronic commerce Web site.

<table>
<tr><td>

**SESSION
8.1**

</td><td>

In this session, you will learn about how to create an effective marketing strategy and advertising approach for an electronic commerce Web site. By identifying potential customer groups and creating a targeted message for each group, you can design a Web site that satisfies the needs of each group. You will also learn about new research into the behavior of Web site visitors that suggests ways in which Web sites can respond to visitors who arrive at a site with different needs at different times.

</td></tr>
</table>

Elements of Marketing Strategy

In your first meeting with Amanda, you explain that **marketing mix** is the combination of elements that a company uses to achieve its goals for selling and promoting its products or services. When a company decides which elements it will use, it calls that particular marketing mix its **marketing strategy**. Most marketing classes teach the **four Ps of marketing**: product, price, promotion, and place. **Product** is the physical item or service that a company is selling. The intrinsic characteristics of the product are important, but as you learned in Tutorial 2, customers' perceptions of the product, called the product's **brand**, can be as important as the actual characteristics of the product.

The **price** element of the marketing mix is the amount the customer pays for the product. In recent years, marketing experts have argued that companies should think of price in a broader sense, that is, the total of all financial costs that the customer pays (including transaction costs) to obtain the product. This total cost is subtracted from the benefits that a customer derives from the product to yield an estimate of the **customer value** obtained in the transaction. As you learned in Tutorial 1, the Web creates new opportunities for creative pricing and price negotiations through online auctions, reverse auctions, and group buying strategies. These opportunities might help companies find new ways to create increased customer value.

Promotion includes any means of spreading the word about the product. On the Internet, new possibilities abound for communicating with customers and potential customers. Tutorial 2 included a number of communication techniques that companies are using to promote their products, including affiliate marketing, building virtual communities, and engaging in meaningful dialog (using e-mail and other means) with customers.

For years, marketing managers dreamed of a world in which instant deliveries would give all customers exactly what they wanted when they wanted it. The problem of **place** (also called **distribution**), which is the need to have product available in many different locations, has plagued companies since commerce began. Although the Internet does not solve all logistics and distribution problems, it can certainly help. Digital products (software, music, e-books) can be delivered almost instantly on demand through the Internet. For goods that have physical characteristics and must be shipped, the Internet has allowed much better tracking and control over shipments.

The Four Ps of Marketing and the Internet

The Internet has expanded the potential range of each of marketing's traditional four Ps, but it has also added new elements to the marketing mix. The Internet's ability to facilitate communication has opened the door to interactivity and customization in ways that marketers had never before imagined. Before the Internet, companies would spend years creating a brand, honing pricing strategies, promoting the product, and arranging distribution and delivery. This laborious process included much trial and error. For example, product development engineers might spend years redesigning and adding features to a product only to find that customers were not interested in those features. The Web allows customers to communicate their needs directly and efficiently so that each customer (or group of customers) can participate in the design of products.

By participating in the design, redesign, and feature selection process, customers develop a heightened level of commitment to a product. In the past, companies worked hard to promote products that they had designed and hoped that customers would accept. By including customers in the product creation process, companies have been able to reduce the need for large promotion efforts. However, companies still need to choose whether to follow a product-based marketing strategy or a customer-based marketing strategy.

Product-Based Marketing Strategies

In Tutorial 2, you learned about the importance of a company's Web presence and how it must integrate with the brand or other established images the company has chosen to use in its promotional activities. Personal Touch Gifts and Awards offers a variety of products that appeal to different groups. In this session, you will learn how Amanda might appeal to the group of individual (as opposed to business) customers that buy from Personal Touch. In the next session, you will learn how to do the same thing for business customers.

Managers at most companies often think of their businesses in terms of the products and services they sell. This is a logical way to think of a business, because companies spend a great deal of effort, time, and money to design and create those products and services. At Personal Touch, Amanda thinks of her business as a collection of trophies, plaques, medals, and other awards. That is, she thinks of them as physical objects. When you ask Amanda to describe her business, she presents you with a list of products organized into categories that reflect the manufacturing or design process—the list that appears in Figure 8-1.

Figure 8-1	PERSONAL TOUCH PRODUCTS

Boxes	**Buttons and Ribbons**	**Clocks**	**Desktop**	**Display Cases**
Business card holders	1" metal button	Acrylic	Acrylic	Counter-top
Cigar boxes	2" metal button	Metal	Glass	Free-standing floor
Desktop accessories	Flat stock ribbon	Wood	Marble	Shadow boxes
Golf ball boxes	Rosette style ribbon		Metal	Wall-mounted
Keepsake boxes			Wood	

Medals	**Mugs**	**Paper**	**Pen and Pencil Sets**	**Pins**
Acrylic	Glass	Card size	Acrylic	Cast metal
Cast metal	Pewter	Mounted or framed	Marble	Enameled
Engraved metal		Padded diploma covers	Metal	Engraved metal
Medal frames		Parchment	Wood	Letter pins
Neck ribbons				

Plaques	**Trays**	**Trophies**
Acrylic	Bronze	Cups
Glass	Pewter	Columns
Marble	Stainless steel	Figures
Metal		Symbols
Wood		

For customers who are likely to buy items from particular product categories or who are likely to think of their needs in terms of product categories, this type of product-based organization makes sense. In the trophies and awards business, a number of companies use this approach in their print catalogs and on their Web sites.

To examine product-based Web site designs:

1. Start your Web browser, and then go to the Online Companion page by entering the URL **http://www.course.com/NewPerspectives/EC** in the appropriate location of your Web browser. Click the hyperlink for your book, click the **Tutorial 8** link, and then click the **Session 8.1** link. Click the **Awards4u.com** link and wait while your browser loads the Awards4u home page shown in Figure 8-2.

Figure 8-2   AWARDS4U.COM ENGRAVING AND AWARDS HOME PAGE

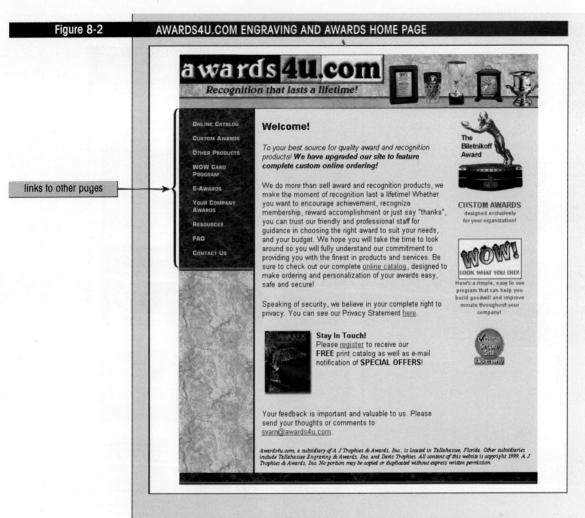

links to other pages

2. Click the **Online Catalog** link, and then click the **Award Clocks** image or the **Award Clocks** link located on the left side of the page to open the catalog page for products in this category, as shown in Figure 8-3. Note that the page includes links to various types of clocks that Awards4u.com offers for sale, including clocks made of acrylic, jade, metal, wood, and marble.

Figure 8-3   AWARD CLOCKS PRODUCT CATALOG PAGE

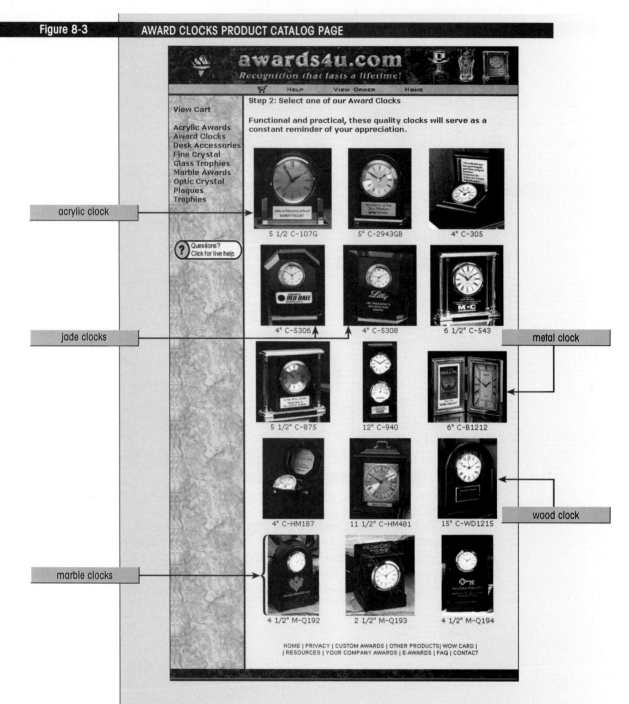

acrylic clock

jade clocks

metal clock

marble clocks

wood clock

3. Click your browser's **Back** button to return to the Online Catalog page. Explore the links to the company's other products to see how the company has arranged them into product categories. When you are finished exploring the site, click your browser's **Back** button to return to the company's home page.

4. Click your browser's **Back** button or use its history list to return to the Online Companion page for Session 8.1, and then click the **Southern California Trophy Company** link to open the home page for another product-based Web site. Southern California Trophy has fewer product categories, but the products it offers are listed as navigation links down the left side of the page. See Figure 8-4. Again, the products are arranged by type (such as Desk Accessories, Clocks, and Pins/Medals) and by material (such as Acrylic/Astrolite, Lucite, and Crystal/Etched Glass).

Figure 8-4	SOUTHERN CALIFORNIA TROPHY COMPANY HOME PAGE

Southern California Trophy Company

73 years in business giving you the quality you need.

Welcome to Southern California Trophy Company's AWARDS BY INTERNET Web Site

product-oriented promotional message

NEW Plaques, Jade Glass, Crystal and Trophies added to our On-Line Trophy Store
Browse, Select, Engrave and Purchase your awards and trophies via the web!

Home
Online Store
About Us
Custom Designs
Desk Accessories
Clocks
Acrylic / Astrolite
Perma-Plaque
Lucite Embedments
Pins / Medals
Famous Awards
Crystal / Etched Glass
Plaques
Elegant Trophy Cups
Bronze Cast Plaques
Time Capsules
Promotional Products
Ad Specialty Products
Request Information

links to product categories

Within these pages you will find information on creating and ordering awards, gifts and promotional items direct from the West Coast's largest full service awards company. Browse our site to gain insight into our company's diverse product lines. View our storied past through **FAMOUS AWARDS by SCTC**, and contact us for any of our free full color product brochures and / or information on creating your own special needs.

The items pictured are just a few samples of what you will find while browsing our site. Use the navigation bar on the left to find more information about all we have to offer, or contact SCTC directly.

This page has been visited **O O 8 8 O 5** times since our online launch in 1997

Contact Southern California Trophy Company for more information.

5. Explore the links to the company's product pages to see how they have arranged them into product categories.

6. When you are finished exploring the site, click your browser's **Back** button or use its history list to return to the Online Companion page for Session 8.1.

Both of these companies are using a product-based strategy. They have organized their Web sites from an internal viewpoint, that is, according to the way that the companies have organized their product design and manufacturing processes. If customers arrive at these Web sites looking for a specific type of product, such as an acrylic clock, this product-based approach will work well for these companies. Alternatively, customers who are looking to fulfill a specific need, such as a need for a golf trophy or for a debate tournament award, might not find these Web sites as useful. You explain to Amanda that many marketing researchers and consultants advise companies when designing their Web sites to think as if they were their own customers.

Customer-Based **Marketing Strategies**

One of the key lessons you learned in Tutorial 2 is that the Web creates an environment that allows buyers and sellers to engage in complex communication modes. The communication structures on the Web can become much more complex than those in traditional mass media outlets such as broadcast and print advertising. When Personal Touch takes its business to the Web, the company can create a Web site that is flexible enough to meet the needs of many different customers and other site visitors. Instead of thinking of its Web site as a collection of products, Personal Touch can build the site to meet the needs of various types of customers.

Communicating with Different Market Segments

Although dividing Personal Touch's customers into business and individual consumer groups is a good first step, you explain to Amanda that several subgroups probably exist within each of those groups. Amanda will need to use her experience in her business to think about how Personal Touch can break down each group into subgroups and then develop marketing strategies and tactics that will reach customers in each subgroup effectively. In Tutorial 2, you learned that these subgroups are called **market segments**. Many companies develop specific marketing strategies for each segment. Even companies that use the same medium for communicating with each market segment can tailor their messages to each segment. Creating separate messages for specific market segments is called **segment marketing** or **targeted marketing**.

Marketers have traditionally used three categories of variables to identify market segments. One variable is location. Firms divide their customers into groups by where they live or work. In this type of segmentation, called **geographic segmentation**, companies create different combinations of marketing efforts for each geographical group of customers. The grouping can be by nation, state (or province), city, or even by neighborhood. Alternatively, companies can develop one marketing strategy for urban customers, another for suburban customers, and yet a third for rural customers.

The second category uses information about age, gender, family size, income, education, religion, or ethnicity to group customers. This type of segmentation is called **demographic segmentation**. Traditional marketers frequently use demographic variables because research has shown that customer needs and usage of products are strongly related to these types of variables. Demographic segmentation also exists on the Web. For example, there are numerous sites that are devoted to women's issues or that are directed at specific age groups (such as teenagers) whose members tend to purchase music CDs and trendy clothing. Often demographic and geographic segmenting strategies are combined. For example, an airline might target middle-income families living in Wisconsin and Michigan with mid-winter advertising for vacation trips to Florida.

In **psychographic segmentation**, marketers try to group customers by variables such as social class, personality, or approach to life. For example, an auto company might direct advertising for a sports car to customers who are gregarious and goal-oriented. The use of psychographic segmentation has increased dramatically in recent years as marketers attempt to identify the characteristics of specific lifestyles. Marketers can then craft advertising to reach people who see themselves as having a particular lifestyle.

Companies that advertise on television often create messages designed to reach the likely audiences of various types of programs. These audiences represent one or more market segments. The market segments can be geographic, demographic, psychographic, or a combination. Figure 8-5 presents some examples from the television medium that show how companies do this.

Figure 8-5	TELEVISION ADVERTISING MESSAGES TAILORED TO PROGRAM AUDIENCES

Type of Television Program	Type of Advertising
Children's cartoons	Children's toys and games
Daytime dramas	Household and laundry goods; pet foods
Late-night talk shows	Snack foods and nonprescription drugs
Golf tournaments	Golf equipment, investments, and life insurance
Baseball, football, hockey games	Snack foods, beer, automobiles and trucks
Documentary films	Books, CDs, educational videotape

Children's television shows are likely to feature advertising for products that will appeal to children. Ads on daytime dramas are directed at people who are home during the day and who thus might be interested in household and laundry-care products. These people are also more likely than others to own pets, so they will see ads for pet foods. Advertisers on late-night talk shows often direct their ads at people who are having trouble getting to sleep. Advertisers also believe that this late-night audience is receptive to promotions for snack foods to eat while watching these programs or for non-prescription medications to overcome whatever might be keeping them up so late.

Advertisers use sports programming as a vehicle for two different market segments. Some sports shows, such as golf or tennis coverage, appeal to higher income groups. Other sports shows, such as baseball or football game coverage, appeal to more moderate income groups. As a result, programs that cover golf or tennis are more likely to include ads for investment and insurance products than are baseball or football programs. Also, since viewers of golf tournaments and tennis matches are likely to play the sport, these programs will include ads for game equipment.

Programs that show documentary films will often carry ads for books, book clubs, CDs, or even educational videotapes. Advertisers believe that these types of products will appeal to the intellectual, arts-loving audiences of these programs.

Companies do much more than just match advertising messages to market segments. They also build a sales environment for their product or service that corresponds to the market segment they are trying to reach. In the physical world, store design and layout are often directed at specific market segments. If you walk through a shopping mall, you can observe that colors, displays, lighting, background music, and even the clothes worn by sales clerks will vary with the targeted segment. For example, a clothing store for young women will present a completely different experience to its customers than will a clothing store that sells expensive, conservative evening gowns.

The Web gives companies an opportunity to present different store environments in the virtual marketspace too. Figures 8-6 and 8-7 show the home pages of Old Navy and Eddie Bauer, respectively.

Figure 8-6	OLD NAVY HOME PAGE

Figure 8-7	EDDIE BAUER HOME PAGE

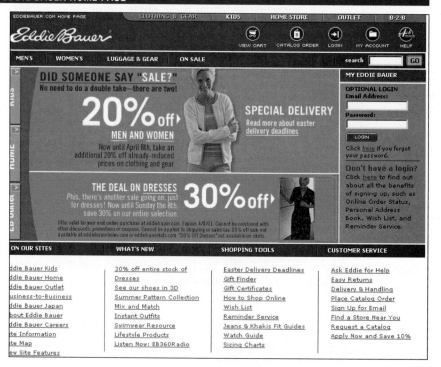

Both pages are well designed and functional. However, you can see that they are each addressed to different market segments. The Old Navy site is targeted at young, fashion-conscious buyers. The site uses a wide variety of typefaces and bold colors to convey its tone. The emphasis on the page is to "get this look" and, presumably, become the envy of your friends. In contrast, the Eddie Bauer page is rendered in muted, earthy tones. The page is designed for older, more practical folks. The messages emphasized on the page are the price reductions—messages that appeal to a market segment full of people looking for good clothing values.

In the physical world, retail stores have limited floor and display space. These limitations often force physical stores to decide on one particular message to convey. Exceptions do exist, such as a music store that has a separate room for classical CDs (with different background music than the rest of the store) or a large department store that can use lighting and display space differently in each department. Smaller retail stores usually must choose the one image that will appeal to most of their customers. On the Web, retailers can provide separate virtual spaces for different market segments. Some Web retailers provide the ultimate in targeted marketing—they allow their customers to create their own stores. One example of an awards and trophies Web store that uses this type of targeted marketing is **Trophies2Go.com**.

To explore targeted marketing at Trophies2Go.com:

1. Make sure your browser has loaded the Online Companion page for Session 8.1, and then click the **Trophies2Go.com** hyperlink and wait while your browser loads the Trophies2Go.com home page shown in Figure 8-8.

| Figure 8-8 | TROPHIES2GO.COM HOME PAGE |

link to pages for sports market segment customers

link to pages for corporate market segment customers

link to login for customers who have created their own customized stores

2. Click the **Sports** link on the tab located near the top of the page to open the part of the Web site that is targeted at customers who are interested in sports awards. The page that opens includes a number of pictures that depict sports and other related categories, such as Coaches and Victory, and some non-sports categories, such as Cheerleading and Scholastics. See Figure 8-9. These pictures are links to separate sections of the Web site that offer trophies and awards for those sports and activities. Below each graphic is a drop-down list box control that allows the customer to select a specific type of award for the activity depicted in the picture.

Figure 8-9   TROPHIES2GO.COM SPORTS AWARDS PAGE

drop-down list boxes include lists of specific award types for each activity

pictures are links to catalog pages of awards for each type of activity

3. Click several of the drop-down list arrows to see the product types offered for each activity. The categories are the same for each activity, except that some activities, such as Victory and Coaches, do not have as many product type categories.

4. Click the drop-down **list arrow** under the Baseball graphic, and then select **Acrylics**. The top portion of the page that appears is shown in Figure 8-10. Note that the awards are all specific to the sport of baseball. Trophies2Go.com has decided that showing specific award designs instead of showing a generic award will help make their products more appealing to specific market segments. Also, note that the top of the page now contains a second row of tabs that include links to each of the product types for that sport or other activity.

TROUBLE? Depending on how your browser is configured, you might see a warning dialog box with a message about sending unencrypted information. Click the **OK** or **Continue** button to close the dialog box. Then continue with Step 5.

| Figure 8-10 | TROPHIES2GO.COM ACRYLIC BASEBALL AWARDS PAGE |

tabs with links to each type of award for baseball

acrylic awards for baseball

featured items list includes only baseball awards

5. Click your browser's **Back** button to return to the Trophies2Go.com home page. You can explore the picture links and the drop-down list box links to see how the company has customized each product offering for the sport or other activity. Note that many of the products are quite similar for the various activities, but that Trophies2Go.com has presented the products on each activity page to highlight how they will look when created for that activity. This site clearly demonstrates the power of the Web to tailor the customer experience. When you are finished exploring the site, click your browser's **Back** button to return to the company's home page.

6. Click the **Corporate** link in the tab located near the top of the page to open the section of the Web site that is customized for that market segment. The page that opens includes three links, Corporate, Promotional, and Your Store. The Corporate link leads to pages that are targeted to business customers. Below the Corporate link is a drop-down list box that includes links to product categories within the Corporate pages. The Promotional link leads to pages that feature "give-away" products that carry the customer's logo for distribution at trade shows and to customers. The Your Store link leads to pages with products that Trophies2Go.com has designed for specific clients. Many Web sites use this customized store approach to provide their best customers with a shopping site that is tailored to the specific needs of each customer. Often these sites are password-protected and offer prices that have been negotiated with the specific customer.

7. When you have finished exploring the Corporate section of the Trophies2Go.com site, click your browser's **Back** button or use its history list to return to the Online Companion page for Session 8.1.

Amanda agrees that the Personal Touch Web site should include features that target specific market segments. You explain that targeting specific market segments will require that Personal Touch first analyze its customers and identify its main market segments.

Identifying Customer-Based Market Segments

Amanda explains that Personal Touch organizes its catalogs by product type. The largest category of products they sell is sports awards. These range from small medals to large trophies. The other types of awards include scholastic, merit, and service awards. Schools give scholastic awards to everyone from spelling bee winners to champion debate teams. Companies give their employees recognition awards that include merit awards (such as salesperson of the year) and service awards (such as 20-year pins). Companies also buy engraved gift items that they give to customers.

You note that these categories all focus on the type of product, so you ask Amanda to describe which of her customers buy which products. She explains that some of the awards appeal to children and others to adults. Among children's awards, some are more popular with older children. Also, schools seem to spend more money on the awards for older children and teenagers. Some of the corporate sales are sports awards, but most of them are either gifts for customers or merit and service awards for employees. Individuals buy a fairly unpredictable mix of all the products.

Larger companies, schools, and not-for-profit organizations buy the same kinds of products as smaller companies, but these larger entities usually demand special price schedules and often have very strict delivery date requirements. Currently, Personal Touch prints one set of catalogs, but the catalogs that it sends to larger customers either have a separate price sheet included or a letter reminding them to contact their assigned sales representative for special pricing information. As Amanda describes which of her customers are likely to buy specific products, you sketch an outline of her descriptions in the diagram that appears in Figure 8-11.

Figure 8-11   **ORGANIZING PERSONAL TOUCH CUSTOMERS INTO MARKET SEGMENTS**

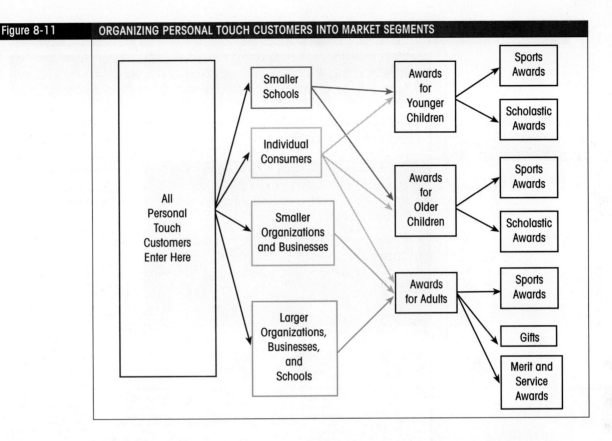

You show Amanda the diagram and explain that it provides a roadmap for building the Personal Touch electronic commerce Web site. All customers will enter the site at the Personal Touch home page, which is at the left side of the diagram. The home page includes links to three different stores, each designed to meet the needs of a specific market segment. Within each store, customers can select from product categories and then specific products that are offered to meet their particular needs. Note that Personal Touch can make the same products available in more than one store—one of the benefits of using hyperlinked Web pages to build a product catalog that you learned about in Tutorial 3.

Amanda likes your ideas, but is concerned that some customers might know exactly what they want when they open the site's home page and might be discouraged by having to work through layers of stores and categories to get what they want. You explain that Personal Touch can offer the best of both worlds to its customers. By including links on the site's home page to popular products or product categories, Personal Touch can meet the needs of those customers too. To help Amanda see how this can work, you will show her how **Dell Computer Corporation** uses this approach on its site.

To explore multiple market segments used at Dell's Web site:

1. Make sure your browser has loaded the Online Companion page for Session 8.1, and then click the **Dell** link and wait while your browser loads the Dell home page shown in Figure 8-12. This home page includes links along the right side to separate stores for each of Dell's major market segments in the United States, a drop-down list box near the top of the page that offers links to specific sites for Dell's international customers, and links at the bottom of the page to specific product categories.

Figure 8-12   **DELL HOME PAGE**

links to separate stores for each international market segment

links to separate stores for each market segment

links to specific product categories

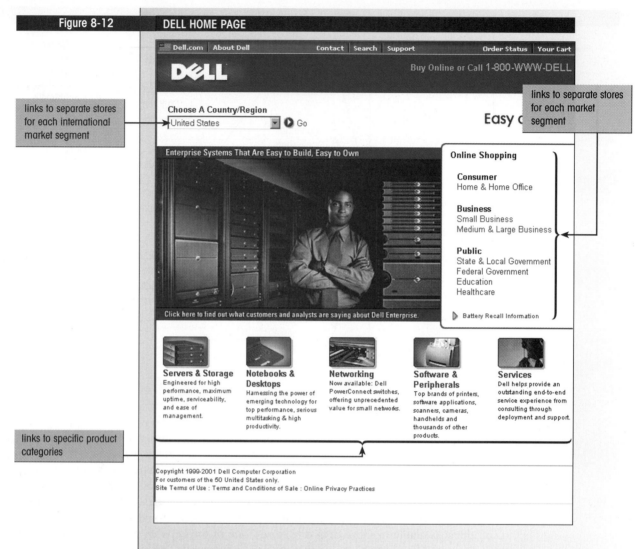

2. Click two or three of the market segment links (**Home & Home Office**, **Small Business**, **Medium & Large Business**, **State & Local Government**, **Federal Government**, **Education**, or **Healthcare**) on the right side of the page, and explore the Dell stores for each segment. Note that each link opens to a page that is customized to the needs of customers in that segment. Each page features different products and offers different services.

3. Click your browser's **Back** button to return to the Dell home page. Click the **Education** link to open the Dell store for that market segment. Note that this segment is subdivided by education level (K-12 or higher education) and by type of customer (institutions or faculty and staff). Explore each of these links to the four stores. Note that the largest difference in page layout and design is between the types of customer. That is, the pages for the two institutional customer types look more like each other than do the pages for the two types of K-12 customers.

4. Click your browser's **Back** button to return to the previous page, and then click the **Medium & Large Business** link to open the Dell Business Center page. On the right side of the page near the top, you will see a link that allows Dell's Premier customers to log in.

5. Click the **What is Premier?** link to learn more about this program.

6. Click the **Launch Tour** link on the page that opens to obtain more details on the Premier accounts that Dell offers to its larger business customers. A window opens and offers two choices for the tour; if you are certain that your computer can display Flash animations, click the **Flash Version**. Otherwise, click the **HTML Version** to begin the tour. No matter which version you select, you can exit the tour by clicking the window's **Close** button.

7. When you have finished exploring the Dell site, click your browser's **Back** button or use its history list to return to the Online Companion page for Session 8.1.

You explain to Amanda that the Dell Premier accounts are the ultimate level of customer-based market segmentation. In these accounts, Dell offers each customer its own Dell Web site. Dell can customize a company's Premier account pages to show product selections for which price and terms have already been negotiated. As you went through the tour, you found that Dell even allows the employees of its customers to create personalized pages within their company's Premier pages. This highly customized approach to offering products and services that match the needs of a particular customer is called **one-to-one marketing**. Thus, the Internet gives marketers the best opportunity for highly customized interactions with customers that they have had since rising costs made the door-to-door salesperson obsolete in the 1960s.

Market Segmentation Using Customer Behavior

In addition to targeting groups of customers as market segments, the Web allows companies to target the same customers in different ways at different times. A similar kind of targeting, called **behavioral segmentation**, is sometimes possible in the physical world. For example, a company might decide that its mission is to serve hungry people. A given person will respond to hunger in different ways at different times. If a person is hungry in the morning, but late for work, that person might drive through a fast food restaurant or grab a quick cup of coffee at the train station. Lunch might be a sandwich ordered and delivered to the office, or lunch could require a nice restaurant if a client needs to be entertained. Dinner could be at a restaurant with friends, take-out from a neighborhood Chinese restaurant, or a delivered pizza. The point is that the same person will require different combinations of products and services depending on the occasion. This type of behavioral segmentation is sometimes called **occasion segmentation**.

In the physical world, businesses tend to specialize in meeting one or a few of these needs. For example, the Chinese restaurant might offer dining room service and take-out service, but this same restaurant would not offer a drive-through window or a morning coffee kiosk. Very few, if any, restaurants offer everything from fast food through a five-course dinner. In the online world, it is much easier to design a Web site that meets the needs of visitors that arrive in different modes. Thus, a Web site design can include elements that appeal to different behavioral market segments.

Marketing researchers are beginning to study how people desire different combinations of products, services, and Web site features depending on their mode of interaction with the site. These researchers are finding that people need Web sites that offer a range of interaction possibilities. Remember that a single person might visit one Web site at different times and search for different interactions each time. Customizing visitor experiences to match the site usage behavior patterns of each visitor or type of visitor is called **usage-based market segmentation**.

The Browser

You explain to Amanda that some visitors to the Personal Touch Web site will be surfing or browsing. The job of the Web site for potential customers in this mode is to offer them something that will pique their interest. The site should include words that are likely to jog the memory of visitors and remind them of something they want to buy on the site.

These key words are often called **trigger words** because they prompt a visitor to stay and investigate the products or services offered on the site. Links to explanations about the site or instructions for how to use the site are particularly helpful to this type of customer. A site should include extra content related to the product or service the site sells. This content can keep a visitor that is in browser mode interested long enough to stay at the site, develop a favorable impression of the company, and buy on this visit or bookmark the site for a return visit.

The Buyer

Visitors that arrive in buyer mode are ready to make a purchase right away. The best thing a site can offer to a buyer is to be certain that nothing will get in the way of the purchase transaction. For visitors who have chosen a product from a printed catalog, many Web sites include a text box control on their home pages that allow visitors to enter the catalog item number. This places that item in the site's shopping cart and takes the buyer directly to the shopping cart page.

The shopping cart page should offer a link that takes the visitor back into the shopping area of the site, but the primary goal is to get the buyer to the shopping cart as quickly as possible—even if the buyer is at the site for the first time. The shopping cart should allow the buyer to create an account and log in *after* placing the item into the cart. The site should not ask visitors to log in until they near the end of the shopping cart procedure.

The Shopper

Some customers will arrive at the Web site knowing that Personal Touch offers items for sale in which they are interested. These visitors are motivated to buy, but they are looking for more information before they make a purchase decision. For the visitor who is in shopper mode, a site should offer comparison tools, product reviews, and lists of features. You tell Amanda about a site that offers many useful features for shopper mode visitors, the **Crutchfield** consumer electronics Web store.

To visit a shopper-oriented site at Crutchfield:

1. Make sure your browser has loaded the Online Companion page for Session 8.1, and then click the **Crutchfield** link and wait while your browser loads the Crutchfield home page. Crutchfield is a Web store that sells home and car audio and video products.

2. Click the link to **Home & Portable A/V** in the Shop by Category list of links on the page, and then click the **Portables** link under the CD Players subheading in the product listing. The page that is displayed offers visitors a short description of the product category, a list of products with inventory status information and prices, and a telephone number to call for more information. The list is sorted by brand; however, a visitor that is in shopper mode wants the ability to manipulate the information. This page offers that ability. The visitor can click links that sort the product list by price or show only the best-selling items. Another link changes the page to include product photos, and each product name is a link to detailed information about that product. The top portion of the page, which shows these features, appears in Figure 8-13.

Figure 8-13	INFORMATION MANIPULATION FEATURES OF THE CRUTCHFIELD WEB SITE

link to customer service page with telephone number for immediate help

short description of prodcuct category

controls that allow the visitor to manipulate information

product list

3. Click the **Sort by Price** link that appears at the top of the list. The page reloads and lists the products in ascending price order.

4. Click the **Show Only Best Sellers** link to have the page reload and display a shorter list that includes only the portable CD players that are most popular with Crutchfield customers.

5. Click one of the product links to view descriptive information about one of the CD players. Note that the product pages have links to even more detailed information about the product, including The Nitty Gritty, What's in the Box? and All Accessories for this item. Through these links, Crutchfield is trying to provide all of the information you would find in a physical retail store by looking at the product on display and reading the box.

6. Click your browser's **Back** button to return to the Crutchfield home page. Some categories have a **Click to Compare** option in the product listings. Search the site until you find one of these categories, click the check boxes for two or more of the products, and then click the **Click to Compare** button. Your browser should return to a page similar to the one shown in Figure 8-14, which compares two DVD players. Note that each feature name is also a link to a page that explains that feature.

Figure 8-14	PRODUCT COMPARISON FEATURES OF THE CRUTCHFIELD WEB SITE

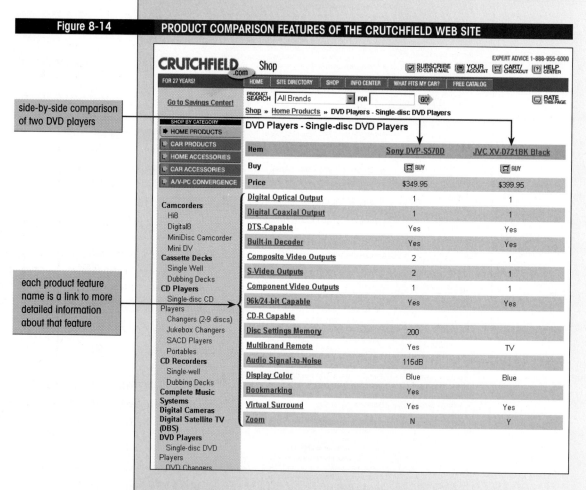

side-by-side comparison of two DVD players

each product feature name is a link to more detailed information about that feature

Item	Sony DVP-S570D	JVC XV-D721BK Black
Buy	BUY	BUY
Price	$349.95	$399.95
Digital Optical Output	1	1
Digital Coaxial Output	1	1
DTS-Capable	Yes	Yes
Built-in Decoder	Yes	Yes
Composite Video Outputs	2	1
S-Video Outputs	2	1
Component Video Outputs	1	1
96k/24-bit Capable	Yes	Yes
CD-R Capable		
Disc Settings Memory	200	
Multibrand Remote	Yes	TV
Audio Signal-to-Noise	115dB	
Display Color	Blue	Blue
Bookmarking	Yes	
Virtual Surround	Yes	Yes
Zoom	N	Y

7. When you have finished exploring the Crutchfield site, click your browser's **Back** button or use its history list to return to the Online Companion page for Session 8.1.

You explain to Amanda that, although researchers have identified these three main visitor modes, their work is still in the preliminary stages. Much of Web site visitor behavior is not yet well understood. One recent study conducted by the major consulting firm McKinsey & Co. examined the behavior of 50,000 users in 2000 and identified six different groups of active Internet users. These six market segments and their characteristic behavior traits are:

■ **Simplifiers** are users who like convenience. They are attracted by sites that make doing business easier, faster, or otherwise more efficient for them than is possible in the physical world.

■ **Surfers** use the Web to find information, explore new ideas, and shop. They like to be entertained, and they spend far more time on the Web than other people. To attract surfers, sites must offer a wide variety of content that is attractive, well displayed, and constantly updated.

■ **Bargainers** are in search of a good deal. Although they make up less than 10 percent of the online population, they make up over half of all visitors to eBay. They enjoy searching for the best price or shipping terms and are willing to move among sites to do that.

■ **Connectors** use the Web to stay in touch with other people. They are intensive users of chat rooms, electronic greeting card sites, and Web-based e-mail. Connectors tend to be new to the Web, are less likely than other people to purchase on the Web, and are actively trying to learn what the Web has to offer them.

■ **Routiners** return to the same sites over and over again. They use the Web to obtain news, stock quotes, and other financial information. Routiners like the comfort of working with a user interface that they know well.

■ **Sportsters** are similar to routiners, but they tend to spend time on sports and entertainment sites rather than at news and financial information sites. Because they view the Web as an entertainment vehicle, sportsters are attracted by sites that are interactive and vibrant.

The challenge for Web businesses today is to identify which of these (or similar) groups is visiting their sites and to formulate ways of generating revenue from each segment. As more researchers study Web site visitor behavior, perhaps researchers will learn how to recognize the various modes in which visitors arrive and then channel them into the appropriate sections of the site. Until then, many Web sites will use Dell's approach, in which visitors are asked to identify themselves as belonging to a particular category of customer when they enter the site.

Intensity of the Customer Relationship

You explain to Amanda that one goal of marketing is to create strong relationships between the company and its customers. The reason that one-to-one marketing and usage-based segmentation are so valuable is that they help to strengthen companies' relationships with their customers. You learned in Tutorial 2 that many companies also invest much time and money in creating brands. The combination of branding and good customer experiences can create an intense feeling of loyalty toward the company and its products or services. Researchers have identified several stages of loyalty as customer relationships develop over time. A five-stage model of customer loyalty appears in Figure 8-15.

Figure 8-15   **FIVE STAGES OF CUSTOMER LOYALTY**

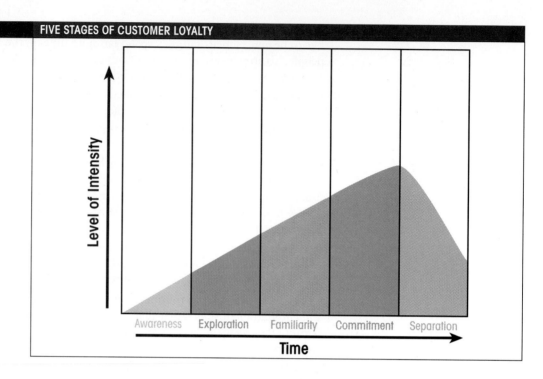

This model shows the increase in intensity of the relationship as the customer moves through the first four stages. In the fifth stage, a decline occurs and the relationship terminates. Not all customers go through the full five stages; some will stop at each stage and continue the relationship at that level of intensity or terminate the relationship at that point. The characteristics of the five stages are outlined in the next sections.

Awareness

Customers who recognize the name of the company or one of its products are in the **awareness** stage of customer loyalty. They know that the company or product exists, but have not had any interaction with the company. Advertising a brand or a company name is a common way for companies to achieve this level of relationship with potential customers.

Exploration

In the **exploration** stage, potential customers learn more about the company or its products. The potential customer might visit the company's Web site to learn more, and the two parties often will communicate via telephone or e-mail. A large amount of information interchange can occur between the parties at this stage.

Familiarity

Customers who have completed several transactions and are aware of the company's policies regarding returns, credits, and pricing flexibility are in the **familiarity** stage of their relationship with the company. In this stage, customers are as likely to shop and buy from competitors as they are from the company.

Commitment

After having a considerable number of highly satisfactory experiences with a company, some customers develop a fierce loyalty or strong preference for the products or brands of that company. These customers have reached the **commitment** stage and are often willing to tell others about how happy they are with their interactions. To lure customers from the familiarity stage to the commitment stage, companies sometimes make concessions on price or terms. Usually, the value of the strong relationship is worth more to the company than these concessions.

Separation

Over time, the conditions that made the relationship valuable might change. The customer may be severely disappointed by changes in levels of service or product quality. The company can also evaluate the relationship and conclude the loyal, committed customer is costing too much to maintain. As the intensity of the relationship fades, the parties enter a **separation** stage.

You explain to Amanda that one important goal of her marketing strategy should be to move customers into the commitment stage as rapidly as possible and keep them there as long as possible. Further, she should try to make sure that the only customers to move into the separation stage are those that Personal Touch determines to be costing more to serve than they are worth.

An analysis of how customers' behavior changes as they move through the five stages can yield information about how they interact with the company and its products in each stage. The five stages are sometimes called the **customer life cycle** and using those stages to create groups of customers that are in each stage is called **life-cycle segmentation**. Two companies that undertake continuing research into market segmentation and how companies can use segment information to develop better relationships with their customers are **Claritas** and **Donnelley Marketing**.

To explore market segmentation tools and information at Claritas and Donnelley Marketing:

1. Make sure your browser has loaded the Online Companion page for Session 8.1, and then click the **Claritas** link and wait while your browser loads the Claritas home page.

2. Click the **Claritas Products** link on the left side of the page, and then click the **Segmentation** link at the top of the page that loads. This segmentation page contains general information about the software and information products that Claritas offers. See Figure 8-16.

Figure 8-16	CLARITAS MARKET SEGMENTATION TOOLS

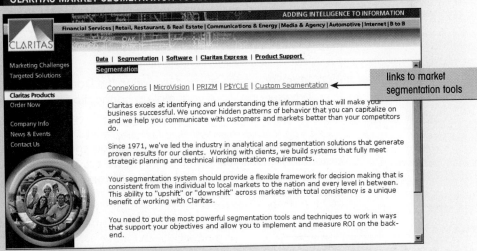

3. Follow the **ConneXions, MicroVision, PRIZM**, and other links to learn more about the Claritas products.

4. When you are finished exploring the site, use your browser's **Back** button or use its history list to return to the Online Companion page for Session 8.1.

5. Click the **Donnelley Marketing** link to open the home page for that company, and then click the **Analytical Services** link near the left edge of the page. The page that loads, which appears in Figure 8-17, describes Donnelley's approach to creating market segments that combine customer behavior with demographic and lifestyle data to appropriately segment customers.

| Figure 8-17 | DONNELLEY MARKETING ANALYTICAL SERVICES PAGE |

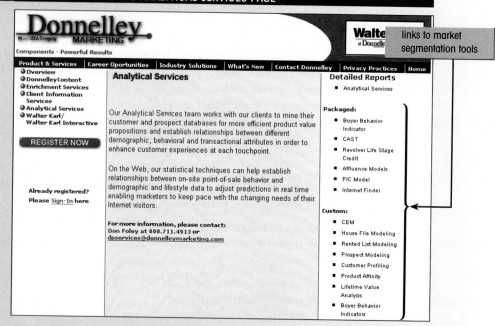

6. Click the links to market segmentation tools that appear on the right side of the Analytical Services page to learn more about the software tools and information offered by Donnelley. A number of these products include combinations of multiple market segments. Each link will open in a separate browser window. To return to the Analytical Services page from any of these pages, click the window's **Close** button.

7. When you have finished exploring the Donnelley Marketing site, close your browser and close your dial-up connection if necessary.

Amanda appreciates all of the information you have found about ways to organize her customers into markets segments. In the next session, you will learn how to create advertising and promotion strategies that Amanda can use to target the customers in each of those market segments.

Session 8.1 QUICK CHECK

1. True or False: Customers' perceptions of a product make up the product's brand.

2. The combination of elements that a company uses to achieve its goals for selling and promoting its products and services is called its _____.

3. When customers are likely to buy items by product category, a(n) _____ marketing strategy makes sense.

4. Companies that create separate messages for different groups of customers are engaging in _____.

5. True or False: In the physical world, store design and layout are seldom designed to appeal to members of specific market segments.

6. A highly customized approach to offering products and services that match the needs of particular customers is called _____.

7. Visitors to a Web site that are ready to make a purchase right away are said to be in _____ behavior mode.

8. Customers who are willing to tell others about their satisfactory dealings with a company are in the _____ stage of customer loyalty.

SESSION 8.2

In this session, you will learn how companies use the Web for advertising and for other promotional activities such as sending e-mail, developing affiliate relationships with other Web sites, creating coupons on the Web, and increasing the likelihood of appearing in the results lists of search engines and Web directories. Companies must focus their marketing and advertising efforts to achieve desired results. You will learn which tools to use for specific messages and audiences on the Web and how to integrate marketing efforts for businesses that have both a Web presence and a physical presence.

Advertising on the Web

You explain to Amanda that advertising is all about communication. The communication might be with current customers, with potential customers, or even with former customers that you would like to regain. To be effective, Personal Touch should send a different message to each of these audiences.

The five-stage customer life-cycle model shown in Figure 8-16 (in the previous session) can be helpful in determining the message to convey to each of these audiences. In the Awareness stage, the advertising message should inform. The message could describe a new product, suggest new uses for your existing products, or describe specific improvements that you have made to a product. Audiences in the Exploration stage should receive messages that explain how a product or service works and encourage switching to your brand. In the Familiarity stage, the advertising message should be persuasive—convincing customers to purchase your products or request that a salesperson call. Customers in the Commitment stage should be sent reminder messages. These ads should reinforce customers' good feelings about the brand and remind them to buy products or services. Companies do not typically target ads at customers who are in the Separation stage.

Amanda tells you that Personal Touch has an established advertising program in traditional media, including ads in print publications—sports magazines and publications targeted at teachers and school coaches—and some limited television and radio advertising on professional soccer match broadcasts. Amanda has found that children who play soccer (and their parents) are often avid professional soccer fans. You point out that any online advertising should be coordinated with existing advertising efforts. For example, print ads should include the Personal Touch URL.

About Banner Ads

The predominant form of advertising on the Web is through banner ads. A **banner ad** is a small rectangular object on a Web page that displays a stationary or moving graphic and includes a hyperlink to the advertiser's Web site. Banner ads are versatile advertising vehicles—their graphic images can help increase awareness and build brand, yet users can click them to open the advertiser's Web site and learn more about the product. Thus, banner ads can serve both an informative function and a persuasive function.

Early banner ads used a simple graphic, usually in GIF format, which loaded with the Web page and remained on the page until the user moved to another page or closed the browser. Today, Web designers can create attention-grabbing ads with animated GIFs and a variety of Shockwave, Java, and Flash rich object media. These ads can be rotated so that each time the Web page is loaded into a browser the ad changes. Banner ads come in a variety of sizes and shapes, as you can see in the Britannica.com home page shown in Figure 8-18.

Figure 8-18   BANNER ADS ON THE BRITANNICA.COM HOME PAGE

Although Web sites can create banner ads in any dimensions they choose, advertisers decided early in the life of electronic commerce that it would be easier to standardize the sizes. The three banner ads on the Web page shown in Figure 8-19 are among the most common sizes, the **full banner** (468 × 60 pixels), the **half banner** (234 × 60 pixels), and the **square button** (125 × 125 pixels). The standard banner sizes that most Web sites have voluntarily agreed to use are called **interactive marketing unit (IMU) ad formats**.

To learn more about IMU ad formats:

1. Start your Web browser, and then go to the Online Companion page by entering the URL **http://www.course.com/NewPerspectives/EC** in the appropriate location of your Web browser. Click the hyperlink for your book, click the **Tutorial 8** link, and then click the **Session 8.2** link. Click the **Internet Advertising Bureau** (IAB) link, and wait while your browser loads the IAB home page. The IAB is a not-for-profit organization that promotes the use of Internet advertising and encourages effective Internet advertising. This organization has established voluntary standards for IMUs.

2. Scroll down the main frame to see the section titled IAB Ad Standards, and then click the **IAB/CASIE Advertising Banner Sizes** link to open the Ad Standards page. This page includes a brief explanation of the voluntary IMU guidelines and usually includes examples of newly approved IMUs. The page also includes a drop-down list box with links to pages that contain the remaining IMU ad formats.

3. Click the drop-down **list arrow**, and then select **Banners and Buttons** to open the page shown in Figure 8-19.

Figure 8-19   BANNER AND BUTTON IMU AD FORMATS

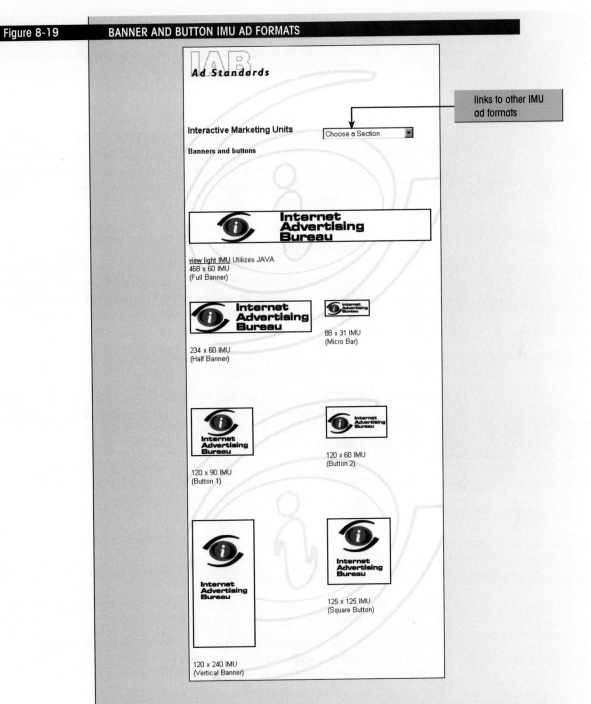

4. Use the drop-down list box to select the other pages with IMU formats. The sky-scraper formats are usually placed along the right side of a Web page that requires the user to scroll down to read.

5. When you have finished exploring the IAB site, use your browser's **Back** button or its history list to return to the Online Companion page for Session 8.2.

In its simplest form, a banner ad is nothing more than a graphic image combined with a hyperlink. The size of the ad's graphic file is important, because sites that carry your banner ad load the graphic as part of their Web page. Most sites prefer that the banner ad be less than 16K so that the page-loading process is not slowed down too much.

Creating Banner Ads

To create your own banner ads, you simply create a GIF or JPEG format file using any graphics editor, and then reference the file in the Web page along with a link to the site that you want your visitors to open when they click the graphic. The HTML for a banner ad that uses a GIF file named BannerGraphic.gif and that links to the start page at www.myStore.com would be:

<a href="http://www.myStore.com/"><img src="BannerGraphic.gif"></a>

A number of advertising agencies create banner ads for clients as part of their service. Web site designers frequently offer banner creation services, too. The cost of having a banner ad built by a professional designer ranges from under $100 up to $1,500. If you cannot afford a professionally created graphic and do not have a graphics editor available on your computer, you can use an online banner creation site to build your own animated GIF file to use in a banner ad.

To create a banner ad graphic online:

1. Make sure your browser has loaded the Online Companion page for Session 8.2, and then click the **ABCBanners** link and wait while your browser loads the site's start page. ABCBanners is an advertising-supported Web site that offers free, downloadable graphics.

2. Click the large graphic in the middle of the page labeled **Click Here to Start** to open the first of many pages that contain banner backgrounds. Click the banner background that you want to use for your ad.

3. Click the option button control next to the font that you would like to use, scroll to the bottom of the page, and then click the **Next** button.

4. Type the text you would like to appear in your banner in the text box control, and then click the **Next** button.

5. Click the option button control next to the texture or solid color you want to use for your text, and then click the **Next** button.

6. Click the spot in the banner background at which you want the upper-left corner of the text to begin. The page that loads contains a link to another Web page on which your banner resides. See Figure 8-20.

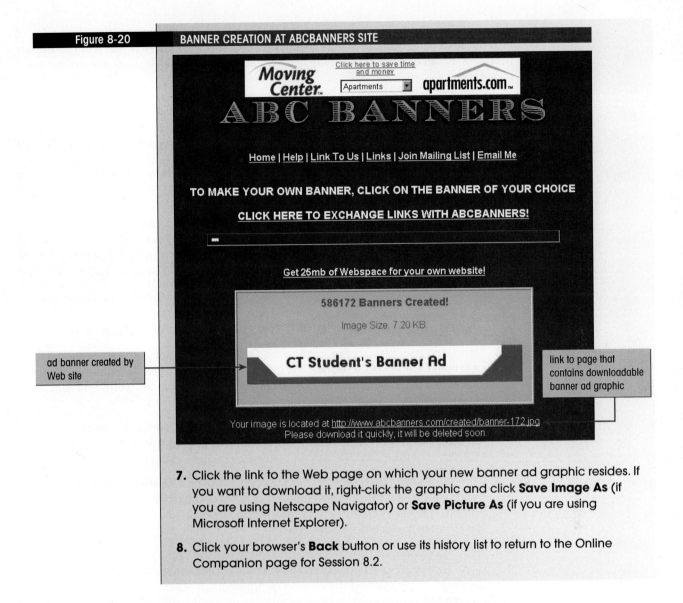

Figure 8-20   BANNER CREATION AT ABCBANNERS SITE

ad banner created by Web site

link to page that contains downloadable banner ad graphic

7. Click the link to the Web page on which your new banner ad graphic resides. If you want to download it, right-click the graphic and click **Save Image As** (if you are using Netscape Navigator) or **Save Picture As** (if you are using Microsoft Internet Explorer).

8. Click your browser's **Back** button or use its history list to return to the Online Companion page for Session 8.2.

Using Banner Ads

You explain to Amanda that there are three different ways to arrange for other Web sites to load Personal Touch banner ads. The first is to use one of the banner exchange networks described in Tutorial 3. A **banner exchange network** coordinates ad-sharing so that sites run other exchange members' ads, and vice versa. Usually, the exchange requires that each site accept two ads for every one of its ads that run on the network. The exchange makes a profit by selling the extra ad space to other businesses. Since banner exchanges are free, many Web businesses do use them; however, it is often difficult to find a group of other Web sites that have formed an exchange or that belong to an exchange that are not direct competitors. This limitation prevents many businesses from using link exchange programs.

The second way is to find a Web site that appeals to one of Personal Touch's market segments and pay that site to carry its ads. This requires considerable time and effort. Smaller sites may not have an established pricing policy for advertising. Larger sites usually have fairly high standard rates that are discounted for larger customers. Smaller customers must pay the standard rates. You explain to Amanda that she can have an advertising agency represent Personal Touch in this effort. In fact, a full-service advertising agency can help design the ads, create the banners, and find appropriate Web sites. An agency that does a lot of Internet advertising work can often negotiate lower fees with the sites that will run the ads because they can consolidate their clients' budgets and buy large blocks of advertising space at one time.

A third way to place banner advertising is to use a banner advertising network. A **banner advertising network** serves as a broker between advertisers and Web sites that carry ads. There is a wide range of companies in this business. The larger firms offer many of the same services as comprehensive ad agencies and often sell space primarily on larger Web sites such as Yahoo! that have high traffic rates and are, thus, more expensive. The smaller firms, on the other hand, often sell only leftover discounted space. Many of these smaller firms have fallen on hard times with the decline in advertising purchases that has occurred recently, and many have gone out of business.

Individual banner ad networks usually specialize in selling ad space either by impression or by click-through. As you learned in Tutorial 2, an **impression** is counted each time an ad loads into a Web page (some Web sites allow multiple banner ads to load repeatedly as long as the user keeps the page open), and a **click-through** occurs when a user clicks the ad and is taken to the advertiser's page.

To learn more about the two types of banner ad networks:

1. Make sure your browser has loaded the Online Companion page for Session 8.2, and then click the **DoubleClick** link and wait while your browser loads the site's start page. DoubleClick is the largest banner ad network in the world and sells ad space by impression.

2. Move your mouse pointer over the **Marketers** link near the top of the page. On the drop-down list that appears, click the **Media Buying** link to open a page that describes DoubleClick's online advertising approaches.

3. Click the **Brand Network** link to learn more about how DoubleClick can associate a company's product with sites that have an established brand. When you are finished exploring this section of the site, click your browser's **Back** button to return to the Media Buying page.

4. Click the **Audience Network** link, and then click the **TARGET** link to open the page shown in Figure 8-21. DoubleClick's DART program uses a number of demographic, psychographic, and behavioral variables to create advertising targeted at very specific segments.

| Figure 8-21 | DOUBLECLICK'S TARGETED ADVERTISING SERVICES |

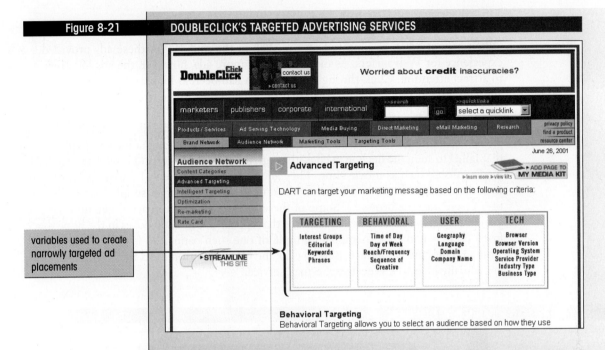

variables used to create narrowly targeted ad placements

5. When you have finished exploring the DoubleClick site, click your browser's **Back** button or its history list to return to the Online Companion page for Session 8.2.

6. Click the **ValueClick** link and wait for the start page for that company to load (this might take a few seconds).

7. Click the **Performance Advertising** link, and then click the **Advertiser** link on the right side of the page (or click the **Advertisers** link at the top of the page) to open the page that describes ValueClick's approach to selling Web advertising. ValueClick-placed ads are not priced by impression, but by click-through.

8. Click the other links to explore the site and learn more about how ValueClick approaches market segmentation in placing ads for its clients.

9. When you are finished, click your browser's **Back** button or use its history list to return to the Online Companion page for Session 8.2.

You discuss the banner ad placement options with Amanda and decide that the best approach for Personal Touch will be to use the advertising agency that is currently handling the account and ask them to identify individual Web sites and banner ad networks to carry banner ads for the firm.

After reviewing strategy for placing banner ads for Personal Touch, you encourage Amanda to consider placing banner ads for other sites on the Personal Touch site to generate some extra revenue. Since the Personal Touch site will not have large amounts of traffic even if it is highly successful, the impression-based ad networks will not be interested in buying ad space on the site for their customers. However, the click-through networks might have advertisers that will pay some amount to run ads on the Personal Touch site.

The rate that Personal Touch could charge is probably around 50 cents per click-through. If the Personal Touch site achieves 200,000 impressions per month and achieves a .50 percent click-through rate, the advertising could generate several hundred dollars per month (after paying the brokerage fee to the banner ad network).

Effectiveness of Banner Ads

When banner ads first appeared on the Web in the mid-1990s, these ads provided a new experience for Web surfers. As more users saw more ads, however, the ads lost their ability to attract attention. Click-through rates, which had been as high as 2 percent when banner ads were first introduced, have steadily dropped and now range from .30 percent to .50 percent, depending on the site's content.

To battle this decrease, banner ad designers first introduced animated GIFs with moving elements that might attract the user's eye more frequently than stationary graphics. When that failed to stem the decline in click-through rates, designers created ads that displayed rich media effects, such as movie clips. They added interactive effects by writing Java programs that could respond to a user's click with some action (other than simply loading the advertiser's page into the browser). Some of these interactive ads even acted like miniature video games. Designers also created banner ads that appear to be dialog boxes in the hope that confused users would click them. An example of one such banner ad is shown in Figure 8-22. This ad is designed to induce users to click the Correct button to fix the "error," but the banner actually links to a Web-based e-mail service.

Figure 8-22	BANNER AD DISGUISED AS A DIALOG BOX

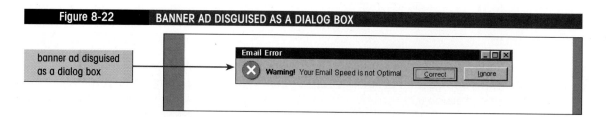

banner ad disguised as a dialog box

Periodically, advertisers would create new banner ad sizes and place the ads in page locations other than at the top or bottom. For example, the skyscraper ad was designed to be placed on the side of a Web page and remain visible as the user scrolls down.

Unfortunately for the advertisers, none of these efforts prevented the inexorable decline in click-through rates. In what some observers see as a last ditch attempt to make advertising work on the Web, banner ad designers have turned to the alternative ad formats described in the next section.

Other Web Ad Formats

The steady decline in the effectiveness of banner ads has prompted advertisers to explore other formats for Web ads. One of these formats is the pop-up ad. A **pop-up ad** is an ad that appears in its own window when the user opens or closes a Web page. The window in which the ad appears does not include the usual browser controls. The only way to dismiss the ad is to click the small close control in the upper-right corner of the window's frame. Many users find pop-up ads to be extremely annoying.

A particularly irritating variation on the pop-up ad technique occurs at Web sites that open more than one pop-up ad when the user leaves the site or closes the browser. Another variation on the pop-up ad is the **pop-behind** ad, which opens a new ad-laden browser window (or windows) very quickly and then reopens the browser window with the desired content in front of it. Most computers are too slow to display the ad windows before reloading the content windows. Users do not see the windows with the ads until they close the content-laden browser window. Then they see one or more windows with ads that seem to have just magically appeared out of thin air.

Despite user objections to the use of pop-up ads, an increasing number of Web sites have started using them as a way of delivering a larger advertising image in a more forceful way. Some users have responded by using ad-blocking software that prevents banner ads and pop-up ads from loading (see the Online Companion's Additional Information section for links to Web sites that distribute or sell ad-blocking software).

Another intrusive ad format is the **interstitial ad**, which opens in its own browser window when a user clicks a link instead of the page that the user intended to load (the general meaning of the word "interstitial" is something that comes between two other things). Many interstitial ads close automatically, allowing the intended page to open in the existing browser window. Other interstitials require the user to click a button before they will close. Since they open in a full-sized browser window, interstitial ads offer the advertiser even more space than the pop-up ad format. Many users find interstitials to be more annoying than pop-up ads because interstitials are larger and because they are an even more forceful interruption of the Web-browsing experience.

A fourth ad format is the active ad. **Active ads** generate graphical activity that "floats" over the Web page itself instead of opening in a separate window. One of the first active ads featured the figure of a little man who walked into the displayed Web page, unrolled a movie poster, and then pasted the poster onto the Web page (covering up part of the Web page content—content that a user might have been reading!). After about 10 seconds, the figure walked off the page and the poster disappeared. While it was open on the page, the poster was an active link to the movie's Web site. Another active ad has the image of a Ford Explorer driving into the Web page. The Web page is animated to shake with the vibrations of the Explorer as it drives through. Figure 8-23 shows an example active ad for the Gap that has opened on the Clubs page of portal site theglobe.com.

| Figure 8-23 | ACTIVE AD FOR THE GAP OPENED ON THE CLUBS PAGE AT THEGLOBE.COM |

The Gap ad even includes a form that the user can complete to request a Gap catalog! Active ads are certainly attention getting and are even more intrusive than pop-ups or interstitials because active ads occur in the Web page itself and offer no obvious way to dismiss them. Advertisers will likely continue to create new ad formats as users become accustomed to seeing active ads and they lose their effectiveness.

After learning more about the types of advertising that can be placed on or linked to Web pages, Amanda decides that using less-intrusive banner ads on the Personal Touch site is a good idea. Many of the site visitors will be established customers of the company, and Amanda does not want to do anything that will annoy them or provide an uncomfortable experience.

E-Mail Marketing

Sociologists and cultural anthropologists have proclaimed e-mail one of the greatest tools for human communication to be developed in the 20th century. Since advertising is a process of communication, using e-mail in a company's advertising strategy will add a very powerful element. As you learned in Tutorial 2, e-mail can be an important part of customer relationship management strategies. You also learned about e-mail's role in permission marketing strategies in that tutorial.

Amanda is interested in using e-mail effectively, but she would like to avoid sending unwanted e-mails (or "spam") to Personal Touch customers. You explain to Amanda that the key element in any e-mail marketing strategy is to obtain customers' approval before sending them any e-mail that includes a marketing or promotional message. Thus, Personal Touch should get customers to "opt-in" for specific topics about which they would like to receive e-mail.

Combining Content and Advertising

One successful strategy that many companies use is combing content with an advertising message. This is an example of the rational branding approach to customer relationships you learned about in Tutorial 2. The customer makes a rational decision to accept advertising messages in return for getting the content.

Amanda is planning to target some of the market segments you identified earlier by creating content that will appeal to those segments. Personal Touch already has two employees who write articles for the quarterly print catalogs. Amanda is certain that they can collect information that would be valuable to many of their customers. You explain that a good way to send content is to insert hyperlinks in the e-mail messages. The hyperlinks should take the customers to the content that is stored on the Personal Touch Web site. Once customers are viewing pages on the Web site, it is easier to induce them to stay on the site and consider purchases.

Outsourcing E-mail Processing

Amanda expects that the number of customers who opt-in to these information-laden e-mails will grow rapidly and is concerned that the job of handling the e-mail lists and mass-mailing software could quickly exceed the capabilities of the Personal Touch information technology staff. You explain that a number of companies offer e-mail management services and that most companies like Personal Touch outsource their e-mail processing operation. The Additional Information section of the Online Companion pages for this tutorial includes links to several companies that offer such services.

To learn more about outsourcing e-mail:

1. Make sure your browser has loaded the Online Companion page for Session 8.2, and then click the **MessageMedia** hyperlink and wait while your browser loads the site's start page.

2. Click the **solutions** link located near the top of the page to explore the information about MessageMedia's online marketing and messaging services. See Figure 8-24.

Figure 8-24   **MESSAGEMEDIA: SOLUTIONS PAGE**

3. Click the **M³ Platform** link, and then read the information provided about MessageMedia's e-messaging solutions. When you are finished, click your browser's **Back** button to return to the MessageMedia: Solutions page. From there, you can follow the SurveySolutions, UnityMail, and MailKing links to learn more about MessageMedia's other services.

4. When you are finished exploring the site, click your browser's **Back** button or use its history list to return to the Online Companion page for Session 8.2.

Amanda is convinced that an e-mail management firm could do an excellent job with the promotional and informational e-mail she is planning for several of Personal Touch's market segments.

Affiliate Marketing Programs

In Tutorial 2, you learned that in affiliate marketing, one firm, the affiliate, displays links to a seller on its Web site that allow Web site visitors to buy things at the seller's site. The affiliate receives a commission on sales that results from visitors that arrive at its site. Because the links on the affiliate's sites are usually related to the content on the site, the visitors to the site are often more likely to be interested in the product or service being offered in the affiliate ad. Thus, click-through rates for affiliate marketing links are, on average, significantly higher than click-through rates for banner ads. Some affiliate marketing programs report click-through rates as high as 4 percent, which is about eight times current click-through rates for banner ads.

Affiliate commissions can be based on several variables. In the **pay-per-click** model, the affiliate earns payment each time a site visitor clicks the link and loads the seller's page. This is similar to the click-through model of charging for banner advertising.

In the **pay-per-conversion** model, the affiliate earns payment each time a site visitor is converted from a visitor into either a qualified prospect or a customer. An example of a seller that might use the qualified prospect definition is a credit-card issuing bank. The bank might decide that its best strategy is to pay affiliates only when the visitor turns out to be a good credit risk. Alternatively, the bank may decide it only wants to pay the affiliate if the visitor is approved for the credit card and then accepts the card (that is, the visitor completes the sale). A site that pays its affiliates on completed sales usually pays a percentage of the sale amount rather than a fixed amount per conversion. Some sites use a combination of these methods to pay their affiliates.

You can learn more about affiliate programs offered by different sites by going to the Web site and looking for a link to information about its affiliate program. Alternatively, you can visit an **affiliate program broker** site that offers affiliate program opportunities for a number of Web sites. Amanda is interested in having Personal Touch participate in an affiliate program with a Web florist because people often consider sending flowers when they are ordering awards. The two products are complementary, not competitive, since few customers will decide to send flowers instead of buying an award.

To learn about affiliate marketing at Proflowers.com:

1. Make sure your browser has loaded the Online Companion page for Session 8.2, and then click the **Proflowers.com** hyperlink and wait while your browser loads the site's start page.

2. Scroll down the list on the left, and then click the **Affiliate Program** link to load the page that appears in Figure 8-25.

| Figure 8-25 | PROFLOWERS.COM AFFILIATE PROGRAM INFORMATION PAGE |

3. Click the **Frequently Asked Questions** link to learn more about the affiliate program. You can follow the other links to examine the affiliate agreement and visit some of Proflowers.com's existing affiliate sites.

4. When you are finished exploring the site, you can close your browser and close your dial-up connection, if necessary.

Amanda is interested in learning more about affiliate program broker sites. She noticed that the **Proflowers.com** affiliate site was administered by another company, **Be Free, Inc.** You explain that Be Free provides software, management consulting, and brokerage services to firms like Proflowers.com and Personal Touch. The Additional Information section of the Online Companion contains a link to Be Free and other affiliate brokers such as **Commission Junction** and **LinkShare**. You can explore these links to learn more about broker-intermediated affiliate programs.

Session 8.2 QUICK CHECK

1. True or False: Companies should send advertising messages to customers who are in the Exploration stage that remind them to buy the company's products or services.

2. Usually, companies do not target advertising messages at customers who are in the _____ stage.

3. Banner ads can serve both a(n) _____ function and a(n) _____ function.

4. In its simplest form, a banner ad is a graphic image combined with a(n) _____.

5. True or False: One way to place banner advertising is to use the services of a banner advertising network.

6. Designers have continually added new attention-getting features to banner ads to combat the steady decline in _____.

7. True or False: An affiliate site is always owned by the company that creates the affiliate marketing program.

CASE PROBLEMS

Case 1. Market Segmentation at Buy.com **Buy.com** is a major Web retailer of more than one million different computer, consumer electronics, office, sports, and other entertainment products.

1. Start your Web browser, and then go the Online Companion page by entering the URL http://www.course.com/NewPerspectives/EC in the appropriate location of your Web browser. Click the Tutorial 8 link, and then click the Case Problems link. Click the Buy.com link and wait while your browser loads that company's home page.

2. The Buy.com site is divided into about 10 different stores that you can access through the links across the top of the home page. Click each link and examine the structure of each store's site.

3. From your examination, determine whether Buy.com has organized its site using a product-based or a customer-based marketing strategy. In approximately 100 words, describe your conclusion and support that conclusion with at least two examples.

4. Assume that you are outfitting your dorm room or apartment with the essentials of student life. Use the Buy.com site to select a laptop computer, a small color television, a stapler, a telephone, and a good dictionary. In approximately 300 words, describe your shopping experience. Explain how the Buy.com site helped or hindered you, and then provide suggestions for improving the site based on your shopping experience.

Case 2. Different Market Segments at VH1.com **VH1.com** is the Web site related to the MTV-owned cable television channel VH1.

1. Start your Web browser, and then go to the Online Companion page by entering the URL http://www.course.com/NewPerspectives/EC in the appropriate location of your Web browser. Click the Tutorial 8 link, and then click the Case Problems link. Click the VH1.com link to open the home page for the site. The VH1.com home page contains links to more than 20 categories of information, products, and services.

2. Follow the links on the home page to learn more about VH1. Select three of the link categories that appear somewhere on the home page and examine them in depth.

3. Write a report of approximately 300 words that includes three paragraphs. In each paragraph, describe one of the categories that you have examined, and then describe the psychographic characteristics of a site visitor that would find that category particularly appealing.

Case 3. Web Ad Scavenger Hunt In this case, you will explore the Web to learn more about what types of ads are currently being used for specific purposes.

1. Start your Web browser, and then go to the Online Companion page by entering the URL http://www.course.com/NewPerspectives/EC in the appropriate location of your Web browser. Click the Tutorial 8 link, and then click the Case Problems link. Click the refdesk.com link to open the refdesk.com home page.

2. Scroll down the page until you see the Current News / Weather / Business / Sports category in the center column, locate the Weather subcategory, and then click the more >> link to open the Weather Resources page. This page contains approximately 100 links to various Web sites that offer weather-related information.

3. Follow any of the links that you choose, but select five of the links that are for-profit sites and that carry advertising. Write a report that describes, for each of the five links, the number of ads that run on the site's home page (or that pop up or otherwise appear

as you enter or leave the home page). For each ad, indicate the following: format (banner, pop-up, interstitial, active, or other), size (if it is a banner ad, you might want to refer to the Internet Advertising Bureau, site IAB, and the name of the company or product that is being advertised.

Case 4. An Alternative to Streaming Media   You are the assistant advertising manager for Sloppy Joe's, a supplier of prepared meat products to restaurants. The company's marketing director, Susan Li, is interested in adding rich media features to Sloppy Joe's banner ads that now run on a number of restaurant supply portals and distributor sites. She has asked you to evaluate an alternative to streaming media for these banner ads that is offered by a Web technology company called **burst.com**.

1. Start your Web browser, and then go to the Online Companion page by entering the URL http://www.course.com/NewPerspectives/EC in the appropriate location of your Web browser. Click the Tutorial 8 link, and then click the Case Problems link. Click the burst.com link to open that company's home page.

2. Follow the links on the home page to learn more about burst.com and its burstware technology. Remember that the information on the burst.com site will present the product in the best possible light; you may want to use your favorite search engine to find reviews or independent evaluations of burstware.

3. Write a report to Susan of approximately 200 words that outlines the advantages and disadvantages of using burstware for the specific purpose of enriching banner ads.

QUICK | CHECK ANSWERS

Session 8.1
1. True
2. marketing mix
3. product-based
4. segment marketing or target marketing
5. False
6. one-to-one marketing
7. buyer
8. commitment

Session 8.2
1. False
2. separation
3. informative, persuasive
4. link or hyperlink
5. True
6. click-through rates
7. False

what you get out of this course

1. building an online store
2. security
3. marketing
4. Payment
5. Laws (state and international)
6. Planning

PLANNING FOR THE ONLINE BUSINESS

Developing Ideas and Creating Business Plans for Web Enterprises

CASE

OBJECTIVES

In this tutorial you will:

- Learn about business plans and the process of creating them

- Find help on the Web for building a business plan

- Learn how to use brainstorming and Web searches to identify e-business ideas

- Evaluate the e-business ideas that result from brainstorming sessions and Web searches

- Find sample business plans on the Web

- Write portions of a business plan

Corey's Souvenir World

Your friend Corey Admundson started a small souvenir stand in Niagara Falls while she was in college more than 10 years ago. It was a great business for a student who wanted to work in the summers when Niagara Falls' tourism is at its peak. Corey continued to operate the business after her college years, and Corey's Souvenir World (CSW) has grown to become a well-established business in Niagara Falls.

CSW sells all kinds of souvenir items, including key chains, coffee mugs, maps, stuffed animals, thimbles, spoons, plaques, refrigerator magnets, bumper stickers, and many more items. Although most of the items sold have individual prices ranging from $2 to $35, the store's inventory includes items priced as low as $1 and as high as $980 (for oil paintings of Niagara Falls scenes done by local artists).

Corey enjoys the souvenir business and wants to expand. However, because the tourist season is limited in Niagara Falls and because there is a lot of strong competition there, she does not think that opening more stores in Niagara Falls would be a very good idea. So Corey has started to think about other ways to expand her business. She considered selling franchises to people who would like to take her business expertise to other markets, but she is worried that the merchandising techniques she has developed might not work in other tourist areas. She also is not sure that she has developed a distinctive brand that would command high franchise fees. Corey has also thought about opening other stores in other tourist areas, but there are no other major tourist areas very close to Niagara Falls, and she is reluctant to take on the travel demands and the other difficulties that come with operating a widely dispersed operation.

Corey's customers have often expressed concerns about getting souvenirs back home safely. They are worried about packing them in suitcases that will be checked onto airplanes or stuffed into the back of the family station wagon. CSW does offer a shipping service for an extra charge, and about 20 percent of customers have at least one item shipped home.

Corey has noticed that a common reason that customers decide not to buy an item, other than their worries about transporting their souvenirs home, is uncertainty. Shoppers in retail stores often like to examine merchandise, go home to think about how it would fit in with existing décor or, if it is a gift, how the recipient will enjoy it, and then come back and make the purchase. Unfortunately for CSW, most of their customers are just passing through the area and cannot easily return to the store. In the face of uncertainty, shoppers tend to forego purchases. Corey believes that some kind of follow-up marketing would generate significant sales to customers who had second thoughts about buying while in the store.

Corey has been reading about the Internet and electronic commerce on the Web. She is not a very technologically savvy person and has been reluctant to consider doing business on the Web. She is, however, seeing many other small businesses move to the Web with some success. She has asked you to help her sketch out a business plan that she can use to evaluate the idea of taking CSW to the Web while continuing to operate CSW's location in Niagara Falls.

SESSION 9.1

In this session, you will learn what a business plan is and why a businessperson creates one. You will find resources on the Web that can help you create a good business plan. You will see how CSW can use brainstorming to generate ideas for its Web-based business and how CSW can evaluate the business ideas that emerge from the brainstorming session. You will also learn what key elements should be included in a business plan and how to go about gathering information that you can use to create a good business plan.

What Is a Business Plan?

In your first meeting with Corey, you explain to her that a **business plan** is an organized document that summarizes the expected future activities of an existing or proposed business. This document includes sections that describe the business, identify and evaluate competitors, explain how it attracts or will attract customers, and outline product or service creation processes. The business plan should also include a marketing plan, an operations plan, and a financial plan. Most business plans include an executive summary at the beginning of the document for people who want to get a quick overview or who want to decide whether to read the rest of the plan. The main sections of a typical business plan appear in Figure 9-1.

Figure 9-1	MAIN SECTIONS OF A TYPICAL BUSINESS PLAN

Executive Summary

Description of Business

Analysis of Competitors

Marketing Plan

Operations Plan

Financing Plan

Who Needs A Business Plan?

Although many people do start small businesses without a formal business plan, most business advisors strongly suggest that anyone thinking of starting a new business—or significantly expanding or otherwise changing an existing business—develop a written plan. A business plan forces the entrepreneur or business manager to think carefully about what the goals of the business are, how the business will accomplish those goals, and what obstacles the business will need to overcome to be successful.

If the business will require funds from external sources such as investors or banks, a business plan will have to be submitted before any money is committed. Investors and banks will study the plan carefully and examine key assumptions made in the plan. Thus, the business plan should always clearly state assumptions and provide logical or factual support for any critical assumptions or estimates included in the plan. Investors and banks will focus on the financing plan, but they will read other parts of the business plan carefully because the marketing plans, operations plans, and environment (industry and competitors) can have significant effects on the reasonableness of estimates made in the financing plan.

If the business will need to ask vendors to extend credit on purchases, those vendors will ask to see the business plan. Vendors will be interested in the financing plan because they do not want to extend credit if the company is unable to make timely payments. Vendors will also be interested in reviewing the operations plan to see how their products or services will be used in the new business. Vendors often can identify opportunities for selling additional products to the company by understanding its operations.

Any strategic partners that the business asks to make commitments of time or reputation to the enterprise will also ask to see a business plan. Established companies do not want to waste their resources or their reputations with companies that are not going to be successful.

You tell Corey that she will be the primary beneficiary of a business plan. By going through the structured process of creating a business plan, Corey will learn much about her business and will be forced to think specifically about the problems she will face and the issues that will arise as she takes CSW to the Web.

Finding Help for Business Planning on the Web

You explain to Corey that there are many books on the subject of business planning. You may be able to find some of them in your school's library or at the local public library. There are also a number of software packages that you can buy that will help you create a standard business plan. In addition, there are many resources for the business plan writer on the Web. Some of these sites contain general overview information; others are more specific in their coverage. *The Wall Street Journal* sponsors a site that contains useful general information for people who are starting a business. Much of the information on this site can be helpful to the business plan writer.

To examine general business plan information at StartupJournal:

1. Start your Web browser, and then go to the Online Companion page by entering the URL **http://www.course.com/NewPerspectives/EC** in the appropriate location of your Web browser. Click the **Tutorial 9** link, and then click the **Session 9.1** link. Click the **StartupJournal** link, and wait while your browser loads the home page shown in Figure 9-2.

| Figure 9-2 | STARTUPJOURNAL HOME PAGE |

links to detailed information for business plan writers

link to business plan writing software

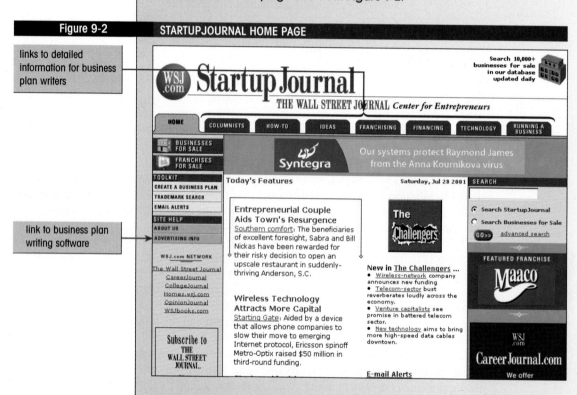

2. Click the **Ideas** tab near the top of the page to open the Ideas page. The center of the page contains links to articles from *The Wall Street Journal* and other publications about a broad range of ideas for new businesses or improving existing businesses by undertaking new ventures. The left side of the page includes links to specific categories of ideas. Because Corey is interested in taking her retailing business to the Web, you want to explore the retailing category.

3. Click the **Retailing** link at the left side of the page to open the retailing page. Click one or more of the links in the center section to read articles about business ideas for the retailing industry.

4. Click your browser's **Back** button twice to return to the StartupJournal home page, and then click the **Financing** tab to open the page that appears in Figure 9-3.

Figure 9-3   STARTUPJOURNAL FINANCING INFORMATION PAGE

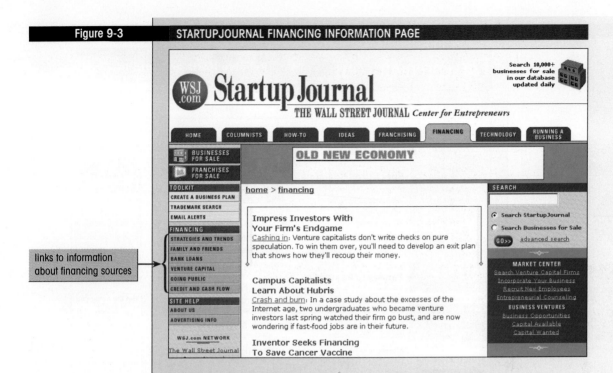

links to information
about financing sources

5. As noted in the figure, the left side of the page includes links to advice on how to approach different sources of financing for the new business venture including family and friends, banks, venture capitalists, the public capital markets, and vendors (who can finance the business by extending credit). Click one or more of those links, and examine several of the articles on those subjects.

6. When you are finished exploring the StartupJournal site, click your browser's **Back** button or use its history list to return to the Online Companion page for Session 9.1.

The StartupJournal site includes information that can be useful once the business is beyond the planning stage. Another site that is sponsored by a business publication and that is very useful to the business planner is the Smallbizsearch.com site operated by *Entrepreneur Magazine*.

To search for business plan information using Smallbizsearch:

1. Make sure your browser has loaded the Online Companion page for Session 9.1, and then click the **Smallbizsearch** hyperlink and wait while your browser loads the Entrepreneur.com home page.

2. Click the **Web Directory** link just below the row of tabs near the top of the page to load the Smallbizsearch tool page shown in Figure 9-4.

Figure 9-4	SMALLBIZSEARCH DIRECTORY AND SEARCH TOOL

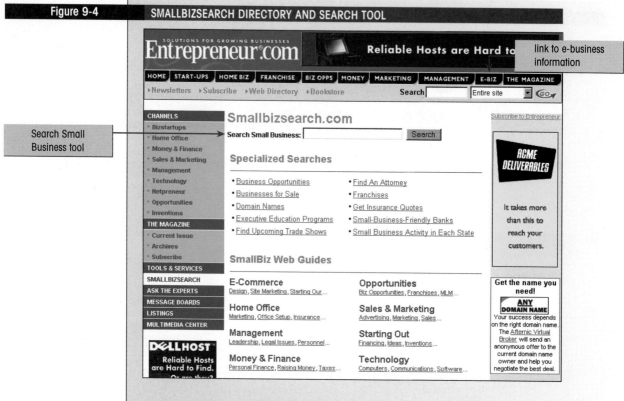

Search Small
Business tool

link to e-business
information

TROUBLE? Close any pop-up window that opens. You may have to close pop-up windows as you move from site to site.

3. Type the words **business plans** in the Search Small Business box, and then click the **Search** button. You should obtain a large number of results. You can follow any of these links to articles about business plans that have appeared in *Entrepreneur Magazine*.

4. When you are finished examining articles, click your browser's **Back** button or use its history list to return to the Smallbizsearch tool page. The tabs near the top of the page are links to categories of information on the site. You might want to explore the e-biz tab or the links in the Web Site Directories section of the page. When you have finished exploring the site, click your browser's **Back** button or use its history list to return to the Online Companion page for Session 9.1.

One of the most comprehensive sources on the Web for people starting a business is the U.S. Government's Small Business Administration (SBA) site. The SBA is a government agency that was created in 1953 to aid, counsel, and protect small businesses in the United States. As part of that mission, the SBA provides a number of resources for small businesses and new businesses. The SBA Web site includes a wide variety of resources created by the agency and many links to other useful sites. In particular, the SBA site includes quite a bit of information about business plans and the process of creating business plans.

To explore business planning resources at the SBA Web site:

1. Make sure your browser has loaded the Online Companion page for Session 9.1, and then click the **SBA** hyperlink and wait while your browser loads the agency's home page, shown in Figure 9-5. Two links on this page, the Starting Your Business and Financing Your Business links, lead to information that is especially helpful to business planners. These two links are noted in Figure 9-5.

Figure 9-5	SBA HOME PAGE

links to information that can help business planners

2. Click the **Starting Your Business** link to load that page and begin your search in that section of the SBA Web site.

3. Click the **Business Plans** link on the left side of the Starting Your Business page. This page displays the tutorial titled "The Business Plan—Road Map to Success," which the SBA has been using in workshops throughout the country for a number of years. The Business Plans page also includes a link to a downloadable version of the tutorial. Take a few minutes to skim the contents of the Road Map. If you are using a computer that permits you to download files, you can download the tutorial for later reference.

4. Click the **Startup Kit** link on the left side of the page to find a broader set of information about starting a new business. The page that loads includes links to an HTML version and to a downloadable PDF version of the Startup Kit. This kit includes some information about business plans, but it also includes a broad array of related information about how to obtain financing, what resources the SBA and state governments offer to new businesses, and a section that you can use to assess whether or not you would make a good entrepreneur.

5. When you are finished reviewing the Startup Kit, scroll down the window, and then click the **Shareware** link near the bottom of the list of links on the left side of the page. The page that opens has links to the SBA Online Library Reading Room.

6. Click the **Files for Starting Your Business** link to open that page in the reading room, shown in Figure 9-6. Note that the links on the left side of the page have changed to show other reading rooms in the online library. This page offers links to business plan writing programs and templates for creating business plans in various software products. The software and templates are somewhat dated, but they are free. The templates are designed to work with versions of software that are no longer in general use. However, some of the templates can be loaded into currently available software using the file conversion utilities included with most current word processing and spreadsheet programs. You can download and try out some of the programs and templates if you want.

Figure 9-6	SBA SHAREWARE FOR STARTING YOUR BUSINESS PAGE

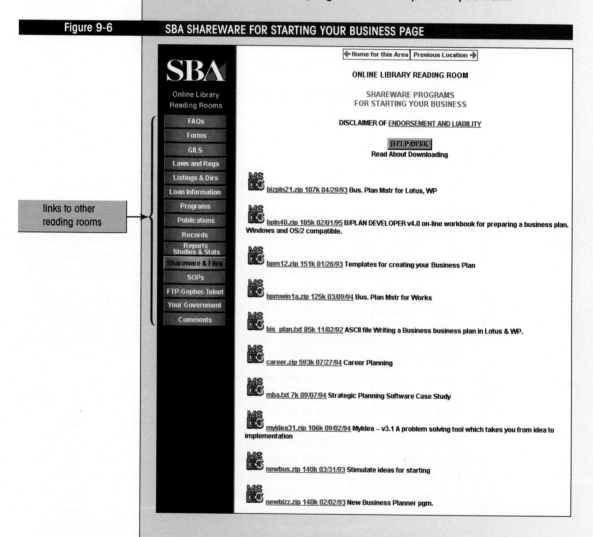

7. After you have examined the shareware available on the SBA site, spend some time exploring the other resources on the site. When you are finished, click your browser's **Back** button or use its history list to return to the Online Companion page for Session 9.1.

Corey really appreciates the leads to these Web sites and will review the downloaded materials carefully before the two of you get together for your first brainstorming session.

Generating and Evaluating Business Ideas

In your next meeting with Corey, you want to explore a number of ideas for CSW's online business. You also need to learn a bit about the business. Corey explains to you that she is thinking of building a Web site that will give customers a way to stay in touch with CSW and order additional souvenirs after they get home. You tell Corey that it might be better not to focus on specific goals for the Web business just yet.

Brainstorming to Identify Issues

You begin asking Corey questions about the business so you can learn more about it and so that the two of you can engage in a brainstorming exercise. **Brainstorming** is an exercise in which two or more people talk about ideas and write them down without evaluating them. The purpose of brainstorming is to generate bursts of creativity and to think of new ideas. Many businesspeople develop limited ways of thinking about their businesses because they tend to do the same things in the same ways for years. After the brainstorming session is over, you can sit down and evaluate each idea. You should include in the brainstorming session people who can help with new ideas and insights about the business; however, you do not want to include people who might take the results and use them to start their own businesses. Because Corey is worried that some of her employees might do just that, you have decided to do the brainstorming session with just the two of you.

Customer Behavior

To begin the brainstorming, you ask Corey to talk about her experiences over the years in selling CSW's products. She begins by telling you that a lot of customers return each year or every few years and are disappointed to find that the products that they liked are no longer in the store. She also tells you that customers also have concerns about transporting purchased items home.

You ask if she noticed any other barriers to sales. Corey says that sometimes customers are reluctant to buy higher-priced items—such as the paintings—because they are afraid they will not like them when they get them home. CSW charges customers the exact cost of shipping for this service; that is, CSW does not make a profit on the shipping service.

Returns Policy

You ask about CSW's return policy, and Corey explains that it is a very liberal policy that offers a 30-day money-back guarantee. Not many customers return items, and Corey is convinced that is not because they are all completely happy with their purchases, but because customers find it time-consuming and inconvenient to re-pack and ship items back to CSW.

Inventory

You ask Corey about the store's inventory and find that Corey thinks of the inventory items in general categories that reflect where she buys them. CSW buys from importers and distributors because most of the products are made in other countries, including Taiwan, Malaysia, and the People's Republic of China. Corey has found it easier to work with Canadian and U.S. vendors than to make buying trips to Asia—especially for the relatively small quantities she buys. The importers and distributors usually specialize in handling a particular type of product. One will sell stuffed animals, another will sell coffee mugs, and others will sell key chains, spoons, as well as these other items. Therefore, Corey talks to you about soft goods, metal goods, engraved items, silk-screened clothing, and similar categories of items. You recall that the store is laid out in these same categories.

As you both continue to discuss inventory, it becomes clear that many of these vendors could supply CSW with items that are customized for many different tourist destinations. For example, the coffee mug distributor could easily provide CSW with a full line of coffee mugs labeled "I Love NY" or with pictures of the Golden Gate Bridge, Florida palm trees or images of many other popular tourist destinations in addition to the Niagara Falls mugs that the distributor currently provides.

Warehouse and Shipping Facilities

You ask Corey about her warehouse and shipping facilities, and she explains that because CSW ships only about 20 percent of its sales, it does not have a very large shipping department. Niagara Falls streets are narrow and have heavy traffic during tourist season. The rental rates for shop space in the town's tourist areas are relatively high. To make it easier for large trucks to make deliveries and to save on rental costs, CSW does have a small warehouse near the edge of town for receiving shipments from vendors, sending out shipments to customers, and storing inventory that will not fit into the retail location. Corey tells you that the warehouse could be expanded easily because there is vacant space for rent in the warehouse building and in other buildings in that part of town. The customer shipments often go out on the same trucks (often FedEx or UPS) that make deliveries of vendor shipments to the warehouse.

Gross Profit Margins

You ask Corey about her gross profit margins. A **gross profit margin** (also called **gross margin** or **profit margin**) is the difference between the selling price of an item and its cost, expressed as a percentage of the selling price. Some retailers talk about **markups**, which is the difference between the selling price of an item and its cost expressed as a percentage of the item's cost. Neither gross margins nor markups include the costs of operating the business, just the cost of the inventory item, including any inbound freight charges.

Corey explains that the profit margins do vary considerably with the retail price of the item. Margins are highest on the lowest-priced items. For example, a key chain that sells for $2 would cost CSW about 50 cents, yielding a profit of $1.50. The markup on the key chain is 300 percent ($1.50 divided by $.50 equals 3.0 or 300 percent) and the gross margin is 75 percent ($1.50 divided by $2.00 equals .75, or 75 percent). For higher-priced items, gross margins are lower up to a point. For the very high-priced items, the gross margins go back up, but not as high as for the lowest-priced items. Items in the $8 to $20 price range, which make up the largest part of the store's volume, yield gross margins of about 40 percent. Higher-priced items yield about 60 percent. Overall, the store's average gross margin for the past three years has been 45 percent.

Competition

You ask Corey if she knows of any other souvenir stores in Niagara Falls that are planning to open Web storefronts or create any business-enhancing Web sites. She tells you that she is not aware of any. Corey belongs to several business organizations, including the local Chamber of Commerce, and she assures you that she would probably have heard if anyone else were planning a Web launch soon.

Brainstorming Session Idea List

You have been taking notes during this discussion so that you can review the ideas generated with Corey and evaluate them. The list appears in Figure 9-7 and will be the basis for the evaluation discussion you will have with Corey when you turn these ideas into parts of the business plan.

Figure 9-7 | **BRAINSTORMING SESSION IDEA LIST**

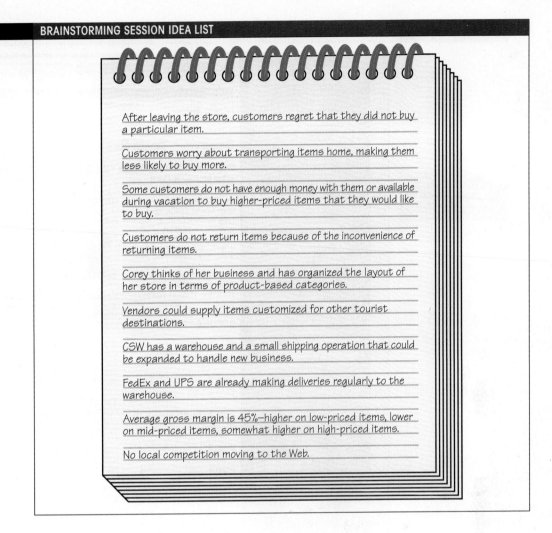

After leaving the store, customers regret that they did not buy a particular item.

Customers worry about transporting items home, making them less likely to buy more.

Some customers do not have enough money with them or available during vacation to buy higher-priced items that they would like to buy.

Customers do not return items because of the inconvenience of returning items.

Corey thinks of her business and has organized the layout of her store in terms of product-based categories.

Vendors could supply items customized for other tourist destinations.

CSW has a warehouse and a small shipping operation that could be expanded to handle new business.

FedEx and UPS are already making deliveries regularly to the warehouse.

Average gross margin is 45%—higher on low-priced items, lower on mid-priced items, somewhat higher on high-priced items.

No local competition moving to the Web.

Finding Ideas on the Web

Corey is happy with the results of your brainstorming session and figures that if two heads are better than one in a brainstorming session, then the millions of heads on the Web might offer even more value. You explain to Corey that many of the business ideas she will find on the Web will be general suggestions that tend to be limited to small geographic areas—after all, if they were ideas that would work on a national or global scale, the person proposing the idea would have created a business plan and done it instead of posting it on a Web site.

However, since the Web is a low-cost way to explore opportunities (the only cost is the time you invest searching the Web), you tell Corey that you can explore some business idea Web sites to see if they can contribute anything to your brainstorming session results.

To explore business idea Web sites:

1. Make sure your browser has loaded the Online Companion page for Session 9.1, and then click the **Idea Café** link and wait while your browser loads the Starting Your Business—Small Business Information page shown in Figure 9-8. You can explore the links in the body of this page to identify business ideas, names, legal issues, and other startup information. Note that the page includes information about general business ideas. The focus of this page is not specific to Web business ideas.

Figure 9-8	IDEA CAFÉ STARTING YOUR BUSINESS PAGE

IDEACAFE ®
SMALL BUSINESS ONLINE

"A FUN APPROACH TO SERIOUS BUSINESS!"™

REGULARS◆ENTER HERE   NOT A REGULAR? ◆JOIN HERE   FREE NEWSLETTER [your email] GO

one of the biggest names in IP service + one of the biggest names in IP hardware

◆ Sprint.   Upgrade to Sprint Dedicated Internet Access and receive a Cisco router   [click here]

BIZ GRANT CENTER

CYBERSCHMOOZ
◆ Ask Questions ▶ Share Tips
◆ People in Biz - Profiles
◆ Coffee Talk with Experts

STARTING YOUR BIZ
◆ Idea ▶ Name ▶ Plan ▶ $ ▶ Do It!

links to more information about starting a business →

RUNNING YOUR BIZ
◆ Marketing | Sales | Customers
◆ Financing Your Business
◆ HR | Employees | Contractors
◆ Tech | Reviews | Tips | Ideas
◆ Legal | Biz Forms
◆ Managing | Operations
◆ eCommerce | Work the Web

THE 'YOU' IN YOUR BIZ
◆ Gen X Biz
◆ Work @ Home
◆ Take Out Info
◆ Feed Your Mind ◀ Biz Books ▶
◆ The Fridge - Biz Info on Ice
◆ Biz Communication Zone

DE-STRESS & HAVE FUN
◆ Contest & Winners!
◆ Send Awards & Greetings
◆ Your Biz Horoscope
◆ Yoga @ Your Desk
◆ Guide to Find FUN Online

TELL A FRIEND
Email this info or hint to someone you know who could use it.

FIND IT ▶
◆ Biz Web Guide ▶
◆ Search CyberSchmooz ▶
Search Idea Cafe [   ] GO

NEW! CLASSIFIEDS

STARTING YOUR BIZ

Before You Start • Biz Idea • Biz Name • Biz Plan • Legal Setup • Get Money & Do It

So you want to be your own boss! You're ready to take control of your worklife and create your own business. You'll work where, when, and how you want. Great goal, but how do you make it happen?

Start here: take it step-by-step at Idea Cafe.

BEFORE YOU START

Step 1: YOUR BUSINESS IDEA

Step 2: NAME YOUR BUSINESS

Step 3: PLAN YOUR BUSINESS

Step 4: LEGAL SET-UP

Step 5: GET MONEY & DO IT!

STARTING A BUSINESS IDEAS: Q& A with Idea Cafe Experts

BEFORE YOU START
If you have a job now, here's what to do before you kiss your paycheck goodbye. Idea Cafe's Pre-Pink Slip Action Plan: Or Seven Steps to Take While You've Still Got a Job. from Idea Cafe CEO Francie Ward.

[Francie Ward]

Next attack the steps ahead. First skim though to see the whole picture; then work out your thoughts on paper; then act!

If you get stuck, discouraged, or stymied, just come back to Idea Cafe. Bounce your queries off others in CyberSchmooz or use our search to hook up with specifically what you need.

Take Out Info®
Here's an online collection of digital resources bursting with ideas to help you start your business!

Order up some instant, low-cost entrepreneurship tips to find out what ingredients equal success.

A menu of entrees for evaluating and enhancing your leadership skills.

Uncover the leadership qualities and styles that can make your biz idea a reality.

Hot Buy! Nearly 175 pages of How to Start and Run a Small Business

2. When you are finished exploring the Idea Café Idea and Name Page, click your browser's **Back** button or use its history list to return to the Online Companion page for Session 9.1. Click the **Idea Site for Business** link to explore another site devoted to collecting business ideas. Follow some of the links on the page to see if this site has any suggestions or ideas that Corey can use. You should read at least one of the featured articles.

3. When you are finished exploring the Idea Site for Business, use your browser's **Back** button or use its history list to return to the Online Companion page for Session 9.1. Click the **About.com Electronic Commerce Start-Up Ideas** link to open that page. Examine the links on that page and the pages to which it links to see if you can find any ideas that might help Corey with her planned business.

4. After you have examined this site and its links, click your browser's **Back** button or use its history list to return to the Online Companion page for Session 9.1.

After examining some of the top business idea sites on the Web, you conclude that these sites do not have many useful ideas for entrepreneurs. The sites that look the most promising usually turn out to be sites that are selling some kind of creativity enhancement or business plan writing tool. You explain to Corey that the free ideas you were able to find on the Web did not seem very relevant to her business. You both decide to move on and work with the ideas you generated in the brainstorming session.

Evaluating the Ideas Identified in the Brainstorming Session

After a brainstorming session, you should take the list of ideas and evaluate them. As you do this evaluation, you can identify patterns in the issues and create business elements from those ideas. You can decide to ignore some ideas because they would cost too much or be too difficult to address. You might combine several ideas to create a new solution that addresses all of the issues. Most important, you can look for new insights into business processes and how you can improve them.

Improving Customer Service

As you look over the results of your brainstorming session with Corey, you both begin to see some ideas emerge. The first thing you notice is that CSW could use a more customer-focused approach overall. Its current product-based organization and store layout has let some customer service issues go unaddressed. Customers' regrets about not buying a particular item when they visited the store, their concerns about transporting items, their inability to afford certain items that they would like to buy because they are spending money on their vacations at the time, and their reluctance to return items with which they are not satisfied are all opportunities that CSW can address in some way with its new Web presence.

As you talk with Corey about some of these issues, you both begin thinking that solutions for these customer service issues might present additional business opportunities. For example, the Web site will give customers a chance to buy items months after their visit when they have recovered financially from the costs of their vacations. This addresses one of the customer service issues identified in the brainstorming session, and it will also give people who have never visited Niagara Falls a chance to buy Niagara Falls themed products too.

Expanding the Product Line

Corey explains that CSW spends a significant amount of money in advertising and store location costs to attract customers. Once customers are in CSW's retail store, they might walk out with a $3 key chain—or nothing at all—even if they had a good experience in the store. There are many reasons that a customer might not buy on a first visit to the store. For example, a customer might be low on cash or worried about transporting an item back home. Unlike a store that the customer can visit again easily, CSW loses the goodwill it has established on a customer's first visit if that customer does not buy on the first visit.

Corey agrees and explains that many tourists who return regularly to Niagara Falls do come back to CSW because they like the products and the friendly salespeople. You explain that if CSW can serve these loyal customers even when they are not in Niagara Falls, it will generate more income because the cost of acquiring the customer for the first time is already invested and does not need to be spent again.

Corey mentions that CSW's vendors can supply products that are customized for many different destinations, and wonders if CSW could sell souvenirs for a number of popular tourist destinations. You explain that by opening a Web store and selling souvenirs for not only Niagara Falls but also many different tourist destinations, CSW could become a regular year-round shopping destination for a group of loyal customers.

Using Existing Logistics Capabilities

Because CSW already has a warehouse and shipping operation, the Web business can use that existing infrastructure to handle fulfillment and logistics for its Web site. **Fulfillment** is the process of pulling items from the warehouse shelves, packing those items, and shipping them to customers. Although CSW might have to increase its warehouse space and add some employees, it should be able to do both without making any major investments in new buildings. **Logistics** is getting the right item to the right place at the right time. Because CSW is already receiving regular FedEx and UPS deliveries, it can easily arrange for those companies to handle the new volume of outbound shipping that the Web site will generate. Again, CSW will not incur any major investment to do this.

Expanding the Customer Base

Corey tells you that she believes that some of her customers would buy souvenirs before or after trips. She has talked to many of her customers who travel on business and like to bring back souvenirs for their children, spouses, and friends. A common concern of these customers is that they often are very busy on their trips and do not have time to shop for souvenirs. Corey believes that these customers would be interested in shopping at a Web site before they leave on their trips to purchase souvenirs for their destinations. Other potential customers could use the Web site to learn more about the kinds of souvenirs that are available in the area and check prices before leaving home.

Integrating the Existing Business With the Web Business

Corey is thinking about the additional warehouse capabilities and realizes that there may be another advantage to adding the Web business to CSW's operations. She explains to you that if the Web business does increase the volume of souvenirs that she buys, CSW will be able to negotiate lower unit prices for inventory. Even if many of the items, such as coffee mugs imprinted with "I Love NY," are not items that the store carries currently, many of CSW's vendors will group items with different imprints when calculating quantity discounts.

This buying power could increase CSW's overall gross profit margins (by lowering costs while prices remain constant) or could allow CSW to reduce prices on items sold in its retail store. Either way, the Web business could help the existing business become more profitable, more price-competitive locally, or both.

Another synergy between the two businesses could be generated by asking customers at the retail store if they would like to be on the Web site's e-mail list. You explain to Corey that she should always ask customers if they want to receive offers via e-mail before putting them on the list and that CSW should limit the number of e-mails sent. Each e-mail message should include a link to a Web page that will give customers the ability to cancel the e-mail subscription at any time.

Offering Shipping Services to Local Competitors

You suggest one last business idea based on the brainstorming list. Because no local competitors appear to be interested in opening a Web site, CSW might consider offering a drop-ship service to their competitors. A **drop-ship** service is a warehouse facility that ships goods to other companies' customers directly. This type of service helps those companies avoid incurring the costs of creating their own fulfillment and logistics operations. Corey explains that some of her competitors already have warehouses and shipping operations, but some of the smaller stores do not. The local retail environment is quite competitive, so other stores might not be willing to give CSW a way to increase its business. Alternatively, the smaller stores may find CSW's service to be appealing enough that they might overlook the issue. Corey explains that it would cost very little to determine the level of interest in this service, so CSW should include it in the business plan.

Corey is very happy with the results of the brainstorming session and the evaluation of the ideas it generated. A summary of the ideas that Corey has agreed to include in CSW's Web business plan appears in Figure 9-9.

Figure 9-9	SUMMARY OF BUSINESS PLAN IDEAS

Improve customer service

Use a customer-focused approach instead of a product-focused approach to designing the Web site

Give customers in the retail store an opportunity to have the Web site follow up with merchandise offers after they have returned home—especially for high-priced items such as paintings

Expand the product line

Add souvenirs for popular tourist destinations other than Niagara Falls

Use existing fulfillment and logistics infrastructure

Existing warehouse and shipping operations can be expanded without requiring significant investment

FedEx and UPS are already making regular deliveries

Expand the existing customer base

Sell to business travelers who would like to order souvenirs before/after business trips

Offer shipping services to local competitors

Session 9.1 QUICK CHECK

1. The _____ portion of a business plan is useful to people who want a quick overview of the plan.

2. Most business plans include three separate plans, one each for _____, _____, and _____.

3. True or False: The only time a business really needs a business plan is when it is applying for a loan or trying to raise money from investors.

4. True or False: The Web is a good place to find help when you are creating a business plan.

5. An exercise in which two or more people talk about ideas and write them down without evaluating them is called _____.

6. If a retailer buys an item for $2 and sells it for $5, which would be higher when expressed as a percentage, the item's markup or its gross profit margin?

7. The process of pulling items from warehouse shelves, packing the items, and shipping them to customers is called_____.

8. True or False: A physical store can benefit from improved customer service provided by its companion Web business.

SESSION 9.2

In this session you will learn how to create significant portions of a business plan for CSW. After describing the business, you will conduct a competitive analysis and summarize your findings. Then you will create key elements of a marketing plan, an operations plan, and a financing plan for the business. Finally, you will create the executive summary and cover letter that will be placed at the front of the business plan.

Learning More About Business Plans

Few business owners or managers have ever written a business plan. Small business owners are often too busy with the details of daily operations to worry about the big picture. Managers in larger organizations usually only work with part of the business. Their need to focus on the parts of the business that they must manage keeps them from seeing the overall picture. To write a good business plan requires a broad knowledge of everything that affects the business. That is why preparing a business plan can be a good learning exercise for any business owner or manager. It can give them insights that they would never get in the course of their normal activities.

You tell Corey that many top business executives will admit that plans (of any kind) often have little value, but these same people will argue strongly that the process of planning is invaluable. Thus, even if the business plan is not used to obtain loans or interest potential investors, the creation of the plan can be a valuable experience.

Reading Sample Business Plans

You explain to Corey that business plan writers often read other business plans before starting their own plans. Although each business plan will contain unique information that describes the particular business being proposed in the plan, most business plans do look very much alike. They contain similar sections and similar types of content. Becoming familiar with the typical styles and layouts that others have used in their business plans can help you create a plan that readers will recognize and find easy to read and understand. There are a few sites on the Web that have sample business plans that you can review.

To find sample business plans on the Web:

1. Start your Web browser, and then go to the Online Companion page by entering the URL **http://www.course.com/NewPerspectives/EC** in the appropriate location of your Web browser. Click the **Tutorial 9** link, and then click the **Session 9.2** link. Click the **Interactive Business Planner** link, and wait while your browser loads the Canada Business Service Centre's Interactive Business Planner home page. Click the **English** button to open the page shown in Figure 9-10.

Figure 9-10   INTERACTIVE BUSINESS PLANNER ENGLISH-LANGUAGE HOME PAGE

Canada Business Service Centres

Canada

Interactive Business Planner

Français

Welcome to the IBP - the Interactive Business Planner

The **IBP** is the first business planning software product designed specifically to operate on the World Wide Web. The **IBP** uses the capabilities of the Internet to assist entrepreneurs prepare a 3 year business plan for their new or existing business.

With the **IBP**, you will:

- be guided through each section of your business plan using a question and answer format;
- learn definitions and tips, and view sample business plans to help you to write your own plan;
- have financial projections prepared for you, based upon the information you provide; and
- use the power of the Internet to assist you in researching your business plan.

Introduction to the IBP

About Business Planning

Create New Plan or Continue Existing Plan

link that leads to sample business plans

Canada Business Service Centres

NUNAVUT NWT YUKON BC AB SASK MAN ONT QUE NB NS PEI NFLD

Nunavut | YK | NWT | BC | AB | Sask | Man | Ont | Que | NB | NS | PEI | Nfld

[About This Site] [Important Notices]

2. Scroll down the page and then click the button labeled **Create New Plan or Continue Existing Plan**. On the page that loads, click the **New Users Click here** link to open the New User Sign-In Screen. The site requires free registration to enter the area that contains the sample business plans. Type your information into the boxes provided on the form. If you are concerned about your privacy, you can enter an assumed name and e-mail address. When you have completed the form, click the **Enter** button. On the next screen, type the **Username** and **Password** you just created in the boxes provided, and then click the **Enter** button to open the page shown in Figure 9-11.

Figure 9-11   INTERACTIVE BUSINESS PLANNER DIRECTORY PAGE

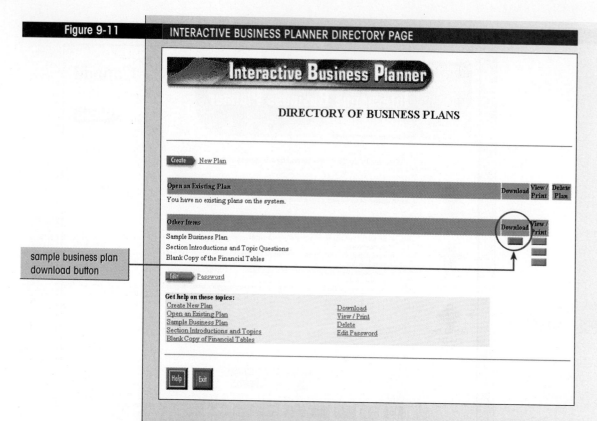

sample business plan
download button

3. Click the **Download** button in the Sample business plan row (as indicated in the figure). On the page that opens, select **Retail** sector, if necessary, and **Ontario** sector (since Niagara Falls is in Ontario) in the drop-down list boxes, scroll down the window, and then, if necessary, click the **Rich Text Format** option button near the bottom of the page. Click the **Enter** button at the bottom of the page. On the page that opens, click the **Enter** button. On the next page that opens, click the link labeled **Your sample business plan**. This link will be the e-mail address you submitted when you registered in Step 2 with ".rtf" added. Click that link to open the sample business plan. Depending on how your browser is configured, it will either open the business plan in a browser window or provide an option to download the file.

TROUBLE? If your browser opens a dialog box that asks if you want to download the file, you can instruct the browser to place the file in a folder of your choosing. You can then open the RTF (rich text format) file that downloads with almost any word processing program, such as Microsoft Word or WordPad, or WordPerfect.

4. When you have finished reading the sample business plan, use your browser's **Back** button or its history list to return to the Online Companion page for Session 9.2.

5. Click the **Bplans.com** link to open the home page for that site, and then click the **Sample Plans** link near the top of the page to open the page that appears in Figure 9-12.

Figure 9-12   **BPLANS.COM SAMPLE PLAN CENTER PAGE**

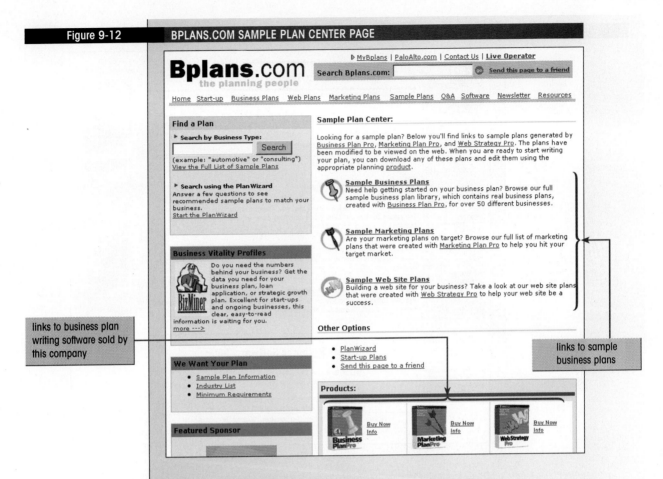

links to business plan writing software sold by this company

links to sample business plans

6. Click the **Sample Business Plans** link to open a page that contains links to more than 100 business plans. These plans were created using the business plan writing software sold by PaloAlto Software, the company that sponsors the Bplans.com site. Choose several links to follow, and read through the business plans. Because these plans were all created with the same software, they all have a similar appearance. Recall, however, that most business plans do contain the same elements and tend to look alike even when they are not created using the same software tool.

7. When you have finished reviewing the business plans, click your browser's **Back** button to return to the Sample Plan Center page. From this page, you can click the links to **Sample Marketing Plans** and **Sample Web Site Plans** to explore those example plans too.

8. When you have finished exploring the resources available at the Bplans.com site, use your browser's Back button or history list to return to the Online Companion page for Session 9.2.

9. Click the **Business Plan Center** link to open the page that appears in Figure 9-13. This site is also sponsored by a company that sells business plan writing software.

Figure 9-13   **BUSINESS PLAN CENTER HOME PAGE**

10. Click the **Example Business Plans** link to open a page with links to more than 20 business plans prepared by MBA students. These plans have been selected for inclusion on this site as part of an annual business plan competition. You can examine any of the plans by clicking the link that leads to it.

11. When you are finished exploring the resources at the Business Plan Center site, click your browser's **Back** button or use its history list to return to the Online Companion page for Session 9.2.

Corey tells you that the tour through other companies' business plans has been very helpful. She has learned a great deal about formatting, length, and what to include in CSW's plan and is ready to get started on the job of writing the business plan with you.

Writing the Business Plan

Most business consultants advise that creating a complete business plan will take the average businessperson between 20 and 50 hours. Because this tutorial is designed to take much less time than that, outlines are provided that you can use to create portions of the business plan for CSW. You will draw from the knowledge you have gained in earlier tutorials as you create the marketing plan and the operations plan.

Some parts of the business plan require the business plan writer to have considerable legal and accounting knowledge. Few businesspeople have sufficient knowledge in these areas, and they will often consult with legal and accounting professionals to obtain assistance with those tasks. The parts of the business plan that require such knowledge are marked in the outline with "consult a lawyer" or "consult an accountant". You will not be asked to complete those parts of the business plan.

Description of Business

You explain to Corey that the first section of the business plan that you will write is a description of the business. This section should describe the business, how it is or will be organized, what licenses or permits it will need, what products or services will be offered, and who will be part of the management team. The managers' qualifications should be included in this description. Because Corey is planning a Web business, that fact should also be included in the description section.

In describing the business, you should emphasize the factors that will help the business be successful and profitable. It is especially important to identify factors that will ensure the future growth of the business. The description should explain what physical facilities the business will need.

The description should include a review of the risks that the business will face. The people who will read the business plan, bankers and investors, are very knowledgeable people. If they see a business plan that does not identify risks, they will assume that the planner is unaware that all businesses face risks. An unaware businessperson is not the kind of person with whom banks and investors want to trust their money. So, acknowledge the risks and explain how the business will minimize the impact of those risks.

Some companies include a mission statement in this section of their business plans. A **mission statement**, also called a **vision statement**, is a summary of the company's philosophy. This statement should include the company's long-term goals and a general description of how it intends to reach its goals. Some critics argue that mission statements are nothing more than platitudes that make obvious statements—and some mission statements certainly warrant that criticism. However, a good, succinct mission statement can help managers of a company stay focused on long-term goals.

To write the Description of Business section of CSW's business plan:

1. Open the word processing software that you normally use to create documents.

2. Review the CSW business description outline that Corey has prepared for you. It appears in Figure 9-14.

Figure 9-14	CSW DESCRIPTION OF BUSINESS SECTION OUTLINE

Description of the Business

Name of the business
- Explain why you chose the particular name you will use for the online business
- The name does not identify the business as being in Niagara Falls, so customers will not be confused and think that the site only sells Niagara Falls souvenirs.

Legal form of the business, permits and licenses required
- Consult a lawyer

Products and services to be sold
- Describe the products that CSW will sell on the Web site
- Explain why these products are suitable to be sold on the Web
  - High value-to-weight ratio
  - Easy to pack for shipment (and we have experience doing that)

Explain that the business is an extension of the existing retail store
- How the products carried by the online store will be similar to and different from those carried in the retail store

Advantages of selling souvenirs online
- Reduces the seasonal fluctuations in the business
- Provides better customer service
  - Include some examples here

Management team
- Describe Corey's experience in the retail souvenir business here

3. Using the outline, the information about CSW contained in this tutorial, and the knowledge you have gained from studying earlier tutorials in this book, write the Description of Business section for CSW's business plan. Make any assumptions necessary to complete this task. Remember to omit any section that requires legal or accounting advice. This section of the plan should be about 300 to 800 words in length.

4. Follow your instructor's specific directions for saving or submitting this assignment, and then exit your word processing program.

Analysis of Competitors

Corey is concerned about working on the analysis of competitors for the plan. She explains to you that although she understands the nature of local competition very well, she has no idea what kind of competitors exist on the Web. You explain that the searchable nature of the Web makes a competitive analysis quite easy to do.

To search for competitors on the Web:

1. Make sure your browser has loaded the Online Companion page for Session 9.1, and then click the **Yahoo!** hyperlink and wait while your browser loads the Yahoo! Web directory main page.

2. Type **souvenir** in the search box, then click the **Search** button. The page that loads will contain search results for the term souvenir. Your page will look similar to the page that appears in Figure 9-15. Because Web directory sites update their contents every day, your results will be somewhat different.

Figure 9-15   YAHOO! SEARCH RESULTS FOR SOUVENIR

link to results from Yahoo! store registrants

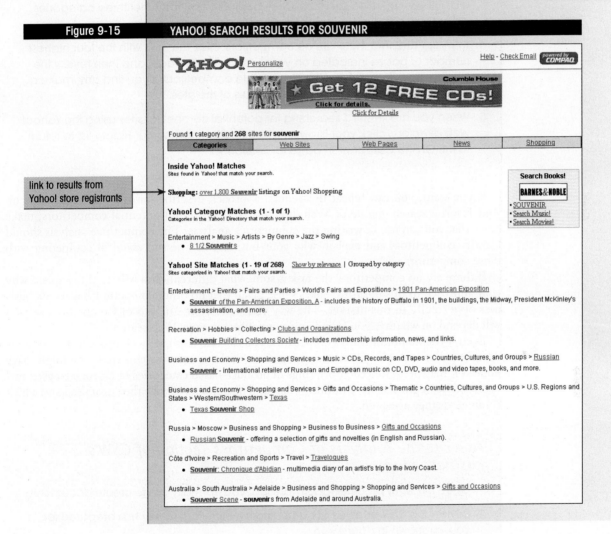

3. Click the first link that appears in the search results list, which will be the results obtained from within the Yahoo! Shopping sites. In return for their registration fees, Yahoo! gives these businesses preferential listing through this link at the top of any relevant search results page. As you examine the page that loads, look for potential competitors. Corey is happy to see that none of the links in this results category appear to be to stores that would be competitors to CSW's Web business. The subcategories (which appear with the number of links in each subcategory along the left side of the page) with the largest number of links are Sports & Outdoors, Flowers & Gifts, Books, and Arts & Collectibles. CSW is definitely not in the sports souvenir business, and the other three categories do not appear likely to include competitors.

4. To make sure that there are no competitors, click the links with the four highest number of pages indicated on your search results page, and then review the results pages for each to identify possible competitors. If you find any, make a note of their URLs and outline key features of the sites.

5. When you are finished searching for potential competitor sites using the Yahoo! Web directory, click your browser's **Back** button or use your History list to return to the Online Companion page for Session 9.2.

If you want, you can repeat the general approach described in the preceding steps on your favorite search engine or Web directory. If you do find potential competitors, make notes that you can use in writing the competitive analysis. The competitive analysis should identify competitors and explain why your business will be successful in competing with those competitors.

If there are no competitors, the task is somewhat different. You will need to explain why your approach to this business makes sense given that no other competitor has seen a business opportunity in this market. The way you write your Analysis of Competitors section will depend on whether you found any competitors in your Web search.

Even if you do not find any competitors, you can still learn from companies that sell similar items. For example, when examining some of the sports souvenir sites, you might have noticed if they presented their offerings in product-based categories or customer-based categories. You might also have noticed what kind of shipping service they promised and which credit cards they accepted.

To write the Analysis of Competitors section of CSW's business plan:

1. Open the word processing software that you normally use to create documents.

2. Review the CSW analysis of competitors outline that Corey has prepared for you, as shown in Figure 9-16.

Figure 9-16	CSW DESCRIPTION OF COMPETITORS SECTION OUTLINE

Analysis of Competitors

No direct competitors to CSW's proposed business currently exist on the Web.

Some sites sell sports souvenirs, historical or antique souvenirs, or souvenirs from a specific location

Some sites that are affiliated with museums or tourist attractions do sell souvenirs

CSW's goal is to sell souvenirs for a number of different tourist destinations

By focusing on the customer (one customer can buy souvenirs from many different destinations) rather than on the product (the souvenirs themselves), CSW can create a completely different Web business opportunity than any existing site

Why hasn't somebody else done this already?

CSW is already in the business and has an awareness of the Web that other retail souvenir stores may not have

What we have learned by examining similar sites (even those that are not direct competitors)

Use of graphics on the site

Payment and shipment options offered

Items on the site in product-based categories, customer-based categories, and sometimes both

3. Using the outline, the information about CSW contained in this tutorial, and the knowledge you have gained from studying earlier tutorials in this book, write the Analysis of Competitors section for CSW's business plan. Make any assumptions necessary to complete this task. This section of the plan should be about 100 to 400 words in length.

4. Follow your instructor's specific directions for saving or submitting this assignment, and then exit your word processing program.

Marketing Plan

The marketing plan for a new business endeavor can be its most important part. The business cannot be successful without successful marketing. If customers never find out that CSW's Web site exists, they will never buy from it. In Tutorial 2, you learned how to design user interfaces that create a Web presence consistent with the mission of the company. In Tutorial 8, you learned how to use advertising and other marketing techniques to build a marketing strategy for a Web-based business. Now you can apply that knowledge to CSW's business plan.

To write the Marketing Plan section of CSW's business plan:

1. Open the word processing software that you normally use to create documents.

2. Review the CSW marketing plan outline that Corey has prepared for you, as shown in Figure 9-17.

| Figure 9-17 | CSW MARKETING PLAN SECTION OUTLINE |

Marketing Plan

Web Presence
> What will CSW do to create a Web presence that is consistent with the existing store's reputation?

Branding
> How will CSW create and maintain its brand on the Web?

Affiliate Marketing
> Should CSW sign up affiliates?
> Should CSW become an affiliate to any major Web sites? Which ones? Why?

Web Site Name
> What domain name(s) are available? Which of those will the site use?

Major Market Segments
> What are CSW's main market segments for the Web store and what methods will best reach each segment?

Advertising
> What types of advertising will the site use to promote itself?
>> Online ads
>> Physical world ads
> What types of ads, if any, will the site include from other Web merchants or services?

E-Mail marketing
> What, if any, types of e-mail marketing will CSW use?
> Will the e-mail programs include content? If so, who will provide the content?

3. Using the outline, the information about CSW contained in this tutorial, and the knowledge you have gained from studying earlier tutorials in this book, write the Marketing Plan section for CSW's business plan. Make any assumptions necessary to complete this task. This section of the plan should be about 500 to 1,000 words in length.

4. Follow your instructor's specific directions for saving or submitting this assignment and close your word processing program.

Operations Plan

The operations plan section of a business plan includes information about how a business will manufacture products (if it is a manufacturer), sell products or services, and collect payments from its customers. It also includes warehousing and other logistics. For CSW, the operations plan must include a description of how the Web site will be created and maintained, how Corey will buy products and have them shipped to the CSW warehouse, how the warehouse will be managed, and how shipments will be made. CSW's operations plan should also include information about which payments CSW will accept from customers and how it will process them. You have learned about all of these topics in earlier tutorials, so the operations plan gives you an opportunity to review that material and apply what you have learned to CSW's business plan.

For Web businesses, the business plan usually includes screen images of sample, or "mock up," Web pages that will be used in the site. These pages do not need to contain all of the design features that will appear in the completed site, but they should convey an idea of the kinds of interaction a customer could expect when shopping on the site.

To write the Operations Plan section of CSW's business plan:

1. Open the word processing software that you normally use to create documents.

2. Review the CSW operations plan outline that Corey has prepared for you, as shown in Figure 9-18.

Figure 9-18	CSW OPERATIONS PLAN SECTION OUTLINE

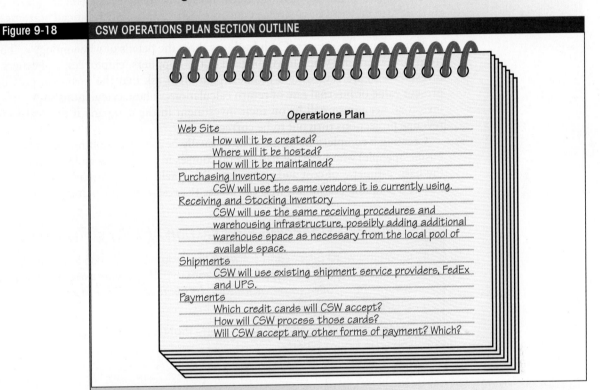

Operations Plan

Web Site
    How will it be created?
    Where will it be hosted?
    How will it be maintained?
Purchasing Inventory
    CSW will use the same vendors it is currently using.
Receiving and Stocking Inventory
    CSW will use the same receiving procedures and
    warehousing infrastructure, possibly adding additional
    warehouse space as necessary from the local pool of
    available space.
Shipments
    CSW will use existing shipment service providers, FedEx
    and UPS.
Payments
    Which credit cards will CSW accept?
    How will CSW process those cards?
    Will CSW accept any other forms of payment? Which?

3. Using the outline, the information about CSW contained in this tutorial, and the knowledge you have gained from studying earlier tutorials in this book, write the Operations Plan section for CSW's business plan. Make any assumptions necessary to complete this task. This section of the plan should be about 300 to 600 words in length. You should create a sample home page for the Web site and one sample of each type of page that the site will use, such as product description pages, order form, contact information, and any content pages that you might decide to include in the design. These pages will be included in the appendix to the business plan.

4. Follow your instructor's specific directions for saving or submitting this assignment, and then exit your word processing program.

Financing Plan

The financing plan is the part of the business plan that explains how much the business operation will cost to launch and keep operating. It also includes projections of revenue, usually including detailed calculations and statements of the assumptions used in creating the projections.

The financing plan shows the amounts of borrowing, if any, that are necessary to make the business solvent. Many business plans are created for the main purpose of applying for loans or inducing people to invest in the business. Thus, this section is often the most detailed in the entire plan.

A complete financing plan includes pro-forma financial statements and budgets that show how money will flow through the operation. **Pro-forma financial statements** are the financial statements that result if the business planner's cost estimates and revenue projections turn out to be correct. **Cash budgets** show the details of when money will be received from customers and when it will be paid out to suppliers, employees, and others. Potential investors who are reviewing a business plan often ask that the financing plan include net present value or internal rate of return calculations. These calculations show how much the investors' net return will be on their investment in the company if the cost estimates and revenue projections turn out to be correct.

Creating a complete financing plan is usually beyond the abilities of students (and many businesspeople) who have not had several courses in accounting and finance. You can create the basic estimates of cost and revenue and then take that information to an accountant or business planning consultant who can create the rest of the financing plan.

> ### To write the Financing Plan section of CSW's business plan:
>
> 1. Open the word processing software that you normally use to create documents. *Note: Your instructor might direct you to complete this activity using a spreadsheet software program such as Microsoft Excel instead of your word processing program.*
>
> 2. Review the CSW financing plan outline that Corey has prepared for you, as shown in Figure 9-19.

Figure 9-19	CSW FINANCING PLAN SECTION OUTLINE

Financing Plan

Initial costs estimates
- Web site creation
- Initial stocks of inventory items
- Additional shipping equipment
- Introductory advertising campaign

Ongoing costs estimates
- Cost of goods sold
  - Which items will sell on the Web site?
  - How many additional items will sell each month?
- Inbound freight
- Fulfillment staff salaries
- Web site maintenance staff (content and technical)
- Ongoing advertising programs

Revenue Estimates
- Which items will sell on the Web site?
- How many additional items will sell each month?

Pro-forma financial statements—income statement, balance sheet, statement of changes in financial position
- Consult an accountant

Cash flow projections, master budget, loan repayment schedules
- Consult an accountant

Tax payments budget
- Consult an accountant

Net present value and rate of return calculations
- Consult an accountant

3. Using the outline, the information about CSW contained in this tutorial, and the knowledge you have gained from studying earlier tutorials in this book, write the portions of the Financing Plan section that you are able to complete without obtaining professional accounting counsel. Make any assumptions necessary to complete this task. This section of the plan should be under 200 words in length. *Note: If your course has prerequisites that include the necessary accounting and finance classes, your instructor might assign you the task of creating a complete financing plan.*

4. Follow your instructor's specific directions for saving or submitting this assignment, and then exit your word processing or spreadsheet program.

Executive Summary and Cover Page

The last part of the business plan to be written appears at the front of the completed plan. The executive summary is an important part of the plan, but it is usually easier to write after you have completed the other sections of the plan. The executive summary includes highlights from each other section. You should choose elements of the business plan that you would like to emphasize or that might encourage a reader to spend more time and read the rest of the plan. Thus, the executive summary is as much a sales tool as it is a summary.

The cover page should include the name of the company, contact information, and a statement regarding the confidential nature of the plan. Your lawyer can suggest the exact wording, but the confidentiality statement should make clear that the plan is intended for the recipient only and should preclude copying or further distribution without your consent. Many business plans are either numbered (so the company can keep a record of who received which numbered copy) or are addressed to a specific person on the cover page.

To write the Executive Summary and Cover Page for CSW's business plan:

1. Open the word processing software that you normally use to create documents.

2. Review the sections of the business plan that you have already written.

3. Write a summary that includes the important points made in each section. Be sure to write in a style that helps Corey sell the idea to potential lenders and investors. This section of the plan should be under 200 words in length.

4. Follow your instructor's specific directions for saving or submitting this assignment, and then exit your word processing program.

With a little additional help from her lawyer and accountant, Corey can take the business plan draft you have prepared for her and create a complete business plan. She can use the business plan to apply for bank loans or interest potential investors. She can also use it as a roadmap and guide as she launches CSW's online business.

Session 9.2 QUICK CHECK

1. True or False: Most business plans contain similar sections and similar types of content.

2. Most Web sites that offer sample business plans are sponsored by _____.

3. The _____ section of a business plan should include a review of the risks that the business will face.

4. A statement of a company's long-term goals that includes a general description of how it intends to reach those goals is called a(n) _____.

5. One good way for a prospective Web business to identify possible competitors is to _____.

6. The _____ section of a business plan will include an explanation of how the business will collect payments from its customers.

7. True or False: The executive summary of a business plan should include a confidentiality statement that explains the restricted permitted distribution of the plan.

CASE PROBLEMS

Case 1. Web-Aided Brainstorming. With one or more other students (as assigned by your instructor), identify a product or service that could be sold on the Web.

1. Start your Web browser, and then go to the Online Companion page by entering the URL http://www.course.com/NewPerspectives/EC in the appropriate location of your Web browser. Click the Tutorial 9 link, and then click the Case Problems link. Click one or more of the links to Web directories and search engines listed for Case Problem 1 to find companies that offer products or services on the Web that are similar to the one you have chosen. If group members are familiar with other Web directories or search engines, they might use those tools instead of those listed. Each group member should undertake these searches independently.

2. Meet as a group with the search results. Spend at least 15 minutes talking about the features of the sites you have found. Identify what works and what does not work on these sites. If none of the group members were able to find any sites that sell your product or service, discuss the features that should be included in your site.

3. Create an idea list based on your discussion. Write a short paragraph for each idea on your list in which you explain the idea. Submit your annotated idea list to your instructor.

Case 2. Marketing Plan for a B2B Web site. Trusty Power Tools (TPT) sells small power tools, such as drills, power screwdrivers, and power saws, to builders and other companies in the construction industry.

1. Start your Web browser, and then go to the Online Companion page by entering the URL http://www.course.com/NewPerspectives/EC in the appropriate location of your Web browser. Click the Tutorial 9 link, and then click the Case Problems link. Scroll to the Case Problem 2 listings, then click the Black & Decker link to open its home page. Black & Decker is one of TPT's main competitors in the construction industry, but it also sells a large number of products to the consumer market.

2. Explore the Black & Decker site to learn how they present their products.

3. After you have examined the site, use your browser's Back button to return to the Case Problem 1 section of the Online Companion, and then click the Makita link. Makita is another of TPT's competitors. Makita's main market is also the construction industry. Explore the site to see how its approach differs from that of Black & Decker.

4. Use your browser's Back button to return to the Case Problem 2 section of the Online Companion, and then click the Snap-on link and explore that site. Snap-on sells more to auto repair shops and manufacturing plants than to the construction industry, but it does compete with TPT to some extent. Examine its approach to presenting tools on its site.

5. TPT is creating a business plan for a complete overhaul of its current Web site. Write approximately 300 words that would become part of the marketing plan section for TPT in which you describe how TPT should present its tools on the new site. Support your arguments with what you learned from the three sites you visited. Remember to make adjustments as necessary for differences between the construction industry market and the markets served by Black & Decker and Snap-on.

Case 3. Corporate Coffee Service. The founders of Corporate Coffee Service are preparing a business plan that they can take to their bank to borrow money for a major expansion of their small business. Corporate Coffee installs and maintains coffee brewing and serving equipment to companies in the Indianapolis metropolitan area. Its service also includes supplying coffee, tea, cups, and other consumable items. Companies sign a contract that specifies service levels, but most companies want to be permitted to modify those service levels from time to time (for example, when they have a large sales presentation in house).

Corporate Coffee wants to streamline ordering by encouraging customers to use the planned new Corporate Coffee Web site to monitor and change orders as necessary.

1. Start your Web browser, and then go to the Online Companion page by entering the URL http://www.course.com/NewPerspectives/EC in the appropriate location of your Web browser. Click the Tutorial 9 link, and then click the Case Problems link. Click the Case Problem 3 link and use the links to coffee service companies to review the sites to learn more about this business.

2. Write the operations plan for the order control portion of Corporate Coffee's new site. Include a description of how the site will display customer accounts and how it will handle authorization to ensure that only the person authorized by the customer can change orders. State any assumptions you believe are necessary to make.

Case 4. Analysis of Business Plans. In this case, you will compare the persuasiveness of two different business plans.

1. Start your Web browser, and then go to the Online Companion page by entering the URL http://www.course.com/NewPerspectives/EC in the appropriate location of your Web browser. Click the Tutorial 9 link, and then click the Case Problems link. Click either or both of the links listed under Case Problem 4, and examine several of the sample business plans provided on these sites.

2. Choose two of the business plans from either site. For each plan, carefully review the executive summary.

3. Write a report of approximately 150 words for each executive summary in which you rate the persuasiveness of the summary. Explain why the executive summary made you want to read the rest of the plan (or why it did not).

QUICK | CHECK ANSWERS

Session 9.1

1. executive summary
2. False
3. marketing, operations, and financing
4. True
5. brainstorming
6. markup would be higher than gross margin (in this example, the item's gross profit margin is 60 percent and its markup is 150 percent)
7. Fulfillment
8. True

Session 9.2

1. True
2. companies that sell software for creating business plans
3. description of business; business description; executive summary
4. mission statement; vision statement
5. use a Web directory; use a search engine; search the Web
6. operations plan
7. False

In this appendix you will:

- Explore career opportunities in electronic commerce

- Discover the different technology careers in electronic commerce

- Discover the different business careers in electronic commerce

- Learn about electronic commerce careers that combine business and technology skills

- Examine the different types of electronic commerce employers

CAREERS IN ELECTRONIC COMMERCE

What Careers Exist in Electronic Commerce?

Electronic commerce is truly creating a revolution in the way people do business. When a revolution occurs, even if it is an economic revolution, major changes occur. The information revolution has changed many people's lives and it will continue to change many more people's lives in the near future. For a person studying electronic commerce, one of the most interesting changes is the creation of new career opportunities. Although electronic commerce is eliminating jobs in many traditional businesses, it is opening up many new careers for persons who want to work with the new ways of doing business that have become possible using the Web and Internet technologies.

Electronic commerce is a combination of technology and business. Thus, some of the new career opportunities are open to people who have technology education and skills. Other career opportunities are open to people who have business education and skills. Some of the most interesting new careers are open only to people who have obtained knowledge in both technology *and* business.

Technology Careers in Electronic Commerce

The foundations of electronic commerce are the computing and networking technologies on which the Internet exists. Many companies have created intranets to provide employees working within the company the same efficiencies that the Internet and Web have provided to the population as a whole. These technologies must be designed, specified, installed, and maintained by people. Electronic commerce offers careers in both hardware and software technologies, including networking, systems, programming, systems analysis, and databases.

Network and Systems Technology Jobs

Electronic commerce is built on the Internet, which is a network of networks. Thus, it is not surprising that many jobs in electronic commerce concern the design, installation, maintenance, and administration of computer networks. **Network technicians** run cable, connect computers to the cable, and repair cables and connectors. Many network technicians learn job skills through on-the-job training, but some of them obtain certificates or associate degrees before starting to work in this area.

Network administrators have knowledge of network operating software. They set up accounts for new users on the network and monitor network traffic to ensure that the network does not become congested. Many network administrators began their careers as network technicians and continued their education while working. Some network administrators hold bachelor's or associate degrees, but most have taken examinations to become certified in the network software packages that run on their systems.

Network designers must know what networking products are available, what the specifications are for those products, and how to use them to create local or wide area networks. Network designers often are certified to work on the products manufactured by one or more vendors. Some network designers have bachelor's degrees; however, many have associate degrees or hold specialized certificates.

Another job that involves the computers that are connected by the network is a **systems technician**. A systems technician performs preventive maintenance on computers and repairs them as needed. Systems technicians usually have specialized training and often hold certificates or associate degrees. **Systems administrators** are responsible for the reliable and secure operation of the computers on the network and the network itself. This management position is usually filled by a person who holds a bachelor's degree and has many years of experience as a systems technician and in one or more network-related jobs.

Programming and Systems Analyst Jobs

Traditional businesses hire many programmers and analysts to ensure that their computing systems operate effectively. A **programmer** writes instructions, or program code, in a language that the computer can understand. A **systems analyst** outlines the structure of those instructions and makes sure that the resulting program will accomplish the needs of its users. Systems analysts work closely with teams of programmers to ensure that the program code accomplishes its objectives.

Electronic commerce requires systems that enable many people using many different kinds of computers to work together efficiently. Electronic commerce creates many jobs for programmers who can write good code in languages such as Java or C++. Programmers who can work with markup languages, such as HTML or XML (extensible markup language), are also in high demand in electronic businesses.

Programmers who know several languages and are familiar with multiple operating systems are especially valuable in electronic commerce. Electronic commerce sites tend to have many types of computers running various operating systems and application software packages. A programmer who can write CGI scripts or Perl for a company's UNIX Web server one day, and then add JavaScript instructions to a Web page's HTML code the next day, is highly valued and compensated in most electronic business environments. Programmers with knowledge of DHTML (dynamic HTML) are also in high demand. A good programmer is one who can learn new programming and markup languages quickly. Programmers who can work with the many languages that are frequently used to build electronic commerce systems are sometimes called **Web programmers**.

Programmers often have associate degrees, but many have bachelor's degrees in computer science or information systems. Systems analysts usually have bachelor's degrees. Many systems analysts begin their careers as programmers and are promoted from that position.

Database Jobs

Many electronic commerce sites make extensive use of databases. A **database** is a collection of information organized in a way that allows users to obtain useful summaries of that information. For example, an online travel agency might keep information about its customers in a database. If the agency wants to promote a reduced airfare to persons flying from Denver, the agency could extract from its database a list of customers who live in or near Denver. It could then send e-mail messages to all of those customers with information about the reduced airfare. When most people talk about databases, they use the term *database* to mean the collected information *and* the software used to organize and manage that information collection.

The process of extracting information from a database is called **querying**, and it is accomplished by writing a **query**, which is a set of instructions that tells the database what data to extract. Large databases can have millions of records. A **record** is the collection of information about a particular entity. An **entity** is a person, place, object, event, or idea. For example, in a customer database, each record contains information about a particular customer. Each record in a database can have many fields. Each database **field** contains one characteristic about the entity. For example, in a customer database, each customer record might have fields for the customer's name, street address, city, state, telephone number, e-mail address, date of last purchase, and so on.

Creating and managing a database effectively requires many different skills. To create a database that is useful for business purposes, such as marketing and strategic planning, companies hire database analysts. A **database analyst** must have training in two areas: the theory of database design and the creation of data models that represent objects and processes in the real world. Database analysts often obtain their knowledge of database theory and their modeling skills in college-level database courses. Most database analysts hold an associate or bachelor's degree in computer science or information systems.

Creating the structure for storing information in a database is important; however, the real value of having a large quantity of stored information is that companies can extract the information in many different ways. **Database programmers** write queries that extract portions of the data. These queries provide the answers to questions that managers have about their business operations. In electronic commerce, managers want to know how many site visitors click particular banner ads, for example. If visitors have registered with the site and have provided information about themselves, the database will contain many interesting combinations of information about click-through behavior. The most common language that database programmers use is called **SQL** (often pronounced "sequel"), which is an acronym for **structured query language**. Although SQL versions can vary from one specific database management program to another, virtually all database management programs include an implementation of SQL. Database programmers often hold associate or bachelor's degrees in computer science or information systems. Many of them can write programs in other languages, too. For example, when you search for a book at Amazon.com, the search process generates the Web page for each book from a database. The database management system at Amazon.com is closely integrated with the software that generates its Web pages. Thus, even database programmers who do not work with other programming languages must understand some of the features and capabilities of those other languages. In smaller organizations, programmers frequently work in a position that combines the responsibilities of database programmer and Web programmer.

Because a database can be an important organizational resource, most companies that have sizable databases put one person in charge of them. This person, called a **database administrator (DBA)**, is responsible for the design and maintenance of the company's database. Database analysts and database programmers often report to the DBA. The DBA has final say regarding what entities will be included in the database and what fields will be stored for each entity. The DBA works with systems administrators and network administrators to make sure that the computer hardware and networking capabilities will be sufficient to ensure smooth operation of the database and its database management software. DBAs usually have bachelor's degrees in computer science or information systems. Many of them also hold advanced degrees, such as a master of business administration (MBA) or other master's degrees in information systems. Most DBAs worked as database programmers or database analysts before becoming DBAs.

Business Careers in Electronic Commerce

For persons who have education and experience in business, electronic commerce offers career paths that are similar to those that exist in traditional business. However, because electronic business is growing much more rapidly than traditional business, electronic business careers often offer more challenges, rewards, and opportunities for rapid advancement. For persons with business degrees, electronic commerce offers careers in management, marketing, sales, and customer service.

Management Jobs

Every business, as it grows, needs managers to monitor and control its increasingly complex and numerous processes. Firms engaging in electronic commerce need people to manage the processes that create the products or services they offer for sale and to manage the people who make those processes work. Most management positions require a bachelor's degree and some experience in the business process they manage. Some management positions require an MBA degree. In companies that engage in electronic commerce, managers must be conversant with strategic electronic business models. They must understand how technology can help them create new opportunities for managing their supply chains, interacting with vendors, identifying new customers, and increasing the efficiency of their internal operations.

Companies sometimes hire or promote employees to management positions with associate degrees or specialized certificates, especially for first-line supervisor positions. Many managers in Web businesses came up through the technical job ranks. Many management positions in electronic commerce require a combination of technical and business knowledge.

Marketing and Sales Jobs

Sales are the lifeblood of any business; electronic commerce businesses are no different. Because many marketing and sales activities in Web businesses are conducted via the Internet, marketing and sales jobs require candidates who have a higher-than-usual familiarity with the Internet and its technologies.

Marketing department employees in electronic commerce must work with Web site designers to make sure that the company's brands and its overall image are appropriately represented in the Web site's presence. They must develop advertising strategies, including ad design and ad placement, that will work on the Web. They must also be able to identify new opportunities for creating or identifying new customers using strategies such as disintermediation and reintermediation. **Marketing strategies** are the comprehensive set of plans that businesses use to achieve their branding and market share objectives.

Jobs in marketing include **marketing staff assistants**, who help implement marketing plans. Marketing staff assistants often hold associate degrees or bachelor's degrees in business administration or marketing. **Marketing analysts** devise and test plans to implement marketing strategies and usually have bachelor's degrees or several years of experience as marketing staff assistants. **Market researchers** conduct and analyze tests of advertising plans or other marketing efforts. Market researchers usually hold bachelor's degrees in marketing or statistics; many of them hold advanced degrees in marketing or MBA degrees.

Marketing managers devise the strategies that their companies will follow and work with marketing analysts to develop the plans that will carry out these strategies. Marketing managers usually have years of experience as marketing analysts or market researchers, hold bachelor's degrees in marketing, and often hold MBA degrees.

Sales department employees in Web businesses devise specific sales approaches that accomplish the objectives of their organizations' marketing plans. These sales approaches might include e-mail campaigns, personal selling, permission marketing, and many other ways of communicating with prospective and current customers. **Sales assistants** and **salespeople** write text for promotional e-mail messages, telephone prospects, and reply to inquiries from prospective customers using e-mail, the telephone, and regular mail. Sales assistants and salespeople may have attended different kinds of sales training programs and they often hold associate or bachelor's degrees.

Sales managers supervise the activities of sales assistants and salespersons and ensure that the sales approaches as implemented do achieve the goals of their organizations' marketing plans. Sales managers often have many years of experience as salespersons and often have worked in marketing, as well. Sales managers generally hold bachelor's degrees and often have earned MBA degrees.

Customer Service Jobs

Marketing and sales employees are responsible for customer contact up to the point of sale. Once a customer purchases a product or service, the customer service department takes over. In many electronic business activities, customers do not have any personal contact with employees of the company before making a purchase. Therefore, if anything goes wrong with the purchase, the customer service department becomes the customer's initial point of contact with the organization. The customer service department helps customers with complaints or questions to resolve their problems. If the customer service department doesn't respond appropriately and satisfactorily to customer complaints and questions, the organization risks losing those customers forever.

Most Web businesses hire a large number of **customer service representatives (CSRs)**. CSRs handle calls from customers who need information about their purchases. Order status, shipping inquiries, and defective merchandise returns are among the many information requests to which CSRs must respond. CSRs usually hold certificates, associate degrees, or bachelor's degrees. Many companies require all of their sales and marketing employees to work as CSRs for some length of time as part of their training. These companies believe that sales and marketing staff members who have learned what makes customers unhappy after the sale will do a better job identifying customer needs before the sale. **Customer service managers** supervise the activities of CSRs. Most customer service managers hold bachelor's or MBA degrees and also have experience as a CSR.

Business/Technology Careers in Electronic Commerce

Electronic commerce companies are unusual in that they have many jobs in which people must have a combination of technology and business skills to be successful. These career paths seldom exist in traditional companies and thus are among the most difficult to fill in the rapidly growing electronic business sector. Pure technology positions and pure business positions do exist in traditional companies, and electronic businesses have been able to hire many of the best technology and business employees away from traditional companies. Persons who have a combination of technology and business skills are much harder to find. Some careers in this combined electronic commerce position are for people with skills in Web page design, Web page content, and project management.

Web Page Design Jobs

The job of **Web page designer** has existed for less than a decade because the Web itself is that young. All types of companies need Web pages, so the demand for Web page designers is very high. Most Web page designers have multiple skills and broad knowledge about design, graphics, and business. Good Web page designers must be able to combine graphic elements on a page with colors that convey their company's image and reflect its branding strategies. Thus, they must have a combination of design skills and business knowledge.

To implement their designs as actual Web pages, Web page designers must know how to create graphic effects using Web technology. Web page designers have a wide variety of educational backgrounds and employment histories. Many hold certificates or degrees at the associate or bachelor's level. These credentials might be in any of a wide variety of fields, including art, graphic design, programming, markup languages, business, or computer science. Web page design jobs can be found in almost any part of an organization. Frequently, they are in marketing departments, but many Web page designers work for systems administrators or other technology managers.

Web Page Content Jobs

Web page writers and **Web page editors** work together to create the content that appears on an organization's Web pages. People in these jobs may have either technical or creative writing skills and they usually have a good understanding of markup languages. Web page designers usually hold bachelor's degrees and have writing or editing experience.

As more Web businesses add audio and video media clips to their pages, they must hire audio and video engineers, producers, and directors to create the clips. Most of these employees have experience in creating television and radio productions before entering the electronic commerce sector.

Project Management Jobs

In electronic commerce, many of the business activities that make a company successful are organized and conducted as projects. A **project** is a business activity that draws together employees from a number of different functional areas to accomplish a specific objective within a given time frame. For example, the activities required for launching a new Web site are usually organized as a project.

Electronic business projects require that business goals be accomplished by deploying technologies in an organized and controlled manner. Thus, **project managers** must know something about business, something about technology, and a great deal about budgeting, managing people, and coordinating activities. Most project managers hold bachelor's degrees in business, industrial or civil engineering, or project management. Many of them hold certificates in project management or several of its component disciplines. Most project managers have experience in jobs that are performed in the types of projects that they currently manage. Project management is one of the most interesting and challenging jobs in electronic commerce.

Types of Electronic Commerce Employers

As you have seen, electronic commerce provides job opportunities for people who have a wide variety of educational backgrounds, experience levels, and skill sets. Electronic commerce jobs exist in many different types of organizations. Three main categories of organizations in which you can find an electronic business job include companies that engage in electronic commerce (Web businesses and traditional companies that have electronic commerce initiatives), the consulting firms that advise those companies, and service providers (companies that provide technical and business services on an ongoing basis to those companies).

Web Businesses and Traditional Companies

Web businesses, increasingly called **dot-com businesses**, are companies that conduct all or most of their business on the Web. Most of these companies are young because the Web has only existed for a relatively short time. Traditional companies have been in business for many years. Many traditional companies have launched electronic commerce initiatives to expand their business or compete with newer companies that have started competing with them using a Web business approach. Both types of companies offer excellent job opportunities for people who have technology skills, business knowledge, and an understanding of how electronic commerce works.

Consulting Firms

Traditionally, executives of large companies have used **consulting firms** to advise them on business strategy issues. In recent years, however, consulting firms have begun providing advice to companies on a wide range of business strategies, processes, and decisions. Many of these consulting firms provide extensive services related to technology planning and implementation. To do this, they need people with outstanding technology and management skills. As the Web has grown, these consulting firms have become very active in advising their clients on electronic commerce strategy and implementation. Consulting firms offer excellent jobs to people with electronic commerce skills. Consulting firms hire people to be strategy consultants, implementation advisors, and trainers.

Service Providers

Internet service providers (ISPs), application service providers (ASPs), and commerce service providers (CSPs) all sell their services to electronic businesses. These Web service providers must have employees who understand electronic commerce and who have very good technology skills. For example, when 200 Web businesses rely on one CSP to operate their Web servers and make sure that their connection to the Internet is maintained **24/7** (open 24 hours a day and seven days a week), they expect that CSP to have employees who are highly competent technically. Web businesses cannot afford lengthy downtimes or server failures. In general, the technical employees of a CSP have better technical skills than the employees at the companies to which they provide service. Having good technical skills creates very good job opportunities for persons at these Web service providers. In addition, Web service providers must hire people with many of the same business and business-technology talents that are in demand at their customers' businesses.

Summary

Electronic commerce offers many job opportunities for people who have the necessary technical and business skills. With the knowledge you have obtained about electronic commerce, you can now plan your career and begin to study the subjects that will lead to one of the interesting and challenging jobs described in this appendix. The Online Companion page for the Appendix includes many useful links for locating jobs in the electronic commerce field. You might wish to follow some of these links to identify the different jobs available in your personal field of interest.

1-800-flowers.com

(http://www.1800flowers.com/) Outgrowth of FTD's telephone flower order business

24/7 Media

(http://www.247media.com/) Web site that provides banner ad and e-mail services

A

ABCBanners

(http://www.abcbanners.com/) An advertising-supported Web site that offers free downloadable graphics

absolute paths

Information that shows the location of a file on a computer; in HTML, a path begins with a slash (/)

acceptance

The expression of willingness to take an offer, including all of its stated terms

accounts receivable

A system that contains information about money owed to a merchant or company, which is money that should flow into the merchant's account

ACLU

(http://www.aclu.org/) The American Civil Liberties Union, a non-profit organization that disseminates information, conducts fund-raising activities, and provides a two-way contact channel for reporting violations

acquiring bank

See merchant bank

active ads

Ads that generate graphical activity that "floats" over the Web page itself instead of opening in a separate window

active content

A term that refers to programs that are embedded transparently in Web pages and cause some action to occur

ActiveX control

An object that contains programs and properties that Web designers place in their Web pages to perform particular tasks

ActiveX Controls Library

(http://download.cnet.com/ downloads/ 0-10081.html) A Web page hosted by CNET providing categories of ActiveX controls for just about any task

Adbility

(http://www.adbility.com/) A Web directory of resources for online advertising

addressable media

A category of mass media that is directed at a known addressee and that may include direct mail, telephone calls, and e-mail messages

AdKiller

(http://www.adkiller.com/) Banner ad blocking software

Adobe PageMill

(http://www.adobe.com/products/ pagemill/main.html) A WYSI-WYG Web site development software program

AdRelevance

(http://www.adrelevance.com/) Online company that measures online advertising activity so you can make the best possible marketing and advertising decisions

AdResource

(http://adres.internet.com/) A Web site that provides Internet advertising and Web site promotion resources

AdSubtract

(http://www.adsubtract.com/) Software that blocks banner ads, protects privacy, and speeds up the Web

ad view

A term that refers to each Web page loaded by a visitor that contains an ad

affiliate marketing

A marketing tool where one firm's Web site includes descriptions, reviews, ratings, or other information about a product that are linked to another firm's site, which offers the item for sale

Alice's Antiques of SoHo

(http://www.dir-dd.com/ alices-antiques.html/) Online store specializing in European and American antiques

alignment property

HTML tag that tells the browser how to align text in the document content

Allaire Cold Fusion

(http://www.allaire.com/Products/ coldfusion/) A complete application server and Web site development tool

Alta Vista

(http://www.altavista.com/) A Web search engine

alternative tag

An HTML tag that includes a text description of a graphic object

Amazon.com

(http://www.amazon.com/) A large online store that sells books, music, electronics, toys, hardware, and other items

Amazon.com Auctions

(http://auctions.amazon.com/) The auction Web site of Amazon.com

American Greetings

(http://www.americangreetings. com/) The Web site for American Greetings that you can use to send electronic greetings

Amnesty International

(http://www.amnesty.org/) A not-for-profit organization that campaigns on human rights issues

anchor

An HTML tag that links one point in an HTML document to another point in the same document

Apache HTTP Server

(http://www.apache.org/) The most popular HTTP server on the Internet

applet

A program written in Java programming language that is embedded in a Web page that you download and display

Art.com

(http://www.art.com/) A poster art and framing company

asymmetric encryption

A type of encryption that encodes messages by using two mathematically related numeric keys; also known as public-key encryption

Auctions.com

(http://www.auctions.com/) An auction Web site

augmented linear structure

Storyboarding feature that links each page directly back to the first page, while keeping links that allow you to move to the next and previous pages

authentication

The process of establishing the validity of one's claimed identity

authorization

The process of giving an individual access to information based on his or her identity after a person's true identity is established

Authorize.Net

(http://www.authorizenet.com/) A Web site that provides online, real-time credit card processing services

Autobytel.com

(http://www.autobytel.com/) A Web site that provides information about vehicles for sale and related consumer information

Automated Clearing House (ACH) Network

A network where checks from consumers are credited to merchant accounts and deducted from consumer checking accounts

automated fulfillment system

A common function of an electronic commerce site that notifies customers that their orders were received and then ships the orders to the correct locations

awareness

Stage in the five-stage model of customer loyalty at which customers recognize the name of the company or one of its products

B

B & D Gourmet Coffee

(http://www.bdcoffee.com/) Sells coffees and related supplies

Baan

(http://www2.baan.com/) An ERP software publisher

Backflip

(http://www.backflip.com/) Provides a bookmarking tool on its Web site to maintain bookmarks in one common area for viewing from any browser or computer

bankonewallet

(http://www.bankonewallet.instabuy.com/) Completes forms and holds credit cards for Bank One customers

banner ad

A small rectangular object on a Web page that displays a stationary or moving graphic and includes a hyperlink to the advertiser's Web site

banner advertising network

A company that serves as a broker between advertisers and Web sites that carry ads

banner exchange

A service in which members post banner advertisements on each other's sites, providing a highly visible form of advertising for a low-cost investment

BannerExchange

(http://www.bannerexchange.com/) A banner exchange advertising organization

banner exchange network

A network that coordinates ad-sharing so that sites run other exchange members' ads, and vice versa

bargainers

Web site visitor behavior of users who enjoy searching for the best price or shipping terms and are willing to move among sites to do that

beenz

(http://www.beenz.com/home.html) A brand of scrip that is marketed as a loyalty reward program for Internet customers

Be Free

(http://www.befree.com/) An affiliate program broker

behavioral segmentation

Mareketing segmentation that targets the same customers in different ways at different times

Berkman Center for Internet and Society

(http://eon.law.harvard.edu/property/) Harvard Law School organization that tackles tough Internet intellectual property issues

Berlitz

(http://www.berlitz.com/) Provides language training and translation products and services

Better Business Bureau

(http://www.bbbonline.org/) An organization that promotes trust and confidence in online merchants

BetterWhois.com

(http://www.betterwhois.com/) Domain search and registry services covering the shared domain registry

Beyond.com

(http://www.beyond.com/) Mega-shopping Web site

bid

An agreement by a buyer to a seller to purchase one unit of a salable item

Big Brother

(http://pauillic.inria.fr/~fpottier/bb.html.en) Link-checking software

BigStep

(http://www.bigstep.com/) Online store building software and Web site

blind signature

A cryptographic modification of an owner's digital money to validate electronic cash without revealing the payer's identity

BoldFish

(http://www.boldfish.com/) Market-leading software and services for e-mail delivery

bolero.net

(http://www.bolero.net/) An association dedicated to creating a set of interoperable electronic commerce applications

brainstorming

An exercise in which two or more people talk about ideas and write them down without evaluating them

brand

Customers' perceptions of the product

Britannica.com

(http://www.britannica.com/) Online full, searchable version of Britannica's print edition plus Web-integrated tools and features

broadcast media

A category of mass media that is directed at the general public and may include television, radio, and newspaper advertising

Brodia

(http://www.brodia.com/) A server-side electronic wallet

burst.com

(http://www.burst.com/) A Web technology company that provides an alternative to streaming media for banner ads

Business 2.0

(http://www.business2.com/marketing/index.htm) Web site that displays Internet marketing articles

business plan

An organized document that summarizes the expected future activities of an existing or proposed business

business policies

The elements of a country's culture that have become ingrained in the everyday business practices of a particular company

business unit

See strategic business unit

buy.com

(http://www.buy.com/) An Internet superstore

cannibalization

The process of taking away sales from a print edition of a newspaper or other media by providing the same content on the Web at little or no charge

card not present

A term that refers to making online purchases when the merchant's location and the purchaser's location are different

card processors

Fee-for-services organizations that handle all of the details of processing credit cards

CareerSite.com

(http://www.careersite.com/) An employment firm focusing on technology and higher-level jobs

Cars.com

(http://www.cars.com/) A themed portal site displaying ads for new and used cars, financing, leasing, and other car-related products and services

cash budgets

Portion of a busniess plan that shows the details of when money will be received from customers and when it will be paid out to suppliers, employees, and others

catalog

A common feature of an electronic commerce site that may contain detailed information about each product sold by the company, including the item's name, description, price, shipping cost, size, color, and sometimes a picture

CDnow

(http://www.cdnow.com/) Online seller of music CDs

certification authority (CA)

Issues a digital certificate, including information about an entity, expiration date, and public key, to an organization or individual

character tags

HTML tags (logical character tags or physical character tags) that can be applied to an individual character to modify its characteristics

charge card

A card that carries no preset spending limit where the entire amount charged is due at the end of the month

Charge Solutions

(http://www.chargesolutions.com/) Provides Internet-based real-time credit card processing

CheckFree Corporation

(http://www.checkfree.com/) Online bill paying service using electronic checks

CheMatch

(http://www.chematch.com/) Bulk petrochemicals auction Web site targeting the industrial chemicals market

ChemConnect

(http://www.chemconnect.com/) Auction Web site targeting the entire chemicals market

Chemdex

(http://www.chemdex.com/) Research chemicals auction Web site targeting the industrial chemicals market

circuits

Specific telephone lines connected to create a single path between caller and receiver

circuit switching

A centrally controlled model of connecting specific telephone lines to create a single path between caller and receiver

Cisco Systems

(http://www.cisco.com/) A large company that specializes in end-to-end networking hardware and software solutions

Claritas, Inc.

(http://www.claritas.com/index.html) A company that undertakes continuing research into market segmentation and how companies can use segment information to develop better relationships with their customers

click

A term that refers to each time a visitor clicks a banner ad to open an advertiser's page

Clickshare

(http://www.clickshare.com/) Electronic check processing service

click-through

See click

click-through rate

The percentage of site visitors that click banner ads

ClickZ Network

(http://www.clickz.com/) Web site for Internet-related articles

client-side electronic wallets

Electronic storage devices that store a customer's information on the consumer's computer

client-side storage

The practice of storing cash on a consumer's computer, thereby reducing electronic cash's portability

closing tags

The HTML tag that tells the browser to turn off a feature

CNET

(http://www.cnet.com/) A world leading new media company providing information about computers

Coca-Cola

(http://www.coke.com/) A market-leading beverage company

Coin Universe

(http://www.coin-universe.com/) Auction Web site specializing in coins and coin-related items

commerce

A negotiated exchange of valuable objects or services between at least two parties (a buyer and a seller), including all activities that each of the parties undertakes to complete the transaction

commerce service providers (CSPs)

See Web hosting services

Commission Junction

(http://www.cj.com/ An affiliate program broker

commitment

Stage in the five-stage model of customer loyalty at which customers demonstrate fierce loyalty or strong preference for the products or brands of a company and are willing to tell others about how happy they are with their interactions

commodities

Standard items that buyers usually select using price as their main criterion

CompUSA Auctions

(http://www.compusaauctions.com/) Auction Web site primarily targeting its technology inventory to mid-sized and smaller businesses

computer security

The protection of assets from unauthorized access, use, alteration, or destruction

connectors

Web site visitor behavior of users who use the Web to stay in touch with other people

contamination

See data alteration

contract

An agreement between two or more legal entities that provides for an exchange of value between or among them

conversion rate

In advertising, the percentage of recipients who respond to an ad or promotion

cookie

A small data file, including information such as a user name and password, that some Web sites write to your hard drive when you view the Web site

Cookie Central

(http://www.cookiecentral.com/) A Web site devoted to the topic of electronic cookies

copyright

The protection of expression that covers someone's or some entity's intellectual property

Copyright Clearance Center

(http://www.copyright.com/) The largest licenser of photocopy reproduction rights in the world

Copyright Website, The

(http://www.benedict.com/contents.htm) A Web site that provides real-world, practical, and relevant copyright information

cost per thousand (CPM)

A pricing metric that is used when companies purchase mass media advertising; companies pay a dollar amount for each thousand persons in the estimated audience

countermeasure

A general name for a procedure, either physical or logical, that recognizes, reduces, or eliminates a threat

CPM

See cost per thousand

credit card

A card that has a preset spending limit based on the user's credit limit

CREDITNET.COM

(http://www.creditnet.com/) A credit card authorization service

Crutchfield

(http://www.crutchfield.com/) A consumer electronics Web store

cryptography

The science that studies encryption

customer life cycle

The five stages that can yield information about how customers interact with the company and its products in each stage

Customer Profile Exchange (CPEX)

A standard that governs the way companies collect customer information and share it with others

customer value

This total cost is subtracted from the benefits that a customer derives from the product

customs duties

Taxes levied by a country on certain commodities when they are imported into that country

CyberCash

(http://www.cybercash.com/) Electronic cash and electronic check processing service

CyberSource Payment Services

(http://www.cybersource.com/services/payment/) A credit card payment service company

cybersquatting

The practice of registering a domain name that is the trademark of another person or company with the hope that the trademark's owner will pay huge sums to purchase the domain name

Cybersquatting and the Law

(http://www.patents.com/resource.htm) A Web page that contains the latest information about cybersquatting

cyber vandalism

The electronic defacing of an existing Web site's pages

D

data alteration

A destructive practice of unauthorized users changing data as it passes over a network from a user to a commerce site

Data Encryption Standard (DES)

An encryption standard adopted by the U.S. government for encrypting sensitive or commercial information

data loss

The problem that occurs when a thief removes electronic information while it is in transit; also known as denial attack

decryption program

A program that reverses an encryption procedure

defamation

The act of making a false statement that injures the reputation

defamatory statement

A statement that is false and injures the reputation of another person or company

definition lists

Lists of terms, each followed by a definition line and usually indented slightly to the right, that appear when the browser encounters the HTML <DL> tag

degrading service

A disruption in service that can cause critical, time-sensitive transactions to falter; also known as delay

delay

See degrading service

Dell

(http://www.dell.com/) Leading computer manufacturer offering a high degree of configuration flexibility to its customers

Della Weddings

(http://www.dellaweddings.com/) A wedding registry service that connects to many local and national department and gift stores

demographic segmentation

Information about age, gender, family size, income, education, religion, or ethnicity to group customers psychographic segmentation, marketers try to group customers by variables such as social class, personality, or their approach to life

denial attack

See data loss

Digimarc Corporation

(http://www.digimarc.com/) Digital watermarking software company

digital certificate

An electronic signature that verifies the identity of a user or Web site; also known as a digital ID

digital envelope

A type of security that uses two layers of encryption to protect a message

digital ID

See digital certificate

digital signature

The electronic equivalent of a personal signature that cannot be forged

digital watermark

A pattern of bits inserted into a digital image, audio, or video file that identifies the file's copyright information

disintermediation

The process of one company removing another company from an industry value chain

distribution place

See place

divisibility

A property that distinguishes electronic cash from real currency and determines the size of payment units

document content

The parts of a Web document that you want the user to see on the screen, such as text and graphics

Donnelley Marketing

(http://www.donnelleymarketing. com/) A company that undertakes continuing research into market segmentation and how companies can use segment information to develop better relationships with their customers

DoubleClick

(http://www.doubleclick.net/us/) The largest banner ad network in the world and it sells ad space by impression

DoubleClick Privacy Statement

(http://www.doubleclick.net/ company_info/about_doubleclick/ privacy) A Web page that contains an example cookie policy statement

double spending

The problem that occurs when the same electronic cash is paid to two different merchants

Dow Jones Interactive

(http://bis.dowjones.com/) A Web service that provides business-focused subscriptions to digitized newspaper, magazine, and journal content

dropship

A warehouse facility that ships goods to other companies' customers directly

E

eavesdropper

In the context of the Internet, a person or device that is able to listen to and copy transmissions

eBay

(http://www.ebay.com/) One of the first auction Web sites

e-card

An electronic greeting card

eCash

(http://www.digicash.com/) A brand of electronic cash for the Internet shopper

eCoin

(http://www.ecoin.net/) A brand of electronic cash that issues VIRC eCoins

electronic cash

Currency that you purchase with a credit card and then download to your computer or smart card

electronic check

The digital equivalent of a conventional paper check

electronic commerce

The conduct of selling, buying, logistics, or other organization-management activities via the Web

electronic data interchange (EDI)

A transaction that occurs when one business transmits computer-readable data in an agreed-upon format to another business

electronic funds transfer (EFT)

The process of exchanging account information electronically over private communications networks; also known as wire transfers

Electronic Privacy Information Center (EPIC)

(http://www.epic.org/) A public-interest research center in Washington, D.C.

electronic wallet

An electronic storage device that stores electronic currency and information about the wallet's owner, such as the owner's name, address, phone number, and credit card numbers

eMarketer

(http://www.emarketer.com/) A Web site for Internet market research and statistics

encapsulation

See tunneling

encryption

The process of encoding information using a secret key to produce a string of unintelligible characters

EPIC

See Electronic Privacy Information Center

escrow service

A third party in a transaction that holds the buyer's payment until he or she receives and is satisfied with the purchased item

ESPN

(http://espn.go.com/) An organization that provides sports-related news and information

eToys

(http://www.etoys.com/) An Internet toy company offering affiliate programs

Europages

(http://www.europages.com/) European business directory with content in six languages

European Banner Exchange

(http://www.eurobanner.com/) A banner exchange advertising organization

eWallet

(http://www.ewallet.com/) The EntryPoint electronic wallet

Exchange-it

(http://www.exchange-it.com/) A banner exchange advertising organization

Excite

(http://www.excite.com/) A portal site and search directory on the Web

Expedia

(http://www.expedia.com/) Microsoft's online travel agency

explicit warranty

A statement that provides specific descriptions of warranty terms

Exploration

Stage in the five-stage model of customer loyalty at which potential customers learn more about the company or its products

external image

A graphic image that must be displayed on the Web page by the browser using a file viewer program

extranet

A Web-based network that connects a company's network to the networks of its business partners, selected customers, or suppliers

eyeblaster creates active ads

(http://www.eyeblaster.com/) Online company that helps publishers, agencies, and advertisers to create and manage out-of-banner advertsing campaigns

 F

fair use

The practice of allowing limited use of copyrighted material when certain conditions are met

familiarity

Stage in the five-stage model of customer loyalty at which customers who have completed several transactions and are aware of the company's policies regarding returns, credits, and pricing flexibility

Fatbrain.com

(http://www.fatbrain.com/) A large online bookstore targeting computer, technical, and business books

Federal Trade Commission (FTC)

The main federal agency responsible for enforcing a variety of consumer protection laws

FedEx

(http://www.fedex.com/) A company that ships packages around the world; its Web site offers freight-tracking capabilities

file viewer

A program that a browser uses to display an external image on a Web page

flat-rate access

A system where the consumer or business pays one monthly fee for unlimited telephone line usage

float

Money that is deposited in an electronic merchant's account and is earning interest temporarily until that money is paid to the ultimate vendor

Flooz

(http://www.flooz.com/) A Web site that lets you send server scrip as an e-mail attachment

forum selection clause

A statement that a contract will be enforced according to the laws of a particular state

fraud

An intentional lie or distortion of truth intended to convince another person or company to part with something of value or to surrender a legal right

FreeTranslation.com

(http://www.freetranslation.com/) A Web site offering free Web-based translation tools

front page

The first page of a Yahoo! online store, or the main entrance to your catalog or portfolio of goods on a Bigstep online store

FTC Consumer Protection Page

(http://www.ftc.gov/ftc/consumer. htm) Information available on the Web and maintained by the FTC about consumer protection laws and assistance

FTD.com

(http://www.ftd.com/) The Web business of FTD that started in 1994

fulfillment

The process of pulling items from the warehouse shelves, packing those items, and shipping them to customers

full banner

One of the standardized sizes of banner ads displayed on Web page (468 × 60 pixels)

 G

Gateway

(http://www.gateway.com/) A leading computer manufacturer

Gator

(http://www.gator.com/) A Web site offering a client-side electronic wallet

GeoCities

(http://www.geocities.yahoo.com/ home) A Web site that provides free Web space

geographic segmentation

Marekting efforts created for each geographical group of customers

Golf Club Exchange

(http://www.golfclubexchange.com/) An auction Web site specializing in golf-related equipment and supplies

Google

(http://www.hotbot.lycos.com/) A Web search engine

Grainger.com

(http://www.grainger.com/) The Web site of one of the largest MRO suppliers in the world

gross profit margin (also called gross margin or profit margin)

The difference between the selling price of an item and its cost

group purchasing site

A Web site that receives bids from multiple buyers on an item and negotiates a better price with the item's provider

Guidescope

(http://www.guidescope.com/ home/) An ad blocking software

 H

Haggle Online

(http://www.haggle.com/) An auction Web site specializing in computer equipment

half banner

One of the standardized sizes of banner ads displayed on Web page (234 × 60 pixels)

hash function

A procedure that creates a fixed length number–often 128 bits (16 characters) long–that summarizes a message's contents in an attempt to eliminate electronic message alterations

hierarchial structure

Storyboarding feature that organizes Web pages so that the first page starts with a general topic that includes links to more specific topics on other Web pages

Hewlett-Packard

(http://www.hp.com/) A large manufacturer of computer and computer-related products

HitExchange

(http://www.hitexchange.net/) A banner exchange advertising organization

home page

The first page of a Web site or store

Hotbot

(http://www.hotbot.lycos.com/) A Web search engine

hyperlinks

See hypertext links

hypertext links

Specially formatted text in a document or on a Web page that you click to instantly view another topic or document

I

IBM Home Page Reader

(http://www.austin.ibm.com/sns/hpr.html) A product that provides spoken Internet browsing software for the blind or visually impaired

IBM Micro Payments

(http://www-4.ibm.com/software/webservers/commerce/payment/mpay/) Provides cash for micropayments as low as one cent

ICVERIFY

(http://www.icverify.com/) Electronic transaction processing software

Idiom

(http://www.idiominc.com/) Software to help maintain Web sites in multiple languages

implied warranty

A promise that is not expressly stated but that a buyer may infer from the seller's advertising or from a generally existing understanding of the product's use

impression

A term that refers to each time a banner ad loads an ad into a Web page

income taxes

Taxes levied by national, state, and local governments on the net income generated by business activities

index

A search engine's database of Web pages

industry value chain

See value system

Information Technology Association of America (ITAA)

(http://www.itaa.org/) A trade organization representing U.S. information technology companies

Infoseek

(http://infoseek.go.com/) A portal site and search directory on the Web

inline image

A graphic image that appears directly on a Web page when the page is loaded

InstaBuy

(http://www.instabuy.com/) A CyberCash product (client-side)

integrated security

A concept that ensures that all security measures work together to prevent unauthorized disclosure, destruction, or modification of assets

integrity

A term that refers to preventing unauthorized data modification

integrity threat

A term that refers to unauthorized parties altering message streams of information

Intel

(http://www.intel.com/) One of the world's largest manufacturers of computer processor chips

intellectual property

The ownership of ideas and control over the tangible or virtual representation of those ideas

interactive marketing unit (IMU) ad formats

The standard banner sizes that most Web sites have voluntarily agreed to use

interface

On a Web site, the view it offers to visitors and includes its layout, colors, hyperlinks, images, ad controls (such as buttons)

intermediaries

Companies in an industry value chain that occupy an intermediate step between the manufacturer and the final consumer

Internal Revenue Service

(http://www.irs.gov/) The government agency that administers U.S. federal tax laws

International Securities Exchange

(http://www.iseoptions.com/) Electronic securities exchange targeting low-cost trading in a few hundred most actively traded stocks options contracts

Internet Advertising Bureau

http://www.iab.net/ A not-for-profit organization that promotes the use of the Internet and encourages effective Internet advertising

Internet infrastructure

The computers and software connected to the Internet and the communications networks over which the message packets travel

Internet Protocol (IP)

An Internet protocol developed to establish rules for routing individual data packets from their sources to their destinations; IP also handles all the addressing details for each packet, ensuring that each is labeled with the correct destination

Internet Traffic Report

(http://www.internettrafficreport.com/) An Internet site that checks the quality and capacity of electronic equipment exchanging electronic mail from country to country

InternetSecure

(http://www2.internetsecure.com/) A company that provides secure credit card processing

InterNIC

(http://www.internic.net/regist.htlm) An Internet site that provides domain name services

INTERSHOP

(http://www.intershop.com/Products/) A company that provides electronic commerce software for mid-range businesses

interstitial ad

An ad that opens in its own browser window when a user clicks a link instead of the page that the user intended to load (the general meaning of the word "interstitial" is something that comes between two other things)

intranet

A Web-based private network that hosts Internet applications on a local area network

issuing bank

The bank that issues a cardholder's credit card

item page

An individual product, service, or piece or artwork that is sold or displayed in a catalog or portfolio of a Bigstep online store

items

Products for sale in an online store

J

J.B. Hunt Transport Services

(http://www.jbhunt.com/) Logistical information management and freight carrier firm

Java Security

(http://java.sun.com/sfaq/) Sun Microsystems' frequently asked questions Web page about Java security

JOBTRAK.COM

(http://www.jobtrak.com/) An employment firm focusing on technology and higher-level jobs

John Marshall Law School Cyberspace Law Index

(http://www.jmls.edu/cyber/index/index.html) A Web page that includes articles about jurisdiction and other Internet-related areas

Jupiter Communications

(http://www.jup.com/) A company that conducts market research and an analysis of the online consumer market

Jupiter Media Metrix

(http://www.jmm.com/) A Web site that provides Internet marketing resources

jurisdiction

The ability of a government to exert control over a person or corporation

K

KPMG

(http://www.kpmgca.com/) A well-known certification authority

L

L.L. Bean

(http://www.llbean.com/) A large clothing retailer with a Web presence

Lands' End

(http://www.landsend.com/) A large clothing retailer with an Web presence

Legal Information Institute

(http://www.law.cornell.edu/index.html) A Web site that includes pages about the Uniform Commercial Code and other laws governing business contracts and transactions within the U.S. jurisdiction

Lernout & Hauspie

(http://www.lhs.com/) A company that provides speech recognition, translation, and text-to-speech technologies

LEXIS-NEXIS Xchange

(http:///web.lexis.com/xchange) An online legal research tool

life-cycle segmentation

Marketing strategy that stages in the customer life cycles to create groups of customers that are in each stage

linear structure

Storyboarding feature that links each page to the next and previous pages in an ordered chain of pages

Linkbot Pro

(http://www.linkbot.com/products/linkbot.htm) Link-checking software

links

See hypertext links

LinkScan

(http://www.elsop.com/) Link-checking software

LinkShare

(http://www.linkshare.com/) An affiliate program broker

liquidation broker

A firm that finds buyers for the unusable and excess inventory of another firm

local area network (LAN)

A computer network that spans a geographically small area

localization

A translation that considers multiple elements of the local environment, such as business and cultural practices, in addition to local dialect variations in the language

logical character tags

HTML tags that can be applied to an individual character to indicate how you want use the character, not how you want to display it

logical security

A type of security that protects assets using nonphysical mechanisms, such as antivirus software and passwords

logistics

Delivery and warehousing activities that will provide the right goods in the right quantities in the right place at the right time

long-arm statutes

Laws that can create personal jurisdiction for the courts

Los Angeles Times

(http://www.latimes.com/) A large newspaper that includes an online version of its print newspaper

Lycos

(http://www.lycos.com/) A portal site and search directory on the Web

M

Macromedia Dreamweaver

(http://www.macromedia.com/software/dreamweaver/) Web site development software

Macromedia Flash

(http://www.macromedia.com/shockwave/download/) A browser plug-in that you need in order to view certain Web pages

maintenance, repair, and operating (MRO) supplies

Supplies and other overhead expenses incurred by a business in addition to the main materials and labor costs of creating a product or service

many-to-many communications model

A model in which buyers communicate via the Web with individuals working for the seller and with other potential buyers

many-to-one communications model

A model in which buyers communicate via the Web with individuals working for the seller

Maricopa

(http://www.mcli.dist.maricopa.edu/tut/lessons.html) Web site that provides free online tutorials on HTML

marketing mix

The combination of elements that a company uses to achieve its goals for selling and promoting its products or services

marketing strategy

The combination of elements that a company decides to use to achieve its goals for selling and promoting its products or services

market segmentation

The practice of dividing a pool of potential customers into segments and targeting them with specific advertising messages

market segments

Marketing strategies and tactics that will reach customers in each sub-group effectively

marketspace

A term used to describe commerce in the information world, as opposed to commerce in the physical world

markups

The difference between the selling price of an item and it's cost expressed as a percentage of the item's cost

mass media approach

A business's approach to identifying and reaching customers by preparing advertising and promotional materials about the company and its products or services, and delivering these messages to potential customers by broadcasting them on television or radio, printing them in newspapers or magazines, posting them on highway billboards, or mailing them

Matrix Information and Directory Services (MIDS)

(http://tracemap.mids.org/) A Web site that checks the quality and capacity of electronic equipment connecting to the Internet from country to country

McAfee

(http://www.mcafee.com/) A popular antivirus software publisher

McKinsey Quarterly, The

(http://www.mckinseyquarterly.com/) Quarterly magazine that publishes articles about Internet marketing

Mercata

(http://www.mercata.com/) A group purchasing Web site

merchandising

In retail store environments, the knowledge of merchants about store design, layout, and product display

merchant account

An account that conventional and online businesses have that allows them to accept credit card payments and receive authorization to process those payments by the bank that issued the credit card

merchant bank

A bank that does business with online and offline merchants that accept credit cards; also known as an acquiring bank

merchant service providers

Providers that process credit card accounts and with whom businesses have merchant accounts

message digest

A number computed from a message that is a summary of the entire message

MessageMedia

(http://www.messagemedia.com/) A company that offers e-mail management services

META tags

HTML tags inserted in a Web page that contain information to describe its contents for Web search engines

MicroAge

(http://www.microage.com/) Web-based sales training programs for new Internet technology products

micro marketing

The practice of targeting very small market segments for specific advertising and promotion efforts

micropayment

An electronic payment of less than one dollar that you might use to purchase a single track on a music album, a newspaper article, or a complicated literature search

Microsoft bCentral

(http://www.bcentral.com/) A banner exchange advertising organization

Microsoft FrontPage

(http://www.microsoft.com/frontpage/) Web site development software

Microsoft Internet Information Server

(http://www.microsoft.com/ntserver/web/exec/feature/Datasheet.asp) A popular Web server

MilliCent

(http://www.millicent.digital.com/home.html) Compaq's electronic cash system providing micropayments as low as one cent

MILPRO

(http://www.milpro.com/) An MRO supplier

misappropriation

Rerouting of payments from customers to an unauthorized person or persons

mission statement (or vision statement)

Summary of the company's philosophy

MNBA wallet

(http://www.mnbawallet.com/) An electronic wallet that securely stores multiple addresses, credit card numbers, and passwords

Mondex

(http://www.mondex.com/) A Web site that provides electronic cash and a smart card to store the cash

Mondex card

An electronic cash system in which money is held in a smart card that contains a computer chip with memory to store user information

Monster.com

(http://www.monster.com/) A Web site providing employment ads focusing on technology and higher-level jobs

MRO

See maintenance, repair, and operating (MRO) supplies

Museum of Modern Art (MoMA)

(http://www.moma.org/) One of the first museums in the world to use the Web to help introduce interested visitors to its collections, creating congruence with its present image

MyOneWallet

(http://www.myonewallet.com/) An electronic wallet from Capital One

MyPoints

(http://www.mypoints.com/) An online marketing reward program

mySimon

(http://www.mysimon.com/) Bot-based comparison shopping site

N

NACHA

(http://www.nacha.org/) The organization that develops operating rules and business practices for the Automated Clearing House (ACH) Network

NCSA

(http://archive.ncsa.uiue.edu/General/Internet/WWW/HTMLPrimerAll.htm) Web site that provides a comprehensive list of HTML codes and descriptions on their functionality

necessity

A category of computer security that prevents data delays or denials (removals)

necessity threat

A threat that disrupts or denies normal computer processing; also known as delay or denial threats

NECX Online Exchange

(http://www.necx.com/) Business-to-business trade auction Web site

negotiation

The communication between a Web browser and a server to decide on the best encryption method to use in an exchange

NetCheque

(http://www.netcheque.org/) A research prototype electronic check system developed by the University of Southern California

Netscape Composer

(http://home.netscape.com/communicator/composer/v4.0/) An easy-to-use Web site publishing tool

Netscape Corporation

(http://www.netscape.com/) Web browser and server publisher

Netscape Enterprise Server

(http://home.netscape.com/enterprise/v3.6/index.html) A Web server

Network Solutions

(http://www.networksolutions.com/) A firm providing domain name registry and related services

New York Times

(http://www.nyt.com/) A large newspaper that provides online versions of its print newspaper

NextCard Concierge

(http://www.nextcard.com/wallets/) An electronic wallet that completes online forms and remembers passwords

nexus

The connection between a taxpaying entity and a government with taxing authority

Nielsen//NetRatings Internet marketing research

http://www.nielsen-netratings.com/ A joint venture that sets the benchmark for best practices in panel-based research and real-time tracking and collection of Internet audience behavior

nonrepudiation

A process that ensures that a message sender's digital signature is proof the sender was the true author of the message

Northern Light

(http://www.northernlight.com/) A Web search engine that also searches its own database of acquired journals and other publications

Norton

(http://www.symantec.com/nav/indexA.html) A popular antivirus software publisher

not-for-profit organization

An organization that is devoted to a goal other than generating revenue, such as promoting the sciences, the arts, humanitarian causes, education, political interests, or the general welfare

 O

occasion segmentation

Type of marketing segmentation in which the same person will require different combinations of products and services depending on the occasion

offer

A declaration of willingness to buy or sell a product or service that includes sufficient details to be firm, precise, and unambiguous

Office Depot

(http://www.officedepot.com/) Market leader in office equipment and supplies

offline purchases

Purchases that occur in physical stores

one-to-many communications model

A model in which communication flows from one advertiser to many potential customers

one-to-one communications model

A model in which a wide-ranging interchange occurs within the framework of an existing trust relationship and both the seller and the buyer actively participate in this exchange of information

one-to-one marketing

This highly customized approach to offering products and services that match the needs of a particular customer

Online Benefits

(http://www.online-benefits.com/) A service that provides password-protected accessibility to employees' benefits information and performs complex benefit option calculations

online purchases

Purchases that occur on the Internet

Onsale

(http://www.onsale.com/) An auction Web site specializing in selling its own refurbished computers and computer-related items

opening tags

The first HTML tag that tells the browser to turn on the feature and apply it to the document content that follows

opt-in email

The practice of sending e-mail messages to people who have requested information on a particular topic or about a specific product

ordered lists

Lists that appear in numeric order when the browser encounters the HTML <OL> tag

O'Reilly Software

(http://website.oreilly.com/) Web server software publisher

P

packet-switching network

A network that utilizes an efficient and inexpensive technique by which files and messages are broken down into packets that are labeled electronically with codes indicating both their origins and destinations

page view

A term that refers to each Web page loaded by a visitor

paragraph property

An HTML tag that tells the browser to adds a blank line

Passport Wallet

(http://www.passport.com/) An electronic wallet

PayPal

(http://www.paypal.com/) A Web site that provides electronic cash that you can send to a recipient via e-mail

pay-per-click

The affiliate earns payment each time a site visitor clicks the link and loads the seller's page

pay-per-conversion

An affiliate earns a commission each each time a site visitor clicks the link and loads the seller's page

Pepsi

(http://www.pepsiworld.com/) A major beverage company

permission marketing

Marketing by sending information only to those potential customers who have requested such information

personal contact approach

A business's approach to identifying and reaching customers by individually searching, qualifying, and contacting potential customers

personal jurisdiction

Jurisdiction that is generally determined by the residence of the parties involved in a dispute

physical character tags

HTML tags that can be applied to an individual character to indicate how to format the character

physical security

A type of security that includes tangible protection devices, such as alarms, guards, fireproof doors, security fences, safes or vaults, and bombproof buildings

place

The need to have product available in many different locations (also called distribution)

pop-behind ad

An ad that opens a new ad-laden browser window (or windows) very quickly and then reopens the browser window with the desired content in front of it

populating the catalog

A phrase that refers to placing items for sale in an online store

pop-up ad

An ad that appears in its own window when the user opens or closes a Web page

portability

The ability of electronic cash to be freely transferable between any two parties

Price

The amount the customer pays for the product

Price Watch

(http://www.pricewatch.com/) A search engine that indexes and compares items for sale on Web sites

primary activities

In a business unit value chain, includes the activities of designing, purchasing, producing, promoting, marketing, delivering, and providing after-sale support for products and services

privacy

The protection of individual rights to nondisclosure

privacy policy

A company's statement on what information its Web site is collecting, how it will use that information, and with whom (if anyone) it will share that information

private-key encryption

See symmetric encryption

private network

A private, leased-line connection between two companies that physically connects their intranets to one another

Procter & Gamble

(http://www.pg.com/) A major manufacturer of food, beverages, healthcare products, laundry and cleaning supplies, and paper goods

procurement

A description of the purchasing activities of a business plus the monitoring of all elements of purchase transactions and the management and development of relationships with key suppliers

product

The physical item or service that a company is selling

product disparagement

Occurs when a defamatory statement injures the reputation of a product or service

Proflowers.com

(http://www.proflowers.com/) A Web site that lets customers order flowers online

pro-forma financial statements

The financial statements that result if the business planner's cost estimates and revenue projections turn out to be correct

Promotion

Includes any means of spreading the word about the product

properties

Additional information that controls how an HTML tag is used

property taxes

Taxes levied by states and local governments on the personal property and real estate used in a business

ProQuest

(http://www.proquest.com/) A Web site that specializes in online digital copies of published and unpublished works, such as doctoral dissertations, masters theses, newspapers, journals, other specialized academic publications

prospecting

See personal contact approach

proxy server

A computer inserted into a network between Web clients in a specific domain and Web servers outside of that domain

public-key encryption

See asymmetric encryption

public network extranet

An extranet that exists when an organization allows the public to access its intranet from any public network, such as the Internet, or when two or more companies agree to link their intranets using a public network

Publish

(http://www.publish.com/) Provides Web site design and Internet marketing articles

Qpass PowerWallet

(http://www.qpass.com/) A server-side electronic wallet

Quaker Oats

(http://www.quakeroats.com/) A major food products manufacturer

rational branding

A marketing strategy that substitutes an offer to help Web users in some way in exchange for viewing an ad

real time

A term that refers to immediate processing of an online purchase

Reel.com

(http://www.reel.com/) A online seller of movies

refdesk.com

(http://www.refdesk.com/) A portal site and search directory on the Web

registering

The process of creating a user ID and entering a name, address, phone number, and e-mail address into a form on a Web site

Registrars.com

(http://registrars.com/) A firm providing domain name registry and related services

reintermediation

The process of one company entering an industry value chain with a new way of providing value to the other participants in the industry value chain

relatives paths

Information that indicates the location of a file in relationship to the current Web

repeat visits

A term that refers to subsequent Web site page loads after the initial visit

request header

The part of a message that contains information about the browser software, including the browser's default language setting

Reuters

(http://www.reuters.com/) A news wire service

reverse auction

A type of auction in which the role of the bidder as buyer is reversed to bidder as seller

RewardsPrograms.com

(http://rewardsprograms.com/) A Web site that tracks marketing rewards programs

routers

Computers that determine the best way to move a packet forward to its destination

Routiners

Web site visitor behavior of users who return to the same sites over and over again

routing algorithms

The programs that determine the best way to move a packet forward to its destination

RSA Data Security, Inc.

(http://www.rsasecurity.com/) A firm that offers solutions to electronic commerce security problems

S

Sabre Group

(http://www.sabre.com/) A firm that provides information technology solutions for the travel and transportation industry

Salon.com

(http://www.salon.com/) An online magazine publisher

SAP E-Business Solutions

(http://www.sap.com/) An ERP software publisher

Schneider Logistics

(http://www.schneiderlogistics. com/) A logistical information management and freight carrier firm

SciQuest

(http://www.sciquest.com/) A Web auction site that provides laboratory instruments and supplies

scrip

A form of electronic cash that is stored on your computer and that you obtain by depositing money at a scrip vendor's server; also known as server scrip

search engine spamming

The activity of submitting the same URL an excessive number of times to the same search engine

secrecy

A term that refers to protection from inadvertent information disclosure without regard to existing legislation

sections

Categories of related products in an online store

secure commerce site

A commerce site that uses encryption techniques to protect transactions

security policy

A written statement that describes what assets a company wants to protect, why the company wants to protect these assets, who is responsible for that protection, and acceptable and unacceptable employee behaviors

segment marketing

Marketing strategy that creates separate messages for specific market segments (also called target marketing)

segments

Groups of potential customers divided in terms of demographic characteristics, such as age, gender, marital status, income level, and geographic location

separation

Stage in the five-stage model of customer loyalty at which the intensity of the customer-company relationship fades and the company must evaluate whether or not maintaining the relationship with the customer is costing too much to maintain

server scrip

See scrip

server-side electronic wallets

Electronic storage devices that store consumer information on a remote server belonging to a particular merchant or belonging to the wallet's publisher

shopping cart

A common feature of an electronic commerce site that keeps track of the items a customer has selected to purchase and that lets the customer view and update the contents of the cart, add new items to it, or remove items from it

signature

Any symbol executed or adopted for the purpose of authenticating a writing

Simplifiers

Web site visitor behavior of users who like convenience

SiteOwner

(http://www.siteinspector.com/) Link-checking software

Slate

(http://www.slate.com/) An e-zine published by Microsoft

Smart card

A plastic card containing a computer chip that stores electronic currency and information about the card's owner

SmartCart

(http://www.smartcart.com/) Versatile shopping cart software

SmartClicks

(http://www.smartage.com/ promote/smartclicks/) A banner exchange advertising organization

SmartShip

(http://www.smartship.com/) A company that integrates shipping options into Web sites or software applications

sniffer programs

Software that provides the means to tap into the Internet and record information that passes through a particular computer (router) from its source to its destination

SoftLock.com

(http://www.softlock.com/) A firm that provides digital watermarking to enable downloadable digital content

SoftQuad HoTMetaL PRO

(http://www.hotmetalpro.com/) A Web site development tool

software metering

The process of tracking the number of times someone uses a digital item

Southern California Trophy Company

(http://www.socaltrophy.com/) An online awards and trophies business

spam

A term that refers to unsolicited e-mail messages

spammers

Companies or people that issue spam

spamming

A term that refers to the action of sending unsolicited e-mail messages

spiders

Information retrievers that crawl through the Web and index Web sites and their pages

Spinfrenzy.com Mud Brick Awards

(http://www.spinfrenzy.com/muddies/) Awards given to the worst offenders of Web site design

Sportsters

Web site visitor behavior of users who tend to spend time on sports and entertainment sites rather than at news and financial information sites

square button

One of the standardized sizes of banner ads displayed on Web page (125 × 125 pixels)

StampAuctions

(http://www.stampauctions.com/) Auction Web site specializing in stamps and stamp-related supplies

Staples

(http://www.staples.com/) Market leader in office equipment and supplies

static Web page

A Web page that displays content and provides links to related pages containing additional information

Stealthencrypt.com

(http://www.stealthencrypt.com/index2.html) A firm providing steganography and encryption products

steganography

The art and science of hiding information by embedding messages within other messages or graphics

stickiness

The ability of a Web site to keep visitors at the site and to attract repeat visitors

stored value cards

Cards with magnetic strips to record electronic currency balances

storyboarding

Technique for mapping exactly how Web pages relate (or are linked) to one another for navigation purposes

strategic business unit

One particular combination of product, distribution channel, and customer type in a large company that is used to organize work; also known as business unit

subject-matter jurisdiction

A court's authority to decide a type of dispute

Submit It!

(http://www.submit-it.com/) A search engine submission service

supporting activities

In a business unit value chain, the activities of finance and accounting, human resource management, and technology development

Surfers

Web site visitor behavior of users who use the Web to find information, explore new ideas, and shop

symmetric encryption

A type of encryption that encodes a message by using a single key—which is usually a large integer number—to encode and decode data; also known as private-key encryption

 T

tags

The HTML codes that control the appearance of the document content

Tallahassee Engraving and Awards

(http://www.awards4u.com/) An online trophies and awards business

target marketing

See segment marketing

technology-enabled customer relationship management

The process by which a firm obtains detailed information about a customer's behavior, preferences, needs, and buying patterns, and then uses that information to set prices, negotiate terms, tailor promotions, add product features and otherwise customize its entire relationship with that customer; customer relationship management (CRM)

technology infrastructure

A country's business and government telecommunications networks that carry and route computer data traffic in that country

theft

The unauthorized taking or use of goods or services

theglobe.com

(http://www.theglobe.com/) Virtual community that was the outgrowth of a class project at Cornell University

threat

Any act or object that poses a danger to computer assets

thumbnails

Small images that can be clicked to open a larger version of the image

tort

An action taken by one legal entity that causes harm to another legal entity; also known as a tortious action

tortious action

See tort

TouchScape

(http://www.touchscape.com/) Web site that provides e-mail marketing services

Toyota

(http://www.toyota.com/) A major auto manufacturer Web site

trademark dilution

The reduction of the distinctive quality of a trademark by alternative uses

transaction and payment processing

A common function of an electronic commerce site that occurs when the shopper proceeds to the virtual checkout where volume discounts, sales tax, shipping costs, and total costs are calculated and the customer's payment is processed

transaction costs

The total of all costs that a buyer and a seller incur as they gather information and negotiate a purchase-sale transaction; may include brokerage fees, sales commissions, and the costs of information search and acquisition

transaction taxes

Taxes, including sales taxes, use taxes, and excise taxes, levied on the products or services that a company sells or uses

Transmission Control Protocol (TCP)

An Internet protocol developed to establish fundamental rules about how data is moved across networks and how network connections are established and broken; TCP also controls the assembly of a message into smaller packets before it is transmitted over the Internet and the reassembly of packets when they reach their destination

Transparent Language

(http://www.transparent.com/) A Web site providing language-related services, products, and free features

TravelBids

(http://ww.travelbids.com/) Reverse-auction Web site (bidder as seller)

Travelocity

(http://www.travelocity.com/) An online travel agency

trial visit

A term that refers to the first time that a particular visitor loads a Web site page

trigger words

Key words

Trojan horse

A program hidden inside another program or Web page that masks its true purpose

Trophies2Go.com

(http://www.trophies2go.com/) Online store for awards and trophies

TRUSTe

(http://www.truste.org/) A firm that establishes privacy principles to which members must ascribe

tunneling

A system that secures sensitive data messages from eavesdroppers

two-sided tags

HTML tags that require opening tags and closing tags

U

uBid

(http://www.ubid.com/) An auction Web site specializing in computer-related items

Uniform Resource Locator (URL)

The location (or address) of a file on the Web

United Nations

(http://www.un.org/) A global organization that provides peacekeeping and humanitarian services

unordered lists

Lists that appear in no particular order and usally appear with a bullet symbol when the browser encounters the HTML <UL> tag

UPS

(http://www.ups.com/) A major transporter of packages and freight

URL

See Uniform Resource Locator

usability test

An observation or monitoring of persons' actions as they use a Web site

usage-based market segmentation

Customizing visitor experiences to match the site usage behavior patterns of each visitor or type of visitor

U.S. Bank wallet

(http://www.usbank.com/wallet/) An electronic wallet

U.S. Copyright Office

(http://www.loc.gov/copyright/circs/) The official Web site of the U.S. Copyright Office

U.S. Federal Trade Commission

(http://www.ftc.gov/) Regulations and helpful guidelines for businesses to comply with the law

U.S. Patent and Trademark Office

(http://www.uspto.gov/) Provides trademark and patent information, and a search available for trademarks

V

value chain

A way of organizing the activities that each strategic business unit undertakes

ValueClick

(http://www.valueclick.com/) Online service that provides global Internet advertising solutions for online advertisers and website publishers

value system

The larger stream of activities into which a particular business unit's value chain is embedded; also known as industry value chain

Verance Corporation

(http://www.verance.com/verance.html) A firm providing digital audio watermarking systems

VeriSign

(http://www.versign.com/) A well-known certification authority

VH1.com

(http://www.vh1.com/) Web site for music, television, and movie entertainment information

virtual community

A gathering place for people and businesses that does not have a physical existence but helps companies, their customers, and their suppliers to plan, collaborate, transact business, and otherwise interact in ways that benefit all of them; also known as a Web community or an online community

virtual private network (VPN)

An extranet that uses public networks and their protocols to send sensitive data to partners, customers, suppliers, and employees by using a system called tunneling or encapsulation

viruses

Malevolent programs that hide within other programs or in e-mail messages

vision statement

See mission statement

visit

A term that refers to a visitor loading a page from a Web site

VitaminShoppe.com

(http://www.vitaminshoppe.com/) Major vitamin and health food Web site

W

W3C Web Accessibility Initiative

(http://www.w3.org/WAI/) A Web page with links to information for making more Web pages accessible to the disabled

Wall Street Journal

(http://www.wsj.com/) A large newspaper that provides online versions of its print newspaper

warranty disclaimer

A statement that the seller will not honor some or all implied warranties

Washington Post

(http://www.washingtonpost.com/) A large newspaper that provides an online version of its print newspaper

Waterford Crystal

(http://waterford-usa.com/) Major Crystal manufacturer

Webby Awards

(http://www.webbies.com/) Awards given to some of the best Web sites on the Web

Web client

A computer that uses its Internet connection to become part of the Web

Web hosting services

Services that allow businesses to jump into electronic commerce easily and affordably by providing the necessary hardware, Web server software, and electronic commerce software to create a sight quickly; also known as commerce service providers (CSPs)

Webmonkey

(http://www.webmonkey.com/) Web site that provides information about all things related to the Internet and to the development of Web pages

Web portal

A site that includes free features such as a search engine, directory, a free e-mail site, or chat rooms with the intention of attracting a large number of visitors and becoming a doorway for those visitors to the Internet

Web profiling

The collection of marketing information about visitors to a Web site

Webwasher

(http://www.webwasher.com/windowing) Banner ad blocking software

WELL, The

(http://www.well.org/) One of the first Web communities

Wine.com

(http://www.wine.com/) Web site based in California that sells wine and other products

Winebid

(http://www.winebid.com/) An auction Web site specializing in wine and wine-related products and supplies

Wire transfers

See electronic funds transfer

World Intellectual Property Organization

(http://www.wipo.org/eng/main.htm) An organization that promotes and oversees international digital copyright issues

World Wide Learn

(http://www.worldwidelearn.com/webdesign-courses.htm) Web site that provides access to Webmaster certificate programs, Web design courses, free online HTML tutorials, and Web authoring guides

World Wide Web Consortium (W3C)

(http://www.w3.org/) Web site that provides examples of special character symbols and the way they are coded

worm

An Internet attack that automatically propagates versions of itself to other computers

writing

The terms of a contract in a tangible form

X

X:drive

(http://www.xdrive.com/) A Web site that provides up to 100MB of free Web space to members

Y

Yahoo!

(http://www.yahoo.com/) A portal site and search directory on the Web

Yahoo! Auctions

(http://auction.yahoo.com/) An auction Web site

Yahoo! Mail

(http://mail.yahoo.com/) A Web site that provides a free e-mail account and storage space for messages

Yahoo! Store Listings

(http://stores.yahoo.com/) Yahoo! Store's index of Web sites

Yahoo! Wallet

(http://wallet.yahoo.com/) A server-side electronic wallet

Yahoo! Web Page Design and Layout

(http://dir.yahoo.com/Arts/Design_Arts/Graphic_Design/Web_Page_Design_and_Layout/) A Web page that contains links to many of the top resources for how to build a Web site

yesmail.com

(http://www.yesmail.com/) A Web site that provides permission marketing e-mail services